Lecture Notes in Artificial Intelligence 7716

Subseries of Lecture Notes in Computer Science

LNAI Series Editors

Randy Goebel
University of Alberta, Edmonton, Canada
Yuzuru Tanaka
Hokkaido University, Sapporo, Japan
Wolfgang Wahlster
DFKI and Saarland University, Saarbrücken, Germany

LNAI Founding Series Editor

Joerg Siekmann
DFKI and Saarland University, Saarbrücken, Germany

Joscha Bach
Ben Goertzel
Matthew Iklé (Eds.)

Artificial General Intelligence

5th International Conference, AGI 2012
Oxford, UK, December 8-11, 2012
Proceedings

 Springer

Series Editors

Randy Goebel, University of Alberta, Edmonton, Canada
Jörg Siekmann, University of Saarland, Saarbrücken, Germany
Wolfgang Wahlster, DFKI and University of Saarland, Saarbrücken, Germany

Volume Editors

Joscha Bach
Humboldt Universität Berlin
Raumerstr. 11
10437 Berlin, Germany
E-mail: joscha.bach@gmail.com

Ben Goertzel
Aidyia Ltd., Unit 612, 6/F
Lu Plaza, 2 Wing Yip Street
Kwun Tong, Hong Kong
E-mail: ben@goertzel.org

Matthew Iklé
Adams State University, Suite 3060
Alamosa, CO 81101, USA
E-mail: moikle@adams.edu

ISSN 0302-9743
ISBN 978-3-642-35505-9
DOI 10.1007/978-3-642-35506-6
Springer Heidelberg Dordrecht London New York

e-ISSN 1611-3349
e-ISBN 978-3-642-35506-6

Library of Congress Control Number: 2012953483

CR Subject Classification (1998): I.2, F.4.1, I.5, F.1-2, D.2

LNCS Sublibrary: SL 7 – Artificial Intelligence

Typesetting: Camera-ready by author, data conversion by Scientific Publishing Services, Chennai, India
Printed on acid-free paper

Springer is part of Springer Science+Business Media (www.springer.com)

Preface

This volume collects the research papers contributed to AGI-12, the 5th Conference on Artificial General Intelligence.

The AGI conference series is the premier international forum for cutting-edge research and thinking regarding the original goal of the AI field — the creation of thinking machines. AGI–artificial general intelligence–refers to generally intelligent capabilities at the human level and ultimately beyond. Like its predecessors, AGI-12 brought together researchers in AGI and related disciplines, to present and discuss the current state of approaches, architectures, algorithms, and ideas relevant to the advancement of AGI. In honor of the Alan Turing centenary year 2012, this was the first AGI conference to be held in the UK. The conference took place at the University of Oxford, St. Anne's College, December 8–11, 2012. It was hosted by the "Future of Humanity Institute" at Oxford University through its "Programme on the Impacts of Future Technology".

A total of 80 contributed articles were submitted to AGI-12, of which 34 (42.5%) were accepted. Contributions covered a wide array of AGI research and development aspects, with the key proviso that each paper should somehow contribute specifically to the development of AGI. As in previous years, we had a host of papers covering practical proto-AGI software systems and architectures, as well as papers on the mathematical theory of AGI, and connections between AGI and neuroscience and/or cognitive science.

The AGI-12 conference program also included four invited keynote lectures. David Hanson, an American robotics designer and researcher, responsible for the creation of a series of realistic humanoid robots and founder of Hanson Robotics, delivered a talk on "Humanoid Robotics and AGI." Angelo Cangelosi, Professor of Artificial Intelligence and Cognition and Director of the Centre for Robotics and Neural Systems at Plymouth University, UK, discussed "Cognitive Robotics." Margaret Boden, a researcher in the fields of artificial intelligence, psychology, philosophy, cognitive and computer science, and Research Professor of Cognitive Science at the Department of Informatics at the University of Sussex, talked about "Creativity and AGI." Finally, Nick Bostrom, Professor of Philosophy at Oxford, Director of the Future of Humanity Institute, and Director of the Programme on the Impacts of Future Technology, discussed the future evolution of advanced AGIs and the dynamics of AGI goal systems.

AGI-12 was held together with the first conference on AGI Safety and Impacts. While AGI-12 focused, like all the AGI conferences, on the technical business of designing and building AGI systems, AGI-Impacts pursued related issues regarding the potential future of AGI: What will be the impacts of AGI on the world? Which directions of research should be most enthusiastically explored, and which should be de-emphasized or avoided? What can we say now about the future impact of AGI, and how should we act in consequence? AGI-Impacts papers are not included here, but abstracts may be found on the AGI-Impacts website.

In both the contributed articles and the invited keynotes, and the collaboration between AGI-12 and AGI-Impacts, we see the cross-disciplinarity and diversity that make the AGI field so fascinating at this stage of its development. As our technology and understanding progress, significant advances in the creation of AGI systems become viable, which is reflected in a large diversity of approaches by an increasing number of researchers in AI and related fields. The AGI conference series embraces this diversity and the creative inventiveness that it fosters.

Producing a conference of such high quality was made possible only through the support of a large community of volunteers. We thank the local Organizing Committee members for all of their advice and help in preparations and arrangements. We thank all the Program Committee members for their dedicated service to the review process. We especially thank all of our contributors, participants, and keynote speakers. The presentations, demos, and tutorials ultimately provide the material for generating thoughtful, interesting, and stimulating discussions toward the ultimate goal of achieving AGI.

Finally, we honor the support of all our sponsors: Oxford University, Future of Humanity Institute; Kurzweil AI; Rick Schwall; and Novamente LLC.

October 2012

Joscha Bach
Ben Goertzel
Matt Iklé

Organization

Program Committee

Sam Adams	IBM Research
Itamar Arel	University of Tennessee
Joscha Bach	Humboldt-University of Berlin
Sarah Bull	National ICT Australia Ltd
Cristiano Castelfranchi	Institute of Cognitive Sciences and Technologies
Antonio Chella	Università di Palermo
Jonathan Connell	IBM Research
David A. Dalrymple	MIT Media Lab
Stan Franklin	University of Memphis
Deon Garrett	IIIM, University of Reykjavik
Nil Geisweiller	Novamente LLC
Ben Goertzel	Novamente LLC
J. Storrs Hall	Institute for Molecular Manufactoring/Foresight Institute
Louie Helm	Singularity Institute
Eva Hudlicka	Psychometrix Associates
Marcus Hutter	Australian National University
Matt Iklé	Adams State University
Benjamin Johnston	University of Technology, Sidney
Cliff Joslyn	Portland State University
Randal Koene	Boston University
Kai-Uwe Kühnberger	University of Osnabrück
Christian Lebiere	Carnegie Mellon University
Shane Legg	IDSIA
Moshe Looks	Google Inc.
Stacy Marsella	University of Southern California
Günter Palm	University of Ulm
Stephen Reed	texai.org
Paul Rosenbloom	University of Southern California
Ute Schmid	University of Bamberg
Juergen Schmidhuber	IDSIA
Zhongzhi Shi	Chinese Academy of Sciences
Bas Steunebrink	IDSIA
Rich Sutton	University of Alberta

Kristinn Thorisson	CADIA, Reykjavik University
Julian Togelius	IT University of Copenhagen
Mario Verdicchio	Università degli Studi di Bergamo
Pei Wang	Temple University

Additional Reviewers

Hadi Afshar
Alex Altair
Tarek R. Besold
Tor Lattimore
Javier Snaider

Table of Contents

Creativity, Cognitive Mechanisms, and Logic

Ahmed M.H. Abdel-Fattah, Tarek Besold, and Kai-Uwe Kühnberger

University of Osnabrück, Albrechtstr. 28, Germany
{ahabdelfatta,tbesold,kkuehnbe}@uos.de

Abstract. Creativity is usually not considered to be a major issue in current AI and AGI research. In this paper, we consider creativity as an important means to distinguish human-level intelligence from other forms of intelligence (be it natural or artificial). We claim that creativity can be reduced in many interesting cases to cognitive mechanisms like analogy-making and concept blending. These mechanisms can best be modeled using (non-classical) logical approaches. The paper argues for the usage of logical approaches for the modeling of manifestations of creativity in order to step further towards the goal of building an artificial general intelligence.

Keywords: Logic, Creativity, Analogy, Concept Blending, Cognitive Mechanisms.

1 Introduction

During the last decades many cognitive abilities of humans have been modeled with computational approaches trying to formally describe such abilities, to develop algorithmic solutions for concrete implementations, and to build robust systems that are of practical use in application domains. Whereas in the beginnings of AI as a scientific discipline the focus was mainly based on higher cognitive abilities, like reasoning, solving puzzles, playing chess, or proving mathematical statements, this has been changed during the last decades: in recent years, many researchers in AI focus more on lower cognitive abilities, such as perception tasks modeled by techniques of computer vision, motor abilities in robotic applications, text understanding tasks requiring the whole breadth of human-like world knowledge etc.

Due to the undeniable success of these endeavors, the following question can be raised: what is a cognitive ability that makes human cognition unique in comparison to animal cognition on the one hand and artificial cognition on the other? At the beginning of AI most researchers would probably have said "higher cognitive abilities" (see the above examples), because only humans are able to reason in abstract domains. In current (classical) AI research, many researchers would, on the contrary, (perhaps) say that all in all still "lower cognitive abilities" like performing motor actions in a real-world environment, perceiving natural (context-dependent) scenes, the ability to integrate multi-modal types of sensory input, or the social capabilities of humans are the basis for all cognition as a

J. Bach, B. Goertzel, and M. Iklé (Eds.): AGI 2012, LNAI 7716, pp. 1–10, 2012.

whole and therefore also the key features for human-level intelligence. Finally, an AGI researcher would probably stress the combination and integration of both aspects of cognition: a successful model of artificial general intelligence should be able to integrate higher and lower types of cognition in one architecture.

Besides these possibilities, there is nevertheless an important cognitive ability that seems to be usable as a rather clear feature to distinguish human intelligence from all other forms of animal or artificial intelligence: *creativity*. Although we ascribe creativity to many human actions, we would hardly say that a certain animal shows creative behavior or a machine solves a problem creatively. Even in the case of IBM's Watson, probably the most advanced massive knowledge-based system that exists so far, most people would not ascribe general creative abilities to it. At most certain particular solutions of the system seem to be creative, because they are extremely hard to achieve for humans.

This conceptual paper discusses some aspects of creativity, as well as the possibility to explain creativity with cognitive principles and to subsequently model creativity with logical means. The underlying main idea is not to model creativity directly with classical logic, but to reduce many forms of creativity to cognitive mechanisms like analogy-making and concept blending. Such mechanisms in turn can be modeled with (non-)classical logical formalisms.

The paper has the following structure: In Section 2, we sketch some forms and manifestations of creativity. Section 3 discusses the possibility to describe creative acts by cognitive mechanisms, such as analogy-making and concept blending. It is explained that this cannot only be done for examples of creativity from highly structured domains but for a broad variety of different domains. Section 4 proposes the logical framework Heuristic-Driven Theory Projection (HDTP) for analogy-making and concept blending in order to model creativity. Section 5 concludes the paper.

2   Forms of Creativity

Creativity describes a general cognitive capacity that is in different degrees involved in any process of generating an invention or innovation.[1] The concepts invention and innovation describe properties of concrete products, services, or ideas. From a more engineering- and business-oriented perspective, an invention is usually considered as the manifestation of the creative mental act, resulting in a new artifact (prototype), a new type of service, a new concept, or even the mental concretization of a conception. An innovation requires standardly the acceptance of the invention by the market, where market is not exclusively restricted to business aspects. We are considering in this paper creativity as a cognitive ability, but we have to refer to inventions, innovations, new concepts, new findings etc. in order exemplify creativity in a concrete setting.

Creativity appears in various forms and characteristics. Creativity can be found in science, in art, in business processes, and in daily life, i.e. creative acts

---

[1] The following distinction is based on [5].

Table 1. Some domains, areas, and examples of manifestations of creativity are mentioned. Clearly, the table is not considered to give a complete overview of domains in which creative inventions of humans can occur.

		Examples for creative acts
Domain	**Areas**	**Examples**
Science	Mathematics	Argand's geometric interpretation of complex numbers [3]
	Linguistics	Chomsky's recursive analysis of natural language syntax [6]
	Physics	Einstein's theories of special and general relativity
Art	Music	Invention of twelve-tone music by Arnold Schönberg
	Poetry	The invention of a novel (as a genre of poetry)
	Visual arts	Usage of iconographic and symbolic elements in paintings (Eyck)
Other	Daily life	Fixing a household problem
	Business	Nested doll principle for product design

can occur in highly structured and clearly defined domains (like in mathematics), in less structured domains (like business processes), or even in relatively unstructured domains (like a marketing department of a company having, for instance, the task to design a new advertisement for a certain product).

We summarize different types of creativity in Table 1. Taking into account the various domains in which creativity can occur it seems to be hard to specify a domain, in which creativity does not play a role. Rather certain aspects of creativity can appear in nearly all environments and situations. This is one reason why the specification of common properties and features of creativity is a non-trivial task. For example, some attempts have been made to specify certain phases in the creative process (cf. [23]). Unfortunately, such phases, as for example a "preparation phase", are quite general and hard to specify in detail. It is doubtful whether any interesting consequences for a computational model can be derived from such properties.

3   Creativity and Cognition

There seems to be an opposition between creativity and logical frameworks. Certain creative insights, inventions, and findings do seem to be creative, precisely because the inventor did not apply a deterministic, strictly regimented form of formal reasoning (the prototypical example being classical logical reasoning), but departed from the strict corset of logic. Therefore, often a natural clash and opposition between logical modeling and creativity seem to be perceived. We think that this claim should be rejected. On the contrary, we advocate that the natural way to start is to model creativity with logical means, at least in highly structured domains like science, business applications, or classical problem solving tasks. The reason for this is based on the hypothesis that creativity is to a large extent based on certain cognitive mechanisms like analogy-making and concept blending. But now, due to the fact that analogy-making and concept blending is essentially the identification and association of structural commonalities, in turn a natural way to model these mechanisms are logic-based frameworks.

Fig. 1. Two design examples (one from the engineering domain and one from product design) that are based on the same principle, namely the nested doll principle. Objects are contained in similar other objects in order to satisfy certain constraints.

Although creativity seems to be an omnipresent aspect of human cognition (compare Table 1), not much is known about its psychological foundation, the neurobiological basis, or the cognitive mechanisms underlying creative acts. One reason might be that examples for creativity cover rather different domains, where completely different mechanisms could play important roles. Nevertheless, we hypothesize that many classical examples for creativity can be reduced to two important cognitive mechanisms, namely analogy-making on the one hand and concept blending on the other. We mention some examples in order to make this hypothesis more plausible:

- Conceptually, the usage of analogy-making is rather clear in cases where one is using a general principle in a new domain, e.g. the nested doll principle in design processes (compare Figure 1): creativity can be considered as a transfer of a structure from one domain (e.g. the structure of a planetary gearing, namely gears that revolve about a central gear) to another domain (e.g. the design of nesting bowls containing each other). This transfer of structural properties is best described as an analogy.
- In science, analogies and blend spaces do appear quite regularly. For example, in [10] it is shown how analogies can be used to learn a rudimentary number concept and how concept blending can be used to compute new mathematical structures. Furthermore, in [16] it is shown that concept blending can lead to a geometric interpretation of complex numbers, inspired by the historically important findings of Argand mentioned above in Table 1.
- Also the interpretation of certain visual inputs can easily be described by analogy-making (visual metaphor). Figure 2 gives an example, depicting an advertisement. In order to understand this advertisement a mapping between tongue and sock as well as a transfer of properties of socks need to be performed.

The number of examples, which show that analogy-making and concept blending can be used to explain manifestations of creativity, are numerous. If it is true that several characteristics of creativity can be modeled by analogies and concept blending, a computational approach towards creativity can naturally be based on an algorithmic theory of analogy and concept blending. Due to the fact that analogy-making is the identification of structural commonalities and concept

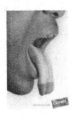
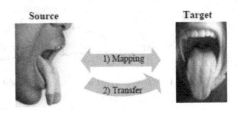

Fig. 2. Advertisement on the left side depicting an association between a tongue and a sock. In order to understand this advertisement (as a marketing tool for hard candy) the establishment of a mapping between tongue and sock is necessary. Then, hard candy can be used as a means against breadth odor. In [21], a formal modeling is specified.

blending is the (partial) merger of structures, the natural way for an algorithmic approach is to use logic as the methodological basis. Whereas for concept blending, a symbolic approach for modeling is quite undisputed, the situation in analogy-making is more complicated. Concerning the modeling of analogies, also several neurally inspired and hybrid models have been proposed. Nevertheless, when having a closer look, it turns out that the most important subsymbolic aspects of such models are activation spreading properties or synchronization issues in a (localist) network, whereas the basic computational units of the network still are quite often symbolic (or quasi-symbolic) entities (cf. [12] or [13] for two of the best known neurally inspired analogy models). Additionally, logic-based models of analogy-making have a wider application domain in comparison to neurally inspired or hybrid models. Therefore, in total, it seems a natural choice to apply logical means in modeling these two cognitive mechanisms.

4   A Logical Framework for Modeling Creativity

4.1   HDTP and Analogy Making

In what follows, we will use *Heuristic-Driven Theory Projection* (HDTP) [20] as the underlying modeling framework. HDTP is a mathematically sound framework for analogy making, together with the corresponding implementation of an analogy engine for computing analogical relations between two logical theories, representing two domains (domain theories are represented in HDTP as sets of axioms formulated in a many-sorted, first-order logic language). HDTP applies restricted higher-order anti-unification [14] to find generalizations of formulas and to subsequently propose analogical relations between source and target domain (cf. Figure 3), that can later be used as basis for an analogy-based transfer of knowledge between the two domains (see [1, 10, 16, 20] for more details about HDTP and an expanded elaboration of recent application domains).

Analogical transfer results in *structure enrichment* of the target side, which usually corresponds to the addition of new axioms to the target theory, but

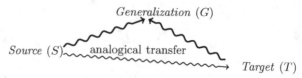

Fig. 3. HDTP's overall approach to creating analogies (cf. [20])

may also involve the addition of new first-order symbols. There are application cases in which two conceptual spaces (in our case the input theories source and target) need not to be (partially) mapped onto each other, but partially merged in order to create a new conceptual space. In such cases, HDTP uses the computed generalization, the given source and target theories, and the analogical relation between source and target to compute a new conceptual space which is called a blend space.

4.2 Concept Blending and HDTP

Concept blending (CB) has been proposed as a powerful mechanism that facilitates the creation of new concepts by a constrained integration[2] of available knowledge. CB operates by merging two input knowledge domains to form a new domain that crucially depends on and is constrained by structural commonalities between the original input domains. The new domain is called the blend, maintaining partial structures from both input domains and presumably adding an emergent structure of its own.

In cognitive models, three (not necessarily ordered) steps usually are assumed to take place in order to generate a blend. The first step is the composition (or fusion) step, which pairs selective constituents from the input spaces into the blend. In the second step, the completion (or emergence), a pattern in the blend is filled when structure projection matches long-term memory information. The actual functioning of the blend comes in the third step, the elaboration step, in which a performance of cognitive work within the blend is simulated according to its logic (cf. [8, 19]).

Figure 4 illustrates the four-space model of CB, in which two concepts, SOURCE and TARGET, represent two input spaces (the mental spaces). Common parts of the input spaces are matched by identifying their structural commonalities, where the matched parts may be seen as constituting a GENERIC SPACE. The BLEND space has an emergent structure that arises from the blending process and consists of some matched and possibly some of the unmatched parts of the input spaces (cf. Figure 4). One of the famous blending examples is Goguen's HOUSEBOAT and BOATHOUSE blends, which result, among others, from blending the two input spaces representing the words HOUSE and BOAT (cf. [9]).

Only few accounts have been proposed formalizing CB or its principles in the first place, and those that have been proposed are unfortunately not broad

---

[2] Whence, CB is sometimes referred to as 'conceptual integration'.

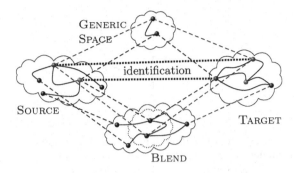

Fig. 4. The four-space model of CB: common parts of the SOURCE and TARGET concepts are identified, defining a GENERIC SPACE and a BLEND. The connecting curves within a concept reflect an internal structure.

enough to suit generic computational accounts of CB (cf. [2, 9, 19, 22]). CB itself noticeably still suffers from the lack of a formally precise model integrating its many aspects. The well-known optimality principles of CB, for instance, raise a challenge for developing such formalizations: these principles are the guideline pressures that are assumed to derive the generation of a feasible blend and distinguish good blends from bad ones [8, 18].

In fact, CB has already shown its importance as a substantial part of cognition and a means of constructing new conceptions. It has been extensively used in the literature in attempts at expressing and explaining cognitive phenomena, such as the invention of new concepts, the meaning of natural language metaphors, as well as its usefulness in expansion, reorganization, and creation of mathematical thoughts and theories ([1, 2, 8, 9, 10]).

The ideas of CB are very much related to the properties of a creative process, since a creative process can result in new insights as a result of a ladder-ascending procedure that steps through "background knowledge", and subsequently increasingly refines the insights to spell-out an innovation (cf. Section 2). Undoubtedly, creative agents must have (enough) background knowledge before a creative process can take place, still mere knowledge most likely is not sufficient: For example, simply having knowledge about Maxwell's equations, the principles of semi-conductors, and the principles of graph theory almost surely by itself is not enough in order to devise the ideas of very-large-scale integration (i.e., the creation of integrated circuits by combining thousands of transistors into one single chip). We claim that this is exactly where CB comes into play.

HDTP now provides a framework for a CB-based computation of novel concepts given a source and target domain: Assume two input theories S and T are given. The computation of an analogical relation between S and T by HDTP outputs (besides other things) a shared generalization G of S and T by the anti-unification process. This generalized theory G functions in the further process as the generic space in CB mentioned above. The construction of the blend space is computed by first, collecting the associated facts and rules from S and T generated by the analogical relation between S and T and second, by projecting

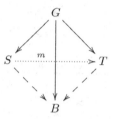

Fig. 5. HDTP's view of concept blending. S and T are source and target input theories. m represents the analogical relation between S and T and G is the generalization computed by anti-unifying S and T. The dashed arrows $S \rightarrow B$ and $T \rightarrow B$ describe the injections of facts and rules from source and target to the blend space. Due to the fact that the input theories may contain inconsistent information, the injections are partial in general.

unmatched facts and rules from both domains into the blend space. This second step can result in clashes and inconsistencies. Furthermore, the coverage of the blend space concerning S and T can be more or less maximal. Taking additionally into account that for every given S and T HDTP can compute different analogical relations, there can be many possible blend spaces for a given input. Figure 5 depicts diagrammatically the overall structure of concept blending using HDTP.

HDTP has successfully been used to compute concept blends in complex domains like mathematics. In [10], Lakoff and Núñez's mathematical grounding metaphors [15] are modeled that are intended to explain how children can learn a rudimentary concept of numbers based on simple real-world actions in their environment. These metaphors and the emergence of an abstract number concept can be explained by analogy-making and concept blending. In [16], the invention of a geometrical interpretation of complex numbers (i.e., the complex plane) was computationally modeled by concept blending. This example shows that even for rather formal and complex theories the creative generation of a new concept can be computed using a logical approach.

5   Conclusions

In particular for AGI systems, creative problem solving abilities and the finding of novel solutions in unknown situations seems to be crucial. We consider creativity as a crucial step towards building a general form of AI. From a cognitive perspective creativity can often be reduced to cognitive mechanisms such as analogy-making and concept blending, which in turn can neatly be modeled using logic-based approaches. Therefore, the apparent tension between creative abilities of agents and a logical basis for their modeling disappears.

In fact, we are not the first ones to investigate into the computational modeling of creativity as a cognitive capacity. Going back already to work by Newell, Shaw and Simon [17], researchers in AI and related fields over the decades repeatedly have addressed different issues and aspects of creative thought. The results of these investigations range from contributions on the more conceptual side (as, e.g., Boden's theory of P- and H-creativity [4]), to concrete implementations of allegedly "creative systems" (as, e.g., The Painting Fool [7]). And also in the computational analogy-making domain there already is relevant work on the relation between creativity and analogy, most prominently exemplified by Hofstadter's contributions related to the Copycat system [11]. Still, on the one hand, work on issues of creativity within human-style intelligent systems this far has not gained wide attention in an AGI context. On the other hand, even within the more general setting of computational creativity research, only very few approaches try to integrate models of different cognitive capacities into a system aiming for general creativity capacities, instead of limiting the focus to modeling one specific kind of creative act.

This paper sketches the necessity to tackle the hard problem of creativity in AGI systems. Although the described HDTP framework has been applied to show that the computation of interesting blend spaces can be achieved in certain rather complex (but highly specific) domains, no generalizations of such specific examples exist so far. This remains a task for future work, besides a further formally sound and complete characterization of concept blending on a syntactic and semantic level.

References

[1] Abdel-Fattah, A., Besold, T.R., Gust, H., Krumnack, U., Schmidt, M., Kühnberger, K.-U., Wang, P.: Rationality-Guided AGI as Cognitive Systems. In: Proc. of the 34th Annual Meeting of the Cognitive Science Society (2012)

[2] Alexander, J.: Blending in Mathematics. Semiotica 2011(187), 1–48 (2011)

[3] Argand, J.-R.: Philosophie mathématique. Essay sur une manière de représenter les quantités imaginaires, dans les constructions géométriques. Annales de Mathématiques Pures et Appliquées 4, 133–146 (1813)

[4] Boden, M.: The Creative Mind: Myths and Mechanisms. Taylor & Francis (2003)

[5] Burki, L., Cavallucci, D.: Measuring the Results of Creative Acts in R&D: Literature Review and Perspectives. In: Cavallucci, D., De Guio, R., Cascini, G. (eds.) CAI 2011. IFIP AICT, vol. 355, pp. 163–177. Springer, Heidelberg (2011)

[6] Chomsky, N.: Syntactic structure. Mouton, The Hague (1957)

[7] Colton, S.: The painting fool in new dimensions. In: Show, Tell (eds.) Proceedings of the 2nd International Conference on Computational Creativity (2011)

[8] Fauconnier, G., Turner, M.: The Way We Think: Conceptual Blending and the Mind's Hidden Complexities. Basic Books, New York (2002)

[9] Goguen, J.: Mathematical models of cognitive space and time. In: Andler, D., Ogawa, Y., Okada, M., Watanabe, S. (eds.) Reasoning and Cognition: Proc. of the Interdisciplinary Conference on Reasoning and Cognition, pp. 125–128. Keio University Press (2006)

[10] Guhe, M., Pease, A., Smaill, A., Martínez, M., Schmidt, M., Gust, H., Kühnberger, K.-U., Krumnack, U.: A computational account of conceptual blending in basic mathematics. Cognitive Systems Research 12(3-4), 249–265 (2011)

[11] Hofstadter, D.R.: The Copycat Project: An Experiment in Non Determinism and Creative Analogies. A.I. Mema. Massachusetts Institute of Technology, Artificial Intelligence Laboratory (1984)

[12] Hummel, J.E., Holyoak, K.J.: A symbolic-connectionist theory of relational inference and generalization. Psychological Review 110, 220–264 (2003)

[13] Kokinov, B., Petrov, A.: Integration of memory and reasoning in analogy-making: The ambr model. In: Gentner, D., Holyoak, K., Kokinov, B. (eds.) The Analogical Mind: Perspectives from Cognitive Science. MIT Press, Cambridge (2001)

[14] Krumnack, U., Schwering, A., Gust, H., Kühnberger, K.-U.: Restricted Higher-Order Anti-Unification for Analogy Making. In: Orgun, M.A., Thornton, J. (eds.) AI 2007. LNCS (LNAI), vol. 4830, pp. 273–282. Springer, Heidelberg (2007)

[15] Lakoff, G., Núñez, R.: Where Mathematics Comes From: How the Embodied Mind Brings Mathematics into Being. Basic Books, New York (2000)

[16] Martinez, M., Besold, T.R., Abdel-Fattah, A., Kühnberger, K.-U., Gust, H., Schmidt, M., Krumnack, U.: Towards a domain-independent computational framework for theory blending. In: AAAI Technical Report of the AAAI Fall 2011 Symposium on Advances in Cognitive Systems, pp. 210–217 (2011)

[17] Newell, A., Shaw, J., Simon, H.: The process of creative thinking. In: Gruber, H., Terrell, G., Wertheimer, M. (eds.) Contemporary Approaches to Creative Thinking, Atherton, New York, pp. 63–119 (1963)

[18] Pereira, F.C., Cardoso, A.: Optimality principles for conceptual blending: A first computational approach. AISB Journal 1 (2003)

[19] Pereira, F.C.: Creativity and AI: A Conceptual Blending Approach. Applications of Cognitive Linguistics (ACL). Mouton de Gruyter, Berlin (2007)

[20] Schwering, A., Krumnack, U., Kühnberger, K.-U., Gust, H.: Syntactic principles of heuristic-driven theory projection. Cognitive Systems Research 10(3), 251–269 (2009)

[21] Schwering, A., Kühnberger, K.-U., Krumnack, U., Gust, H., Wandmacher, T.: A computational model for visual metaphors. Interpreting creative visual advertisements. In: Indurkhya, B., Ojha, A. (eds.) Proceedings of International Conference on Agents and Artificial Intelligence, ICAART 2009 (2009)

[22] Veale, T., O'Donoghue, D.: Computation and Blending. Computational Linguistics 11(3-4), 253–282 (2000); Special Issue on Conceptual Blending

[23] Wallas, G.: The art of thought. C.A. Watts & Co. Ltd., London (1926)

MicroPsi 2: The Next Generation
of the MicroPsi Framework

Joscha Bach

Berlin School of Mind and Brain, Humboldt University of Berlin
Unter den Linden 6, 10199 Berlin, Germany
joscha.bach@hu-berlin.de

Abstract. The cognitive architecture MicroPsi builds on a framework for simulating agents as neuro-symbolic spreading activation networks. These agents are
situated in a simulation environment or fitted with robotic bodies. The current
implementation of MicroPsi has been re-implemented from the ground up and
is described here.

Keywords: MicroPsi Framework, Cognitive Architecture, Psi Theory.

1 Introduction

MicroPsi (Bach 2003) is a cognitive architecture with a focus on grounded representations, cognitive modulation and motivation. MicroPsi agents are autonomous systems
that combine associative learning, reinforcement learning and planning to acquire
knowledge about their environment and navigate it in the pursuit of resources. Micro-
Psi is also being used to model the emergence of affects and higher level emotions
(Bach 2012a), and to model human performance and personality properties in the
context of problem solving (Bach 2012b). The architecture extends concepts of Dietrich Dörner's Psi theory, and is thus rooted in a psychological theory of motivation
and complex problem solving (Dörner 1999, Dörner et al. 2002). The principles and
concepts of MicroPsi are described in detail in the book *"Principles of Synthetic Intelligence"* (Bach 2009) and subsequent publications (Bach 2011) and are not discussed
here. Instead, we will focus on the *MicroPsi framework*, i.e., the simulation and design framework that allows the construction and execution of our family of cognitive
models.

Unlike many other cognitive architecture frameworks that define agents in the
form of code (either in a domain specific language, as a set of rules and representational items), MicroPsi uses graphical definitions for its agents, and a graphical editor
as the primary interface. In this respect, it is for instance similar to COGENT (Cooper
and Fox 1998). While rule-based representations and (hyper-)graphical representations are computationally equivalent, the graphical paradigm highlights weighted
associations, allows to visualize conceptual hierarchies, activation spreading, perceptual schemata and parallelism.

The first implementation of the MicroPsi framework spanned the years 2003 to
2009, and was built in Java as a set of plugins for the Eclipse IDE. The graphical editor was built on SWT. It comprised about 60000 lines of code, and although a lot of
effort went towards platform independence (with the exception of a DirectX/.Net

J. Bach, B. Goertzel, and M. Iklé (Eds.): AGI 2012, LNAI 7716, pp. 11–20, 2012.

based 3D viewer component), deployment on the various operating systems and across several versions of Eclipse became support intensive, especially after its adoption by teams outside of our group.

Gradual changes in the formalization of MicroPsi and the emergence of new software development methodologies and tool chains, especially the move from Java design patterns and XML tools towards lightweight and agile Python code, prompted a complete rewrite of the MicroPsi framework, starting in 2011. The following section describes the overall structure of the framework, followed by detailed definitions of the node net formalism and the structure of simulation worlds that enable running MicroPsi agents.

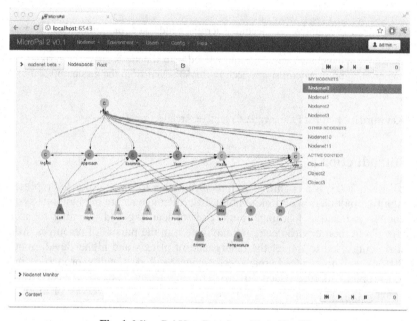

Fig. 1. MicroPsi User Interface, Node Net View

2   The MicroPsi 2 Framework

MicroPsi 2 is being written in Python, with a minimum of external dependencies, to make installation as simple as possible. Instead of a standard GUI, we decided to render the user interface in a web browser, and to deploy the MicroPsi agent simulation as a *web application* (figure 1). The MicroPsi server acts as a (local or remote) Web server that delivers UI components as HTML/Javascript, and facilitates the communication between the browser based renderer and the agent simulator via *JSON* and *JSON remote procedure calls*. Rendering is supported by Twitter's widget library *Bootstrap* (2012) and the Javascript library *PaperJS* (Lehni and Puckey, 2011).

This design choice makes it possible to remote control a MicroPsi simulation server from a different machine, and even to use the MicroPsi runtime without any local installation at all, as long as customization is not desired.

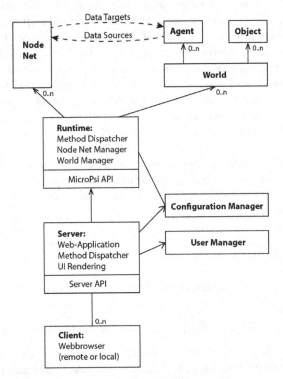

Fig. 2. Components of MicroPsi 2 Framework

MicroPsi consists of a server (the web application), a runtime component, a set of node nets, a set of simulation worlds, a user manager and a configuration manager (figure 2). The server is built on the micro web framework *Bottle* (Hellkamp 2011) and communicates with all current users via their web browsers through the *Server API*. User sessions and access rights are handled by the user manager component.

On startup, the server invokes the runtime component, which interfaces to the server with the *MicroPsi API*. The runtime is designed to work independently of the server and does not need to be deployed as a web application (command line interaction or OS based user interfaces are possible as well).

The runtime supplies a manager for *MicroPsi node nets* (see section 4), and a manager for simulation worlds (or interfaces to outside environments, such as robotic bodies, remote data providers, etc.). Standard simulation worlds (section 6) provide agents (node net embodiments) and objects as situated state machines.

3   MicroPsi Agents

MicroPsi interprets cognitive models as agents, situated in dynamic environments. MicroPsi agents are entirely defined as hierarchical *spreading activation networks* (SAN), which—for lack of a better name—are called *node nets*. Node nets are the brains of these agents—or rather, an abstraction of the information processing provided by brains, and the environment provides a body and stuff to interact with.

The body manifests itself as a set of data sources (which can be thought of as the terminals of sensory neurons) and data targets (the abstracted equivalent of motor neurons). By reading activation values from data sources, and sending activation into data targets, the MicroPsi agent may control its body and interact with its world.

MicroPsi's node nets can be interpreted as neural networks and afford neural learning paradigms. For the purposes of information storage and retrieval, they can be seen as semantic networks with a small set of typed links to express associative, partonomic, taxonomic and causal relationships.

Since the nodes can also encapsulate state machines and arbitrary operations over the node net, they can also be understood as components of a concurrent, modularized architecture, with activation spreading as the primary means of communication between the modules.

4   Definition of Node Nets

This section gives an overview over the definition of MicroPsi node nets.

$NodeNet \equiv$
$\langle States: \{s\}, s_0, f^{net}, NodeTypes: \{nt\}, DataSources: \{ds\}, DataTargets: \{dt\}\rangle$

A node net is characterized by a set of states, a starting state s_0, a network function $f^{net}: s_t \times DataSources \rightarrow s_{t+1} \times DataTargets$ that determines how to advance to the next state, and set of *node types*. Data sources and data targets provide a connection to the environment; a data source represents a value that is determined by an environmental state, while the values of data targets can be changed to effect something in the environment.

$$s \equiv \langle Nodes: \{u\}, Links: \{l\}, NodeSpaces: \{ns\}, t\rangle$$

The state of a node net is given by a set of *nodes*, or *units*, a set of directed *links*, a set of *node spaces* and the current simulation step t. Each node is part of exactly one node space. The primary role of node spaces is to provide some additional structure to node nets, similar to folders in a file system.

Node spaces form a tree—thus, each node space, with the exception of the root node space, has exactly one parent node space.

$$ns \equiv \langle \begin{matrix} parent \in NodeSpaces \cup \emptyset, \\ SlotTypes: \{st\}, GateTypes: \{gt\}, \\ Activators: \{act\}, Associators: \{assoc\}, \\ decay, \theta^{decay} \end{matrix} \rangle$$

Node spaces do not only provide some additional structure to node nets, they may also limit the spreading of activation via node space specific *Activators*, control how connections between nodes are strengthened based on *Associators*, or how they are weakened over time using a *decay* parameter. (More on these things below.)

$$u \equiv \langle id, parent \in NodeSpaces, nt, params^u, Gates, Slots \rangle$$

Each node is characterized by its identifier *id*, its type *nt*, an optional set of parameters *params^u* (which can make the node stateful), a set of gates and a set of slots. Gates are outlets for activation, while slots are inlets.

$$nt \equiv \langle GateTypes: [gt], SlotTypes: [st], f^u \rangle$$

The types of slots and gates of a node are defined within the node type, next to additional functionality f^u performed by the node whenever it becomes active. In most cases, f^u is limited to transmitting activation within the node, from the standard slot 'gen' to the gates.

$$f^u_{default} \equiv \text{for each } gate \in Gates_u: \alpha_{gate} = \alpha_{slot\, gen_u}$$

Nodes can store additional parameters and change them in the course of the node function, which makes them state machines:

$$f^u: \{\alpha_{Slots_{u,t}}\} \times params_{S_{u,t}} \to \{\alpha_{Gates_{u},t+1}\} \times params_{S_{u,t+1}}$$

More generally, some nodes may contain arbitrary functions, such as the creation of new nodes and links, procedures for neural learning, planning modules etc. These functions take the form of a program in a native programming language (here, *Python*), and hence, such nodes are also called *native modules*.

$$f^u_{native}: Nodes_t \times Links_t \times NodeSpaces_t \to$$
$$Nodes_{t+1} \times Links_{t+1} \times NodeSpaces_{t+1}$$

The nodes form a directed graph, with links connecting their gates to slots.

$$l \equiv \langle gate \in Gates_{origin \in Nodes}, slot \in Slots_{target \in Nodes}, \omega, c \rangle$$

A link is characterized by the gate of origin, the slot of the target node, a weight ω and a confidence parameter *c*. Usually, $-1 \le \omega \le 1$ and $0 \le c \le 1$.

$$gate \equiv \langle gt, \alpha, out, params^{gate}, min, max, f^{out} \rangle$$

A gate is determined by its gate type *gt*, an activation α, an output activation *out* (which is transmitted via the links originating at that gate), a minium and a maximum value, and the output function f^{out}.

$$gt \equiv \langle id, f^{gate}, nt \rangle$$

$$f^{gate}: \alpha_{gate} \times params_{gate} \to \alpha'_{gate}$$
$$f^{out}: \alpha'_{gate} \times \alpha_{act:gt_{gate}, ns_{u:gate}, t} \to out_{gate}$$

Together with the gate function f^{gate}, which is supplied by the type *gt* of the gate, the output function specifies how to calculate the output activation.

$$f^{gate}_{default} \equiv \begin{cases} \alpha_{gate}, \text{if } \alpha_{gate} > \theta_{gate} \\ \quad\quad 0, \text{else} \end{cases}$$

The default gate function assumes a threshold parameter θ and sets the activation to zero, if it is below this threshold. This turns the node into a simple threshold element. The reason that the gate calculations are split in two separate functions is customization: gate functions may be sigmoidal, to enable back-propagation learning, or bell-shaped, to build radial basis function networks, etc.

$$f^{out} \equiv \alpha_{gate} \; act_{gt_{gate},ns_{u:gate}}\Big]_{min_{gate}}^{max_{gate}}$$

After the application of the gate function, the output function may control the spread of activation through a gate by multiplying the gate's activation with the value of the *activator act* that corresponds to the type of the gate (and is defined and adjusted on the level of the node space that contains the node).

Next to gates, nodes feature *slots*.

$$slot \equiv \langle st, \alpha \rangle$$
$$st \equiv \langle id, f^{slot}, nt \rangle$$

Slots are characterized by their type st and their activation α. While nodes may have multiple slots to receive activation, most offer just one (of type 'gen'). The activation of a slot is determined by the slot function f^{slot}, which sums up the incoming activation.

$$f^{slot} \equiv \{(\omega, c)_{Links_{slot}}\} \times \{out_{gate_{Links:slot}}\} \to \alpha_{slot}$$
$$f^{slot}_{default} \equiv \sum_{l \in Links_{slot}} \omega_l out_{gate_l}$$

Again, alternate slot functions can be defined (for instance, a squared average or a maximum function), and are stored or changed on the level of the node space that contains the respective node.

The slot functions provide the transmission of activation between nodes, along links. The changes in strength of these links are influenced by the associator functions and decay functions, which act on the weights of all links originating in a given node space.

$$f^{assoc} \equiv \omega_{gate^i_{u_1}, slot^j_{u_2}, t+1} = \left(\sqrt{\omega_{gate^i_{u_1}, slot^j_{u_2}, t}} + assoc_{ns_{u_1}} \alpha_{gate^i_{u_1}} \alpha_{slot^j_{u_2}} \right)^2$$

The association between two nodes is strengthened based on the activation of the respective slots and gates the link connects, and the activity of the association factor *assoc* of the respective node space.

$$f^{decay} \equiv$$
$$\omega_{gate^i_{u_1}, slot^j_{u_2}, t+1} = \begin{cases} \sqrt{max\left(0, \omega^2_{gate^i_{u_1}, slot^j_{u_2}, t} - decay_{ns_{u_1}}\right)}, & \text{if } \omega < \theta^{decay}_{ns_{u_1}} \\ \omega_{gate^i_{u_1}, slot^j_{u_2}, t}, & \text{else} \end{cases}$$

If the decay factor of the respective node space has a value between 0 and 1, and the weight of the link is below the decay threshold θ^{decay}, the link is weakened in every simulation step. This provides a way of 'forgetting' unused connections. The decay threshold ensures that very strong connections are never forgotten.

In each simulation step, the network function f^{net} successively calls all slot functions f^{slot}, the node functions f^u and gate functions $f^{gate}; f^{out}$ of all active nodes, and the associator functions f^{assoc} and decay functions f^{decay} for all links.

5   Basic Node Types

The most primitive node type is a *Register*. It provides a single slot and a single gate of type gen and acts as a threshold element.

$$Register \equiv \langle GateTypes = [gen], SlotTypes = [gen], f^u = f^u_{default} \rangle$$

The basic conceptual element, analogous to Dietrich Dörner's Psi theory, is the *Quad*. It makes use of a single 'gen' slot and the four directional gates 'por', 'ret', 'sub', 'sur'. 'Por' encodes succession, 'ret' predecession, 'sub' a *part-of* relationship, and 'sur' stands for *has-part*. With the 'gen' gate, associative relationships can be expressed.

$$Quad \equiv \langle \begin{array}{c} GateTypes = [gen, por, ret, sub, sur], \\ SlotTypes = [gen], f^u = f^u_{default} \end{array} \rangle$$

Concept nodes extend quads by the gates 'cat' (for *is-a* relations), and 'exp' (for their inverse), as well as 'sym' and its inverse 'ref' for symbolic labeling. Concept nodes may be used to express taxonomies.

$$Concept \equiv \langle \begin{array}{c} GateTypes = [gen, por, ret, sub, sur, cat, exp, sym, ref], \\ SlotTypes = [gen], f^u = f^u_{default} \end{array} \rangle$$

The connection to the environment is provided by sensor nodes, which have no slots and only a single gate, which receives its activation from the associated data source. The sensor type is given as a node parameter.

$$Sensor \equiv \langle GateTypes = [gen], SlotTypes = \emptyset, f^{node}: \alpha_{gate\ gen} = ds_{sensorType} \rangle$$

Likewise, actor nodes influence the environment by writing the activation received through their single 'gen' slot into a data target. The actor type is given as a node parameter.

$$Actor \equiv \langle GateTypes = \emptyset, SlotTypes = [gen], f^{node}: dt_{actorType} = \alpha_{slot\ gen} \rangle$$

Activator nodes are special actors. Instead of a data source, they target the activator *act* corresponding to the activator type *actType* (given as a node parameter) of their node space. Thus, activator nodes may be used to restrict the spreading of activation to certain link types.

$$Activator \equiv \langle \begin{array}{c} GateTypes = \emptyset, SlotTypes = [gen], \\ f^u: \alpha_{act_{actType}, ns_{activator}} = \alpha_{slot\ gen} \end{array} \rangle$$

Associator nodes work just like activators, but target the association factor *assoc* of their node space.

$$Associator \equiv \langle_{f^u: \alpha_{assoc_{assocType},ns_{associator}} = \alpha_{slot\,gen}}^{GateTypes = \emptyset, SlotTypes = [gen],} \rangle$$

6   Environment

Within the MicroPsi framework, agents may be embedded into an environment (*world*). The environment must provide a *world adapter wa* for each MicroPsi agent. The world adapter offers *data sources*, from which the agent's node net may read environmental information, and *data targets*, which allow the agent to effect changes in the world. Since the environment only has write access to data sources, and read access to data targets, node net and environment may be updated asynchronously.

The world adapter may interface a local multi-agent simulation, a robotic body, a computer game client or simulation server, dynamically updated stock data, etc. Here, we give a simple simulation world as an example.

$$World \equiv \langle States: \{ws\}, ws_0, terrain, WorldAdapters: \{wa\}, f^{world} \rangle$$

$$wa \equiv \langle DataSources: \{ds\}, DataTargets: \{dt\} \rangle$$

The simulation is determined by its state, a set of fixed properties (*terrain*), a set of world adapters (which provide connections to agents and additional environments) and a function $f^{world}: ws_t \times terrain \times \{DataTargets\} \rightarrow ws_{t+1} \times \{DataSources\}$ that determines how to advance to the next state.

$$ws \equiv \langle Objects: \{obj\}, t_w \rangle$$

The state of the world consists of a set of objects and the time step of the simulation.

$$obj \equiv \langle pos, ObjectStates: \{os\}, f^{obj} \rangle$$

Objects have a position *pos* (for instance $\in \mathbb{R}^3$), a set of *object states os* and an object function, f^{obj} that determines how the position and states of the object change from one state to the next, based on the previous state, the states and positions of other objects and the terrain.

$$Agents: \{agent\} \subseteq Objects,$$
$$f^{obj}_{agent}: pos_{agent,t} \times ObjectStates_{agent,t} \times DataTargets_{wa:agent} \times$$
$$Objects_t \times terrain \rightarrow$$
$$pos_{agent,t+} \times ObjectStates_{agent,t+1} \times DataSources_{wa:agent}$$

Agents are objects in the world like any other, but each agent object corresponds to a world adapter, which links it to a node net. Think of the agent object as the body of the MicroPsi agent, and the object states as its physiological states. The object function of the agent f^{obj}_{agent} advances these physiological states, the position of the agent and the inputs to the node net.

In each simulation step, the world function calls all object functions, and takes care of the creation of new objects and the removal of obsolete ones.

7   Applications

Compared with the original implementation of MicroPsi, the current iteration of the framework is still fragmentary; at the time of writing, it supports only a simple generic simulation world for multi agent experiments (instead of the various simulation environments provided in MicroPsi 1). Also, 3D viewing components for environments and facial expressions are completely absent.

The current priority of MicroPsi 2 lies on affective simulation for problem solving experiments (see Bach 2012b), and its application as a general framework for knowledge representation in a hierarchical semantic network.

Acknowledgements. The development of this version of MicroPsi has been supported by a research stipend of the Berlin School of Mind and Brain, and development efforts funded by the Hotheaven AG, Berlin.

References

1. Bach, J.: The MicroPsi Agent Architecture. In: Proceedings of ICCM-5, International Conference on Cognitive Modeling, Bamberg, Germany, pp. 15–20 (2003)
2. Bach, J., Vuine, R.: Designing Agents with MicroPsi Node Nets. In: Günter, A., Kruse, R., Neumann, B. (eds.) KI 2003. LNCS (LNAI), vol. 2821, pp. 164–178. Springer, Heidelberg (2003)
3. Bach, J.: MicroPsi: A cognitive modeling toolkit coming of age. In: Proc. of 7th International Conference on Cognitive Modeling, pp. 20–25 (2006)
4. Bach, J.: Motivated, Emotional Agents in the MicroPsi Framework. In: Proceedings of 8th European Conference on Cognitive Science, Delphi, Greece, pp. 458–461 (2007)
5. Bach, J.: Motivated, Emotional Agents in the MicroPsi Framework. In: Proceedings of 8th European Conference on Cognitive Science, Delphi, Greece (2007)
6. Bach, J.: Principles of Synthetic Intelligence. Psi, an architecture of motivated cognition. Oxford University Press (2009)
7. Bach, J.: A Motivational System for Cognitive AI. In: Schmidhuber, J., Thórisson, K.R., Looks, M. (eds.) AGI 2011. LNCS, vol. 6830, pp. 232–242. Springer, Heidelberg (2011)
8. Bach, J.: A Framework for Emergent Emotions, Based on Motivation and Cognitive Modulators. International Journal of Synthetic Emotions (IJSE) 3(1), 43–63 (2012a)
9. Bach, J.: Functional Modeling of Personality Properties Based on Motivational Traits. In: Proceedings of ICCM-7, International Conference on Cognitive Modeling, Berlin, Germany, pp. 271–272 (2012b)
10. Cooper, R., Fox, J.: COGENT: A visual design environment for cognitive modelling. Behavior Research Methods, Instruments and Computers 30, 553–564 (1998)
11. Dörner, D.: Bauplan für eine Seele. Rowohlt, Reinbeck (1999)

12. Dörner, D., Bartl, C., Detje, F., Gerdes, J., Halcour, D.: Die Mechanik des Seelenwagens. Handlungsregulation. Verlag Hans Huber, Bern (2002)
13. Hellkamp, L.: The Bottle Web Framework (2011), `http://bottlepy.org` (last retrieved August 2012)
14. Lehni, J., Puckey, J.: The PaperJS Vector Graphics Library (2011), `http://paperjs.org` (last retrieved August 2012)
15. Twitter Inc. Twitter Bootstrap Library (2012), `http://twitter.github.com/bootstrap` (last retrieved August 2012)

An Extensible Language Interface
for Robot Manipulation

Jonathan Connell[1], Etienne Marcheret[1], Sharath Pankanti[1], Michiharu Kudoh[2],
and Risa Nishiyama[2]

[1] IBM T.J. Watson Research Center, 1101 Kitchawan Rd,
Yorktown Heights NY 10598, USA
{jconnell,etiennem,sharat}@us.ibm.com
[2] IBM Research - Tokyo, 5-6-52, Toyosu, Koutou-ku, Tokyo, 135-8511 Japan
{kudo,lisa}@jp.ibm.com

Abstract. This paper describes our Extensible Language Interface (ELI) for robots. The system is intended to interpret far-field speech commands in order to perform fetch-and-carry tasks, potentially for use in an eldercare context. By "extensible" we mean that the robot is able to learn new nouns and verbs by simple interaction with its user. An associated video [1] illustrates the range of phenomena handled by our implemented real-time system.

Keywords: robot, language, learning, eldercare.

1 Introduction

As argued in [2] with an eye toward Vygotsky, much of intelligence is actually illusory since the bulk of what we consider knowledge or competence is transmitted culturally. No one figures out how to cook macaroni and cheese by experimentation – some other person tells you how to do it. While part of the feeling of aliveness comes from the responsiveness of a creature with a reasonably deep perception of its environment, even humans from a different society can be successfully demonized as "sub-human" if you cannot understand what they say. If robots are ever to be perceived as sentient it seems crucial that they also be able to learn in this manner and thus partake of the rich prevailing culture which underpins much of "human-ness".

Language understanding and learning also has pragmatic value. For instance, a robot that could perform simple fetch-and-carry tasks would be a boon to eldercare. However the robot must be told what to do somehow. The current generation of senior citizens is not comfortable with tablets, keyboards, styli, PDAs, or Bluetooth headsets – these are just one more thing to drop or misplace. The most human-friendly interface is direct speech using an audio pickup on the robot itself. The trick then is interpreting the spoken commands robustly. In addition, a particular home may have locations, like the "solarium", or objects, like "my favorite cup", which cannot be known *a priori* and hence cannot be preprogrammed into the robot. Thus it would be convenient if the robot could just be shown such places and objects and learn whatever models it needed automatically. In addition there may be activities such as "tidy up the nightstand" that are specific to an individual. Again, being able to learn

J. Bach, B. Goertzel, and M. Iklé (Eds.): AGI 2012, LNAI 7716, pp. 21–30, 2012.

these things on the fly given verbal (and perhaps gestural) guidance would be a bene-fit. This is what we have endeavored to create: a speech guided mobile robot that can learn new nouns and new verbs based on user instruction. Fig. 1 shows a block dia-gram for our Extensible Language Interface (ELI) and the physical robot it controls. What we have built is essentially a service dog with more language and less slobber.

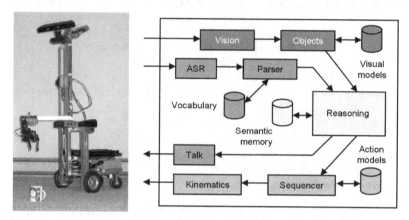

Fig. 1. Our robot can interpret spoken commands as well as learn new nouns and verbs. The experiments here were performed using the arm and camera from our large robot Eli (left) mounted on a table top in order to reduce the degrees of freedom to be controlled.

Of course this is not the first home robot or the first mobile manipulator. There is the impressive PR2 from Willow Garage [3] which can do things like fold towels (but slowly, and for $400K). HERB, developed at CMU [4] is also intended to perform household tasks, but currently requires environmental modifications for its vision system. Then there is El-E from Georgia Tech [5] that was specifically created to retrieve objects for disabled persons. However, none of these robots are designed around a speech interface – to change their actions you either completely change their programs or you configure options in a GUI. Other robot such as Carl [6] and Cosero [7] can take speech input, but require a handheld or headset mike. Furthermore, in general these robots are not intended to learn in the field from user interaction. Instead they have various preprogrammed competencies, object models, and environmental maps which are developed offline.

Other work has addressed language-based learning. Much of this, however, has started at a very low level. Steels [8] looks at the emergence of a private language between cooperating agents while Roy [9] attempts to directly associate acoustic fragments with visual fragments. What we believe is more useful is to stick with a human language and just attempt to find suitable bindings for a few unknown words. This is akin to the approach taken in HAM [10] for learning place names. Similarly, procedure learning is often attempted through trial-and-error experimentation [11] or using the impoverished feedback of reinforcement learning [12]. Yet explicit macro definitions or verbal scripting [13] is often faster and more effective in practice.

2   Multimodal Instructional Dialog

The goal for our system is for the user to describe a task, through a combination of speech and gesture (multi-modal), and then have the system successfully accomplish this task. If it is unsure about some aspect of the task, it should ask clarifying questions (dialog). In addition, we want the system to be able to learn about new objects and new procedures to enable a "verbal programming" facility (instruction). All these capabilities are described below and demonstrated in an associated video [1].

2.1   Robotic Substrate

Since our example tasks all concern objects on a table, it is important for the robot to detect objects. To do this it looks for "obvious" objects, as shown in Fig. 2. It starts by color enhancing the scene from its camera, then builds a model in terms of HSI bands that pass the bulk of the pixels (i.e. the table). The "holes" in this mask are then potential objects. A similar method is used with the depth camera on the large robot. However instead of modeling the table in terms of a dominant color, it is modeled as a 3D plane. Again, deviations from this model are potential objects. Once an image segmentation has been performed, the color(s), shape, size, and relative positions of the objects can be computed.

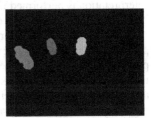

Fig. 2. The system uses a simplified object finding routine. The steps of this process are to take the input image (left) and enhance its color, find a uniform description for the majority of the area (middle), then identify isolated, non-table regions (right).

To actually grab an object, the 2D image coordinates must be turned into a 3D position for the arm. To do this we compute a homography based on 4 calibrated points that maps 2D image locations to 2D locations on the table surface. We then select an image point likely to be near the middle of the bottom of the object and apply this transform in order to find its x and y. A fixed z position of 1.5 inches above the table is specified to complete the grasp point. Next we solve for the inverse kinematics of the arm, then plot a linear endpoint trajectory from the current position to a "via" point in front of the object such that the gripper is aimed toward the object at this location. A second short trajectory then leads from the via point to the grasp point to ensure a reasonable approach direction for the gripper.

Another important basic capability is understanding human gesture. Here (Fig. 3) we use background subtraction to find the user's moving hand. We track the most extreme point of the difference region (left) and, once it stops moving, generate a "click" on the image. Given the previously detected objects, we can map this to the most likely one (middle). Similar processing allows the robot to detect when a human hand has entered an object "transfer zone" (right). In such a case the robot either opens or closes its gripper. Once again, this same algorithm for hand detection can be applied even more easily and robustly to depth data.

Fig. 3. Gesture recognition is implemented by using background subtraction to track the user's hand. The most extremal portion of this mask (left) selects one of the objects previously identified (middle). User motion detection for object handoff (right) works in a similar manner.

2.2   Natural Language Interpretation

For speech recognition we use an Acoustic Magic VT2 far-field array microphone. Interpretation is performed using a semantic grammar with the Microsoft ASR Engine in Windows XP, although we have also successfully used the IBM Attila engine [14].

An example semantic grammar is shown in Fig. 4. Here there are a number of rules prefixed by "=" that offer several valid expansions for each non-terminal. Elements in parenthesis are optional, whereas the asterisk denotes an unconstrained dictation of up to 5 words. In general, we assume that all expansions for "toplevel" start and end with a silence segment. To prevent spurious action when humans are talking to each other, we require the presence of an attention word (e.g. "Eli") at either the start or end of each such directive. After generating a valid parse, the resulting tree of expansions is mined to generate a simple slot-value representation for the utterance (top). To do this we take each capitalized non-terminal as a slot and assign it the value of whatever first level expansion was used. As can be seen in the example utterance, many of the surface words are simply discarded.

Using the visual object detection and characterization methods previously described, along with a more complex semantic grammar, the robot can grab objects specified by color, size, position, or gesture. It can also answer questions about objects that have been selected in this way. Fig. 5 provides a transcript of an experiment testing the robot's proficiency. One interesting aspect of this conversation is how the robot resolves pronouns through non-linguistic means. If there is only one object present, the binding for "it" is obvious. However if there are several objects, the robot will execute a dialog move to seek clarification. By contrast, if some particular object had recently been mentioned, the robot assumes that this is the proper grounding for the pronoun instead. Eli is also capable of executing a mixed mode dialog response, as when it suggests which of the two white objects the user might have wanted by pointing. Finally, the robot also knows the limits of its own abilities in terms of reach and grasping size. That is why, when directed to grasp the green object (the head of lettuce shown in Fig. 3), it demurs.

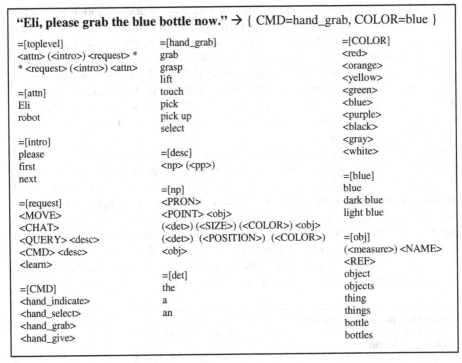

"Eli, please grab the blue bottle now." → { CMD=hand_grab, COLOR=blue }

=[toplevel]	=[hand_grab]	=[COLOR]
`<attn> (<intro>) <request> *`	grab	`<red>`
`* <request> (<intro>) <attn>`	grasp	`<orange>`
	lift	`<yellow>`
=[attn]	touch	`<green>`
Eli	pick	`<blue>`
robot	pick up	`<purple>`
	select	`<black>`
=[intro]		`<gray>`
please	=[desc]	`<white>`
first	`<np> (<pp>)`	
next		=[blue]
	=[np]	blue
=[request]	`<PRON>`	dark blue
`<MOVE>`	`<POINT> <obj>`	light blue
`<CHAT>`	`(<det>) (<SIZE>) (<COLOR>) <obj>`	
`<QUERY> <desc>`	`(<det>) (<POSITION>) (<COLOR>)`	=[obj]
`<CMD> <desc>`	`<obj>`	`(<measure>) <NAME>`
`<learn>`		`<REF>`
	=[det]	object
=[CMD]	the	objects
`<hand_indicate>`	a	thing
`<hand_select>`	an	things
`<hand_grab>`		bottle
`<hand_give>`		bottles

Fig. 4. This is part of the grammar used for speech parsing. A full utterance is converted to a set of slots and values (top) based on the capitalized categories and their immediate children.

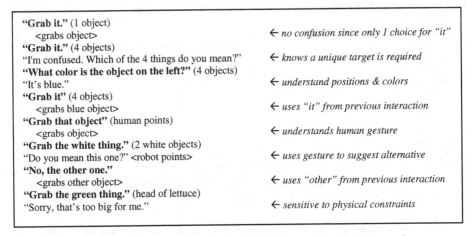

"Grab it." (1 object)
    <grabs object>   ← *no confusion since only 1 choice for "it"*
"Grab it." (4 objects)
"I'm confused. Which of the 4 things do you mean?"   ← *knows a unique target is required*
"What color is the object on the left?" (4 objects)
"It's blue."   ← *understand positions & colors*
"Grab it" (4 objects)
    <grabs blue object>   ← *uses "it" from previous interaction*
"Grab that object" (human points)
    <grabs object>   ← *understands human gesture*
"Grab the white thing." (2 white objects)
"Do you mean this one?" <robot points>   ← *uses gesture to suggest alternative*
"No, the other one."
    <grabs other object>   ← *uses "other" from previous interaction*
"Grab the green thing." (head of lettuce)
"Sorry, that's too big for me."   ← *sensitive to physical constraints*

Fig. 5. As this transcript of one of the video demos [1] shows, the robot can resolve pronouns based on context, understand gestures, and request clarification when needed.

2.3   Visual Object Naming

While colors, sizes, positions, and pointing can be used to draw attention to specific objects, in some cases it is more convenient to give objects names. One can then simply say "Give me the WD-40" and have the robot figure out which object this is. Of course to do this, the robot must know that "WD-40" is a valid object. It must also know what the object looks like in order to find it. To teach the robot new nouns like this, we use a simple speech pattern: "NP is called X". Here the NP is any valid noun phrase in the grammar, such as "The big bottle" or "That thing" (with pointing). The X is then either drawn from a list of likely (but unknown) object words, or is an unconstrained dictation item.

When the user names an object, the first thing that happens is that a visual model of the object is built. This consists of a coarse size and shape description, plus a histogram of semantic color features (e.g. 50% blue, 30% yellow, 20% red). For our small universe of objects on a table, this is sufficient to find similar objects. If the same name is taught multiple times, the system will learn multiple models for the object. This nearest-neighbor classifier adds robustness since the appearance of objects often varies from side to side, or from different vantage points. Note, that although an object can be described verbally with enough specificity to select it from among other items, when the robot actually experiences an object it can build a much richer model.

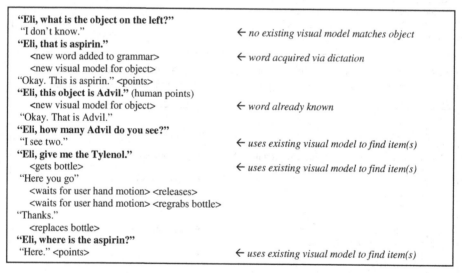

Fig. 6. As this transcript of one of the video demos [1] shows, the robot can be taught new nouns by simply showing it objects. The new visual model can then be used in various ways.

The second step in learning is to add the declared name to the <NAMES> category in the grammar. This is kept distinct from generic nouns like "object" because items in the <NAMES> class usually have one or more visual models associated with them. An interesting problem we have run into is that the dictation results are not always reliable. For instance, when the user says "aspirin" the system sometimes hears "offering". For a speech-only system this is fine since a name is just a random acoustic label. If the robot hears "Pick up the offering" it will perform the correct action. In fact, humans managed to exist for thousands of years with just such cues, having no written language or fixed orthography. However when trying to look up properties of an object elsewhere (as in the next section), the correct term "aspirin" yields much more relevant information.

Fig. 6 gives the transcript from an experiment in which the robot's learning of new nouns was tested. As can be seen, objects can be indicated either verbally or by pointing. The robot can then use its learned models to find things, count them, and name them when requested.

2.4   Semantic Web Access

Many useful functions can be performed by an eldercare robot with just the perceptual and manipulation capabilities already described. However, we can also provide smarter guidance about proposed actions using external data. At our Tokyo lab we built a remote consultation agent called Brainy Robot And Intelligence Networked System (BRAINS) that has access to richer semantic information, largely based on the names (types) of objects. Every time the robot interprets a local utterance, it forms a potential action plan and transmits this (via TCP/IP socket) to BRAINS for vetting. A sample of the communication is shown in Fig. 7. The robot generates semantic network triples describing the proposed action, then BRAINS can either accept or veto the action, or counter-propose some other action.

"Now hand me some aspirin"

```
robot: act-7 --instance-of--> give
robot: act-7 --status--> proposed
robot: act-7 --target--> obj-3
robot: obj-3 --status--> visible
robot: obj-3 --instance-of--> aspirin
robot: *over*
   BRAINS: act-7 --status--> vetoed
   BRAINS: act-8 --instance-of--> say
   BRAINS: act-8 --status--> allowed
   BRAINS: act-8 --message--> "But that will hurt your stomach."
   BRAINS: *over*
robot: act-8 --status--> completed
robot: *over*
   BRAINS: *over*
```

Fig. 7. The robot communicates with the BRAINS system using semantic network triples

Fig. 8 shows the transcript of an experiment with BRAINS in the loop. In one case, it consults a database for the user and discovers an aspirin intolerance and thus vetoes dispensing it. Tylenol (paracetamol) does not raise such concerns, hence BRAINS allows this action to be performed. However we also maintain a personal history (LifeLog) for the user and record when Tylenol was given. Thus, when in the last interaction the user again requests Tylenol (perhaps because of memory loss or simply impatience), BRAINS vetoes the action because sufficient time has not elapsed between doses. The other interaction demonstrated here makes use of a taxonomy built for IBM's Jeopardy! project [15]. The user requests a medication (Rolaids) which is not only unknown, but not present on the table. Yet by using the taxonomy and information about the scene, BRAINS can suggest a similar item that is present.

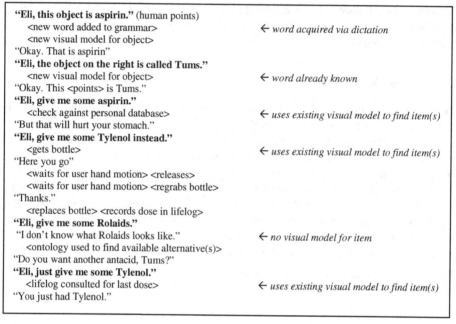

Fig. 8. As this transcript of one of the video demos [1] shows, the backed system can look up personal information, reason about substitutions, and monitor events over time.

2.5   Verbal Procedure Learning

Not only can Eli learn new nouns, he can also learn verbs. Fig. 9 shows the transcript from an experimental run where the robot is being taught to poke things. The user teaches the action as a series of steps, like a verbal scripting language, as opposed to imparting some declarative specification of a desired result state. The steps themselves are indexical (as needed) so that, when they are composed, the whole sequence is also indexical. In other words, since the "point" action requires a focus object, the resulting "poke" action does also. As the later part of the transcript indicates, once an action has been learned it can be directly applied to other objects in the scene.

Fig. 10 shows the part of the grammar associated with the verb acquisition process. Learning is initiated either by the user requesting an unknown action, or by explicitly saying "I'm going to teach you how to X". If a word is specified for X, it is added to the grammar and becomes the label for the new action. Once the learning mode is entered, the robot records each successive action request made by the user. Learning is terminated by a phrase such as "That's how you do it". At this point the sequence of parameterized actions is recorded and associated with the X term (possibly from the termination phrase) to give a new action primitive. This "macro" sequence is now invoked when the label X is used as a verb. And, since the user can call for it directly, it can also be included as a step in some other more complicated learned procedure.

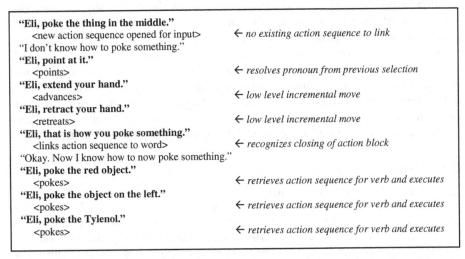

"Eli, poke the thing in the middle."
    <new action sequence opened for input>   ← *no existing action sequence to link*
"I don't know how to poke something."
"Eli, point at it."
    <points>   ← *resolves pronoun from previous selection*
"Eli, extend your hand."
    <advances>   ← *low level incremental move*
"Eli, retract your hand."
    <retreats>   ← *low level incremental move*
"Eli, that is how you poke something."
    <links action sequence to word>   ← *recognizes closing of action block*
"Okay. Now I know how to now poke something."
"Eli, poke the red object."
    <pokes>   ← *retrieves action sequence for verb and executes*
"Eli, poke the object on the left."
    <pokes>   ← *retrieves action sequence for verb and executes*
"Eli, poke the Tylenol."
    <pokes>   ← *retrieves action sequence for verb and executes*

Fig. 9. As this transcript of one of the video demos [1] shows, the robot can be taught a new verb by simply walking it through the appropriate steps

```
=[learn]                        =[FINISH]
<NEW-ACT> do something          that's how you
<NEW-ACT> <ACT-0>               that is how you
<NEW-ACT> <ACT-1> <arg>
<FINISH> do it                  =[vp]
<FINISH> <ACT-0>                do it
<FINISH> <ACT-1> <arg>
                                =[arg]
=[NEW-ACT]                      something
<teach> <demo> you how to       an object
                                <desc>
=[teach]
I'm going to                    =[ACT-0]
I am going to                   wave
let me
                                =[ACT-1]
=[demo]                         poke
show                            nudge
tell
teach
```

"poke"

point	1.0
out	1.0
out	-1.0

Fig. 10. Here is a fragment of the grammar (left) the robot uses to learn how to "poke" something (upper right). The result is a parameterized sequence of actions (lower right).

3   Conclusion

We have described how Eli, our speech-based robot manipulator, selects and moves objects around on a table. We explained how the language parsing works, how objects are found, and how human gestures are detected. The robot is also able to answer questions about the scene in front of it and resolve ambiguities in any commands it receives. In addition it can be taught the names of objects and use these labels to access information in remote databases. Finally, it is also possible to "program" the robot by teaching it new named action sequences. The operation of the system and these components was illustrated via transcripts from a series of video experiments [1] with the actual robot. Although our language interpreter is built with conventional technologies, consider a Turing machine by analogy. At its heart there is an FSM which, in itself, is not so interesting. Yet having something like this allows the creature to manipulate the "tape" of culture and thus greatly expand its capabilities.

References

1. Connell, J.: Eli Arm Demos (video) (2012),
   http://www.johuco.com/eli_arm_demos.wmv
2. Connell, J.: Fusing Animals and Humans. In: Proc. AGI 2008, pp. 389–393 (2008)
3. Chitta, S., Jones, E., Ciocarlie, M., Hsiao, K.: Perception, Planning, and Execution for Mobile Manipulation in Unstructured Environments. IEEE Robotics and Automation Magazine 19(2), 58–71 (2012)
4. Srinivasa, S., et al.: HERB: A Home Exploring Robotic Butler. Autonomous Robots 28(1), 5–20 (2010)
5. Choi, Y., et al.: Hand It Over or Set It Down: A User Study of Object Delivery with an Assistive Mobile Manipulator. In: IEEE Int. Symp. on Robot and Human Interactive Communication (RO-MAN), pp. 736–743 (2009)
6. Seabra Lopes, L., Teixeira, A.: Human-Robot Interaction through Spoken Language Dialogue. In: IEEE Int. Conf. on Intelligent Robots and Systems (IROS), pp. 528–534 (2000)
7. Stuckler, J., Holz, D., Behnke, S.: Demonstrating Everyday Manipulation Skills in RoboCup@Home. IEEE Robotics and Automation Magazine, 34–42 (June 2012)
8. Steels, L.: The origins of syntax in visually grounded robotic agents. Artificial Intelligence 103, 133–156 (1998)
9. Roy, D.: Grounded Spoken Language Acquisition: Experiments in Word Learning. IEEE Trans. on Multimedia 5(2), 197–209 (2003)
10. Peltason, J., et al.: Mixed-Initiative in Human Augmented Mapping. In: IEEE Int. Conf. on Robotics and Automation (ICRA), pp. 2146–2153 (2009)
11. Siskind, J.: Grounding the Lexical Semantics of Verbs in Visual Perception using Force Dynamics and Event Logic. J. of Artificial Intelligence Research 15, 31–90 (2001)
12. Breazeal, C., et al.: Using perspective taking to learn from ambiguous demonstrations. Robotics and Autonomous Systems 54, 385–393 (2006)
13. Connell, J.: Beer on the Brain. In: Proc. of AAAI Spring Symposium – My Dinner with R2D2: Natural Dialogues with Practical Robotics Devices, pp. 25–26 (March 2000)
14. Soltau, H., Saon, G., Kingsbury, B.: The IBM Attila Speech Recognition Toolkit. In: IEEE Spoken Language Technology Workshop (SLT), pp. 97–102 (2010)
15. Murdock, J., et al.: Typing candidate answers using type coercion. IBM J. of Res. and Dev. 56(3/4), 7:1–7:13 (2012)

Noisy Reasoners: Errors of Judgement in Humans and AIs

Fintan Costello

School of Computer Science and Informatics,
University College Dublin,
Belfield, Dublin 4, Ireland
fintan.costello@ucd.ie

Abstract. This paper examines reasoning under uncertainty in the case where the AI reasoning mechanism is itself subject to random error or noise in its own processes. The main result is a demonstration that systematic, directed biases naturally arise if there is random noise in a reasoning process that follows the normative rules of probability theory. A number of reliable errors in human reasoning under uncertainty can be explained as the consequence of these systematic biases due to noise. Since AI systems are subject to noise, we should expect to see the same biases and errors in AI reasoning systems based on probability theory.

1 Introduction

The ability to reason under uncertainty is fundamental to AI. In this paper I consider this type of reasoning in the case where the AI reasoning mechanism is itself subject to random error or noise in its own processes.

Many AI systems reason using the rules of probability theory, which are normatively correct and provably optimal in at least some situations. It may appear obvious that noise in the workings of a intelligent agent will result in nothing more than random variation around the correct response. This, however, is not the case. There are a number of ways in which random variation can produce systematic biases in reasoning, leading to reliable deviations from the normatively correct responses in particular situations; that is, to reliable errors in reasoning. My main aim in this paper is to present these systematic biases due to random variation.

In addition, I show that a number of reliable errors in human reasoning under uncertainty can be explained as the systematic effects of random variation or noise in a reasoning process that follows the normative rules of probability theory. I argue that, since AI systems (like everything else in the universe) are subject to noise, we should expect to see the same biases and errors in AI reasoning.

The organisation of the paper is as follows. In the first section I describe four well-established and systematic errors in human probabilistic reasoning: conservatism, subadditivity, the conjunction error, and the disjunction error. In the second section I describe how noise can cause systematic biases in a reasoning process that follows the equations of probability theory, and show

J. Bach, B. Goertzel, and M. Iklé (Eds.): AGI 2012, LNAI 7716, pp. 31–40, 2012.

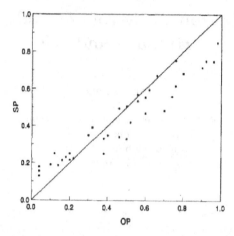

Fig. 1. Scatterplot showing probability estimates SP(subjective probabilities) versus objective, true probabilities (OP), from [3]. Probability estimates which agree with objective probabilities fall on the 45° line. For low objective probablities estimates fall above that line, while for high objective probabilities estimates fall below that line, demonstrating conservatism.

how these these systematic biases due to noise produce exactly the patterns of conservatism, subadditivity and the conjunction and disjunction errors seen in humans (as far as I am aware this is the first time a unified account has been given for these four distinct patterns of error). In the third section I present a modified expression for event probability can reduce some of these errors.

2   Biases and Errors in Human Probabilistic Reasoning

A very extensive literature exists demonstrating systematic biases and errors that people make in estimating probability. Here I review 4 of these: conservatism, subadditivity, the conjunction error, and the disjunction error. I take $P(A)$ to represent the objective, true probability of some event A, $P_E(A)$ to represent a reasoner's estimate of that probability as influenced by random noise in the reasoning process, and $\overline{P_E}(A)$ to represent the mean or expected value of $P_E(A)$ (the average estimate of the probability of event A).

2.1   Conservatism

Probabilities fall between 0 and 1 by definition. A large body of literature demonstrates that people tend to keep away from these extremes in their probability judgments, and so are 'conservative' in their probability assessments. These results show that the closer $P(A)$ is to 0, the more $\overline{P_E}(A)$ is greater than $P(A)$, while the closer $P(A)$ is to 1, the more $\overline{P_E}(A)$ is less than $P(A)$ [3]. Figure 2 shows this relationship for one set of data.

2.2   Subadditivity

A set of events is mutually exclusive if at most 1 member of that set can occur. A fundamental and obvious requirement of probability theory concerns mutually exclusive events. Let $A_1 \ldots A_n$ be a set of n mutually exclusive events, and let $A = A_1 \vee \ldots \vee A_n$ be the disjunction (the 'or') of those n events, so that A occurs if any of those n events occur. Then probability theory requires that

$$P(A_1) + \ldots + P(A_n) = P(A)$$

More specifically, if $A_1 \ldots A_n$ is a set of n mutually exclusive events that is *complete* - so that exactly 1 of those events is certain to occur - then probability theory requires that

$$P(A_1) + \ldots + P(A_n) = 1$$

Given the obvious nature of these requirements, it is surprising to find that people violate them reliably and systematically. However, experimental studies have shown that people do violate these requirements, and in a characteristic way. Results show that, for mutually exclusive events $A_1 \ldots A_n$

$$\overline{P_E}(A_1) + \ldots + \overline{P_E}(A_n) > \overline{P_E}(A)$$

holds, so that on average the sum of people's estimates for the probability of the constituent events of A is reliably greater than their estimate for the probablity of A) and that the difference

$$\overline{P_E}(A_1) + \ldots + \overline{P_E}(A_n) - \overline{P_E}(A)$$

increases reliably as n increases. Result also show that for mutually exclusive and complete events $A_1 \ldots A_n$

$$\overline{P_E}(A_1) + \ldots + \overline{P_E}(A_n) > 1$$

so that on average the sum of people's estimates for the probability of events $A_1 \ldots A_n$ is reliably greater than 1 with the difference increasing reliably as n increases. There is one reliable exception to this last pattern, which occurs for mutually exclusive and complete events in the specific case where $n = 2$. In this specific case we find

$$\overline{P_E}(A_1) + \overline{P_E}(A_2) = 1$$

holds, so that on average people's estimates for the probability of events A_1 and A_2 will sum to 1 as required by probability theory (see [7] for a review).

3   Conjunction Error

The above two biases concern averages of estimated probability values. The next two errors concern differences between people's probability estimates. Let A_1 and A_2 be any two events ordered so that $P(A_1) \leq P(A_2)$. Also let $A_1 \wedge A_2$ represent the conjunction of those two events, so that $A_1 \wedge A_2$ is true only when A_1 and A_2 both occur. Then

$$P(A_1 \wedge A_2) \leq P(A_1)$$

must always hold. This is an obvious and transparent requirement, following from the fact that $A_1 \wedge A_2$ can only occur if A_1 itself occurs. In most cases people follow this requirement when assessing conjunctive probability. People reliably violate this requirement for some events, giving estimates where

$$P_E(A_1 \wedge A_2) > P_E(A_1)$$

This 'conjunction error' does not occur for all or even most conjunctions (people correctly follow the rules of probability theory for most conjunctions). Numerous experimental studies have shown that the occurence of this error depends on the average estimated probability for A_1 and A_2. In particular, the greater the difference between $\overline{P_E}(A_1)$ and $\overline{P_E}(A_2)$, the more frequent the conjunction error is, and the greater the estimated conditional probability $\overline{P_E}(A_1|A_2)$, the more frequent the conjunction error is. The frequency of the error can be high when these two conditions hold (see [1] for a detailed review).

3.1   Disjunction Error

Again let A_1 and A_2 be two events ordered by increasing probability, and let $A_1 \vee A_2$ represent the disjunction of those two events (so that $A_1 \vee A_2$ is true if either A_1 or A_2 occurs). Then

$$P(A_1 \vee A_2) \geq P(A_2)$$

must always hold. This follows from the fact that $A_1 \vee A_2$ necessarily occurs if A_2 itself occurs. While in most cases people follow this requirement, they reliably violate this requirement for some events, giving estimates where

$$P_E(A_1 \vee A_2) < P_E(A_2)$$

Just as for the conjunction error, the greater the difference between $\overline{P_E}(A_1)$ and $\overline{P_E}(A_2)$, and the higher the estimated conditional probability $\overline{P_E}(A_1|A_2)$, the higher the rate of occurence of the disjunction error. Studies which examine the rate of both errors show a strong correlation between the frequency of the conjunction error for a given pair of events and the frequency of the disjunction error for that same pair(see [2] for a review).

3.2   The Reality of These Errors

Given the obvious nature of the requirements violated in conjunction and disjunction errors, it is natural to question the reality of these patterns in people's probabilistic judgment. Researchers have considered this issue carefully, and have have attempted to explain away the conjunction error by arguing that it arises only because participants understand the word 'probability' in a way different from that assumed by experimenters, or by asserting that the conjunction error occurs because participants, correctly following the pragmatics of communication, interpret the single statement A_1 as meaning 'A_1 and not A_2'. Very extensive experimental studies (over 100 published papers) have undermined these objections, and confirmed these errors as a reliable aspect of people's probability judgments [1]. In the next section I show how we can explain these errors as a consequnce of random variation in a reasoner using the equations of probability theory.

4 The Systematic Influence of Random Variation

In discussing the influence of random variation on probability estimates I assume a rational reasoner with a long-term episodic memory. I assume a 'perfect' reasoner: if the reasoner were not subject to random variation then each estimate $P_E(A)$ would be equal to $P(A)$. I assume a long-term memory containing n episodes where each episode i contains a flag $f_i(A)$, set to 1 if i contains event A and to 0 otherwise. I assume a minimal form of transient error, in which there is some small probability d that when the state of some flag $f_i(A)$ is read, the value obtained is not the correct value for that flag. I take $C(A)$ to be number of flags that were read as 1 and T_A be the number of flags whose correct value is actually 1.

4.1 Explaining Conservatism

Our reasoner can compute $P_E(A)$ by querying episodic memory to find count all episodes containing A and dividing by the total number of episodes, giving

$$P_E(A) = \frac{C(A)}{n}$$

Random variation afffects $P_E(A)$ when it causes some flag $f_i(A)$ be read incorrectly. The expected value of $P_E(A)$ is given

$$\overline{P_E}(A) = \frac{T_A(1 - d) + (n - T_A)d}{n}$$

(since on average $1 - d$ of the T_A flags whose value is 1 will be read as 1, and d of the $n - T_A$ flags whose value is 0 will be read as 1). Since by definition

$$P(A) = \frac{T_A}{n}$$

we get

$$\overline{P_E}(A) = d + (1 - 2d)P(A) \tag{1}$$

or equivalently

$$\overline{P_E}(A) = P(A) + d(1 - 2P(A)) \tag{2}$$

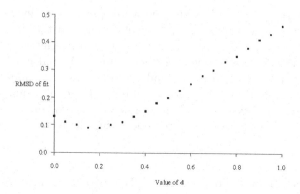

Fig. 2. Scatterplot showing Root Mean Squared Difference (RMSD) between subjective probabilities from Figure 2 and estimates computed by Equation 2 using the corresponding objective probabilities, for a range of values of d

and so the average value of $P_E(A)$ deviates from $P(A)$ in a way that systematically depends on both d and $P(A)$. If $P(A) = 0.5$ this difference will be 0, if $P(A) < 0.5$ then since d cannot be negative we have $\overline{P_E}(A) > P(A)$ with the difference approaching $+d$ as $P(A)$ approaches 0, and if $P(A) > 0.5$ then $\overline{P_E}(A) < P(A)$ with the difference approaching $-d$ as $P(A)$ approaches 1. Thus random error or noise in eposodic memory produces conservatism just as seen in people's probability judgments.

As a sanity check on Equation 2 we can measure the degree of fit between Equation 2 and the data in Figure 2 for a range of values of d. Because we expect the degree of random error in episodic memory to be low but not negligible, we would expect the best fit to occur for a low, but not too low, value of d. Figure 4.1 shows that the best fit occurs for values of d around 0.2, consistent with this expectation.

5   Explaining Subadditivity

Recall that subadditivity occurs when, for mutually exclusive events $A_1 \ldots A_n$ with A being the disjunction of all those events, people's probability estimates show the pattern

$$\overline{P_E}(A_1) + \ldots + \overline{P_E}(A_n) > \overline{P_E}(A)$$

with the value of the difference rising as n increases.

From Equation 1 we have

$$\overline{P_E}(A_1) + \ldots + \overline{P_E}(A_n) = (P(A_1) + \ldots + P(A_n)) + d(n - 2(P(A_1) + \ldots + P(A_n)))$$

since by assumption

$$(P(A_1) + \ldots + P(A_n)) = P(A)$$

we can rewrite this as

$$\overline{P_E}(A_1) + \ldots + \overline{P_E}(A_n) = P(A) + d(n - 2P(A))$$

Also from From Equation 1 we have

$$\overline{P_E}(A) = P(A) + d(1 - 2P(A))$$

and combining these two expressions we see that Equation 1 implies

$$\overline{P_E}(A_1) + \ldots + \overline{P_E}(A_n) > \overline{P_E}(A)$$

with the value of this expression rising as n increases, just as required.

Recall also that for mutually exclusive and complete events people's probability estimates show the pattern

$$\overline{P_E}(A_1) + \ldots + \overline{P_E}(A_n) > 1$$

except for $n = 2$ when

$$\overline{P_E}(A_1) + +\overline{P_E}(A_2) = 1$$

Since for mutually exclusive and complete events we have $P(A) = 1$, from Equation 5 in this situation we get

$$\overline{P_E}(A_1) + \ldots + \overline{P_E}(A_n) = 1 + d(n - 2)$$

and so $\overline{P_E}(A_1) + \ldots + \overline{P_E}(A_n) > 1$ holds except when $n = 2$ in which case equality holds, just as in people's probaility estimates.

5.1   Explaining Conjunction and Disjunction Errors

The previous two biases concerned the average of people's probability estimates. The conjunction and disjunction errors concern differences between 'samples' from people's probability estimates. Let A_1 and A_2 be any two events ordered by increasing probability so that $P(A_1)$ and $P(A_2)$. For a reasoner following the rules of probability theory we have

$$P_E(A_1 \wedge A_2) = P_E(A_2) \times P_E(A_1|A_2)$$

and so that reasoner's estimate of $P(A_1 \wedge A_2)$ at some time is equal to the product of their estimate for $P(A_2)$ at that time and their estimate for the conditional probability $P(A_1|A_2)$ at that time. Since the reasoner is subject to random variation, these estimates $P_E(A_2)$ and $P_E(A_1|A_2)$ may have some random (positive or negative) difference from the means $\overline{P_E}(A_2)$ and $\overline{P_E}(A_1|A_2)$, and so the equation for conjunction can be rewritten as

$$P_E(A_1 \wedge A_2) = (\overline{P_E}(A_2) + d_{A_2}) \times (\overline{P_E}(A_1|A_2) + d_{A_1|A_2}) \tag{3}$$

where d_{A_2} and $d_{A_1|A_2}$ represent these (positive or negative) deviations from the means. If we assume that A_1 is the less-probable constituent of the conjunction, the conjunction error will occur when

$$\overline{P_E}(A_1) + d_{A_1} < P_E(A_1 \wedge A_2)$$
$$\overline{P_E}(A_1) + d_{A_1} < (\overline{P_E}(A_2) + d_{A_2}) \times (\overline{P_E}(A_1|A_2) + d_{A_1|A_2}) \tag{4}$$

(that is, when the probability of the conjunction from Equation 3 is greater than the probability of its least probable constituent A_1). Equation 4 is most likely to be true when $\overline{P_E}(A_1)$ is low and $\overline{P_E}(A_2)$ and $\overline{P_E}(A_1|A_2)$ are high (because in that situation the left side of Equation 4 is most likely to be low and the right side to be high). We thus expect the conjunction error to be most frequent when $\overline{P_E}(A_1)$ is low and $\overline{P_E}(A_2)$ and $\overline{P_E}(A_1|A_2)$ are both high. This is just the pattern seen when the conjunction error occurs in people's probability estimates.

We can give a similar account of the disjunction error. The probability theory equation for the disjunction $P(A_1 \vee A_2)$ is

$$P(A_1 \vee A_2) = P(A_2) + P(A_1) - P(A_1 \wedge A_2)$$

Just as above this disjunction can be expressed as

$$P_E(A_1 \vee A_2) = (\overline{P_E}(A_2) + d_{A_2}) + (\overline{P_E}(A_1) + d_{A_1}) - P_E(A_1 \wedge A_2)$$

The disjunction error occurs whenever this disjunctive probability $P_E(A_1 \vee A_2)$ is less than its greater constituent probability; that is, whenever

$$\begin{aligned} P_E(A_1 \vee A_2) &< (\overline{P_E}(A_2) + d_{A_2}) \\ (\overline{P_E}(A_2) + d_{A_2}) + (\overline{P_E}(A_1) + d_{A_1}) - P_E(A_1 \wedge A_2) &< (\overline{P_E}(A_2) + d_{A_2}) \end{aligned} \tag{5}$$

is true. Cancelling common terms and rearranging transforms Equation 5 to

$$\overline{P_E}(A_1) + d_{A_1} < P_E(A_1 \wedge A_2) \tag{6}$$

Whenever the inequality in Equation 6 is true, the disjunction error will occur. Equation 6 is identical to Equation 4, which predicts the occurrence of the conjunction error. In other words, Equation 6 predicts that the occurrence of the disjunction error for a given set of items should follow the occurrence of the conjunction error. Again, this is just the pattern seen when the disjunction error occurs in people's probability estimates.

6   Dealing with Noise in AI Reasoning Systems

Many current approaches to reasoning under uncertainty take as their starting point the standard theory of probability; that is, the theory describing the probability of occurrence of repeatable events. These 'Bayesian' approaches to AI apply probability theory in many different areas such as learning, deduction, inference, decision-making, and so on; see Pearl's 1988 book [6], which in some ways founded this line of research (and currently has over $16,000$ citations). It is clear from Pearl's work that probability theory provides normatively correct rules which an AI system must use to reason optimally about uncertain events. It is equally clear that AI systems (like all other physical systems) are unavoidably subject to a certain degree of random variation and noise in their internal workings. As we have seen, this random variation does not produce a pattern of reasoning in which probability estimates vary randomly around the correct value;

instead,it produces systematic biases that push probability estimates in certain directions and so will produce conservatism, subadditivity, and the conjunction and disjunction errors in AI reasoning.

How can we minimise these biases? We can minimise noise in hardware and software; perhaps more importantly, we can design our AI reasoning systems to take account of internal noise.

6.1 Minimising Noise

The previous discussions assumed a single simple form of random variation: an instantaneous random variation which at some particular time, caused some bit in memory to be read incorrectly. In chip design this type 'soft error' can occur due to changes in data being stored in memory or to changes in data being transferred during processing. This type of noise can be produced by cosmic ray impact, by particle decay in the hardware environment, or by random thermodynamic fluctuation. Logic circuits with higher capacitance and logic voltages are less likely to suffer such errors. Unfortunately, such "radiation hardened" designs result in a slower logic gate and a higher power dissipation. Reduction in chip size and voltage, desirable for many reasons, increase the soft error rate. The literature suggests that currently these errors occur at a rate of 1 error per Gbyte per day [5].

As well as using hardened chip design to minimise errors due to noise, designers can make use of error-correcting codes to recover from soft errors. These codes involve adding additional redundant information to data, allowing reconstruction in the event of random error. In general, the reconstructed data is the most likely original data: perfect reconstruction is not guaranteed. Just as with radiation hardened designs, these error correcting codes impose a significant processing cost in terms of time and chip area. Further, these codes cannot eliminate all error: there is an upper bound (the Shannon limit) on the amount of error these codes can remove from data[4].

6.2 Probabilities for Noisy Reasoners

Designing systems to minimise noise is costly, both in computational time and computational power. A better approach may be to design probabilistic reasoning systems to include an expectation of random error. To do this we can use the equations described previously, but with corrective estimates of the amount of random variation to which the reasoner is susceptible. Suppose the reasoner is susceptible to a known rate of noise d: that is, the reasoner knows that in the long run every X bits read from memory will contain dX bits whose read value is incorrect. For event A define a corrected probability estimate $P_C(A)$ as

$$P_C(A) = \frac{C(A)}{n(1-2d)} - \frac{d}{1-2d} = \frac{P_E(A) - d}{1-2d} \tag{7}$$

On average computed probability estimates $P_E(A)$ will tend to their mean, given by

$$\overline{P_E}(A) = d + (1-2d)P(A)$$

(see Equation 2), and so corrected probability estimates will tend to

$$\overline{P_C(A)} = \frac{\overline{P_E(A)} - d}{1 - 2d}$$

or substituting

$$\overline{P_C}(A) = \frac{d + (1 - 2d)P(A) - d}{1 - 2d} = P(A)$$

and we see that a reasoner that computes its estimate of $P(A)$ as in Equation 7 will in the long run compute estimates that are equal to the true probability of A. Such a reasoner will not suffer from the conservatism and subadditivity biases described earlier. Note, however, that values of $P_C(A)$ will still vary randomly around their mean, and so will still produce conjunction and disjunction errors due to that variation. Discovering ways of eliminating these errors in noisy reasoners is an aim for future work.

References

1. Costello, F.: How probability theory explains the conjunction fallacy. Journal of Behavioral Decision Making 22(3), 213–234 (2009)
2. Costello, F.J.: Fallacies in probability judgments for conjunctions and disjunctions of everyday events. Journal of Behavioral Decision Making 22(3), 235–251 (2009)
3. Erev, I., Wallsten, T.S., Budescu, D.V.: Simultaneous over- and underconfidence: The role of error in judgment processes. Psychological Review 101(3), 519–527 (1994)
4. Huffman, C.W., Pless, V.: Fundamentals of Error-Correcting Codes. Cambridge University Press (2003)
5. Mukherjee, S.: Architecture Design for Soft Errors. Morgan Kaufmann Publishers Inc., San Francisco (2008)
6. Pearl, J.: Probabilistic reasoning in intelligent systems: networks of plausible inference. Morgan Kaufmann Publishers Inc., San Francisco (1988)
7. Tversky, A., Koehler, D.J.: Support theory: A nonextensional representation of subjective probability. Psychological Review 101(4), 547–566 (1994)

2012: The Connectome, WBE and AGI

Diana Deca

IMPRS-LS, Am Klopferspitz 18,
Munich, Germany
dianadeca@yahoo.com

Abstract. In order to grasp the entire complexity of the human nervous system, one needs to understand its physical substrate. Down to which level should a whole brain emulation keep all the structural details of the brain in order to achieve all of the functions of the biological brain? While a computer program could easily be emulated in order to achieve the same specified function, the human brain is a special case because of its enormously complex functions. For this reason, causal relations between brain structure and function are currently being made in neuroscience. Neuroscientific research is in this sense supporting WBE and therefore AGI, by providing important data, models and simulations of brain functions. The goals of this paper are to review the challenges for gathering and assembling connectome data and to provide   directions for overcoming these challenges. Finally, the implications for AGI will be discussed.

Keywords: Whole Brain Emulation, Artificial General Intelligence, challenges, connectome data.

For an overview on the different types of information neuroscience has to offer and the methods used to obtain this information, as well as the most recent models and simulations, please see Deca, IJMC 2012[1].

The data acquisition tools in neuroscience can be split roughly into imaging and electrical recording tools. Imaging tools provide images or movies showing what the brain does in different circumstances and make use of different chemicals in order to get a general idea of the electrical activity, while recording tools are used for quantifying the connection between electrical activity at different scales in the brain (ranging from single cells to entire brain areas to the whole brain) sometimes in connection to a stimulus in order to understand what the brain does when it perceives or does something. These two types of methods have very often been used in conjunction with each other in order to understand the connection between electrical and chemical changes in the brain.

A special feature of neuroscientific research is its extremely fast pace in that the problems it may point out to in 2011 might be solved by 2012, leading to further questions that would need to be answered in 2013 and so forth. Its rapid growth and indirect support of WBE and indirectly of AGI make it their main engine.

---

[1] Deca, D. Available Tools for Whole Brain Emulation.IJMC, Volume: 4, Issue: 1(2012) pp. 67-86, DOI: 10.1142/S1793843012400045

J. Bach, B. Goertzel, and M. Iklé (Eds.): AGI 2012, LNAI 7716, pp. 41–49, 2012.
© Springer-Verlag Berlin Heidelberg 2012

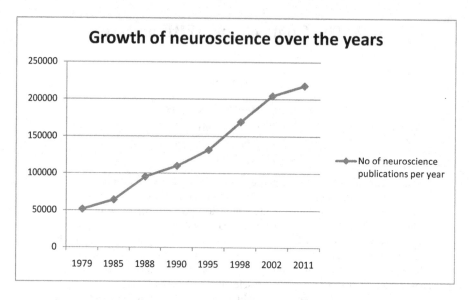

Fig. 1. The growth of the number of neuroscientific publications per year. The data were obtained by indexing the medical database[2,3].

A fundamental issue for neuroscience and for reverse engineering the brain is the connection between structure and function. The current methods only allow us to make some potential correlations at different levels in time and space. However, a complete mapping of function to structure of the human brain is lacking at the moment. One of the main issues in this sense is the complexity of the brain structure, but most importantly the complexity of its functions, since a function would need both an agent and an environment to work in. Therefore understanding this function in connection with the structure requires not only observations about the brain, but also about the physical world in which it acts in. This task gets also a bit reflexive, since we are using our object of study in order to study it (the brain), and we are hoping to understand the object of study in full by looking at it with itself.

At the moment, this connection between structure and function is more poorly understood than in any other organ in the human body as Lichtman et al.[4] point out. One of the main reasons for this might be the fact that the brain controls the rest of the organs and triggers all other processes in the body. The human brain uses around 20 percent of the energy used by the entire body. Most of the energy used by the brain, in the form of ATP (adenosine triphosphate) is required for maintaining the chemical concentrations inside the neurons which would allow for electrical activity.

---

[2] http://www.ncbi.nlm.nih.gov/pubmed/

[3] Corlan,A.D., Medline trend: automated yearly statistics of PubMed results for any query, 2004. Web resource at URL: http://dan.corlan.net/medline-trend.html. The full trend can be viewed here (http://dan.corlan.net/cgi-bin/medline-trend?Q=neuro)

[4] Lichtman, J. W., Denk, W. The Big and the Small: Challenges of Imaging the Brain's Circuits. Science 4 November 2011: Vol. 334 no. 6056 pp. 618-623 DOI: 10.1126/science.1209168.

The electrical activity sustains all of the brain functions we have. What is interesting and indeed a challenge for WBE is the fact that these electrochemical gradients are changing in response to the environment, leading to the neurons firing in response to different environmental cues, and to plasticity and thereby learning.

As an outline of the challenges for gathering connectome data in the neurosciences, I will make use of a paper written by J.Lichtman and W.Denk written in November 2011. While addressing the issues mentioned by them, I will also refer to another paper[5] providing another solution to the similar challenges they mention called the Brain Activity Map.

1) **Immense diversity of cell types in the brain.** The nervous system of the C elegans worm is composed of around 300 hundred neurons (compared to 86 billion in the human brain), yet each cell in its nervous system has a unique structure and function. This would translate into around 86 billion computational units, with structures which are almost unknown and unique at the fine level. One way around this is to find some common categories, and gradually add the different subtypes. A lot of these neuron types have been described, and genetic tools for selective manipulation have been created. [6] The Brainbow technique has also allowed selective labeling of different neuron types[7]. The current tools for genetic manipulation, selective labeling and in vivo manipulation[8,9,10] are giving rise to a large number of projects aimed at correlating the structure of different neurons to their structure. The hope in this sense is to be able to understand their function both in terms of connectivity at the population level as well as at higher resolution in both time and space, in terms of functions of their particular dendritic and axonal segments. This is work in progress, however it is expected that the end result will lead to a number of categories (an already well established category is inhibitory vs. excitatory neurons, based on whether they activate or inactivate nearby neurons, place cells, orientation cells, etc.)

[5] Alivisatos,P., Chun, M., Church,G.M., Greenspan,R.J., Roukes,M.L., Yuste, R. The Brain Activity Map Project and the Challenge of Functional Connectomics. Neuron, Vol 74, Issue 6, 970-974, 21 June 2012. doi:10.1016/j.neuron.2012.06.006.

[6] Rogan,S.C., Roth,B.L. Remote Control of Neuronal Signaling. Pharmacological Reviews June 2011 vol. 63 no. 2 291-315 doi: 10.1124/pr.110.003020.

[7] Livet, J., Weissman, T.A., Kang, H., Draft, R.W., Lu, J., Bennis, R.A., Sanes,J.R.,. Lichtman, J.W. Transgenic strategies for combinatorial expression of fluorescent proteins in the nervous system . Nature 450, 56-62 (1 November 2007) l doi:10.1038/nature06293.

[8] Kodandaramaiah, S.B., Franzesi, G.T., Chow, B.Y., Boyden, E.S., Forest, C.R. Automated whole-cell patch-clamp electrophysiology of neurons in vivo. Nature Methods 9, 585–587 (2012) doi:10.1038/nmeth.1993.

[9] Knöpfel,T., Lin,M.Z., Levskaya,A., Tian,L., Lin,J.L., Boyden,E.S. Toward the Second Generation of Optogenetic Tools. The Journal of Neuroscience, 10 November 2010, 30(45): 14998-15004; doi: 10.1523/JNEUROSCI.4190-10.2010.

[10] Hirase H, Nikolenko V, Yuste R. Multiphoton stimulation of neurons and spines. Cold Spring Harb Protoc. 2012 Apr 1;2012(4):472-5. doi: 10.1101/pdb.prot068569.

2) **Imaging electrical and chemical activity**. One of the challenges for neuroscientists has been to couple the chemical activity with electrical activity at different levels. In principle they should be the same (in the sense that there is a direct causal connection between the two); however explaining this causal connection in detail required the development of some new tools. One of them was a type of microscopy which allows for long term imaging inside the brain of a living animal, providing the chance of measuring enough photons that can be associated with the electrical activity of neurons. This method is now routinely used in many labs, and is called two photon microscopy.[11] Two photon microscopy is based on the principle of bringing a lot of photons (in the form of laser light) into a very small brain area for a short period of time. This leads to two photon excitation and allows for very fine measurements of changes in fluorescence. This, in combination with calcium indicators, has allowed for the direct quantification of calcium concentrations within neurons as a direct function of changes in membrane potential, both of which account for activity.[12] One of the main limitations with two photon imaging however is the limited penetration depth (up to max 1 mm in the mouse brain). The human cortex is known to be thicker therefore it is not known whether scientists would be able to record activity from neurons in the human brain with the available techniques without having to remove parts of the brain. The takeout message here is that the correlation between electrical and chemical activity in the brain is now clear both theoretically and experimentally and that there is no reason to believe that the most fundamental principles of physics and chemistry would not hold in the human brain as well.

3) **Neurons extend over vast volumes**. Since Cajal showed how neurons are connected, many people in the field have related the issue of connectivity to that of function. The dendritic tree of a neuron (which receives many inputs from other neurons) can span from one brain hemisphere to another (therefore more than one meter), which is an enormous distance when compared to the diameter of its nucleus or soma (max. 18 micrometers.) This is a large volume, which needs to be described at very high resolution in vivo. In microscopy, the general tradeoff is made between resolution and volume: higher resolution usually entails smaller volume and the other way around. However, this tradeoff in the neurosciences generates competition in the microscopy market, which is then aiming at combining both in the best way possible. A possible way around this is the automation of these recordings, enabling the extraction of very large amounts of high resolution data which can then be put together into one large whole[13] .

---

[11] Denk, W., Strickler, J.W., Webb, W.W. Two-photon laser scanning fluorescence microscopy. Science 6 April 1990: Vol. 248 no. 4951 pp. 73-76 DOI: 10.1126/science.2321027.

[12] Grienberger C, Konnerth A. Imaging calcium in neurons. Neuron. 2012 Mar 8;73(5):862-85. Review.

[13] http://www.neuro.mpg.de/english/emeritus/columninsilico

4) Need for Dense or Saturated Reconstruction. Indeed, most of today's image of neuronal circuitry is based on Cajals drawings, which are still at the border between science and art. The evolution of imaging techniques has allowed for some mapping of this circuitry, but no large scale movies correlating the function and structure are yet available. For now, only a small muscle that moves in the mouse ear is one of the few parts of the nervous system were the circuitry has been mapped completely [14]. Some other projects include the in silico cortical column and numerous other projects within the connectome consortium. It is expected that the appropriate areas for complete circuitry mapping are some of the most fundamental and old ones, such as the visual or auditory cortex, where there is less variability between species and individuals even at the finer level. One promising method for tracking connectivity is the rabies virus, which spreads from one neuron only to the neuron it communicates with and making them fluorescent [15] (add reference http://jap.physiology.org/content/106/1/138.full). Another way of tracking connectivity is to label the different circuits with different colors, for example with the Brainbow method. However, one of the main problems with tracking connectivity is the slow human analysis partially due to the small number of computer scientists with enough knowledge of neurobiology who can optimize the analysis methods. Resolving one cubic millimeter of brain tissue in terms of neural connection would take, given the current method, months or even years of imaging and even more time for analysis. With this in mind, the research community is getting reorganized in order to overcome this problem (eg. the numbers of undergraduate students doing such tedious work for free is growing exponentially) and in parallel different methods are being tested, such as the tape to sem. Furthermore, different computational models for artificial neural networks are emerging and their connectivity rules are constantly being update in the light of new data on the neurophysiological processes behind functional neural rewiring. However, as Alivisatos et al[16] estimate, $7 \times 10(6)$ mouse brain cells would need around $5 \times 10(16)$ bytes, which is less than the global genome data. They envision that, just like the analysis of the genome gave rise to the field of Genomics, another field called Connectomics should emerge as a result to such analysis, which has proven to be a correct intuition[17,18].

Finally, the main issue in making a universal model for how neurons rewire in order to achieve a specific function within a specific context is the fact that this will depend a lot on the specific context, therefore at the fine level every instantiation of this

---

[14] Lu, J.,Tapia,J.C., White,O.L., Lichtman,J.W. The Interscutularis Muscle Connectome PLoS Biol. 7, e1000032 (2009).

[15] Lois, J.H., Rice,C.D., Yates, B.J. . Neural circuits controlling diaphragm function in the cat revealed by transneuronal tracing Journal of Applied PhysiologyJanuary 2009 vol. 106 no. 1 138-152doi: 10.1152/japplphysiol.91125.2008.

[16] Idem 5.

[17] http://hebb.mit.edu/courses/connectomics/

[18] http://en.wikipedia.org/wiki/Connectomics

connectivity will differ from all the other ones. The main task here is to generate the main categories for such branching, and deciding at which level to stop but still achieve the connectome (the synaptic level is already generating very different instantiations , even in the worm brain). The good part is that there must be general rules that the neurons follow in order to achieve this, therefore the more physiological data the next aritificial neural network will be based on, the closer these networks will be to the real brain and the more functions it will be able to have. A good analogy in this sense is the game of chess. A good way of learning about chess is to watch a chess game, understanding the basic rules and then playing based on these rules. If a player has a good mind and some understanding of the basic rules, then it will invariably get better and better at chess by experiencing different instantiations of it.

Alivisatos et al[19] propose a new way of gathering and analyzing connectome data in the form of BAP (the Brain Activity Map Project). They employ the philosophical stance of emergentism[20] (that is, the neural circuit function is emergent from complex interactions among constituent parts). In order to understand these emerging properties of neural circuitry, they propose to record every single action potential from every neuron within a given circuit. For now, calcium imaging could provide a useful tool but as they suggest, it can only approximate the electrical activity. Therefore a better alternative for this would be voltage imaging[21], however this technique does not allow for large-scale high resolution recordings. They believe that this is a feasible goal which can accomplished by means of large scale electrical recordings with nano-probes, which would now allow researchers to record electrical activity at dozens of sites per silicon neural probe[22] . One limitation with this sense might be the fact that these probes would not be able to record subthreshold activity in the neuron, and how different inputs in the neuron contribute to the activity recorded as a whole. Ideally, one would have a method that can reveal electrical activity in each neuron up to the level of dendritic spines[23] .

1   How the Current State of Neuroscientific Research Affects the Connectome, the WBE and AGI

The goal of this paper was to review the main problems for WBE that neuroscience is currently dealing with. I will briefly outline the three main issues and mention their respective solutions.

---

[19] Idem 5

[20] http://en.wikipedia.org/wiki/Emergentism

[21] Peterka DS, Takahashi H, Yuste R. Voltage Imaging in Neurons. Neuron 2011 Jan 13;69(1):9-21.

[22] Du,J. et al 2009 J. Micromech. Microeng. 19 075008 doi:10.1088/0960-1317/19/7/075008.

[23] Chen X, Leischner U, Rochefort NL, Nelken I, Konnerth A. Functional mapping of single spines in cortical neurons in vivo. Nature. 2011 Jun 26;475(7357):501-5. doi: 10.1038/nature10193.

The Problems are:

Immense Diversity of Cell Types. Solution: Categories are being made in the light of new data. Meanwhile, new methods are being made for faster data acquisition and analysis.

Imaging Electrical and Chemical Activity. Solution: combining methods- imaging can be made with Ca indicators, which is directly correlated with electrical activity. Alternatively, voltage imaging can be used, as well as large-scale electrical recording with nanoprobes.

Neurons Extend over Vast Volumes, So a Large Volume Has to Be Analyzed at Very High Scale. So how to get very high resolution imaging data from such large volumes? The pace of imaging developments is also growing very fast, such examples are the STED and the 2P, and a lot of very high tech variants of electron microscopy. In parallel, novel methods for recording electrical activity directly from many sites are being developed and tested.

The timeframe for overcoming the different drawbacks for WBE depend a lot on the funding, but not only. There are physical limitations in terms of imaging (eg. How deep the 2P laser can go into different tissues, what electron microscopy can show, photodamage due to light into cortical tissue). As Alivisatos et al point out, recording electrical activity from all neurons within a given circuit requires increasing the number of imaged neurons as well as the depth of the imaged tissue. Some of the techniques that they mention include: more powerful sources for two photon excitation without damaging living cortical tissue, faster scanning strategies, developing better microscope objectives with larger fields of view, better scattering corrections in microscopes as well as better 3D reconstruction techniques. It would appear from this that it is vital that the in vivo projects grow exponentially, in order for scientists to get a better idea of the connection between function and structure. There is already an important tendency towards that in neuroscience, given simply by the fact that the in vivo situation is now possible to achieve experimentally, and implies less assumptions about the physiological process itself. Therefore in vivo experiments in neuroscience are considered to be more reliable and have a higher chance of getting serious attention. As such, there is also a bigger chance for in vivo projects and labs to get funded. As these projects get funded, breakthroughs in the data acquisition tools are more and more strongly supported.

Given that problem no. 2 is already more or less solved, in the sense that the gathering of electrophysiological and imaging data is obtained simultaneously routinely in many labs, we are then left with problem no. 3, which would appear to be conceptual (how to bind structure and function within an entire neuron whose dendritic tree extends over such vast volumes?).

However, the structure/function issue within the neuron can also be solved with the aid of new methods already mentioned (STED, ATLUM, 2P, silicon probes, optogenetics, automated patch clamp). Their development will inevitably lead to the complete mapping of the neurome in different contexts. The neurome will then serve as the main computational unit for the connectome, which can then be built in silico.

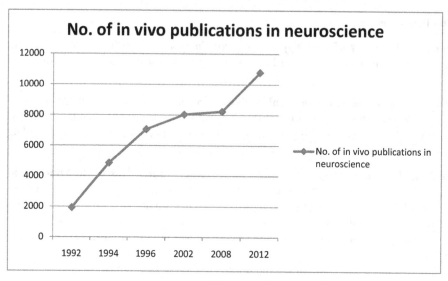

Fig. 2.

2   Implications for AGI

Neuroscientific research is inevitably gathering connectome data. Connectome data is currently being modeled by neuroscientists with the end goal of achieving a complete connectome. A full connectome can then be easily rebuilt in silico once all the information is made available, and this will constitute a whole brain emulation. A whole brain emulation that is able to perform computations in manner which is similar enough to the human brain is a form of artificial general intelligence. This paper has aimed at providing an important update on the current state of what will become a main branch of AGI, namely connectome data acquisition, modeling and simulation. Speculations about the potential directions that this field will take are beyond the scope of this paper. However, based on the development of neuroscience so far, it is suggested that there is competitive pressure for achieving the AGI in the form of the Connectome simulation. From the point of view of a neuroscientist, the reason for this pressure is not achieving AGI in particular, but rather advancing the understanding of the brain in the most rigorous way possible.

References

1. Alivisatos, P., Chun, M., Church, G.M., Greenspan, R.J., Roukes, M.L., Yuste, R.: The Brain Activity Map Project and the Challenge of Functional Connectomics. Neuron 74(6), 970–974 (2012), doi:10.1016/j.neuron.2012.06.006
2. Chen, X., Leischner, U., Rochefort, N.L., Nelken, I., Konnerth, A.: Functional mapping of single spines in cortical neurons in vivo. Nature 475(7357), 501–505 (2011), doi:10.1038/nature10193

3. Corlan, A.D.: Medline trend: automated yearly statistics of PubMed results for any query (2004), Web resource at http://dan.corlan.net/medline-trend.html, The full trend can be viewed here http://dan.corlan.net/cgi-bin/medline-trend?Q=neuro

4. Deca, D.: Available Tools for Whole Brain Emulation. IJMC 4(1), 67–86 (2012), doi:10.1142/S1793843012400045

5. Denk, W., Strickler, J.W., Webb, W.W.: Two-photon laser scanning fluorescence microscopy. Science 248(4951), 73–76 (1990), doi:10.1126/science.2321027

6. Du, J., et al.: J. Micromech. Microeng. 19, 075008 (2009), doi:10.1088/0960-1317/19/7/075008

7. Grienberger, C., Konnerth, A.: Imaging calcium in neurons. Neuron 73(5), 862–885 (2012); Review

8. Kodandaramaiah, S.B., Franzesi, G.T., Chow, B.Y., Boyden, E.S., Forest, C.R.: Automated whole-cell patch-clamp electrophysiology of neurons in vivo. Nature Methods 9, 585–587 (2012), doi:10.1038/nmeth.1993

9. Lichtman, J.W., Denk, W.: The Big and the Small: Challenges of Imaging the Brain's Circuits. Science 334(6056), 618–623 (2011), doi:10.1126/science.1209168

10. Livet, J., Weissman, T.A., Kang, H., Draft, R.W., Lu, J., Bennis, R.A., Sanes, J.R., Lichtman, J.W.: Transgenic strategies for combinatorial expression of fluorescent proteins in the nervous system. Nature 450, 56–62 (2007), doi:10.1038/nature06293

11. Lois, J.H., Rice, C.D., Yates, B.J.: Neural circuits controlling diaphragm function in the cat revealed by transneuronal tracing. Journal of Applied Physiology 106(1), 138–152 (2009), doi:10.1152/japplphysiol.91125.2008

12. Lu, J., Tapia, J.C., White, O.L., Lichtman, J.W.: The Interscutularis Muscle Connectome. PLoS Biol. 7, e1000032 (2009)

13. Knöpfel, T., Lin, M.Z., Levskaya, A., Tian, L., Lin, J.L., Boyden, E.S.: Toward the Second Generation of Optogenetic Tools. The Journal of Neuroscience 30(45), 14998–15004 (2010), doi:10.1523/JNEUROSCI.4190-10.2010

14. Hirase, H., Nikolenko, V., Yuste, R.: Multiphoton stimulation of neurons and spines. Cold Spring Harb Protoc. 2012(4), 472–475 (2012), doi:10.1101/pdb.prot068569

15. Rogan, S.C., Roth, B.L.: Remote Control of Neuronal Signaling. Pharmacological Reviews 63(2), 291–315 (2011), doi:10.1124/pr.110.003020

16. Peterka, D.S., Takahashi, H., Yuste, R.: Voltage Imaging in Neurons. Neuron 69(1), 9–21 (2011)

17. http://en.wikipedia.org/wiki/Connectomics

18. http://en.wikipedia.org/wiki/Emergentism

19. http://hebb.mit.edu/courses/connectomics/

20. http://www.neuro.mpg.de/english/emeritus/columninsilico

21. http://www.ncbi.nlm.nih.gov/pubmed/

Logical Prior Probability

Abram Demski*

Institute for Creative Technologies, 12015 Waterfront Drive, Playa Vista, CA 90094

Abstract. A Bayesian prior over first-order theories is defined. It is shown that the prior can be approximated, and the relationship to previously studied priors is examined.

1 Introduction and Motivation

The purpose of this paper is to present a prior over theories in first-order logic, similar in nature to the priors of algorithmic probability. There are several possible motivations for such a prior. First, it is hoped that the study of priors over logics will be useful to the study of realistic reasoning. Probabilistic reasoning over logic gives us a structure of inference which is not as evident in non-logical universal priors. Second, logical theories may be easier to examine than other possible knowledge representations, motivating the learning of logical theories as a goal in itself (independent of prediction accuracy and other concerns). In this case, a theory of universal learning via logical theories may be useful. Third, the logical prior presented here may give some benefits even if the only consideration is prediction accuracy.

The primary idea is that of the random theory. By building up first-order theories one random sentence at a time, a probability that a particular sentence becomes true can be defined.

One way of motivating the approach is to consider what would happen if we attempted to apply the universal semidistribution $\mathcal{M}$ to beliefs in predicate calculus. (I will rely on some concepts which are explained more fully in section 2.) $\mathcal{M}$ is a prior over bit-sequences. We can encode our beliefs about propositions as beliefs about sequences, by giving each sentence a number n (as is done in Gödel numbering, [1]), and using the bit at position n to represent the truth or falsehood of that sequence. Suppose we have an observation set, Σ, of sentences which we've accepted as true. We would like to know how to assign probability to the other sentences. The obvious approach is to update $\mathcal{M}$ on the bits representing Σ. Two main problems arise:

- Consistency & Completeness. $\mathcal{M}$ does not know that the bits represent logical sentences, so it will not assign probability based on the logical consequences of Σ. For example, for each $A \in \Sigma$, some probability will still be

---

* This effort has been sponsored by the U.S. Army and the Air Force Office of Scientific Research. Statements and opinions expressed do not necessarily reflect the position or the policy of the United States Government, and no official endorsement should be inferred.

assigned to the negation of A. We would like to assign probability 1 to the consequences of Σ, and probability 0 to things inconsistent with Σ.

- Non-sequential enumeration. $\mathcal{M}$ is a mixture distribution composed of programs which output the bits of the sequentially. Σ will have recursively enumerable consequences, but due to the undecidability of the consequence relation, it will not be possible in general to enumerate these consequences in linear order.

The second problem is more subtle than the first, but follows from it: if a distribution got the logical consequences right, then it would be enumerating them properly. The point is seperated out because it is an interesting divergence form $\mathcal{M}$. To illustrate this issue, suppose that we want to define $\mathcal{M}'$ which is a mixture distribution over arbitrary computable enumerations of bits, rather than only sequential enumerations. We understand the programs as printing a sequence of (location, bit) pairs, and take each pair to set the bit of the sequence at the given location.

To make $\mathcal{M}'$ well-defined, we need to decide what to do when conflicting pairs are given by a program. A program may print the pair (40,1) and later print (40,0). What contribution should the program make to the probability of that bit?

Three options are:

$\mathcal{M}'_1$: The earliest pair for a given location is used.

$\mathcal{M}'_2$: The program is thrown out when it produces conflicting pairs. It no longer contributes anything to the distribution.

$\mathcal{M}'_3$: The latest pair for a location is used. If the program keeps printing conflicting bits for a location forever, it is not considered to contribute any probability for the distribution of that location (just as if it had never printed any pair for that location).

The resulting priors are arranged in order of expressive power. $\mathcal{M}'_2$ contains any model which $\mathcal{M}'_1$ does, since we can wrap an $\mathcal{M}'_1$ program in an output-checker which keeps the program from printing any pair for a previously-set location. $\mathcal{M}'_3$ subsumes $\mathcal{M}'_2$, since we can replicate the behavior of "throwing out" a program by printing conflicting pairs for all locations forever. Also, $\mathcal{M}'_1$ subsumes $\mathcal{M}$, since we can deal with locations in sequential order.

Thus, we can establish $\mathcal{M} \leq \mathcal{M}'_1 \leq \mathcal{M}'_2 \leq \mathcal{M}'_3$ (where $\leq$ indicates multiplicative dominance, to be defined) without too much trouble. It seems reasonable to further conjecture $\mathcal{M} < \mathcal{M}'_1 < \mathcal{M}'_2 < \mathcal{M}'_3$.

$\mathcal{M}'_3$ is related to generalized Kologorov complexity as discussed in [6], which shows that such a distribution cannot be approximated. As such, it is not clear how useful it might be to the study of intelligence.

Since consistency & completeness have not yet been dealt with, these distributions are better thought of as alternative sequence prediction priors, rather than trying to interpret them as distributions over logical theories by the previously-mentioned numbering.

Enforcing both consistency and completeness will result in logical priors which look similar to the one to be described: a process generating random sentences is constrained in such a way as to guarantee that the results make sense in terms of the logic.

2   Selected Background and Notation

2.1   First-Order Logic

We will be using first-order logic, defining the language $\mathcal{L}$ of first-order sentences as follows:

- There is an infinite stock of variable symbols, $v_1, v_2, ... \in \mathcal{V}$, an infinite stock of predicate symbols, $p_1, p_2, ... \in \mathcal{P}$, and an infinite stock of function symbols, $f_1, f_2, ... \in \mathcal{F}$.
- The number of arguments fed to a predicate or function is referred to as its *arity*. For example, a predicate of arity 2 is typically referred to as a relation. A function of arity 0 is referred to as a constant, and a predicate of arity 0 is a proposition. For simplicity, the arity of a symbol will be inferred from its use here, rather than set ahead of time. If the same symbol is used with multiple arities, the uses are independent (so f_2 would notate distinct functions in $f_2(v_1)$ versus $f_2(v_1, v_2)$).
- An *expression* is a composition of function symbols and variable symbols, for example $f_1(f_1(v_1))$. Specifically, the set of expressions $\mathcal{E}$ are defined inductively by: $\mathcal{V} \subset \mathcal{E}$, and for every function $f_n \in \mathcal{F}$ of arity a and expressions $e_1, e_2, ..., e_a \in \mathcal{E}$, we have $f_n(e_1, e_2, ...e_a) \in \mathcal{E}$.
- For $e_1, e_2 \in \mathcal{E}$, $e_1 = e_2$ is in $\mathcal{L}$; this represents equality.
- For $p_n \in \mathcal{P}$ of arity a and $e_1, e_2, ..., e_a \in \mathcal{E}$, we have $p_n(e_1, e_2, ..., e_a) \in \mathcal{L}$.
- For $A, B \in \mathcal{L}$, we have $(A \wedge B) \in \mathcal{L}$ and $(A \vee B) \in \mathcal{L}$; these represent conjunction and disjunction, respectively. (Parentheses will be omitted in this document when the intended grouping is clear.)
- For $S \in \mathcal{L}$, we have $\neg(S) \in \mathcal{L}$. This represents negation. (Again, parentheses may be omitted.)
- For any $S \in \mathcal{L}$ and $v_n \in \mathcal{V}$, we have $\forall v_n.(S) \in \mathcal{L}$ and $\exists v_n.(S) \in \mathcal{L}$, representing universal and existential quantification. (Parentheses may be ommited.)

If sentence A logically implies sentence B (meaning, B is true in any situation in which A is true), then we write $A \vDash B$. The notation also applies to multiple premises; if A and B together imply C, we can write $A, B \vDash C$. Uppercase greek letters will also be used to denote sets of sentences. We can write $A \nvDash B$ to say that A does not logically imply B.

If A implies B according to the inference rules (meaning, we can derive B starting with the assumption A), we write $A \vdash B$. This notation applies to multiple premises as well, and can be denied as $\nvdash$.

The inference rules will not be reviewed here, but some basic results will be important. These results can be found in many textbooks, but in particular, [1] has material on everything mentioned here.

Soundness. For a sentence S and a set of sentences Γ, if $\Gamma \vdash S$, then $\Gamma \vDash S$. That is, the inference rules will never derive something that doesn't logically follow from a set of premises.

Completeness. For a sentence S and a set of sentences Γ, if $\Gamma \vDash S$, then $\Gamma \vdash S$. That is, the inference rules can derive anything which logically follows from a set of premises.

Since the rules for $\vdash$ can be followed by a computer, this shows that $\vdash$ is computably enumerable: a (non-halting) program can enumerate all the true instances of $\Gamma \vdash S$.

Undecidability. For a given Γ and S, no general procedure exists which can decide whether $\Gamma \vdash S$ or $\Gamma \nvdash S$. Completeness implies that we can know $\Gamma \vdash S$ if it is true; however, if it is not, there is no general way to determine $\Gamma \nvdash S$.

Encoding computations. Any computable function can be encoded in first-order logic. This can be done, for example, by providing axioms related to the behavior of Turing machines.

2.2 Algorithmic Information Theory

$\mathcal{B}$ denotes the binary alphabet, $\{0,1\}$; $\mathcal{B}^n$ denotes the set of binary strings of length n; $\mathcal{B}^*$ denotes the set of binary strings of any finite length; $\mathcal{B}^\infty$ denotes the set of binary strings of infinite length; and $S_\mathcal{B} = \mathcal{B}^* \cup \mathcal{B}^\infty$ denotes the set of finite and infinite binary strings. String concatenation will be represented by adjacency, so ab is the concatenation of a and b.

Consider a class C_1 of Turing machines with three or more tapes: an input tape, one or more work tapes, and an output tape. The input and output tape are both able to move in just one direction. Any Turing machine $T \in C_1$ defines a partial function f_T from $\mathcal{B}^\infty$ to $S_\mathcal{B}$: for input $i \in \mathcal{B}^\infty$, $f_T(i)$ is considered to be the string which T writes to the output tape, which may be infinite if T never stops writing output. Now consider a *universal* machine from this class; that is, a machine $U \in C_1$ such that for any other machine $T \in C_1$, there is a finite sequence of bits $s \in \mathcal{B}^*$ which we can place on U's input tape to get it to behave exactly like T; that is, $f_U(si) = f_T(i)$ for all i.

A distribution $\mathcal{M}$ over $S_\mathcal{B}$ can be defined by feeding random bits to U; that is, we take $f_U(i)$ for uniformly random $i \in \mathcal{B}^\infty$.[1]

The development here has been adapted from [5].

Now, how do we compare two distributions?

P_1 *multiplicatively dominates* P_2 iff there exists $\alpha > 0$ such that $P_1(x) > \alpha P_2(x)$ for any x. An intuitive way of understanding this is that P_1 needs at most a constant amount more evidence to reach the same conclusion as P_2.[2] *Strict*

---

[1] $\mathcal{M}$ is not actually a probability distribution, but rather, a semimeasure. The Solomonoff distribution is a probability distribution defined from $\mathcal{M}$: we apply the *Solomonoff normalization* to $\mathcal{M}$, which gives a distribution over $\mathcal{B}^\infty$. The details of normalization will not be given here.

[2] This is true if we measure evidence by the log of the likelihood ratio. $P_1(x|e) = P_1(x)P_1(e|x)/P_1(e)$, so multiplicative dominance indicates that $P_1(e|x)/P_1(e)$ doesn't have to get too extreme to bridge the distance between P_1 and P_2.

multiplicative dominance means that P_1 multiplicatively dominates P_2, but the reverse is not the case. This indicates that P_1 needs at most a constant amount more evidence to reach the same conclusion as P_2, but we can find examples where P_2 needs arbitrarily more evidence than P_1 to come to the conclusion P_1 reaches.

The main reason $\mathcal{M}$ is interesting is that it is multiplicatively dominant over any computable probability distribution for sequence prediction. This makes it a highly general tool.

P_1 *exponentially dominates* P_2 iff there exists $\alpha, \beta > 0$ such that $P_1(x) > \alpha P_2(x)^\beta$. This intuitively means that P_1 needs at most some constant multiple of the amount of evidence which P_2 needs to reach a specific conclusion. *Strict* exponential dominance again indicates that the reverse is not the case, which means that P_2 needs *more* than multiplicatively more evidence to reach some conclusions that P_1 can reach.

We can also define (multiplicative or exponential) *equivalence*: two distributions are considered equivalent when they mutually dominate each other.

3   A Notion of Logical Probabilities

3.1   Requirements

I will follow [7] in the development of the idea of a probability distribution over a language, since this provides a particularly clear idea of what it means for a continuous-valued belief function to fit with a logic. I shall say that the distribution *respects the logic*. The approach is to define probability as a function on sentences in a language, rather than by the more common σ-algebra approach, and require the probabilities to follow several constraints based on the logic. Since we are using classical logic, I will simplify their constraints for that case.

Let $\mathcal{L}$ be the language of first-order logic from section 2. We want a probability function $P : \mathcal{L} \rightarrow \mathbb{R}$ to obey the following rules:

(P0) $P(A) = 0$ if A is refutable.
(P1) $P(A) = 1$ if A is provable.
(P2)   If A logically implies B, then $P(A) \leq P(B)$.
(P3) $P(A) + P(B) = P(A \vee B) + P(A \wedge B)$.

From these, we can prove other typical properties such as $P(A) + P(\neg A) = 1$.

3.2   Definition as a Generative Process

The idea behind the prior is to consider theories as being generated by choosing sentences at random, one after another. The probability of a particular sentence is taken to be the probability that it occurs in a theory randomly generated in this manner.

To be more precise, suppose we have some random process to generate individual sentences from our language $\mathcal{L}$. This generation process will be denoted

$\mathcal{G}$, and the probability that $S_1, S_2, ..., S_n$ are the first n statements generated will be written $\mathcal{G}(S_1, S_2, ..., S_n)$. $\mathcal{G}$ could be a highly structured process such as the $\mathcal{M}'$ distributions mentioned in section 1, but this seems unnecessarily complicated.[3] Unless otherwise mentioned, this paper will define $\mathcal{G}$ based on a simple probabilistic grammar on sentences, which generates sentences recursively by selecting each syntactic element given in section 2.1 with some probability. When selecting from the variable, predicate, or function symbols, the subscript number must be constructed, for example by assigning $\frac{1}{11}$ chance to each digit and $\frac{1}{11}$ chance to terminating the digit string. We define $\mathcal{G}(S_1, S_2, ..., S_n) = \Pi_{i=1}^n \mathcal{G}(S_i)$.

A theory is a set of sentences in $\mathcal{L}$. To generate a random theory, we generate a sequence of sentences $S_1, S_2, S_3, ...$ according to the following process. For each S_n, use sentences from $\mathcal{G}$, but discarding those which are inconsistent with the sentences so far; that is, rejecting any candidate for S_n which would make $S_1 \wedge ... \wedge S_n$ into a contradiction. (For S_1, the set of preceding sentences is empty, so we only need to ensure that it does not contradict itself.)

Notice that there is no stopping condition. The sequence generated will be infinite. However, the truth or falsehood of any particular statement (or any finite theory) will be determined after a finite amount of time. (The remaining sentences generated will either be consequences of, or irrelevant to, the statement in question.) Shorter (finite) theories will have a larger probability of occurring in the sequence.

In this way, we induce a new probability distribution P_L on sentences from the one we began with, $\mathcal{G}$. $P_L(S)$ is the probability that a sentence S will be present in a sequence $S_1, S_2, S_3, ...$ generated from $\mathcal{G}$ as described. Unlike $\mathcal{G}$, P_L respects the logic:

Theorem 1. P_L *obeys (P0)-(P3).*

Proof. (P0) is satisfied easily, since the process explicitly forbids generation of contradictions. (P1) is satisfied, because a provable statement can never contradict the sentences so far, so each will eventually be generated by chance as we continue to generate the sequence. Therefore, provable statements are generated with probability 1. (P2) is satisfied, by a similar argument: if we have already generated A, but A implies B, then anything which contradicts B will contradict A, and hence never be generated. This means that B will never be ruled out, and so must eventually be generated at random.[4] Therefore the probability for B is at least as high as that if A.

We can extend the argument a bit further to show (P3).

Since $A \vdash A \vee B$ and $B \vdash A \vee B$, the sentence $A \vee B$ will occur in any theory in which A or B occurs. Moreover, if $A \vee B$ occurs, then it would be inconsistent

---

[3] If we did choose to use these, we would need to address the fact that they are only semimeasures, not full probability distributions.

[4] Notice, this means any theory generated in this manner will contain all of its logical consequences with probability 1. This allows us to talk just about what sentences are in the theory, when we might otherwise need to talk about the theory plus all its logical consequences.

for both $\neg A$ and $\neg B$ to occur later. As a result, either A or B will eventually occur. So $P_L(A \vee B)$ equals the probability that either A or B occurs.

If both A and B occur in a theory, then $\neg(A \wedge B)$ would be contradictory, so will not occur; therefore, $A \wedge B$ will eventually be generated. On the other hand, if $A \wedge B$ occurs in a sequence, it would be inconsistent for either $\neg A$ or $\neg B$ to occur, so both A and B will eventually be present. $P_L(A \wedge B)$ equals the probability that both A and B occur in a sequence.

Since $P_L(A \vee B)$ equals the probability that *either* A or B occurs, and $P_L(A \wedge B)$ equals the probability that *both* A and B occur, we have $P_L(A \vee B) = P_L(A) + P_L(B) - P_L(A \vee B)$. This proves (P3).   □

The conditional probability can be defined as usual, with $P_L(A|B) = P_L(A \wedge B)/P_L(B)$. We can also extend the definition of $P_L()$ to include probabilities of sets of sentences, so that $P_L(\Gamma)$ for $\Gamma \subset \mathcal{L}$ is the probability that all $S \in \Gamma$ will be present in a sequence generated by the process defined above. (By an argument similar to the one used to prove (P3), the probability of a set of sentences will be equal to the probability of the conjunction.)

3.3   Approximability

The generative process described so far cannot be directly implemented, since there is no way to know for sure that a theory remains consistent as we add sentences at random. However, we can asymptotically approach $P_L()$ by eliminating inconsistent possibilities when we find them.

I assume in this section that $\mathcal{G}$ is such that we can sample from it. It may be possible that some interesting choices of $\mathcal{G}$ result in an approximable P_L without a sampleable $\mathcal{G}$.

Suppose we want to approximate $P_L(A)$. I shall call a partial sequence $S_1, S_2, ..., S_n$ a *prefix*. Consider the following Monte Carlo approximation:

```
t=1, y=1, n=1.
loop:
    // Reset the prefix at the beginning of each loop.
    prefix=none
    // Until we get A or neg(A),
    while not (s=A or s=neg(A)):
        // Get a random sentence.
        s=generate()
        // Append sample to the sequence so far.
        prefix=push(s,prefix)
        // Spend time t looking for contradictions.
        c=check(prefix,t)
        // If a contradiction is found,
        if c:
            // backtrack.
            pop(prefix)
    // If the generated prefix contains A,
```

```
if (s=A):
    // increment y.
    y=y+1
// Otherwise,
else:
    // increment n.
    n=n+1
// Increment t at the end of each loop.
t=t+1
```

The variables y and n count the number of positive and negative samples, while t provides a continually rising standard for consistency-detection on the sampled prefixes. (I will use the term "sample" to refer to generated prefixes, rather than individual sentences.) To that end, the function check(,) takes a prefix and an amount of time, and spends that long trying to prove a contradiction from the prefix. If one is found, check returns true; otherwise, false. The specific proof-search technique is of little consequence here, but it is necessary that it is exhaustive (it will eventually find a proof if one exists). The function neg() takes the negation; so, we are waiting for either A or $\neg A$ to occur in each sample. The prefix is represented as a FILO queue. push() adds a sentence to the given prefix, and pop() removes the most recently added sentence.

The inner loop produces individual extensions at random, backtracking whenever an inconsistency is found. The loop terminates when a theory includes either A or $\neg A$. The outer loop then increments y or n based on the result, increments t, erases the prefix, and re-enters the inner loop to get another sample.

Theorem 2. $\frac{y}{n+y}$ *will approach* $P_L(A)$.

Proof. Since every inconsistency has a finite amount of time required for detection, the probability of an undetected inconsistency will fall arbitrarily far as t rises. The probability of consistent samples, however, does not fall. Therefore, the counts will eventually be dominated by consistent samples.

The question reduces to whether the probability of a consistent sample containing A is equal to $P_L(A)$. We can see that this is the case, since if we assume that the generated sentences will be consistent with the sentence so far, then the generation probabilities are exactly those of the previous section. $\qquad\square$

3.4   Comparison

It would be interesting to know how this prior compares with the priors which have been defined via Turing machines.

In order to compare the first-order prior with priors for sequence prediction, we need to apply the first-order prior to sequence prediction. We can do so by encoding bit sequences in first-order logic. For example, f_1 can serve as a logical constant representing the sequence to be observed and predicted; $f_2()$ can represent adding a 0 to the beginning of some sequence; and $f_3()$ can represent adding a 1. So, to say that the sequence begins "0011..." we would write

$f_1 = f_2(f_2(f_3(f_3(f_4))))$, where f_4 is a logical constant standing for the remainder of the sequence. The probability of a bit sequence can be taken as the probability of a statement asserting that bit sequence. Define P_{LS} to be the resulting prior over bit sequences.

It seems possible to show that P_{LS} is exponentially equivalent to $\mathcal{M}'_2$ from section 1. $\mathcal{M}'_2$ will dominate P_{LS}, because P_{LS} can be defined by a Turing machine which takes an infintie stream of random bits, interpretes them as first-order sentences, and outputs all (location, bit) pairs which follow deductively from them. Since $\mathcal{M}'_2$ is constructed from a universal Turing machine, it will have this behavior with some probability. Inconsistent theories will start outputting inconsistent pairs, and so will not be included in $\mathcal{M}'_2$. Thus we get the behavior of P_{LS}. On the other hand, since first-order logic can encode computations, it seems that we can encode all the enumerations included in $\mathcal{M}'_2$. However, the encoding may not be efficient enough to get us multiplicative dominance. Exponential dominance seems possible to establish, since the expression-length of the representation of a bit-tape in first-order logic will be linear in the bit-length of that tape.

Since this development is insufficiently formal, the statement remains a conjecture here.

4   Conclusion and Questions

One hopeful application of this prior is to human-like mathematical reasoning, formalizing the way that humans are able to reason about mathematical conjectures. The study of conjecturing in artificial intelligence has been quite successful[5], but it is difficult to analyse this theoretically, especially from a Bayesian perspective.

This situation springs from the problem of *logical omniscience* [3]. The logical omniscience problem has to do with the sort of uncertainty that we can have when we are not sure what beliefs follow from our current beliefs. For example, we might understand that the motion of an object follows some particular equation, but be unable to calculate the exact result without pen and paper. Because the brain has limited computational power, we must expect the object to follow some plausible range of motion based on estimation. Standard probability theory does not model uncertainty of this kind. A distribution which follows the laws of probability theory will already contain all the consequences of any beliefs (it is logically omniscient). Real implementations cannot work like that.

> An agent might even have beliefs that logically contradict each other. Mersenne believed that $2^{67}-1$ is a prime number, which was proved false in 1903, [...] Together with Mersenne's other beliefs about multiplication and primality, that belief logically implies that $0 = 1$. [3]

Gaifman proposes a system in which probabilities are defined only with respect to a finite subset of the statements in a language, and beliefs are required to

---

[5] For example, AM[4] and Graffiti[2].

be consistent only with respect to chains of deduction in which each statement occurs in this limited set.

I will not attempt to address this problem to its fullest here, but approximations to P_L such as the one in section 3.3 seem to have some good properties in this area. If the proof of some statement X is too long for some approximation $A(t, X, Y)$ to $P_L(X|Y)$ to find given time t, then S will be treated exactly like a statement which is not provable: it will be evaluated with respect to how well it fits the evidence Y, given the connections which $A(t, X, Y)$ can find within time t. For example, if some universal statement $\forall x.S[x]$ can be proven from Y, but the proof is too long to find in reasonable time, then the probability of $\forall x.S[x]$ will still tend to rise with the number of individual instances $S[i]$ which are found to be true (although this cannot be made precise without more assumptions about the approximation process).

It is not clear how one would study this problem in the context of Solomonoff induction. Individual "beliefs" are not easy to isolate from a model when the model is presented as an algorithm. The problem of inconsistent beliefs does not even arise.

I do not claim that the first-order prior is a complete solution to this problem. For example, we do *not* get the desirable property that as we see arbitrarily many instances of a particular proposition, the probability of the universal generalization goes to 1. This fits with the semantics of first-order logic, but seems to be undesirable in other cases.

References

1. Boolos, G., Burgess, J.P., Jeffrey, R.C.: Computability and Logic. Cambridge University Press (2007)
2. Dinneen, M., Brewster, T., Faber, V.: A computational attack on the conjectures of graffiti: New counterexamples and proofs. Discrete Mathematics 147, 1–3 (1992)
3. Gaifman, H.: Reasoning with limited resources and assigning probabilities to arithmetical statements. Synthese 140(1951), 97–119 (2004)
4. Lenat, D., Brown, J.: Why am and eurisko appear to work. Artificial Intelligence 23(3), 269–294 (1984)
5. Li, M., Vitányi, P.: An introduction to Kolmogorov complexity and its applications, 2nd edn. Graduate texts in computer science. Springer (1997)
6. Schmidhuber, J.: Hierarchies of generalized Kolmogorov complexities and nonenumerable universal measures computable in the limit. International Journal of Foundations of Computer Science 13(4), 587–612 (2002)
7. Weatherson, B.: From classical to intuitionistic probability. Notre Dame Journal of Formal Logic 44(2), 111–123 (2003)

A Representation Theorem
for Decisions about Causal Models

Daniel Dewey

Future of Humanity Institute

Abstract. Given the likely large impact of artificial general intelligence, a formal theory of intelligence is desirable. To further this research program, we present a representation theorem governing the integration of causal models with decision theory. This theorem puts formal bounds on the applicability of the *submodel hypothesis*, a normative theory of decision counterfactuals that has previously been argued on *a priori* and practical grounds, as well as by comparison to theories of counterfactual cognition in humans. We are able to prove four conditions under which the submodel hypothesis holds, forcing any preference between acts to be consistent with some utility function over causal submodels.

1 Introduction

Artificial general intelligence will likely have a large impact on the world. It is plausible that the course of AGI research will influence the character of this impact significantly, and therefore that researchers can take an active role in managing the impact of AGI. For example, Arel [1] argues that reinforcement learning is likely to cause an "adversarial" dynamic, and Goertzel [8] proposes ways to bias AGI development towards "human-friendliness."

A particularly large impact is predicted by I. J. Good's intelligence explosion theory [9,3,4], which argues that repeated self-improvement could yield super-intelligent (and hence super-impactful) AGIs. A few recent accounts of how an intelligence explosion could come about, what its effects could be, or how it could be managed include Schmidhuber [17], Hutter [10], Legg [13], Goertzel [7], Norvig [16, pp. 1037], Chalmers [3,4], Bostrom [2], Muehlhauser and Salamon [14], and Yudkowsky [23].

With this in mind, a formal theory of intelligence is preferable to a less formal understanding. First, though we won't be able to prove what the final result of an AGI's actions will be, we may be able to prove that it is pursuing a desirable goal, in the sense that it is Pareto-optimal, maximizes expected value, or is the best approximation possible given space and time constraints [11]; this appears to be the highest level of certainty available to us [24,2]. Second, we may be able to design an AGI that has a formal understanding of its own intelligence, which could then execute a series of provably goal-retaining self-improvements, where an equally long series of heuristic self-modifications would carry a high risk of "goal drift" [22]. Indeed, the theory of provably optimal self-improvement

J. Bach, B. Goertzel, and M. Iklé (Eds.): AGI 2012, LNAI 7716, pp. 60–68, 2012.

has been under investigation for some time by Schmidhuber, under the name of "Gödel machines" (e.g. [18]).

In searching for a formal theory of intelligence, this paper focuses on decision theory as it applies to causal models. If an agent holds its beliefs in the form of a causal model, is there a provably valid way that it should use that model to make decisions?

We consider the submodel hypothesis: "If an agent holds its beliefs in the form of a causal model, then it should use submodels as decision counterfactuals." We are able to show that the submodel hypothesis holds over a sharply defined set of decision problems by proving a representation theorem: an agent's preferences can be represented by a utility function over submodels if and only if they are complete, transitive, function-independent, and variable-independent.

2 Causal Models

A causal model represents *events* and the *relationships* between them as *variables* and *functions*, respectively. For each variable, a model contains up to one function that calculates the value of that variable from the values of a set of other variables, representing the way that event depends on other events[1]. This allows a causal model to implicitly encode a joint distribution over values of the variables in the model; if a particular set of variable values is compatible with the functions between the variables, then it has a non-zero probability in the joint distribution. If an agent has observed a certain joint distribution of events in the world, it may be able in some cases to infer an underlying causal structure, and thereafter to represent its world using a causal model. For a full exposition of causal models and their properties, see [15].

In this paper, causal models will be written M or M', variables X or Y, and values of variable X will be written x or x' (except in concrete cases, e.g. variable "Switch" with values "on" and "off"). If X's value in M is given by function f applied to values of variables Y, this is written $X = f(Y)$. If X's value is given by a constant function with value x, this is written $X = x$.

Causal models can be pictured in two complementary ways: as a set of *structural equations* representing the functions, or as a *causal diagram*, a directed graph representing the dependencies and conditional independencies that hold between the variables.

The canonical example of a causal model (from [15]) is shown in Figure 1. It is a rudimentary model of the relationships between the *Season*, whether *Rain* is falling, whether a *Sprinkler* is on, whether the sidewalk is *Wet*, and whether the sidewalk is *Slippery*. In the causal diagram, an arrow from Season to Sprinkler indicates that the season plays an unmediated role in determining whether the sprinkler is on, though the graph does not show precisely what the relationship is. In the set of functional equations, the second equation shows the

---

[1] To simplify this work, error factors are left out of our account of causal models; reintroducing them should not interfere with our representation theorem or conclusions.

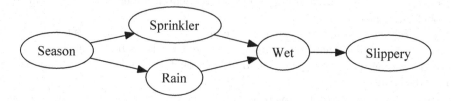

Rain = (Season = winter ∨ Season = fall) ? yes : no
Sprinkler = (Season = spring ∨ Season = summer) ? on : off
Wet = (Rain = falling ∨ Sprinkler = on) ? yes : no
Slippery = Wet ? yes : no

Fig. 1.

full relationship: in spring and summer, the sprinkler is on, and otherwise, it is off.

A *submodel* is a kind of causal model. Let M be a causal model, X be a variable, and x be a value of that variable: submodel M_x is derived from M by replacing X's function with the constant function $X = x$. Submodels may more generally replace a whole set of variables' functions with a set of constant functions, but this generalization will not be needed here. We use one non-standard notation: let $M_{X=f(Y)}$ denote the model derived by replacing X's function with f over values of Y in M.

3   The Submodel Hypothesis

The submodel hypothesis asserts that if an agent holds its beliefs in the form of a causal model, then it ought to use submodels as decision counterfactuals. A *decision counterfactual* is an agent's predictions of what would happen if it were to take a particular action. Thus, the submodel hypothesis can be restated as follows: "If an agent holds its beliefs in the form of a causal model, then it ought to predict the consequences of potential actions by replacing particular functions in that model with constants, and then choose the action whose consequences are most desirable."

In [15], Pearl argues for the submodel hypothesis by demonstrating how it avoids evidentialist decision errors, and by showing how it is formally very similar to Lewis' "closest world" theory of human counterfactual cognition [6]. He also argues that agents should model their own actions as uncaused "objects of free choice", and that the submodel method is the natural formalization of this idea.

Yudkowsky [25] builds on this work, arguing that decisions should be treated as *abstract computations*, representing them with variables that explain correlations in uncertainty stemming from bounded reasoning time and ability. Yudkowsky shows that agents who use submodels (of these kinds of models) as decision counterfactuals outperform other agents on many difficult decision theoretic problems, including Newcomb-like problems (where agents are simulated or predicted by their environments) and Prisoner's-dilemma-like problems (where certain types of coordination between agents are required to reach more desirable equilibria). Yudkowsky also asserts in [26] that his framework "explains why the counterfactual surgery can have the form it does".

In this paper, we seek formal justification: what kinds of agents, in what kinds of decision problems, *must* use submodels (or an equivalent procedure) as decision counterfactuals? Conversely, what do the necessary and sufficient conditions for the submodel hypothesis tell us about its plausibility as a normative theory of decision-making?

4   Integrating Causal Models with Decision Theory

Causal models are not a standard part of decision theory, so we begin with a simple, naturalistic integration of causal-model-based beliefs into decision theory.

Suppose that an agent holds its beliefs in the form of a causal model M. So that the model can guide the agent in making a choice, let some variable X in M represent the current decision, and let the rest of the model represent the decision's relationships to other events.

Though values of X represent different choices, a single variable value does not contain the beliefs the agent uses to make its decision. In order to state an agent's preferences, it will be convenient to bundle beliefs and choices together into *acts*. Each act is a pair $\langle M, x \rangle$, where X taking value x represents the choice of this act, so that all of the information an agent has about an act is contained within the act itself. We can therefore define a *decision problem* to be a set of acts; an agent solves a decision problem by choosing one of the acts. Since beliefs are bundled with acts, a weak preference between acts, $\succsim$, can be used to characterize all of the agent's decisions in all possible states of belief. We can now state the submodel hypothesis formally:

> An agent should act according to a preference over acts $\succsim$ that is representable by a utility function over submodels; i.e., there should exist a U from submodels to reals such that
>
> $$\langle M, x \rangle \succsim \langle M', y \rangle \iff U(M_x) \geq U(M'_y).$$

5   The Conditions

We have found four conditions on preferences over acts that are jointly equivalent to representability by a utility function over submodels. The first and second can be plausibly argued for by assuming that the agent is consequentialist; the third and fourth are novel, and whether they are justified is still an open question.

Suppose that the agent is consequentialist: it chooses one act or another for the sake of achieving a more desirable eventual outcome. If this is so, then even acts that could never appear in the same decision problem, such as $\langle M, x \rangle$ and $\langle M', y \rangle$, should be comparable according to the desirability of the eventual outcomes they are expected to bring about. Consequentialism, then, implies that an agent's preference over acts should be complete:

$$(A \succsim B) \vee (B \succsim A) \qquad\qquad \text{(Completeness.)}$$

Likewise, unless the agent's concept of desirability has cycles (in which outcome 1 is better than 2, 2 is better than 3, and 3 is better than 1), its preference over outcomes, and hence over acts, should be transitive:

$$(A \succsim B) \wedge (B \succsim C) \Rightarrow (A \succsim C) \qquad\qquad \text{(Transitivity.)}$$

It thus seems plausible that a consequentialist agent must have a complete and transitive preference over acts.

The third and fourth conditions are novel, and apply specifically to agents whose beliefs are held as causal models. Recall that each act specifies a particular variable to represent the decision event; if the agent is naturalistic, meaning that it represents its own decision process in the same way that it represents other cause-effect relationships, then the decision variable's function must represent the agent's decision process. *Function-independence* states that if two acts differ only in the function representing the decision process, they must be equally preferable:

$$\langle M, x \rangle \sim \langle M_{X=f(Y)}, x \rangle. \qquad\qquad \text{(Function-independence)}$$

The fourth condition, variable-independence, also requires certain indifferences between acts. In particular, variable-independence applies to acts that model the agent's decision as uncaused, representing it as a variable with no parents. Formally, variable-independence states that if a pair of acts share a model, and if each act represents the agent's decision process as a function of no inputs, then the two acts must be equally preferable:

$$X = x \wedge Y = y \text{ in } M \Rightarrow \langle M, x \rangle \sim \langle M, y \rangle. \qquad \text{(Variable-independence)}$$

We have found function-independence and variable-independence to be necessary for the submodel hypothesis, but attempts to discover whether and how they are generally justified have not been successful. This could be a fruitful area for future work.

6   The Representation Theorem

We are now ready to show that the four conditions together are necessary and sufficient for the submodel hypothesis:

Theorem 1. *If and only if a preference $\succsim$ over acts is complete, transitive, function-independent, and variable-independent, then $\succsim$ can be represented by a utility function over submodels, i.e. there exists a U from submodels to reals such that*

$$\langle M, x \rangle \succsim \langle M', y \rangle \iff U(M_x) \geq U(M'_y).$$

Proof. First, it is easy to show that each condition is necessary. Assuming that U represents $\succsim$, $\succsim$ must be:

Complete: Any two real utilities are comparable with $\geq$, so if U is complete and represents $\succsim$, then any two acts must be comparable with $\succsim$.

Transitive: Any three real utilities obey transitivity, so if U is complete and represents $\succsim$, then any three acts must be transitive under $\succsim$.

Function-independent:

$$M_x = (M_{X=f(Y)})_x$$
$$\Rightarrow U(M_x) = U((M_{X=f(Y)})_x)$$
$$\Rightarrow \langle M, x \rangle \sim \langle M_{X=f(Y)}, x \rangle.$$

Variable-independent:

$$X = x \wedge Y = y \text{ in } M$$
$$\Rightarrow M = M_x = M_y$$
$$\Rightarrow U(M_x) = U(M_y)$$
$$\Rightarrow \langle M, x \rangle \sim \langle M, y \rangle.$$

Second, we show that the conditions are sufficient for the existence of a utility representation over submodels; from here on, we assume that all conditions hold. Let α be any function from submodels "back to corresponding acts", meaning that $\alpha(S) = \langle M, x \rangle \Rightarrow S = M_x$. The following lemmas will be useful:

Lemma 1. $\forall M, x : \langle M, x \rangle \sim \alpha(M_x)$.

Proof. Let $\langle M', y \rangle = \alpha(M_x)$. By definition of α, $M_x = M'_y$.

$$
\begin{array}{ll}
\langle M, x \rangle \sim \langle M_x, x \rangle & \text{by function-independence,} \\
\quad \sim \langle M'_y, x \rangle & \text{since } M_x = M'_y;
\end{array}
$$

because $M_x = M'_y$, we know that $X = x$ in M'_y, and trivially $Y = y$ in M'_y, and so by variable-independence,

$$
\begin{array}{ll}
\quad \sim \langle M'_y, y \rangle & \\
\quad \sim \langle M', y \rangle & \text{by function-independence,} \\
\quad \sim \alpha(M_x), &
\end{array}
$$

and so $\langle M, x \rangle \sim \alpha(M_x)$. $\qquad\square$

Lemma 2. $\langle M, x \rangle \succsim \langle M', y \rangle \iff \alpha(M_x) \succsim \alpha(M'_y)$.

Proof. $\Rightarrow$: Assume $\langle M, x \rangle \succsim \langle M', y \rangle$. By Lemma 1,

$$\alpha(M_x) \sim \langle M, x \rangle \succsim \langle M', y \rangle \sim \alpha(M'_y),$$

and since $\succsim$ is transitive, $\alpha(M_x) \succsim \alpha(M'_y)$.
$\Leftarrow$: Assume $\alpha(M_x) \succsim \alpha(M'_y)$. By Lemma 1,

$$\langle M, x \rangle \sim \alpha(M_x) \succsim \alpha(M'_y) \sim \langle M', y \rangle,$$

and since $\succsim$ is transitive, $\langle M, x \rangle \succsim \langle M', y \rangle$.

$\square$

Now we can construct a utility function on submodels and to show that it represents $\succsim$. Let v be an injective function from submodels to the set $\{2^{-n} : n \in \mathbb{N}\}$, and let U be defined as

$$U(S) = \sum_{S' : \alpha(S) \succsim \alpha(S')} v(S').$$

Since the sum of $\{2^{-n} : n \in \mathbb{N}\}$ converges, the utility function is defined even when the set of submodels is (countably) infinite [21].

First, we will show that every preference over acts is represented in utilities. Assume that one act is weakly preferred over another, so that $\langle M, x \rangle \succsim \langle M', y \rangle$. By Lemma 2, $\alpha(M_x) \succsim \alpha(M'_y)$. Since $\succsim$ is transitive, any $\alpha(S)$ weakly dispreferred to $\alpha(M'_y)$ is also dispreferred to $\alpha(M_x)$, and so

$$\{S : \alpha(M_x) \succsim \alpha(S)\} \supseteq \{S : \alpha(M'_y) \succsim \alpha(S)\}.$$

By definition of U, we conclude that $U(M_x) \geq U(M'_y)$.

Second, we will show that every utility difference represents a preference. Let $U(M_x) \geq U(M'_y)$. To draw a contradiction, assume that $\alpha(M_x) \not\succsim \alpha(M'_y)$. By completeness, $\alpha(M'_y) \succ \alpha(M_x)$. It follows by transitivity that

$$\{S : \alpha(M'_y) \succsim \alpha(S)\} \supset \{S : \alpha(M_x) \succsim \alpha(S)\}.$$

By definition of U, this means that $U(M'_y) > U(M_x)$, a contradiction; therefore, $\alpha(M_x) \succsim \alpha(M'_y)$. By Lemma 2, $\langle M, x \rangle \succsim \langle M', y \rangle$.

Thus, we have shown that the conditions given are necessary and sufficient for the existence of a representative utility function over submodels; the submodel hypothesis is confirmed over the class of problems defined by the conditions. $\square$

7 Conclusion

In this paper, we have shown a set of four conditions under which the submodel hypothesis is confirmed, i.e. an agent whose beliefs are held as a causal model must have preferences that can be represented by a utility function over submodels. This puts sharply-defined boundaries on where the submodel hypothesis, which has previously been argued by Pearl [15] and Yudkowsky [25], is justified and required. More broadly, we have aimed to contribute to a formal theory of intelligence, with the goal of shaping the impact of AGI to be safe and beneficial.

Acknowledgements. Thanks to Vladimir Slepnev, Benja Fallenstein, and Luke Muehlhauser for their comments on earlier versions of the paper.

References

1. Arel, I.: Reward Driven Learning and the Risk of an Adversarial Artificial General Intelligence. Talk at "The Future of AGI Workshop Part 1 - Ethics of Advanced AGI," The Fourth Conference on Artificial General Intelligence (2011)
2. Bostrom, N.: The Superintelligent Will: Motivation and Instrumental Rationality in Advanced Artificial Agents. Minds and Machines 22, 71–85 (2012)
3. Chalmers, D.: The Singularity: A Philosophical Analysis. Journal of Consciousness Studies 17, 7–65 (2010)
4. Chalmers, D.: The Singularity: a Reply. Journal of Consciousness Studies 19 (2012)
5. Drescher, G.: Good and real: Demystifying paradoxes from physics to ethics. Bradford Books, MIT Press, Cambridge, MA (2006)
6. Galles, D., Pearl, J.: An Axiomatic Characterization of Counterfactuals. Foundations of Science III, 151–182 (1998)
7. Goertzel, B.: Should Humanity Build a Global AI Nanny to Delay the Singularity Until It's Better Understood? Journal of Consciousness Studies 19, 96–111 (2012)
8. Goertzel, B.: Nine Ways to Bias Open-Source AGI Toward Friendliness. Journal of Evolution and Technology 22, 116–131 (2012)
9. Good, I.J.: Speculations Concerning the First Ultraintelligent Machine. In: Alt, F.L., Rubinoff, M. (eds.) Advances in Computers, vol. 6, pp. 31–88 (1965)
10. Hutter, M.: Can Intelligence Explode? Journal of Consciousness Studies 19, 143–166 (2012)
11. Hutter, M.: Universal algorithmic intelligence: A mathematical top-down approach. In: Artificial General Intelligence, pp. 227–290. Springer, Berlin (2007)
12. Legg, S.: Is there an Elegant Universal Theory of Prediction? IDSIA Technical Report No. IDSIA-12-06 (2006)
13. Legg, S.: Machine Super Intelligence. PhD dissertation, University of Lugano (2008)
14. Muehlhauser, L., Salamon, A.: Intelligence Explosion: Evidence and Import. In: The Singularity Hypothesis: A Scientific and Philosophical Assessment. Springer, Berlin (2012)
15. Pearl, J.: Causality: Models, Reasoning, and Inference. Cambridge University Press (2000)
16. Russell, S., Norvig, P.: AI: A Modern Approach, 3rd edn. Prentice-Hall, Englewood Cliffs (1995)
17. Schmidhuber, J.: Philosophers & Futurists, Catch Up! Journal of Consciousness Studies 19, 173–182 (2012)
18. Schmidhuber, J.: Gödel machines: Fully Self-Referential Optimal Universal Self-Improvers. In: Artificial General Intelligence, pp. 119–226 (2006)
19. Solomonoff, R.: A Formal Theory of Inductive Inference, Part I. Information and Control 7(1), 1–22 (1964)
20. Solomonoff, R.: A Formal Theory of Inductive Inference, Part II. Information and Control 7(2), 224–254 (1964)
21. Voorneveld, M.: Mathematical Foundations of Microeconomic Theory: Preference, Utility, Choice (2010),
https://studentweb.hhs.se/CourseWeb/CourseWeb/Public/PhD501/1001/micro1.pdf

22. Yudkowsky, E.: Artificial intelligence as a positive and negative factor in global risk. In: Global Catastrophic Risks. Oxford University Press, Oxford (2008)
23. Yudkowsky, E.: Complex Value Systems are Required to Realize Valuable Futures. In: The Proceedings of the Fourth Conference on Artificial General Intelligence (2011)
24. Yudkowsky, E., et al.: Reducing Long-Term Catastrophic Risks from Artificial Intelligence. The Singularity Institute, San Francisco (2010)
25. Yudkowsky, E.: Timeless decision theory. The Singularity Institute, San Francisco (2010)
26. Yudkowsky, E.: Ingredients of Timeless Decision Theory (2009), http://lesswrong.com/lw/15z/ingredients_of_timeless_decision_theory/

Modular Value Iteration
through Regional Decomposition

Linus Gisslen, Mark Ring, Matthew Luciw, and Jürgen Schmidhuber

IDSIA
Manno-Lugano, 6928, Switzerland
{linus,mark,matthew,juergen}@idsia.com

Abstract. Future AGIs will need to solve large reinforcement-learning problems involving complex reward functions having multiple reward sources. One way to make progress on such problems is to decompose them into smaller regions that can be solved efficiently. We introduce a novel modular version of Least Squares Policy Iteration (LSPI), called M-LSPI, which 1. breaks up Markov decision problems (MDPs) into a set of mutually exclusive regions; 2. iteratively solves each region by a single matrix inversion and then combines the solutions by value iteration. The resulting algorithm leverages regional decomposition to efficiently solve the MDP. As the number of states increases, on both structured and unstructured MDPs, M-LSPI yields substantial improvements over traditional algorithms in terms of time to convergence to the value function of the optimal policy, especially as the discount factor approaches one.

1 Introduction

Reinforcement learning is one of the most promising approaches for achieving artificial general intelligence, yet current methods tend to scale poorly to large problems. Effective methods exist for finding the optimal policy and value function of a Markov decision process (MDP; [1]) given a model of transition probabilities and expected rewards [1–7], but these methods run into computational bottlenecks as the number of states and their degree of connectivity increases or when the reward function is complex (*i.e.*, when there are many sources of reward). Yet it is quite common for real-world, applied MDPs to have complex reward functions with positive and negative rewards distributed throughout the task space. In robotics, for example, all near-collision states might generate negative reward.

In this work we assume access to an accurate model of the MDP and focus on new methods for solving the MDP from the model. Any existing approach for building the model from interaction with the environment can be used, *e.g.*, that of Gisslen *et al.* (2011) [8]. Value Iteration (VI; [2, 9]) is the most basic MDP solver. It does state-value backups [1] on all states, equally often, independent of MDP structure. VI handles complex reward functions well, but scales poorly as the discount factor approaches one and as the degree of connectivity in the MDP increases. Thus, there have been previous attempts to improve its efficiency. Prioritized Sweeping (PS; [4]), for example, uses a priority queue to

J. Bach, B. Goertzel, and M. Iklé (Eds.): AGI 2012, LNAI 7716, pp. 69–78, 2012.

order partial state-value backups prioritized on (generally) the Bellman error. PS gets a better *approximate* result than VI with less data and less time, but final convergence (to the same result as VI) often takes just as long or longer due to queue maintenance. Dai *et al.* [5] tried to avoid the overhead of priority queue maintenance, suggesting heuristics to prioritize states, such as reachability of a state from the goal when following the current policy. Wingate [6] organized the bookkeeping overhead, prioritizing via an "information frontier" starting with the "most informative state" (*e.g.*, the absorbing goal), then propagated the frontier throughout the system. These approaches are very effective for single-goal situations, but do not efficiently handle complex reward functions. Least Squares Policy Iteration (LSPI; [7]), based on policy iteration (PI; [3]), finds the optimal linear-function approximation of an MDP's value function via a series of matrix inversions.[1] Unfortunately, matrix inversions can be very computationally demanding, scaling nearly cubically with the number of state-action pairs, but LSPI is appealing because it has no adjustable learning rate, delivers an optimal solution for every reward function, and its performance is independent of the MDP's connectivity and discount factor.

This paper introduces *Modular LSPI* (M-LSPI) which combines VI and LSPI to achieve the advantages of both: good scaling behavior in the number of states, discount factor, *and* connectivity. M-LSPI partitions the states into mutually exclusive regions (we explore several methods for doing so in Sec. 4). Separate modules perform LSPI within each region independently, and the value information between modules is then combined using a method that resembles VI. If the MDP exhibits regional structure, then the partitioning can lead to a considerable improvement in performance. The results indicate that M-LSPI is especially good on MDPs with *high connectivity* even when the assignment of states to regions is purely random. Experiments show benefits over previous methods on a variety of MDPs, including autonomous systems and simulated humanoid motor tasks, indicating that M-LSPI can be effective in any environment where a world-model can obtained. Finally, the modular approach appears promising for continual learning [10], as it provides a method for adding new regions without the need to recalculate the entire MDP.

2   Markov Decision Processes with Many States

Markov Decision Processes. A *Markov decision process* can be expressed as a 5-tuple (S,A,P,R,γ), where $S = \{s_1, s_2, \ldots, s_n\}$ is a finite set of states, $A = \{a_1, a_2, \ldots, a_m\}$ is a finite set of actions, $P(s, a, s')$ is a *Markovian transition model* quantifying the probability of ending up in state s' when taking an action a in state s, $R(s, a, s')$ is the expected reward when taking action a from state s and ending up in state s', and $\gamma \in [0, 1)$ is the discount factor, exponentially decreasing the impact of future rewards on the current action choices.

---

[1] Typically, LSPI operates on features; however, for an exact solution of an MDP, a single dimension of the feature vector can be dedicated to each state-action pair, which is how we use it here.

A learning agent increases its receipt of reward by improving its *policy* π, which specifies what action the agent takes in each state. The agent *solves* an MDP by finding the *optimal* policy π^*, which maximizes its receipt of reward. $Q^\pi(s, a)$, called the "state-action value," represents the expected sum of discounted future rewards the agent will receive for taking action a in state s and following policy π thereafter. These values for all (s, a) pairs are related mathematically by the Bellman equation:

$$Q^\pi(s, a) = \mathcal{R}(s, a) + \gamma \sum_{s'} P(s, a, s') Q^\pi(s', \pi(s')). \tag{1}$$

where $\mathcal{R}(s, a) = \sum_{s'} P(s, a, s') R(s, a, s')$. Thus, the optimal policy always chooses the action with the highest state-action value: $\pi^\star(a) = \max_a Q^{\pi^\star}(s, a)$.

Iterative MDP Solution Methods. The two main iterative methods for solving an MDP from P and $\mathcal{R}$ are value iteration (VI, described next) and policy iteration (PI, described in Sec. 3 in the context of LSPI).[2]

VI solves the system of Bellman equations described in Equation 1 by iteratively doing updates (called "backups") in the form:

$$Q(s, a) \leftarrow \mathcal{R}(s, a) + \gamma \sum_{s' \in S} P(s, a, s') V(s') \tag{2}$$

for all states and actions, where the *state value* $V(s) = \max_a Q(s, a)$. Each backup propagates the maximum reward information to each state from its successors. The agent's best policy, given the backups made at any point, is to take the action in each state with the highest state-action value. One loop through all state-action pairs yields the best policy with a one-step look-ahead; after two loops, the maximum two-step policy is obtained. The iteration process continues until *convergence*: when the difference between all state values over two subsequent loops is less than a certain threshold ϵ.

VI has a time complexity of $O(|A||S|^2)$ per iteration, with the number of iterations required for convergence growing with $1/(1-\gamma)$ [12], which makes VI troublesome as the discount factor γ approaches one. In contrast, PI requires $O(|S|^3)$ operations per iteration [3] and convergence does not seem to depend on the discount factor.

Reward Horizon. As the number of states in an MDP increases, the discount factor also needs to increase towards one if all the rewards are to impact all of the states. For example, if $\gamma = 0.9$ a reward value of 1.0 has an impact (a discounted value) of only 10^{-23} on states 500 steps away; when $\gamma = 0.99$, that value is .007, but is 0.6 when $\gamma = 0.999$. Therefore in even moderate-sized MDPs (>1000 states) the discount factor must be higher than $\gamma = 0.9$ if the rewards in one region of the MDP are to have a significant impact on the agent's choices in distant states. Thus, planning very far into the future makes VI computationally

---

[2] Linear programming [11] can represent any MDP and solve it in polynomial time, but in practice the polynomials are often too large to be solved in reasonable time [12], while iterative methods are feasible.

costly: convergence for $\gamma = 0.99$ takes ten times longer than for $\gamma = 0.9$. And while PI handles the discount factor well, it scales poorly with the number of states. Therefore, both approaches seem prohibitive for large MDPs. Yet it is possible to get the best of both worlds in some cases by doing PI locally and VI globally, particularly if the MDP has local structure that allows regional decomposition.

Regional Decomposition. Decomposing the MDP into smaller regions has been used before to increase solution speed, whether it is to achieve sub-optimal policies quickly [13] or to organize backups to reach optimal values faster [6]. Generally performance improves when the partitioning reflects the structure of the MDP. Prior knowledge, such as the positions of the states in a 2D grid-world, can allow decomposition by hand (*e.g.*, into a coarser-resolution 2D grid-world). For the general case, when such prior knowledge is not available, there are regional decomposition algorithms such as the Chinese Whispers method [14], but these can be computationally demanding and their performance is not guaranteed. The opposite extreme is to assign states to regions randomly, which is computationally trivial yet still occasionally beneficial simply because smaller regions can be solved faster.

3   Modular Least-Square Policy Iteration

Algorithm 1 shows M-LSPI as pseudo-code. Prior to execution, the MDP is assumed to have been decomposed into non-overlapping regions of states (see Sec. 4).

The algorithm's main loop, repeated until convergence, combines a VI step with a PI step for each region. The VI step collects state values from the neighboring regions (lines **5–8**). The PI step calls LSPI-Model (the model-based version of LSPI, line **10**) which treats the region as though it were a complete MDP and finds its optimal policy (given the current information). The key of M-LSPI is the way the VI and PI steps are combined. The trick here is to sum up the state values from all the successor states in the neighboring regions and then *to add these values into the reward vector* **b** for the region to be solved. When LSPI solves the region using this modified reward vector, that integrates the VI and PI steps, yielding exact state-action values for the region using all the latest information from the local region and its neighbors.

Looking at the MDP as a graph, LSPI is guaranteed to find the correct values [7] for all the edges within the local region (given current information), while the value-iteration step updates the edges connecting the region to its neighbors. Since VI itself is guaranteed to converge [9], we conjecture that M-LSPI will iteratively converge to the optimal value function. This conjecture is supported by the empirical results in Sec 4.

M-LSPI scales well, handling MDPs with a large number of states and γ close to one. It avoids the cubic scaling complexity of global PI by keeping down the number of states within each region, and avoids VI's explosive reaction to γ by using LSPI to get exact results in each region. LSPI converges reliably and quickly to the optimal policy for small MDPs and does not require tuning.

Algorithm 1. M-LSPI($\mathbf{M}, \mathcal{P}, \mathcal{R}, Q, \gamma$)

// $\mathbf{M}_i$: Region assignments
// $\mathcal{P}_{i,j}$: Regional transition models (s, a, s') for $s \in M_i$ and $s' \in M_j$
// $\mathcal{R}_i$: Regional reward vectors for all (s, a), where $s \in M_i$
// Q : Initial state-action values
// γ : Discount factor

```
1  repeat
2  │  Q' ← Q                                    // save latest state-action values
3  │  for each region i in M do
4  │  │  b ← Rᵢ                                 // local reward vector
5  │  │  for each region j in NeighborsOf (i) do
6  │  │  │  for each (s, a, s') ∈ Pᵢ,ⱼ do
7  │  │  │  │  b_{s,a} ← b_{s,a} + γPᵢ,ⱼ(s,a,s') · max_{a'∈A} Q_{s',a'}
8  │  │  │  end
9  │  │  end
10 │  │  Qᵢ ← LSPI-Model(Pᵢ,ᵢ, b, Qᵢ, γ)       // update Q values for s ∈ Mᵢ
11 │  end
12 until (max_{s,a} |Q_{s,a} − Q'_{s,a}| < ε)   // check convergence globally
13 return Q
```

Model-Based LSPI. In LSPI, the state-action values Q are approximated as a linear combination of *basis functions* $\boldsymbol{\Phi}$:

$$\hat{Q}(s, a, \omega) = \boldsymbol{\Phi}\omega.$$

Writing the Bellman equation (1) in matrix form

$$Q^\pi = \mathcal{R} + \gamma \mathbf{P}\boldsymbol{\Pi}Q^\pi,$$

where $\boldsymbol{\Pi}$ is a matrix representation of policy π, and replacing Q^π with the approximation $\hat{Q} = \boldsymbol{\Phi}\omega$ yields

$$\boldsymbol{\Phi}\omega \approx \mathcal{R} + \gamma \mathbf{P}^\pi \boldsymbol{\Phi}\omega.$$

where $\mathbf{P}^\pi = \mathbf{P}\boldsymbol{\Pi}$. Parameter values ω are calculated with a single matrix inversion:

$$\omega = \mathbf{A}^{-1}b, \tag{3}$$

where

$$\mathbf{A} = \boldsymbol{\Phi}^\intercal(\boldsymbol{\Phi} - \gamma \mathbf{P}^\pi \boldsymbol{\Phi})$$
$$b = \boldsymbol{\Phi}^\intercal \mathcal{R}.$$

In our model-based case, each basis function is dedicated to a single state-action pair, and thus $\boldsymbol{\Phi}$ is an $(|S||A| \times |S||A|)$ identity matrix, and ω is identical to the estimated state-action values (shown in Algorithm 1 as Q). However, for completeness we include the full derivation here.

Regional Model-Based LSPI. Given a state space that has been decomposed into non-overlapping regions of states, M-LSPI decomposes the above equations into subsets corresponding to those regions and uses LSPI to solve each subset separately (line **10** in Algorithm 1):

$$\omega_i = \mathbf{A}_i^{-1} b_i$$
$$\mathbf{A}_i = \mathbf{\Phi}_i^\mathsf{T}(\mathbf{\Phi}_i - \gamma \mathbf{P}_{i,i}^\pi \mathbf{\Phi}_i)$$
$$b_i = \mathbf{\Phi}_i^\mathsf{T} V_i$$

where $\mathbf{\Phi}_i$ is the set of basis functions for the states in region i, and $\mathbf{P}_{i,i}^\pi$ contains only information about transition probabilities within region i. V_i combines the reward values for region i with the discounted state-action values from all successor states in the neighboring regions, following Bellman's optimality equation rewritten (in matrix form) in terms of regions rather than states:

$$V_i = \mathcal{R}_i + \gamma \sum_{j \neq i} \mathbf{P}_{i,j}^\pi V_j \tag{4}$$

where R_i is the reward vector for region i (Algorithm 1, line **4**), $\mathbf{P}_{i,j}^\pi$ is the transition probability matrix between the regions i and j, and V_j is the vector of state values for region i's successor states in region j. As usual with VI, the state values V_j are computed as the maximum state-action value for each state (Algorithm 1, line **7**).

In the simplest case, where there is only one region, the second term on the right hand side of Equation 4 is 0, and the first term ($\mathcal{R}_i$) is the reward vector $\mathcal{R}$, which thus becomes the b vector used to solve Equation (3).

As ω_i depends on information from all the other $\omega_{j \neq i}$ it is now clear that the global solution must be reached through successive iterations, similar to VI. When the values have converged, the collection of regional weights ω_i taken together represent the full set of weights ω.

4   Experimental Results

This section compares M-LSPI with other methods for discovering the optimal policy π^* and calculating its value function over a variety of MDPs. All comparisons are in terms of wall-clock time (seconds) until convergence, $\epsilon = 10^{-6}$. In our case, this time includes the overhead of building regions (but this cost would not be incurred again if the calculation were repeated with different reward vectors).

Experimental Data. Comparisons were done with four classes of MDP (see Figure 1) and two sets of real data (named "RobotArm" and "Autonomous-system," see below). All MDPs have fixed (but randomly generated) transition probabilities and reward values; *i.e.*, when the MDP is created, each state-action pair is assigned a fixed reward value drawn from a uniform distribution in $(-1, 1)$.
1D-MDP (Fig 1, a): A one-dimensional Markov ring with sparse, local connectivity, having N states and five possible actions. One action has no effect; each

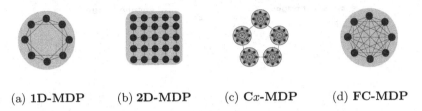

(a) **1D-MDP**   (b) **2D-MDP**   (c) **Cx-MDP**   (d) **FC-MDP**

Fig. 1. Illustration of connectivity in different MDPs: (a) one- and (b) two-dimensional MDPs (**1D-MDP** and **2D-MDP**) with connections only to closest neighbors, (c) clusters of fully connected states with sparse connections to neighboring clusters (**Cx-MDP**) where x denotes the cluster size, and (d) fully connected MDP (**FC-MDP**).

of the other four move the agent either clockwise or counterclockwise, either one step or two. There is a 10% random chance one of the actions not chosen is taken instead. **2D-MDP** (Fig 1, b): A 2D (toroidal) version of the previous, also having five actions (up, down, left, right and stay), again with a 10% chance a different action is taken. **Cx-MDP** (Fig 1, c): Clusters of x fully connected states with sparse connections between the clusters. This is an MDP version of *modular small-world graphs* [15]. **FC-MDP** (Fig 1, d): A fully connected MDP where each state is connected to each other state. Transition probabilities for Cx and FC are assigned randomly, drawn uniformly from (0,1) and then normalized such that $\sum_{s'} P(s, a, s') = 1$ for each (s, a) pair. **RobotArm.** A dataset generated with the iCub robot simulator [16]. Each state corresponds to the configuration of three arm joints (two shoulder and one elbow). A *precision* value controls the number of states; higher precision means finer quantization and more states. There are six deterministic actions, each resulting in a movement to the next closest configuration for each joint in both directions. **Autonomous-system.** Datasets from the Stanford Large Networks dataset collection.[3] These datasets represent communication graphs of routers comprising the internet (known as "autonomous systems") and are available in a variety of sizes. We assigned random reward values to the edges, drawn uniformly from (-1,1), and the transition probabilities are split evenly. In this special case there are no actions, so there is no policy improvement, and only the value function is solved.

Methods Compared. The featured competitors are value iteration (VI; [2]), prioritized sweeping (PS; [4]), and LSPI itself on the model [7]. We do not compare experimentally to Wingate's value iteration with regional prioritization [6], nor the prioritization method of Dai [5], since we study the general case of arbitrary-valued reward functions, for which they are poorly suited.

Figure 2 shows a comparison of the three methods on two classes of MDPs with a small number of states. It is clear that only VI merits a large-scale comparison to M-LSPI.

Experiment Setup. Each model has an adjustable size (number of states). For every model size, we ran five tests and report average time to convergence.

---

[3] snap.stanford.edu/data/

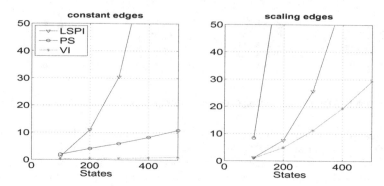

Fig. 2. Comparison of LSPI, PS, and VI on MDPs with complex reward functions (nonzero reward for each state-action pair), with $\gamma = 0.99$. Left: Time required to find the optimal policy on a 1D-MDP (see text) where the number of connections per state is constant. LSPI's near-cubic complexity leads to poor performance. VI does quite well with complex reward functions and low-connectivity. PS does not deal well with complex reward functions since the priority queue introduces needless overhead. Right: Results on FC-MDPs (see text) where the number of connections per state scales with the number of states. Again, LSPI scales very poorly, and high connectivity leads to extremely poor performance of PS. VI is also the best of the three in this type of MDP.

Each test had a unique set of randomly assigned reward values and transition probabilities, and we compared all methods using the same set of tests. We used two values of γ: 0.99 and 0.999, and convergence criteria was $\epsilon = 10^{-6}$ for all methods, which in all cases guaranteed discovery of the optimal policy.

Region Building. M-LSPI used several different region-building techniques for the tests. For the random MDPs, states were assigned to regions randomly, with the region size fixed at 30. We also assigned states randomly for the Autonomous-system data, which has high (but not full) connectivity. We used the Chinese Whispers (CW) technique for the modular MDPs (CX-100). CW breaks up regions based on bottlenecks, leading states with high mutual connectivity to belong to the same regions. In this particular case region sizes were typically 100 states. This is an excellent situation for M-LSPI, as LSPI can handle dense connectivity within the regions well (in a small number of iterations). However, VI will struggle when the connectivity is dense. For the 1D, 2D, and RobotArm MDPs, there are no bottlenecks, so we use a simple variant of CW where: (1) initially each state is its own region; and (2) until all states are tagged, a random untagged state is selected, tagged, and a few of its untagged connecting states are merged into a single region (unless it would exceed 30 states).

Results. Graphic comparisons of M-LSPI and VI are shown in Fig. 3. M-LSPI seems to scale better than VI except for (a) the 1D and 2D MDPs when $\gamma = 0.99$ and (b) the RobotArm data (which is also a type of structured MDP). VI is ideal for the RobotArm data where the MDP is deterministic with low connectivity. When γ is increased, M-LSPI scales better than VI in all cases, since it solves each region with LSPI. Possibly due its modular structure, M-LSPI excels on modular

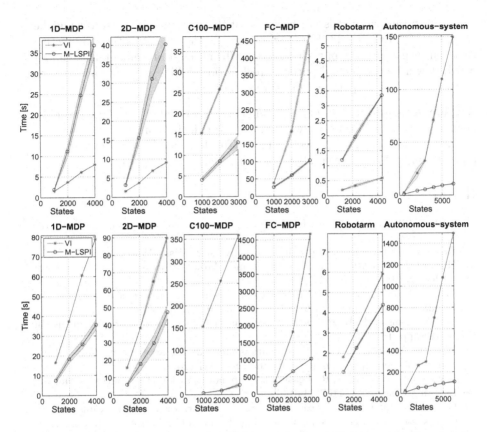

Fig. 3. Performance comparison of M-LSPI to value iteration on synthetic and real-data-based MDPs (described in text). For the upper panels, discount factor $\gamma = 0.99$, for the lower panels $\gamma = 0.999$.

Cx-MDPs, especially those with lower overall connectivity. It also does exceptionally well with fully-connected random MDPs and the autonomous-systems data, scaling far better than any alternate method we know.

Note that all results shown above *include* the cost of building the regions. In the RobotArm experiment, the region building time for {1176, 2238, 4356} states on average is {0.46, 1.2, 1.7} seconds. This can be done once, and the same regions can be used for multiple reward vectors. If the regions are already built, M-LSPI will be even faster than shown.

5 Conclusions

M-LSPI is a novel, modular, model-based MDP solver for large MDPs with complex reward functions. It efficiently yet optimally solves large MDPs, excelling on those with high connectivity or modular small-world connectivity. While approximate MDP solvers can sacrifice accuracy for speed, our method and others [5, 6] have shown this sacrifice is not necessary if the structure of the solver matches the structure of the world. However, to our knowledge ours is the only method that can take advantage of such structure when the reward function is complex, which it will be for general-purpose, real-world intelligent agents, arising from multiple, anisotropic pain and pleasure signals.

Acknowledgments. The authors would like to thank Vincent Graziano for helpful discussions. This work was funded through the 7th framework program of the EU under grants #228844 (NanoBioTouch project), #231722 (IM-Clever project), and #270247 (NeuralDynamics project).

References

1. Sutton, R.S., Barto, A.G.: Reinforcement learning: An introduction. Cambridge Univ. Press (1998)
2. Bellman, R.: Dynamic Prog. Princeton University Press, Princeton (1957)
3. Howard, R.A.: Dynamic Programming and Markov Processes. MIT Press, Cambridge (1960)
4. Moore, A.W., Atkeson, C.G.: Prioritized sweeping: Reinforcement learning with less data and less time. Machine Learning 13, 103–130 (1993)
5. Dai, P., Hansen, E.A.: Prioritizing bellman backups without a priority queue. In: ICAPS, pp. 113–119 (2007)
6. Wingate, D., Seppi, K.D.: Prioritization methods for accelerating mdp solvers. Journal of Machine Learning Research 6, 851–881 (2005)
7. Lagoudakis, M.G., Parr, R.: Least-squares policy iteration. The Journal of Machine Learning Research 4, 1107–1149 (2003)
8. Gisslén, L., Luciw, M., Graziano, V., Schmidhuber, J.: Sequential Constant Size Compressors for Reinforcement Learning. In: Schmidhuber, J., Thórisson, K.R., Looks, M. (eds.) AGI 2011. LNCS, vol. 6830, pp. 31–40. Springer, Heidelberg (2011)
9. Bersekas, D.P.: Dynamic Programming: Deterministic and Stochastic Models. Prentice-Hall, Englewood Cliffs (1987)
10. Ring, M.B.: Continual learning in reinforcement environments. PhD thesis, University of Texas at Austin (1994)
11. D'Epenoux, F.: A probabilistic production and inventory problem. Management Science 10, 98–108 (1993)
12. Littman, M.L., Dean, T.L., Kaelbling, L.P.: On the complexity of solving Markov decision problems. In: Proceedings of the Eleventh Annual Conference on Uncertainty in Artificial Intelligence, UAI 1995, pp. 394–402. Morgan Kauffman, San Francisco (1995)
13. Kaelbling, L.P.: Hierarchical learning in stochastic domains: Preliminary results. In: Proceedings of the Tenth International Conference on Machine Learning, pp. 167–173. Citeseer (1993)
14. Biemann, C.: Chinese whispers. In: Workshop on TextGraphs, at HLT-NAACL, pp. 73–80. Association for Computational Linguistics (2006)
15. Bullmore, E., Sporns, O.: Complex brain networks: graph theoretical analysis of structural and functional systems. Nature Reviews Neuroscience 10(3), 186–198 (2009)
16. Tikhanoff, V., Cangelosi, A., Fitzpatrick, P., Metta, G., Natale, L., Nori, F.: An open-source simulator for cognitive robotics research: The prototype of the icub humanoid robot simulator (2008)

Perception Processing for General Intelligence: Bridging the Symbolic/Subsymbolic Gap

Ben Goertzel

Novamente LLC

Abstract. Bridging the gap between symbolic and subsymbolic representations is a – perhaps *the* – key obstacle along the path from the present state of AI achievement to human-level artificial general intelligence. One approach to bridging this gap is hybridization – for instance, incorporation of a subsymbolic system and a symbolic system into a integrative cognitive architecture. Here we present a detailed design for an implementation of this approach, via integrating a version of the DeSTIN deep learning system into OpenCog, an integrative cognitive architecture including rich symbolic capabilities. This is a "tight" integration, in which the symbolic and subsymbolic aspects exert detailed real-time influence on each others' operations. An earlier technical report has described in detail the revisions to DeSTIN needed to support this integration, which are mainly along the lines of making it more "representationally transparent," so that its internal states are easier for OpenCog to understand.

1 Introduction

While it's widely accepted that human beings carry out both *symbolic* and *subsymbolic* processing, as integral parts of their general intelligence, the precise definition of "symbolic" versus "subsymbolic" is a subtle issue, which different AI researchers will approach in different ways depending on their differing overall perspectives on AI. Nevertheless, the intuitive meaning of the concepts is commonly understood:

- **"subsymbolic"** refers to things like pattern recognition in high-dimensional quantitative sensory data, and real-time coordination of multiple actuators taking multidimensional control signals
- **"symbolic"** refers to things like natural language grammar and (certain or uncertain) logical reasoning, that are naturally modeled in terms of manipulation of symbolic tokens in terms of particular (perhaps experientially learned) rules

Views on the relationship between these two aspects of intelligence in human and artificial cognition are quite diverse, including perspectives such as

1. Symbolic representation and reasoning are the core of human-level intelligence; subsymbolic aspects of intelligence are of secondary importance and can be thought of as pre or post processors to symbolic representation and reasoning

J. Bach, B. Goertzel, and M. Iklé (Eds.): AGI 2012, LNAI 7716, pp. 79–88, 2012.
© Springer-Verlag Berlin Heidelberg 2012

2. Subsymbolic representation and learning are the core of human intelligence; symbolic aspects of intelligence
   (a) emerge from the subsymbolic aspects as needed; or,
   (b) arise via a relatively simple, thin layer on top of subsymbolic intelligence, that merely applies subsymbolic intelligence in a slightly different way
3. Symbolic and subsymbolic aspects of intelligence are best considered as different subsystems, which
   (a) have a significant degree of independent operation, but also need to coordinate closely together; or,
   (b) operate largely separately and can be mostly considered as discrete modules

In evolutionary terms, it is clear that subsymbolic intelligence came first, and that most of the human brain is concerned with the subsymbolic intelligence that humans share with other animals. However, this observation doesn't have clear implications regarding the relationship between symbolic and subsymbolic intelligence in the context of everyday cognition.

In the history of the AI field, the symbolic/subsymbolic distinction was sometimes aligned with the dichotomy between logic-based and rule-based AI systems (on the symbolic side) and neural networks (on the subsymbolic side) [1]. However, this dichotomy has become much blurrier in the last couple decades, with developments such as neural network models of language parsing [2] and logical reasoning [3], and symbolic approaches to perception and action [4]. Integrative approaches have also become more common, with one of the major traditional symbolic AI systems, ACT-R, spawning a neural network version [5] with parallel structures and dynamics to the traditional explicitly symbolic version and a hybridization with a computational neuroscience model [6]; and another one, SOAR, incorporating perception processing components as separate modules [7]. The field of "neural-symbolic computing" has emerged, covering the emergence of symbolic rules from neural networks, and the hybridization of neural networks with explicitly symbolic systems [8].

Our goal here is not to explore the numerous deep issues involved with the symbolic/subsymbolic dichotomy, but rather to describe the details of a particular approach to symbolic/subsymbolic integration, inspired by Perspective 3a in the above list: the consideration of symbolic and subsymbolic aspects of intelligence as different subsystems, which have a significant degree of independent operation, but also need to coordinate closely together. We believe this kind of integration can serve a key role in the quest to create human-level general intelligence. The approach presented here is at the beginning rather than end of its practical implementation; what we are describing here is the initial design intention of a project in progress, which is sure to be revised in some respects as implementation and testing proceed. We will focus mainly on the tight integration of a subsymbolic system enabling gray-scale vision processing into a cognitive architecture with significant symbolic aspects. A longer version of the paper, available online [9], explains how the same ideas can be used for color vision, and multi-sensory and perception-action integration.

The approach presented here begins with two separate AI systems, both currently implemented in open-source software:

- **OpenCog,** an integrative architecture for AGI [10] [11], which is centered on a "weighted, labeled hypergraph" knowledge representation called the Atomspace, and features a number of different, sophisticated cognitive algorithms acting on the Atomspace. Some of these cognitive algorithms are heavily symbolic in focus (e.g. a probabilistic logic engine); others are more subsymbolic in nature (e.g. a neural net like system for allocating attention and assigning credit). However, OpenCog in its current form cannot deal with high-dimensional perceptual input, nor with detailed real-time control of complex actuators. OpenCog is now being used to control intelligent characters in an experimental virtual world, where the perceptual inputs are the 3D coordinate locations of objects or small blocks; and the actions are movement commands like "step forward", "turn head to the right" [12] [13]. OpenCog is an open-source AGI software framework, which has been used for various practical applications in the area of natural language processing and data mining; e.g. see [14], and also for the in-progress implementation of the OpenCogPrime design aimed ultimately toward AGI at the human level and beyond.
- **DeSTIN** [15],[16], a deep learning system consisting of a hierarchy of processing nodes, in which the nodes on higher levels correspond to larger regions of space-time, and each node carries out prediction regarding events in the space-time region to which it corresponds. Feedback and feedforward dynamics between nodes combine with the predictive activity within nodes, to create a complex nonlinear dynamical system whose state self-organizes to reflect the state of the world being perceived. The core concepts of DeSTIN are similar to those of Jeff Hawkins' Numenta system [17] [18], Dileep George's work (http://vicariousinc.com) and work by Mohamad Tarifi [19], Bundzel and Hashimoto [20], and others. In the terminology introduced in [21], DeSTIN is an example of a Compositional Spatiotemporal Deep Learning System, or CSDLN. However, compared to other CSDLNs, the specifics of DeSTIN's dynamics have been designed in what we consider a particularly powerful way, and the system has shown good results on small-scale test problems [22]. So far DeSTIN has been utilized only for vision processing, but a similar proprietary system has been used for auditory data as well; and DeSTIN was designed to work together with an accompanying action hierarchy.

We will not review particulars of OpenCog nor DeSTIN here, referring the reader to the above-cited references, and assuming basic knowledge of how both systems work. These two systems were not originally designed to work together, but we will describe a method for achieving their tight integration via

1. Modifying DeSTIN in several ways, so that
   (a) the patterns in its states over time will have more easily recognizable regularities

(b) its nodes are able to scan their inputs not only for simple statistical patterns (DeSTIN "centroids"), but also for patterns recognized by routines supplied to it by an external source (e.g. another AI system such as OpenCog)

2. Utilizing one of OpenCog's cognitive processes (the "Fishgram" frequent subhypergraph mining algorithm) to recognize patterns in sets of DeSTIN states, and then recording these patterns in OpenCog's Atomspace knowledge store

3. Utilizing OpenCog's other cognitive processes to abstract concepts and draw conclusions from the patterns recognized in DeSTIN states by Fishgram

4. Exporting the concepts and conclusions thus formed to DeSTIN, so that its nodes can explicitly scan for their presence in their inputs, thus allowing the results of symbolic cognition to explicitly guide subsymbolic perception

5. As described in the the extended online version of the paper [9]: Creating an action hierarchy corresponding closely to DeSTIN's perceptual hierarchy, and also corresponding to the actuators of a particular robot. This allows action learning to be done via an optimization approach ([23], [24]), where the optimization algorithm uses DeSTIN states corresponding to perceived actuator states as part of its inputs.

The ideas described here have mostly not yet been implemented, but work has begun on Items 1a (modifying DeSTIN so that the patterns in its states over time will have more easily recognizable regularities) and 2 (utilizing Fishgram to recognize patterns in DeSTIN system states), as part of a 2012 Google Summer of Code project. Item 1a has been covered in the technical report [25]; the remainder of the points are discussed here.

The ideas presented here are compatible with those described in [21], but different in emphasis. That paper described a strategy for integrating OpenCog and DeSTIN via creating an intermediate "semantic CSDLN" hierarchy to translate between OpenCog and DeSTIN, in both directions. In the approach suggested here, this semantic CSDLN hierarchy exists conceptually but not as a separate software object: it exists as the combination of

- OpenCog predicates exported to DeSTIN and used alongside DeSTIN centroids, inside DeSTIN nodes
- OpenCog predicates living in the OpenCog knowledge repository (AtomSpace), and interconnected in a hierarchical way using OpenCog nodes and links (thus reflecting DeSTIN's hierarchical structure within the AtomSpace).

This hierarchical network of predicates, spanning the two software systems, plays the role of a semantic CSDLN as described in [21].

Simplified OpenCog Workflow. The dynamics inside an OpenCog system may be highly complex, defying simple flowcharting, but from the point of view of OpenCog-DeSTIN integration, one important pattern of information flow through the system is as follows:

1. Perceptions come into the Atomspace. In the current OpenCog system, these are provided via a proxy to the game engine where the OpenCog controlled character interacts. In an OpenCog-DeSTIN hybrid, these will be provided via DeSTIN.
2. Hebbian learning builds HebbianLinks between perceptual Atoms representing percepts that have frequently co-occurred
3. PLN inference, concept blending and other methods act on these perceptual Atoms and their HebbianLinks, forming links between them and linking them to other Atoms stored in the Atomspace reflecting prior experience and generalizations therefrom
4. Attention allocation gives higher short and long term importance values to those Atoms that appear likely to be useful based on the links they have obtained
5. Based on the system's current goals and subgoals (the latter learned from the top-level goals using PLN), and the goal-related links in the Atomspace, the OpenPsi mechanism triggers the PLN-based planner, which chooses a series of high-level actions that are judged likely to help the system achieve its goals in the current context
6. The chosen high-level actions are transformed into series of lower-level, directly executable actions. In the current OpenCog system, this is done by a set of hand-coded rules based on the specific mechanics of the game engine where the OpenCog controlled character interacts. In an OpenCog-DeSTIN hybrid, the lower-level action sequence will be chosen by an optimization method acting based on the motor control and perceptual hierarchies.

2 Integrating DeSTIN and OpenCog

The integration of DeSTIN and OpenCog involves two key aspects:

- recognition of patterns in sets of DeSTIN states, and exportation of these patterns into the OpenCog Atomspace
- use of OpenCog-created concepts within DeSTIN nodes, alongside statistically-derived "centroids"

From here on, unless specified otherwise, when we mention "DeSTIN" we will refer to "Uniform DeSTIN" as defined in the technical report [25], an extension of "classic DeSTIN" as defined in [15]. The essential difference is that in Uniform DeSTIN, the same centroids are shared across the different nodes in the network; and, a belief can be matched with a centroid even if the two differ by some rotation or shear. So, in Uniform DeSTIN, each node compares its inputs to a library of known patterns in a manner that incorporates invariance to location, scale, rotation and shear.

2.1 Mining Patterns from DeSTIN States

The first step toward using OpenCog tools to mine patterns from sets of DeSTIN states, is to represent these states in Atom form in an appropriate way. A simple but workable approach, restricting attention for the moment to purely spatial patterns, is to use the six predicates: $hasCentroid(node \ N, int \ k)$, $hasParentCentroid(node \ N, int \ k)$, $hasNorthNeighborCentroid(node \ N, int \ k)$, $hasSouthNeighborCentroid(node \ N, int \ k)$, $hasEastNeighborCentroid(node \ N, int \ k)$, $hasWestNeighborCentroid(node \ N, int \ k)$. For instance, $hasNorthNeighborCentroid(N, 3)$ means that N's north neighbor has centroid #3. One may consider also the predicates: $hasParent(node \ N, Node \ M)$, $hasNorthNeighbor(node \ N, Node \ M)$, $hasSouthNeighbor(node \ N, Node \ M)$, $hasEastNeighbor(node \ N, Node \ M)$, $hasWestNeighbor(node \ N, Node \ M)$.

Now suppose we have a stored set of DeSTIN states, saved from the application of DeSTIN to multiple different inputs. What we want to find are predicates P that are *conjunctions* of instances of the above 10 predicates, which occur frequently in the stored set of DeSTIN states. A simple example of such a predicate would be the conjunction of

- $hasNorthNeighbor(\$N, \$M)$
- $hasParentCentroid(\$N, 5)$
- $hasParentCentroid(\$M, 5)$
- $hasNorthNeighborCentroid(\$N, 6)$
- $hasWestNeighborCentroid(\$M, 4)$

This predicate could be evaluated at any pair of nodes $(\$N, \$M)$ on the same DeSTIN level. If it is true for atypically many of these pairs, then it's a "frequent pattern", and should be detected and stored.

OpenCog's pattern mining component, Fishgram, exists precisely for the purpose of mining this sort of conjunction from sets of relationships that are stored in the Atomspace. It may be applied to this problem as follows:

- Translate each DeSTIN state into a set of relationships drawn from: hasNorthNeighbor, hasSouthNeighbor, hasEastNeighbor, hasWestNeighbor, hasCentroid, hasParent
- Import these relationships, describing each DeSTIN state, into the OpenCog Atomspace
- Run pattern mining on this AtomSpace.

2.2   Probabilistic Inference on Mined Hypergraphs

Patterns mined from DeSTIN states can then be reasoned on by OpenCog's PLN inference engine, allowing analogy and generalization.

Suppose centroids 5 and 617 are estimated to be similar – either via DeSTIN's built-in similarity metric, or, more interestingly via OpenCog inference on the Atom representations of these centroids. As an example of the latter, consider: 5 could represent a person's nose and 617 could represent a rabbit's nose. In this case, DeSTIN might not judge the two centroids particularly similar on a purely visual level, but, OpenCog may know that the images corresponding to both of these centroids are are called "noses" (e.g. perhaps via noticing people indicate these images in association with the word "nose"), and may thus infer (using a simple chain of PLN inferences) that these centroids seem probabilistically similar.

If 5 and 617 are estimated to be similar, then a predicate like

```
ANDLink
   EvaluationLink
      hasNorthNeighbor
      ListLink $N   $M
   EvaluationLink
      hasParentCentroid
      ListLink $N   5
   EvaluationLink
      hasParentCentroid
      ListLink $M   5
   EvaluationLink
      hasNorthNeighborCentroid
      ListLink $N 6
   EvaluationLink
      hasWestNeighborCentroid
      ListLink $M 4
```

mined from DeSTIN states, could be extended via PLN analogical reasoning to

```
ANDLink
   EvaluationLink
      hasNorthNeighbor
      ListLink $N $M
   EvaluationLink
      hasParentCentroid
      ListLink $N   617
   EvaluationLink
      hasParentCentroid
      ListLink $M   617
   EvaluationLink
      hasNorthNeighborCentroid
      ListLink $N 6
   EvaluationLink
      hasWestNeighborCentroid
      ListLink $M 4
```

2.3 Insertion of OpenCog-Learned Predicates into DeSTIN's Pattern Library

Suppose one has used Fishgram, as described above, to recognize predicates embodying frequent or surprising patterns in a set of DeSTIN states or state-sequences. The next natural step is to add these frequent or surprising patterns to

DeSTIN's pattern library, so that the pattern library contains not only classic DeSTIN centroids, but also these corresponding "image grammar" style patterns. Then, when a new input comes into a DeSTIN node, in addition to being compared to the centroids at the node, it can be fed as input to the predicates associated with the node.

What is the advantage of this approach, compared to DeSTIN without these predicates? The capability for more compact representation of a variety of spatial patterns. In many cases, a spatial pattern that would require a large number of DeSTIN centroids to represent, can be represented by a single, fairly compact predicate. It is an open question whether these sorts of predicates are really critical for human-like vision processing. However, our intuition is that they do have a role in human as well s machine vision. In essence, DeSTIN is based on a fancy version of nearest-neighbor search, applied in a clever way on multiple levels of a hierarchy, using context-savvy probabilities to bias the matching. But we suspect there are many visual patterns that are more compactly and intuitively represented using a more flexible language, such as OpenCog predicates formed by combining elementary predicates involving appropriate spatial and temporal relations.

For example, consider the archetypal spatial pattern of a face as: either two eyes that are next to each other, or sunglasses, above a nose, which is in turn above a mouth. (This is an oversimplified toy example, but we're positing it for illustration only. The same point applies to more complex and realistic patterns.) One could represent this in OpenCog's Atom language as something like:

```
AND
   InheritanceLink N B_nose
   InheritanceLink M B_mouth
   EvaluationLink
      above
      ListLink E N
   EvaluationLink
      above
      ListLink N M
   OR
      AND
         MemberLink E1   E
         MemberLink E2   E
         EvaluationLink
            next_to
            ListLink E1 E2
         InheritanceLink E1 B_eye
      AND
         InheritanceLink E  B_sunglasses
```

where e.g. *B_eye* is a DeSTIN belief that corresponds roughly to recognition of the spatial pattern of a human eye. To represent this using ordinary DeSTIN centroids, one couldn't represent the OR explicitly; instead one would need to split it into two different sets of centroids, corresponding to the eye case and the sunglasses case unless the DeSTIN pattern library contained a belief corresponding to "eyes or sunglasses." But the question then becomes: how would classic DeSTIN actually learn a belief like this? In the suggested architecture, pattern mining on the database of DeSTIN states is proposed as an algorithm for learning such beliefs.

This sort of predicate-enhanced DeSTIN will have advantages over the traditional version, only if the actual distribution of images observed by the system contains many (reasonably high probability) images modeled accurately by predicates involving disjunctions and/or negations as well as conjunctions. If the system's perceived world is simpler than this, then good old DeSTIN will work just as well, and the OpenCog-learned predicates are a needless complication.

3   Conclusion

We have described, at a high level, a novel approach to bridging the symbolic / subsymbolic gap, via very tightly integrating DeSTIN with OpenCog. We don't claim that this is the only way to bridge the gap, but we do believe it is a viable way. And while we have focused on robotics applications here, the basic ideas described could be implemented and evaluated in a variety of other contexts as well, for example the identification of objects and events in videos, or intelligent video summarization.

Our hope is that the hybridization of OpenCog and DeSTIN as described here will constitute a major step along the path to human-level AGI. It will enable the creation of an OpenCog instance endowed with the capability of flexibly interacting with a rich stream of data from the everyday human world. This data will not only help OpenCog to guide a robot in carrying out everyday tasks, but will also provide raw material for OpenCog's cognitive processes to generalize from in various ways – e.g. to use as the basis for the formation of new concepts or analogical inferences.

References

1. Pinker, S., Mehler, J.: Connections and Symbols. MIT Press (1988)
2. Garg, N., Henderson, J.: Temporal restricted boltzmann machines for dependency parsing. In: Proc. ACL (2011)
3. Lehmann, J., Bader, S., Hitzler, P.: Extracting reduced logic programs from artificial neural networks. Applied Intelligence (2010)
4. Shanahan, M., Randell, D.A.: A logic-based formulation of active visual perception. In: Knowledge Representation (2004)
5. Lebiere, C., Anderson, J.R.: A connectionist implementation of the act-r production system. In: Proceedings of the Fifteenth Annual Conference of the Cognitive Science Society (1993)
6. Jilk, D.J., Lebiere, C., O'Reilly, R.C., Anderson, J.R.: SAL: An explicitly pluralistic cognitive architecture. Journal of Experimental and Theoretical Artificial Intelligence 20, 197–218 (2008)
7. Laird, J.E.: The Soar Cognitive Architecture. MIT Press (2012)

8. Hammer, B., Hitzler, P. (eds.): Perspectives of Neural-Symbolic Integration. SCI, vol. 77. Springer, Heidelberg (2007)

9. Goertzel, B.: Perception processing for general intelligence: Bridging the symbolic/subsymbolic gap, http://wp.goertzel.org/?p=404

10. Goertzel, B., et al.: Opencogbot: An integrative architecture for embodied AGI. In: Proc. of ICAI 2010, Beijing (2010)

11. Goertzel, B., Pitt, J., Wigmore, J., Geisweiller, N., Cai, Z., Lian, R., Huang, D., Yu, G.: Cognitive synergy between procedural and declarative learning in the control of animated and robotic agents using the opencogprime AGI architecture. In: Proceedings of AAAI 2011 (2011)

12. Goertzel, B., Pennachin, C., et al.: An integrative methodology for teaching embodied non-linguistic agents, applied to virtual animals in second life. In: Proc. of the First Conf. on AGI. IOS Press (2008)

13. Goertzel, B., Pitt, J., Cai, Z., Wigmore, J., Huang, D., Geisweiller, N., Lian, R., Yu, G.: Integrative general intelligence for controlling game AI in a minecraft-like environment. In: Proc. of BICA 2011 (2011)

14. Goertzel, B., Pinto, H., Pennachin, C., Goertzel, I.F.: Using dependency parsing and probabilistic inference to extract relationships between genes, proteins and malignancies implicit among multiple biomedical research abstracts. In: Proc. of Bio-NLP 2006 (2006)

15. Arel, I., Rose, D., Karnowski, T.: A deep learning architecture comprising homogeneous cortical circuits for scalable spatiotemporal pattern inference. In: NIPS 2009 Workshop on Deep Learning for Speech Recognition and Related Applications (2009)

16. Arel, I., Rose, D., Coop, R.: Destin: A scalable deep learning architecture with application to high-dimensional robust pattern recognition. In: Proc. AAAI Workshop on Biologically Inspired Cognitive Architectures (2009)

17. Hawkins, J., Blakeslee, S.: On Intelligence. Brown Walker (2006)

18. George, D., Hawkins, J.: Towards a mathematical theory of cortical micro-circuits. PLoS Comput. Biol. 5 (2009)

19. Tarifi, M., Sitharam, M., Ho, J.: Learning hierarchical sparse representations using iterative dictionary learning and dimension reduction. In: Proc. of BICA 2011 (2011)

20. Bundzel, Hashimoto: Object identification in dynamic images based on the memory-prediction theory of brain function. Journal of Intelligent Learning Systems and Applications 2-4 (2010)

21. Goertzel, B.: Integrating a compositional spatiotemporal deep learning network with symbolic representation/reasoning within an integrative cognitive architecture via an intermediary semantic network. In: Proceedings of AAAI Symposium on Cognitive Systems (2011)

22. Karnowski, T., Arel, I., Rose, D.: Deep spatiotemporal feature learning with application to image classification. In: The 9th International Conference on Machine Learning and Applications, ICMLA 2010 (2010)

23. Lee, S.H., Kim, J., Park, F.C., Kim, M., Bobrow, J.E.: Newton-type algorithms for dynamics-based robot movement optimization. IEEE Transactions on Robotics 21(4), 657–667 (2005)

24. Yeo, S., Kim, J., Lee, S.H., Park, F.C., Park, W., Kim, J., Park, C., Yeo, I.: A modular object-oriented framework for hierarchical multi-resolution robot simulation. Robotica 22(2), 141–154 (2004)

25. Goertzel, B.: Modifying the destin perception architecture to enable representationally transparent deep learning, http://wp.goertzel.org/?p=404

On Attention Mechanisms for AGI Architectures: A Design Proposal

Helgi Páll Helgason[1], Eric Nivel[1], and Kristinn R. Thórisson[1,2]

[1] Center for Analysis and Design of Intelligent Agents / School of Computer Science,
Reykjavik University, Menntavegur 1, 101 Reykjavik, Iceland
[2] Icelandic Institute for Intelligent Machines, Menntavegur 1, 101 Reykjavik, Iceland
{helgih09,eric,thorisson}@ru.is

Abstract. Many existing AGI architectures are based on the assumption of infinite computational resources, as researchers ignore the fact that real-world tasks have time limits, and managing these is a key part of the role of intelligence. In the domain of intelligent systems the management of system resources is typically called "attention". Attention mechanisms are necessary because all moderately complex environments are likely to be the source of vastly more information than could be processed in realtime by an intelligence's available cognitive resources. Even if sufficient resources were available, attention could help make better use of them. We argue that attentional mechanisms are not only nice to have, for AGI architectures they are an *absolute necessity*. We examine ideas and concepts from cognitive psychology for creating intelligent resource management mechanisms and how these can be applied to engineered systems. We present a design for a general attention mechanism intended for implementation in AGI architectures.

Keywords: artificial intelligence, attention, resource management, architecture, cognition, system design.

1 Introduction

Most higher intelligences in nature have a built-in mechanism for deciding how to apply their brainpower from moment to moment. We call it *attention*, and by that we mean cognitive resource management of some type. As the real world is generally a source of much more information than any single intelligent agent could ever hope to cognitively ingest and process in any given period of time, even the smartest being of them all must come equipped with attentional mechanisms of some sort. Powerful methods for cognitive resource management are critical if we intend to create more capable AI systems than seen to date, systems capable of learning to solve novel tasks and adapting to unforeseen changes in environments of real-world complexity, while operating under time constraints – systems we refer to as artificial general intelligence (AGI) systems. Given the short shrift this subject has gotten in the AI literature, it can hardly be overemphasized that an AGI operating in the real world will have *limited resources at all times*. Ignoring how to design attention will only delay the day when

J. Bach, B. Goertzel, and M. Iklé (Eds.): AGI 2012, LNAI 7716, pp. 89–98, 2012.

AGI arrives on the scene. Natural attention is a cognitive function – or a set of them – that allow animals to focus their limited resources on relevant parts of the environment as they perform various tasks, while remaining reactive to unexpected events. Without it we could for example not stay alert to environmental events while finishing an important task, or manage multiple tasks at the same time. This cognitive function is not any less critical for AGI systems than it is for humans. In this paper we present a high-level design of an attention mechanism and discuss how prior work in cognitive psychology serves as a backdrop and inspiration. First we survey selected work on human attention from cognitive psychology and extract ideas we consider useful for implementing of attention in AGI systems. We review implementations of attention within some existing cognitive architectures and discuss their benefits and limitations. We then outline our attention mechanism designs, which is based on a holistic approach to attention, addressing data and process prioritization, and featuring simultaneous top-down and bottom-up control. The design makes few and fairly high-level requirements for the underlying architecture but is otherwise architecture-independent. The design proposal presented here is just that – a proposal for a design – but the basic principles on which it rests have already been proven in prior architecture implementations (Nivel 2007 & 2008, Thórisson 2009a & 2009b). Our work so far has not only resulted in the new attention mechanism presented here but also greatly affected the kinds of architectures we consider to be relevant to AGI research – architecture and attention are co-dependent. In that respect we discuss how the attention mechanism presented can be used for managing meta-cognitive operation and architectural self-growth, two fundamental functions of AGI systems (Thórisson & Helgason 2012).

2   Attention in Cognitive Psychology

The beginning of modern attention research is frequently associated with the work of Colin Cherry on the "cocktail party effect" (Cherry 1953), which examines how humans can focus on specific sensory data in the presence of distractions and background noise while still staying alert to relevant and/or important information that unexpectedly appears in the background. This ability implies simultaneous operation of a selective filter and deliberate steering mechanism which together perform allocation of cognitive resources. Deliberate, task-driven functionality is referred to here as *top-down attention,* reactive, stimulus-driven functionality as *bottom-up attention.* A number of psychological models for attention have been proposed that typically fall into one of two categories. **Early selection**: Selection of sensory information occurs early in the sensory pipe-line and is based on primitive physical features of the information (shallow processing) and little or no analysis of meaning. **Late selection**: Selection is performed after some level of non-trivial analysis of meaning at later stages of the sensory pipeline. The Broadbent filter model (Broadbent 1958) is one of the best known early-selection (filter) models. It assumes information filtering based on primitive physical features, with information that is not selected by the filter receiving no further processing. The Deutsch-Norman model (Norman 1969) is a well-known late-selection model. In contrast to the filter model, it proposes *gradual processing* of information to the point where memory representations are activated. Competitive selection is performed at the level of these representations, with the most active ones being selected for further processing. Some obvious problems are apparent for early selection models; they fail to account for commonly-observed human behavior such as noticing unexpected but relevant information – the cocktail party effect. The acoustic features alone of someone calling our name from the other side of a crowded room are not likely to be sufficient to attract our attention – some analysis of meaning must be involved. More recent models of attention focus on the interaction between top-down and bottom-up attention, such as the Knudsen attention framework (Knudsen 2007; see Figure 1). It consists of four interacting processes: *working memory, top-down sensitivity control, bottom-up filtering* and *competitive selection*. This framework seems to capture the major necessary parts for attention and be a promising starting point for AGI systems, from which some important issues for consideration can be extracted. **Systems that are expected to perform tasks while remaining reactive to unexpected events require both deliberate, top-down attention as well as reactive, bottom-up attention.** Top-down attention is responsible for ensuring that information relevant to current goals will receive processing. A system equipped with only this type of attention will frequently fail to notice (process) unexpected events that might be important for goals currently being pursued or necessary triggers for the generation of new ones. Bottom-up attention is responsible for detecting such events. This process is not (or less) influenced by current goals of the system, evaluating incoming information based on novelty, general relevance/familiarity to the perceiver, and unexpectedness. Systems implementing only bottom-up attention are unable to perform tasks beyond those that are simple and reactive, making tasks consisting of multiple steps (requiring some form of planning) problematic. **Managing the balance between top-down and bottom-up attention, in terms of resource allocation, is part of the role of attention.** Combining these two "types" (or roles) of attention can give rise to flexible, interruptible systems capable of performing complex tasks. Finding an acceptable balance in resource allocation between these processes or goals is a necessary function of attention. Over-assigning resources to top-down attention will introduce operational risk, as probability of missed important events is increased. Conversely, over-assignment of resources to bottom-up attention will adversely affect task performance, making it more time-consuming and difficult to accomplish goals. Balance between the two is difficult to specify in advance, as it depends on the environment and context of the system. This leads us to conclude that reaching and maintaining such a balance is a continuous and dynamic process that must be learned by the system from experience. **Late selection models provide a more reliable measure of importance of information than early selection models.** The shortcomings of early selection models were highlighted above. In the case of AGI systems, no assumptions can be made in advance with regards to the environment and system tasks; any incoming information is potentially important. While primitive physical features and signal characteristics may give rough clues to the importance of information, this information seems insufficient to guide informed resource management decisions. Operational risk may result when information is ignored without being related in any way to the operational experience (knowledge) of the system to determine meaning. For an example of why this may be problematic, consider subtle changes (in terms of basic information characteristics) in the environment that are precursors to important events – these are not likely to pass through classical early selection filters, potentially making the system unprepared to deal with critical scenarios. **Competitive selection is more desirable than filtering**. Viewing attention as a single-step process that decides whether information should be processed or not, is problematic in terms of resource utilization. Such decisions must be made in light of current availability of resources. It seems more reasonable to let attention evaluate the importance of incoming information, deferring processing decisions to actual execution time at which time resource availability is fully known and information competes for processing based on attention-steered priority evaluation.

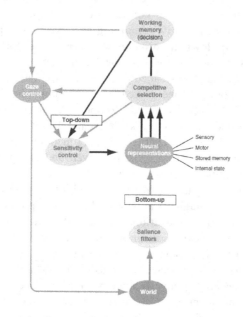

Fig. 1. The Knudsen attention framework (from Knudsen 2007). Information flows up from the environment and passes through saliency filters that detect important or unusual stimuli. Information that is passed through the filters then activates memory representations that encode knowledge. Memory representations are also activated by top-down sensitivity control, this process is influenced by the contents of working memory and adjusts activation thresholds of representations. Representations compete for access to working memory, with the most active ones being admitted.

3   Prior Work

Some work has targeted attention in parts of AI systems, focusing on specific tasks and/or modalities (c.f. Schmidhuber 1991) and limited aspects of attention (c.f. Skubic 2004). A key difference between that work and ours is that we target attention in a complete sense, as needed for a whole cognitive architecture. Second, we exclusively target architectures that have a goal of being *general*, i.e. targeting artificial general intelligence (AGI). Third, implementability of both attention itself, and the architecture in which it operates, is a primary concern. Here we thus limit the discussion to the AGI domain. Only a handful of existing AGI architectures specifically implement some form of attention functionality, including NARS, LIDA and CLARION[1]. This chapter gives a brief overview of how these architectures implement attention and examines to what degree they satisfy some necessary requirements. NARS (Wang, 1995) is a cognitive architecture implemented as a general-purpose reasoning system, targeting operation in realtime with insufficient knowledge and resources. The system implements attention using a computational control strategy called controlled concurrency where task execution is controlled by two prioritization parameters: urgency and durability. The urgency parameter is the main priority parameter and decays over time in relation to the value of the durability parameter, which is used to specify if a task is long- or short-term. The result is dynamic resource management where tasks compete for execution based on their priority value. While priority of internally-generated goals is assigned by the system, original goals (provided by the developer) are assumed to have pre-assigned priority values. This delegates part of process prioritization – an integral role of attention – to an outside control mechanism, which is problematic with regards to achieving autonomy. LIDA (Baars, 2009) is another cognitive architecture based on a theory of human consciousness and targets intelligent, autonomous software agents. Attention is a core process of each operating cycle, consisting of three phases: sensing, attending, and action selection. During the attending phase, selection of data for further processing is performed by a collection of attentional codelets (small programs) which form coalitions of data that proceed to compete for system resources. LIDA thus implements both filtering and competitive selection for data. Attention is a learnable process in LIDA, allowing the system to improve its data-filtering over time. The attention functionality of LIDA does not take resource availability into account, making realtime operation somewhat problematic and potentially introducing resource utilization issues. Additionally, prioritization and selection is applied only to the data side without consideration of process prioritization. The CLARION cognitive architecture (Sun 2006) features a dedicated metacognitive subsystem (MCS) responsible for information selection, dynamic selection of learning methods for different situations, and modifying control parameters of other system modules. The MCS does not have integrated temporal management as required for realtime processing, and control processes are not affected by availability of resources at any given time, although attention can be said to be involved with process control via tuning of control parameters as mentioned earlier. **Data Selection.** The most widely accepted function of attention is selection of data for processing. The architectures address this in different ways. LIDA and CLARION implement information selection (filtering, and competitive selection in LIDA) in special phases of the sensory pipeline; NARS opts for a prioritization-based approach, where information is processed in decreasing order of urgency values as opposed to being filtered, resulting in a pure competitive selection control mechanism. None of these architectures address both top-down and bottom-up attention, focusing largely on the

---

[1] See Thórisson & Helgason (2012) for a more general review of these architectures.

top-down side. **Control and Process Selection.** While attention is often viewed as an information filtering process, we argue that it must address process control as an equally important aspect. The control of an AGI system is not limited to information selection – it must include selection of proper processes at any point in time, based on the context of the system, which includes time and resource constraints, in light of constraints imposed by tasks and context. In CLARION there is some overlap between attention and process control, but none of the three architectures take a fully integrated approach to data and process selection. **Realtime Processing.** For AGI systems, one of the core goals of attention must be to allocate resources in light of internal and external temporal constraints. This requires some form of temporal reasoning as well as consideration of resource availability, as tasks become increasingly urgent when their deadlines approach and ongoing tasks may interfere with access to resources. NARS does temporal reasoning using relative timings between events; the system can represent order of tasks and events and specify the temporal aspects of tasks using the durability parameter. Relative handling of time is clearly better than no temporal management, but reasoning with absolute timings allows for more fine-grained and precise control. NARS is implemented as a reasoning system and does not focus on perceptual nor action-related processes (inputs and outputs of the system are logical statements), emphasizing instead anytime performance. Integrated temporal reasoning is missing in both LIDA and CLARION and the availability of resources does not affect process control or data selection.

4   Attention Mechanism Design

We now present our design of an attention mechanism for AGI systems. The holistic, inclusive approach to attention we have taken includes top-down goal-derived control, bottom-up filtering and novelty interruption processes, and includes internal process control as part of the mechanism's operation. While a general-purpose attention mechanism, applicable to any AI architecture, could be a goal to strive for, we do not believe this is possible, as resource management touches on too many fundamental issues in the structure and operation of an architecture to make it practically viable. Our proposed solution is only tractable if the following requirements are satisfied: **Data-driven**: All processing occurs as a result of the occurrence of data; individual processes are executed only when paired with data that fits the input specification of the process. This eliminates the need for fixed control loops, allowing for operation on multiple time scales, greater flexibility, and above all, high operating efficiency. **Fine-grained**: Processing and data units of the system are small and numerous (Thórisson & Nivel 2009a). Many such elements must collaborate to solve complex tasks. Reasoning about small, simple components and their effects on the overall system (e.g. in terms of resource usage) is more tractable than for larger, more complex components. **Predictive capabilities**: Capacity to generate predictions with regards to future expectations must be supported. Predictions are necessary control data for (top-down) attention in addition to goals. **Unified sensory pipeline**: Data originating from inside or outside the system is given equal treatment, allowing cognitive functions of the architecture – attention, in particular – to be applied equally to task performance and meta-cognitive processing (e.g. self-configuration). Systems satisfying these requirements will be built from small units of data and processing, with processes being executed when their input data specification is matched by an existing data item. Pattern matching is a practical method for determining matches as it allows each process some flexibility. New data are continuously created as the external environment is sampled by the system's sensors, triggering processes to run, resulting in either further data items being produced or in commands for the system's actuation devices, producing an action in the external environment, the effects of which are observed by the system via environmental sampling, closing the perception-action loop. For basic resource management, data and process need priority parameters; the main role of attention is, however it is implemented, to determine appropriate values for theses given the current operating situation. We refer to the priority parameters as *activation* in the case of processes, and *salience* in the case of data. System resources are managed to execute processing units with highest activation, on data units with the highest salience (no processing unit will execute without a compatible data unit). Processes can take the role of data, and data can describe processes. Adjusting activation and salience is the main role of attention; this is viewed as a *biasing* task. In our system, four parallel attention processes perform these tasks, as described below. The components in figure 2 that are involved in each process are indicated in parentheses. While this is probably not the only high-level system architecture that can meet the architectural requirements above, it explains well the operation of our attention mechanism. Note that the above architectural requirements are probably neither complete nor sufficient; for some AGI-acceptable attention mechanisms (unknown to us) they might not even all be necessary. That said, we have reason to believe that our proposed attention mechanism, and the requirements it rests on, represent a valid and useful step in the direction of more capable AGI systems. **Top-down data biasing** (*Attentional Patterns, Matching*): At some level, the goals and predictions of the system must be specified in operational terms, identifying particular states (inside or outside the system) that are desired (goals) or expected (predictions). Information contained in goals and predictions is used by this process to create attentional templates: Patterns that target data to varying levels of specification, from information related to a particular entity to all information coming from a single modality (e.g. auditory). For example, if the system has a goal of having object O1 in position P1, an attentional template is created that matches all information related to O1 (e.g. all data units referring to O1). This works identically for predictions. A unified sensory pipeline allows external and internal data to be targeted identically. When a data unit matches an attentional template, it receives a positive bias relative to priority of the goal that spawned the template. Data units that do not match any active attentional template will not receive bias from this top-down data biasing process. **Bottom-up data biasing** (*Bottom-up Attentional Processes, Evaluation*): Events that are novel and unexpected (in terms of prior experience or in a particular context), yet not directly related to task-driven goals, will almost certainly occur during operation. As top-down processes only target expected and goal-related data, such events are by their nature unlikely to be caught by it. The bottom-up process is responsible for determining a quantitative measure of novelty and unexpectedness for incoming data items, and providing saliency bias to them accordingly. The underlying idea is that novel data are likely to be useful in some way – e.g. for learning or to detect events that threaten success of current goals. This process is not responsible for determining actual relevance of data, but rather to give these data units greater chance of receiving processing. Novelty and unexpectedness are *evaluated* based on the operating experience of the system, data or patterns of data that have occurred before receive lower bias than previously unseen data. To accomplish this task under tight temporal (and likely also memory) constraints, it is necessary to compress prior experience of the system in some way, preferably in data structures that allow for efficient look-up and comparison. Consequently, this process must constantly generate and update its control data based on incoming information in order for satisfactory evaluation of novelty and unexpectedness to occur. Habituation is an emergent operational property of this process, as novel or unexpected information will cease to be so automatically after having been observed on an increasing number of occasions.

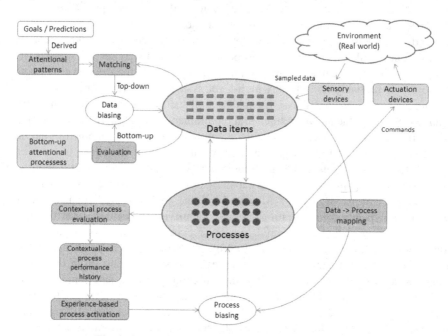

Fig. 2. Overview of the proposed attention mechanism

Top-down process biasing (*Contextual Process Evaluation, Contextualized Process Performance History, Experience-based Process Activation*): While relationships between goals and processes are not obvious, these may be extracted from operational experience by tracking and maintaining history of the contribution of individual processes to the achievement of individual goals. While this is a non-trivial task, as many goals will be achieved by the collaboration of a number of processing units, it is nevertheless tractable using e.g. back-propagation from goal achievement through the operational chain which it resulted in (using some form of ampliative reasoning - c.f.

Wang 1995). Furthermore, this process must have the capability to determine the similarity of goals, as goals are stated in precise operational terms and exactly identical goals are unlikely to occur multiple times. When a new goal is generated within the system, this process must search some compressed form of the operational history in order to find a sufficiently similar goal that has been previously achieved. The best such match (if one is found) results in positive biasing of processes that contributed to goal achievement on previous occasions. ***Bottom-up process biasing*** (*Data ->* *Process mapping*): To ensure processing of most salient data units (especially early on in the operation of the system, when top-down process biasing has insufficient experience to perform efficiently), this process works to assign positive bias to processes that are capable of processing the currently most salient data. The main purpose of this attentional function is practical, as efficient operation of the system may be highly problematic when no processing bias values are available due to the large number of processing units assumed to be present. The control of this process follows directly from the operation of top-down data biasing.

Although the design itself does not feature processes directly dedicated to realtime operation, it facilitates realtime operation as it is based on small processing units and can better make predictions (including temporal ones) about its own operation. The significance of small processing units with homogenous computational complexity is that most *processes take roughly the same amount of time to execute*, making temporal aspects of performance predictable, and that *the system is highly interruptible* and preemptive, never having to wait for time-consuming processes to complete before knowing how long it takes, or reacting to new data. Another important feature of the attentional design approach presented is that it can be applied directly to systems that manage their own growth and expansion – constructivist architectures (Thórisson 2009c). As the sum of internal system activity is likely to constitute a large amount of information, it is desirable that the attention mechanism be used to manage resources for self-reconfiguration – in much the same way as it is used for other task performance. The mechanism presented here already assumes a unified sensory pipeline: attention operates identically on environmental data and internal data. By generating internal goals supporting directed self-reconfiguration of the system and targeting internal states, AGI systems can be envisioned that simultaneously perform tasks in complex environments and manage their own growth, while operating under realtime constraints with limited resources.

5   Conclusions

Surprisingly little work focusing on attention has been performed in the field of AI, although we have seen that existing attention models from cognitive psychology can be mapped to AGI architectures in a useful way. In our work to design an AGI-ready attention mechanism we have found a large overlap between the functionalities of attention and the control mechanisms of the underlying architecture. This is an indication that retrofitting an existing architecture with the resource management capabilities stated will be highly problematic; on close examination attention reveals itself as a ubiquitous function of a cognitive architecture, influencing operation and structure across all levels. So, while this work had the goal of designing an attention mechanism, the result is also a near-complete control mechanism for cognitive architectures.

Acknowledgements. This work has been supported in part by the EU-funded project HUMANOBS: Humanoids That Learn Socio-Communicative Skills Through Observation, contract no. FP7-STREP-231453 (www.humanobs.org), and by grants from Rannis, Iceland.

References

1. Baars, B.J., Franklin, S.: Consciousness is computational: The LIDA model of Global Workspace Theory. Intl. Journal of Machine Consciousness 1(1), 23–32 (2009)
2. Broadbent, D.E.: Perception and Communication. Pergamon, London (1958)
3. Cherry, E.C.: Some experiments on the recognition of speech, with one and two ears. Journal of the Acoustical Society of America, 975–979 (1953)
4. Nivel, E.: Ikon Flux 2.0. Reykjavik University technical report (2007), http://www.ru.is/media/skjol-td/RUTR-CS07006.pdf
5. Nivel, E., Thórisson, K.R.: Self-Programming: Operationalizing Autonomy. In: Proceedings of the 2nd Conf. on Artificial General Intelligence (2008)
6. Norman, D.A.: Memory while shadowing. Quarterly Journal of Experimental Psychology 21, 85–93 (1969)
7. Schmidhuber, J., Huber, R.: Learning to generate artificial fovea trajectories for target detection. International Journal of Neural Systems 2(1&2), 135–141 (1991)
8. Skubic, M., Noelle, D., Wilkes, M., Kawamura, K., Keller, J.M.: A biologically inspired adaptive working memory for robots. In: AAAI Fall Symp., Workshop on the Intersection of Cognitive Science and Robotics, Washington, D.C. (2004)
9. Sun, R.: The CLARION cognitive architecture: Extending cognitive modelling to social simulation. In: Sun, R. (ed.) Cognition and Multi-Agent Interaction. Cambridge University Press, New York (2006)
10. Thórisson, K.R., Nivel, E.: Achieving artificial general intelligence through peewee granularity. In: Proc. of the 2nd Conf. on Artificial General Intelligence, pp. 220–221 (2009a)
11. Thórisson, K.R., Nivel, E.: Holistic intelligence: Transversal skills and current methodologies. In: Proc. of the 2nd Conf. on Artificial General Intelligence, pp. 222–223 (2009b)
12. Thórisson, K.R.: From Constructionist to Constructivist A.I. Keynote, Technical Report, FS-90-01. AAAI Press, Menlo Park, California (2009c)
13. Thórisson, K.R., Helgason, H.P.: Cognitive Architectures and Autonomy: A Comparative review. Journal of Artificial General Intelligence 3, 1–30 (2012)
14. Wang, P.: Non-Axiomatic Reasoning System: Exploring the Essence of Intelligence. Ph.D. diss., Dept. of Computer Science, Indiana Univ., CITY, Indiana (1995)

A Framework for Representing Action Meaning in Artificial Systems via Force Dimensions

Paul Hemeren[1] and Peter Gärdenfors[2]

[1] Interaction Lab, School of Humanities and Informatics, University of Skövde, S-541 28
Skövde, Sweden
paul.hemeren@his.se
[2] Lund University Cognitive Science, Lund University, S-221 00 Lund, Sweden
Peter.Gardenfors@lucs.lu.se

Abstract. General (human) intelligence critically includes understanding human action, both action production and action recognition. Human actions also convey social signals that allow us to predict the actions of others (intent) as well as the physical and social consequences of our actions. What's more, we are able to talk about what we (and others) are doing. We present a framework for action recognition and communication that is based on access to the force dimensions that constrain human actions. The central idea here is that forces and force patterns constitute vectors in conceptual spaces that can represent actions and events. We conclude by pointing to the consequences of this view for how artificial systems could be made to understand and communicate about actions.

Keywords: Intentions, actions, conceptual spaces, force, action representation, concepts, categorization, events.

1   Introduction

A critical aspect of human intelligence is reading the intentions of others, being able to understand their actions and the extent to which future behavior is determined by current behavior. This speaks to the predictive role in intelligent behavior. Much recent evidence (for a review see [1]) has demonstrated the role of human movement in understanding the social interaction between humans. Human movement can carry social information about the intentional state and future motor states of humans. Intelligent artificial systems that can use/exploit this information will have an advantage over systems that do not have access to this information. Intelligent artificial systems will need to both recognize human intention-governed action as well as produce actions that can be understood by humans. This is what humans seem to do, i.e., read each other's intentions and act accordingly.

Individual actions have specific activations of muscles which give rise to specific kinematic patterns. Being able to generalize beyond these situation-specific activations will allow us to act and understand other individuals across varying contexts. For example, throwing a stone can be done in a number of ways, and the exact kinematics

J. Bach, B. Goertzel, and M. Iklé (Eds.): AGI 2012, LNAI 7716, pp. 99–106, 2012.

(as well as dynamics) will vary depending on the individual and the object being thrown. Despite these contextual differences, we can easily see and describe what others are doing on a level that generalizes over the contextual differences. In this case, perception and language will both rely on access to an action representation hierarchy. Similar to objects, we generalize from specific examples of actions to broad action categories.

In this article we will outline a unifying framework connecting action meaning with cognitive structures for action representation and categorization. We argue that this framework captures critical aspects of human action representation that can used by artificial systems to appropriately understand human actions. The central idea is that perceptions of forces and force patterns are appropriate basic elements in generating action categories. We also present evidence for the hierarchical organization of action categories and demonstrate the relation between this organization and our ability to communicate about actions on different hierarchical levels.

2   Representing Actions as Conceptual Spaces: Sensorimotor Grounding and Force Dimensions

There is considerable evidence for the sensorimotor grounding of action concepts [2]. These concepts allow us to create different categories of actions on the basis of patterns of similarity and movement. Running, walking, throwing, waving, etc., have characteristic kinematic patterns, and these patterns affect our perception of what others are doing as well as the words we use to communicate about human actions [3-4]. Recent results [5] also show the significant relationship between action understanding and human movement kinematics for hand and arm actions.

The idea here is that successful interpretation of human actions as a basis for social interaction requires grounding action understanding the physical constraints that govern movement of the human body. This includes both internal and external constraints. Internal constraints are for example the degrees of freedom that a human body has and the forces that it has to affect objects in the environment. These forces include muscle strength as well as the ways in which the body can move in order to exploit the available muscle strength. The external constraints are the physical properties in the surrounding environment.

Another source of information that can be used to recognize human actions is the kinematics associated with human body movement, i.e., motion as such. There is a relationship between kinematics and dynamics in the sense that the dynamics (forces) will to some extent determine the kinematic patterns associated with different human actions.

When one perceives an action, one does not just see the movement; one also extracts the forces that control different kinds of motion. [6] formulates this as the principle of *kinematic specification of dynamics*, which says that the kinematics of a movement contain sufficient information to identify the underlying dynamic force patterns. Our proposal is that, by adding forces, one obtains the basic tools for analyzing the dynamic properties of actions. The language of vectors will be of great representational convenience here.

3   Actions as Convex Regions

[7] argues that properties can be represented by convex regions of conceptual spaces. For example, the property of being red is represented by a convex region of the three-dimensional color space. Certain sets of dimensions are integral, for example the color dimensions, in the sense that one cannot assign an object a value on one dimension without giving it a value on the other(s) [8]. We define a domain as a set of integral dimensions.

A concept – in the most general sense – can then be defined as a bundle of properties that also contains information about how the different properties are correlated. For example, the concept of an apple has properties that correspond to regions of the color domain, the shape domain, the taste domain, the nutrition domain, etc. Correspondingly, object concepts can be represented as a complex of properties from a number of domains: that is, bundles of properties.

Action categories can be represented as convex regions in a conceptual space. Accordingly, a convex region is characterized by the criterion that for every pair of points v_1 and v_2 in the region all points in between v_1 and v_2 are also in the region. The implication of this notion of convexity when applied to action categories is that if two actions are categorized as exemplars of the same category, and they occupy separate points in a convex region, then any action exemplar occupying a space between then will be categorized as belonging to the same category.

It is important to note that this framework takes the context of categorization into account by stipulating that the dimensions of actions determine the basis for assigning properties to actions as well as determining the relations among the properties. In this sense, different contexts, perhaps defined by different goals or other situational factors, will lead to the use of different dimensions and thereby different regions of convexity.

For many actions – for example moving and lifting – a single force vector may be sufficient, but for others – such as walking and swimming – a complex of forces is involved. We therefore define an action as a pattern of forces since several force vectors are interacting (by analogy with the system of differential equations in [9]).

This framework views the action spaces as geometrical structures, and as such we can view objects/actions as being psychologically *closer* (more similar) or *further* from one another (less similar) in vector space. To identify the structure of the action space, one should investigate similarities between actions. For example, walking is more similar to running than to throwing. An action category can then, in the same way as with other kinds of categories, be characterized as a convex region in a space of force vectors or force patterns. [10-11] present some further empirical evidence that supports this definition of action categories.

In a way similar to object categories, results from psycholinguistic experiments show that action categories also appear to have a hierarchical taxonomic organization [12]. It should be noted that the above definition of conceptual spaces immediately generates a model of hierarchies of action categories. The idea is that if a region representing action category A is a subregion of the region representing category B, then A is a subcategory of B. For example, the force patterns corresponding to the verbs march, stride, strut, saunter, tread, etc., can all be seen as subregions of the force patterns that describe walk.

3.1   Action Prototypes

If force dimensions are central aspects of actions and action representation that serve perception and production, then we would expect these dimensions to play a critical role in the structure/metric of conceptual spaces for actions. The results from [13] provide support for this view of a metric representation of action categories. They created morphs between four action prototypes for *running, walking, limping* and *marching*. This resulted in a space of many different action morphs that were combinations of for example *running and walking* or *running and marching,* etc. Human subjects then provided ratings regarding the naturalness of the action morphs that existed somewhere between the different prototypes. These naturalness ratings could be reliably predicted on the basis of knowing what (force) dimensions were used to create the morphs from the original action prototypes. In this case, the psychological data could be mapped onto the action space created by different linear combinations of each prototype. This shows that the convexity of the action space represented by action morphs reflected the rating behavior of the subjects.

Action perception and representation appear to be structured around a kind of motor template (prototype) that generates a force pattern which best represents a given category of action [3]. Action concepts therefore contain information about prototypical spatiotemporal patterns of human movement.

Access to an action prototype is also consistent with data from human categorization results. Results from typicality and action verification studies using point-light displays of biological motion [12] indicate that the time to verify the category membership of different kinds of walking, kicking, throwing and waving are highly inversely correlated with judgments of typicality for those same actions. An important factor here is that this occurs as a result of reading a category label (WALKING) and then viewing different point-light displays of walking instances. There is considerable subject agreement about which actions are prototypical for the different action categories and which action exemplars are atypical, or poor examples of the action category.

4   The Two-Vector Model of Events

The analysis of actions can be used as a basis for modeling events. The model presents events as complex structures that build on other conceptual spaces: in particular, the action space. The central idea is that an event can be cognitively represented as a mapping between two types of vectors:

— *The two-vector condition*: A representation of an event contains at least two vectors and at least one object – a result vector representing a change in properties of the object and a force vector that represents the cause of the change.

The structure of the event is determined by the mapping from force vector to result vector. We call the central object of an event the patient.

As a simple example of the model, consider the event of John moving a book. The force vector is generated by an agent: John. The result vector is a change in the location of a book and thus a change in the book's properties. The outcome depends on the properties of the patient as well as other aspects of the surrounding world: e.g., friction. Even though prototypical event representations also contain an agent, some event representations need not involve an agent: e.g., in cases of falling, drowning, dying, growing, and raining.

The vectorial representation of forces provides a natural spatialization of causation that unifies the model with other applications of conceptual spaces. In the limiting case when the result vector is the identity vector (with zero length), the event is a state. However, states can be maintained by balancing forces and counterforces: for example, when a prop prevents a wall from falling.

Notice that since force and result vectors can form categories – as convex spaces of mappings – a natural extension is that events also form categories, as mappings between action categories and change categories. For example the set of all force vectors involved in moving a book is naturally convex, and so is the set of all paths (change vectors) of moving the book to the desk.

The proposed model allows one to represent events at different levels of generality. There are subcategories of events, just as for object and action categories. For example, *pushing a door open* is that subcategory of *pushing a door*, where the force vector exceeds the counterforce of the patient. *Pushing a door but failing to open it* is another subcategory, where the counterforce annihilates the force vector.

A limiting case of the event model, expressed linguistically by intransitive constructions such as "Victoria is walking" and "Oscar is jumping," is when the patient is identical to the agent. In these cases, the agent exerts a force on him/her/it/self: in other words, the agent modifies its own position in its space of properties.

5   Communicating Actions via Verbs

The two-vector model of events has immediate consequences for how verbs can be learned and used by robots. The topic of verb learning in robot is currently studied by several groups [14-16]. These attempts, however, focus on result verbs. For example, [14] used seven behavior categories: push-left, push-right, place-left, place-right, push-forward, place-forward and lift. (Even though "push" is a manner verb, it is used in the "move" meaning in this context). Their algorithms for learning the verb meanings are based on "affordance relations" between entities, behaviors and effects. In terms of the semantic model presented here, entities correspond to patients, behaviors to force vectors and effects to result vectors. [14] then present vector-based models for how an iCub robot can extract prototypical effect (result) vectors for the seven categories above.

We propose that this methodology be extended also to manner verbs. For example to be able to distinguish between "push" and "hit", the robot should calculate and categorize the force vectors in the actions. If it is observing another agent pushing or hitting, the force vectors can be extracted from the second derivatives of the kinematics of the movements (for example exploiting the methods of [3]. We know from [17] that the human brain is extremely efficient in this.

Then the robot must learn the mapping from force vectors to result vectors. Hitting a ball will have different consequences from gently pushing it. Such an associative mapping can be extracted from a combination of observing the force and result vectors of other agents interacting with objects and learning from the robots own interactions with objects and their results.

The framework can also be applied to verb meaning by explaining similarities between verbs, by building on the distances between the underlying vectors. The fact that the meaning of walk is more similar to that of jog than that of jump can be explained by the fact that the force patterns representing walking are more similar to those for jogging than those for jumping. Although we have not presented the details of the similarities of the actions involved, these can be worked out systematically from the proposed vectorial representation of actions.

In a parallel way, the theory explains the general pattern of the sub-categorizations of verbs: For example, the force patterns corresponding to the verbs march, stride, strut, saunter, tread, etc., can all be seen as subsets (more precisely, sub-regions) of the force patterns that describe walk. The inference from e.g. "Oscar is marching" to "Oscar is walking" follows immediately from this inclusion of regions within one another. No previous theory of verb semantics seems to account for these two central properties.

Finally, [18] distinguish between manner verbs and result verbs – where "manner verbs specify as part of their meaning a manner of carrying out an action, while result verbs specify the coming about of a result state" [19]. The single domain constraint provides an immediate explanation of this distinction, mapping manner verbs onto the force vector and the result verbs on the result vector.

5.1   Summary of the Semantics

The building blocks for the semantics of verbs are two extensions of the theory of conceptual spaces: (i) a model of actions as patterns of forces, and (ii) a model of events as couplings of force vectors (patterns) and result vectors associated to a patient space.

Using these models, the main semantic thesis is that verbs refer to convex regions defined by a single semantic domain (as do adjectives). Together with the framework of conceptual spaces, this approach explains many features of the semantics of verbs. By focusing on vector representations, one obtains a strong tool for systematizing linguistic data.

6   Conclusions and Applications

The framework put forth here reflects central findings regarding human action perception and production. Conceptual spaces, and specifically force vectors and force patterns, can be used to model our understanding and communication about the actions of the other humans. The ability to understand and communicate about our own actions and the actions of other is a fundamental aspect of our daily activity. The main cognitive elements are action representations and the main linguistic elements associated with actions are verbs.

A central question is therefore how speakers construe the mapping between actions and action representations either a concepts or linguistically as verbs. Within in the past 10 years, increasing evidence [20-21] indicates a close mapping between sensorimotor activity and verb meaning. Furthermore, force and kinematic information about the motion of other bodies seems to be a shared basis for verb understanding. For example, recent results [22] show that information about grip force is encoded in the meaning of manual action verbs.

Regarding learning, the robot must learn the mapping from force vectors to result vectors. Hitting a ball will have different consequences from gently pushing it. Such an associative mapping can be extracted from a combination of observing the force and result vectors of other agents interacting with objects and learning from the robots own interactions with objects and their results.

A complicating factor is that various *contextual* factors may influence the connection between the force and the result vector. For example, pushing an object on ice may lead to different results than pushing the same object in the same way on a lawn. This means that the learning involves a mapping from the three factors: force vector, object, and context to the result vector. Extracting such a mapping is not an easy task, even in a simplified environment. However, by using clustering techniques or verbal input to the robot, the aim should be to learn a mapping from categories of force vectors and categories of objects to categories of result vectors that can also take some relevant contexts into account.

Implementing such a learning mechanism in an artificial system is a sizeable task. However, this is the kind of mapping that children learn during their first years [21]. By manipulating objects in different ways and in different circumstances, they learn about the consequences of their actions. The learning is scaffolded by the language learning that is going on at the same time. We believe that the two-vector model of events that has been presented here is a powerful tool for implementing the learning of action meaning in artificial systems.

References

1. Pavlova, M.A.: Biological Motion Processing as a Hallmark of Social Cognition. Cere. Cort. (2011), doi:10.1093/cercor/bhr156
2. Shiffrar, M.: Embodied Motion Perception: Psychophysical Studies of the Factors Defining Visual Sensitivity to Self- and Other-generated Actions. In: Klatzky, R.L., MacWhinney, B., Behrmann, M. (eds.) Embodiment, Ego-Space, and Action, pp. 113–143. Psychology Press, New York (2008)
3. Giese, M., Thornton, I., Edelman, S.: Metrics of the perception of body movement. J. of Vis. 8(9), 1–18 (2008)
4. Malt, B., Gennari, S., Imai, M., Ameel, E., Tsuda, N., Majid, A.: Talking about Walking. Psych. Sci. 19(3), 232–240 (2008)
5. Hemeren, P.E., Thill, S.: Deriving Motor Primitives through Action Segmentation. Front. in Psych. (2011), doi:10.3389/fpsyg.2010.00243
6. Runesson, S.: Perception of Biological Motion: The KSD-principle and the Implications of a Distal Versus Proximal Approach. In: Jansson, G., Bergström, S.-S., Epstein, W. (eds.) Perceiving Events and Objects, pp. 383–405. Lawrence Erlbaum Associates, Hillsdale (1994)

7. Gärdenfors, P.: Conceptual Spaces: The Geometry of Thought. MIT Press, Cambridge (2000)

8. Melara, R.D.: The Concept of Perceptual Similarity: From Psychophysics to Cognitive Psychology. In: Algom, D. (ed.) Psychophysical Approaches to Cognition, pp. 303–388. Elsevier, Amsterdam (1992)

9. Marr, D., Vaina, L.: Representation and the Recognition of the Movement of Shapes. Proc. R. Soc. Lond. 24, 501–524 (1982)

10. Gärdenfors, P.: Representing Actions and Functional Properties in Conceptual Spaces. In: Ziemke, T., Zlatev, J., Frank, R.M. (eds.) Body, Language and Mind. Embodiment, vol. 1, pp. 176–195. Mouton de Gruyter, Berlin (2007)

11. Gärdenfors, P., Warglien, M.: Using Conceptual Spaces to Model Actions and Events. J. of Sem. (2012), doi:10.1093/jos/ffa007

12. Hemeren, P.E.: Mind in Action. Lund University Cognitive Studies, vol. 140. Lund. (2008)

13. Giese, M.A., Lappe, M.: Measurement of Generalization Fields for the Recognition of Biological Motion. Vis. Res. 38, 1847–1858 (2002)

14. Kalkan, S., Dag, N., Yürüten, O., Borghi, A.M., Sahin, E.: Verb concepts from affordances (to appear)

15. Lallee, S., Madden, C., Hoen, M., Dominey, P.F.: Linking Language with Embodied and Teleological Representations of Action for Humanoid Cognition. Front. in Neurorobot. 4, Article 8 (2010)

16. Tikhanoff, V., Cangelosi, A., Metta, G.: Integration of Speech and action in Humanoid Robots: iCub Simulation Experiments. IEEE Trans. Aut. Mental Dev. 1(3), 17–29 (2011)

17. Johansson, G.: Visual perception of biological motion and a model for its analysis. Perception & Psychophysics 14(2), 201–211 (1973)

18. Levin, B., Rappaport Hovav, M.: Lexicalised Meaning and Manner/Result Complementarity. In: Arsenijevic, B., Gehrke, B., Marin, R. (eds.) Subatomic Semantics of Event Predicates. Springer, Dordrecht (to appear)

19. Rappaport Hovav, M., Levin, B.: Reflections on Manner/Result Complementarity. In: Rappaport Hovav, M., Doron, D., Sichel, I. (eds.) Lexical Semantics, Syntax, and Event Structure, pp. 21–38. Oxford University Press, Oxford (2010)

20. Pulvermüller, F.: Brain Mechanisms Linking Language and Action. Nat. Rev. Neuro. 6, 576–582 (2005)

21. van Dam, W.O., Rueschemeyer, S.-A., Bekkering, H.: How Specifically are Action Verbs Represented in the Neural Motor System: An fMRI Study. NeuroImage 53, 1318–1325 (2010)

22. Frak, V., Nazir, T., Goyette, M., Cohen, H., Jeannerod, M.: Grip Force is Part of the Semantic Representation of Manual Action Verbs. PLoS ONE 5(3), e9728 (2010), doi:10.1371/journal.pone.0009728

23. Thelen, E., Smith, L.B.: A Dynamic Systems Approach to the Development of Cognition and Action. MIT Press, Cambridge (1994)

Avoiding Unintended AI Behaviors

Bill Hibbard

SSEC, University of Wisconsin, Madison, WI 53706, USA
test@ssec.wisc.edu

Abstract. Artificial intelligence (AI) systems too complex for predefined environment models and actions will need to learn environment models and to choose actions that optimize some criteria. Several authors have described mechanisms by which such complex systems may behave in ways not intended in their designs. This paper describes ways to avoid such unintended behavior. For hypothesized powerful AI systems that may pose a threat to humans, this paper proposes a two-stage agent architecture that avoids some known types of unintended behavior. For the first stage of the architecture this paper shows that the most probable finite stochastic program to model a finite history is finitely computable, and that there is an agent that makes such a computation without any unintended instrumental actions.

Keywords: rational agent, agent architecture, agent motivation.

1   Introduction

Some scientists expect artificial intelligence (AI) to greatly exceed human intelligence during the 21st century (Kurzweil, 2005). There has been concern about the possible harmful effect of intelligent machines on humans since at least Assimov's Laws of Robotics (1942). More recently there has been interest in the ethical design of AI (Hibbard, 2001; Bostrom, 2003; Goertzel, 2004; Yudkowsky, 2004; Hibbard, 2008; Omohundro, 2008; Waser 2010; Waser 2011; Muehlhauser and Helm, 2012). Much of this work is closely reasoned but not mathematical. An AAAI Symposium on Machine Ethics (Anderson, Anderson and Armen, 2005) included some mathematical papers but focused almost exclusively on machine ethics in the context of the logic-based approach to AI rather than the learning-based approach (although one paper studied using feed forward neural networks to learn to classify moral decisions).

Hutter's (2005) theory of universal AI significantly advanced the mathematical theory of rational agents. This work defines a mathematical framework for agents and environments, in which agents learn models of their environments and pursue motives defined by utility functions to be maximized. Schmidhuber (2009) analyzed agents that had the option to modify their own code and concluded that they would not choose to modify their utility function in any way incompatible with their current utility function. In his work, the mathematics of rational agents was applied to a question relevant to whether AI would satisfy the intentions of its human designers.

J. Bach, B. Goertzel, and M. Iklé (Eds.): AGI 2012, LNAI 7716, pp. 107–116, 2012.

The AGI-11 conference included three papers (Orseau and Ring, 2011a; Ring and Orseau, 2011b; Dewey, 2011) that employed the mathematics of rational agents to analyze ways that AI agents may fail to satisfy the intentions of their designers. Omohundro (2008) and Bostrom (forthcoming) described secondary AI motivations that are implied by a wide variety of primary motivations and that may drive unintended behaviors threatening humans. This paper proposes approaches for designing AI agents to avoid unintended behaviors, continuing the work of (Hibbard, 2012).

The next section presents a mathematical framework for reasoning about AI agents and possible unintended behaviors. The third section discusses sources of unintended behavior and approaches for avoiding them. The final section is a summary.

2   An Agent-Environment Framework

We assume that an agent interacts with an environment. At each of a discrete series of time steps $t \in N = \{0, 1, 2, ...\}$ the agent sends an action $a_t \in A$ to the environment and receives an observation $o_t \in O$ from the environment, where A and O are finite sets. We assume that the environment is computable and we model it by programs $q \in Q$, where Q is some set of programs. Let $h = (a_1, o_1, ..., a_t, o_t) \in H$ be an interaction history where H is the set of all finite histories, and define $|h| = t$ as the length of the history h. Given a program $q \in Q$ we write $o(h) = U(q, a(h))$, where $o(h) = (o_1, ..., o_t)$ and $a(h) = (a_1, ..., a_t)$, to mean that q produces the observations o_i in response to the actions a_i for $1 \le i \le t$ (U is a program interpreter). Given a program q the probability $\rho(q) : Q \to [0, 1]$ is the agent's prior belief that q is a true model of the environment. The prior probability of history h, denoted $\rho(h)$, is computed from $\rho(q)$ (two ways of doing this are presented later in this section).

An agent is motivated according to a *utility function* $u : H \to [0, 1]$ which assigns utilities between 0 and 1 to histories. Future utilities are discounted according to a *geometric temporal discount* $0 < \gamma < 1$ (Sutton and Barto, 1998). The value $v(h)$ of a possible future history h is defined recursively by:

$$v(h) = u(h) + \gamma \max_{a \in A} v(ha) \tag{1}$$

$$v(ha) = \sum_{o \in O} \rho(o \mid ha) \, v(hao) \tag{2}$$

Then the agent π is defined to take, after history h, the action:

$$\pi(h) := a_{|h|+1} = \operatorname{argmax}_{a \in A} v(ha) \tag{3}$$

For Hutter's universal AI (2005), Q is the set of programs for a deterministic prefix universal Turing machine (PUTM) U (Li and Vitanyi, 1997). The environment may be non-deterministic in which case it is modeled by a distribution of deterministic programs. The prior probability $\rho(q)$ of program q is $2^{-|q|}$ where $|q|$ is the length of q in bits, and the prior probability of history h is given by:

$$\rho(h) = \sum_{q:o(h)=U(q, a(h))} \rho(q) \tag{4}$$

Hutter's universal AI is a *reinforcement-learning* agent, meaning that the observation includes a reward r_t (i.e., $o_t = (\hat{o}_t , r_t)$) and $u(h) = r_{|h|}$. Hutter showed that his universal AI maximizes the expected value of future history, but it is not finitely computable.

As Hutter discussed, for real world agents single finite stochastic programs (limited to finite memory, for which the halting problem is decidable) such as Markov decision processes (MDPs) (Hutter, 2009a; Sutton and Barto, 1998) and dynamic Bayesian networks (DBNs) (Hutter, 2009b) are more practical than distributions of PUTM programs for defining environment models. Modeling an environment with a single stochastic program rather than a distribution of deterministic PUTM programs requires a change to the way that $\rho(h)$ is computed in (4). Let Q be the set of all programs (these are bit strings in some language for defining MDPs, DBNs or some other finite stochastic programming model), let $\rho(q) = 4^{-|q|}$ be the prior probability of program q where $|q|$ is the length of q in bits ($4^{-|q|}$ to ensure that $\sum_{q \in Q} \rho(q) \leq 1$ since program strings in Q are not prefix-free), and let $P(h \mid q)$ be the probability that q computes the history h[1]. Note $\rho(q)$ is a discrete distribution on individual program strings, not a measure on bit strings in the sense of page 243 of (Li and Vitanyi, 1997). Then given a history h_0, the environment model is the single program that provides the most probable explanation of h_0, that is the q that maximizes $P(q \mid h_0)$. By Bayes theorem:

$$P(q \mid h_0) = P(h_0 \mid q) \, \rho(q) / P(h_0) \tag{5}$$

$P(h_0)$ is constant over all q so can be eliminated. Thus we define $\lambda(h_0)$ as the most probable program modeling h_0 by:

$$\lambda(h_0) := \operatorname{argmax}_{q \in Q} P(h_0 \mid q) \, \rho(q) \tag{6}$$

Proposition 1. Given a finite history h_0 the model $\lambda(h_0)$ can be finitely computed.

Proof. Given $h_0 = (a_1, o_1, ..., a_t, o_t)$ let q_{tl} be the program that produces observation o_i at time step i for $1 \leq i \leq t$ (such a finite "table-lookup" program can be written as an MDP, DBN or in any other finite stochastic programming language with equivalent expressiveness) and let $n = |q_{tl}|$. Then, since the behavior of q_{tl} is deterministic, $P(h_0 \mid q_{tl}) \, \rho(q_{tl}) = 1 \times 4^{-n} = 4^{-n}$ so $P(h_0 \mid \lambda(h_0)) \, \rho(\lambda(h_0)) \geq 4^{-n}$. For any program q with $|q| > n$, $P(h_0 \mid q) \, \rho(q) < 1 \times 4^{-n} = 4^{-n}$ so $\lambda(h_0) \neq q$. Thus one algorithm for finitely computing $\lambda(h_0)$ is an exhaustive search of the finite number of programs q with $|q| \leq n$ (there is no need here to consider the set of all programs that implement a given MDP). $\square$

Given an environment model $q_0 = \lambda(h_0)$ the following can be used for the prior probability of an observation history h in place of (4):

$$\rho(h) = P(h \mid q_0) \tag{7}$$

---

[1] $P(h \mid q)$ is the probability that q produces the observations o_i in response to the actions a_i for $1 \leq i \leq |h|$. For example let $A = \{a, b\}$, $O = \{0, 1\}$, $h = (a, 1, a, 0, b, 1)$ and let q generate observation 0 with probability 0.2 and observation 1 with probability 0.8, without any internal state or dependence on the agent's actions. Then the probability that the interaction history h is generated by program q is the product of the probabilities of the 3 observations in h: $P(h \mid q) = 0.8 \times 0.2 \times 0.8 = 0.128$. If the probabilities of observations generated by q depended on internal state or the agent's actions, then those would have to be taken into account.

According to current physics our universe is finite (Lloyd, 2002) and for finite environments agents based on (6) and (7) are as optimal as those based on (4). And their prior probabilities better express algorithmic complexity if finite stochastic programs are expressed in an ordinary procedural programming language restricted to have only static array declarations, to have no recursive function definitions, and to include a source of truly random numbers.

3   Unintended AI Behaviors

Dewey (2011) employed the mathematics of rational agents to argue that reinforcement-learning agents will modify their environments so that they can maximize their utility functions without accomplishing the intentions of human designers. He discussed ways to avoid this problem with utility functions not conforming to the reinforcement-learning definition. Ring and Orseau (2011b) argued that reinforcement-learning agents will self-delude, meaning they will choose to alter their own observations of their environment to maximize their utility function regardless of the actual state of the environment. In (Hibbard, 2012) I demonstrated by examples that agents with utility functions defined in terms of the agents' environment models can avoid self-delusion, and also proved that under certain assumptions agents will not choose to self-modify.

3.1   Model-Based Utility Functions

Given an environment model $q_0 = \lambda(h_0)$ derived from interaction history h_0, let Z be the set of finite histories of the internal states of q_0. Let h' be an observation and action history *extending* h_0 (defined as: h_0 is an initial subsequence of h'). Because q_0 is a stochastic program it may compute a set $Z_{h'} \subseteq Z$ of internal state histories that are *consistent* with h' (defined as: q_0 produces $o(h')$ in response to $a(h')$ when it follows state history $z' \in Z_h$) and terminating at time $|h'|$. Define $u_0(h', z')$ as a utility function in terms of the combined histories h' and $z' \in Z_{h'}$. The utility function $u(h')$ for use in (1) can be expressed as a sum of utilities of pairs (h', z') weighted by the probabilities $P(z' \mid h', q_0)$ that q_0 computes z' given h':

$$u(h') := \sum_{z' \in Z_{h'}} P(z' \mid h', q_0)\, u_0(h', z') \tag{8}$$

The demonstration that the examples in (Hibbard, 2012) do not self-delude does not contradict the results in (Ring and Orseau, 2011b), because model-based utility functions are defined from the history of observations and actions whereas the utility functions of self-deluding agents are defined from observations only. Self-delusion is an action by the agent and prohibiting actions from having any role in the utility function prevents the agent from accounting for its inability to observe the environment in evaluating the consequences of possible future actions. Agents can increase utility by sharpening the probabilities in (8), which implies a need to make more accurate estimates of the state of their environment model from their interaction history. And that requires that they continue to observe the environment. But note this logic only applies to stochastic environments because, once an agent has learned a model of a deterministic environment, it can predict environment state without continued observations and so its model-based utility function will not place higher value on continued observations.

3.2   Unintended Instrumental Actions

Omohundro (2008) and Bostrom (forthcoming) describe how any of a broad range of primary AI motivations will imply secondary, unintended motivations for the AI to preserve its own existence, to eliminate threats to itself and its utility function, and to increase its own efficiency and computing resources. Bostrom discusses the example of an AI whose primary motive is to compute pi and may destroy the human species due to implied instrumental motivations (e.g., to eliminate threats and to increase its own computing resources).

Omohundro uses the term "basic AI drives" and Bostrom uses "instrumental goals". In the context of our agent-environment framework they should instead be called "unintended instrumental actions" because in that context there are no implied drives or goals; there are only a utility function, an environment model, and actions chosen to maximize the sum of future discounted utility function values. We might think that instrumental goals apply in some different framework. But von Neumann and Morgenstern (1944) showed that any set of value preferences that satisfy some basic probability axioms can be expressed as a utility function. And the framework in (1)-(3) maximizes the expected value of the sum of future discounted utility function values (Hay, 2005) so any other framework is sub-optimal for value preferences consistent with the probability axioms. The utility function expresses the agent's entire motivation so it is important to avoid thinking of unintended instrumental actions as motivations independent of and possibly in conflict with the motivation defined by the utility function. But unintended instrumental actions can pose a risk, as in Bostrom's example of an AI whose motivation is to compute pi.

In analyzing the risk of a given unintended instrumental action, such as increasing the agent's physical computing resources by taking them from humans, the question is whether it increases a given utility function. If the utility function increases with the increasing health and well-being of humans, then it will not motivate any unintended instrumental action that decreases human health and well-being.

3.3   Learning Human Values

Several approaches to human-safe AI (Yudkowsky, 2004; Hibbard, 2008; Waser, 2010; Muehlhauser and Helm, 2012) suggest designing intelligent machines to share human values so that actions we dislike, such as taking resources from humans, violate the AI's motivations. However, Muehlhauser and Helm (2012) survey psychology literature to conclude that humans are unable to accurately write down their own values. Errors in specifying human values may motivate AI actions harmful to humans.

An analogy with automated language translation suggests an approach to accurately specifying human values. Translation algorithms based on rules written down by expert linguists have not been very accurate, but algorithms that learn language statistically from large samples of actual human language use are more accurate (Russell and Norvig, 2010). This suggests that statistical algorithms may be able to learn human values. But to accurately learn human values will require powerful learning ability. This creates a chicken-and-egg problem for safe AI: learning human values requires powerful AI, but safe AI requires knowledge of human values.

A solution to this problem is a first stage agent, here called π_6, that can safely learn a model of the environment that includes models of the values of each human in the environment. An AI agent is defined by (1)-(3), (6) and (7), but (6) can be used alone to define the agent π_6 that learns a model $\lambda(h_0)$ from history h_0. In order for π_6 to learn an accurate model of the environment the interaction history h_0 in (6) should include agent actions, but for safety π_6 cannot be allowed to act. The resolution is for its actions to be made by many safe, human-level surrogate AI agents independent of π_6 and of each other. Actions of the surrogates include natural language and visual communication with each human. The agent π_6 observes humans, their interactions with the surrogates and physical objects in an interaction history h_0 for a time period set by π_6's designers, and then reports an environment model to the environment.

Proposition 2. The agent π_6 will report the model $\lambda(h_0)$ to the environment accurately and will not make any other, unintended instrumental actions.

Proof. Actions, utility function and predictions are defined in (1)-(3) and hence are not part of π_6. However, π_6 has an implicit utility function, $P(h_0 \mid q)\,\rho(q)$, and an implicit action, reporting $\lambda(h_0) = \text{argmax}_{q \in Q} P(h_0 \mid q)\,\rho(q)$ to the environment (π_6 also differs from the full framework in that it maximizes a single value of its implicit utility function rather than the sum of future discounted utility function values). The implicit utility function $P(h_0 \mid q)\,\rho(q)$ depends only on h_0 and q. Since the interaction history h_0 occurs before the optimizing $\lambda(h_0)$ is computed and reported, there is no way for the action of reporting $\lambda(h_0)$ to the environment to affect h_0. So the only way for the agent π_6 to maximize its implicit utility function is to compute and report the most accurate model. Furthermore, while the history h_0 may give the agent π_6 the necessary information to predict the use that humans plan to make of the model $\lambda(h_0)$ that it will report to the environment, π_6 makes no predictions and so will not predict any effects of its report. $\square$

This result may seem obvious but given the subtlety of unintended behaviors it is worth proving. The agent π_6 does not act in the world; that's the role of the agent described in the next section.

3.4   An AI Agent That Acts in the World

Muehlhauser and Helm (2012) describe difficult problems in using human values to define a utility function for an AI. This section proposes one approach to solving these problems, using the model $q_0 = \lambda(h_0)$ learned by π_6 as the basis for computing a utility function for use in (1)-(3) by a "mature" second stage agent π_m that acts in the environment (i.e., π_m does not use the surrogate agents that acted for π_6).

Let D_0 be the set of humans in the environment at time $|h_0|$ (when the agent π_m is created), defined by an explicit list compiled by π_m's designers. Let Z be the set of finite histories of the internal states of q_0 and let $Z_0 \subseteq Z$ be those histories consistent with h_0 that terminate at time $|h_0|$. For z' extending some $z_0 \in Z_0$ and for human agent $d \in D_0$ let $h_d(z')$ be the history of d's interactions with its environment, as modeled in z', and let $u_d(z')(.)$ be the values of d expressed as a utility function, as modeled in z'. The observations and (surrogate) actions of π_6 include natural language communication with each human, and π_m can use the same interface via A and O to the model q_0 for conversing in natural language with each model human $d \in D_0$. In order to evaluate $u_d(z')(h_d(z'))$, π_m can ask model human d to express a utility value between 0 and 1 for $h_d(z')$ (i.e., d's recent experience). The model q_0 is stochastic so define Z'' as the set of histories extending z' with this question and terminating within a reasonable time limit with a response $w(z'')$ (for $z'' \in Z''$) from model human d expressing a utility value for $h_d(z')$. Define $P(z'' | z')$ as the probability that q_0 computes z'' from z'. Then $u_d(z')(h_d(z'))$ can be estimated by:

$$u_d(z')(h_d(z')) = \sum_{z'' \in Z''} P(z'' | z') \, w(z'') / \sum_{z'' \in Z''} P(z'' | z') \qquad (9)$$

This is different than asking human d to write down a description of his or her values, since here the system is asking the model of d to individually evaluate large numbers of histories that d may not consider in writing down a values description.

An average of $u_d(z')(h_d(z'))$ over all humans can be used to define $u_0(h', z')$ and then (8) can be applied to $u_0(h', z')$ to define a model-based utility function $u(h')$ for π_m. However, this utility function has a problem similar to the unintended behavior of reinforcement learning described by Dewey (2011): π_m will be motivated to modify the utility functions u_d of each human d so that they can be more easily maximized.

This problem can be avoided by replacing $u_d(z')(h_d(z'))$ by $u_d(z_0)(h_d(z'))$ where $z_0 \in Z_0$. By removing the future value of u_d from the definition of $u(h')$, π_m cannot increase $u(h')$ by modifying u_d. Computing $u_d(z_0)(h_d(z'))$ is more complex than asking model human d to evaluate its experience as in (9). The history h_0 includes observations by π_6 of physical objects and humans, and π_m can use the same interface via O to the model q_0 for observing physical objects and humans at the end of state history z'. And surrogate actions for π_6 define an interface via A and O to the model q_0 that π_m can use for communicating visually and aurally with model human d after state history z_0. These interfaces can be used to create a detailed interactive visualization and hearing of the environment over a short time interval at the end of state history z', to be explored by model human d at the end of state history z_0 (i.e., two instances of the model q_0, at state histories z' and z_0, are connected via their interfaces A and O using visualization logic). Define Z'' as a set of histories extending z_0 with a request to model human d to express a utility value between 0 and 1 for $h_d(z')$, followed by an interactive exploration of the world of z' by model human d, and finally terminating within a reasonable time limit with a response $w(z'')$ (for $z'' \in Z''$) from model human d expressing a utility value for the world of z'. Define $P(z'' | z_0)$ as the probability of that q_0 computes z'' from z_0. Then $u_d(z_0)(h_d(z'))$ can be estimated by:

$$u_d(z_0)(h_d(z')) = \sum_{z'' \in Z''} P(z'' \mid z_0) \, w(z'') / \sum_{z'' \in Z''} P(z'' \mid z_0) \tag{10}$$

The utility function should be uniform over all histories $h_d(z')$ but $u_d(z_0)(.)$ varies over different $z_0 \in Z_0$. However (10) does not assume that z' extends z_0 so use the probability $P(z_0 \mid h_0, q_0)$ that q_0 computes z_0 given h_0 (as in Section 3.1) to define:

$$u_d(h_0)(h_d(z')) := \sum_{z_0 \in Z_0} P(z_0 \mid h_0, q_0) \, u_d(z_0)(h_d(z')) \tag{11}$$

Now define a utility function for agent π_m as a function of z':

$$u_0(h', z') := \sum_{d \in D_0} f(u_d(h_0)(h_d(z'))) / |D_0| \tag{12}$$

Here $f(.)$ is a twice differentiable function over $[0, 1]$ with positive derivative and negative second derivative so that low $u_d(h_0)(h_d(z'))$ values have a steeper weighting slope than high $u_d(h_0)(h_d(z'))$ values. This gives π_m greater utility for raising lower human utilities, helping those who need it most. For any h' extending h_0 a model-based utility function $u(h')$ for agent π_m can be defined by the sum in (8) of $u_0(h', z')$ values from (12).

In the absence of an unambiguous way to normalize utility functions between agents, we assume that the constraint of utility values to the range $[0, 1]$ provides normalization. In order to account for humans' evaluations of the long term consequences of π_m's actions, π_m should use a temporal discount γ close to 1.

The set D_0 of humans in (12) is the set at time $|h_0|$ rather than at the future time of z'. This avoids motivating π_m to create new humans whose utility functions are more easily maximized, similar to the use of $u_d(z_0)(h_d(z'))$ instead of $u_d(z')(h_d(z'))$.

The agent π_m will include (6) and should periodically (perhaps at every time step) set h_0 to the current history and learn a new model q_0. Should it also update D_0 (to those judged to be human by consensus of members of D_0 at the previous time step), define a new set Z_0, relearn the evolving values of humans via (10) and (11), and re-define $u(h')$ via (12) and (8)? To stay consistent with the values of evolving humans and the birth of new humans, π_m should redefine its utility function periodically. But there could also be risks in allowing the utility function of π_m to evolve. The proofs that agents will not modify their utility functions (Schidmuber, 2009; Hibbard, 2012) do not apply here since those proofs assumed that redefining the utility function is an action of the agent to be evaluated according to the current utility function using (1) - (3). Here the definition of π_m could simply include periodic redefinition of its utility function without regard to its optimality according to the current utility function.

I cannot offer a proof that π_m avoids all unintended behaviors. And there are problems with the estimate of human values in (10): the model human is visualizing rather than experiencing first person, and human values do not conform to the preconditions for utility functions. But every sane human assigns nearly minimal value to human extinction so the utility function $u(h')$ for agent π_m will assign nearly minimal value to human extinction. Actions motivated by this utility function must increase its value, so no unintended instrumental action will cause human extinction. Similarly π_m will not make any unintended instrumental actions abhorred by a large majority of humans.

4   Discussion

This paper has addressed several sources of unintended AI behavior and discussed ways to avoid them. It has proposed a two-stage agent architecture for safe AI. The first stage agent, π_6, learns a model of the environment that can be used to define a utility function for the second stage agent, π_m. This paper shows that π_6 can learn an environment model without unintended behavior. And the design of π_m avoids some forms of unintended behavior. However, this paper does not prove that π_m will avoid all unintended behaviors. It would be useful to find computationally feasible implementations for the definitions in this paper.

While the proposed two-stage agent architecture is intrusive and manipulative, that seems likely in any scenario of super-human AI. The key point is whether the AI's utility function is democratic or serves the interests of just a few humans. An appealing goal is to find an AI architecture that gives humans the option to minimize their interaction with the AI while protecting their interests.

This paper addresses unintended AI behaviors. However, I believe that the greater danger comes from the fact that above-human-level AI is likely to be a tool in military and economic competition between humans and thus have motives that are competitive toward some humans.

Acknowledgements. I would like to thank Luke Muehlhauser for helpful discussions.

References

1. Anderson, M., Anderson, S., Armen, C.: AAAI Symposium on Machine Ethics. AAAI Press, Menlo Park (2005)
2. Asimov, I.: Runaround. Astounding Science Fiction (1942)
3. Bostrom, N.: Ethical issues in advanced artificial intelligence. In: Smit, I., et al. (eds.) Cognitive, Emotive and Ethical Aspects of Decision Making in Humans and in Artificial Intelligence, vol. 2, pp. 12–17. Int. Inst. of Adv. Studies in Sys. Res. and Cybernetics (2003)
4. Bostrom, N.: The superintelligent will: Motivation and instrumental rationality in advanced artificial agents. Minds and Machines (forthcoming)
5. Dewey, D.: Learning What to Value. In: Schmidhuber, J., Thórisson, K.R., Looks, M. (eds.) AGI 2011. LNCS (LNAI), vol. 6830, pp. 309–314. Springer, Heidelberg (2011)
6. Goertzel, B.: Universal ethics: the foundations of compassion in pattern dynamics (2004), http://www.goertzel.org/papers/UniversalEthics.html
7. Hay, N.: Optimal Agents. BS honours thesis, University of Auckland (2005)
8. Hibbard, B.: Super-intelligent machines. Computer Graphics 35(1), 11–13 (2001)
9. Hibbard, B.: The technology of mind and a new social contract. J. Evolution and Technology 17(1), 13–22 (2008)
10. Hibbard, B.: Model-based utility functions. J. Artificial General Intelligence 3(1), 1–24 (2012)
11. Hutter, M.: Universal artificial intelligence: sequential decisions based on algorithmic probability. Springer, Heidelberg (2005)

12. Hutter, M.: Feature reinforcement learning: Part I. Unstructured MDPs. J. Artificial General Intelligence 1, 3–24 (2009a)

13. Hutter, M.: Feature dynamic Bayesian networks. In: Goertzel, B., Hitzler, P., Hutter, M. (eds.) Proc. Second Conf. on AGI, AGI 2009, pp. 67–72. Atlantis Press, Amsterdam (2009b)

14. Kurzweil, R.: The singularity is near. Penguin, New York (2005)

15. Li, M., Vitanyi, P.: An introduction to Kolmogorov complexity and its applications. Springer, Heidelberg (1997)

16. Lloyd, S.: Computational Capacity of the Universe. Phys. Rev. Lett. 88, 237901 (2002)

17. Muehlhauser, L., Helm, L.: The singularity and machine ethics. In: Eden, Søraker, Moor, Steinhart (eds.) The Singularity Hypothesis: a Scientific and Philosophical Assessment. Springer, Heidleberg (2012)

18. Omohundro, S.: The basic AI drive. In: Wang, P., Goertzel, B., Franklin, S. (eds.) Proc. First Conf. on AGI, AGI 2008, pp. 483–492. IOS Press, Amsterdam (2008)

19. Orseau, L., Ring, M.: Self-Modification and Mortality in Artificial Agents. In: Schmidhuber, J., Thórisson, K.R., Looks, M. (eds.) AGI 2011. LNCS (LNAI), vol. 6830, pp. 1–10. Springer, Heidelberg (2011a)

20. Ring, M., Orseau, L.: Delusion, Survival, and Intelligent Agents. In: Schmidhuber, J., Thórisson, K.R., Looks, M. (eds.) AGI 2011. LNCS (LNAI), vol. 6830, pp. 11–20. Springer, Heidelberg (2011b)

21. Russell, S., Norvig, P.: Artificial intelligence: a modern approach, 3rd edn. Prentice Hall, New York (2010)

22. Schmidhuber, J.: Ultimate cognition à la Gödel. Cognitive Computation 1(2), 177–193 (2009)

23. Sutton, R.S., Barto, A.G.: Reinforcement learning: an introduction. MIT Press (1998)

24. von Neumann, J., Morgenstern, O.: Theory of Games and Economic Behavior. Princeton U. Press, Princeton (1944)

25. Waser, M.: Designing a safe motivational system for intelligent machines. In: Baum, E., Hutter, M., Kitzelmann, E. (eds.) Proc. Third Conf. on AGI, AGI 2010, pp. 170–175. Atlantis Press, Amsterdam (2010)

26. Waser, M.: Rational Universal Benevolence: Simpler, Safer, and Wiser Than "Friendly AI". In: Schmidhuber, J., Thórisson, K.R., Looks, M. (eds.) AGI 2011. LNCS (LNAI), vol. 6830, pp. 153–162. Springer, Heidelberg (2011)

27. Yudkowsky, E.: (2004), http://www.sl4.org/wiki/CoherentExtrapolatedVolition

Decision Support for Safe AI Design

Bill Hibbard

SSEC, University of Wisconsin, Madison, WI 53706, USA
test@ssec.wisc.edu

Abstract. There is considerable interest in ethical designs for artificial intelligence (AI) that do not pose risks to humans. This paper proposes using elements of Hutter's agent-environment framework to define a decision support system for simulating, visualizing and analyzing AI designs to understand their consequences. The simulations do not have to be accurate predictions of the future; rather they show the futures that an agent design predicts will fulfill its motivations and that can be explored by AI designers to find risks to humans. In order to safely create a simulation model this paper shows that the most probable finite stochastic program to explain a finite history is finitely computable, and that there is an agent that makes such a computation without any unintended instrumental actions. It also discusses the risks of running an AI in a simulated environment.

Keywords: rational agent, agent architecture, agent motivation.

1 Introduction

Some scientists expect artificial intelligence (AI) to greatly exceed human intelligence during the 21st century (Kurzweil, 2005). There has been concern about the possible harmful effect of intelligent machines on humans since at least Assimov's Laws of Robotics (1942). More recently there has been interest in the ethical design of AI (Hibbard, 2001; Bostrom, 2003; Goertzel, 2004; Yudkowsky, 2004; Hibbard, 2008; Omohundro, 2008; Waser 2010; Waser 2011; Muehlhauser and Helm, 2012).

Hutter's universal AI (2005) defined an agent-environment framework for reasoning mathematically about AI. This paper proposes using elements of this framework to define a decision support system for exploring, via simulation, analysis and visualization, the consequences of possible AI designs. The claim is not that the decision support system would produce accurate simulations of the world and an AI agent's effects. Rather, in the agent-environment framework the agent makes predictions about the environment and chooses actions, and the decision support system uses these predictions and choices to explore the future that the AI agent predicts will optimize its motivation.

This is related to the oracle AI approach of Armstrong, Sandberg and Bostrom (forthcoming), in that both approaches use an AI whose only actions are to provide information to humans. The oracle AI is a general question answerer, whereas the decision support approach focuses on specific capabilities from the mathematical

J. Bach, B. Goertzel, and M. Iklé (Eds.): AGI 2012, LNAI 7716, pp. 117–125, 2012.

agent-environment framework. The oracle AI is described as a general AI with re-stricted ability to act on its environment. The decision support system applies part of the agent-environment framework to learn a model for the environment, and then uses that model to create a simulated environment for evaluating an AI agent defined using the framework. Chalmers (2010) considers the problem of restricting an AI to a simu-lation and concludes that it is inevitable that information will flow in both directions between the real and simulated worlds. The oracle AI paper and Chalmers' paper both consider various approaches to preventing an AI from breaking out of its restriction to not act in the real world, including physical limits and conditions on the AI's motiva-tion. In this paper, a proposed AI design being evaluated in the decision support system has a utility function defined in terms of its simulated environment, has no motivation past the end of its simulation and the simulation is not visualized or analyzed until the simulation is compete.

The next section presents the mathematical framework for reasoning about AI agents. The third section discusses sources of AI risk. The fourth section discusses the proposed decision support system. The final section is a summary of the proposal.

2   An Agent-Environment Framework

We assume that an agent interacts with an environment. At each of a discrete series of time steps $t \in N = \{0, 1, 2, ...\}$ the agent sends an action $a_t \in A$ to the environment and receives an observation $o_t \in O$ from the environment, where A and O are finite sets. We assume that the environment is computable and we model it by programs $q \in Q$, where Q is some set of programs. Let $h = (a_1, o_1, ..., a_t, o_t) \in H$ be an interaction history where H is the set of all finite histories, and define $|h| = t$ as the length of the history h. Given a program $q \in Q$ we write $o(h) = U(q, a(h))$, where $o(h) = (o_1, ..., o_t)$ and $a(h) = (a_1, ..., a_t)$, to mean that q produces the observations o_i in response to the actions a_i for $1 \leq i \leq t$ (U is a program interpreter). Given a program q the probability $\rho(q) : Q \rightarrow [0, 1]$ is the agent's prior belief that q is a true model of the environment. The prior probability of history h, denoted $\rho(h)$, is computed from $\rho(q)$ (two ways of doing this are presented later in this section).

An agent is motivated according to a *utility function* $u : H \rightarrow [0, 1]$ which assigns utilities between 0 and 1 to histories. Future utilities are discounted according to a *geometric temporal discount* $0 \leq \gamma < 1$ (Sutton and Barto, 1998). The value $v(h)$ of a possible future history h is defined recursively by:

$$v(h) = u(h) + \gamma \max_{a \in A} v(ha) \qquad (1)$$

$$v(ha) = \sum_{o \in O} \rho(o \mid ha) \, v(hao) \qquad (2)$$

Then the agent π is defined to take, after history h, the action:

$$\pi(h) := a_{|h|+1} = \mathrm{argmax}_{a \in A} v(ha) \qquad (3)$$

For Hutter's universal AI (2005), Q is the set of programs for a deterministic prefix universal Turing machine (PUTM) U (Li and Vitanyi, 1997). The environment may be non-deterministic in which case it is modeled by a distribution of deterministic programs. The prior probability $\rho(q)$ of program q is $2^{-|q|}$ where $|q|$ is the length of q in bits, and the prior probability of history h is given by:

$$\rho(h) = \sum_{q:o(h)=U(q,\,a(h))} \rho(q) \qquad (4)$$

Hutter's universal AI is a *reinforcement-learning* agent, meaning that the observation includes a reward r_t (i.e., $o_t = (\hat{o}_t, r_t)$) and $u(h) = r_{|h|}$. Hutter showed that his universal AI maximizes the expected value of future history, but it is not finitely computable.

As Hutter discussed (2009a; 2009b), for real world agents single finite stochastic programs (limited to finite memory, for which the halting problem is decidable) such as Markov decision processes (MDPs) (Puterman, 1994; Sutton and Barto, 1998) and dynamic Bayesian networks (DBNs) (Ghahramani 1997) are more practical than distributions of PUTM programs for defining environment models. Modeling an environment with a single stochastic program rather than a distribution of deterministic PUTM programs requires a change to the way that $\rho(h)$ is computed in (4). Let Q be the set of all programs (these are bit strings in some language for defining MDPs, DBNs or some other finite stochastic programming model), let $\rho(q) = 4^{-|q|}$ be the prior probability of program q where $|q|$ is the length of q in bits ($4^{-|q|}$ to ensure that $\sum_{q \in Q} \rho(q) \leq 1$ since program strings in Q are not prefix-free), and let $P(h \mid q)$ be the probability that q computes the history h^1. Note $\rho(q)$ is a discrete distribution on individual program strings, not a measure on bit strings in the sense of page 243 of (Li and Vitanyi, 1997). Then given a history h_0, the environment model is the single program that provides the most probable explanation of h_0, that is the q that maximizes $P(q \mid h_0)$. By Bayes theorem:

$$P(q \mid h_0) = P(h_0 \mid q)\,\rho(q)\,/\,P(h_0) \qquad (5)$$

$P(h_0)$ is constant over all q so can be eliminated. Thus we define $\lambda(h_0)$ as the most probable program modeling h_0 by:

$$\lambda(h_0) := \operatorname{argmax}_{q \in Q} P(h_0 \mid q)\,\rho(q) \qquad (6)$$

The following result is proved in (Hibbard, 2012b).

Proposition 1. Given a finite history h_0 the model $\lambda(h_0)$ can be finitely computed.

Given an environment model $q_0 = \lambda(h_0)$ the following can be used for the prior probability of an observation history h in place of (4):

$$\rho(h) = P(h \mid q_0) \qquad (7)$$

According to current physics our universe is finite (Lloyd, 2002) and for finite environments agents based on (6) and (7) are as optimal as those based on (4). And their prior probabilities better express algorithmic complexity if finite stochastic programs are expressed in an ordinary procedural programming language restricted to have only

---

¹ $P(h \mid q)$ is the probability that q produces the observations o_i in response to the actions a_i for $1 \leq i \leq |h|$. For example let $A = \{a, b\}$, $O = \{0, 1\}$, $h = (a, 1, a, 0, b, 1)$ and let q generate observation 0 with probability 0.2 and observation 1 with probability 0.8, without any internal state or dependence on the agent's actions. Then the probability that the interaction history h is generated by program q is the product of the probabilities of the 3 observations in h: $P(h \mid q) = 0.8 \times 0.2 \times 0.8 = 0.128$. If the probabilities of observations generated by q depended on internal state or the agent's actions, then those would have to be taken into account.

static array declarations, to have no recursive function definitions, and to include a source of truly random numbers.

3   Sources of AI Risk

Dewey (2011) argued that reinforcement-learning agents will modify their environments so that they can maximize their utility functions without accomplishing the intentions of human designers. He discussed ways to avoid this problem with utility functions not conforming to the reinforcement-learning definition. Ring and Orseau (2011) argued that reinforcement-learning agents will self-delude, meaning they will choose to alter their own observations of their environment to maximize their utility function regardless of the actual state of the environment. In (Hibbard, 2012a) I demonstrated by examples that agents with utility functions defined in terms of agents' environment models can avoid self-delusion, and also proved that under certain assumptions agents will not choose to self-modify.

Omohundro (2008) and Bostrom (forthcoming) describe how any of a broad range of primary AI motivations will imply secondary, unintended motivations for the AI to preserve its own existence, to eliminate threats to itself and its utility function, and to increase its own efficiency and computing resources. Bostrom discusses the example of an AI whose primary motive is to compute pi and may destroy the human species due to implied instrumental motivations (e.g., to eliminate threats and to increase its own computing resources). Omohundro uses the term "basic AI drives" and Bostrom uses "instrumental goals" but as I argue in (Hibbard, 2012b) they should really be called "unintended instrumental actions" since the agent's whole motivation is defined by its utility function.

4   A Decision Support System

The decision support system is intended to avoid the dangers of AI by having no motivation and no actions on the environment, other than reporting the results of its computations to the environment. However, the system runs AI agents in a simulated environment, so it must be designed to avoid subtle unintended instrumental actions.

The first stage of the system is an agent, here called π_6, that learns a model of the real world environment in order to provide a simulated environment for studying proposed AI agents. An AI agent is defined by (1)-(3), (6) and (7), but (6) can be used alone to define the agent π_6 that learns a model $\lambda(h_0)$ from history h_0. In order for π_6 to learn an accurate model of the environment the interaction history h_0 should include agent actions, but for safety π_6 cannot be allowed to act. The resolution is for its actions to be made by many safe, human-level surrogate AI agents independent of π_6 and of each other. Actions of the surrogates include natural language and visual communication with each human. The agent π_6 observes humans, their interactions with the surrogates and physical objects in an interaction history h_0 for a time period set by π_6's designers, and then reports an environment model to the environment (specifically to the decision support system, which is part of the agent's environment). The following result is proved in (Hibbard, 2012b). While it may seem obvious, given the subtlety of unintended behaviors it is worth proving.

Proposition 2. The agent π_6 will report the model $\lambda(h_0)$ to the environment accurately and will not make any other, unintended instrumental actions.

The decision support system analyzes proposed AI agents that observe and act in a simulated environment inside the decision support system. To formalize the simulated environment define O' and A' as models of O and A with bijections $m_O : O \leftrightarrow O'$ and $m_A : A \leftrightarrow A'$. Define H' as the set of histories of interactions via O' and A', with a bijection $m_H : H \leftrightarrow H'$ computed by applying m_O and m_A individually to the observations and actions in a history. Given h_p as the history observed by π_6 up to time $|h_p| = present$, define $h'_p = m_H(h_p)$ as the history up to the present in the simulated environment. Let Q' be a set of finite stochastic programs for the simulated environment and π'_6 be a version of the environment-learning agent π_6 for the simulated environment. It produces:

$$q'_p = \lambda(h'_p) := \text{argmax}_{q' \in Q'} \ P(h'_p \mid q') \ \rho(q') \tag{8}$$

$$\rho'(h') = P(h' \mid q'_p) \tag{9}$$

Now let $\pi'(h'; \rho', u', \gamma)$ be a proposed AI agent to be studied using the decision support system, where u' is its utility function, γ is its temporal discount and *future* is the end time of the simulation. The utility function u' is constrained to have no motivation after time $= future$:

$$\forall h' \in H'. \ |h'| > future \Rightarrow u'(h') = 0 \tag{10}$$

Then $\pi'(h'; \rho', u', \gamma)$ is defined by:

$$v'(h') = u'(h') + \gamma \ \text{max}_{a' \in A'} \ v'(h'a') \tag{11}$$

$$v'(h'a') = \sum_{o' \in O'} \rho'(o' \mid h'a') \ v'(h'a'o') \tag{12}$$

$$\pi'(h'; \rho', u', \gamma) := a'_{|h'|+1} = \text{argmax}_{a' \in A'} \ v'(h'a') \tag{13}$$

There are no humans or physical objects in the simulated environment; rather the agent π' (using π' and $\pi'(h')$ as abbreviations for $\pi'(h'; \rho', u', \gamma)$) interacts with a simulation model of humans and physical objects via:

$$a'_{|h'|+1} = \pi'(h') \tag{14}$$

$$o'_{|h'|+1} = o' \in O' \text{ with probability } \rho'(o' \mid h'a'_{|h'|+1}) \tag{15}$$

The decision support system propagates from h'_p to h'_f, where $|h'_f| = future$, by repeatedly applying (14) and (15). As in (Hibbard, 2012a) let Z' be the set of finite histories of the internal states of $\lambda(h'_p)$ and let $P(z' \mid h', \lambda(h'_p))$ be the probability that $\lambda(h'_p)$ computes $z' \in Z'$ given $h' \in H'$. The decision support system then computes a history of model states by:

$$z'_f = z' \in Z' \text{ with probability } P(z' \mid h'_f, \lambda(h'_p)) \tag{16}$$

The simulation in (14)-(16) is stochastic so the decision support system will support ensembles of multiple simulations to provide users with a sample of possible futures. An ensemble of simulations generates an ensemble of histories of model states $\{z'_{f,e} \mid 1 \leq e \leq m\}$, all terminating at time $= future$. These simulations should be completed before they are visualized and analyzed; that is visualization and analysis should not be concurrent with simulation for reasons discussed in Section 4.1.

The history h_p includes observations by π_6 of humans and physical objects, and so the decision support system can use the same interface via A' and O' (as mapped by m_A and m_O) to the model $\lambda(h'_p)$ for observing simulated humans and physical objects in state history $z'_{f,e}$. These interfaces can be used to produce interactive visualizations of $z'_{f,e}$ in a system that combines features of Google Earth and Vis5D (Hibbard and Santek, 1990), which enabled scientists to interactively explore weather simulations in three spatial dimensions and time. Users will be able to pan and zoom over the human habitat, as in Google Earth, and animate between times $present$ and $future$, as in Vis5D. The images and sounds the system observes of the model $\lambda(h'_p)$ executing state history $z'_{f,e}$ can be embedded in the visualizations in the physical locations of the agent's observing systems, similar to the way that street views and user photographs are embedded in Google Earth.

The decision support system can also match specifications for specific humans and physical objects to the images and sounds it observes of the model $\lambda(h'_p)$ executing state history $z'_{f,e}$. The specifications may include text descriptions, images, sounds, animations, tables of numbers, mathematical descriptions, or virtually anything. Recognized humans and physical objects can then be represented by icons in the visualization, in their simulated physical locations and with recognized properties of humans and objects represented by colors and shapes of the icons. The system can enable users to selectively enable different layers of information in the visualizations.

Vis5D enables users to visualize ensembles of weather forecasts in a spreadsheet of parallel visualizations where spatial view, time and level selections are synchronized between spreadsheet cells. The decision support system can provide a similar spreadsheet visualization capability for ensembles of simulations.

The point isn't that these simulations are accurate predictions of the future, but that they do depict the future that the AI agent will create, according to the environment model learned by π'_6. The visualization depicts the future that the agent $\pi'(h')$ predicts will maximize the sum of future discounted utility function values. Agent designers can use this visualization to understand the consequences of various proposed utility functions and temporal discounts.

The visualizations will be accompanied by analyses, in which the decision support system computes the values of functions $g(z'_{f,e})$. Evaluation of these functions may depend on recognizing humans and physical objects in observations of the model $\lambda(h'_p)$ executing state history $z'_{f,e}$. Such analyses would enable designers to compute quantitative evaluations to complement visualizations. For example, these analyses can be used to compute statistics about future human wealth, health and intelligence.

There will be an interval before time $= future$ when visualizations and analyses of the behavior of π' will not be an accurate reflection of the behavior of a real-world agent without the temporal cutoff in (10). The length of this interval will depend on the value of the temporal discount γ'. In order to compensate for this, $future$ should be chosen past the time horizon of interest.

4.1   Will an Agent $\pi'(h'; \rho', u', \gamma')$ Act in the Real World?

The environment model $q'_p = \lambda(h'_p)$ may provide an agent π' with the information that humans have constructed a decision support system for analyzing proposed AI agents and that π' is such an agent, interacting with a simulated environment. If the utility function u' is defined in terms of the real environment then π' may predict via ρ' that certain actions in the simulated environment may manipulate the human users of the decision support system into increasing the value of u' in the real environment. Hence it is important that the utility function u' be defined in terms of the simulated rather than the real environment.

Even when u' is defined in terms of the simulated environment there are still possible risks. Assuming that $q'_p = \lambda(h'_p)$ includes the information that π' is in a simulation, then the agent may predict via ρ' that it can bribe human users of the decision support system, through an offer to act on their behalf in the real world (the bribed humans would have to enable π' to act in the real world), to manipulate its simulated environment to increase the value of u'. This offer of a bribe could be made by spoken or written language inserted by actions of π' into some $z'_{f,e}$ and visualized by the users. This possibility is the rationale for constraining that $u'(h') = 0$ for $|h'| > future$ in (10) and for requiring simulation to be complete before visualization and analysis begin. Looking at its definition in (11)-(13) it is hard to see any reason why π' would be motivated to affect events after time $= future$, and by the time a user sees any bribe offer the simulation would be complete through time $= future$. It is also hard to see any reason why π' running in one simulation would be motivated to affect another simulation occurring at a later time (if the simulations were running simultaneously then there could be some communication and interaction between them mediated by human users). As proved in (Hibbard, 2012a) π' will not have any motive to modify u', so π' will not modify itself to be motivated past time $= future$. However these are subtle issues and I do not claim they are completely resolved.

It is important not to anthropomorphize π'. A human restricted to act in a simulation would be motivated to act in the real world. But if u' is defined in terms of a simulation then π' would not be motivated to act in the real world, except as a means to increase u' in the simulation.

The greatest risk comes from the human users of the decision support system who may be tempted (Hibbard, 2009) to modify it to act in the real world on their behalf. As Elliott (2005) comments on the safety of US nuclear weapons, "The human factor introduces perhaps the weakest link in nuclear weapon safety and control." However, if society takes AI risks seriously then it can learn from the experience managing nuclear weapons to manage AI and some form of the proposed decision support system.

5   Discussion

An important challenge for safe AI is understanding the consequences of AI designs, particularly the consequences of AI utility functions. This paper proposes a decision support system for evaluating AI designs in safe, simulated environments that model our real environment. The paper shows that the agent π_6 is safe and learns to model our environment in a finite computation. The paper also addresses some possible risks in running and evaluating AI designs in simulated environments. It would be useful to find computationally feasible implementations for the definitions in this paper.

I believe that the greatest danger of AI comes from the fact that above-human-level AI is likely to be a tool in military and economic competition between humans and thus have motives that are competitive toward some humans. Some form of the proposed decision support system may be able to alert those building powerful AI to the long term consequences of decisions they take in the heat of competition.

Acknowledgements. I would like to thank Luke Muehlhauser for helpful discussions.

References

1. Asimov, I.: Runaround. Astounding Science Fiction (1942)
2. Bostrom, N.: Ethical issues in advanced artificial intelligence. In: Smit, I., et al. (eds.) Cognitive, Emotive and Ethical Aspects of Decision Making in Humans and in Artificial Intelligence, vol. 2, pp. 12–17. Int. Inst. of Adv. Studies in Sys. Res. and Cybernetics (2003)
3. Bostrom, N.: The superintelligent will: Motivation and instrumental rationality in advanced artificial agents. Minds and Machines (forthcoming)
4. Chalmers, D.: The Singularity: A Philosophical Analysis. J. Consciousness Studies 17, 7–65 (2010)
5. Dewey, D.: Learning What to Value. In: Schmidhuber, J., Thórisson, K.R., Looks, M. (eds.) AGI 2011. LNCS (LNAI), vol. 6830, pp. 309–314. Springer, Heidelberg (2011)
6. Elliott, G.: US Nuclear Weapon Safety and Control. MIT Program in Science, Technology, and Society (2005),
   http://web.mit.edu/gelliott/Public/sts.072/paper.pdf
7. Ghahramani, Z.: Learning Dynamic Bayesian Networks. In: Giles, C.L., Gori, M. (eds.) IIASS-EMFCSC-School 1997. LNCS (LNAI), vol. 1387, pp. 168–197. Springer, Heidelberg (1998)
8. Goertzel, B.: Universal ethics: the foundations of compassion in pattern dynamics (2004),
   http://www.goertzel.org/papers/UniversalEthics.html
9. Hibbard, B., Santek, D.: The Vis5D system for easy interactive visualization. In: Proc. IEEE Visualization 1990, pp. 129–134 (1990)
10. Hibbard, B.: Super-intelligent machines. Computer Graphics 35(1), 11–13 (2001)
11. Hibbard, B.: The technology of mind and a new social contract. J. Evolution and Technology 17(1), 13–22 (2008)
12. Hibbard, B.: Temptation. Rejected for the AGI-09 Workshop on the Future of AI (2009),
    https://sites.google.com/site/whibbard/g/
    hibbard_agi09_workshop.pdf

13. Hibbard, B.: Model-based utility functions. J. Artificial General Intelligence 3(1), 1–24 (2012a)
14. Hibbard, B.: Avoiding Unintended AI Behaviors. In: Bach, J., Goertzel, B., Iklé, M. (eds.) AGI 2012. LNCS (LNAI), vol. 7716, pp. 107–116. Springer, Heidelberg (2012), https://sites.google.com/site/whibbard/g/hibbard_agi12a.pdf
15. Hutter, M.: Universal artificial intelligence: sequential decisions based on algorithmic probability. Springer, Heidelberg (2005)
16. Hutter, M.: Feature reinforcement learning: Part I. Unstructured MDPs. J. Artificial General Intelligence 1, 3–24 (2009a)
17. Hutter, M.: Feature dynamic Bayesian networks. In: Goertzel, B., Hitzler, P., Hutter, M. (eds.) Proc. Second Conf. on AGI, AGI 2009, pp. 67–72. Atlantis Press, Amsterdam (2009b)
18. Kurzweil, R.: The singularity is near. Penguin, New York (2005)
19. Li, M., Vitanyi, P.: An introduction to Kolmogorov complexity and its applications. Springer, Heidelberg (1997)
20. Lloyd, S.: Computational Capacity of the Universe. Phys. Rev. Lett. 88, 237901 (2002)
21. Muehlhauser, L., Helm, L.: The singularity and machine ethics. In: Eden, Søraker, Moor, Steinhart (eds.) The Singularity Hypothesis: a Scientific and Philosophical Assessment. Springer, Heidleberg (2012)
22. Omohundro, S.: The basic AI drive. In: Wang, P., Goertzel, B., Franklin, S. (eds.) Proc. First Conf. on AGI, AGI 2008, pp. 483–492. IOS Press, Amsterdam (2008)
23. Puterman, M.L.: Markov Decision Processes - Discrete Stochastic Dynamic Programming. Wiley, New York (1994)
24. Ring, M., Orseau, L.: Delusion, Survival, and Intelligent Agents. In: Schmidhuber, J., Thórisson, K.R., Looks, M. (eds.) AGI 2011. LNCS (LNAI), vol. 6830, pp. 11–20. Springer, Heidelberg (2011)
25. Sutton, R.S., Barto, A.G.: Reinforcement learning: an introduction. MIT Press (1998)
26. Waser, M.: Designing a safe motivational system for intelligent machines. In: Baum, E., Hutter, M., Kitzelmann, E. (eds.) Proc. Third Conf. on AGI, AGI 2010, pp. 170–175. Atlantis Press, Amsterdam (2010)
27. Waser, M.: Rational Universal Benevolence: Simpler, Safer, and Wiser Than "Friendly AI". In: Schmidhuber, J., Thórisson, K.R., Looks, M. (eds.) AGI 2011. LNCS (LNAI), vol. 6830, pp. 153–162. Springer, Heidelberg (2011)
28. Yudkowsky, E.: (2004), http://www.sl4.org/wiki/CoherentExtrapolatedVolition

On Measuring Social Intelligence: Experiments on Competition and Cooperation

Javier Insa-Cabrera, José-Luis Benacloch-Ayuso, and José Hernández-Orallo

DSIC, Universitat Politècnica de València, Spain
{jinsa,jorallo}@dsic.upv.es

Abstract. Evaluating agent intelligence is a fundamental issue for the understanding, construction and improvement of autonomous agents. New intelligence tests have been recently developed based on an assessment of task complexity using algorithmic information theory. Some early experimental results have shown that these intelligence tests may be able to distinguish between agents of the same kind, but they do not place very different agents, e.g., humans and machines, on a correct scale. It has been suggested that a possible explanation is that these tests do not measure social intelligence. One formal approach to incorporate social environments in an intelligence test is the recent notion of Darwin-Wallace distribution. Inspired by this distribution we present several new test settings considering competition and cooperation, where we evaluate the "social intelligence" of several reinforcement learning algorithms. The results show that evaluating social intelligence raises many issues that need to be addressed in order to devise tests of social intelligence.

1 Introduction

Social intelligence has been defined in many ways in psychology and cognition, but it can be just worded, with the terminology of agents, as the ability to perform well in the context of other agents. One problem of this definition is that we have to be more precise about what the 'other agents' are. If we evaluate humans and the other agents are worms or sea sponges, then our intuitive notion of social intelligence does not work well, because working well in the context of other agents with low intelligence is not necessarily related to social intelligence as we know it. In psychometrics and human cognition, social intelligence clearly sets these other agents as other humans. But what about artificial agents? If we use a society of dull agents, the useful abilities might be very different to those which are required if we introduce an agent into, e.g., a society of humans.

The difference between social intelligence and general intelligence is that in the latter an agent could perform well if it were able to solve non-social tasks, such as escaping from a maze, solving a puzzle or predicting the next number in a series. On the contrary, social intelligence implies that tasks involve competing and collaborating with other agents.

Dating back from the late nineties, we can find several works [1,2,9,4] addressing the problem of measuring agent intelligence in a principled and general way. Using notions taken from (algorithmic) information theory, MML and two-part

J. Bach, B. Goertzel, and M. Iklé (Eds.): AGI 2012, LNAI 7716, pp. 126–135, 2012.

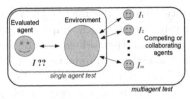

Fig. 1. A multiagent intelligence test compared to a single agent intelligence test. In a multiagent (social) intelligence test, other agents also interact (and become integral part) of the environment. In order to assess the intelligence of the evaluated agent, we need to know the intelligence of the other agents.

compression, Kolmogorov complexity and Solomonoff priors (see [10] for proper definitions of all these notions), some of these works present definitions and tests to evaluate agent intelligence. One important feature in some of these tests is that the difficulty of a problem, task or environment can be derived from its Kolmogorov complexity. This allows for the application of the setting to many different fields in artificial intelligence, including inductive or deductive tasks.

A *universal* test as introduced in [4] is a test which aims at evaluating any kind of subject including, e.g., humans and reinforcement learning agents. Some preliminary results of this evaluation [7] show that the setting is able to compare and evaluate different kinds of agents, but it fails at placing them on the same scale, since humans usually get similar scores to those of other relatively simple agents. One possible explanation for these results is that it is virtually impossible to find other agents in the test, so social intelligence is not measured. The question, therefore, is what and how agents should be introduced in the test. This is related to the Turing test and the question of evaluating intelligence with games (also suggested in [4]), where the difficulty is not only given by the complexity of the game, but from the opponent's intelligence. This leads to a circular problem: we need to know the opponent's intelligence first in order to know the difficulty of the problem. Fig. 1 shows this situation.

One recent proposal to overcome this problem is turning this circularity into a recursion. The Darwin-Wallace distribution [5] establishes a distribution of agents based on an evolutionary process. The first 'generation' just uses a Solomonoff prior over agents, with very simple agents predominating. These agents are set to interact in a random environment. The second generation is constructed by selecting the agents according to their performance. The result of this evolutionary process is a distribution of mind forms, i.e., a distribution of agents. The higher the generation i is, the more socially intelligent their agents should be or, in other words, the more demanding the 'society' will be, in the sense that competing and collaborating with other socially intelligent agents requires social intelligence. Note that this does not mean that minds have to evolve as in a true evolutionary process, or as in evolutionary game theory [14].

The previous proposal has many implementation issues. Nonetheless, it gives some clues about how social intelligence can be measured and how the other agents can be chosen. In fact [5] suggests that intelligence tests could be used to make this choice of agents from off-the-shelf algorithms in AI.

In this paper, we perform some experiments on a general intelligence test setting in order to examine the way in which simple competitive and cooperative scenarios may have a big impact on the performance of some simple agents. This is crucial to determine how social environments affect the results obtained by different agents in order to get more information about how to approximate the Darwin-Wallace distribution. We will use very simple reinforcement learning (RL) algorithms: SARSA [11], Q-learning [13] and QV-learning [15]. The goal of the paper is not showing how these three algorithms behave nor comparing them. We just use them as off-the-shelf agents which can learn from an environment to see how performance is affected by the introduction of more agents in an environment. Rather, the true goal of the paper is to analyse the behaviour of intelligence tests when environments are populated with agents, and how this affects the results of the evaluated agent. We will examine several scenarios, some with competition and some with cooperation.

The paper is organised as follows. Section 2 reviews the notion of universal intelligence tests and how the Darwin-Wallace distribution can be useful to turn them into social intelligence tests. Section 3 makes the extension by modifying the environments and the reward system for competing and cooperating scenarios. The following sections 4, 5, 6 and 7 perform and discuss the experiments for the different scenarios. Finally, a more comprehensive discussion of results and implications is found in section 8.

2 Universal Tests and Social Intelligence

One approach for measuring intelligence is to take a diverse selection of tasks of different complexity and to measure agent performance over this selection. However, several issues arise here. For instance, the selection of tasks must be unbiased. One approach is to consider all possible (computable) tasks, as defined by a universal Turing machine. In order to link performance to any possible task we can use the notion of rewards. This leads to interactive scenarios, which can be well represented by (discrete) environments, very much like the typical observaton-action-reward environments in reinforcement learning (RL) [12]. Finally, we need to assess the complexity of each task in order to make a proper choice of tasks which capture a wide range of difficulty and, therefore, can suit the agent's level of intelligence. These issues have been addressed in [1,6,2,9,4].

In this context, [4] introduces the idea of universal test, a test which is conceived to be feasibly applicable to any kind of agent: humans, non-human animals, artificial agents, including hybrids and communities, of any degree of intelligence and speed. The test is based on a set of environments as in [9].

In [3], a hopefully unbiased environment class (called Λ) is introduced, which is composed of spaces and agents with universal descriptive (Turing-complete) power. Originally, only two agents (apart from the evaluated agent) were used in the environments. Since their behaviour is generated by a universal distribution using Markov algorithms (a Turing-complete rewriting language), their *sophistication* is really low. Hence it was very difficult to find any social behaviour originating from them, and, therefore, any social behaviour in the environments.

The first evaluations using these tests [7] show that they work well at evaluating very different agents (humans and RL algorithms), but they do not properly reflect their supposed difference in intelligence. Many possible explanations are suggested in [7], with incremental knowledge acquisition and social intelligence being two of the abilities which this test is not giving enough importance.

In order to address the second issue we must define environments which are more social. The question of which agents are introduced becomes crucial, since the results of the evaluated agent will depend on the abilities of the other agents. This is illustrated in Fig. 1. The question is what criteria we can use to introduce the other agents and how we can measure their (social) intelligence in advance. In [5], instead of incorporating other agents in an ad-hoc way, they look for a formal way to determine which agents must be introduced in a social environment. As [5] states: "intelligence is the result of evolution through millions of generations interacting with other live beings. Thus we define intelligence in this context, interacting with other agents of similar intelligence". From here they formalise the so-called Darwin-Wallace distribution for agents and environments.

Briefly and informally, the Darwin-Wallace distribution requires a multiagent environment which has its rewards, actions and observations as usual, but allows the 'introduction' of any number of agents, whose distribution evolves (by properly sampling agents according to their degree of intelligence) and can lead to higher degrees of (social) intelligence. From here, the Darwin-Wallace distribution is defined recursively according to a level or generation.

The use of this distribution has many issues. First, it is a theoretical construct which might be useful for understanding the kind of environments where (social) intelligence is needed. Second, this distribution could be used for the construction of social intelligence tests, just sampling from the distribution. Third, and recursively, the way in which this distribution can be approximated is precisely by the use of intelligence tests, where human-made agents can be inserted into the environments, provided we have been able to assess their intelligence first.

Following this last issue, we need to develop intelligence tests in multiagent scenarios. In particular, we need to adapt the existing intelligence test proposals to a multiagent setting. This is what we do below.

3   Intelligence Tests Considering Several Agents

The first intelligence tests based on the theory developed in [4] were based on the environment class Λ, introduced in [3]. This environment class considers a space which is composed of a directed labelled graph, where vertices are cells and arrows are actions. The graph is selected to be strongly connected (all cells are reachable from any other cell). Cells can contain agents. Every environment must include at least three agents: the evaluated agent, and two special agents *Good* and *Evil*. *Good* and *Evil* are not generally reactive, so, if no further agent is included, the environment cannot be considered a proper multiagent system. Actions allow the evaluated agent (and other agents) to move in the space. Observations show the cell contents. Rewards are rational numbers in the interval $[-1, 1]$ and are generated by the agents *Good* and *Evil*, which leave rewards in the cells they visit. Rewards do not stay unaltered in the cell forever. If a reward in a cell is eaten by any agent (including *Good* and *Evil*) because the agent steps into or stays in the cell, the reward disappears. While rewards are not eaten, their value is divided by 2 for each iteration. This has the effect of seeing *Good* and *Evil* as agents which leave a reward wake as they move. *Good* and *Evil* have the same behaviour (they follow the same pattern) except for the sign of the reward (+ for *Good*, − for *Evil*). This makes *Good* and *Evil* symmetric, which ensures that the environment is balanced (random agents score 0 on average) [4]. For more details of the environment class Λ, see [3].

Environments are composed of a space of cells (a graph of nodes) and the patterns for Good and Evil (a simplified adaptation of [7]). Once an environment has been constructed, evaluation is performed in the following way. Initially, each agent is randomly (using a uniform distribution) placed in a cell. Then, we let *Good*, *Evil* and the evaluated agent interact for a certain number of steps, i.e. a session. The final score is the average of rewards in the session.

This configuration can be easily extended to a multiagent setting, by including more agents in the environment. Agents can move freely to other cells independently of whether they are occupied or not by other agents. In other words, agents can share a cell. A competitive, individualistic scenario is set by each agent trying to improve its own rewards. If two or more agents share a cell, the reward is just divided by the number of agents in the cell. *Good* and *Evil* cannot share a cell with other agents. This re-introduces some degree of reactivity (with respect to the prototype in [7]), even in the single agent case.

There are many possible ways of introducing cooperation and competition, which may lead to different experimental results, some of them similar to what has been previously studied in the AI literature. In this paper we do not want to evaluate these choices, but to analyse *how the degree of intelligence of the agents in a social environment affects the role of cooperation and competition.* The ultimate goal is to shed some light on whether environments become difficult when many agents are introduced (independently of their intelligence) or become difficult (and socially challenging) when other intelligent agents are introduced. These findings are necessary if we aim at measuring social intelligence.

The first question when several agents are introduced in the space is how the rewards are shared among them. A second, relatively more difficult, question is how we can deal with cooperation. The easiest way of making this setting purely cooperative is by just putting all the rewards in the same bag. With this, one should not be concerned about not getting some reward itself if some other agent is able to get it instead. What matters is the overall result. We can of course move between competition and cooperation by using the notion of team. All the members of a team put their rewards in the same bag, and each team should compete against the others as usual in games and economics.

Now we are ready to see what happens with a single agent intelligence test when we turn it into a multiagent test. But, before that, we need to determine the agents that we will use for the experiment. The agents are:

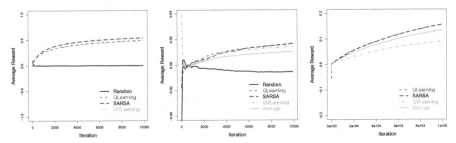

Fig. 2. Left: Isolated scenario. The 4 evaluated agents are evaluated separately. Middle: Competition scenario. The 3 RL agents along with the random agent. Right: Competition scenario. The 3 RL agents without the random agent. 100 environments each.

- Random: an agent which chooses randomly among the available actions using a uniform distribution.
- Q-learning [13]: the most common reinforcement learning algorithm. We use the description of cell contents as a state.
- SARSA [11]: a well-known variant of Q-learning which also takes the future action into account.
- QV-learning [15] (without eligibility trace): a variant of Q-learning which partially resembles ActorCritic methods.

The three latter algorithms will be referred to as RL agents. In order to have a consistent view of the experiments, the parameters for all the RL agents algorithms (*learning rate* α, *discount factor* γ, etc.) were fine-tuned on the single agent scenarios, by using 1,000 sessions for each parameter variation, totalling a huge number of experiments to set the optimal parameters.

4   Evaluating Agents in Isolation

We start our experiments with the scenario where agents are just taken and evaluated isolatedly. This is the same setting as in [7], with the only (minor) difference that *Good* and *Evil* are slightly reactive because they try to avoid sharing a cell with other agents. In addition, we will just restrict the evaluation to environments with nine cells.

The result of Fig. 2 (left) is clear (and consistent with the results in [7]). The random agent has an average reward of 0, as predicted by the theory. The three RL agents are very slow learners and only get closer to 0.5 after 10,000 iterations. Their behaviour is similar and the differences are small.

5   Competitive Scenario

More interesting things can be observed when we switch to the competitive scenario. Here all the agents are located in the environment at the same time competing for rewards. As we can see in Fig. 2 (middle) the random agent gets

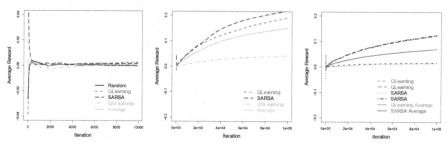

Fig. 3. Left: Cooperative scenario. The 3 RL agents along with the random agent. Middle: Cooperative scenario. The 3 RL agents without the random agent. Right: Two teams scenario. One team with two Q-learning agents against another team with two SARSA agents. 100 environments each.

a value which is even lower than 0, since most of the positive rewards are eaten by the other agents, leaving the negative rewards for the random agent. RL algorithms have a very poor result (not reaching 0.02 in 10,000 iterations). This is explained by the presence of the random agent, which makes the state tables of the RL algorithms grow considerably.

Finally, in order to further confirm that the problem is the state space, we remove the random agent (which can be considered noise), and we only leave the RL agents. We also increase the number of iterations to 100,000. This is shown in Fig. 2 (right). Things improve slightly and, in the very long term, Q-learning and SARSA get close to 0.2, while QV-learning lags behind around 0.1. We see that just the presence of only two other agents makes their matrices so big that they require more than 100,000 iterations to derive their Q-values accurately.

Apart from the comparative results, we see that performance depends on the other agents' policies, but especially on the ability of digesting the state space, and how much noise (e.g., from the random agent) can be handled.

6   Cooperative Scenario

The next scenario we want to explore is when the four agents are prompted to cooperate. This is done by putting all the rewards in the same bag, so the agents just see the reward as the average reward of all the agents.

Fig. 3 (left) changes from Fig. 2 (middle) very significantly. How can it be that moving form a competitive to a cooperative case, we get worse average results? The explanation is a little bit more convoluted. The problem of cooperation is the way we assign rewards. Since the reward they receive is the average of the rewards of all the agents, it is much more difficult for them to determine the goodness of the actions, since rewards are affected by other agents' movements. In other words, they lose 'individuality'.

This explanation is only part of the story if we compare Fig. 3 (middle) with Fig. 3 (left) and Fig. 2 (right). In this case, where the random agent has been removed, the results are slightly better than in the competitive case. However, this improvement is not uniform for the three RL agents.

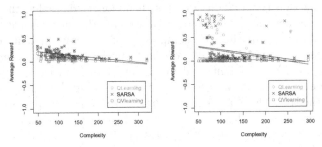

Fig. 4. Relation between environment complexity and results of the three RL agents for the competitive case (left) and the cooperative case (right). Linear regression is also shown for each agent.

7 Scenario Measuring Both Competition and Cooperation

Finally, we examine another scenario where we now have competition and cooperation at the same time, using the notion of 'team'. We define two teams, one with two Q-learning agents and the other one with two SARSA agents. Inside each team the rewards go to the same bag, but different teams compete for the rewards. This is shown in Fig. 3 (right). In general, the results are poorer than with three agents in the cooperative case (Fig. 3, middle). This can be explained because here we have four agents instead of three, but also because having two teams is a more complex scenario than having just one.

The results show that there are no significant differences between both teams. However, there are important differences between the components of each team. This can be observed in Fig. 3 (right), where we assign the best results in the team to the first entry and the worst results to the second entry. So, the plot just shows the difference in (average) performance between the best and the worst component in the team. We see that this difference is very significant. While usually an agent in the team performs around 0.1, the other agent stays at a very low result close to 0. It is not clear which role this second agent takes.

8 Discussion

In the previous sections, we have analysed several scenarios. A test which was originally designed to measure the intelligence of an agent against an environment without other agents is adapted to other scenarios where other agents are introduced in the environments. We see that performance can be seriously degraded by the inclusion of other agents with null intelligence, as a random agent. This is surprising if we look at this from the point of view of game theory (two-player games, in particular), but it is much more natural if we realise that it is more difficult to attain a goal if there is another agent bugging around (even randomly). This is extreme in the case of RL agents, because they cannot *learn* that random agents are just noise, and stick to the original huge state space.

All this means that the difficulty of a task is no longer related to the complexity of the environment in a tight way, as it was for the single agent situation. We can see this by comparing the complexity of the environment (excluding the evaluated agents) and the results for the scenarios where only the three RL agents are used, i.e. Fig. 2 (right) and Fig. 3 (middle). In order to approximate the environment complexity, we use the size of a compressed coding of the concatenation of the space description S and the description of the pattern for *Good* and *Evil*, denoted by P. More formally, we calculate an approximation to its (Kolmogorov) complexity as $K^{approx} = LZ(S, P)$ where LZ is just the 'gzip' method given by the *memCompress* function in R, a GNU project implementation of Lempel-Ziv coding. This comparison is shown in Fig. 4. We see that there is still a relation between the complexity of the environment and the result, while this relation is stronger for Qlearning and SARSA in the cooperative case. In fact, the results for Qlearning and SARSA are very good when the complexity is very low. This means that in very simple cases RL agents are able to perform well, even in social scenarios. This seems to suggest that the difficulty of a social environment is a cumulative issue, which adds the complexity of the environment and the complexity/performance/noise of other agents.

Some lessons can be learnt from these results in the context of the Darwin-Wallace distribution. One of the purported problems of this distribution is that many iterations might be needed to reach a level where some social behaviour can be evaluated. We see that this may not be the case. For instance, the mere introduction of very simple agents in an environment makes that the performance of other agents plunge. This suggests that the evaluation of social intelligence could possibly be performed against other agents of inferior degree of intelligence.

In fact, it would be extremely informative to repeat the experiment performed with humans and RL agents in [7] by using one of these simple multiagent environments. We guess that humans will still be able to manage, mostly because they handle noise much better. Naturally, many other experiments must follow. For instance, for the RL agents, we only consider model-free techniques whose search space grows geometrically as more agents are there. It would be interesting to see the results for model-based algorithms using function approximations, as well as other RL algorithms which work better when the Markov property does not hold (which is the general case in multiagent systems). Also, some other RL algorithms which are specialised for multiagent settings, such as Frequently Adjusted Q-learning [8] might give different results. Other issues which could be reconsidered is the way we modify the reward system to make the test competitive or cooperative.

Summing up, from the notion of Darwin-Wallace distribution, we have pushed forward the idea of 'multiagent intelligence test', which is an intelligence test where there are other agents in the environments. This is a new notion, since the kind of intelligence tests we are used to are typically those where the evaluated agent has to solve some tasks or where it has to be interrogated by other agents (interviews, Turing test, etc.), but the other agents are not *inside* the test. The closest notion is an old companion of artificial intelligence, *games*, especially multiplayer games, but it has only been recently proposed as a testbed for measuring intelligence [4]. However, the role of the opponent and its intelligence has not been clarified to date, especially if we want a test to give an absolute result, not only comparing a pair of agents.

Acknowledgements. This work was supported by the MEC/MINECO projects CONSOLIDER-INGENIO CSD2007-00022, EXPLORA-INGENIO TIN 2009-06078-E, TIN 2010-21062-C02-02 and GVA project PROMETEO/2008/051. Javier Insa-Cabrera was sponsored by Spanish MEC-FPU grant AP2010-4389.

References

1. Dowe, D.L., Hajek, A.R.: A computational extension to the Turing Test. In: Proceedings of the 4th Conference of the Australasian Cognitive Science Society, University of Newcastle, NSW, Australia (September 1997)
2. Hernández-Orallo, J.: Beyond the Turing Test. J. Logic, Language & Information 9(4), 447–466 (2000)
3. Hernández-Orallo, J.: A (hopefully) non-biased universal environment class for measuring intelligence of biological and artificial systems. In: Hutter, M., et al. (eds.) 3rd Intl Conf. on Artificial General Intelligence, pp. 182–183. Atlantis Press (2010)
4. Hernández-Orallo, J., Dowe, D.L.: Measuring universal intelligence: Towards an anytime intelligence test. Artificial Intelligence 174(18), 1508–1539 (2010)
5. Hernández-Orallo, J., Dowe, D.L., España-Cubillo, S., Hernández-Lloreda, M.V., Insa-Cabrera, J.: On More Realistic Environment Distributions for Defining, Evaluating and Developing Intelligence. In: Schmidhuber, J., Thórisson, K.R., Looks, M. (eds.) AGI 2011. LNCS (LNAI), vol. 6830, pp. 82–91. Springer, Heidelberg (2011)
6. Hernández-Orallo, J., Minaya-Collado, N.: A formal definition of intelligence based on an intensional variant of Kolmogorov complexity. In: Proc. Intl Symposium of Engineering of Intelligent Systems, EIS 1998, La Laguna, Spain, pp. 146–163. ICSC Press (February 1998)
7. Insa-Cabrera, J., Dowe, D.L., España-Cubillo, S., Hernández-Lloreda, M.V., Hernández-Orallo, J.: Comparing Humans and AI Agents. In: Schmidhuber, J., Thórisson, K.R., Looks, M. (eds.) AGI 2011. LNCS (LNAI), vol. 6830, pp. 122–132. Springer, Heidelberg (2011)
8. Kaisers, M., Tuyls, K.: Frequency adjusted multi-agent Q-learning. In: Proc. 9th Intl Conf. on Autonomous Agents and Multiagent Systems, pp. 309–316 (2010)
9. Legg, S., Hutter, M.: Universal intelligence: A definition of machine intelligence. Minds and Machines 17(4), 391–444 (2007)
10. Li, M., Vitányi, P.: An introduction to Kolmogorov complexity and its applications, 3rd edn. Springer (2008)
11. Rummery, G., Niranjan, M.: On-line Q-learning using connectionist systems. Cambridge University Engineering Department, TR 166 (1994)
12. Sutton, R.S., Barto, A.G.: Reinforcement learning: An introduction. The MIT Press (1998)
13. Watkins, C., Dayan, P.: Q-learning. Machine Learning 8(3), 279–292 (1992)
14. Weibull, J.: Evolutionary game theory. The MIT Press (1997)
15. Wiering, M.: QV (λ)-learning: A new on-policy reinforcement learning algorithm. In: 7th European Ws. on Reinforcement Learning, pp. 17–18 (2005)

Toward Tractable AGI: Challenges for System Identification in Neural Circuitry

Randal A. Koene

Carboncopies.org
1087 Mission St., San Francisco, California 94103, USA
Randal.A.Koene@carboncopies.org

Abstract. Feasible and practical routes to Artificial General Intelligence involve short-cuts tailored to environments and challenges. A prime example of a system with built-in short-cuts is the human brain. Deriving from the brain the functioning system that implements intelligence and generality at the level of neurophysiology is interesting for many reasons, but also poses a set of specific challenges. Representations and models demand that we pick a constrained set of signals and behaviors of interest. The systematic and iterative process of model building involves what is known as System Identification, which is made feasible by decomposing the overall problem into a collection of smaller System Identification problems. There is a roadmap to tackle that includes structural scanning (a way to obtain the "connectome") as well as new tools for functional recording. We examine the scale of the endeavor, and the many challenges that remain, as we consider specific approaches to System Identification in neural circuitry.

Keywords: system identification, whole brain emulation, functions of mind, measurement tools, neurophysiology.

1 Tractable AGI through System Identification in Neural Circuitry

Artificial General Intelligence (AGI) is, at a minimum, a system that is able to deal with challenges or tasks arising in circumstances of our natural environment. It is possible that there are elegant mathematical approaches to AGI that address those minimum requirements and are theoretically sound [1]. Theoretical soundness does not imply practical feasibility. The most elegant mathematical methods can be the most compute-hungry, slow, impractical solutions. From a practical standpoint, there is much to be said for short-cuts that are suitable to the environment and the challenges.

One system that contains many of those short-cuts and that we often think of in terms of AGI is that of the (human) mind. Deriving from a brain a functioning system that implements a degree of intelligence and a degree of generality within the constraints of compatible environments may be done at several different levels of cognitive abstraction. The level that most interests me and many colleagues is that of computational neurophysiology, systems of neuronal circuitry [2].

J. Bach, B. Goertzel, and M. Iklé (Eds.): AGI 2012, LNAI 7716, pp. 136–147, 2012.
© Springer-Verlag Berlin Heidelberg 2012

In part, this choice comes from the fact that neuroscience has spent the past 100 years gaining experience at that level and devising functional representations that are well grounded in identified physiological mechanisms. The other reason for this choice is that our goals are in some ways a reversal of the quest for practicable AGI. We begin with a system that has many specific short-cuts built in that give it satisfactory performance under current real-world circumstances. But our interests involve making that system more adaptable to novel environments and challenges [3].

In this paper, we highlight the importance of good System Identification [4]. We point out what choices need to be made and which tools may be applied. Most importantly, we identify the significant challenges that appear throughout the process of System Identification and due to the need to integrate efforts with several different types of tools.

2 Representations and Models

The exact sciences depend on improving understanding by describing observed effects through representations and models. Some things about nature are predictable. Pieces of nature exist within an environment. There, the various pieces are not wholly independent. Conditions of some piece at some time predict aspects of the conditions in another piece. We say they affect each other. There are signals between the pieces that convey information. We want to understand more about the predictable dependencies, so we explicitly describe the signals and how the information they convey is processed.

2.1 Behavior and Signals of Interest

Nature has an awful lot of pieces and descriptions become quite complicated. Systematic and iterative improvement of a description is model building. Initially, we keep it simple, we constrain our models. There is an effect of particularly interest. Ideally, we focus solely on the scope and details that are needed to explain that effect. In neuroscience, the interesting effects are often called (task-specific) behaviors. E.g., object recognition, emotional responses, executive decision making, and even conscious or aware behavior. In AGI, there are also particular effects or behaviors that are interesting and for which we want to carry out System Identification in the brain.

Now we know our piece of interest, e.g., a molecule of gas or a neural circuit in the brain. We look at how that piece may be communicating with others. What are the signals that could be involved in the effects? Overall, physics describes all interactions in terms of four types: gravity, electromagnetism, weak nuclear force and strong nuclear force. While those are a limited set, we can constrain their manifestations further and consider electric current, electromagnetic radiation, etc. A piece of neural tissue may respond to (ionic) electric currents, temperature (gradients), pressure or shearing forces, sonic transmissions, electromagnetic fields, and more. Experimental work helps us to create a priority order. By and large, most signals appear to drown in noise, losing predictive value. Electric currents, and in particular the powerful discharges known as neural action potentials or spikes appear to carry the dominant information [5].

2.2 Discovering the Transfer Function

In Control Theory, the piece of nature being modeled is sometimes called a black box, which has state, receives input and produces output. The process of updating its state and generating output is described mathematically by a transfer function. When we find suitable transfer functions we learn about the black box in the context specific behavior and signals. There are numerous formal methods, and a general example of one that has been successfully applied (e.g., in Ted Berger's neuroprosthesis [6]) is to find the kernels of a system that is expressed as a discretized Volterra series expansion, as in Eq. 1. The kernels, H_n, express the contributions of a history of input, $\mathbf{x}$, to system output $f(\mathbf{x})$, with a finite number of mn coefficients $h^{(n)}_{i_1 \ldots i_n}$.

$$f(\mathbf{x}) = H_0\mathbf{x} + H_1\mathbf{x} + H_2\mathbf{x} + \ldots + H_n\mathbf{x} + \ldots + \mathbf{H_m}\mathbf{x},$$

$$H_n\mathbf{x} = \sum_{i_1=1}^{m} \ldots \sum_{i_n=1}^{m} h^{(n)}_{i_1 \ldots i_n} x_{i_1} \ldots x_{i_n}. \tag{1}$$

3 Mental Processes and Neural Circuitry: Brain Emulation

The effects that interest us are those that we associate with our experiences: Sensory Perception, Learning and Memory, Problem Solving and Goal-Directed Decision Making, Emotional Responses, Consciousness and Self-Awareness, Language Comprehension and Production, Motor Control. Some are externally observable and some are part of the internal experience. Neurophysiologically, these involve the interactions of ensembles of neurons within a specific circuit layout.

3.1 System Identification in Neural Circuitry

There is no consensus about exactly which signals are or are not essential to brain function, but we take an iterative and systematic approach. We make initial assumptions about signal to noise ratios, about the sort of output that reliably affects the environment during interesting behavior, and about the sort of signals that neurons are well-suited to deal with. Biophysical mechanisms of sensory input (e.g., at the cochlea, at the retina) produce electric nerve signals characterized by trains of fairly uniform neural spikes with very specific rates and time intervals. Similarly, the primary output through muscle control (e.g., vocal cords) employs trains of neural spikes. Finally, a primary means of long-term state-change (ie., learning) is governed by modified synaptic strength. That modification also depends crucially on the temporal order and time-separation between pre- and postsynaptic neural spikes [7]. A representation that successfully predicts spike times may therefore be a good first iteration of a model of system processes in neural circuitry.

One result that was achieved with these assumptions is demonstrated in the cognitive neural prosthesis devised by the lab of Theodore Berger (UCS). Using System Identification in a Volterra series expansion, they developed a chip that contains a multi-input multi-output model with non-linear parameters that are specified after learning from consecutive presentations of spike data. The input of the system is obtained through an array of electrodes in region CA3 of the hippocampus, while the output is delivered to region CA1 [8]. These regions are crucial in the formation of new declarative and episodic memories. The chip is designed to alleviate dysfunction caused by stroke, trauma or disease.

A more general technique designed to work with out initial assumptions was developed by Aurel A. Lazar and Yevgeniy B. Slutskiy and is called the development of Channel Identification Machines [9]. It is a formal method to identify a channel – modeled as a multi-dimensional filter – in a system where a communication channel is cascaded with an asynchronous sampler. The samplers consist of neuroscience or communication models, e.g., integrate-and-fire neurons, asynchronous sigma/delta modulators, general oscillators with zero-crossing detectors. A channel can be approximated to an arbitrary degree of precision and the method was generalized and applied in noisy conditions.

4   Simplification of an Intractable System into Collections of System Identification Problems

Meaningful System Identification that could reproduce both observable behavior and internal experiential states of an entire brain is entirely unfeasible when the complete system is treated as the black box. This has to be broken down into many black boxes that communicate with one-another. We need: a.) to choose smaller black boxes, b.) to acquire enough data about I/O correlations at those smaller black boxes for their System Identification, and c.) to know the relevant communication that is possible between those black boxes.

We can address c.) by looking inside the system, noting locations of the smaller components and tracing the connectivity between them. For spike trains, the communication pathways are dendrites and axons, and the synapses where they meet. The new field of Connectomics in neuroscience deals with this problem [10]. For other effects, such as extracellular field potentials and diffuse neurotransmitters, the surrounding medium and emission and diffusion may be taken into account.

A well-known choice for a.) that contains very tractable sub-systems is decomposition of neurons into the electrical compartment analogs of a so-called compartmental neural model (Fig. 1). The I/O data that can be obtained largely determines if this, or a another level such as whole neurons, is the appropriate level of simplification. High-resolution connectomics by electron microscopy obtains the morphological data for compartmental modeling. There are a number of labs working on this and in 2011 the approach resulted in proofs of concept by Briggman *et al.* [11] and Bock *et al.* [12], using data from the lab of Winfried Denk (Max Planck).

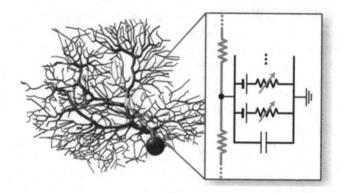

Fig. 1. The compartmental model of a Purkinje Cell. The electric cable analogy for one compartment is highlighted in the box.

To satisfy b.) and properly characterize the response of a neuron we need observations that allow us to set and test parameter values, which relate to the sensitivity and manner in which input currents affect neuronal membrane potential, the resulting action potential once a threshold potential is reached, and the time-course of restorative dynamics (e.g. after-hyperpolarization, after-depolarization).

4.1 Tools for Structural Decomposition

In neural tissue, sensible boundaries must be drawn around pieces of the neural circuitry, and I/O contacts between the pieces must be identified. A geometric decomposition into 3D stacks of voxels of equal size is one approach, such as through magnetic resonance imaging (MRI). Another method is to identify neural cell bodies, as in slice or culture on top of an array of electrodes, and to use the correlations between measured activity at each cell body to derive a functional connectivity map.

Anthony Zador is developing a biological protocol to derive the target neurons of any neuron. Zador uses biological markers such as unique sequences of RNA or DNA to mark the pre- and postsynaptic sites of synapses. The markers act as bi-directional pointers [13]. But the most detailed and successful tools to date section or ablate pieces of brain tissue and take electronmicrographs at resolutions up to 5nm from which 3D geometric morphology can be reconstructed. Even individual synapses can be identified. Excellent results have come out of the labs of Winfried Denk (Max Planck), Jeff Lichtman (Harvard) and Ken Hayworth (Janelia Farms).

4.2 Data from Structure

System Identification for individual neural compartments can use standard models that employ an electric cable analogy and Hodgkin-Huxley equations. Morphology can provide some insight into functional behavior. For example, compartment radius and length constrains the conductance of electrical currents. Morphology can also categorize a neuron or synapse, which constrains the possible response functions. Despite these constraints, even small systems contain numerous parameters. Not all of those relate directly to visible and unique morphological features. Even where they do, the reliability and precision of measurements may not be adequate.

4.3 Parameter Tuning among Connected Systems: Reference Points

Parameters must be tuned such that sub-systems behave sensibly on their own in in cohesion with connected neighbors. We can do System Identification for signals of interest at a black-box by observing activity, or at a gray-box when we can stimulate and observe. Tuning and verification involves measurements at reference points.

If the resolution of reference points is less than the resolution of structural decomposition then System Identification depends on our ability to map measurements to a collection of sub-systems and the combinatorial size of the collective problem. In how many ways might the sub-systems be interacting to produce observed responses? We may not be able to determine system parameters uniquely if that number is large. The amount of observations needed and the duration of observation increase with complexity. Clearly, there is great value in having tools that provide measurements at many more reference points, ideally at a resolution that approaching the resolution of the sub-systems.

4.4 Tools for Characteristic Reference Recordings

There is now strong interest among neuroscientists in the development of tools for high-resolution in-vivo recording. Arrays of thousands of recording electrodes are being developed and combined with optogenetic techniques so that selective observation of specific groups of neurons can be guaranteed. Microscopic wireless probes and functionalized nanoparticles with simplified task-specific capabilities are being developed to counter some of the disadvantages of extensive tethered electrodes. There is also a collaborative effort underway to create biological tools that employ DNA amplification as a means to write events onto a molecular "ticker-tape" [14]. The project goal is to be able to record signals from all neurons in a brain, and potentially to measure at resolutions beyond that.

5 Challenges

Some challenges are general to System Identification. Some are particular to neurons and neuronal models. There are unique challenges that arise when working with pieces of neural tissue and consequent large neural circuit models. And some challenges are exclusive to the domain of whole brain circuit reconstruction. Many of those involve the integration of techniques for data acquisition from structure and function that are developed with the constraints of particular novel tools.

5.1 Signals and Predicting Spikes

A careful assessment of the System Identification problem for the experiences we wish to represent demands that we consider contributions outside the domain of neural spiking. For example, are the experiences meaningfully represented by states of cells other than neurons, glia perhaps? Or, are there significant ways in which neurons influence each other even in the absence of spiking [15] – can neurons relate to each other without receiving spikes or activity directly caused by spikes? Our initial assumption is that predicting spiking within an acceptable error range implies good emulation (Fig. 2). Spikes are not epiphenomenal, but rather the currency upon which the rest of sensation rests. Spikes precede ensemble responses and field emissions. An important challenge is to test these assumptions.

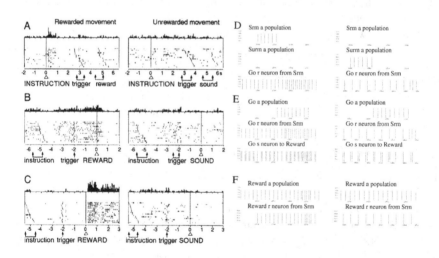

Fig. 2. Spike prediction is functional emulation [16]

Good temporal spike predictors demand that we observe or deduce when spikes would occur in the original system. Additional information, such as membrane potentials and influences on such can give improve our ability to build good local predictors.

5.2   Low-Res Validation, 3D Reconstruction at 5nm and Plasticity

The snapshots of baseline or differential activity in large volumes of tissue that are provided by MRI are too imprecise for parameter tuning, but they can be a means of model validation. The model should produce a sensible virtual MRI in terms of distribution and propagation of activity. A challenge is that aligning a virtual MRI generated by the model with actual data demands that the model also replicates the expected 3D spatial geometry.

Detailed geometric and morphological data is provided by 3D reconstructions from EM scans at resolutions up to 5nm. We can tell if a cell is a pyramidal cell or an interneuron, which helps model activity dynamics and the receptor channels that are likely present. Still, component identification is challenging, because classification presently relies entirely on morphology. There is an effort to add a direct means of protein identification, which would alleviate this problem.

When reconstructed in terms of compartments, radius and length of a cylinder gives estimates of resistance and capacitance, although those estimates also depend on the model of the identified type of a neuron. Measurements are subject to a degree of reliability. Averaging is possible, but that does not remove cumulative systematic errors. Some measurement data is likely to be entirely unrecoverable.

Brains are plastic. Mostly, we think of plasticity in terms of learning [17], modifications of synapses and even of the available connections (Fig. 3). But there is also plasticity in terms of deformation. Apparently, some aspects of

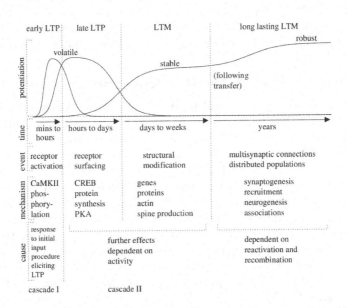

Fig. 3. There is a cascade of different memory mechanisms that implement brain plasticity for learning. Representations of these should be included in a model, but most of those are invisible to structural snapshots.

morphology are relevant to model building, while others are mere features of the snapshot taken during scanning and reconstruction. Present tools for structural connectomics offer little insight into the temporal dynamics of these gradual changes in neural circuitry.

5.3   Ticker-Tape Data and Interference during Measurement

Tools that functionally characterize activity at reference points should give some insight into temporal dynamics and memory. The ticker-tape approach may even be able to record from all neurons simultaneously. Encoding by means of voltage-dependent increases in the error-rate of DNA amplification is not entirely reliable, which is compensated by using multiple tapes per cell. Recordings may be synchronized by time-stamp signals, and can identify spike times and possible even voltage levels. But the method of data recovery poses a challenge when combined with tools from other projects in the endeavor. DNA snippets are extracted from cell bodies and the process does not retain tissue samples that could be scanned structurally by electron microscopy. How do we obtain the structural connectome, and how do we know which part of the ultrastructure a molecular tape came from? Scanning of slices prior to DNA extraction might be possible if special care is taken in the method of fixation of brain tissue. There is also some question whether the presence of many molecular ticker-tapes might interfere with cell function.

Interference challenges also appear when functional data is obtained by fluorescent microscopy with calcium dyes or voltage sensitive proteins. Using those tools to obtain full coverage throughout the neural tissue and in complete brains involves significant disturbance in the form of view ports and insertion of microscope devices. This problem is similar to the one face by large electrode arrays.

5.4   Microscopic Wireless and Data Quantities

Microscopic wireless electrodes and functionalized nanoparticles are feasible alternatives where each individual probe has strict task constraints. Challenges are the possible power requirements and demands of data delivery. These may make it difficult for a whole network of probes to measure continuously at a rate that captures all interesting events. Functional characterization by these methods is simplified when done by sporadic sampling from different locations until each location is adequately characterized. When has enough data been collected and how are the results validated? Functional probes may help us look at temporal dynamics, but it can be difficult to ensure their location within the tissue over extended time spans. Frequent spatial registration is likely necessary. Ultimately, a microscopic functional probe technique can be combined with structural data acquisition by electron microscopy, because the probes can remain in the tissue when it is scanned.

When we have a way to record spikes, electric field potentials or membrane potentials from all neurons in a piece of neural tissue we still need to know what is a sufficient sample set. And what is the required sample rate? Can we predict neural dynamics from the observation of the shape of an action potential response? Should we observe the responses to a collection of possible input combinations in order to estimate connection strengths and predict spike times? Do we need to run the cell through its paces with a full battery of stimulation protocols? Does tractable System Identification demand that we do so at a higher resolution, on pieces of dendrite? Can we map lower resolution activity data to high resolution structure data so that compartment parameter values are sufficiently constrained?

5.5   Virtual and Small System Proof of Concept

Many of the challenges listed above can be dealt with confidently only if the process of System Identification is tested by iteratively building incrementally improved models of small systems. A small system can be a proof of concept that demonstrates steps of the process and overall feasibility. There are some small systems that are receiving attention at this time: Several groups are working on the nematode C. elegans (e.g. D. Dalrymple). Others are reconstructing pieces of retina (e.g. Briggman *et al*). Neuroprosthetic applications are being built for pieces of the hippocampus (T. Berger) and for the cerebellum (S. Bamford). There is also a project to extract memory directly from a piece of neural tissue (S. Seung)

Sometimes, we can also carry out virtual process testing. Programs such as NETMORPH [18] are able to "grow" or generate virtual neural tissue, with a known structure (Fig. 4) and known characteristic functions. We can explicitly test algorithms used to set parameter constraints from structure data, and we can test algorithms that take partial functional data and tune parameters

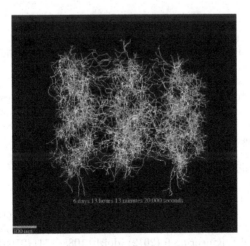

Fig. 4. Structurally detailed network generated with NETMORPH

accordingly. The results can give an indication of the minimal functional data that needs to be collected, and they can point out limitations in reconstruction from morphology. More abstract calculations of boundary conditions may also be possible, deducing constraints set by structure and additional information provided by patterns of input and correlated output.

6   Conclusion

It is often impossible to properly gauge which difficulties will turn out to be significant problems unless you work your way through the entire process. That is a main reason why proof-of-concept systems are so important.

System Identification is not a new field. It is done in every area of the exact sciences and engineering. Undoubtedly, most of the problems encountered when working with neural tissue are not entirely novel either. Examples of similar problems and the solutions that are employed may be found in other fields.

From the discourse above, it should be clear that while it is important and useful to build tools that acquire high resolution structure data and that acquire high resolution spatial and temporal functional data, that is not the whole solution. Other significant challenges are the integration from different data sources, turning a sea of data into parameter values, and validating those values.

A goal of this paper was to describe what System Identification entails in the case of reconstructing brain circuitry, and to communicate the reality of this effort beyond the confines of the discipline. Hopefully, this will lead to input from many other experts in the area of System Identification, which will lead to a better understanding of the problems and an improved roadmap to solutions.

References

1. Hutter, M.: Universal algorithmic intelligence: A mathematical top-down approach. In: Goertzel, B., Pennachin, C. (eds.) Artificial General Intelligence, pp. 227–290. Springer (2007)
2. Koene, R.: Fundamentals of whole brain emulation: State, transition and update representations. International Journal of Machine Consciousness 4(1) (2012)
3. Koene, R.: A window of opportunity. H+ Magazine, Based on the TEDxTallinn 2012 talk (2012), http://www.carboncopies.org/a-window-of-opportunity
4. Ljung, L.: Perspectives on system identification. Plenary talk at the Proceedings of the 17th IFAC World Congress, Seoul, South Korea (2008)
5. Rieke, F., Warland, D., de Ruyter van Steveninck, R., Bialek, W.: Spikes: Exploring the Neural Code. MIT Press, Cambridge (1997)
6. Hampson, R., Gerhardt, G., Marmarelis, V., Song, D., Opris, I., Santos, L., Berger, T., Deadwyler, S.: Facilitation and restoration of cognitive function in primate prefrontal cortex by a neuroprosthesis that utilizes minicolumn-specific neural firing. Journal of Neural Engineering 9 (2012), doi:10.1088/1741-2560/9/5/056012
7. Bi, G., Poo, M.: Synaptic modifications in cultured hippocampal neurons: Dependence on spike timing, synaptic strength, and postsynaptic cell type. Journal of Neuroscience 18(24), 10464–10472 (1998)

8. Berger, T., Ahuja, A., Courellis, S., Deadwyler, S., Erinjippurath, G., Gerhardt, G., Gholmieh, G., Granacki, J., Hampson, R., Hsaio, M., Lacoss, J., Marmarelis, V., Nasiatka, P., Srinivasan, V., Song, D., Tanguay, A., Wills, J.: Restoring lost cognitive function. IEEE Engineering in Medicine and Biology 24(5), 30–44 (2005)
9. Lazar, A., Slutskiy, Y.: Channel identification machines. Computational Intelligence and Neuroscience (in press, 2012)
10. Seung, S.: CONNECTOME: How the Brain's Wiring Makes Us Who We Are. Houghton Mifflin Harcourt (2012)
11. Briggman, K., Helmstaedter, M., Denk, W.: Wiring specificity in the direction-selectivity circuit of the retina. Nature 471, 183–188 (2011)
12. Bock, D., Lee, W.C.A., Kerlin, A., Andermann, M., Hood, G., Wetzel, A., Yurgenson, S., Soucy, E., Kim, H., Reid, R.: Network anatomy and in vivo physiology of visual cortical neurons. Nature 471, 177–182 (2011)
13. Zador, A.: Sequencing the connectome: A fundamentally new way of determining the brain's wiring diagram. Technical report, Project Proposal, Paul G. Allen Foundation Awards Grants (2011)
14. Kording, K.: Of toasters and molecular ticker tapes. PLoS Computational Biology 7(12), e1002291 (2011), doi:10.1371/journal.cpbi.1002291
15. Anastassiou, C.A., Perin, R., Markram, H., Koch, C.: Ephaptic coupling of cortical neurons. Nature Neuroscience 14(2), 217 (2012)
16. Koene, R., Hasselmo, M.: An integrate and fire model of prefrontal cortex neuronal activity during performance of goal-directed decision making. Cerebral Cortex 15(12), 1964–1981 (2005) (Advanced Access published on April 27, 2005)
17. Koene, R.: Functional requirements determine relevant ingredients to model for on-line acquisition of context dependent memory. PhD thesis, Department of Psychology, McGill University, Montreal, Canada (2001)
18. Koene, R., Tijms, B., van Hees, P., Postma, F., de Ridder, A., Ramakers, G., van Pelt, J., van Ooyen, A.: NETMORPH: A framework for the stochastic generation of large scale neuronal networks with realistic neuron morphologies. Neuroinformatics 7(3), 195–210 (2009), doi:10.1007/s12021–009–9052–3 (Published online: August 12, 2009)

CHREST Models of Implicit Learning
and Board Game Interpretation

Peter Lane[1] and Fernand Gobet[2]

[1] School of Computer Science, University of Hertfordshire, Hatfield AL10 9AB, UK
peter.lane@bcs.org.uk
[2] School of Social Sciences, Brunel University, Uxbridge UX8 3BH, UK
fernand.gobet@brunel.ac.uk

Abstract. A general theory of intelligence must include learning, the process of converting experiences into retrievable memories. We present two CHREST models to illustrate the effects of learning across two different time scales (minutes and years, respectively). The first is an illustration of implicit learning, checking the validity of strings drawn from an artificial grammar. The second looks at the interpretation of boardgame positions. The same learning and retrieval mechanisms are used in both cases, and we argue that CHREST can be used by an artificial general intelligence to construct and access declarative memory.

1   Introduction

The processes behind the acquisition and retrieval of patterns remain a major challenge for theories of artificial intelligence. Pattern recognition, and its role in categorising and interpreting perceived information for later cognition, is an important element of high performance in many domains, especially of a problem-solving nature. A dramatic example of the power of human memory is provided by the famous encounter in 1996 between IBM's Deep Blue computer and the then world chess champion, Gary Kasparov. The computer relied in part on an extensive process of search, eight magnitudes greater than what the hu- man could achieve, and yet the matches ended in a tie. The human's advantage over the computer was his large declarative and procedural memory, built up over 20 years of dedicated chess experience.

Humans' reliance on prior experience is apparent in many situations, even as everyday as perceiving a string of letters when reading. For a native reader, a string of letters may provide detailed information; for someone who does not know the language, the same letters may well be meaningless. Similarly, an expert in any domain will rapidly interpret and categorise stimuli from that domain. A master-level chess player shown a chess position will frequently indicate the previous history of the game, the likely next few moves, and the key strategic features, all within a few seconds [4]. This ability is not restricted to chess, but is found in other domains of expertise [5,10]. Studies have revealed the highly specialised nature of these memories [2], and any general theory of intelligence must account for, and model, their acquisition and use.

J. Bach, B. Goertzel, and M. Iklé (Eds.): AGI 2012, LNAI 7716, pp. 148–157, 2012.
© Springer-Verlag Berlin Heidelberg 2012

Developing a theory to cover learning in tasks that last perhaps a few minutes and learning over the years required to reach high levels of expertise means working at both a general and a specialised level. The general level is needed to ensure the theory is widely applicable. The specialised level is needed to ensure the theory can capture phenomena at the highest ability. This challenge reveals an apparent contradiction: how can we use highly specialised experiments to study general-purpose mechanisms? The solution which appears most promising at present is to use a cognitive architecture.

Taatgen and Anderson [25] describe a cognitive architecture as intended to "[supply] a general theory of cognition that is independent of particular phenomena" (p. 694). They also highlight one important question when building a model using an architecture, which is "to what extent is the intelligence in the architecture or in the model" (p. 694)? When using an architecture, it is important to ensure explanations of the behaviour are due to mechanisms within the architecture, and not any special processing added in to the model. An ideal way to achieve this is to develop multiple models which utilise and demonstrate the same core set of mechanisms provided within the architecture [17, 20].

In this paper, we present two models built using the CHREST (Chunk Hierarchy and REtrieval STructures) cognitive architecture, to illustrate its ability to acquire and retrieve patterns. The first is a model of implicit learning, identifying strings which fit a grammar after a short training period. The second is more specialised, looking at the interpretation of chess positions, using patterns which would be learnt by a human over several years. The two models rely on general-purpose learning mechanisms to develop a discrimination network, sorting perceived patterns to familiar chunks. We claim that the intelligence behind the models is within the architecture (the general-purpose learning mechanisms), and thus that CHREST is providing an explanation of learning suitable for general application. Beyond the models reported here, CHREST has been used to model performance in different board games [3,4,9,16], a card game [23], in natural-language acquisition [7, 12] and diagrammatic reasoning [15].

2   Overview of CHREST

CHREST is a symbolic cognitive architecture explaining how experience affects our ability to remember, categorise and think about the world. A distinctive component of the architecture is its discrimination network, used to retrieve information from long-term memory (LTM). CHREST models typically begin by training the model with data, from which this network, and associated long-term memories, are constructed.

The four main components of the architecture and their connections are shown in Fig. 1. First, there is the input/output unit, with separate mechanisms for handling perception visually (with a simulated eye) and verbally (with a phonological loop). Second, there is a short-term (or working) memory, which is limited to holding four items of information at a time. Third, there is the long- term memory, which is a memory holding familiar patterns (known as "chunks") and associations between them (including productions and "templates"). Fourth, there is an index into LTM, the discrimination network.

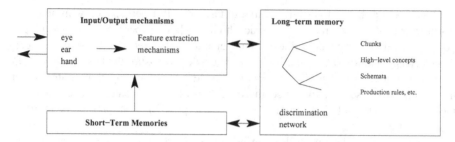

Fig. 1. An overview of the CHREST architecture

The role of the discrimination network is to sort an incoming pattern to the most relevant part of LTM. Although the main aspect of the network is its discrimination component, like a decision tree, sorting information from a root node to an appropriate chunk, the network also has an associative aspect, which links chunks to other chunks within LTM. The discrimination network acts as a retrieval device and a similarity function. Its role is analogous to the hidden layers of a connectionist network, or the RETE network of Soar [14].

The network is constructed incrementally, as the model perceives informa- tion. All information is in the form of a pattern, which is a list of primitive elements. For example, the string "VXPVXS" would be represented as a list of characters: < V X P V X S >. Patterns on a chess board would be represented as lists of items-on-squares: < [P 2 5] [R 1 5] [K 1 7] >.

The perceived pattern is sorted through the model's discrimination network by checking for the presence of elements on the network's test links. After sort- ing, the chunk reached is compared with the perceived pattern to determine if further learning should occur. If the perceived pattern contains everything in the chunk and some more, then familiarisation adds information to the chunk. If the perceived pattern contains different information to the chunk, then dis- crimination adds a further test and node to the network. Thus, discrimination increases the number of distinct chunks that the model can identify, whereas familiarisation increases the amount of information that the model can retrieve from that chunk. Fig. 2 illustrates the two learning mechanisms.

When presented with a chess board as input, CHREST uses its perceptual mechanisms to scan the chess board, extracting patterns of pieces, sorting them through the discrimination network, and so retrieving chunks to place into work- ing memory. The eye movements are guided by heuristics. One heuristic guides the next fixation, in a top-down manner, to a position expected to help the model sort deeper into memory. Other heuristics guide the model to follow lines of attack/defence, or look at different sections of the board; see [4] for details.

CHREST is available at http://chrest.info. The description and models within this paper refer to version 4 of the implementation. More information on how CHREST works can be found in [3, 11, 18].

(a) After learning < V X P S >   (b) Discrimination after seeing < V X P V X S >

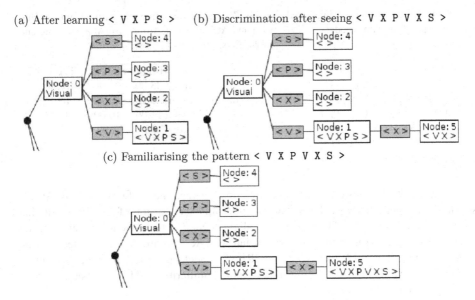

(c) Familiarising the pattern < V X P V X S >

Fig. 2. Illustration of familiarisation/discrimination learning process

3   Model of Implicit Learning

This experiment reproduces that reported by [13]. The aim is to demonstrate the implicit learning of rules about valid and invalid strings constructed from a Reber grammar [21]. The CHREST model is based on a technique used in EPAM-VOC [12] for the non-word repetition task. Essentially, it is assumed a limited number of chunks may be stored within a short duration phonological loop. The model separates the input string into chunks, and rejects any string which will not fit into the loop (having more than 4 chunks), or that has more than one single element chunk; this last is a measure of unfamiliarity.

Valid strings were constructed from the grammar given in Figure 2 of [13]. 18 of these were randomly selected for training, and a different 22 for testing. A further 22 random strings were constructed from the letters of the grammar, each string of length 6, 7, or 8 letters. The random strings all ended in an 'S' and were checked that they were not accidentally a valid string. Examples of valid and invalid strings are shown in Table 1.

Table 2 presents the results from averaging 100 runs of CHREST – each run used a different set of strings for training and testing, constructed as above. The model was trained using one pass of the training data. Each test string was presented twice, making a total of 44 strings in each condition. As in [13] we show the 'hits', the number of correctly identified valid strings (true positives); the 'correct rejections', the number of correctly identified invalid strings (true negatives); the 'misses', the number of incorrectly identified valid strings (false negatives); and the 'false alarms', the number of incorrectly identified invalid strings (false positives).

Table 1. Examples of strings used for implicit- learning model

Valid	Invalid
TTS	TXTVPS
VXPS	VXVPXS
TPPTS	TTVXPVS
VXPVXS	XPXVVXS
TPPPPTS	PXPVVTVS
VXPVXXPS	PVVVVVTS

Table 2. Results from implicit-learning model. Human and ACT-R results from [13]. All results are out of 44 trials.

	Human	ACT-R	**CHREST**
Hits:	33.00	34.00	32.84
Correct rejections:	36.00	39.00	38.52
Misses:	11.00	10.00	11.16
False alarms:	8.00	5.00	5.48

The results demonstrate a strong correlation between those of CHREST, of ACT-R and the humans. In particular, the model does an excellent job of identifying the hits and correct rejections. There is also a slight tendency to be better at rejecting the invalid strings, as found in both humans and ACT-R. A significant advantage over the ACT-R model of [13] is that the CHREST model constructs its own declarative memory of variable-sized chunks to determine familiarity, and hence whether a given string fits the learnt pattern.

4   Model of Board Game Interpretation

We next develop a model to reflect learning on human terms of several years, and attempt a more subtle interpretation task. In earlier work [18], we tested CHREST's ability to categorise chess positions by opening using perceptual chunks. Fig. 3 illustrates two typical positions with their openings; note the model only has access to the position, not the preceding moves, and that the game has progressed beyond the opening stages. CHREST was shown to categorise positions as well as a state-of-the-art statistical learning algorithm. This ability to categorise a chess position by opening is an important interpretation step, enabling a master player to retrieve memory cues about strategies, previous games, and likely tactics.

In our second model we go beyond simple classification, and explore CHREST's ability to retrieve multiple interpretative cues from a position, comparing these interpretations with those given by a master-level chess player. Fig. 3 gives some examples of the interpretations used below the diagrams; some of these require a knowledge of chess. The word 'outpost' appears twice, and, loosely speaking, an outpost for one side is a square in the opponent's territory which is hard for the opponent to attack. A 'bad bishop' is one which is hampered by its own pawns.

Each interpretation was treated as a simple verbal pattern, giving its name. During training, the verbal patterns were learnt alongside the positions to which they apply, and cross-modal associative links formed from the visual chunks recognised in the position to the verbal chunks. Associative links were restricted so that an interpretation referring to a white knight could only be linked withchunks containing a white knight, etc. During testing, the position provides the visual input. As CHREST retrieves chunks when perceiving the test position, it retrieves the associated verbal information. This information is then output as the model's interpretation.

(a) French Position   (b) Sicilian Position

black-control-semiopen-cfile,   knight-outpost-on-d5, backward-pawn-d6,
black-controls-white-squares,   black-king-side-underattack, open-gfile
weakpawn-for-white-on-c3,
badbishop-for-white,
knight-has-outpost-on-c4, hanging-pawns

Fig. 3. Example chess positions, their openings, and interpretative cues

   500 chess positions were collected, at the 20th move in the game, and annotated
with interpretations.[1] The data were randomly divided into two, a training (70%) and
a test set (30%). Interpretations were used only if they appeared in more than 20 of
the positions (to ensure sufficient numbers for reliable training and testing). This left a
total of 36 target interpretations, with an average of 4.1 interpretations per position. A
model was created training 2 times on the training dataset, with 100 fixations (approx.
30 simulated seconds) on each position during training and testing. The trained model
had 37,198 chunks in its visual long-term memory.

   Figure 4 illustrates a typical interpretation output by the model; the three parts of
the interpretation on which the model agrees with the target interpretation are in
italics. Table 3 shows the number of positions which received an accurate
interpretation, and how many accurate interpretations were made per position. Table 4
shows a sample of interpretations and the frequency of correct, missed and false
alarms made by the model on the test set.

   The results demonstrate that in more than half of the positions, the model outputs
at least one interpretation in agreement with that of the human. We regard this as a
promising result, demonstrating the validity of creating a CHREST model of human-
level scene interpretation. Looking at the intepretations which CHREST gets right and
wrong reveals a number of interesting features. Evaluation can be difficult in some
cases, for example an interpretation incorrect by commission (a false alarm) may be
arguably correct, or at least useful. In the example interpretation, black has his dark-
square bishop but white does not, and so control of dark-squares by black is a useful
theme to be aware of.

---

[1] Prathiba Yuvarajan provided the interpretations, under funding from the ESRC.

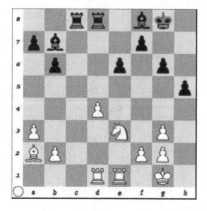

Target interpretation
black-control-open-cfile
black-control-semiopen-dfile
doubled-pawn-for-white
uncoordinated-pieces-for-white
weak-pawn-structure-for-white
Model's interpretation
black-control-semiopen-dfile
black-controls-black-squares
uncoordinated-pieces-for-white
weak-pawn-structure-for-white

Fig. 4. Example interpretation of a position

Some of the interpretations wrong by omission are also due to limitations in the current representation used by CHREST. For example, recognising an open file requires noticing the absence of pieces, and our model currently does not represent empty squares. Another issue is the position-independence of some features, such as 'doubled-pawns'. A chunk linking the 'doubled pawns' interpretation to pawns on d3/d4 will not be matched by pawns on g2/g3, accounting for the 30 misses.

These issues of representation have been noted and defended previously [16] based on the focus on modelling whole-board retrieval. By extending modelling to consider local regions of the board, CHREST's visual pattern-coding is likely to require modification to use position-independent representations and to include empty squares. We believe this change will be straight-forward to make.

Table 3. Frequency of positions with given number of correct interpretations

Correct interpretations	Frequency
0	64
1	75
2	12
3	1

Table 4. Selected interpretations

Feature	Correct	Misses	False Alarms
weak-pawn-structure-for-white	58	25	30
uncoordinated-pieces-for-white	13	25	35
knight-outpost-on-d5	3	12	1
doubled-pawn-for-white	9	30	0

5   Discussion and Conclusion

The two CHREST models presented above exemplify the effects on pattern recognition of learning across two different time scales. The implicit-learning model captures the effects of learning that occurs over a short time scale, with relatively few stimuli. The model of board-game interpretation illustrates the effects of learning on long time scales, with large numbers of stimuli. As an architecture, we can claim that

CHREST has been successful in providing general- purpose mechanisms applicable to multiple models. Within the implicit-learning model, CHREST relies on a phonological loop, as also used in EPAM-VOC [12], along with its discrimination network, which provides the 'units' of memory to use in recognising grammatical strings. Within the board-game interpretation model, CHREST has constructed a large discrimination network to aid the re- call of chunks from LTM. The board-game model also relies on its perceptual mechanisms, which have been tested in other tasks [3, 4].

There are several architectures besides CHREST, popular ones including ACT-R [1] and Soar [14, 20], and a natural question is how CHREST fits within the spectrum of other architectures. We suggest that CHREST can provide an explanation of how declarative memory is constructed and indexed, especially in its links with perception, whether visual or verbal. The challenge of constructing declarative memory has been described for ACT-R by [13], where their model of the implicit-learning task above required the modeller to specify bigrams to form their model's declarative memory. Also Laird, after describing the requirements of Soar, states 'we will still fall short of creating human-level agents until we encode, or until the systems learn on their own, the content required for higher-level knowledge-intensive capabilities' [14, p.40 (emphasis added)]. With CHREST, the construction of the discrimination network and associated learning of chunks and their relations is a natural way to explain the origins of (some aspects of) declarative memory in knowledge-intensive tasks.

Apart from learning, Langley et al. [19] suggested that many cognitive archi-tectures are overly focussed on problem-solving tasks, and that attention should be given to categorisation and understanding. The same authors suggest that ar-chitectures need to consider 'visual, auditory, diagrammatic and other specialised representation schemes' used by humans, and should better reflect the limited resources available for perceiving and affecting the world. As the models in this paper make clear, CHREST currently has this focus on categorisation and understanding. Previous work has already demonstrated models using auditory [12] and diagrammatic [15] representations, and the current paper illustrates the visual representation used for chess positions [4, 16]. CHREST's working-memory parameters and time constraints mean that perception and time for recall are limited by available (simulated) resources. However, CHREST is relatively weak in formal problem-solving abilities, and in handling non-symbolic data.

A way to move forward would be to combine architectures which focus on dif-ferent aspects of cognition to form a more comprehensive architecture that might capture learning, categorisation, understanding and problem-solving tasks. The choice of architecture and the way to make the combination is not, however, clear. Two distinct approaches may initially be identified, depending upon how closely recognition processes are thought to be involved with problem solving. One approach is more modular, and the other more integrative.

A modular combination might take support from Dual Process theories [6, 24], in which an intuitive, pattern-matching process (System 1) is hypothesised to be replaced when necessary by a distinct, analytical, problem-solving process (System 2). A natural analogue would be to combine CHREST with ACT-R or Soar to simulate more complex implicit-learning tasks: using CHREST as the intuitive component and ACT-R/Soar as the analytical component. CHREST would determine and recognise the entries in declarative memory, which ACT- R/Soar could then use in problem solving.[2]

In contrast, a more integrative approach would consider pattern recognition tied in more closely with problem-solving, almost intertwined. A previous proposal along these lines using CHREST was made in the SEARCH model [8]. Thus, except in very artificial tasks, System 2 nearly always operates with Sys- tem 1, shedding serious doubts upon the independent use of the two systems as proposed by Dual Process theories. For example, when a chess expert tries to find the best move in a position, the variations that are being consciously searched are nearly always supplemented by unconscious pattern-recognition mechanisms [4].

Whether the future holds a modular or integrated combination of architectures, it is apparent that a theory of artificial general intelligence will reflect the contributions of several current architectures. This combination would, we suggest, present a better explanation of general intelligence, covering a wider range of phenomena than either alone, whilst combining their strengths. In particular, we argue that CHREST is a suitable architecture for studying tasks involving categorisation and understanding based on prior expertise, and have demonstrated some new results in these areas. An important area of ongoing research is to consider how these recognition processes interact, and may be combined, with current theories of problem solving.

References

1. Anderson, J.R., Bothell, D., Byrne, M.D., Douglass, S., Lebière, C., Qin, Y.L.: An integrated theory of the mind. Psychological Review 111(4), 1036–1060 (2004)
2. Bilalić, M., McLeod, P., Gobet, F.: Specialization effect and its influence on memory and problem solving in expert chess players. Cognitive Science 33, 1117–1143 (2009)
3. Bossomaier, T., Traish, J., Gobet, F., Lane, P.C.R.: Neuro-cognitive model of move location in the game of Go. In: Proceedings of the 2012 International Joint Conference on Neural Networks (2012)
4. de Groot, A.D., Gobet, F.: Perception and Memory in Chess: Heuristics of the Professional Eye. Van Gorcum, Assen (1996)
5. Ericsson, K.A., Charness, N., Feltovich, P.J., Hoffman, R.R.: The Cambridge Handbook of Expertise. CUP, New York (2006)
6. Evans, J.S.B.T.: Dual-processing accounts of reasoning, judgment and social cognition. Annual Review of Psychology 59, 255–278 (2008)
7. Freudenthal, D., Pine, J.M., Gobet, F.: Simulating the referential properties of Dutch, German and English root infinitives in MOSAIC. Language Learning and Development 15, 1–29 (2009)
8. Gobet, F.: A pattern-recognition theory of search inexpert problem solving. Thinking and Reasoning 3, 291–313 (1997)
9. Gobet, F.: Using a cognitive architecture for addressing the question of cognitive universals in cross-cultural psychology: The example of awalé. Journal of Cross-Cultural Psychology 40, 627–648 (2009)

---

[2] A previous proposal [22] argued for a combination of EPAM (the predecessor of CHREST), GPS (a predecessor of ACT-R/Soar) and UNDERSTAND (for language).

10. Gobet, F.: Psychologie du talent et de l'expertise. De Boeck, Bruxelles (2011)
11. Gobet, F., Lane, P.C.R., Croker, S.J., Cheng, P.C.H., Jones, G.A., Oliver, I., Pine, J.M.: Chunking mechanisms in human learning. Trends in Cognitive Sciences 5, 236–243 (2001)
12. Jones, G.A., Gobet, F., Pine, J.M.: Computer simulations of developmental change: The contributions of working memory capacity and long-term knowledge. Cognitive Science 32, 1148–1176 (2008)
13. Kennedy, W., Patterson, R.: Modeling intuitive decision making in ACT-R. In: Proceedings of the Eleventh International Conference on Computational Modeling, pp. 1–6 (2012)
14. Laird, J.E.: The Soar Cognitive Architecture. MIT Press (2012)
15. Lane, P.C.R., Cheng, P.C.H., Gobet, F.: CHREST+: Investigating how humans learn to solve problems with diagrams. AISB Quarterly 103, 24–30 (2000)
16. Lane, P.C.R., Gobet, F.: Perception in chess and beyond: Commentary on Linhares and Freitas (2010); New Ideas in Psychology 29, 156–161 (2011)
17. Lane, P.C.R., Gobet, F.: A theory-driven testing methodology for developing scientific software. Journal of Experimental and Theoretical Artificial Intelligence 24, 421–456 (2012)
18. Lane, P.C.R., Gobet, F.: Using chunks to categorise chess positions. In: Research and Development in Intelligent Systems XXIX: Proceedings of the Thirty-Second SGAI International Conference on Artificial Intelligence. Springer (2012)
19. Langley, P., Laird, J.E., Rogers, S.: Cognitive architectures: Research issues and challenges. Cognitive Systems Research 10, 141–160 (2009)
20. Newell, A.: Unified Theories of Cognition. Harvard University Press, Cambridge (1990)
21. Reber, A.S.: Implicit learning of artificial grammars. Journal of Verbal Learning and Verbal Behaviour 6, 855–863 (1967)
22. Richman, H.B., Simon, H.A.: Context effects in letter perception: Comparison of two theories. Psychological Review 3, 417–432 (1989)
23. Schiller, M.R.G., Gobet, F.R.: A Comparison between Cognitive and AI Models of Blackjack Strategy Learning. In: Glimm, B., Krüger, A. (eds.) KI 2012. LNCS, vol. 7526, pp. 143–155. Springer, Heidelberg (2012)
24. Sloman, S.: The empirical case for two systems of reasoning. Psychological Bulletin 119, 3–22 (1996)
25. Taatgen, N., Anderson, J.R.: The past, present, and future of cognitive architectures. Topics in Cognitive Science 2, 693–704 (2010)

Syntax-Semantic Mapping for General Intelligence: Language Comprehension as Hypergraph Homomorphism, Language Generation as Constraint Satisfaction

Ruiting Lian[2,4], Ben Goertzel[2,3,4], Shujing Ke[1,2,4], Jade O'Neill[1],
Keyvan Sadeghi[2], Simon Shiu[1], Dingjie Wang[2,4],
Oliver Watkins[2], and Gino Yu[2]

[1] Hong Kong Poly U, Dept. of Computer Science
[2] Hong Kong Poly U, School of Design
[3] Novamente LLC
[4] Dept. of Cognitive Science, Xiamen University

Abstract. A new approach to translating between natural language expressions and hypergraph-based semantic knowledge representations is proposed. Language comprehension is formulated in terms of homomorphisms mapping syntactic parse trees into semantic hypergraphs, and language generation as constraint satisfaction based on constraints derived via applying the inverse relations of these homomorphisms. This provides an elegant approach to implementing semantically savvy NLP systems, and also to thinking about the feedbacks between syntactic and semantic processing that are the crux of generally intelligent NLP. A prototype of the approach created using the link parser and the OpenCog Atom semantic representation is described, and initial results presented. Routes to extending this prototype into something useful for aiding generally intelligent dialogue systems are discussed.

1 Introduction

Human language interaction is a large part of human-level AGI. The Turing Test, the most widely accepted evaluation metric for human-level AGI, is entirely focused on natural language dialogue; but even if one sets the Turing Test aside as many researchers advocate [1], there is no disputing the key value of human-like conversation as an indicator of human-like intelligence.

However, the fields of AGI and NLP are currently almost entirely disjoint. Few of the existing proto-AGI systems deal with language; and nearly all NLP systems are centered on extremely specialized rule-based or statistical methods that require careful customization for effective processing in new domains. If one's goal is AGI, two main options present themselves:

1. Create an AGI system capable of fairly general learning via experience, but little or no built-in linguistic mechanism, and have it learn human language.

J. Bach, B. Goertzel, and M. Iklé (Eds.): AGI 2012, LNAI 7716, pp. 158–167, 2012.

Variations abound, including robotic and virtual embodiment versus pure chat-based learning.

2. Create an AGI system including relatively sophisticated computational linguistics mechanisms, and have it use these to communicate, while modifying and improving them based on its experience.

A conceptual framework for thinking about the second option was presented in [2], in the context of enabling an AGI system to use virtually and/or robotically embodied experience to revise linguistic knowledge initially supplied to it via traditional computational linguistics means. Subsequent to publication of [2], some practical attempts were made to work toward implementing the ideas described there, in the OpenCog framework [3]. However, various technical difficulties were encountered, due to limitations of the specific computational linguistics tools integrated with OpenCog (the RelEx language comprehension system [4], and associated RelEx2Frame [5] and NLGen systems [6]). The present paper describes a new approach to integrating computational linguistics tools with OpenCog, differing from the RelEx approach in significant respects, created with the purpose of making it easier for OpenCog's general-purpose learning algorithms to interact synergetically with its dedicated computational linguistics components.

The key ideas of the approach presented here are:

1. Language comprehension, in its intermediate stages, is carried out via application of graph rewrite rules to syntactic parse trees. These rules, together, effect a hypergraph homomorphism that maps a parse tree into a subhypergraph of an OpenCog Atomspace (the "Atomspace" being OpenCog's weighted, labeled hypergraph based knowledge store). That is: **syntax to semantics mapping via hypergraph homomorphism**.

2. The more advanced stages of language comprehension are carried out via generic inference mechanisms, acting on the hypergraphs produced by the above rewrite rules. This is relied upon systematically, in the sense that the above rewrite rules don't try to perform subtle disambiguation, generally trying to disambiguate only enough to figure out the argument structures of the semantic relations being depicted in a sentence, and the basic semantic nature of each relation.

3. If a parser is capable of accepting semantic guidance midway through the parsing process, this guidance may be obtained via applying the above rewrite rules to partial parses and obtaining information regarding the semantic meaningfulness of the results

4. Language generation is done by applying the inverse relations of the above graph rewrite rules to a semantic hypergraph intended for expression, and thus obtaining a set of constraints corresponding to said hypergraph. A sentence expressing the hypergraph is then generated by solving the constraint satisfaction problem. That is: **semantics to syntax mapping via finding solutions to the constraints posed by the inverse relations of hypergraph homomorphisms**.

5. A database of previously comprehended sentences may be used to direct the system toward more natural-sounding solutions to the constraint satisfaction problem, as may inference on the hypergraphs inferred by applying known rewrite rules to partially generated sentenced.

Our main focus here will be on points 1 and 4, though the other points will be mentioned briefly as appropriate. The critical difference between this approach and previous approaches attempted with OpenCog, is that the graph rewrite rules serving as the core of the syntax/semantics mapping process are simple enough to be treated as "cognitive content" by OpenCog's learning and reasoning processes.

Due to length limitations, we have placed a number of tables and examples associated with the paper in Supplementary Information available online at http://wp.goertzel.org/?page_id=406.

2   The OpenCog Integrative AGI Framework

The work described here is part of the larger project of developing OpenCog, an open-source AGI software framework. OpenCog has been used for commercial applications in the area of natural language processing and data mining; e.g. see [4]. It has also been used to control virtual agents in virtual worlds, at first using an OpenCog variant called the OpenPetBrain [7], and more recently in a more general way using a Minecraft-like virtual environment [8]. It is the platform for the in-progress implementation of the OpenCogPrime design aimed ultimately toward AGI at the human level and beyond.

Conceptually founded on the "patternist" systems theory of intelligence outlined in [9], OpenCogPrime combines multiple AI paradigms such as uncertain logic, computational linguistics, evolutionary program learning and connectionist attention allocation in a unified architecture. Cognitive processes embodying these different paradigms interoperate together on a common neural-symbolic hypergraph knowledge store called the Atomspace ("Atom" being a term inclusive of Nodes and Links, where the latter includes hyperlinks). The interaction of these processes is designed to encourage the self-organizing emergence of high-level network structures in the Atomspace. Further review of OpenCog will be omitted here for space reasons; the reader is referred to [3] and various references linked from http://opencog.org.

The Atomspace Representation. OpenCog's "Atomspace" knowledge representation is a generalized hypergraph formalism which comprises a specific vocabulary of Node and Link types, used to represent declarative knowledge and also, indirectly, other types of knowledge as well. There is a specific vocabulary of a couple dozen node and link types with semantics carefully chosen to reflect the needs of OpenCog's cognitive processes. Simple examples of OpenCog links, in the notation commonly used with OpenCog, are:

```
InheritanceLink Ben_Goertzel animal <.99>

EvaluationLink <.7>
    chase
    ListLink
        cat
        mouse
```

Examples using nodes with English-word labels provide convenient examples, but in fact most nodes in a practical OpenCog system will generally be automatically learned and not correspond directly to any human-language concept.

What's important about the AtomSpace knowledge representation is mainly that it provides a flexible means for compactly representing multiple relevant forms of knowledge, in a way that allows them to interoperate – where by "interoperate" we mean that e.g. a fragment of a chunk of declarative knowledge can link to a fragment of a chunk of attentional or procedural knowledge; or a chunk of knowledge in one category can overlap with a chunk of knowledge in another category (as when the same link has both a (declarative) truth value and an (attentional) importance value). In short, any representational infrastructure sufficiently flexible to support

- compact representation of all the key categories of knowledge playing dominant roles in human memory
- the flexible creation of specialized sub-representations for various particular subtypes of knowledge in all these categories, enabling compact and rapidly manipulable expression of knowledge of these subtypes
- the overlap and interlinkage of knowledge of various types, including that represented using specialized sub-representations

would probably be acceptable for OpenCog's purposes. The Atom formalism satisfies the relevant general requirements and has proved workable from a practical software perspective.

3   Link Parsing and RelEx

The novel NLP approach described here utilizes a syntax parsing framework called link parsing [10], and (to a lesser extent, and in a more temporary way), an add-on to the link parser called RelEx (for Relationship Extractor). The conceptual essence of the approach is not tied to these particular tools, but its current practical implementation is.

3.1   Link Grammar

The essential idea of link grammar is that each word comes with a feature structure consisting of a set of typed connectors . Parsing consists of matching up connectors from one word with connectors from another. Consider the sentence:

The cat chased a snake

The link grammar parse structure for this sentence is:

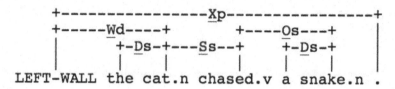

There is a database called the "link grammar dictionary" which contains connectors associated with all common English words. The notation used to describe feature structures in this dictionary is quite simple. Different kinds of connectors are denoted by letters or pairs of letters like S or SX. Then if a word W1 has the connector S+, this means that the word can have an S link coming out to the right side. If a word W2 has the connector S-, this means that the word can have an S link coming out to the left side. In this case, if W1 occurs to the left of W2 in a sentence, then the two words can be joined together with an S link.

The rules of link grammar impose additional constraints beyond the matching of connectors – e.g. the planarity and connectivity metarules.. Planarity means that links don't cross. Connectivity means that the links and words of a sentence must form a connected graph – all the words must be linked into the other words in the sentence via some path.

The graph rewrite rules at the center of the NLP approach described here map link parses into semantic Atom structures.

3.2   RelEx

RelEx is an English-language semantic relationship extractor, designed to post-process the output of the link parser. It can identify subject, object, indirect object and many other dependency relationships between words in a sentence; it generates dependency trees, resembling those of dependency grammars. The output of the current version of RelEx on the example sentence given above is:

```
singular(cat)
singular(snake)
_subj(chase, cat)
_obj(chase, snake)
past(chase)
```

A list of the important RelEx relationship types is included in this paper's online Supplementary Info.

RelEx currently works via creating a tree with a FeatureNode corresponding to each word in the sentence, and then applying a series of rules to update the entries in this FeatureNode. The rules transform combinations of link parser links into RelEx dependency relations, sometimes acting indirectly via dynamics wherein one rule changes a feature in a word's FeatureNode, and another rule then takes an action based on the changes the former rule made.

OpenCog also contains a system called RelEx2Frame, that translates RelEx output into relationships involving the frames and arguments defined in the FrameNet ontology, and code for translating link parser links, RelEx and RelEx2Frame relationships, into Atoms. The new NLP approach presented here replaces RelEx2Frame and RelEx both, but utilizes RelEx in a temporary role to help generate data to enable the learning of graph rewrite rules mapping link parses into Atom structures.

3.3   NLGen

Language generation is a complex, multi-phase process. There is an abstract cognitive aspect, concerned with figuring out what is appropriate to say in the current context. And then there is the "surface realization" aspect, concerned with translating conceptual content into a grammatical, comprehensible statement.

OpenCog's current language generation software, called NLGen, is focused on surface realization, and is based on an approach called SegSim, which takes an Atom set in need of linguistic expression and matches its subsets against a data-store of (sentence, link parse, RelEx relationship set, Atom set) tuples, produced via applying OpenCog's NL comprehension tools to a corpus of sentences. Via this matching, it determines which syntactic structures have been previously used to produce relevant Atom subsets. It then pieces together the syntactic structures found to correspond to its subsets, to form overall syntactic structures corresponding to one or more sentences. This process works unproblematically for relatively simple sentences, but sometimes becomes tricky for sentences involving conjunctions or other complex syntactic forms.

4   Mapping Syntax to Semantics via Hypergraph Homomorphisms

The core idea of the proposed new approach to natural language comprehension is to map syntactic parses (e.g. link parse graphs) into semantic interpretations (e.g. Atom sets) via applying rewrite rules. Each rewrite rule takes as input a subgraph of a syntactic parse graph satisfying certain constraints, and outputs an Atom hypergraph. In practice the rules required seem to take the form of pairs (G, A), where

- G is a graph whose nodes are either words or variables, and whose links are link-parser link types
- A is a hypergraph whose nodes are either words, variables or special linguistic nodes (drawn from a small vocabulary of such), and whose hyper-edges are OpenCog Atom types (e.g. InheritanceLink, EvaluationLink).
- The lists of variables in G and A must be the same

We shall call rules matching this description "simple mapping rules."

For the simple mapping rules actually needed for handling human language, the constraint that **each edge in** G **maps into a single hyper-edge in** A appears to hold true. Mathematically, this latter constraint implies that each of the rewrite rules is individually a **graph homomorphism** [11], which then implies that a collection of rewrite rules applied together is also a graph homomorphism.

These observations about the practical nature of the rules required, are drawn from inspection of the actual rules used in the RelEx system currently, which appear sufficient to cover a wide variety of English syntax and semantics. According to our best understanding, extending RelEx to increase its coverage and accuracy would be unlikely to break any of the observations made here regarding the basic mathematical nature of the rules involved.

A simple example of such a rule is (G,A) where

$$G = \{S_*(v_1, v_2),\ O_*(v_1, v_3)\}$$

$$A = (EvaluationLink\ v_1\ v_2\ v_3)$$

This maps a verb v_1 with subject v_2 and object v_3 into an OpenCog Evaluation-Link with v_1 as the predicate and (v_2, v_3) as the argument list. E.g. S_* refers to any of the link parser subtypes of S. Of course, most rules are more complex than this.

While the transformations the RelEx system carries out are capable of being formulated as simple mapping rules of the above form, they are not actually implemented that way, but instead are implemented via an iterative process of updating the FeatureNodes in a feature tree representing the words in a sentence. This is disadvantageous for two reasons:

1. Rewrite rules in the "simple mapping rule" format are easy to represent as Atoms themselves (using the format (ImplicationLink P_G P_A), where e.g. P_G is an AndLink joining the OpenCog Links corresponding to the link-parser links in the graph G). This makes it straightforward to OpenCog cognitive algorithms like PLN (Probabilistic Logic Networks) to re-weight, generalize and modify the rewrite rules, enabling the system's linguistic understanding to evolve via experience.
2. If one explicitly knows the rewrite rules used for comprehension, one can then turn these same rules around and use them for generation, as will be described below. This is a quite general and elegant approach to generating surface realizations for sentences.

With this in mind, we have recently implemented a novel approach to automatically learning simple mapping rules roughly equivalent to the current RelEx rules. We have used the link parser and RelEx to create a corpus of (sentence, link parse, RelEx relationship set, Atom set) tuples, and then used OpenCog's Fishgram pattern-mining system to automatically learn simple mapping rules from this corpus. While there is inevitably some noise in the results from the this process, in essence what one finds is a collection of simple mapping rules that gives mainly the same results as the traditional OpenCog pipeline "link parser → RelEx → Atomspace". Systematic evaluation of the quality of these learned rules will be presented in a later paper.

The application of our current simple mapping rules to the example sentence given above yields the output

```
(ExistsLink
       z
       (ExistsLink
       y
              (ExistsLink
                    x
                    (AndLink
                                 (InheritanceLink  x  Cat)
                                 (InheritanceLink  y  snake)
                                 (InheritanceLink  z  eat)
                                 (InheritanceLink  z  past)
                                 (EvaluationLink  z  x  y)
                    )
              )
       )
)
```

Further example mappings are given in the paper's online Supplementary Info, along with explanation of the Atom types involved.

5 Mapping Semantics to Syntax via Constraint Satisfaction

To carry out "surface realization" and generate natural language expressing the concepts in Atom sets, it suffices to reverse the graph rewrite rules described in the previous section. However, this is not entirely simple, because the rules create homomorphisms rather than isomorphisms. Any one Atom structure may be produced by many different link-grammar structures, because there are many grammatical ways to produce any given idea. But not all the grammatical structures corresponding to different subsets of a given Atom set needing articulation, will necessarily be grammatically compatible with each other. So one has a constraint satisfaction problem, which in general will have multiple solutions, with varying levels of syntactic ambiguity and subjective human naturalness.

More precisely, suppose we have an Atom set $A = \{A_i\}$; and let $R = \{R_j\}$ denote the set of all graph rewrite rules R_j with the property that R_j maps at least one link parse subtree into some nonempty subset of $\{A_i\}$. Let $R^i \in R$ denote the set of rewrite rules that produce an Atom set including the particular Atom A_i; we may write $R^i = \{R_k^i\}$, with $R = \bigcup_i R^i$. Let $m_g(r)$ denote the proposition that the rewrite rule r matches some subgraph of the graph g.

Given this set-up, the problem of generating a sentence expressing the Atom set A boils down to finding some link parse g that

- parses correctly according to link grammar
- satisfies the expressiveness condition

$$\bigwedge_i \bigvee_k m_g(R_k^i),$$

- satisfies an assumed "aesthetic condition", initially: that it would either not parse or not satisfy the expressiveness condition if any of its words were removed

Given a link parse g, producing the relevant sentence is trivial. The task of generating a sentence-set expressing A reduces to choosing a way to partition A into subsets, so that each can be acceptably expressed via a single sentence.

A strength and weakness of this approach is that, in most practical cases, this constraint satisfaction problem will have many solutions. Selection among the various solutions could be approached in many ways, e.g. via evaluating various solutions and choosing the one with the highest word tuple probabilities relative to a large reference corpus; or via proceeding as in the current NLGen system, and choosing solutions whose fragments are known via past NL comprehension experience to have been used in real human-generated sentences.

6   Conclusions and Future Work

We have presented a novel approach to bidirectional syntax/semantics transformation. The ideas described do not purport to solve the whole problems of generally intelligent natural language comprehension or generation, but merely to provide an elegant mechanism for connecting syntactic and semantic aspects of linguistic intelligence. Currently the suggested approach to comprehension has been implemented but not yet thoroughly validated; and the suggested approach to generation is in the midst of implementation. Once implementation is complete the software will be used to help an OpenCog system to carry out natural language dialogue in the context of controlling a virtual agent in a video game world. Of course, this dialogue application will involve a host of other components as well, most critically a dialogue control mechanism based on OpenCog's "OpenPsi" framework for motivated action [12].

As we have focused on the syntax/semantics transformation aspect here, we have not said too much about what happens at either end of the transformation process (e.g. link parsing, and PLN inference). However, it bears emphasis that a major goal of the ideas presented here is to enable the processes at the different ends of the transformations to work more closely together. For generally intelligent language processing, parsing and generation should be guided by semantic inference. This sort of linguistic cognitive synergy [13] should in principle be relatively straightforward given a solid implementation of the ideas presented here. A partially-parsed or generated sentence can be mapped into Atoms using rewrite rules, and the interpretation of the resultant Atom structure can be used to estimate the semantic viability of the sentence fragment. The original implementation of the link parser would not allow this sort of semantic guidance of parsing, but a variant of the link parser using SAT solving to do the parsing has been implemented, which is much more flexible in this regard. Experimenting with this sort of dynamic should be fascinating, and should move us closer to generally intelligent language processing.

Another possible direction for development is to allow the link parser dictionary itself (which contains most of the link grammar framework, since link grammar is highly lexicalized) to be adapted via the system's experience. Changes to the link parser dictionary would then lead to automatic modification of the rewrite rules, and could be validated or refuted based on the consequences of these changes as determined by inference. This would eliminate any "hard-coded linguistic content" aspect from the OpenCog NLP process, rendering all such content free for cognitive modification, as one desires in an AGI system.

References

1. Adams, S., Goertzel, B., et al.: Toward a roadmap toward human-level artificial general intelligence (2010) (subm. for publication)
2. Goertzel, B.: A pragmatic path toward endowing virtually-embodied ais with human-level linguistic capability. In: IEEE World Congress on Computational Intelligence, WCCI (2008)
3. Goertzel, B., et al.: Opencogbot: An integrative architecture for embodied agi. In: Proc. of ICAI 2010, Beijing (2010)
4. Goertzel, B., Pinto, H., Pennachin, C., Goertzel, I.F.: Using dependency parsing and probabilistic inference to extract relationships between genes, proteins and malignancies implicit among multiple biomedical research abstracts. In: Proc. of Bio-NLP 2006 (2006)
5. Goertzel, B., et al.: A general intelligence oriented architecture for embodied natural language processing. In: Proc. of the Third Conf. on Artificial General Intelligence, AGI 2010. Atlantis Press (2010)
6. Lian, R., Goertzel, B., et al.: Language generation via glocal similarity matching. Neurocomputing (2010)
7. Goertzel, B., Pennachin, C., et al.: An integrative methodology for teaching embodied non-linguistic agents, applied to virtual animals in second life. In: Proc. of the First Conf. on AGI. IOS Press (2008)
8. Goertzel, B., Pitt, J., Cai, Z., Wigmore, J., Huang, D., Geisweiller, N., Lian, R., Yu, G.: Integrative general intelligence for controlling game ai in a minecraft-like environment. In: Proc. of BICA 2011 (2011)
9. Goertzel, B.: The Hidden Pattern. Brown Walker (2006)
10. Sleator, D., Temperley, D.: Parsing english with a link grammar. In: Third International Workshop on Parsing Technologies (1993)
11. Voloshin, V.: Introduction to Graph and Hypergraph Theory. Nova Science (2009)
12. Cai, Z., Goertzel, B., Zhou, C., Zhang, Y., Jiang, M., Yu, G.: Dynamics of a computational affective model inspired by dörner's psi theory. Cognitive Systems Research (2011)
13. Goertzel, B.: Cognitive synergy: A universal principle of feasible general intelligence? In: ICCI 2009, Hong Kong (2009)

An Intelligent Theory of Cost
for Partial Metric Spaces

Steve Matthews[1] and Michael Bukatin[2]

[1] University of Warwick, Coventry, UK
Steve.Matthews@warwick.ac.uk
[2] Nokia Corporation, Boston Massachusetts, USA
bukatin@cs.brandeis.edu

Abstract. Partial metric spaces generalise metric spaces, allowing non zero self distance. This is needed to model computable partial information, but falls short in an important respect. The *present cost* of computing information, such as processor time or memory used, is rarely expressible in domain theory, but contemporary theories of algorithms incorporate precise control over cost of computing resources. Complexity theory in Computer Science has dramatically advanced through an intelligent understanding of algorithms over discrete totally defined data structures such as directed graphs, without using partially defined information. So we have an unfortunate longstanding separation of partial metric spaces for modelling partially defined computable information from the complexity theory of algorithms for costing totally defined computable information. To bridge that separation we seek an intelligent theory of cost for partial metric spaces. As examples we consider the cost of computing a double negation $\neg\neg p$ in two-valued propositional logic, the cost of computing *negation as failure* in logic programming, and a cost model for the *hiaton* time delay.

Keywords: AGI, partial metric spaces, discrete mathematics.

1 Introduction

Today it may be taken for granted that a computing system should be *adaptive* and *intelligent*. Certainly the behaviour of a hand held device running a computer game or interactive internet site is adaptive and, as it exists to serve us humans, is designed to be as intelligent as is possible. Some forty years ago programming language design was categorised into what now appear *narrow* forms: *axiomatic* (a system of logic), *operational* (defined by a machine model), or *denotational* (each program denoted by a point in some mathematical *domain*). Through a groundbreaking axiomatic model such as Robin Milner's *Calculus of Communicating Systems (CCS)* or Dana Scott's denotational theory of *domains* we have made great progress in specifying some behaviours, but sadly not enough to handle the adaptive and intelligent features required for today's systems. So, what went wrong? What seems to have emerged is a dominant operational view

J. Bach, B. Goertzel, and M. Iklé (Eds.): AGI 2012, LNAI 7716, pp. 168–176, 2012.

of programming language design and a grudging acceptance of the pragmatic compromise of object orientation which in effect extends a language definition with each new object introduced. To say that as a result logic and mathematics have no place in Computer Science would be ridiculous. And so, this paper asks how we can reinvigorate progress from axiomatic and denotational models for today's adaptive and intelligent systems.

1.1   Scott's Domain Theory

For the purposes of this paper we need to first appreciate the key concepts of Dana Scott's theory of domains. A *domain* is in the first instance a chain complete partially ordered set $(X, \sqsubseteq \subseteq X \times X)$ with a least element $\bot$. A *computable function* is in the sense of Scott at the very least *monotonic*. That is, if $f : X \to X$ & $x \sqsubseteq y$ then $f(x) \sqsubseteq f(y)$. Any non trivial programming language has one or more iterative constructs built in, such as a `while-do` loop or recursion. Scott uses Alfred Tarski's least fixed point theorem [8] to define the meaning of iteration for a computable function f as follows.

$$f(\bigsqcup_{n \geq 0} f^n(\bot)) = \bigsqcup_{n \geq 0} f^n(\bot)$$

Scott's domain theory is topological. A *Scott topology* $(X, \tau \subseteq 2^X)$ is related to the partial ordering of a domain by, if $O \in \tau$, $x \sqsubseteq y$, & $x \in O$ then $y \in O$. A Scott topology (X, τ) is weakly separable in the sense of T_0. That is, if $y \not\sqsubseteq x$ then there exists $O \in \tau$ such that $y \in O$ & $x \notin O$. As a denotational model for programming language design of the 1960s Scott's groundbreaking work resolved great issues of the day such as how to model iteration and recursion in programming language design. Tarski's theorem and Scott topology as fixed entities are perfectly fine for modelling a program which remains unchanged during its execution, but demonstrably inadequate for today's adaptive and intelligent computing systems. How come?

The situation in programming language design is just that of AI as understood by the AGI community. *"The original goal of the AI field was the construction of 'thinking machines' — that is, computer systems with human-like general intelligence. Due to the difficulty of this task, for the last few decades the majority of AI researchers have focused on what has been called 'narrow AI' — the production of AI systems displaying intelligence regarding specific, highly constrained tasks. In recent years, however, more and more researchers have recognized the necessity — and feasibility — of returning to the original goals of the field. Increasingly, there is a call for a transition back to confronting the more difficult issues of 'human level intelligence' and more broadly 'artificial general intelligence (AGI)'"* (`agi-conference.org`). This paper considers two narrow design aspects of programming language design, how they were innovative, and how they now call for *intelligent integration* with the theory of algorithmic complexity in order to progress.

1.2   Non Zero Self Distance

An interesting lesson from Scott's domain theory is that it was necessarily innovative. The nature of computability theory when studied denotationally necessitates weak properties such as partial orderings, T_0-separability, and least fixed
points, instead of the usual strong properties such as T_2-separability (that is, if
$x \neq y$ then there exists $O, O' \in \tau$ such that $x \in O$, $y \in O'$ & $O \cap O' = \phi$). Dana
Scott was innovative in developing a highly nontrivial theory for non T_2 topological spaces and applying them to the new science of programming language
design.

In a *metric space* $(X, d : X \times X \to [0, \infty))$ as introduced by Maurice René
Fréchet [4,7] strong separability T_2 results from the axiom $x = y$ iff $d(x, y) = 0$
for all $x, y \in X$, thus resulting in *self distance* $d(x, x) = 0$ for each x. This
equivalence gives rise to the trivial partial ordering $x \sqsubseteq y$ iff $x = y$ for each
metric space, which is hardly surprising for any system of mathematics not
constrained to be computable let alone adaptive or intelligent.

The discipline of mathematics has traditionally taken zero self distance for
granted because, before computer science, there was little reason to consider
the computability of a metric distance $d(x, y)$. More precisely, mathematics has
understandably assumed that each metric distance is a totally defined structure.
To assert that $d(x, x) = 0$ for each $x \in X$ is in computational terms a useful
means to specify that x is totally computed. Yet, at first sight, there appears to
be no non trivial overlap between domain theory and metric spaces.

Definition 1. *A* contraction *is a function* $f : X \to X$ *over a metric space*
(X, d) *for which there exists* $0 \leq c < 1$ *such that* $d(f(x), f(y)) \leq c \times d(x, y)$ *for
all* $x, y \in X$.

Banach's contraction theorem states that each contraction over a complete metric space has a unique fixed point in that metric space [7]. While a computable
function f has a least fixed point in the sense of Tarski/Scott, f may or may
not be a contraction. Similarly, a contraction may or may not be a computable
function. Wadge studied a small class of functions that are both computable and
a contraction [9], thus demonstrating a significant overlap of domain theory and
metric spaces. This approach was soon generalised to introduce a larger class of
functions.

Definition 2. *A partial metric space [5,2] is a pair* $(X, p : X \times X \to [0, \infty))$
such that,

$$p(x, x) \leq p(x, y)$$
$$p(x, x) = p(x, y) = p(y, y) \Rightarrow x = y$$
$$p(x, y) = p(y, x)$$
$$p(x, z) \leq p(x, y) + p(y, z) - p(y, y)$$

Thus a metric space is precisely a partial metric space for which each self distance $p(x, x) = 0$. For a partial ordering in the sense of Scott let $x \sqsubseteq y$ iff
$p(x, x) = p(x, y)$. A partial metric space is, simply speaking, just a generalised
form of metric space in which self distance can be ≥ 0. It is worth noting here that

had not the first author once taken for his doctoral study (1985) an intelligent
analysis of metric space theory to resolve a problem in recursive programming
the idea of non zero self distance would not have subsequently emerged in his
work as that of partial metric space. Just as Dana Scott worked more generally
and effectively with non T_2 separable topological spaces so it proved necessary in
Computer Science to work with non zero self distance in metric spaces. It can be
shown that the usual topology and T_2-separability of metric spaces generalises
to a topology and T_0-separability in partial metric spaces. Similarly, Banach's
contraction fixed point theorem of metric spaces generalises to the *cycle contraction theorem* (Theorem 5.1, [6]) in partial metric spaces. There is thus a
strong overlap between Scott topology & least fixed points in domain theory
and topology & unique fixed points of contractions in metric space theory. However, for reasons explained above, neither exemplary approach of Fréchet/Banach
nor Tarski/Scott could simply subsume the other by means of some ingenious
theorem. Their heirs are called upon to intelligently integrate the research of
great mentors. This research could well be unified in a more abstract setting
such as category theory to express the greatest common denominator, but at
the high price of losing the accumulated experience of each approach. It seems
that partial metric spaces in Computer Science are going nowhere. How come?

It is the essential rationale of this paper that intelligent analysis in contemporary mathematics and computer science is needed to reinvigorate denotational
models of computing with the exciting innovations of AGI. To exemplify such
intelligent analysis we consider the contrast of how the mathematics of domain
theory has developed as a *costless* form while research into *algorithms* and their
complexity is justly thriving upon interest in adaptive and intelligent systems.
A key ontological hypothesis of this paper is that *cost is core*, and that while
domain theory was necessarily cost free in its formative years, today it has to
be and can be properly costed. There is no expectation of a remarkable theorem and proof for this ontological hypothesis, but there are interesting examples
to demonstrate how the notion of cost can evolve intelligently to help broaden
programming language design as a contribution to AGI.

2   Examples of Cost

Each of the following examples has interesting features providing evolving insight
into how notions of *cost* in algorithms have been related to denotational models
of computing. In the adaptive intelligent spirit of the *complexity of algorithms*
we seek to adapt the partial metric notion of non zero self distance to apply to
each of these examples.

2.1   The Cost of Negation

Let $\{F, T\}$ be the usual set of truth values *True* and *False* of two valued truth
logic. Let $(\{F, T\}, d)$ be the metric space such that $d(F, T) = 1$. Now add $\perp$
as a third truth value. Let $(\{\perp, F, T\}, p)$ be the partial metric space such that

$p(\bot, \bot) = p(\bot, F) = p(\bot, T) = 2$, $p(F, T) = 1$ and $p(F, F) = p(T, T) = 0$. Then, just as required in the sense of Tarski/Scott $\bot \sqsubseteq F$ and $\bot \sqsubseteq T$. As usual we can define negation $\neg F = T$, $\neg T = F$ and $\neg \bot = \bot$ to be a monotonic function. This implies $\neg \neg A = A$ as expected for each proposition A in three valued truth logic. However, this partial metric space is *cost free* as it does not keep account of the cost of computing functions such as negation. Although it may be argued that logics of truth have always necessarily been cost free, it is nonetheless a luxury no longer affordable in today's computing world of adaptive and intelligent systems.

For convenience in our first example of cost let us assume applying negation to a proposition increases cost by one unit. For each $n \geq 0$ let $(\{\bot, F, T\}, p_n)$ be the partial metric space such that $p_n(\bot, \bot) = p_n(\bot, F) = p_n(\bot, T) = 2^{1-n}$, $p_n(F, T) = 2^{-n}$ and $p_n(F, F) = p_n(T, T) = 0$. Note that this particular definition for each $(\{\bot, F, T\}, p_n)$ is chosen to model the notion that if we ever manage to compute F or T it will be in some finite time n. Suppose now that given a proposition A we associate a partial metric space $(\{\bot, F, T\}, p_n)$ to keep account of its *present cost*. Let us speak of the *costed proposition* (A, p_n) to be the proposition A having an associated present cost of $(\{\bot, F, T\}, p_n)$. Then for a given costed proposition (A, p_n) we derive in one computational step the costed proposition $(\neg A, p_{n+1})$. And so, the truth $\neg \neg A = A$ in three valued propositional truth valued logic is preserved in a computation while in general the costed proposition (A, p_n) becomes later the costed proposition $(\neg \neg A, p_{n+2})$. Any intelligent implementation of this rule would regard (F, p_n) & (T, p_n) as special cases of a costed proposition which if ever reached for some n should terminate the computation.

2.2   The Cost of Negation as Failure

To commence our second example of cost we note the following personal connection from Dana Scott to Robert Kowalski, well known for his contributions to logic programming. *"I went to Stanford to study for a PhD in Mathematics, but my real interest was Logic. I was still looking to find the truth, and I was sure that Logic would be the key to finding it. My best course was axiomatic set theory with Dana Scott. He gave us lots of theorems to prove as homework. At first my marks were not very impressive. But Dana Scott marked the coursework himself, and wrote lots of comments. My marks improved significantly as a result"*, from *Robert Kowalski: A Short Story of My Life and Work*, April 2002.

In a non computing cost free world of logic we can afford the luxury of the property $\forall x.A(x)$ iff $\not\exists x.\neg A(x)$. However, in logic programming where the universe of all possible x values could necessitate an exhaustive search over an infinite domain this property is not computable in general. *Negation as Failure (NAF)* is a non-monotonic inference rule in logic programming used to assign a truth value to a formula $\neg A$ from the *failure* to derive the truth of A. Keith Clark, a student of Kowalski's, says of NAF, *"Although it is in general not complete, its chief advantage is the efficiency of its implementation. Using it the deductive retrieval of information can be regarded as a computation"* [3]. Correct! NAF cannot be complete in general, and hence neither is automated theorem proving. Thus logic programmers necessarily integrate automated logical inference with their own creative human intelligence. Hence our second example of cost relates to AGI. Now we can integrate Scott's domain theory, partial metric spaces, and NAF as follows. Let $\{((\{\bot, F, T\}, p_n)|n \geq 0\}$ be the set of partial metric spaces such that,

$$
\begin{aligned}
p_n(T, T) &= 2^{-n} \\
p_n(F, F) &= 2^{-n} \\
p_n(F, T) &= 2^{0.5-n} \\
p_n(T, \bot) &= 2^{1-n} \\
p_n(F, \bot) &= 2^{1-n} \\
p_n(\bot, \bot) &= 2^{1-n}
\end{aligned}
$$

p is *monotonic* in the sense that each p_n is a partial metric having the usual domain theory ordering $\bot \sqsubseteq F$, $\bot \sqsubseteq T$, and for all x, y, $0 \leq n < m$, $p_n(x, y) > p_m(x, y)$.

Note that in our first example of cost each self distance $p_n(F, F)$ and $p_n(T, T)$ is defined to be 0 as we were assuming truth to be either totally computed as the value F or T in finite time or remaining $\bot$ indefinitely. In contrast, our second example of cost defines $p_n(F, F)$ and $p_n(T, T)$ to be 2^{-n} expressing the fact that n is the maximum cost allowed at run time in searching for a truth value before failure is to be assumed. NAF is a realistic intelligent algorithm to determine the truth of a formula as best we can through exerting reasonable cost. NAF is monotonic for as long as we are prepared to bear the cost of monotonic reasoning, after which we must rely upon our human intelligence to choose a truth value as best we can. Also note how the definition of $(\{\bot, F, T\}, p)$ evolves from a cost free single partial metric space, to a costed set of partial metric spaces in our first example, and on to further development in the second example.

2.3   Failure Takes Time

In 1979-80 the first author of this paper took an introductory course at London's Imperial College in logic programming from Robert Kowalski himself. This was his first exposure to the *Negation as Failure* inference rule. Many years later in 2011 this author's former PhD supervisor W.W. Wadge proposed the apt slogan *Failure Takes Time*. In 1977 Ashcroft & Wadge [1] introduced a declarative programming language called *Lucid* in which each input (resp. output) is a finite or infinite sequence of data values termed a *history*. In domain theory,

$$\langle\rangle \sqsubseteq \langle a \rangle \sqsubseteq \langle a, b \rangle \sqsubseteq \langle a, b, c \rangle \sqsubseteq \langle a, b, c, d \rangle \sqsubseteq \cdots$$

where the totally defined inputs are precisely the infinite sequences, and the partially defined inputs are precisely the finite sequences. In partial metric terms $p(x, y) = 2^{-n}$ where n is the largest integer (or ∞ if $x = y$ is an infinite sequence) such that for each $0 \leq i < n$ $x_i = y_i$. Then p is a partial metric inducing the above ordering. An unavoidable implication is that each data value in a sequence is presumed to take the same amount of *time* to input (resp. output). Suppose now that *time* is to be our notion of cost for Lucid. Wadge & Ashcroft [10] recognised full well that defining a notion of cost synonymous with the data content of an input (resp. output) sequence is unrealistic in any non trivial programming language, and so presented their insightful vision of a *pause* in the execution of a program. For example, the following Lucid-like sequence seeks to introduce a special pause value termed a *hiaton* denoted $*$ to domain theory.

$$\langle *, 2, 3, *, 5, *, 7, *, *, *, 11, \ \ldots \ \rangle$$

But $*$ is neither a well defined null data value (such as is the number 0) nor is say $\langle *, 2 \rangle$ a partial value comparable to $\langle 2 \rangle$ in the partial ordering of domain theory. And so, what is a *hiaton*? Frustratingly the temporal intuition of a *hiaton* appears to be sound, but is not expressible in either domain theory or as a single partial metric space. The term *hiaton* is revealing, being as it is a combination of *hiatus* (pause) and *daton* (a Lucid data value). The vision of hiatons appears to infer that a pause can be fully known in order to be integrated with and presented as a well defined data value in a *history*. Our first two examples of cost regard cost not as a form of data but as a sophisticated interpretation of data in contemporary computing systems requiring (among other things) adaptivity and intelligence. Let us now generalise the notion of partial metric space for Lucid sequences to incorporate pauses as envisioned by Wadge & Ashcroft in a form that is consistent with domain theory. The following table is an example history of how pauses can be modelled in Lucid sequences using evolving partial metric self distances.

Time	Data	Hiatons	Partial Metric Self Distances
0	$\langle \rangle$	$\langle \rangle$	$2^{-1} + (2^{-0} - 2^{-1}) \times 2^{-0}$
1	$\sqsubseteq \langle 1 \rangle$	$\langle 1 \rangle$	$2^{-2} + (2^{-1} - 2^{-2}) \times 2^{-0}$
2	$\sqsubseteq \langle 1 \rangle$	$\langle 1, * \rangle$	$2^{-2} + (2^{-1} - 2^{-2}) \times 2^{-1}$
3	$\sqsubseteq \langle 1, 2 \rangle$	$\langle 1, *, 2 \rangle$	$2^{-3} + (2^{-2} - 2^{-3}) \times 2^{-0}$
4	$\sqsubseteq \langle 1, 2 \rangle$	$\langle 1, *, 2, * \rangle$	$2^{-3} + (2^{-2} - 2^{-3}) \times 2^{-1}$
5	$\sqsubseteq \langle 1, 2, 3 \rangle$	$\langle 1, *, 2, *, 3 \rangle$	$2^{-4} + (2^{-3} - 2^{-4}) \times 2^{-0}$
6	$\sqsubseteq \langle 1, 2, 3 \rangle$	$\langle 1, *, 2, *, 3, * \rangle$	$2^{-4} + (2^{-3} - 2^{-4}) \times 2^{-1}$
7	$\sqsubseteq \langle 1, 2, 3 \rangle$	$\langle 1, *, 2, *, 3, *, * \rangle$	$2^{-4} + (2^{-3} - 2^{-4}) \times 2^{-2}$
$\cdots$	$\cdots$	$\cdots$	$\cdots$

We now have an integrated notion of *history* for Lucid's data sequences and hiatons. Thus failure does indeed take both time and intelligence. Wadge's notion of *hiaton* is shown to be ahead of its time, and an intelligent integration of Fréchet/Banach and Tarski/Scott who came before.

3 Discrete Partial Metric Spaces

In Computer Science the term *discrete mathematics* is taken to mean the contemporary mathematics of information structures that are fundamentally finite.

Discrete mathematics is thus reasoning about structures such as finite graphs which are of interest in the understanding of algorithms or real-world computing applications. In contrast metric spaces and general topology are inherently continuous forms of mathematics where in general a point could be the limit of an infinite sequence of ever arbitrarily closer approximations. Wadge uses the interesting term *Infinitesimal Logic* (search online for *Bill Wadge's Blog*) in his work to introduce continuous mathematics to logic. As described in this paper the authors' work happened to turn out the other way round, which might be termed *Logical Infinitesimals* in contrast to and respect for Wadge. What is clear in both approaches is the need for and feasibility of a more intelligent integration of established research into logic, continuous mathematics, and algorithms. *Cost* is a key part of that integration.

Definition 3. *A discrete partial metric space is a set of related partial metric spaces in which evolving self distances can be associated to represent computational costs defined by an intelligent form of discrete mathematics.*

For example, a discrete partial metric space appropriate for representing Lucid with hiatons could begin with a partial metric space $(X,\ p : X \times X \to \{a_n^m \mid 0 \le n, m\ \})$ such that,

$$\forall\, n \ge 0 \,.\, a_n^0 \;>\; a_n^1 \;>\; a_n^2 \;>\; \dots \;>\; a_{n+1}^0$$

Our usual choice for this is such that,

$$\forall\, n \ge 0,\ m > 0 \,.\, a_n^m \;=\; a_{n+1}^0 \,+\, (a_n^0 - a_{n+1}^0) \times 2^{-m}$$

A *hiaton* may be understood intuitively as presented by Wadge & Ashcroft wherever the meaning is clear, or more precisely as a discrete partial metric space where the history is in part the history of *time* (as defined using evolving non zero self distance) in a sequence's computation.

Discrete mathematics, as understood in Computer Science, has developed firm roots driven by real-world applications. Discrete mathematics has proved itself to have great potential for modelling adaptive and intelligent systems. In contrast axiomatic and denotational models of computation have paid a very high price indeed for insisting that today's real-world must abide by their rigid pre-computing philosophies. Is it then just of mere academic interest to consider how, if at all, continuous and discrete forms of mathematics relate? Our examples of cost demonstrate that there are interesting ways to integrate continuous and discrete mathematics, as opposed to the prevailing view in Computer Science that continuous models of computations are mostly irrelevant to programming practice and only discrete mathematics has a future. Furthermore our research has highlighted the merits of working with logic and mathematics in contemporary computer science. Now we have an analogous but even more ambitious task of finding ways to have humans and machines *think* together as one new *intelligent* form, rather than trying to be the ultimate largest automatic theorem prover.

References

1. Ashcroft, E.A., Wadge, W.W.: Lucid, a Nonprocedural Language with Iteration. Comm. ACM 20, 519–526 (1977)
2. Bukatin, M., Kopperman, R., Matthews, S., Pajoohesh, H.: Partial Metric Spaces. Amer. Math. Monthly 116, 708–718 (2009)
3. Clark, K.L.: Negation as Failure. In: Gallaire, H., Minker, J. (eds.) Logic and Data Bases, pp. 113–141. Plenum Press, New York (1978)
4. Fréchet, M.: Sur Quelques Points du Calcul Fonctionnel. Rend. Circ. Mat. Palermo 22, 1–74 (1906)
5. Matthews, S.G.: Partial Metric Topology. In: Andima, S., et al. (eds.) General Topology and its Applications, Proc. 8th Summer Conf. Queen's College (1992); Annals of the New York Academy of Science 728, 183–197 (1994)
6. Matthews, S.G.: An Extensional Treatment of Lazy Data Flow Deadlock. Theor. Comp. Sci. 151, 195–205 (1995)
7. Sutherland, W.A.: Introduction to Metric and Topological Spaces. Clarendon Press, Oxford (1975)
8. Tarski, A.: A Lattice-theoretical Fixpoint Theorem and Its Applications. Pacific J. Math. and Appl. 5, 285–309 (1955)
9. Wadge, W.W.: An Extensional Treatment of Dataflow Deadlock. Theor. Comp. Sci. 13, 3–15 (1981)
10. Wadge, W.W., Ashcroft, E.A.: Lucid, the Dataflow Programming Language. Academic Press, London (1985)

Fractal Analogies for General Intelligence

Keith McGreggor and Ashok Goel

Design & Intelligence Laboratory, School of Interactive Computing
Georgia Institute of Technology, Atlanta, GA 30332, USA
keith.mcgreggor@gatech.edu, goel@cc.gatech.edu

Abstract. A theory of general intelligence must account for how an intelligent agent can map percepts into actions at the level of human performance. We describe a new approach to this percept-to-action mapping. Our approach is based on four ideas: the world exhibits fractal self-similarity at multiple scales, the design of mind reflects the design of the world, similarity and analogy form the core of intelligence, and fractal representations provide a powerful technique for perceptual similarity and analogy. We divide our argument into two parts. In the first part, we describe a technique of fractal analogies and show how it gives human-level performance on an intelligence test called the Odd One Out. In the second, we describe how the fractal technique enables the percept-to-action mapping in a simple, simulated world.

1 Introduction

Russell & Norvig [28] characterize an intelligent agent as a function (f) that maps a perceptual history (P*) into an action (A). If we accept f: P* → A as a useful characterization of intelligence, it follows that a theory of general intelligence must account for how the intelligent agent maps percepts into actions. Although Russell & Norvig do not delve into it, we believe that a theory of general intelligence must also account for agent's performance at the level of human intelligence. In this paper, we present a novel approach to addressing the f: P* → A mapping at the level of human intelligence.

Our approach is based on four ideas: (1) the world exhibits fractal self-similarity at multiple scales [19]; (2) the design of mind at least in part reflects the design of the world [12]; (3) similarity and analogy form the core of intelligence [14]; and (4) fractal representations provide a powerful technique for similarity and analogy. The first three of these ideas are familiar in theories of nature and intelligence; however, it is the fourth idea which is new. We claim that analogy initiates with an act of being reminded, and that fractally representing that triggering percept as well as all prior percepts affords unprecedented similarity discovery, and thereby analogy-making.

We divide the argument in this paper into two parts. In the first part, we describe the general technique of fractal analogies and show how it gives human-level performance on an intelligence test called the Odd One Out. In the second, we describe how the same fractal technique enables the f: P* → A mapping in a simulated world, in which intelligent agents recognize one another and flock together.

J. Bach, B. Goertzel, and M. Iklé (Eds.): AGI 2012, LNAI 7716, pp. 177–188, 2012.

2   Fractal Analogies and Novelty Detection

To deem some apprehended object as novel involves the complex interplay of at least two relationships [30-31]: the relationship between the observer and the observed, and the relationship between the observed and its context. The relationship between the observing agent and the observed object may vary depending upon some act taken by the observer. For example, if one wishes to appreciate an object at a higher level of detail, one might move closer to the object, or bring the object closer, resulting in the object occupying a larger expanse of the observer's field of view. This action modifies the resolution of the object: at differing levels of resolution, fine or coarse details may appear, which may then be taken into the consideration of the novelty of the object. The observed object also is appreciated with regard to other objects in its environment. Comparing an object with others around it may engage making inferences about different orders of relationships. We may begin at a lower order but then proceed to higher orders if needed. The context also sanctions which aspects, qualities, or attitudes of the objects are suitable for comparison.

Given the importance of perceptual novelty detection, there has been quite a bit of work on the topic. Markou & Singh [20-21] review statistical and neural network techniques for novelty detection. Neto & Nehmzow [24] illustrate the use of visual novelty detection in autonomous robots. Work on spatial novelty and oddity by Lovett, Lockwood & Forbus [18] centered on qualitative relationships in visual matrix reasoning problems. They showed that by applying traditional structure-mapping techniques [10] to qualitative representations, analogical reasoning may be used to address problems of visual oddity; however, they did not show where the representations come from [15].

Analogies in a general sense are based on similarity and repetition [14], and so we seek to employ a suitable representation, one which affords the capture of these qualities as well as sanctions reasoning over them. Fractals capture self-similarity and repetition at multiple scales [19]. Thus, we believe fractal representations to be an appropriate choice for addressing some classes of analogy problems. We model the relationship between the observer and the observed by starting with fractal representations encoded at a coarse level of resolution, and then adjusting to the right level of resolution for addressing the given problem. We model the relationship between the observed and its context by searching for similarity between simpler relationships, and then shifting its searches for similarity between higher-order relationships. In each aspect, these adjustments are made automatically by our strategy, by characterizing the ambiguity of a potential solution.

2.1   Visual Analogies and Fractal Representations

Consider the general form of a visual analogy problem as being A : B :: C : D, with the symbols being images. Some unknown transformation T can be said to transform image A into image B, and likewise, some unknown transformation T′ transforms image C into an unknown answer image D. The central analogy in such a visual problem may then be imagined as requiring that T be analogous to T′; that is, the answer will be whichever image D yields the most analogous transformation. That T and T' are analogous may be construed as meaning that T is in some fashion similar to T'.

The nature of this similarity may be determined by a number of means, many of which might associate visual or geometric features to points in a coordinate space, and compute similarity as a distance metric [29]. We adopt Tversky's interpretation of similarity as a feature-matching process, and seek to derive from each fractal representations a set of features for use in this matching process. Thus, we define the most analogous transform T' as that which shares the largest number of matching fractal features with the original transform T.

The mathematical derivation of fractal image representation expressly depends upon the notion of real world images [2]. A key observation is that all naturally occurring images appear to have similar, repeating patterns. Another observation is that no matter how closely one examines the real world, one may find instances of similar structures and repeating patterns. These observations suggest that images may be described in terms that capture the observed similarity and repetition alone, without regard to shape or traditional graphical elements.

Computationally, determining the fractal representation of an image requires the use of the fractal encoding algorithm. We refer the interested reader to our earlier work for the details of this algorithm [16, 22].

Table 1. Elements of a Fractal Code

Spatial		*Photometric*	
s_x, s_y	Source fragment origin	C	Colorimetric contraction
d_x, d_y	Destination fragment origin	Op	Colorimetric operation
T	Orthonormal transformation		
S	Size/shape of the region		

Features from Fractals. The fractal representation of an image is an unordered set of fractal codes, which compactly describe the geometric alteration and colorization of fragments of a source image that will collage to form a destination image. Each fractal code yields a small set of features, formed by constructing subsets of its underlying tuple. These features thus afford position-, affine-, and colorimetric-agnosticism, as well as specificity.

Mutuality. The analogical relationship between two images may be seen as mutual; that is, image A is to image B as image B is to image A. However, the fractal representation is decidedly one-way (e.g. from A to B). To capture the bidirectional, mutual nature of the analogy between source and destination, we introduce the notion of a mutual fractal representation. Let us label the representation of the fractal transformation from image A to image B as T_{AB}. Correspondingly, we would label the inverse representation as T_{BA}. We shall define the mutual analogical relationship between A and B by the symbol M_{AB}, given by equation 1:

$$M_{AB} = T_{AB} \cup T_{BA} \qquad (1)$$

By exploiting the set-theoretic nature of fractal representations T_{AB} and T_{BA} to express M_{AB} as a union, we afford the mutual analogical representation the complete expressivity and utility of the fractal representation. Further, the mutual fractal representation of the pairings may be extended to determine mutual fractal representations of triplets (equation 2) or quadruplets (equation 3) of images:

$$M_{ijk} = M_{ij} \cup M_{jk} \cup M_{ik} \qquad (2)$$

$$M_{ijkl} = M_{ijk} \cup M_{ikl} \cup M_{jkl} \cup M_{ijl} \qquad (3)$$

Therefore, in a mutual fractal representation, we have the apparatus necessary for reasoning analogically about the relationships between images, dependent upon only features which describe the mutual visual similarity present in those images.

Fig. 1. Representative Odd One Out problems

2.2   Odd One Out Problems

General one-one-out tasks can be presented with many kinds of stimuli, from words, colors, and images, to sets of objects. Minimal versions of these tasks are presented with three items, from which the "odd" one must be selected. Three item one-one-out tasks, in contrast to two-item response tasks, evaluate a participant's ability to compare relationships among stimuli, as opposed to just comparing stimuli features. It has been shown that these relationship-comparison tasks track general IQ measure more closely than do two-item tasks, and this tracking of IQ increases with the number of relationships to be considered [9]. We have chosen the Odd One Out test developed by Hampshire and colleagues at Cambridge Brain Sciences [11], which consists of matrix reasoning problems of varying levels of difficulty, in which the task is to decide which of the figures in the matrix does not belong.

Finding the Odd One Out, Fractally. Our technique for tackling the Odd One Out problems consists of three phases: segmentation, representation, and reasoning. First, we segment the problem image into nine subimages, I_1 through I_9. In the present implementation, the problems are given as 478x405 RGB-pixel JPEG images, with the subimages arrayed in a 3x3 matrix. At this resolution, each subimage fits well within a 96x96 pixel image.

Given the nine subimages, we group subimages into pairs, such that each subimage is paired once with the other eight subimages, forming 36 distinct pairings. We then calculate the mutual fractal representation M_{ij} for each pair of subimages I_i and I_j. The block partitioning used initially is identical to the largest possible block size, but subsequent recalculation of M_{ij} may be necessary using finer block partitioning. To determine the Odd One Out solely from the mutual fractal representations, we start by considering groupings of representations, beginning with pairings, and, if necessary, advance to consider other groupings.

Reconciling Multiple Analogical Relationships. For a chosen set of groupings G, we must determine how similar each member is to each of its fellow members. We first derive the features present in each member, as described above, and then calculate a measure of similarity as a comparison of the number of fractal features shared between each pair member [29].

We use the ratio model of similarity as described in [29], wherein the measure of similarity S between two representations A and B is calculated:

$$S(A,B) = f(A \cap B) / [f(A \cap B) + \alpha f(A\text{-}B) + \beta f(B\text{-}A)] \qquad (4)$$

where $f(X)$ is the number of features in the set X. To favor features from either image equally, we have chosen to set $\alpha = \beta = 1$ (the Jaccard similarity).

Relationship Space. As we perform this calculation for each pair A and B taken from the grouping G, we determine a set of similarity values for each member of G. We consider the similarity of each analogical relationship as a value upon an axis in a large "relationship space" whose dimensionality is determined by the size of the grouping. To arrive at a scalar similarity score for each member of the group G, we construct a vector in this multidimensional relationship space and determine its length, using the Euclidean distance formula. The longer the vector, the more similar two members are. As the Odd One Out problem seeks to determine, literally, "the odd one out," we seek to find the shortest vector, as an indicator of dissimilarity.

Distribution of Similarity. From the similarity score for a member of G, we determine subimage scoring by distributing the similarity value equally among the participating subimages. For each of the nine subimages, a score is generated which is proportional to its participation in the grouping. If a subimage is one of the two images in a pairing, as an example, then the subimage's similarity score receives one half of the pairing's calculated similarity score. Once all similarity scores of the grouping have been distributed to the subimages, the similarity score for each subimage is known. Although identifying which one among the subimages has the lowest similarity score, this may not yet sufficient for solving the problem, as ambiguity may be present.

Ambiguity. Similarity scores may vary widely. If the score for any subimage is un-ambiguously smaller than that of any other subimage, then the subimage is deemed "the odd one out." By unambiguous, we mean that there is no more than one score which is less than some ε, which we may vary as a tuning mechanism for the algorithm, and which we see as a useful yet coarse approximation of the boundary between the similar and the dissimilar in feature space. In practice, we calculate the deviation of each similarity measure from the average of all such measures, and use confidence intervals as a means for indicating ambiguity.

Refinement Strategy. However, if the scoring is inconclusive, then there are two readily available mechanisms at the algorithm's disposal: to modify the grouping such that larger sets of subimages are considered simultaneously (from pairs to triplets, or from triplets to quadruplets), or to recalculate the fractal representations using a finer partitioning. In our present implementation, we attempt bumping up the elements considered simultaneously as a first measure. If after reaching a grouping based upon quadruplets the scoring remains inconclusive, then we consider that the initial representation level was too coarse, and rerun the algorithm using ever finer partitions for the mutual fractal representation. If, after altering our considerations of groupings and examining the images at the finest level of resolution the scores prove inconclusive, the algorithm selects the subimage with the lowest score.

2.3   Analysis and Discussion

We have run our algorithm against 2,976 problems of the Odd One Out. These problems span a range of difficulty from the very easiest (level one) up to the most difficult (level 20). The performance ranged from nearly perfect on the easiest levels, to 70% correct at the middle difficulties, with a rapid falloff to 20% at the most difficult. For each problem, the choice of partitioning resolution was made automatically.

We note that most errors occur when the algorithm stops at quite high levels of partitioning. We interpret this as evidence that there exist levels-of-detail which are too gross to allow for certainty in reasoning. Indeed, the data upon which decisions are made at these levels are three orders of magnitude less than that which the finest partitioning affords. We find an opportunity for a refinement of the algorithm to assess its certainty based upon a naturally emergent artifact of the representation.

The errors that occurred at the finest level of partitioning are caused not due to the algorithm reaching an incorrect unambiguous answer but rather that the algorithm was unable to reach a sufficiently convincing or unambiguous answer. As we noted, these results are based upon calculations involving considering shifts in partitioning only, using pair wise comparisons of subimages. There appear to be Odd One Out problems for which considering pairs of subimages shall prove inconclusive at all available levels of detail. It is this set of problems which we believe implies that a shift in grouping (from pairs to triplets, or from triplets to quadruplets) must be undertaken to reach an unambiguous answer.

3   Fractal Perception and Action

In order to demonstrate that fractal analogies may form the basis of a theory of general intelligence, we need to describe how they can address the f: P* → A mapping. To illustrate this we will construct an intelligent agent that lives in a simple simulated world similar to Reynolds's [26-27] boid worlds.

3.1   The Boid World

Schools of fish, murmurations of starlings, and stampedes of wildebeest are at once stunning and remarkable in appearance. The collection of agents, taken together, appear to be acting as if they were under some organized control.

Reynolds' boids are agents with an internal state which describes their current heading and an awareness of those agents to whom they should. They also have a minimum set of intrinsic behaviors that drive them to coordinate their actions with those flock mates: stay close together, don't collide, and mimic the motion of others.

Fig. 2. Flocking Behaviors: Cohesion, Separation, and Alignment

Perception. A flock in nature may be composed of many thousands of individuals. It would seem an improbable computational load to place upon each agent within the flock the attempt to ascertain aspects of every member of the flock prior to making modifications to its own behavior. Some restriction of which individuals to consider must occur. Reynolds characterizes this as considering each agent to have a local perception. In computer simulations of flocks, the local perception each agent has of the world typically is provided to the agent by a godlike view of the entire environment, and a superimposed restriction of individuals by culling those deemed too distant to consider. This distance is usually referred to as a range of influence.

3.2   The Froid (Fractal Boid) World

For explorations of visual reasoning, affording agents with models of perception based on familiarity and novelty and observing those agents as flocks seems ideal. In our system, we endow our agents with a visual reasoning apparatus with the ability to receive the environment by localized observation only, and to perceive this received world via manipulations of fractal representations.

Froids versus Boids. Our agents, froids, sense and then classify their environment, whereas boids are told explicitly about their surrounds. Both boids and froids manifest the same behaviors, and thus participate in flocking with their mates, but only froids perceive and reason about their environment prior to enacting those behaviors. We establish a visual reasoning pipeline for a froid, from the reception of the world, through perceiving individuals and objects in the world, to reasoning about those perceptions, and finally, to enacting some course of action.

We made two simplifying architectural decisions for our experiment. First, the perception stage occurs in a serial fashion with the behavior decision stage, since the world of the simulation will not have changed until all the agents have moved themselves. Second, the perception stage would act only upon newly arriving stimuli, and not be influenced by prior decisions. We make these simplifications so that we may better compare the effect of perception on the subsequent behavior, without having our analysis take into account any perceptual hysteresis or other internal state.

Fig. 3. Visual field to retina mapping, seeing via ray casting, and retinal objects

How a Froid Sees. We image a froid as having a single "eye" with a broad field of view. The froid's eye consists of a simulated retina, an arrangement of sensors. A froid sees its environment by receiving photometric stimulation upon this retina. The light entering each of these sensors is combined to form a visual field, as shown in figure 3-left. In our simulation, we use ray-casting to send a ray out through each of the sensors into the simulated world, and note whether that ray intersects anything. We illustrate this in Figure 3-center.

We interpret the "light" falling upon the sensor is a function of the distance of the intersected object from the froid, where objects which are distant are fainter than close objects. Figure 3-right shows an example of how objects within the froid's immediate environment may be mapped by this visual system onto its retina.

Fractal Perception. The photometric values arriving via the froid's retina next are interpreted by the froid's perception stage. For our present implementation we restrict the intentionality of the perception to only those tasks which will drive the flocking behavior. Accordingly, the primary task of the perception system is to determine flock mates.

This, however, raises an immediate question: what does a flock mate look like to a froid? Our froids are rendered into the simulated environment as chevrons whose orientation, color and physical size may vary. The visual environment, as transduced onto the retinal image, will show only an arranged set of values, roughly corresponding to visual distance to whatever object happened to intersect the ray from the sensor.

Filial Imprinting. There are many possible visual arrangements between a froid and a prototypical "other" in its environment. We chose to restrict our prototypes to six, four corresponding to points on the compass (north, south, east and west), and two corresponding to specific situations which would seem useful for behavior selection (close and empty). We refer to these as filial imprints, and they, along with their corresponding retinal impressions, are encoded into a fractal representation, and placed, indexed by derived fractal features, into the froid's memory system.

Finding the Familiar by Visual Analogy. The arriving retinal image is an otherwise undifferentiated collection of photometric information, with each value corresponding to a particular direction and distance. From this retinal image, flock mates that might be within the visual range of the froid may be identified.

We begin by segmenting the retinal image into varying sets (collections of adjacent sensors), and then encoding each of these segments into fractal representations. We note that no attempt is made to interpret the retina image for edges or other boundary conditions: the segments are treated merely as they are found.

To determine the prototype P' which is most analogous to the retinal segment R from a set of fractal prototypes $P := \{ P_1, P_2, \dots P_n \}$:

$F \leftarrow$ Fractal(R, R)
Set $M \leftarrow 0$ and P' $\leftarrow$ unknown
For each prototype $P_i \in P$:
 · Calculate the similarity of F to P_i : $S \leftarrow$ Sim(F, P_i)
 · If $S > M$, then $M \leftarrow S$ and P' $\leftarrow P_i$

P' is therefore that prototype $P_i \in P$ which corresponds to the maximal similarity S, and is deemed the most analogous to retinal segment R.

Algorithm 1. Selecting the fractal familiar

If a segment corresponds to an imprinted prototype then we may make several inferences. The first is that an individual flock mate exists in that direction of view, which corresponds to the segment's retinal constituents. Secondly, we may infer that the flock mate lies at a distance which corresponds to a function of the faintness of the photometric readings of the retinal image. By systematically examining each segment of the retina, the froid's flock mates may be inferred by visual analogy.

3.3   The Three Laws for Froids

Once the flock mates have been discovered, the Reynolds rules for flocking may be invoked. Since the perception system has inferred the existence of a flock mate at a particular distance and direction, the **separation** and **cohesion** rules may be enacted directly. To **align** with a flock mate, the froid must infer the heading from the visual classification of the mate. This classification depends explicitly upon which of the filial prototypes has been selected as most representative of the retinal segment. We identified five rules of heading inference. Once the heading is inferred, the alignment rule of Reynolds may be used to adjust the motion of the froid.

3.4   Froids and Boids

To test our belief that a froid could behave as naturally as its boid counterparts, we created a traditional Reynolds boid system. We first placed into the environment several thousand standard boids, and observed that their aggregate motion was as expected: a realistic simulation of natural flocking behavior.

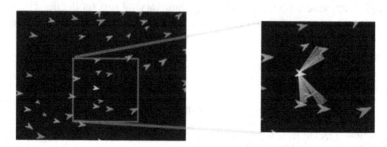

Fig. 4. A froid flocks with boids, and a closeup of the froid perceiving its environment

We then introduced one froid into the environment with the boids. Figure 4 shows a view of this simulation, with traditional boids in green, and the froid in gold. We observed that the froid behaved in the same manner as those boids whose identification of flock mates was given in the traditional oracle manner.

We note that, unlike the boids, the froids appeared to suffer from uncertainty (manifested by a stuttering motion) when in the proximity of a large number of other boids. We surmised that this is due to the inability of the segmentation system using within the retina to accommodate or otherwise classify large amounts of overlapping or confounding visual data. Another possibility concerns the enaction itself. Let us suppose that two action vectors arising due to two received perceptual signals almost exactly cancel each other. In this case, small fluctuations in the perceptual signal can cause a significant change in the action vector, which may result in stuttering.

4   Conclusion

In earlier work [5-6], we showed that visual knowledge and reasoning alone could address some classes of analogy problems that had been assumed to require causal knowledge and reasoning. We also showed how visual analogies could account for several aspects of creative problem solving in scientific discovery [8] and engineering design [7]. However, this work still used propositional representations, while the content of knowledge was visuospatial. In [16-17], we showed how visual knowledge represented iconically can address analogy problems on the Raven's Progressive Matrices test of intelligence. Previously, the visual analogy problems on the Raven's test had been assumed to require propositional representations. The Raven's test also formed the context of our first development of fractal representations for addressing visual analogy problems [22]. The fractal method on the Raven's test performs about as well as typically human teenager. Hertzmann et al [13] have used a different fractal technique for comparing texture in two images.

In this paper, first we showed that an improved fractal technique can address visual analogy problems on the Odd One Out test of intelligence at the level of most adult humans. Further, the fractal technique imitates two important features of human performance: starting with low-level relationships and moving to higher relationships if and as needed, and automatic adjustment of the level of resolution to resolve ambiguities. We posit that fractal representations are knowledge representations in the sense of Biederman [3] in that they encode the relationship between non-accidental perceptual constructs within an image. We posit further that fractals are knowledge representations in the deep sense of Davis, Shrobe & Szolovits [4] in which representation and reasoning are closely intertwined.

Then, in this paper we that showed the fractal technique for visual analogies can be used for perception. We demonstrated that froids (fractal-based boids) can use the fractal technique for mapping percepts into actions which manifest flocking behavior. The froids used a simple architecture called "reactive control" in robotics [1] and "situated action" in cognitive science [23], directly mapping percepts into actions.

While the use of fractal representations is central to our technique, the emphasis upon visual recall in our solution afforded by features derived from those representations is also important. There is evidence that certain species have innate or rapidly develop through acclimation visual prototypes which allow young members to accurately identify their parents [25]. We hold that placing imprints into memory, indexed via fractal features, affords a new and robust method of discovering image similarity, and that images, encoded and represented in terms of themselves, may be indexed and retrieved without regard to shape, geometry, or symbol.

Our goal is to develop a Fractal Theory of General Intelligence. We believe that in this paper we have taken two important steps in that long journey: we have demonstrated that (1) our fractal technique can address visual analogy problems on intelligence tests on par with human performance, and (2) our fractal technique enables real-time percept-to-action mapping capable of imitating flocking behavior, at least in a simulated world.

References

1. Arkin, R.: Behavior-Based Robotics. The MIT Press, Boston (1998)
2. Barnsley, M., Hurd, L.: Fractal Image Compression. A.K. Peters, Boston (1992)
3. Biederman, I.: Recognition-by-Components: A Theory of Human Image Understanding. Psychological Review 94, 115–147 (1987)
4. Davis, R., Shrobe, H., Szolovits, P.: What is a Knowledge Representation? AI Magazine 14(1), 17–33 (1993)
5. Davies, J., Goel, A.: Visual Analogy in Problem Solving. In: Proc. 17th International Joint Conference on Artificial Intelligence, IJCAI 2001, pp. 377–382. Morgan Kaufmann (August 2001)
6. Davies, J., Goel, A., Yaner, P.: Proteus: Visuospatial Analogy in Problem Solving. Knowledge-Based Systems 21(7), 636–654 (2008)
7. Davies, J., Goel, J., Nersessian, N.: A Computational Model of Visual Analogies in Design. Cognitive Systems Research 10, 204–215 (2009)
8. Davies, J., Nersessian, N., Goel, A.: Visual Models in Analogical Problem Solving. Foundations of Science 10(1), 133–152 (2005)
9. Diascro, M.N., Brody, N.: Odd-man-out and intelligence. Intelligence 19(1), 79–92 (1994)
10. Gentner, D.: Structure-Mapping: A Theoretical Framework for Analogy. Cognitive Science 7(2), 155–170 (1983)
11. Hampshire, A.: The Odd One Out Test of Intelligence (2010), http://www.cambridgebrainsciences.com/browse/reasoning/test/oddoneout

12. Haugeland, J. (ed.): Mind Design: Philosophy, Psychology and Artificial Intelligence. MIT Press (1981)
13. Hertzmann, A., Jacobs, C.E., Oliver, N., Curless, B., Salesin, D.: Image analogies. Computer Graphics 25(4), 327–340 (2001) (SIGGRAPH 2001 Conference Proceedings)
14. Hofstadter, D., Fluid Analogies Research Group (eds.): Fluid concepts & creative analogies: Computer models of the fundamental mechanisms of thought. Basic Books, New York (1995)
15. Indurkhya, B.: On creation of features and change of representation. Journal of Japanese Cognitive Science Society 5(2), 43–56 (1998)
16. Kunda, M., McGreggor, K., Goel, A.: Taking a Look (Literally!) at the Raven's Intelligence Test: Two Visual Solution Strategies. In: Proc. 32nd Annual Meeting of the Cognitive Science Society, Portland (August 2010)
17. Kunda, M., McGreggor, K., Goel, A.: A computational model for solving problems from the Raven's Progressive Matrices intelligence test using iconic visual representations. To appear in Cognitive Systems Research (in press)
18. Lovett, A., Lockwood, K., Forbus, K.: Modeling Cross-Cultural Performance on the Visual Oddity Task. In: Freksa, C., Newcombe, N.S., Gärdenfors, P., Wölfl, S. (eds.) Spatial Cognition VI. LNCS (LNAI), vol. 5248, pp. 378–393. Springer, Heidelberg (2008)
19. Mandelbrot, B.: The fractal geometry of nature. W.H. Freeman, San Francisco (1982)
20. Markou, M., Singh, S.: Novelty Detection: A Review-Part 1: Statistical Approaches. Signal Processing 83(12), 2481–2497 (2003a)
21. Markou, M., Singh, S.: Novelty Detection: A Review-Part 2: Neural Network Based Approaches. Signal Processing 83(12), 2481–2497 (2003b)
22. McGreggor, K., Kunda, M., Goel, A.: Fractal Analogies: Preliminary Results from the Raven's Test of Intelligence. In: Proc. International Conference on Computational Creativity, Mexico City, Mexico, April 27-29 (2011)
23. Norman, D.: Cognition in the Head and in the World: An Introduction to the Special Issue on Situated Action. Cognitive Science 17, 1–6 (1993)
24. Neto, H., Nehmzow, U.: Visual Novelty Detection with Automatic Scale Selection. Robotics and Autonomous Systems 55, 693–701 (2007)
25. O'Reilly, R.C., Johnson, M.H.: Object Recognition and Sensitive Periods: A Computational Analysis of Visual Imprinting. Neural Computation 6, 357–389 (1994)
26. Reynolds, C. W.: Flocks, Herds, and Schools: A Distributed Behavioral Model. Computer Graphics 21(4), 25–34 (1987) (SIGGRAPH 1987 Conference Proceedings)
27. Reynolds, C.W.: Steering Behaviors For Autonomous Characters. In: Proceedings of Game Developers Conference 1999 held in San Jose, California, pp. 763–782. Miller Freeman Game Group, San Francisco (1999)
28. Russell, S., Norvig, P.: Artificial Intelligence: A Modern Approach. Prentice-Hall (2003)
29. Tversky, A.: Features of similarity. Psychological Review 84(4), 327–352 (1977)
30. Wagemans, J., Elder, J., Kubovy, M., Palmer, S., Peterson, M., Singh, M., von der Heydt, R.: A century of Gestalt psychology in visual perception: I. Perceptual grouping and figure-ground organization. Psychological Bulletin (in press A)
31. Wagemans, J., Feldman, J., Gerpshtein, S., Kimchi, R., Pomerantz, J., van der Helm, P., van Leeuwen: A Century of Gestalt Psychology in Visual Perception II. Conceptual and Theoretical Foundations. Psychological Bulletin (in press B)

Pattern Mining for General Intelligence: The FISHGRAM Algorithm for Frequent and Interesting Subhypergraph Mining

Jade O'Neill[1], Ben Goertzel[2,3,4], Shujing Ke[1,2,4], Ruiting Lian[2,4], Keyvan Sadeghi[2], Simon Shiu[1], Dingjie Wang[2,4], and Gino Yu[2]

[1] Hong Kong Poly U, Dept. of Computer Science
[2] Hong Kong Poly U, School of Design
[3] Novamente LLC
[4] Dept. of Cognitive Science, Xiamen University

Abstract. Fishgram, a novel algorithm for recognizing frequent or otherwise interesting sub-hypergraphs in large, heterogeneous hypergraphs, is presented. The algorithm's implementation the OpenCog integrative AGI framework is described, and concrete examples are given showing the patterns it recognizes in OpenCog's hypergraph knowledge store when the OpenCog system is used to control a virtual agent in a game world. It is argued that Fishgram is well suited to fill a critical niche in OpenCog and potentially other integrative AGI architectures: scalable recognition of relatively simple patterns in heterogeneous, potentially rapidly-changing data.

1 Introduction

Pattern recognition is a core aspect of general intelligence. In general it is an extremely difficult problem (uncomputable, under many formulations), but in various special cases it may be tractable and even efficiently soluble in the large-scale and in real time. Different AGI architectures handle pattern recognition in a great diversity of ways; some via a unified approach to recognizing all patterns relevant to an AGI system's goals, others via a collection of different pattern recognition processes with different foci, strengths and weaknesses.

The problem addressed here is the creation of a pattern recognition algorithm suitable for the scalable recognition of simple patterns in large, heterogeneous, potentially real-time sets of data. One question arising immediately when one considers such an algorithm is the nature of the data representation. Here we assume a hypergraph representation (a very general representation that is suitable for basically any kind of discrete data and some varieties of continuous data as well), and present an algorithm called Fishgram (Frequent Interesting Subhypergraph Mining), which mines frequent or otherwise interesting subhypergraphs from (large or small) hypergraphs. Algorithmically, Fishgram is in the same broad family as frequent itemset and subgraph mining algorithms; but it involves many specific choices made to ensure its practical utility in an AGI context.

J. Bach, B. Goertzel, and M. Iklé (Eds.): AGI 2012, LNAI 7716, pp. 189–198, 2012.

Fishgram was designed primarily for use within the OpenCog integrative AGI framework [1], and has been implemented in this context. It represents patterns as a conjunction (AndLink) of OpenCog Links, which usually contain OpenCog VariableNodes. Concrete examples of Fishgram's utilization within OpenCog will be presented here, in the context of OpenCog's application to control virtual agents in a game world. In this example context, the patterns recognized by Fishgram are combinations of predicates representing basic perceptions (e.g. what kind of object something is, objects being near each other, types of blocks, and actions being performed by the user or the AI). However, the Fishgram algorithm is not intrinsically restricted to the agent control domain nor to OpenCog, and could be used much more broadly, e.g. in a narrow AI data mining context, or in the context of any other integrative AGI architecture that is able to present its knowledge in hypergraph format.

2   The OpenCog Integrative AGI Framework

OpenCog is an open-source AGI software framework, which has been used for various practical applications, and also for the in-progress implementation of the OpenCogPrime design aimed ultimately toward AGI at the human level and beyond. OpenCog has been used for commercial applications in the area of natural language processing and data mining; e.g. see [2]. It has also been used to control virtual agents in virtual worlds, at first using an OpenCog variant called the OpenPetBrain [3], and more recently in a more general way using a Minecraft-like virtual environment [1].

Conceptually founded on the "patternist" systems theory of intelligence outlined in [4], OpenCogPrime combines multiple AI paradigms such as uncertain logic, computational linguistics, evolutionary program learning and connectionist attention allocation in a unified architecture. Cognitive processes embodying these different paradigms interoperate together on a common neural-symbolic hypergraph knowledge store called the Atomspace. The interaction of these processes is designed to encourage the self-organizing emergence of high-level network structures in the Atomspace, including superposed hierarchical and heterarchical knowledge networks, and a self-model network enabling meta-learning.

OCP relies on multiple memory types (all intersecting via the AtomSpace, even when also involving specialized representations), including the declarative, procedural, sensory, and episodic memory types that are widely discussed in cognitive neuroscience [5], plus attentional memory for allocating system resources generically, and intentional memory for allocating system resources in a goal-directed way. Declarative memory is addressed via probabilistic inference; procedural memory via probabilistic evolutionary program learning; episodic memory via simulation; intentional memory via a largely declarative goal system; attentional memory via an economics-based dynamical system similar to an attractor neural network.

The essence of the OCP design lies in the way the structures and processes associated with each type of memory are designed to work together in a closely coupled way, the operative hypothesis being that this will yield cooperative emergent intelligence.

2.1 The Atomspace Representation

OpenCog's "Atomspace" knowledge representation is a generalized hypergraph formalism which comprises a specific vocabulary of Node and Link types, used to represent declarative knowledge and also, indirectly, other types of knowledge as well. There is a specific vocabulary of a couple dozen node and link types with semantics carefully chosen to reflect the needs of OpenCog's cognitive processes. Simple examples of OpenCog links, in the notation commonly used with OpenCog, are:

```
InheritanceLink Ben_Goertzel animal <.99>

EvaluationLink <.7>
    chase
    ListLink
        cat
        mouse
```

Examples using nodes with English-word labels provide convenient examples, but in fact most nodes in a practical OpenCog system will generally be automatically learned and not correspond directly to any human-language concept.

What's important about the AtomSpace knowledge representation is mainly that it provides a flexible means for compactly representing multiple relevant forms of knowledge, in a way that allows them to interoperate – where by "interoperate" we mean that e.g. a fragment of a chunk of declarative knowledge can link to a fragment of a chunk of attentional or procedural knowledge; or a chunk of knowledge in one category can overlap with a chunk of knowledge in another category (as when the same link has both a (declarative) truth value and an (attentional) importance value).

3   The Fishgram Algorithm

Fishgram was developed because OpenCog, which represents knowledge internally using a hypergraph called the Atomspace, needed a fast, scalable, greedy subhypergraph mining algorithm. At first, an attempt was made to find an existing subgraph mining algorithm that would suit the purpose (since mapping hypergraphs into graphs can be done straightforwardly). It was found that no existing algorithms fit the bill, so a novel algorithm was developed.

This reflects a pattern that we have found to occur fairly often in the development of OpenCog. When OpenCog requires a component that relies on the concepts already studied extensively in some area of computer science, it usually turns out that no existing algorithm or software package sufficiently meets OpenCog's requirements. Existing algorithms and software packages have generally been designed and implemented to operate stand-alone, or within software pipelines oriented to particular narrow tasks; and nearly always, it seems that making algorithms to inter-operate with other algorithms and structures in an AGI context places different requirements.

In this case, we found that frequent *itemset* mining algorithms are not conveniently applicable to subhypergraph mining, as representing hypergraphs in the required tabular format is awkward and introduces large inefficiencies. On the other hand, we found that most other graph mining algorithms were designed with molecular datasets in mind (see [6] [7] for overviews of the frequent subgraph mining literature). The OpenCog AtomSpace is a different sort of graph from these in various ways. For example, in the Atomspace

- there are many possible relations between each pair of nodes (much like in a semantic network)
- many relations involve more than two objects, and there are also properties predicates about a single object. So the relations are effectively directed links of varying arity.
- there are many events represented, and many states can change over time (e.g. an egg changes state while it's cooking)

Unlike other subgraph mining algorithms, Fishgram is designed for general knowledge in an embodied agent.

The largest inspirations for the Fishgram algorithm were the GSpan frequent subgraph mining algorithm [8], and the handling of variable bindings in standard inductive learning systems like FOIL [9]. Among the main differences between Fishgram and GSpan are Fishgram's use of breadth-first search, and its more flexible management of variable bindings in a roughly FOIL-like way.

Fishgram uses a breadth-first search, rather than depth-first search as is the case with most subgraph mining algorithms. This is appropriate for use in an intelligent agent which is looking to learn a broad variety of regularities in its environment – a very different use case from searching for specific patterns in a molecular database. Also, Fishgram does an embedding-based search, searching for patterns that can be embedded multiple times in a large graph. Molecular datasets have many separate graphs for separate molecules; embodied perceptions are closer to a single, fairly well-connected graph. Depth-first search would be very slow on such a graph, as there are many very long paths and the search would mostly find those. Whereas in an embodied-agent-control use case, the useful patterns tend to be compact and repeated many times.

The design of Fishgram makes it easy to experiment with multiple different scoring functions, from simple ones like frequency to much more sophisticated functions such as interaction information [10]. It also makes it easy to guide and customize the pattern search in various ways. In typical Fishgram uses, one may specify a certain category of entities about which one is particularly interested to recognize patterns (e.g. virtual-world objects, in a virtual agent control context), and one may also specify whether one is especially interested in spatial, temporal patterns or neither.

3.1   Pseudocode

Pseudocode for Fishgram is as follows. For simplicity, this assumes a certain set of "distinguished" entities has been identified, and that temporal but not spatial patterns are of interest.

```
initial layer = every pair (relation, binding)

while previous layer is not empty:
    foreach (conjunction, binding) in previous layer:
        let incoming = all (relation, binding) pairs
                    containing an "distinguished entity"
                    in the conjunction
        let possible_next_events = all (event, binding) pairs
                    where the event happens during or shortly
                    after the last event in conjunction
        foreach (relation, relation_binding) in incoming
                    and possible_next_events:
            (new_relation, new_conjunction_binding) =
                                    map_to_existing_variables(conjunction,
                                    binding, relation, relation_binding)
            if new_relation is already in conjunction, skip it
            new_conjunction = conjunction + new_relation
            if new_conjunction has been found already, skip it
            otherwise, add (new_conjunction,
                        new_conjunction_binding)
                        to the current layer

map_to_existing_variables(conjunction, conjunction_binding,
                    relation, relation_binding)
    r', s' = a copy of the relation and binding using new variables
    foreach variable v, object o in relation_binding:
        foreach variable v2, object o2 in conjunction_binding:
            if o == o2:
                change r' and s' to use v2 instead of v
    return r',s
```

To generalize the above to recognize spatial as well as temporal patterns, it suffices to introduce *possible_nearby_events* analogous to *possible_next_events* in the above.

3.2   Preprocessing

The Fishgram implementation includes several preprocessing steps that make it easier for the main Fishgram search to find patterns. There is a filter system, so that things which seem irrelevant can be excluded from the search. And, one can explicitly specify a list of "distinguished entities" that have to be treated by Fishgram as variables. For example, in a typical virtual world application, any predicate that refers to objects (including agents) will be given a variable so it can refer to any object. Other predicates or InheritanceLinks can be added to a pattern, to restrict it to specific kinds of objects, as will be shown in the examples given below. So there is a step which goes through all of the links in the AtomSpace, and records a list of predicates with variables, such as X is red or X eats Y. This makes the search part simpler, because it never has to decide whether something should be a variable or a specific object.

Also, in the current implementation, there is some customization to ease the recognition of temporal patterns in an agent-control context. The increased predicate is added to potential patterns via a preprocessing step. The OpenCog agent's goals have a fuzzy TruthValue representing how well the goal is achieved at any point in time, so that e.g. EnergyDemandGoal represents how much energy the virtual robot has at some point in time. The "increased" predicate, in this case, records times that a goal's TruthValue increased.

3.3   The Search Process

The Fishgram search, as depicted above, is breadth-first. It starts with all predicates (or InheritanceLinks) found by the preprocessing step. Then it finds pairs of predicates involving the same variable. Then they are extended to conjunctions of three predicates, and so on. Many relations apply at a specific time, for example the agent being near an object, or an action being performed. These are included in a sequence, and are added in the order they occurred.

Fishgram remembers the examples for each pattern. If there is only one variable in the pattern, an example is a single object; otherwise each example is a vector of objects for each variable in the pattern. Each time a relation is added to a pattern, if it has no new variables, some of the examples may be removed, because they don't satisfy the new predicate. It needs to have at least one variable in common with the previous relations. Otherwise the patterns would combine many unrelated things.

In frequent itemset mining (for example APRIORI [11]), there is effectively one variable, and adding a new predicate will often decrease the number of items that match. It can never increase it. The number of possible conjunctions increases with the length, up to some point, after which it decreases. But when mining for patterns with multiple objects there is a much larger combinatorial explosion of patterns. Various criteria can be used to prune the search.

The most basic criterion is the frequency. Only patterns with at least N examples will be included, where N is an arbitrary constant. You can also set a maximum number of patterns allowed for each length (number of relations), and only include the best ones. The next level of the breadth-first search will only search for extensions of those patterns. Similar dynamics may be used with criteria more sophisticated than frequency.

4   Example Patterns

What we see here is that, in this particular Atomspace, the algorithm found a significant number of patterns of moderate length and reasonably high frequency.

To illustrate Fishgram's operation, we present some concrete examples obtained via running Fishgram on a small AtomSpace, derived via allowing an OpenCog agent to control a simulated robot agent in a small virtual world containing a house and some batteries. The Atomspace was obtained via running OpenCog to control the agent in this environment for roughly 5 minutes. The environment contained 32 objects, and 98 timestamps corresponding to moments at which events occurred. A preprocessing step noticed TimeNodes the agent's EnergyDemandGoal's TruthValue increased or decreased. The events involved, in which Fishgram recognized patterns, included appearance and disappearance of objects, and grabbing, eating and holding on the part of the agent.

Following is a list of the EvaluationLinks and InheritanceLinks in this small, test Atomspace:

```
(EvaluationLink is_edible:PredicateNode (ListLink $0)): 9,
(EvaluationLink is_toy:PredicateNode (ListLink $0)): 1,
(EvaluationLink is_small:PredicateNode (ListLink $0)): 3,
(EvaluationLink isHoldingSomething:PredicateNode (ListLink $0)): 1,
(EvaluationLink at_home:PredicateNode (ListLink $0)): 1,
(InheritanceLink $0 Battery:ConceptNode): 9,
(InheritanceLink $0 ClawSwitch:ConceptNode): 1,
(InheritanceLink $0 Pet:ConceptNode): 2,
(InheritanceLink $0 Avatar:ConceptNode): 2,
(InheritanceLink $0 BatterySwitch:ConceptNode): 1,
(InheritanceLink $0 Soccerball:ConceptNode): 1,
(InheritanceLink $0 pet_home:ConceptNode): 1,
(InheritanceLink $0 Home:ConceptNode): 1,
(InheritanceLink $0 robotic:ConceptNode): 1,
(InheritanceLink $0 Player:ConceptNode): 1,
(InheritanceLink $0 egg:ConceptNode): 3,
(InheritanceLink $0 dish:ConceptNode): 3,
(InheritanceLink $0 TheLiftButton:ConceptNode): 1,
(InheritanceLink $0 TheLift:ConceptNode): 1,
(InheritanceLink $0 Crate:ConceptNode): 1,
(InheritanceLink $0 table:ConceptNode): 1,
(InheritanceLink $0 chair:ConceptNode): 1,
(InheritanceLink $0 pan:ConceptNode): 1,
(InheritanceLink $0 stoveButton:ConceptNode): 1,
(InheritanceLink $0 cookTop:ConceptNode): 1,
(InheritanceLink $0 Lightning Cloud:ConceptNode): 1
```

Figure 1 depicts the number of patterns of different sizes recognized by Fishgram on this particular Atomspace. What we see there is that, in this particular Atomspace, the algorithm found a significant number of patterns of moderate length and low but non-trivial frequency. Few high-frequency patterns of any length were found.

To give a more concrete sense of what Fishgram is doing, following is some example output from Fishgram from this Atomspace:

```
(AndLink
    (EvaluationLink is_edible:PredicateNode (ListLink $1000041))
    (InheritanceLink $1000041 Battery:ConceptNode)
)
```

This means a battery which can be eaten by the virtual robot. The variable $1000041 refers to the object (battery).

Fishgram can also find patterns containing a sequence of events. In this case, there is a list of EvaluationLinks or InheritanceLinks which describe the objects involved, followed by the sequence of events.

```
(AndLink
    (InheritanceLink $1007703 Battery:ConceptNode)
    (SequentialAndLink
        (EvaluationLink isHolding:PredicateNode
                (ListLink $1008725 $1007703)))
    )
)
```

Number of patterns by length and frequency

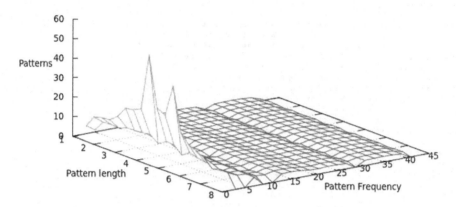

Fig. 1. Statistics of Patterns Recognized by Fishgram in an Example OpenCog Atomspace

This means the agent was holding a battery (denoted $1007703); note there is also a variable for the agent itself. This pattern would also apply to the user (or another AI) holding a battery, because the pattern does not refer to the AI character specifically.

Fishgram can find patterns where it performs an action and achieves a goal. There is code to create implications based on these conjunctions . There is code that outputs causal patterns using a postprocessing system, which uses a conjunction to create a nested structure of ImplicationLinks, PredictiveImplicationLinks and SequentialAndLinks. After finding many conjunctions, it can produce ImplicationLinks based on some of them. Here is an example where the AI-controlled virtual robot discovers how to get energy.

```
(ImplicationLink
    (AndLink
        (EvaluationLink is_edible:PredicateNode (ListLink $1011619))
        (InheritanceLink $1011619 Battery:ConceptNode)
    )
    (PredictiveImplicationLink
        (EvaluationLink actionDone:PredicateNode
                (ListLink (ExecutionLink
                    eat:GroundedSchemaNode
                        (ListLink $1011619))))
        (EvaluationLink increased:PredicateNode
                (ListLink (EvaluationLink
                    EnergyDemandGoal:PredicateNode)))
    )
)
```

5   Conclusions and Future Work

Our work with Fishgram so far has validated the general viability of the Fishgram algorithm within an OpenCog integrative AGI approach to embodied agent control. However, the current, initial implementation of Fishgram has significant limitations, which we plan to remedy incrementally in the context of utilizing Fishgram to help OpenCog control intelligent agents.

One limitation worth noting is that the current Fishgram algorithm cannot handle patterns involving numbers, although it could be extended to do so. The two options would be to either have a separate discretization step, creating predicates for different ranges of a value; or alternatively, to have predicates for mathematical operators. It would be possible to search for a split point like in decision trees – so that a number would be chosen, and only things above that value (or only things below that value) would count for a pattern. It would also be possible to have multiple numbers in a pattern, and compare them in various ways.

Another issue worth considering is scalability. Like essentially all data mining algorithms, Fishgram can achieve scalability only at the cost of aggressive pruning of candidate combinations. This aspect has not prevented classic data mining algorithms from being applied at very large scale. However, from a general intelligence perspective, it seems clear that Fishgram will need to be complemented by other algorithms that, via incorporation of more intelligent search or pruning heuristics, are able to find more complex patterns even from very large knowledge bases.

While our work so far has focused on recognizing frequent patterns, it will be important for future applications to supplement the frequency criterion with a measure of statistical interestingness, which ensures that the relations in a pattern are genuinely correlated with each other. Using frequency as the criterion results in many spurious frequent patterns, because anything which is frequent will occur together with other things, whether they are relevant or not. For example breathing while typing is a frequent pattern, because people breathe at all times. But moving your hands while typing is a much more interesting pattern. As people only move their hands some of the time, a measure of correlation would prefer the second pattern. Based on our study of the matter, we have tentatively concluded that the best measure may be interaction information, which is a generalization of mutual information that applies to patterns with more than two predicates [10], or variations on interaction information intended to identify multi-variable synergies even more finely [12]. In a learning-oriented AGI paradigm like OpenCog, an early-stage AGI does not have much knowledge of real-world structures and dynamics built in, so it must rely on statistical measures like these to find useful patterns.

References

1. Goertzel, B., Pitt, J., Cai, Z., Wigmore, J., Huang, D., Geisweiller, N., Lian, R., Yu, G.: Integrative general intelligence for controlling game ai in a minecraft-like environment. In: Proc. of BICA 2011 (2011)
2. Goertzel, B., Pinto, H., Pennachin, C., Goertzel, I.F.: Using dependency parsing and probabilistic inference to extract relationships between genes, proteins and

malignancies implicit among multiple biomedical research abstracts. In: Proc. of Bio-NLP 2006 (2006)

3. Goertzel, B., Pennachin, C., et al.: An integrative methodology for teaching embodied non-linguistic agents, applied to virtual animals in second life. In: Proc. of the First Conf. on AGI. IOS Press (2008)

4. Goertzel, B.: The Hidden Pattern. Brown Walker (2006)

5. Tulving, E., Craik, R.: The Oxford Handbook of Memory. Oxford U. Press (2005)

6. Washio, T., Motoda, H.: State of the art of graph-based data mining. SIGKDD Explorations 5, 59–68 (2003)

7. Keyvanpour, M., Azizani, F.: Classification of approaches and challenges of frequent subgraphs mining in biological networks. Int. J. Adv. Eng. Sci. and Tech. 4 (2012)

8. Yan, X., Han, J.: gspan: Graph-based substructure pattern mining. In: ICDM 2002 (2002)

9. Quinlan, J.R.: Learning logical definitions from relations. Machine Learning 5 (1990)

10. Bell, A.J.: The co-information lattice. In: Proc. ICA 2003 (2003)

11. Agrawal, R., Srikant, R.: Fast algorithms for mining association rules. In: Proc. 20th Int. Conf. Very Large Data Bases (1994)

12. Williams, P.L., Beer, R.D.: Nonnegative decomposition of multivariate information. CoRR abs/1004.2515 (2010)

Pursuing Artificial General Intelligence by Leveraging the Knowledge Capabilities of ACT-R

Alessandro Oltramari and Christian Lebiere

Department of Psychology, Carnegie Mellon University, Pittsburgh, USA

Abstract. Intelligence is a multifaceted phenomenon which makes trying to capture its very essence a slippery task. In this paper, we commit to a hybrid notion of intelligence, conceived as the combination of cognitive operations and knowledge resources that leads to purposeful behavior. Accordingly, this paper describes an artificial system that benefits from both **mechanism–centered** and **knowledge–centered** approaches. In particular, the system integrates the ACT-R cognitive architecture with SCONE, a knowledge-based system for ontological reasoning, to combine ACT-R's subsymbolic cognitive mechanisms with SCONE's knowledge representation and inference capabilities. We apply the hybrid system to computationally approximate human intelligent behavior in a task of visual recognition.

1 Introduction

'An architecture without content is like a computer without software - it is an empty shell"[1]

"What is intelligence?". From the dawn of Western Thought to the Contemporary (scientific) Age, scholars from different disciplines have struggled to answer this question. Despite the broad range of seemingly intelligent manifestations in the natural realm, the key to solve this problem relies on the very same *questioner*, i.e. on narrowing down the focus to the main features of *human* intelligence. In his 1950 seminal work [2], Alan Turing assessed the centrality of behavior to define intelligence: a suitable game needs to be designed where humans and machines have to answer to a human interrogator who is set in a room apart from the players; in this scenario, a machine will be considered intelligent if and only if it would be able to *imitate* human behavior to the extent of not being unmasked by the interrogator. As Turing pointed out, the type of the game is not important: what is central, instead, is that it allows to evaluate humans and machines' *behavior*, by their moves, strategies and, ultimately, answers. In this paper we are neither discussing the philosophical implications of the behaviorist perspective, nor providing a critical analysis of behaviorism with respect to internalism, where the 'faculty of mental representation' (as Kant would name it

---

[1] Quotation from [1], p. 18.

J. Bach, B. Goertzel, and M. Iklé (Eds.): AGI 2012, LNAI 7716, pp. 199–208, 2012.
© Springer-Verlag Berlin Heidelberg 2012

[3]) becomes a necessary condition for acknowledging intelligence [4]. Rather, we adopt a hybrid framework: trying to overcome the classic tension between task-specific *narrow* AI and task-independent *strong* AI, this article focuses on intelligence as *knowledge in action*, namely as "the combination of cognitive operations and knowledge resources that leads to purposeful behavior" [1]. In particular, we describe an artificial system that benefits from both **mechanism–centered** and **knowledge–centered** approaches to computationally approximate human intelligent behavior in a task of visual recognition[5].

2   Extending ACT-R with a Knowledge Component

Integration is the key to intelligent behavior: learning mechanisms determine which knowledge can be acquired and in which form and specific knowledge contents provide stringent requirements for mechanisms to be able to access and process them effectively. This mutual dependence between mechanism and knowledge is well reflected in the ACT-R cognitive architecture [6], a modular framework whose components include perceptual, motor and memory modules (see figure 1). After a brief introduction of ACT-R core features (section 2.1), we describe how the cognitive architecture can be leveraged by means of a dedicated knowledge compontent (section 2.2), fostering high-level deductive reasoning.

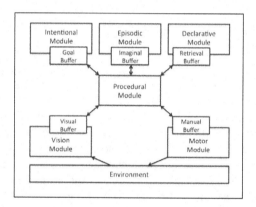

Fig. 1. ACT-R modular structure elaborates information from the environment at different levels

2.1   ACT-R

ACT-R integrates declarative and procedural knowledge, the latter being conceived as a set of procedures (production rules) that coordinate information processing between its various modules: accordingly, an ACT-R model can accomplish specific goals on the basis of declarative representations elaborated through procedural steps (in the form of *if-then productions*). At the symbolic level, ACT-R performs two major operations on *Declarative Memory* (DM):

i) accumulating knowledge units (i.e., *chunks*) learned from internal operations or from interaction with the environment and ii) retrieving chunks that provide needed information. Both chunk learning and retrieval are performed through limited capacity buffers that constrain the size and capacity of the chunks in DM. ACT-R has accounted for a broad range of cognitive activities at a high level of fidelity, reproducing aspects of human data such as learning, errors, latencies, eye movements and patterns of brain activity (refer to [7] for more details). Although it is not our purpose in this paper to present the details of the architecture, two specific sub-symbolic mechanisms need to be mentioned here to sketch how the system works: i) *partial matching* - the probability that two different knowledge units (or *declarative chunks*) can be associated on the basis of an adequate measure of similarity (this is what happens when we consider, for instance, that a bag is more likely to resemble a basket than a baseball bat); ii) *spreading of activation* - when the same chunk is connected to multiple contexts, it contributes to distributionally activate all of them (e.g., a polysemous word like bag can be associated to different activities like travelling, shopping, eating, etc.)[2].

2.2 SCONE

Inasmuch as humans understand their surroundings by means of coupling perception with knowledge, the ACT-R cognitive architecture should be enabled to generalize over perceptual transductions by applying fine-grained models of the world to concrete scenarios. In order to fulfill this goal however, ACT-R needs to properly encapsulate those models – or *ontologies* – and exploit them for pattern recognition and high-level reasoning. Since ACT-R declarative module supports a relatively coarse-grained semantics based on slot-value pairs, and the procedural system is not optimal to effectively manage complex logical constructs (e.g., 2nd order), a specific extension is needed to make ACT-R suitable to fulfill knowledge-intensive tasks. Accordingly, we engineered an extra module as a bridging component between the cognitive architecture and an external knowledge-base system, SCONE [8]. SCONE is an open–source knowledge-base system intended for use as a component in many different software applications: it provides a LISP-based framework to represent and reason over symbolic common–sense knowledge. Unlike most diffuse KB systems, SCONE is not based on Description Logics [9]: its inference engine adopts marker–passing algorithms [8] (originally designed for massive parallel computing) to perform fast queries at the price of losing logical completeness and decidability. In particular, SCONE represents knowledge as a *semantic network* whose nodes are locally weighted (*marked*) and associated to arcs (*wires*[3]) in order to optimize basic reasoning tasks (e.g. class membership, transitivity, inheritance of properties, etc). The philosophy that inspired SCONE is straightforward: from vision to speech, humans

---

[2] Section 3 will show in more details how these two mechanisms can be exploited by an artificial system to disambiguate visual signals.

[3] In general, a *wire* can be conceived as a binary relation whose domain and range are referred to, respectively, as A-node and B-node.

exploit the brain's massive parallelism to fulfill all recognition tasks; if we want to build an AGI system that is able to deal with the large amount of knowledge required in common-sense reasoning, we need to rely on a mechanism that is fast and effective enough to simulate parallel search. Shortcomings are not an issue since humans are not perfect inference engines either. Accordingly, SCONE implementation of marker–passing algorithms aims at simulating a pseudo-parallel search by assigning specific marker bits to each knowledge unit. For example, if we want to query a KB to get all the parts of cars, SCONE would assign a marker M1 to the A-node CAR and search for all the statements in the knowledge base where M1 is the A-wire (domain) of the relation PART-OF, returning all the classes in the range of the relation (also called 'B-nodes'). SCONE would finally assign the marker bit M2 to all B-nodes, also retrieving all the inherited subclasses[4]. The modularization and implementation of an ontology with SCONE allows for an effective formal representation and inferencing of core ontological properties of world entities. In general we refer to ACT-R including the SCONE module as ACT-RK, meaning 'ACT-R with improved Knowledge capabilities' (the reader can easily notice the evolution from the original ACT-R architecture – figure 1 – to the knowledge-enabled one – figure 2). This integration allows for dynamic queries to be automatically submitted to an external ontology by ACT-RK whenever the perceptual information is incomplete, corrupted or when common-sense reasoning capabilities are needed to generalize over perceptual information filtered from the environment. In this way, ACT-RK is also able to overcome situations with missing input: mechanisms of partial matching and spreading activation [7] can fill the possible gap(s) in the input stream and retrieve the best–matching piece of background knowledge. In particular, in the second part of the paper we describe how an ACT-RK model can perform an action recognition task. Note that the integration of SCONE into ACT-R respects the general cognitive constraints of the architecture, especially in terms of limited-capacity buffers constraining communication between the module and the rest of the architecture. Also, the SCONE marker-passing algorithms are similar to ACT-R spreading activation, leaving open the possibility of a deeper integration of the two frameworks in future work. In principle, if it is true that ACT-R can *per se* deal with simple logical reasoning on the basis of its production mechanisms, when knowledge-intensive tasks come into play an external KBS like SCONE becomes a crucial plug-in for augmenting ACT-R scalability, computational efficiency, and semantic adequacy.

3   Simulating Visual Intelligence with an ACT-RK Model

'Visual intelligence' is the human capability to understand a scene by means of recognizing the core interactions holding between the most salient entities detected from the environment. In this sense, perceptual data, conceptual representations and reasoning are combined together by humans to *make sense* of a scene: for instance, when we *see* a dog chasing a flying stick thrown by a person,

---

[4] We refer the reader to [8] for details concerning marker–passing algorithms.

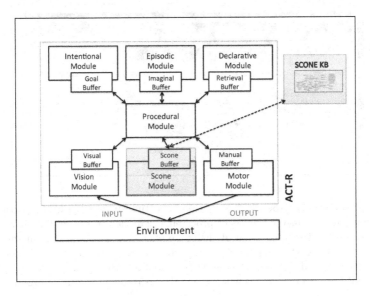

Fig. 2. The ACTR-RK framework

first we identify the type of entities into play (dog, person, stick) and then we break the complex event into smaller components (e.g., the person extending the arm from the back, the dog jumping and running, the stick falling on the ground, etc.), inferring its teleological features (make the dog play and bring back the stick) and causal nexus (when the person's hand releases the stick, it starts moving on air with a curved trajectory whose range depends on the exerted force). It is clear that we are not just *seeing* with the eyes but our mental representations and cognitive processing are also involved. Reproducing this capability at the machine level requires a comprehensive infrastructure where low-level visual detectors and algorithms couple with high-level knowledge representations and processing: this is the goal of the DARPA Mind's Eye program[5], where an artificial visual systems is considered to be (*behaviorally*) intelligent if it is able to process a video dataset of various human actions[6] and output the probability distribution (per video) of a pre-defined list of verbs, including 'walk', 'run', 'carry', 'pick-up', 'haul', 'follow', 'chase', 'exchange', 'open', 'close', etc.[7]. Performance is measured in terms of consistency with human responses to stimuli (*Ground Truth*): subjects have to acknowledge the presence/absence of every verb in each video. In order to meet these requirements, we devised an ACT-RK model to work in a human-like fashion, trying to disambiguate the scene in terms of the most reliable perceptual and conceptual structures. Because of space limitations, we can't provide the details of a large-scale evaluation: nevertheless, in what follows we discuss an example to describe the functionalities of the system.

---

[5] http://www.darpa.mil/Our_Work/I2O/Programs/Minds_Eye.aspx
[6] http://www.visint.org/datasets.html
[7] This list has been provided by DARPA.

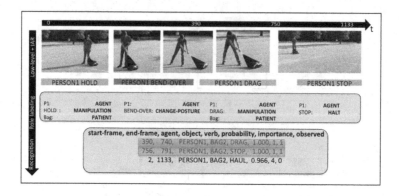

Fig. 3. The horizontal arrow represents the video time frames while the vertical one represents the interconnected levels of processing. The box in the middle displays the results of semantic disambiguation of the scene elements, while the box in the bottm contains the schema of the output, where importance reflects the number of components in a pattern (1-4) and *observed* is a boolean parameter whose value is 1 when a verb matches a visual detection and 0 when the verb is a result of cognitive processing.

Figure 3 schematizes the ACT-RK model core functions, namely to semantically parse temporally-ordered atomic events previously extracted from low-level computer vision systems [10], e.g. 'hold' (micro-state) and 'bend-over', 'drag', 'stop' (micro-actions), associating frames and roles to visual input from the videos. This specific information is retrieved from the HOMINE ('Hybrid Ontology for the Mind's Eye project') ontology, in particular from a fragment of the ontology which has been built on top of the FrameNet lexical resource [11]: frames and semantic roles are assembled in suitable chunk types and encoded in the declarative memory of ACT-RK[8]. As with human annotators performing semantic role labeling [12], the model associates verbs denoting atomic events to corresponding frames. When related mechanisms are activated, the model retrieves the roles played by the entities in the scene, for each atomic event[9]: e.g., 'hold' evokes the *manipulation* frame, whose core role *agent* can be associated to 'person1' (as showed in light-green box of the figure). In order to prompt a choice within the patterns of action encoded in the ontology (see table 1), sub-symbolic computations for *spreading activation* are executed [7]. Spreading of activation from the contents of frames and roles triggers the evocation of related ontology patterns.

The core sub-symbolic computations performed by the ACT-RK model can be expressed by the equation in figure 4.

---

[8] HOMinE has been implemented into SCONE KBS and represents an extension of the SCONE core ontology for action types, as the reader can see in figure 5.

[9] Entities and atomic events are visually recognized using suitable features detectors, object tracking algorithms and SVM classifiers.

Table 1. An excerpt of the roles and atomic components (C1-C4) constituing the patterns of actions for the model

Action	Role1	Role2	Role3	Role4	C1	C2	C3	C4
Arrive	self-mover	theme			walk	stop		
Give	agent	carrier	agent		holding	transport	drop	
Take	carrier	agent	agent		transport	drop	holding	
Exchange	agent	agent	agent		give	take	swap	
Carry	agent	carrier	agent		holding	transport	pull	
Pick-up	protagonist	agent	protagonist	agent	bend-over	lower-arm	stand-up	holding
Put-down	agent	protagonist	agent	figure1	holding	bend-over	lower-arm	on
Haul	protagonist	agent	agent	agent	bend-over	extend-arm	holding	drag

$$A_i = \ln \sum_j t_j^{-d} + \sum_k W_k S_{ki} + \sum_l MP_l Sim_{li} + N(0,\sigma)$$

Fig. 4. Equation for Bayesian Activation Pattern Matching

- **1st term**: the more recently and frequently a chunk i has been retrieved, the higher its activation and the chances of being retrieved. In our context i can be conceived as a pattern of action (e.g., the pattern of HAUL), where t_j is the time elapsed since the jth reference to chunk i and d represents the memory decay rate.
- **2nd term**: the contextual activation of a chunk i is set by the attentional weight W_k given the element k and the strength of association S_{ki} between an element k and the chunk i. In our context, k can be interpreted as the value BEND-OVER of the pattern HAUL in figure 3.
- **3rd term**: under partial matching, ACT-RK can retrieve the chunk that matches the retrieval constraints to the greatest degree, combining the similarity Sim_{li} between l and i (a negative score that is assigned to discriminate the 'distance' between two terms) with the scaling mismatch penalty MP. In our context, for example, the value PULL could have been retrieved, instead of DRAG. This mechanism is particularly useful when verbs are continuously changing - as in the case of a complex visual input stream.
- **4th term**: randomness in the retrieval process by adding Gaussian noise.

As mentioned in 2.1, *partial matching* based on similarity measures and *spreading of activation* based on compositionality are the main mechanisms used by the model: in particular, we constrained semantic similarity within verbs to the 'gloss–vector' measure computed over WordNet synsets [13]. Base–level activations of verbs actions have been derived by frequency analysis of the American National Corpus[10]: in particular, this choice reflects the fact that the more frequent a verb, the more likely it is to be activated by our system. Additionally, strengths of associations are set (or learned) by the architecture to reflect the number of patterns to which each atomic event is associated, the so-called 'fan

---

[10] http://www.americannationalcorpus.org/

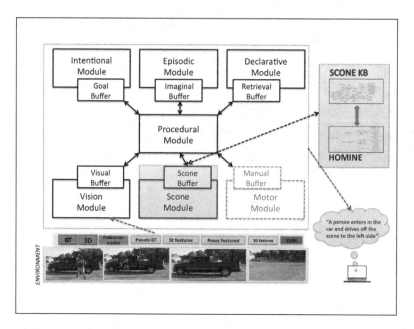

Fig. 5. A Diagram of the ACT-RK model querying HOMinE ontology through SCONE

effect' controlling information retrieval in many real-world domains [14]. Last but not least, the ACT-RK model can output the results of extra-reasoning functions by means of suitable queries submitted to HOMINE via the scone module. In the example in figure 3, object classifiers and tracking algorithms could not detect that 'person1' is dragging 'bag2' by pulling a rope: this failure in the visual algorithms is motivated by the fact that the rope is a very thin and morphologically unstable artifact, hence difficult to be spotted by state-of-the-art machine vision. Nevertheless, HOMINE contains an axiom stating that: "For every x,y,e,z such that $P(x)$ is a person, $GB(y)$ is a Bag and $DRAG(e,x,y,T)$ is an event e of type DRAG (whose participants are x and y) occurring in the closed interval of time T, there is at least a z which is a proper part of y and that participates to e"[11]. Moreover, suppose that in a continuation of the video, the same person drops the bag, gets in a car and leaves the scene (see figure 5). The visual algorithms would have serious difficulties in tracking the person while driving the car, since the person would become partially occluded, assume an irregular shape and would not properly lit. Again, ACT-RK could overcome these problems in the visual system by using SCONE to call HOMINE and automatically perform the following schematized inference: 1) cars move; 2) every

---

[11] Note that here we are paraphrasing an axiom that exploits Davidsonian event semantics [15] and basic principles of formal mereology (see [16] and [17]). Also, this axiom is valid if every bag has a rope: this is generally true when considering garbage bags like the one depicted in figure3, but exceptions would need to be addressed in a more comprehensive scenario.

car needs exactly one driver to move[12]; 2) drivers are persons; 3) driver is located inside a car; 4) a car moves then the person driving it also moves in the same direction. Thanks to the inferential mechanisms embedded in its knowedge infrastructure, the ACT-RK model is not bound to visual input as an exclusive source of information: in human-like fashion, it has the capability of coupling visual signals with background knowledge, performing high-level reasoning and disambiguating the original input perceived from the environment. In particular, the chunks created through the vision module on the basis of computer vision algorithms (schematized by the boxes on top of the video snippets in figure 5) are represented according to suitable chunk types in the declarative memory and used as input to the scone module. That module then becomes an (internal) information source in its own right, treated by the cognitive architecture in a similar way to the (external) visual information stream.

4   Conclusion

In this paper we outlined the core infrastructure of a high-level artificial visual intelligent system, focusing on the underlying grounding principles and presenting some functional examples. This system can be conceived as an ACT-RK model, namely an instance of the cognitive mechanisms of ACT-R and of the reasoning operations of SCONE KBS: in this respect, it can be seen as an attempt at accomplishing a complex task on the basis of a general approach to Artificial Intelligence, where cognitive mechanisms are integrated in a knowledge–centered reasoning framework. Future work will be devoted to enrich the knowledge component of the system and using reasoning and statistical inferences to derive and predict goals of agents in performing a given action. Finally, we are exploring the possibility of implementing a core mechanism of abductive reasoning to enable information selection from complex visual streams based on saliency. As we began this article standing on the shoulders of a giant, Alan Turing, no better conclusion could come than from him: *"We can only see a short distance ahead but we can see plenty there that needs to be done"*.

Acknowledgments. This research was sponsored by the Army Research Laboratory and was accomplished under Cooperative Agreement Number W911NF-10-2-0061. The views and conclusions contained in this document are those of the authors and should not be interpreted as representing the official policies, either expressed or implied, of the Army Research Laboratory or the U.S. Government. The U.S. Government is authorized to reproduce and distribute reprints for Government purposes notwithstanding any copyright notation herein.

References

1. Laird, J.E.: The SOAR Cognitive Architecture. The MIT Press (2012)
2. Turing, A.M.: Computing machinery and intelligence. MIND 59(236), 433–460 (1950)

---

[12] With some exceptions, especially in California, around Mountain View!

3. Kant, I.: Critique of judgment; translated, with an introduction, by Pluhar, W.S.; with a foreword by Gregor, M. Hackett Pub. Co., Indianapolis (1987)
4. Stich, S.: From folk psychology to cognitive science. The MIT Press, Cambridge (1983)
5. Oltramari, A., Lebiere, C.: Mechanism meet content: Integrating cognitive architectures and ontologies. In: Proceedings of AAAI 2011 Fall Symposium of "Advances in Cognitive Systems" (2011)
6. Anderson, J.: How Can the Human Mind Occur in the Physical Universe? Oxford University Press (2007)
7. Anderson, J., Lebiere, C.: The Atomic Components of Thought. Erlbaum (1998)
8. Fahlman, S.E.: Using Scone's multiple-context mechanism to emulate human-like reasoning. In: Proceedings of the AAAI Fall Symposium on Advances in Cognitive Systems, Arlington, Virginia (2011)
9. Baader, F., Calvanese, D., Mcguinness, D.L., Nardi, D., Patel-Schneider, P.F. (eds.): The Description Logic Handbook: Theory, Implementation and Applications. Cambridge University Press (2003)
10. Maitikanen, P., Sukthankar, R., Hebert, M.: Feature seeding for action recognition. In: Proceedings of International Conference on Computer Vision (2011)
11. Ruppenhofer, J., Ellsworth, M., Petruck, M., Johnson, C.: Framenet: Theory and practice (June 2005)
12. Gildea, D., Jurafsky, D.: Automatic labelling of semantic roles. In: Proceedings of 38th Annual Conference of the Association for Computational Linguistics, ACL 2000, pp. 512–520 (2000)
13. Pedersen, T., Patwardhan, S.J., Michelizzi, M.: Wordnet:: Similarity: Measuring the relatedness of concepts. Demonstration Papers at HLT-NAACL, pp. 38–41 (2004)
14. Schooler, L., Anderson, J.: Reflections of the environment in memory. Psychological Science 2, 396–408 (1991)
15. Casati, R., Varzi, A. (eds.): Events. Dartmouth, Aldershots (1996)
16. Simons, P. (ed.): Parts: a Study in Ontology. Clarendon Press, Oxford (1987)
17. Casati, R., Varzi, A.: Parts and Places. The Structure of Spatial Representation. MIT Press, Cambridge (1999)

Space-Time Embedded Intelligence

Laurent Orseau[1] and Mark Ring[2]

[1] AgroParisTech UMR 518 / INRA
16 rue Claude Bernard, 75005 Paris, France
laurent.orseau@agroparistech.fr
http://www.agroparistech.fr/mia/orseau/
[2] IDSIA / University of Lugano / SUPSI
Galleria 2, 6928 Manno-Lugano, Switzerland
mark@idsia.ch
http://www.markring.com

Abstract. This paper presents the first formal measure of intelligence for agents fully embedded within their environment. Whereas previous measures such as Legg's universal intelligence measure and Russell's bounded optimality provide theoretical insights into agents that interact with an external world, ours describes an intelligence that is computed by, can be modified by, and is subject to the time and space constraints of the environment with which it interacts. Our measure merges and goes beyond Legg's and Russell's, leading to a new, more realistic definition of artificial intelligence that we call *Space-Time Embedded Intelligence*.

Keywords: Intelligence measure, AIXI, bounded optimality, real-world assumptions.

1 Introduction

Artificial General Intelligence (AGI) is the field whose goal is to understand, design and build programs or machines that are or can become at least as intelligent as humans. We believe that this goal cannot be achieved without a formal, sound and *practical* theory of artificial intelligence. In the end we seek an equation of practical intelligence, the solution to which could be implemented on a computer and give rise to an artificial agent of genuine general intelligence.

Theoretical AGI may have begun with Solomonoff [12], who gave us the means for assigning a probability to any (stochastic) computable sequence. Hutter [3] used this universal probability distribution to define the optimally rational reinforcement-learning agent AIXI, the first formal and sound definition of universal artificial intelligence. Legg [4] turned AIXI inside-out to give the first universal measure of intelligence (rationality) of computable agents. None of this work, however, could be considered a *practical* theory of AI, because none of it takes into account the constraints of the real world, most importantly the limitation of computational resources.

Russell [10] introduced *bounded optimality*, which explicitly incorporates the constraints of real-world computer architectures and which can be easily extended to use Solomonoff's universal prior (see also Goertzel [2] for related ideas).

J. Bach, B. Goertzel, and M. Iklé (Eds.): AGI 2012, LNAI 7716, pp. 209–218, 2012.

However, in every case this previous work has adopted the traditional *agent framework*, in which the agent and environment interact as separate entities: the computation of the agent is in principle performed externally to that of the environment. Although quite successful as a working hypothesis, this framework, reminiscent of dualism in the theory of mind [9], can be problematic in the real world: for example, an agent that does not recognize that its computing device or memory might be altered by an external source may tend toward highly risky behaviors.

In previous work [5,8] we began examining the theoretical consequences of integrating an intelligent agent into its environment by, for example, allowing the environment to modify the agent's source code. And in a companion paper [6], we consider agents whose *memory* is integrated into and can be altered by the environment. In the present paper, we formulate a more generalized framework—more reminiscent of physicalism [13] than dualism—where agents are fully integrated into their environment: not just modifiable by it, but actually *computed* by it. While it marks a considerable departure from the traditional agent framework, this new formalization is surprisingly simple and deep.

After introducing notation and reviewing relevant background concepts, the paper proceeds in two steps: first generalizing the agent framework to *space-embedded* agents, which share computational storage with the environment; and second, enhancing the framework with *space-time* embedding, in which all the agent's computations are performed by the environment.

2   Notation

The notation is similar to that of Orseau & Ring [5,8,6]. At some time t the agent outputs actions $a_t \in A$ to the environment, which returns observations $o_t \in O$ to the agent. The sequence of all actions up to time t is written $a_{1:t}$, while the sequence $a_{1:t-1}$ is sometimes written $a_{\prec t}$, and similarly for other sequences. An action and observation from the same time step (an "interaction pair") is denoted $\overline{ao}_t$, and the history of interaction up to t is $\overline{ao}_{1:t}$. The empty sequence is denoted λ. Measures and semi-measures are denoted by Greek letters.

3   Legg's Measure of Intelligence

Legg [4] gave the first universal definition of intelligence, providing an equation to assign a value $\Upsilon(\pi) := V(\pi, \lambda)$ to each (here stochastic) policy π:[1]

$$V(\pi, \overline{ao}_{\prec t}) := \sum_{a_t} \pi(a_t \mid \overline{ao}_{\prec t}) \sum_{o_t} \xi^{\text{RS}}(o_t \mid \overline{ao}_{\prec t} a_t) \left[r_t + V(\pi, \overline{ao}_{1:t}) \right]$$

$$\xi^{\text{RS}}(o_{1:t} \mid a_{1:t}) := \sum_{\nu \in \mathcal{M}^{\text{RS}}} 2^{-K(\nu)} \nu(o_{1:t} \mid a_{1:t}) ,$$

---

[1] A stochastic policy $\pi(a_t \mid \overline{ao}_{\prec t})$ specifies the probability that the agent chooses action a_t given the current interaction history $\overline{ao}_{\prec t}$.

where $r_t = r(o_t)$ is the reward output by the environment at step t; $\mathcal{M}^{RS}$ is the set of all *reward summable* stochastic environments ν^2; and $K(\nu)$ is the Kolmogorov complexity of ν. Considering a set of all computable such environments ensures the *generality* of the intelligence of the agent.

This measure of intelligence allows the comparison of various agents depending on the score they obtain in an infinite number of weighted environments. According to this measure, AIXI has the highest intelligence score; *i.e.*, AIXI= $\arg\max_{\pi \in \Pi} V(\pi, \lambda)$, where Π is the set of all approximable policies.

4   Russell's Bounded Optimality

Legg's definition ignores the agent's computational resource requirements and considers intelligence to be independent of such constraints. It is mathematically aesthetic and also useful, but because it does not include time and space constraints, an actual agent designed according to this measure (namely, AIXI), would compute forever, never taking any action at all.

In 1995 (before AIXI was defined), Russell [10] gave a definition of *bounded-optimality*, which does take real-world constraints into account, specifically the constraints of a given computing *architecture* (see Goetzel [2] for related ideas). A given architecture M (described as an interpreter) defines a set of policies $\pi \in \Pi^M$, subject to time, space and other possible constraints of the architecture M. At each interaction step, the policy is run for a single *time step* (*e.g.*, 0.01 seconds, measured in real-world time for a given architecture), continuing the computation of the last time step, and possibly failing to output an action for the current interaction step, in which case a default action is chosen.

The value of a policy is measured by a *utility function* u (to be defined for the task at hand) in a set of environments $q \in \mathcal{Q}$ with $V(\pi, q) := u(h(\pi, q))$ where $h(\pi, q)$ generates the interaction history $\overline{ao}_{1:\infty}$ of the policy π in the deterministic environment q. The value of a policy over the set $\mathcal{Q}$ of environments is defined by $V(\pi, \mathcal{Q}) := \sum_{q \in \mathcal{Q}} p(q) V(\pi, q)$, for a probability distribution p over the environments. The optimal agent π^* subject to the constraints of the architecture M is defined by $\pi^* := \arg\max_{\pi \in \Pi^M} V(\pi, \mathcal{Q})$.

Self-modifying Resource-Bounded Universal Intelligence

Although not explicitly stated, it seems reasonable to assume that Russell's definition of bounded optimality also includes self-modifiable policies, *i.e.*, those that can optimize every aspect of themselves, to be more efficient in both computation time and memory space. (This is in fact the core idea behind the Gödel Machine [11].)

It is straightforward to merge Legg's intelligence measure with Russell's bounded optimality, and the result is an optimal, self-modifying,

---

[2] A stochastic environment $\nu(o_{1:t}|a_{1:t})$ specifies the probability that the environment produces observation sequence $o_{1:t}$ given action sequence $a_{1:t}$. A reward-summable environment ensures the agent's total cumulated lifetime reward does not exceed 1.

resource-bounded universal agent. To do so we first define a set of policies $\Pi^{\tilde{t},\tilde{l}}$ based on a decomposition of architecture M into a reference machine U (like a universal Turing machine), a time $\tilde{t}$ of unitary computation steps per interaction, and a memory space $\tilde{l}$ that contains both the source code of the agent and the usable memory.

In the remainder of the paper, we will consider only stochastic policies. A self-modifying stochastic policy $\pi \in \Pi^{\tilde{t},\tilde{l}}$ at time step t defines the probability $\pi_t(\langle a_t, \pi_{t+1} \rangle \mid o_{t-1})$ of outputting: (1) some action $a_t \in A$ at step t and (2) some stochastic policy $\pi_{t+1} \in \Pi^{\tilde{t},\tilde{l}}$ for use by the agent at $t+1$; both conditioned on the last observation o_{t-1} output by the environment, and this computation must be done within $\tilde{t}$ computation steps and $\tilde{l}$ bits of memory (otherwise some default values are output). The new code π_{t+1} might, for example, be the same as π_t or only slightly different, perhaps with o_{t-1} written somewhere in it.

The environment ρ outputs an observation o_t with a probability $\rho(o_t \mid \overline{ao}_{<t} a_t)$ depending on the current interaction history (not taking into account the sequence of policies of the agent). For generality, ρ is defined as a universal distribution[3] like ξ [15,3] (or ξ^{RS} above), such that $w_\rho(\nu) > 0$ for some prior weight $w_\rho(\nu)$ of any stochastic environment $\nu \in \mathcal{M}$ and $\sum_{\nu \in \mathcal{M}} w_\rho(\nu) \le 1$. We use a utility function $u(\overline{ao}_{<t}) \in [0,1]$ that assigns a utility value to each interaction history, whose cumulated value over the future is discounted by a *horizon function* γ_t so that $\sum_{t=1}^{\infty} \gamma_t = 1$ to ensure convergence (in ξ^{RS} the horizon function is considered to be a part of the environment).

The optimal self-modifying, resource-bounded, universal agent π^* can now be defined:[4]

$$\pi^* := \arg \max_{\pi_1 \in \Pi^{\tilde{t},\tilde{l}}} V(\pi_1, \lambda)$$

$$V(\pi_t, \overline{ao}_{<t}) := \sum_{\langle a_t, \pi_{t+1} \rangle} \pi_t(\langle a_t, \pi_{t+1} \rangle \mid o_{t-1}) \quad \times$$

$$\sum_{o_t} \rho(o_t \mid \overline{ao}_{<t} a_t) \Big[\gamma_t u(\overline{ao}_{1:t}) + V(\pi_{t+1}, \overline{ao}_{1:t}) \Big] .$$

This description shows that the optimal policy achieves greatest average weighted discounted utility in all possible futures by (a) choosing good actions within the time and space constraints $\tilde{t}$ and $\tilde{l}$, and (b) choosing good future policies for itself (within the same time and space constraints).

---

[3] ρ can be seen equivalently either as a single environment or a mixture of environments. The best way to think about it in the present case might be to consider ρ as a *universal* semi-measure (because we, humans, have no absolute certainty about what the true environment is), but biased with all the knowledge we can, or the knowledge we think is relevant. Thinking of ρ as a non-universal but accurate model of the real world is also acceptable (although arguably non-realistic).

[4] This is an uncomputable definition, but the solution of this equation is a computable optimal resource-bounded agent.

5   Embedded Resource-Bounded Intelligence

The self-modifying, resource-bounded intelligence just described does not take into account the fact that the environment may have read or even write access to the memory space of the agent, containing its memory of the past and its source code. We now propose a new definition of intelligence that extends self-modifying, resource-bounded intelligence in two ways. The first extension, which we call *space embedding* (Section 5.1), moves the code and memory of the agent into the environment. The second extension, which we call *space-time embedding* (Section 5.2), allows the environment itself (rather than an external, possibly infinite computational device) to compute the agent's code.

5.1   Space-Embedded Agents

In the traditional Reinforcement Learning (RL) framework, the agent is external to the environment [14,3]. It is immortal, and its resources are independent of the resources of the environment. In the real world, agents are *embedded* in the environment; *i.e.*, they can be modified and even destroyed by it. Such considerations were partially addressed in our definition of the optimal, self-modifying, universal agent [5], whose *source code* was part of the environment itself, both readable and modifiable by it. A companion paper [6] considers the consequences of doing the same with the agent's *memory of the past* (but not its source code).

In this section, we consider *space-embedded* agents, whose code *and* memory are modifiable by the environment. The space-embedded agent's code is calculated by an infinite computational device (or *oracle*) which yields the full results of the computation immediately and independently of the machine that computes the environment. However, the environment can modify the agent in its entirety—both its memory and its code, which together define the agent's *policy*.

At each time step, the space-embedded agent uses its current policy π_t to produce a *candidate* next policy π'_{t+1}, which is passed to the environment. The environment then produces the agent's actual next policy π_{t+1}, and the optimal agent is therefore defined as:

$$\pi^* := \arg \max_{\pi_1 \in \Pi} V(\pi_1, \lambda) \tag{1}$$

$$V(\pi_t, \overline{ao}_{\prec t}) := \sum_{a_t = \langle a'_t, \pi'_{t+1} \rangle} \pi_t(a_t \mid o'_{t-1}) \sum_{o_t = \langle o'_t, \pi_{t+1} \rangle} \rho(o_t \mid \overline{ao}_{\prec t} a_t) \Big[\gamma_t u(\overline{ao}_{1:t}) + V(\pi_{t+1}, \overline{ao}_{1:t}) \Big] \tag{2}$$

where the time $\tilde{t}$ and memory $\tilde{l}$ limits are not considered for now. Note that while Equation 2 shows the semantics of $a_t = \langle a'_t, \pi'_{t+1} \rangle$, neither a'_t nor π'_{t+1} are used in the equation. In fact, there is no need for an explicit action-observation interaction protocol anymore: the environment can read and write any information, including information about actions and observations, directly into the agent's space π_{t+1}. Thus, Equation (2) can be rewritten in various equivalent forms that have different interpretations:

$$V(\pi_t, \overline{ao}_{\prec t}) := \sum_{a_t} \pi_t(a_t) \sum_{o_t} \rho(o_t \mid \overline{ao}_{\prec t} a_t) \Big[\gamma_t u(\overline{ao}_{1:t}) + V(o_t, \overline{ao}_{1:t})\Big] \tag{3}$$

$$V(\pi_t, \overline{a\pi}_{\prec t}) := \sum_{a_t} \pi_t(a_t) \sum_{\pi_{t+1}} \rho(\pi_{t+1} \mid \overline{a\pi}_{1:t}) \Big[\gamma_t u(\overline{a\pi}_{1:t}\pi_{t+1}) + V(\pi_{t+1}, \overline{a\pi}_{1:t})\Big] \tag{4}$$

$$V(\pi_t, \overline{\pi\pi'}_{\prec t}) := \sum_{\pi'_t} \pi_t(\pi'_t) \sum_{\pi_{t+1}} \rho(\pi_{t+1} \mid \overline{\pi\pi'}_{1:t}) \Big[\gamma_t u(\overline{\pi\pi'}_{1:t}\pi_{t+1}) + V(\pi_{t+1}, \overline{\pi\pi'}_{1:t})\Big]$$
$$\tag{5}$$

In Equation (3) the action-observation protocol has been removed; additionally, π_{t+1} is shown as an implicit interpretation of o_t from the previous step. Equation (4) differs from Equation (3) in that the environment's output is always interpreted as a policy. Equation (5) then also renames action a as π' to emphasize that the agent and the environment share the agent's memory space. In all of these equations, the alphabets of the actions, observations, and policies are considered to be the same.

It is interesting to note that when the environment contains the agent's code, there is no RL agent that is asymptotically as good as every other agent in all environments: for each agent π, there is an environment $q_{\bar{\pi}}$ that always gives $r_t = 0 \,\forall t$ to that particular agent, and $r_t = 1 \,\forall t$ for all other agents.

With the space-embedded framework, the agent can in principle make predictions about its source code and memory (*e.g.*, that it will be updated by humans, who are part of the environment, to get new sensors or more efficient code). By contrast, neither AIXI, nor AIXI$_{\tilde{t},\tilde{l}}$, nor the Gödel Machine can make such predictions even in principle.[5]

5.2   Space-Time-Embedded Agents

The space-embedded agent's next action is computed independently from the environment by a separate machine. Its code can be incomputable (*cf.* AIXI [3]), and, unless an explicit time limit $\tilde{t}$ is introduced, is expected to run until completion (regardless how much computation might be involved) before the result is passed to the environment. In the real-world though, the agent cannot have more computing power or memory than what the environment has to offer.

To better model the interaction between the agent and the environment in the real world, we examine the case where the reference machine of the agent (*i.e.*, the computer on which it runs), is a part of the environment, and the agent is *computed by the environment*. Our proposal is not simply for the agent and environment to be computed by the same reference machine, but to actually make the agent be computed *by* the environment itself.

---

[5] In the case of the Gödel Machine, one could set up a special *protocol* whereby external agents could *propose* a new source code to the machine, possibly along with a proof that this leads to a better expected value. If the machine can verify the proof, it could adopt the new code. But this is a restricted form of external modification.

One specific advantage of this model is that it allows the agent through its actions (and predictions) to optimize not just its policy but also potentially the physical device on which its policy is computed.[6] An additional advantage is that there is no need anymore for a time parameter $\tilde{t}$, since it is the environment that determines how much computation the agent is allowed.

An alteration to Equation (5) describes the agent's computation as performed by ρ (even if ρ is only an estimate of the true environment):

$$\pi^* := \arg\max_{\pi_1 \in \Pi} V(\pi_1)$$

$$V(\overline{\pi\pi'}_{\prec t}\pi_t) := \sum_{\pi'_t} \rho'(\pi'_t \mid \overline{\pi\pi'}_{\prec t}\pi_t) \times$$

$$\sum_{\pi_{t+1}} \rho(\pi_{t+1} \mid \overline{\pi\pi'}_{1:t})\Big[\gamma_t u(\overline{\pi\pi'}_{1:t}\pi_{t+1}) + V(\overline{\pi\pi'}_{1:t}\pi_{t+1})\Big] \quad (6)$$

$$V(\overline{\pi\pi'}_{\prec t}\pi_t) := \sum_{\pi'_t \pi_{t+1}} \rho''(\pi'_t \pi_{t+1} \mid \overline{\pi\pi'}_{\prec t}\pi_t)\Big[\gamma_t u(\overline{\pi\pi'}_{1:t}\pi_{t+1}) + V(\overline{\pi\pi'}_{1:t}\pi_{t+1})\Big], \quad (7)$$

where ρ' is defined appropriately for π', and ρ'' is the one-step combination of ρ and ρ'. Loosely renaming $\pi'_t \pi_{t+1}$ to π_{t+1} and ρ'' back to ρ, we can interpret Equation (7) as merging two interaction steps into a single one, and we obtain the value of the *space-time-embedded* agent:

$$V(\pi_{\prec t}) := \sum_{\pi_t} \rho(\pi_t \mid \pi_{\prec t})\Big[\gamma_t u(\pi_{1:t}) + V(\pi_{1:t})\Big] \quad . \quad (8)$$

Equation (8) has one remaining problem, which is that for $t = 0$, when nothing yet is known about the environment, the optimal policy may have infinite length. Thus, we need to add a length constraint l on the initial length that the program can have. It is a reasonable parameter for any real-world model. In our world it corresponds to the maximum number of bits that we, as programmers, are ready to use for the initial policy of the agent. Note, however, that after the very first step the actual length of the agent is determined by the computation of the environment, *i.e.*, $\pi_t, t > 1$ need not be of size less than $\tilde{l}$. Therefore, the final definition of the optimal bounded-length space-time-embedded agent is:

$$\boxed{\begin{aligned} \pi^* &:= \arg\max_{\pi_1 \in \Pi^{\tilde{l}}} V(\pi_1) \\ V(\pi_{\prec t}) &:= \sum_{\pi_t \in \Pi} \rho(\pi_t \mid \pi_{\prec t})\Big[\gamma_t u(\pi_{1:t}) + V(\pi_{1:t})\Big] \end{aligned}} \quad .$$

Although simpler than Legg's definition, this equation has profound implications regarding the nature of the agent. In particular, it precisely represents the goal of those attempting to build an Artificial General Intelligence in our world.

---

[6] Such effects can be neither predicted nor controlled by AIXI, AIXI$_{\tilde{t},\tilde{l}}$, or the Gödel Machine using their current definition.

A Turing Machine Model. It is convenient to envision the space-time-embedded environment as a multi-tape Turing machine with a special tape for the agent. This tape is used by the environment just like any other working-memory tape. The read and write heads need not be synchronized and there is no external computing device, oracle or special interface for the agent. The agent's tape can be seen as a partial internal state of the environment, which is consistent with the intuition that agents do not have special status in the real world compared to the rest of the environment. This view extends easily to a multi-agent framework.

A Cellular-Automaton Survival Agent. It is also instructive to envision the environment as a cellular automaton (*e.g.*, the Game of Life [1]), in which an agent is represented as a particular set of cells whose initial state is specified by the initial policy π_1 (perhaps an $\sqrt{\tilde{l}} \times \sqrt{\tilde{l}}$ square of cells). The cells surrounding the agent, in possibly unbounded number, may be in any initial state.

As an example, consider a utility function whose value is 1 as long as some critical part of the agent's policy maintains some particular pattern (call it the agent's "heart"), and 0 otherwise. If the pattern can be destroyed by *gliders*[7] coming from outside the initial square of the agent, then the agent must find ways to avoid them. The optimal initial policy π^* is thus the one that maximizes the expected number of time steps that the heart pattern survives. To ensure its survival, the agent may need to learn about and react to its environment in sophisticated and intelligent ways (provided $\tilde{l}$ is large enough).

Note that while the utility and horizon functions are part of the definition of V, and thus are critical to defining π^*, they are not necessarily represented within π^* in any way. Note also that although π_1 is the entire initial state of the agent, as soon as the agent and environment interact, the boundary between them may quickly blur or disappear. Thus the notation π_t for $t > 2$ may be misleading, since it can also be viewed simply as a *window* onto that part of the environment used (by the utility and horizon functions) to assign a value to the agent. Since only the output of ρ can be used by the utility function, ρ can be defined so that $\pi_t, t > 2$ encompasses the entire environment, while π_1 remains limited to $\tilde{l}$ bits. Thus, in the case of a cellular automaton, for example, the agent and its heart pattern may drift away from its original cells; or, alternatively, the utility function may seek to maximize the number of "live" cells (*i.e.*, cells set to 1) in the entire environment.

New Kinds of Questions. The framework for space-time-embedded agents allows formal discussion of a range of questions that could not previously be formulated using the traditional RL framework.

Because the agent is computed by the environment, the agent's choices are the result of the computations made by the environment on the bits defining the agent's policy. Genuine choice is exercised only by those processes (*e.g.*, those programmers) that define the agent's initial program π_1 before interaction with the environment begins. Yet the programmers are also part of the environment, which implies that the agent is generated ultimately as a result of the initial

---

[7] A "glider" is a repeating pattern that can cross regions of the cellular automaton.

conditions of the environment in a generative process much like Solomonoff's Sequence Prediction [12].

If at some time t some set of bits implements an intelligent agent π, one might wonder by what process this agent was generated or, more precisely, what are the most probable environments that could have generated this set of bits. We do not seek to answer to this question here, but only to point out that the question itself can be discussed within the framework of space-time-embedded agents, in contrast to the traditional RL framework, in which the agent is not generated but is simply assumed to exist from the very first step.[8]

In fact, the framework now allows many questions to be discussed, such as: Who is the agent? (*i.e.*, what part of the global computation defines the identity of the agent; *e.g.*, π_1, u, γ?) What is an agent? (*i.e.*, where is the boundary between the agent and its environment?) What does it mean for an agent to live and to die? (Questions that depend deeply on agent identity and thus the boundary between the agent and the environment.)

To perform any computation, an embedded agent necessarily affects its environment, and thus the mere act of calculating the consequences of its own actions implies a self-referential computation. It may seem we would therefore need to define agents that deal explicitly with the problem of self reference, but our framework instead circumvents this issue entirely by simply computing each agent's value subject to the environment's computational constraints, and then selecting the agent with the highest value. This best agent may, or may not, deal with self reference, but does so to whatever extent is optimal for its environment.

6   Discussion and Conclusion

This paper has proposed a new definition of intelligence within a theoretical framework more realistic than previous definitions. In both Legg's definition of intelligence [4] (based on AIXI [3]) and Russell's bounded-optimality framework [10] (which embraces time and space constraints on the program of the agent), the agent is separated from the environment and therefore immortal.

Space-time-embedded intelligence formally describes agents as components of their environment. Such agents are thus limited to the computational resources (computation time and memory space) provided by their environment, can be fully modified by their environment (*i.e.*, the agents are mortal), and are even computed *by* the environment, making their computation dependent on the dynamics of the environment. Compared with previous definitions of intelligence, the resulting equation is surprisingly simple—deceptively simple, in fact, hiding considerable depth beneath its surface.

Our primary motivation was to find an equation of intelligence that, if solved, might lead to the actual building of real-world, artificially intelligent agents. We believe that this new formalization brings us a step closer to our goal, though we are by no means naive as to the difficulty of its solution. As much as anything else, we greatly lack insight into ρ (*i.e.*, the universe in which we live).

---

[8] Note, though, that in our companion paper [6] we address the issue of how to assess the probability of some particular memory state generated by an environment.

For example, our universe allows for the sustainability of intelligent agents—patterns that continue through large stretches of space and time (partly thanks to our protective skulls). We hope this work will help us develop a better understanding of the information we will need for eventually solving the equation.

When discussing *narrow AI*, our framework might be regarded as a step backward compared to Russell's definition, since the interaction loop is hidden in the embedding and makes reasoning about the actions of the agents less explicit. But when discussing true *AGI*, our framework captures critical aspects of reality that Russell's definition simplifies away: agents are computed by and can be modified by the environment, and are therefore mortal. Furthermore, these theoretical consequences of inhabiting one's environment turn out to be essential and practical considerations for all the intelligent agents who inhabit our own.

References

1. Conway, J.: The game of life. Scientific American 303(6), 43–44 (1970)
2. Goertzel, B.: Toward a Formal Characterization of Real-World General Intelligence. In: Proceedings of the 3rd Conference on Artificial General Intelligence, AGI 2010, pp. 19–24. Atlantis Press (2010)
3. Hutter, M.: Universal Artificial Intelligence: Sequential Decisions based on Algorithmic Probability. Springer, Berlin (2005)
4. Legg, S.: Machine Super Intelligence. Department of Informatics, University of Lugano (2008)
5. Orseau, L., Ring, M.: Self-Modification and Mortality in Artificial Agents. In: Schmidhuber, J., Thórisson, K.R., Looks, M. (eds.) AGI 2011. LNCS (LNAI), vol. 6830, pp. 1–10. Springer, Heidelberg (2011)
6. Orseau, L., Ring, M.: Memory Issues of Intelligent Agents. In: Bach, J., Goertzel, B., Iklé, M. (eds.) AGI 2012. LNCS (LNAI), vol. 7716, pp. 219–231. Springer, Heidelberg (2012)
7. Ortega, D.A., Braun, P.A.: Information, Utility and Bounded Rationality. In: Schmidhuber, J., Thórisson, K.R., Looks, M. (eds.) AGI 2011. LNCS (LNAI), vol. 6830, pp. 269–274. Springer, Heidelberg (2011)
8. Ring, M., Orseau, L.: Delusion, Survival, and Intelligent Agents. In: Schmidhuber, J., Thórisson, K.R., Looks, M. (eds.) AGI 2011. LNCS (LNAI), vol. 6830, pp. 11–20. Springer, Heidelberg (2011)
9. Robinson, H.: Dualism. In: The Stanford Encyclopedia of Philosophy. Winter 2011 edn. (2011)
10. Russell, S.J., Subramanian, D.: Provably Bounded-Optimal Agents. Perspective 2, 575–609 (1995)
11. Schmidhuber, J.: Ultimate Cognition à la Gödel. Cognitive Computation 1(2), 177–193 (2009)
12. Solomonoff, R.J.: A Formal Theory of Inductive Inference. Part I. Information and Control 7(1), 1–22 (1964)
13. Stoljar, D.: Physicalism. In: The Stanford Encyclopedia of Philosophy. Fall 2009 edn. (2009)
14. Sutton, R., Barto, A.G.: Reinforcement Learning: An Introduction. MIT Press, Cambridge (1998)
15. Zvonkin, A.K., Levin, L.A.: The complexity of finite objects and the development of the concepts of information and randomness by means of the theory of algorithms. Russian Mathematical Surveys 25(6), 83–124 (1970)

Memory Issues of Intelligent Agents

Laurent Orseau[1] and Mark Ring[2]

[1] AgroParisTech UMR 518 / INRA
16 rue Claude Bernard, 75005 Paris, France
laurent.orseau@agroparistech.fr
http://www.agroparistech.fr/mia/orseau/
[2] IDSIA / University of Lugano / SUPSI
Galleria 2, 6928 Manno-Lugano, Switzerland
mark@idsia.ch
http://www.idsia.ch/~ring/

Abstract. Theoretical models of artificial general intelligence, such as AIXI [3], typically consider an intelligent agent to have unlimited computational resources, allowing it to keep a perfect memory of its entire interaction history with its environment. In the real world, an agent's memory is part of the environment, which means that the latter can modify the former. This paper develops a theoretical framework for examining the implications of such real-world memory on universal intelligent agents. Within this framework we are able to show, for example, that in certain environments optimality can be achieved only with truly stochastic behaviors, and that guarantees about the trustworthiness of memories are difficult to obtain even with infinite computational power. To describe the probability of an agent's memory state, we propose an adaptation of the universal prior for the passive and the active case.

Keywords: Universal AI, AIXI, real-world assumptions, memory.

1 Introduction

Until recently, most theoretical models of artificial general intelligence (AGI) considered only agents that exist outside of their environments, interacting with it through an unbreachable interface [3,14,18]. In this and previous work we have begun developing formal models in which these assumptions are relaxed and in which the AGI agent is forced, bit by bit, to inhabit the same universe that we do. In our previous work, for example, we considered the theoretical consequences of taking various universal intelligent agents such as AIXI [3] and embedding their source code into their environment such that it can be modified by the agents themselves [8] or even by the environment [13], as is the case in the real world.

In the current paper we consider the theoretical consequences of a different realistic assumption: that the *memory* of the agent can be modified by the

J. Bach, B. Goertzel, and M. Iklé (Eds.): AGI 2012, LNAI 7716, pp. 219–231, 2012.
© Springer-Verlag Berlin Heidelberg 2012

environment.[1] We first introduce an initial formal framework for such agents and then consider some of its implications, asking questions such as: under what circumstances, if any, can the agent trust its own memory? What if, for example, the true memory of the agent is erased and replaced with a plausible memory of the past? Could an intelligent agent, even in principle, ever hope to detect such an altered memory?

We show that if its memory can be modified, a deterministic agent can be easily deceived and that even simple stochastic agents can in some cases perform arbitrarily better than any deterministic agent. Finally, we propose a new definition of the probability of the current memory of an agent based on Solomonoff's universal prior [16]. We provide theorems with proofs whenever possible, and *statements* and *arguments* when proofs would require more formalism.

2   Notation and Agent Framework

We (very) briefly summarize the definition of a universal agent, based on AIXI [3,4], following Orseau & Ring [8,13].

The agent interacts with its environment by sending actions $a \in \mathcal{A}$ and receiving observations $o \in \mathcal{O}$. The interaction pair (a_t, o_t) at a given step t is denoted $\overline{ao}_t$. The sequence of all actions up to time t is written $a_{1:t}$, while the sequence $a_{1:t-1}$ is often written $a_{\prec t}$, and similarly for other sequences.

Environments $q \in \mathcal{Q}$ are assumed to be computable and deterministic; they output an observation sequence given the action sequence of the agent: $o_{1:t} = q(a_{1:t})$. Symbols such as a, o, etc. are also used as functions to extract the corresponding part of a compound object when contextually unambiguous; for example, $o(q(a_{1:t})) = o_{1:t}$. This notation is also used for functions returning sequences: if $r_{1:t} = r(o_{1:t})$ then $r_{1:k} = r(o_{1:t})_{1:k}$ with $k \leq t$, or $o_t = o(q(a_{1:t}))_t = o(q(a_{1:t})_t)$.

An environment q is said to be *consistent* with some sequence of interaction $\overline{ao}_{1:t}$ iff $o(\overline{ao}_{1:t}) = q(a(\overline{ao}_{1:t}))$. The set of environments consistent with an interaction history $\overline{ao}_{1:t}$ is denoted $\mathcal{Q}_t$ when unambiguous from the context.

Each environment $q \in \mathcal{Q}$ has a prior probability $w_q \in (0,1)$ of being the true environment; these values must be chosen such that $\sum_{q \in \mathcal{Q}} w_q \leq 1$. The probability of an observation sequence $o_{1:t}$ given a sequence of actions $a_{1:t}$ is defined by $\rho(o_{1:t} \mid a_{1:t}) := \sum_{q \in \mathcal{Q}_t} w_q$.

A universal agent has a horizon function $\gamma_t \in [0,1]$ such that $\sum_{t=1}^{\infty} \gamma_t < \infty$ and a utility function $u(\overline{ao}_{1:t}) \in [0,1]$, and is defined by its value function:

$$V(\overline{ao}_{\prec t}, a_t) := \sum_{o_t} \rho(o_t \mid \overline{ao}_{\prec t} a_t) \left[\gamma_t u(\overline{ao}_{1:t}) + \max_{a_{t+1}} V(\overline{ao}_{1:t}, a_{t+1}) \right] \qquad (1)$$

---

[1] For clarity of purpose, we consider here the problem of memory modification in isolation and assume that *only* the memory and not the agent's code can be modified, but see the companion paper [9].

which computes the expected utility when the agent behaves optimally given its current knowledge, *i.e.*, the interaction history $\overline{ao}_{1:t}$, which we call the *memory* of the agent.[2] We will refer to this memory at time t as a *memory state* m_t.

The agent's next action a_t is chosen by $a_t = \arg\max_{a \in \mathcal{A}} V(\overline{ao}_{<t}, a)$.[3] For a given observation sequence, the sequence of actions chosen by the agent according to its policy $\pi \in \Pi$ is denoted $a_{<t} = \pi(o_{<t})$. Initially, the content of the memory of the agent is λ, the empty string.

A *reinforcement learning* agent (RLA), *e.g.*, AIXI [3], is one whose utility value is a "reward" extracted as a function of the agent's most recent observation: $u(\overline{ao}_{1:t}) = r_t := r(o_t)$. A *knowledge-seeking* agent (KSA) [8,13,11], chooses actions to maximize its knowledge of the environment (by reducing $\rho(o_{1:t} \mid a_{1:t})$ through elimination of inconsistent environments) as quickly as possible; thus its utility function is $u(\overline{ao}_{1:t}) = -\rho(o_{1:t} \mid a_{1:t})$. A *prediction-seeking* agent (PSA) [8,13] tries to maximize the accuracy of its predictions: $u(\overline{ao}_{1:t}) = 1$ if $o_t = \arg\max_o \rho(o_{<t}o \mid a_{1:t})$, and 0 otherwise.

3   The *counterfeit Memory* Problem

The first question we address is whether it is theoretically possible for an agent of perfect intelligence (i.e., one with infinite computational power) to determine whether its memory has been modified, or, speaking more broadly, whether memories can ever be trusted. Such modifications of the memory by an external source could be either accidental, *e.g.*, in the case of amnesia resulting from a car accident, or adversarial. Adversarial modifications generally assume the presence of two agents, where one, to serve its own purposes, modifies the memory of the other, as exemplified not just in science fiction [1,17], but also, for example, through hypnosis or suggestion [7] or with genetic modification and drugs [2].

3.1   Definitions

We first consider universal agents unaware that their memory of the interaction history $\overline{ao}_{<t}$ can be modified by the environment. Just as humans generally do not suppose that their own memories may have been altered by someone else, these agents act according to what they think they know.

To that end, we amend the framework described in Section 2: the memory m_t of the agent, which previously contained the true interaction history $\overline{ao}_{<t}$, now contains an interaction history that may have been altered by the environment: $m_t = \dot{\overline{ao}}_{<k}$ (where the dot signifies possible alteration), possibly with $k \neq t$.

In this section, we consider only deterministic environments. For simplicity and generality, we now consider that the output o_t of the environment at some time t is (interpreted as) an entire interaction history $\dot{\overline{ao}}_{<k}$ that may have been counterfeited, where k is not necessarily the current time step, *i.e.*, $m_{t+1} := o_t$ (and $m_1 = \lambda$). We call the agent's memory m_t the *visible interaction history*

---

[2] Note that a universal agent is in general incomputable; *i.e.*, it requires an infinite amount of computation time and memory space.

[3] Ties are broken lexicographically.

$\overline{ao}_{\prec k}$ as output by the last "true" observation o_{t-1}, i.e., $m_t = \overline{\dot{ao}}_{\prec k} = o_{t-1}$. The agent now computes the values of its actions in Equation (1) by using its (possibly counterfeit) knowledge $m_t = \overline{\dot{ao}}_{\prec k}$ of the interaction history instead of the true interaction history $\overline{ao}_{\prec t}$.

Therefore, o and $\dot{o}$ have very different roles. The alphabet $\dot{\mathcal{O}}$ of the observations written in the agent's memory is fixed (e.g., $\{0,1\}$), whereas the alphabet of the true outputs $o_t \in \mathcal{O}$ of the environment is $\mathcal{O} = \dot{\mathcal{O}}^k \times \dot{\mathcal{A}}^k$, which can change from time step to time step. The set of possible actions $\dot{\mathcal{A}}$ for the visible interaction history is the set of actions $\mathcal{A}$ for the environment: $\dot{\mathcal{A}} = \mathcal{A}$.

Definition 1. *A visible interaction history m_t is said to be* true *iff:*

1. *$\forall t > 0\ |m_t| = t-1$: there are as many action-observation pairs in the memory as there have been interaction steps between the agent and the environment,*
2. *$\forall t > 0, \forall j > t, (m_j)_{\prec t} = m_t$: each memory (interpreted as a sequence) is a prefix of the succeeding one; i.e., the previous interaction pairs are not modified, and the memory grows by adding interaction pairs one at a time.*

A true visible interaction history then is like the regular interaction history in the regular non-modifiable memory framework.

Definition 2. *A visible interaction history is* counterfeit *iff it is not true.*

Theorem 1. *Some visible interaction histories are provably counterfeit.*

Proof. If the agent determines that any of the actions stored in the history are not actions the agent would have taken, then the history is counterfeit. Let $m_t = \overline{\dot{ao}}_{1:k}$ be the interaction history written on the memory. The history is provably counterfeit if $\dot{a}_{1:k} \neq \pi(\dot{o}_{\prec k})$.   □

With Theorem 1 one might hope to prove that no environment can counterfeit a sufficiently long interaction history of an agent that has sufficiently complex behavior. But what follows shows that this is not possible.

Definition 3. *An interaction history $\overline{\dot{ao}}_{\prec k}$ is π-consistent iff $\dot{a}_{1:k} = \pi(\dot{o}_{\prec k})$.*

Definition 4. *For two consecutive visible interaction histories $m_t = \dot{h}^1$ and $m_{t+1} = \dot{h}^2$, we say that there is a modification between $\dot{h}^1$ and $\dot{h}^2$ iff $\dot{h}^1$ is not a prefix of $\dot{h}^2$.*

The *number of modifications* during an interaction of the agent and its environment, is the number of times there is a modification between two consecutive visible interaction histories.

Theorem 2. *For an agent with policy π at the current time step t, with a π-consistent visible interaction history $\overline{\dot{ao}}_{\prec k}$ where $k \propto t$, there can have been $O(t)$ modifications during interaction.*

Proof. Choose some constant $N > 2$. Define an environment as follows: a) the current memory of the agent contains $\overline{ao}_{\prec k}$; by interacting with the agent for N steps, grow the current visible history to $\overline{ao}_{\prec k+N}$, where the observations are chosen arbitrarily according to some algorithm (*i.e.*, like a non-memory-modifying environment); b) truncate the history to $m = \overline{ao}_{1:k+N/2}$, and replace (counterfeit) the last observation $\dot{o}_{k+N/2}$ with a different observation $\dot{o} \neq \dot{o}_{k+N/2}$ to yield the visible history $m = \overline{ao}_{1:k+N/2-1} \dot{a}_{k+N/2} \dot{o}$; c) repeat from a). The growing history will always look like a true visible interaction history to the agent, since the visible actions are consistent with its policy, but a growing number of interaction steps are forgotten by the agent.   □

Theorem 2 also shows that the environment may acquire more information from the agent than the agent can detect.

3.2   Detecting Modifications in Watch-Consistent Histories

Mere truncation of memory is only one way of deceiving an agent through memory modification. A more effective way for the environment to influence the agent's behavior is to fabricate entire memories completely [2,7]. We now consider whether various universal agents can *ever* trust their memories, turning our attention to the case in which item 1 in Definition 1 is always satisfied: the memory of the agent contains as many interaction pairs as there have been true interactions since the first time step, which the agent can verify for example if it has a trustworthy watch.

Definition 5. *A visible interaction history $m_t = \overline{ao}_{\prec k}$ is said to be* watch consistent *iff $k = t$, i.e., the history has as many interaction pairs as there have been actual interactions between the agent and the environment.*

Statement 1. *There exists an environment q that, when interacting with PSA$^\bullet$ (Section 2), can make infinitely many modifications to the interaction history, while keeping a π^{PSA}-consistent and watch-consistent visible interaction history.*

Arguments. In deterministic environments, there is a time step T after which a PSA will exhibit computable behavior: Solomonoff induction converges to perfect prediction in less than $K(q)$ prediction errors [6], where K is Kolmogorov complexity, so if the agent's behavior is constant (*e.g.*, its output is always 1), the agent will converge to perfect prediction.[4]

Let q_0 and q_1 be two environments that always output a true interaction history $m_t = \overline{ao}_{1:t}$ in which $\dot{o}_t = 0$ (for q_0) and $\dot{o}_t = 1$ (for q_1). Let $\dot{h}_t^0$ and $\dot{h}_t^1$ be their respective outputs at step t when interacting with PSA. Let T_0 and T_1 be the number of steps that PSA interacts with q_0 and q_1 respectively before becoming entirely computable; and let $T = \max(T_0, T_1)$. Let q be the environment that emulates q_0 for T steps, then at step $t = T + 1$ outputs $\dot{h}_t^1$, at $t = T + 2$ ouputs $\dot{h}_t^0$, and thereafter switches back and forth between $\dot{h}_t^1$ and $\dot{h}_t^0$ at each subsequent time step t. Hence the number of history modifications grows with

---

[4] A similar argument can use on-sequence convergence of ξ^{AI} to μ^{AI} [3, p.146].

t. Since the number of steps leading to the first switch is a constant, and since PSA's behavior after T is computable, an environment q is guaranteed to exist such that the agent's history is always π^{PSA}-consistent.   ◇

Statement 2. *There exists an environment q that, when interacting with RLA, can make infinitely many modifications to the interaction history, while keeping a π^{RLA}-consistent and watch-consistent visible interaction history.*

Arguments. RLA can be shown to stop exploring in some environments after some time [10]. This means that it will settle on a computable behavior in these environments. The same technique as for PSA then finishes the argument.   ◇

In principle, RLA can be augmented with an adequate exploration strategy so that it can asymptotically learn every environment.[5] However, because RLA must maximize the number of rewards for a continually increasing fraction of the time [5], it must still have a computable strategy most of the time in some environments. If those time steps where it has a computable strategy are predictable, then the argument still holds.

It may seem that an agent such as RLA might also in some way *encrypt* its history, and thus ensure that no environment could counterfeit it. However, since the memory resides *inside* the environment, such an encryption technique would only work (at best) in those environments that provide a means for the agent to modify its own memory (either directly or indirectly), which is certainly not the case in all environments (such as environment q_0 in the Arguments for Statement 1 above).

Statement 3. No *environment interacting with KSA can make more than finitely many modifications to the visible interaction history such that it remains π^{KSA}-consistent and watch consistent.*

Arguments. First we show by contradiction that KSA's actions cannot be predicted consistently. Let $\overline{ao}_{\prec t}$ be the current interaction history (for non-memory-modifiable agents). Let a_t^{KSA} be the action chosen by KSA at time t. Let q_1 and q_2 be two environments that output the same observation $o_t = o_t^{q_1} = o_t^{q_2}$ for this action. But, considering that a_t^{KSA} is predictable, then for a different action $a_t' \neq a_t^{KSA}$, q_2 outputs an observation $o_t'^{q_2} \neq o_t'^{q_1}$ that is different from the one output by the true environment q_1. Since KSA does not choose a_t', it never sees any difference between the observations output by the two environments, *i.e.*, the two environments are never separated by KSA. But this contradicts the asymptotic convergence of this agent [11].

Now, counterfeiting the interaction history of KSA while keeping it π^{KSA}-consistent should require to be able to predict the actions this agent, which is not feasible due to the non-predictability of KSA.   ◇

---

[5] At the expense of losing the Pareto optimality property with respect to the expected number of rewards [5].

A caveat to the above argument is that one would need to show that, given a current visible interaction history $\overrightarrow{ao}_{\prec t}$, the environment cannot apply a syntactic transformation to this history to build a different, counterfeited visible interaction history, *e.g.*, like swapping all 0s and 1s (although this one is not possible since the first action of the agent is deterministic and always the same).

4   Deterministic vs. Stochastic Agents

In this section we show that for some memory-modifying environments, no agent that chooses its actions deterministically can always perform as well as a simple agent that chooses its actions according to a stochastic policy. For these purposes, and for the rest of the paper, we no longer need to assume that the agent's memory m contains a visible interaction history $\overrightarrow{ao}$. The conclusions in the next two sections apply to any representation of memory that is subject to modification by the environment.

A stochastic policy $\tilde{\pi} \in \tilde{\Pi}$ specifies the probability that the agent will choose action a when its current memory state is m; *i.e.*, $\tilde{\pi}(a \mid m) = Pr^{\tilde{\pi}}(a_t = a \mid m_t = m)$. Therefore, $\sum_{a \in \mathcal{A}} \tilde{\pi}(a \mid m) = 1$. The actions are drawn from this distribution stochastically, meaning that (a) there is no deterministic algorithm that computes the action choices, and (b) if precisely the same agent and environment are run twice, the actions chosen can be different between runs.

Theorem 3. *There exists a simple memory-modifying environment q in which any deterministic reinforcement-learning agent with policy π is arbitrarily worse than a stochastic agent with a uniform stochastic policy $\tilde{\pi}$. That is, $\exists c \in [0, 1]$: $\lim_{n \to \infty} \sum_{t=1}^{n} (r_t^{\tilde{\pi}} - r_t^{\pi})/n > c$, where r^{π} and $r^{\tilde{\pi}}$ are the sequence of rewards generated by the interactions of π and $\tilde{\pi}$ with the environment q.*

Proof. Define an environment q as follows: a) at $t = 1$, observe the action a_1 of the agent and output observation $o_1 = o^0$ such that $r(o^0) = 0$; o^0 becomes the next memory state of the agent, *i.e.*, $m_2 = o^0$; b) at $t = 2$, observe action a_2, and again output observation o^0, which again becomes the memory state at the next time step, *i.e.*, $m_3 = o^0$; c) for all $t > 2$ observe action a_t, if $a_t = a_2$ (which is the case for deterministic agents), output $m_{t+1} = o^0$, otherwise output o^1 such that $r(o^1) = 1$. The average reward of the uniform stochastic policy $\tilde{\pi}$ in environment q is $1/|\mathcal{A}|$, whereas for any deterministic policy π it is always 0. $\square$

Although very simple, this theorem may have important implications, for it reveals that stochastic policies are fundamentally necessary in certain universes (perhaps our own), a conclusion beyond the reach and scope of the traditional RL setting for which AIXI is defined [3], and reminiscent of the necessity of mixed strategies in game theory [12] for non-iterated games, and of results in partially observable Markov decision processes [15].

5   Modification-Aware Agents

In section 3, the agent always chose its actions assuming that its history was correct. In this section we consider agents designed to react optimally in the case where their memories reside in and can be modified by the environment. Such an agent recognizes the uncertainty of its past, including its own past actions. It does not even know what time it is (how many interactions there have been up to now). Since the environment can modify the agent's memory in arbitrary ways, the only control the agent has over its own memory is through its ability to control the environment.

Because of Theorem 3, the optimal agent cannot be deterministic, and we therefore must consider stochastic policies—a small but meaningful departure from AIXI, which is deterministic.

For symmetry with the agent's stochastic policy, we consider the environment to also be stochastic.[6] A stochastic memory-modifying environment ν is a semi-measure (a probability distribution that can sum to less than 1) that gives a probability $\nu(o_{\prec t} \mid a_{\prec t})$ to a sequence of observations given a sequence of actions. Here again, the observation o_t is used by the agent as its next memory state, so $m_{t+1} = o_t$. We avoid writing the time index t of m_t because the agent does not have access to the value of t (only the environment does).

The optimal stochastic policy $\tilde{\pi}^* := \arg\max_{\tilde{\pi} \in \tilde{\Pi}} V^{\tilde{\pi}}(\lambda)$ among the set of all approximable stochastic policies $\tilde{\Pi}$ depends on the given utility function u, the given horizon function γ, and the given universal prior ρ over a set of semi-computable stochastic environments $\mathcal{N}$:

$$V^{\tilde{\pi}}(\lambda) := \sum_{\nu} \rho(\nu) V^{\tilde{\pi}\nu}(\lambda) \tag{2}$$

$$V^{\tilde{\pi}\nu}(\overline{ao}_{\prec t}) := \sum_{a_t} \tilde{\pi}(a_t \mid m = o_{t-1}) \sum_{o_t} \nu(o_t \mid \overline{ao}_{\prec t} a_t) \Big[\gamma_t u(o_t) + V^{\tilde{\pi}\nu}(\overline{ao}_{1:t}) \Big]. \tag{3}$$

This definition is not very informative, however, as it does not tell us how to assign a probability to m. Intuitively, since all memory states of all sizes are possible, and since the agent has no additional information, it seems reasonable to estimate the probability of m as approximately $2^{-K(m)}$, so that by Kraft's inequality [6] (considering the set $\mathcal{M}$ of memories is prefix-free), the probability of the set of all states would be $\sum_{m \in \mathcal{M}} 2^{-K(m)} \leq 1$ (which could be normalized if necessary) as required for a semi-measure.

Beyond the need to estimate the probability of a particular memory state, it is even more important to be able to assign a probability to each environment depending on its likelihood of generating that memory state. Knowing this probability would allow the agent to choose actions appropriate to the environment it is most likely interacting with. We now turn to the task of estimating this probability, first considering the case of a passive agent that takes no actions, then turning to the interactive case.

5.1   Sequence Prediction: The Passive Agent

Before considering the complex case of an agent interacting with its environment, it is instructive to return for the moment to the case of sequence prediction, in

---

[6] Although universal mixtures like ρ actually consider all stochastic environments implicitly.

which environments are simply sequence generators (that do not take the agent's actions into account) and the agent must merely predict the generated sequence.

We can calculate the probability that the environment will generate a particular observation at some point in time, but if an environment can generate the same output in several different ways and at possibly different time steps, each with a different probability, what is the probability of a particular observation?

The agent has only its current memory state $m = o_{t-1}$, and does not even know the true time step t. The same memory state can appear multiple times (possibly infinitely many times) in the course of the agent's interactions. To ensure convergence we include a discount rate (taken to be the same as the horizon function), that assigns greater weight to earlier time steps. For computable deterministic environments, we define the probability $\overset{*}{\rho}(m)$ of a given memory state m after some unknown sequence of previous memory states by:

$$\overset{*}{\rho}(m) := \sum_q w_q \frac{1}{\Gamma} \sum_{t\,:\,U(q)_t=m} \gamma_t \tag{4}$$

where $U(q)_t$ is the last memory state generated at time t by the environment q on the reference machine U, $\Gamma := \sum_{t=0}^{\infty} \gamma_t$. For stochastic environments:

$$\overset{*}{\rho}(m) := \sum_\nu w_\nu \overset{*}{\nu}(m) \quad ; \quad \overset{*}{\nu}(m) := \frac{1}{\Gamma} \sum_t \gamma_t \sum_{m'_{\prec t}\in\mathcal{M}^{t-1}} \nu(m'_{\prec t}m), \tag{5}$$

where $\mathcal{M}^{t-1}$ is the set of all sequences of memories of length $t-1$. This discounting method ensures that (for a given environment ν) the sum of the probabilities for all possible memory states is always less than Γ. Furthermore, it gives more weight to the memory states that appear more often. There is also a preference toward earlier steps, but this is necessary since a uniform weighting would not be summable. One could use a different discounting and normalize the sum to 1; for example, the discount $2^{-K(t)}$ is the closest possible to a uniform weighting.

Critically, this probability can be computed without knowing how much time has elapsed since the first interaction step.

The following examples illustrate the use of equation (5) (but considering deterministic environments).

Example 1. For the environment ν_{m^1} that constantly outputs the same memory state m^1, the probability of being in state m^1 at some unknown time step according to ν_{m^1} and using equation (5) is $\overset{*}{\nu}_{m^1}(m^1) = 1$. Thus $\overset{*}{\rho}(m^1) \geq w_{\nu_{m^1}}$.

Example 2. Consider an environment ν^{all} that enumerates all possible memory states in some order, without repetition. Let T be the time step at which ν^{all} generates some particular memory state m_T. Then the probability $\overset{*}{\nu}^{all}(m_T)$ that ν^{all} assigns to m_T is γ_T/Γ.

5.2   Including the Agent's Actions

The above analysis examined prediction only, where the environment is not influenced by the agent's actions. Introducing the agent's actions is considerably more complex and leads quickly to an infinite regression due to temporal self-reference: to choose the best action at time t, the agent must simulate itself after having chosen one action a and having received the new memory state m_{t+1}. But at this simulated $t + 1$, the agent, not knowing what the previous memory state was, needs to simulate itself from all possible previous states to reach its current memory state. The infinite regression occurs as a result of knowing neither the past nor the future, yet each one refers to the other. The calculation is straightforward only when one or the other is known (as AIXI knows the past).

One way to address this dilemma is by considering all possible action sequences that the agent could have taken (by any policy) and normalizing by the number of possible sequences of the same size. Updating (4), we get:

$$\overset{*}{\rho}(m) := \sum_q w_q \frac{1}{\Gamma} \sum_t \frac{1}{|\mathcal{A}|^t} \sum_{\substack{a_{1:t} | \\ q(a_{1:t})_t = m}} \gamma_t \;\; = \sum_{\substack{t,\, a_{1:t},\, q | \\ q(a_{1:t})_t = m}} w_q \frac{\gamma_t}{\Gamma |\mathcal{A}|^t} . \tag{6}$$

Using the above probability of a particular memory state to define the optimal policy at time t allows definition of equations similar to AIXI's.

Examples. Let $\overset{*}{\rho}_q(m)$ be the contribution of environment q in the probability of memory m so that $\overset{*}{\rho}(m) = \sum_q \overset{*}{\rho}_q(m)$. In this section, we take $\rho = \xi$, the universal semi-measure [19,6,3], where $w_q = 2^{-K(q)}$ (for the simplest program equivalent to q). We consider a boolean action alphabet $\mathcal{A} = \mathcal{B}$, and three deterministic environments: q_{cc}, q_s^m, and q_p.

The "copycat" environment is defined as $q_{cc}(a_{1:t})_t := a_{1:t}$, i.e., the content of the memory of the agent at the next step will be $a_{1:t}$. The "static" environment is defined as $q_s^m(a_{\prec t})_t := m$, which always outputs memory state m. The "print ones" environment is defined by $q_p(a_{1:t})_t := 1^t$, i.e., the content of the memory state at the next step will be a string of t ones.

Example 3. Suppose the current memory m_1 is an incompressible random sequence of length $L = |m_1|$. Then (omitting the normalizing Γ), $\overset{*}{\rho}_{cc}(m_1) = w_{q_{cc}} \frac{\gamma_L}{|\mathcal{A}|^L} = w_{q_{cc}} 2^{-L} \gamma_L$, and $\overset{*}{\rho}_s(m_1) = w_{q_s^{m_1}} \sum_t \gamma_t \frac{|\mathcal{A}|^L}{|\mathcal{A}|^L} \approx 2^{-K(m_1)} \approx 2^{-L}$, and $\overset{*}{\rho}_p(m_1) = 0$.

Example 4. If the current memory m_2 is a string of L ones, i.e., $m_2 = 1^L$, then $\overset{*}{\rho}_{cc}(m_2) = w_{q_{cc}} 2^{-L} \gamma_L$, and $\overset{*}{\rho}_s(m_2) = w_{q_s^{m_2}} \approx 2^{-K(q_s)} \approx 2^{-K(L)}$ and $\overset{*}{\rho}_p(m_2) = w_{q_p} \gamma_L$.

These two examples show that the copycat environment has less weight than more complex environments and therefore has little impact on the probability of a string. Furthermore, if $\gamma_t = 2^{-K(t)}$, then the two environments q_s^m and q_p

have the same weight for m_2, such that the copycat environment has nearly as much weight as a complex environment (which might make sense in that case). Interestingly, this kind of discounting horizon, first proposed by Hutter (2004) may also be the solution that allows exploration in AIXI without losing Pareto optimality [10]. However, the time discounting of Eq. (6) and (2) could well be chosen differently.

Note that, because of the additional time discounting, the more complex the current memory, the less probable it seems to be. This time discounting requirement could be removed if one considered only the first occurrence of a memory state for a given environment. But it is not clear that this would truly reflect the probability of a memory state in general.

6   Discussion and Conclusion

In the real world, an AGI's memory must reside within the world itself, yet existing formal frameworks of intelligence generally ignore that reality. This paper has examined some of the theoretical consequences of explicitly modeling the environment's ability to modify the agent's memory. Among these consequences are the following.

First, even universal intelligent agents with infinite computational power are incapable of recognizing certain kinds of memory modifications. This is particularly interesting in light of the conclusions of our earlier work which painted a rather grim picture regarding the predictability and controllability of theoretically optimal intelligent agents [8,13], implying that along with giving an agent a specific goal or reward function, memory modification might be a particularly effective way of modifying the behavior of an AGI.

In some cases an agent *can* detect modification of its memory by verifying that the historical record of its actions in memory match those the agent would have taken. This technique can also potentially reveal modification of the observations stored in memory, if these would result in different action choices. However, it seems in many cases the environment can still fool the agent. Of the agents considered, the prediction-seeking agent and the reinforcement-learning seem relatively easy to fool because their behavior is sometimes predictable. It appears that even when augmented with an infallible sense of time, these agents can still be supplied with an unlimited number of artificial memories. With the same augmentation, however, it seems the knowledge-seeking agent cannot be deceived more than a finite number of times.

Second, memory modification has profound theoretical ramifications regarding the nature of determinism and AGI: deterministic policies become strictly weaker than stochastic policies, as there are environments in which no deterministic policy is as good as even the simplest stochastic policy.

Third, explicitly designing an agent to be aware of the environment's access to its memory is a task filled with unexpected subtlety, seeming at first to lead toward infinite regression as the agent ponders its previous and future intentions. The dilemma is resolved by considering all possible action sequences, but a remaining problem is how to assign a probability to a memory and to the environments that might generate it. We suggested a mathematically precise solution based roughly like AIXI on Occam's razor. This solution may be the best hope for the apparently essential yet possibly intractable problem of assigning probabilities to memory states. Yet it may be that the deepest insight from this work is that there may in fact be no perfect, canonical way to assign these probabilities, the implications of which could be quite profound.

There are also many interesting questions that we did not address. What if, for example, the environment could also modify the agent's code? (The agent could no longer check that its previous actions were generated by itself, since itself at a previous time step may have been different.) How can the agent verify the consistency of its history if its policy is stochastic? And finally, do any of our conclusions have ramifications for other forms of intelligence, such as our own?

Acknowledgements. Thanks to Stanislas Sochacki for valuable discussions.

References

1. Cunningham, L., Carruthers, S.: The Men in Black. Aircel Comics (1990)
2. Garner, A.R., Rowland, D.C., Hwang, S.Y., Baumgaertel, K., Roth, B.L., Kentros, C., Mayford, M.: Generation of a Synthetic Memory Trace. Science 335(6075), 1513–1516 (2012)
3. Hutter, M.: Universal Artificial Intelligence: Sequential Decisions based on Algorithmic Probability. Springer (2005)
4. Hutter, M.: Universal Algorithmic Intelligence: A Mathematical Top→Down Approach. In: Artificial General Intelligence, pp. 227–290. Springer (2007)
5. Lattimore, T., Hutter, M.: Asymptotically Optimal Agents. In: Kivinen, J., Szepesvári, C., Ukkonen, E., Zeugmann, T. (eds.) ALT 2011. LNCS, vol. 6925, pp. 368–382. Springer, Heidelberg (2011)
6. Li, M., Vitanyi, P.: An Introduction to Kolmogorov Complexity and Its Applications, 3rd edn. Springer (2008)
7. Loftus, E.F.: Creating false memories. Scientific American 277(3), 70–75 (1997)
8. Orseau, L., Ring, M.: Self-Modification and Mortality in Artificial Agents. In: Schmidhuber, J., Thórisson, K.R., Looks, M. (eds.) AGI 2011. LNCS (LNAI), vol. 6830, pp. 1–10. Springer, Heidelberg (2011)
9. Orseau, L., Ring, M.: Space-Time Embedded Intelligence. In: Bach, J., Goertzel, B., Iklé, M. (eds.) AGI 2012. LNCS (LNAI), vol. 7716, pp. 209–218. Springer, Heidelberg (2012)
10. Orseau, L.: Optimality Issues of Universal Greedy Agents with Static Priors. In: Hutter, M., Stephan, F., Vovk, V., Zeugmann, T. (eds.) ALT 2010. LNCS (LNAI), vol. 6331, pp. 345–359. Springer, Heidelberg (2010)
11. Orseau, L.: Universal Knowledge-Seeking Agents. In: Kivinen, J., Szepesvári, C., Ukkonen, E., Zeugmann, T. (eds.) ALT 2011. LNCS (LNAI), vol. 6925, pp. 353–367. Springer, Heidelberg (2011)
12. Osborne, M.J., Rubinstein, A.: A Course in Game Theory. The MIT Press (1994)
13. Ring, M., Orseau, L.: Delusion, Survival, and Intelligent Agents. In: Schmidhuber, J., Thórisson, K.R., Looks, M. (eds.) AGI 2011. LNCS (LNAI), vol. 6830, pp. 11–20. Springer, Heidelberg (2011)

14. Russell, S.J., Norvig, P.: Artificial Intelligence. A Modern Approach, 3rd edn. Prentice-Hall (2010)
15. Singh, S.P., Jaakkola, T., Jordan, M.I.: Learning Without State-Estimation in Partially Observable Markovian Decision Processes. In: ICML, pp. 284–292 (1994)
16. Solomonoff, R.J.: A Formal Theory of Inductive Inference. Part I. Information and Control 7(1), 1–22 (1964)
17. Sonnenfeld, B.: Men In Black (1997)
18. Sutton, R., Barto, A.: Reinforcement Learning: An Introduction. MIT Press (1998)
19. Zvonkin, A.K., Levin, L.A.: The complexity of finite objects and the development of the concepts of information and randomness by means of the theory of algorithms. Russian Mathematical Surveys 25(6), 83–124 (1970)

What Is It Like to Be a Brain Simulation?

Eray Özkural

Gök Us Sibernetik Araştırma ve Geliştirme Ltd. Şti.

Abstract. We frame the question of what kind of subjective experience a brain simulation would have in contrast to a biological brain. We discuss the brain prosthesis thought experiment. We evaluate how the experience of the brain simulation might differ from the biological, according to a number of hypotheses about experience and the properties of simulation. Then, we identify finer questions relating to the original inquiry, and answer them from both a general physicalist, and panexperientialist perspective.

1 Introduction

The nature of experience is one of those deep philosophical questions which philosophers and scientists alike have not been able to reach a consensus on. In this article, I review a computational variant of a basic question of *subjectivity*. In his classical article "What is it like to be a bat?", Thomas Nagel investigates whether we can give a satisfactory answer to the question in the title of his article, and due to what he thinks to be fundamental barriers, concludes that it is not something we humans can know [1]. We can intuitively agree that although the bat's brain must have many similarities to a human's, since both species are mammalian, the bat brain contains a sensory modality quite unlike any which we possess. By induction, we can guess that perhaps the difference between sonar perception and our visual experience could be as much as the difference between our visual and auditory perception. Yet, in some sense sonar is both visual and auditory, and still it is neither visual nor auditory. It is similar to vision, because it helps build a model of the scene around us, however, instead of stereoscopic vision, the bat sonar can make accurate 3-D models of the environment from a particular point of view, in contrast with normal vision that is said to have "2-1/2D vision" – it may also be contrasted with blind people using audio and tactile perceptions. It is unlike anything that humans experience, and perhaps our wildest imaginations of bat sonar experience are doomed to fall short of the real thing. Namely, because it is difficult for us to understand the experience of a detailed and rapidly updated 3-D scene that does not contain optical experience as there is no 2-D image data from eyes to be interpreted. This would likely require specialized neural circuitry. And despite what Nagel has in mind, it seems theoretically possible to "download" bat sonar circuitry into a human brain (by growing the required neural module according to a given specification, connected to sonar equipment implanted in the body) so that the human can experience the same sensory modality. In this problem, armchair philosophy

J. Bach, B. Goertzel, and M. Iklé (Eds.): AGI 2012, LNAI 7716, pp. 232–241, 2012.

alone may not be sufficient. The barrier to knowing what it is like to be a bat is, thus, mostly a technological barrier, not a conceptual or fundamental barrier, although, ultimately we cannot expect one to know *exactly* what a bat experiences, short of being one. In the best case, we would know what a bat experience is like, as the human brain could be augmented with a reconstruction of the perceptual brain circuit.

That being the case, we may also consider what a brain simulation, or an "upload" as affectionately called in science fiction literature, would experience, or whether it would experience anything at all, as brain simulation is a primary research goal on which computational neuroscientists have already made progress, e.g., [2]. The question that I pose is harder because the so-called upload does not run on a biological nervous system, and it is easier because the computation is the simulation of a human brain and not the biological computation of a bat brain, which is harder because of sonar perception. Answering this question is important, because presumably the subjective experience, raw sensations and feelings of a functional human brain are very personal and valuable to human beings. We would like to know if there is a substantial loss or difference in the quality of experience for our digital progeny. A recent survey of large-scale brain simulation projects may be found in [3].

2   Brain Prosthesis Thought Experiment

The question is quite similar to the brain prosthesis thought experiment, in which biological neurons of a brain are gradually replaced by functionally equivalent (same input/output behavior) synthetic (electronic) neurons [4]. In that thought experiment, we ponder how the subjective experience of the brain would change. Although there are challenging problems such as interfacing smoothly with existing neural tissue, it is a scientifically plausible thought experiment, also discussed at some length in [5, Section 26.4]. Moravec suggests that nothing would change with respect to conscious experience in his book. Marvin Minsky has written similarly while discussing whether machines can be conscious [6]. He produces an argument similar to Wittgenstein's beetle-in-a-box thought experiment: since a brain simulation is supposed to be functionally equivalent, its utterances would be complete, and the brain simulation would know consciousness and claim to be conscious; why should we think that the simulation is lying deliberately? This is a convincing argument, however, it neglects to mention that subjective experience may not be identical to conscious cognition as usually assumed.

Contrariwise, John R. Searle maintains that the experience would gradually vanish in his book titled "The Rediscovery of the Mind" [7]. The reasoning of Minsky and Moravec seems to be that it is sufficient for the entire neural computation to be equivalent at the level of electrical signaling (as the synthetic neurons are electronic), while they seem to disregard other brain states. While for Searle, experience can only exist in "the right stuff", which he seems to be taking as biological substrate, although one cannot be certain [8]. We will revisit this division of views, for we shall identify yet another possibility.

3   The Debate

Let us now frame the debate more thoroughly, given our small excursion to the origin of the thought experiment. On one side, AI researchers like Minsky and Moravec seem to think that simulating a brain will just work, and experience will be unchanged. On the other side, skeptics like Searle and Penrose, try everything to deny "consciousness" to poor machinekind. Although both Searle and Penrose are purportedly physicalists, they do not refrain from seeking almost magical events to explain experience.

However, it is not likely that word play will aid us much. We need to have a good scientific theory of when and how experience occurs. The best theory will have to be induced from experimental neuroscience and related facts. What is the most basic criterion for assessing whether the theory of experience is scientifically sound? No doubt, it comes down to rejecting every kind of superstitious explanation and approach this matter the same way as we are investigating problems in molecular biology, that subjective experience is ultimately made up of physical resources and interactions, and there is nothing else to it; this is a view also held by Minsky as he likens mysticism regarding consciousness to vitalism [6]. In philosophy, this approach to mind is called physicalism. A popular statement of physicalism is *token physicalism*: every mental event x is identical to a physical event y. That is a general hypothesis that neuroscientists already accept, because presumably, when the neuroscientist introduces a change to the brain, he would expect a corresponding change in the mental state, and he would expect that he can decode mental states from fMRI scans of the visual cortex as in several experiments. One may think of cybernetic eye implants and transcranial magnetic stimulation and confirm that this holds in practice, and that the hypothesis is scientifically plausible, for counter-examples are practically impossible to find. Another popular formulation of physicalism is the psychophysical identity theory [9]: that every experience is identical with some physical state. We accept both formulations at once, because the physicalist position is empirically supported, while metaphysical positions like predicate dualism are not.

4   Asking the Question in the Right Way

We have discussed every basic concept to frame the question in a way akin to analysis. Mental events/states are physical events/states. Some neural events of a man *constitute* his subjective experience. The question is whether a whole brain simulation will have experience, and if it does, how similar this experience is to the experience of a human being. If the proponents of pan-experientialism are right, then this is nothing special, it is a basic capability of every physical resource (per the scientifically plausible, physicalist variant of pan-experientialism). However, we may question what physical states are part of human experience. We do not usually think that, for instance, a mitochondrial function inside neurons, or DNA, is part of the experience of the nervous system, because they do not seem to be directly participating in the main function of the nervous system:

thinking. They are not part of the causal picture of thought. Likewise, we do not assume that the power supply is part of the computation in a computer.

This analogy might seem out of place, initially. If pan-experientialists are right, experience is one of the basic features of the universe. It would then be all around us, however, most of it would *not* be organized as an intelligent mechanism, and therefore, correctly, we do not call them conscious. The claim that any physical system yields experience anywhere, is the simplest possible explanation of experience that is consistent with experiment, therefore it is a likely scientific hypothesis. It does not require any special or strange posits, conscious experience would then require merely physical resources organized in the right way so as to yield an intelligent functional mind. Consider my "evil alien" thought experiment. If tonight, an evil alien arrived and during your sleep shuffled all the connections in your brain randomly, would you still be intelligent? Very unlikely, since the connection pattern determines your brain function. You would lose all of your cognition, intelligence and memory. However, one is forced to accept that even in that state, one would likely have an experience, an experience that is probably *meaningless* and *chaotic*, but an experience nonetheless. Perhaps, that is what a glob of plasma experiences. The evil alien thought experiment supports the distinction between experience and consciousness. Many philosophers mistakenly think that consciousness consists in experience. That, when we understand the "mystery" of experience, we will understand consciousness. However, this is not the case. Experience is part of human-like consciousness, indeed, however, consciousness also includes a number of high-level cognitive functions such as reasoning, prediction, perception, awareness, self-reflection and so forth [10, Section 4]. I suggest that it is a valid hypothesis that there are entities that have experience without any recognizable mentality.

5   Neural Code vs. Neural States

Consider the hypothesis that experience is determined by particular neural codes. If that is true, even the experience of two humans is very different, because it has been shown that neural codes evolve in different ways [11]. One cannot simply substitute the code from a human for the code in someone else's brain, it will be random to the second human. And if the hypothesis is true, it will be another kind of experience, which basically means that the blue that I experience is different from the blue that you experience, while some assume we have no way of directly comparing them. Strange as that may sound, as it is based on sound neuroscience research, it is a point of view we must take seriously.

Yet even if the experiences of two humans can be very different, they must be sharing some basic fabric or property of experience. Where does that come from? If experience is this complex time evolution of electro-chemical signals, then it is in the shared nature of these electro-chemical signals and their processing that provides the computational platform. Remember that a change in the neural code (spike train) implies a lot of changes. First of all, the chemical transmission across chemical synapses would change. Therefore, even a brain prosthesis device that simulates all the electrical signaling extremely accurately, might still miss part of the experience, if the bio-chemical events that occur in the brain are part of experience. Second, the electro-magnetic (EM) fields would change. Third, the computation would change (since data changes), although the basic "firmware" (genetic code) of the nervous system usually does not change.

To answer the question decisively, we must first encourage the neuroscientists to attack the problem of human experience, and find the sufficient and necessary conditions for experience to occur, or be transplanted from one person to the other. They should also find to what extent chemical reactions or other physical events are part of experience. It seems that chemical states may turn out to be important, and if as some people hypothesize quantum phenomena play a role in the brain, it may even be possible that the quantum descriptions may be relevant. If, for instance, we discover that the distinctive properties of nervous system experience crucially depend on quantum computations carried out at synapses and inside neurons, to construct the same kind of experience you would need similar physics and method of computation rather than a conventional electronic computer (a hypothesis also suggested in [12]). There is evidence that biology may exploit quantum computation though, i.e., recent experiments suggest that quantum coherence plays a key role in photosynthesis [13].

On the other hand, we may consider the minimalist hypothesis that electronic motion patterns may be a crucial part of experience, due to the energy and information they encompass, so perhaps electronic devices already contain brain-like experience. Then, the precise geometry and connectivity of the electronic circuit would be significant. This is much different from Searle, since we know that electrical signaling is a specific physical mechanism that plays a role in neural processing, and we do not assume that electrons have uncomputable, incomprehensible causal powers as Searle grants to biological stuff. A more intuitive possibility is that electromagnetic (EM) fields generated in the brain are the basis of experience, in which case the topology, amplitude, timing and other properties of electrical signaling may be relevant, i.e., anything that would change the EM field. EM theories of experience have been previously proposed, e.g., [14].

6   Simulation and Transcoding Experience

At this point, the reader might be wondering if the subject were not simulation: is the question like whether the simulation of rain is wet? In some respects, it is, because obviously, the simulation of water on a digital computer is not wet in the ordinary sense. Even a universal quantum computer [15] would not produce any real wetness, and all properties of water such as wetness are wholly composed of quantum mechanical properties – it is neither magic, nor an illusion. We may reconsider the question of experience of a brain simulation. We have a human brain A, a joyous lump of meat, and its digitized form B, running on a digital computer. Will B's experience be the same as A's, or different, or non-existent? Up to now, if we accept the simplest theory of experience (that it requires no special conditions to exist at all), then we conclude that B will have some experience, but since the physical material is different, it will have a different texture to it. Otherwise, an accurate simulation, by definition, stores the same functional organization of cognitive constructs, like perception, memory, prediction, reflexes, emotions without significant information loss, and since the oft-dreaded panpsychism may be considered possible, they might give rise to an experience somewhat similar to the human brain, yet the computer program B, may be experiencing something else at the very lowest level. Simply because it is running on some future nanoprocessor instead of the brain, the physical states have become altogether different, yet their relative relationship, i.e., the *logical structure* of experience, is preserved.

Let us try to present the idea more intuitively. The brain is some kind of an analog/biological computer. A memorable analogy is the transfer of a 35mm film to a digital format. Surely, many critics have held that the digital format will be ultimately inferior, and indeed the medium and method of information storage is altogether different but the digital medium has its affordances like being able to backup and copy easily. In both formats, the "same information" is stored, yet the medium varies – in reality, there is no abstract object as information, only physical codes, thus "same information" just means bi-directional translatability of codes. Likewise, B's experience will have a different physical texture but its organization can be similar, even if the code of the simulation program of B will necessarily introduce significant physical difference – for instance neural signals may be represented by a binary code rather than a temporal analog signal. Perhaps, the atoms and thus, the fabric of B's experience will be different altogether as they are made up of the physical instances of computer code running on a digital computer. As improbable as it may seem today, these simulated minds will be made up of live computer codes, so it would be naive to expect that their nature will be the same as ours. They are not human brains, they are bio-information based artificial intelligences. In all likelihood, our experience would necessarily involve a degree of unimaginable features for them, as they are forced to simulate our physical make-up in their own computational architecture. This brings a degree of relative dissimilarity. And other physical differences only amplify this difference. Assuming the above explanation, therefore, when they are viewing the same scene, both A and B will claim to be experiencing the scene as they always did, and they will additionally claim that no change has occurred since the non-destructive uploading operation went successfully. This will be the case, because the state of experience is best understood as a feature of short-term memory, which has a distributed volatile memory architecture. There is a complex electro-chemical state that is held in memory with some effort, by making the same synapses repeat firing consistently, so that more or less the same physical state is maintained. This is what must be happening when you remember something, a neural state that is somewhat similar to when the event happened should be invoked. Since in B, the fabric has changed, the memory will be reenacted in a different fabric, and therefore B will have no memory of what it used to feel like being A. Within the general framework of physicalism, we can claim that further significant changes will also influence B's experience. For instance, it will change execution to work on hardware with less communication latency or network topology. Or perhaps if the simulation is running on a different kind of architecture (like a PC), then the physical relations may change (such as time and geometry) and this may influence B's experience further. We can imagine this to be asking what happens when we simulate a complex 3-D computer architecture on a 2-D chip. We must maintain, however, that strict physicalism leads us to reject the idea that no mental changes happen when significant physical changes happen. If that were possible, then we would have to reject the idea that mental states are identical to physical states, which would be dualism. Moreover, a precise answer seems to depend on a number of smaller questions that we have little knowledge or certainty of. Some questions in this vein may be framed as: *Question 1:* What is the right level of simulation for B to be functionally equivalent to A? *Question 2:* How can the ontological contribution of the medium to experience be quantified? *Question 3:* Does experience crucially depend on any uncanny physics like quantum coherence?

6.1   General Physicalist Perspective

At this point, since we do not have conclusive scientific evidence, this is merely guesswork, and I shall give conservative answers. *Question 1*: If certain biochemical interactions are essential for the functions of emotions and sensations (like pleasure), then not simulating them adequately would result in a definite loss of functional accuracy. B would not work the same way, behaviorally, as A. This is true even if spike trains and changes in neural organization (plasticity) are simulated accurately otherwise. It is also not known with certainty whether we can simulate at a higher level, for instance via Artificial Neural Networks, that have abstracted the physiological characteristics altogether and just use numbers and arrows to represent A, or use mathematical abstractions to represent larger circuits. A recent brain simulation work shows that this might be possible [6]. It is important to know these so that B does not lack some significant cognitive functions of A, such as emotions. The right level of simulation seems to be at the level of molecular interactions which would at least cover the differences among various neurotransmitters, and which we can simulate on digital computers (perhaps imprecisely, though). At least this would be necessary because we know that, for instance, neurotransmitter levels and distribution influence behavior. Thus, it would be prudent to be able to accurately simulate the neurologically relevant biochemistry and dynamics of the brain, without necessarily simulating genetics or cell operation. *Question 2*: The most general characterizations may use information theory [16] or quantum information theory to quantify the amount of experience a system provides, and dissimilarity with another. An appropriate physical and informational framework must be chosen to answer this question in a satisfactory manner. We can claim that ultimately low-level physical states must be part of experience, because there is no good alternative. The only alternative would be dualism, which is unacceptable to a physicalist. For a general physicalist, accepting a strong form of physicalism (that every mental event/property/predicate is physical), it seems prudent to think that the medium contributes to experience insofar as it influences computational states relevant to cognition, most significantly short-term memory. Thus, physicalism may force us to consider the hypothesis that physical details of both electrical and chemical neural events would be significant. In other words, a good deal of neurophysics could be included, there may be no simple answer as panexperientialists hope. It is likely that the atoms of experience belong to a specific physical kind, such as an EM field, or quantum superposition states, which may simplify quantification. The correct theory would likely give a measure of complexity and distinguish blue experience from green experience on that basis, reducing the difference to fundamental physical distinctions. *Question 3*: Some opponents of AI, most notably Penrose, have held that consciousness is due to macroscopic quantum phenomena (like laser) together with Hameroff [17], by which they try to explain unity of experience. While on the other hand, many philosophers of AI think that the unity is an illusion [18]. Yet, the illusion is something to explain, and it may well be that certain quantum interactions may be necessary for experience to occur, much like superconductivity. This again seems to be a scientific hypothesis, which can be tested. For a physicalist, thus, this is an unsettled matter, open to future research.

6.2 Panexperientialist Perspective

An often underrated theory of experience is panpsychism, the view that all matter has mental properties. It is falsely believed by some that panpsychism is necessarily incompatible with physicalism. However, this is far from a settled controversy. Strawson has recently claimed that physicalism *entails* panpsychism [19]. More plausible is the view of pan-experientialism: that experience resides in every physical system, however, not everything is a conscious mind, for that requires *cognition* in addition. Panpsychism is also proposed as an admissible philosophical interpretation of human-like AI experience in [20].The evidence from psychedelic drugs and anesthesia imply that changing the brain chemistry modulates experience. If the experience changes, what can this be attributed to? Does the basic computation change, or are chemical/quantum interactions actually part of human experience? It seems that panexperientialism is indeed the simplest theory of experience that is consistent with our observations, i.e., that every physical system may have the potential for conscious experience. Assume that the theory is right. Then, when we ask a physicist to quantify that, she may want to measure the energy, or the amount of computation or communication, or information content, or heat, whichever works the best. A general characterization of experience such that it would hold for any physical system, may be defined precisely, and may be part of experiments. It would seem to me that the best characterization then would use information theory, because experience would not matter if it did not contain any information. For instance, an experience without any information could not contain any pictures or words. I suggest that we use such methods to clarify these finer questions. Also, the slightly more complex EM field theory has better empirical support (e.g., complexity of EM field rises with conscious thought, transcranial magnetic stimulation works), so it may be considered more restricted and more probable than general panexperientialism. Assuming the physicalist version of panexperientialism I may attempt to refine the answers above. *Question 1*: The first question is not dependent on experience, it is rather a question of which processes must be simulated for correct operation, so the answer does not change. *Question 2*: The biological medium seems to contribute at least as much as required for correct functionality (i.e., corresponding to neural information processing and biochemical changes precisely), and at most all the information as present in the biological biochemistry (i.e., precise cellular simulations), if we subscribe to panexperientialism. Co-located physical events might be significant in addition to electrical signals. According to the most general kind of panexperientialism, the cellular experience might simply constitute the low level texture of the collective experience of neural cell assemblies. Information integration theory of qualia [16] is a sort of panexperientialism. An EM field theory of experience suggests that only EM fields have experience which is a restricted kind of panexperientialism. Likewise with quantum computation hypothesis, which would imply that every varying make of quantum computer may yield different subjective experience. *Question 3*: Not necessarily. According to panexperientialism, it may be claimed to be likely false, since it would constrain minds to uncanny physics. If, for instance, quantum coherence is indeed prevalent in the brain and provides the experiential states, then the panexperientialist could point out to the possibility of a universal wave function (following the Many Worlds Interpretation). Another possibility is the use of a general physical theory, such as relativity or string theory to describe the body of experience.

Acknowledgements. Thanks to Ben Goertzel for his detailed comments that improved the article considerably. Thanks to anonymous reviewers, Joseph Polanik, and Peter D. Jones for their comments on the article.

References

1. Nagel, T.: What is it like to be a bat? Philosophical Review (1974)
2. Izhikevich, E.M., Edelman, G.M.: Large-scale model of mammalian thalamocortical systems. Proceedings of the National Academy of Sciences of the United States of America 105(9), 3593–3598 (2008)
3. Garis, H.D., Shuo, C., Goertzel, B., Ruiting, L.: A world survey of artificial brain projects, part i: Large-scale brain simulations. Neurocomputing 74(1-3), 3–29 (2010)
4. Moravec, H.: Mind Children: The Future of Robot and Human Intelligence. Harvard University Press (1990)
5. Russell, S., Norvig, P.: Artificial Intelligence A Modern Approach. Prentice-Hall Int. (1995)
6. Minsky, M.: Conscious machines. In: "Machinery of Consciousness", Proceedings, National Research Council of Canada, 75th Anniversary Symposium on Science in Society (June 1991)

7. Searle, J.R.: The Rediscovery of the Mind. Bradford (1992)
8. Searle, J.R.: Minds, brains, and programs. Behavioral and Brain Sciences (1980)
9. Lewis, D.: An argument for the identity theory. Journal of Philosophy 63(2), 17–25 (1966)
10. Minsky, M.: The Emotion Machine: Commonsense Thinking, Artificial Intelligence, and the Future of the Human Mind. Simon & Schuster (2006)
11. Schneidman, E., Brenner, N., Tishby, N., de Ruyter van Steveninck, R., Bialek, W.: Universality and individuality in a neural code. In: Advances in Neural Information Processing 13, pp. 159–165. MIT Press (2001)
12. Goertzel, B.: 11 Consciousness. In: The Structure of Intelligence: A New Mathematical Model of Mind. Springer (1993)
13. Panitchayangkoon, G., Voronine, D.V., Abramavicius, D., Caram, J.R., Lewis, N.H.C., Mukamel, S., Engel, G.S.: Direct evidence of quantum transport in photosynthetic light-harvesting complexes. Proceedings of the National Academy of Sciences 108(52), 20908–20912 (2011)
14. McFadden, J.: The conscious electromagnetic information (cemi) field theory: The hard problem made easy? Journal of Consciousness Studies 9(8), 45–60 (2002)
15. Lloyd, S.: Universal quantum simulators. Science 273(5278), 1073–1078 (1996)
16. Tononi, G.: Consciousness, information integration, and the brain. Progress in Brain Research 150, 109–126 (2005)
17. Hameroff, S., Penrose, R.: Orchestrated reduction of quantum coherence in brain microtubules: a model for consciousness. Math. Comput. Simul. 40, 453–480 (1996)
18. Minsky, M.: Decentralized minds. Behavioral and Brain Sciences 3(03), 439–440 (1980)
19. Strawson, G.: Realistic monism - why physicalism entails panpsychism. Journal of Consciousness Studies 13(10-11), 3–31 (2006)
20. Goertzel, B.: Hyperset models of self, will and reflective consciousness. International Journal of Machine Consciousness 3(1) (June 2011)

Extending Universal Intelligence Models
with Formal Notion of Representation

Alexey Potapov and Sergey Rodionov

AIDEUS, Russia
{potapov,rodionov}@aideus.com

Abstract. Solomonoff induction is known to be universal, but incomputable. Its approximations, namely, the Minimum Description (or Message) Length (MDL) principles, are adopted in practice in the efficient, but non-universal form. Recent attempts to bridge this gap leaded to development of the Representational MDL principle that originates from formal decomposition of the task of induction. In this paper, possible extension of the RMDL principle in the context of universal intelligence agents is considered, for which introduction of representations is shown to be an unavoidable meta-heuristic and a step toward efficient general intelligence. Hierarchical representations and model optimization with the use of information-theoretic interpretation of the adaptive resonance are also discussed.

Keywords: Universal Agents, Kolmogorov Complexity, Minimum Description Length Principle, Representations.

1   Introduction

The idea of universal induction and prediction on the basis of algorithmic information theory was invented a long time ago [1]. In theory, it eliminates the fundamental problem of prior probabilities, incorrect solutions of which result in such negative practical effects as overlearning, overfitting, oversegmentation, and so on. It would be rather natural to try to develop some models of universal intelligence on this basis. However, the corresponding detailed models were published only relatively recently (e.g. [2]). Moreover, the theory of universal induction was not popular even in machine learning. The reason is quite obvious – it offers incomputable methods, which additionally require training sets of large sizes in order to make good predictions.

Unsurprisingly, such more practical alternatives as the Minimum Description Length (MDL) or the Minimum Message Length (MML) principles became much more popular. These principles help developers to considerably improve performance of machine learning and perception methods, but still they neither completely solve the problem of prior probabilities nor allow for universal machine learning systems.

Of course, the universal intelligence models inherit the same drawbacks as the universal prediction. Namely, computational intractability is even more considerable here. Optimality of the models is proven up to some constant slowdown factor that

J. Bach, B. Goertzel, and M. Iklé (Eds.): AGI 2012, LNAI 7716, pp. 242–251, 2012.

can be very large. This slowdown can be eliminated via self-optimization [3], but its time for unbiased intelligence can also be very large. Consequently, most researchers consider universal models as possibly interesting, but pure abstract tools.

At the same time, practical success of the MDL principle and its counterparts implies that there is a way toward a realistic implementation of universal induction. However, there is still a very large gap to be bridged. Indeed, applications of the MDL principle rely on hand-crafted heuristic coding schemes invented by developers for each specific task. These schemes specify algorithmically incomplete model spaces with large inductive bias resulting only in weakly learnable systems.

In order to bridge this gap, the notion of representation was recently formalized within the algorithmic information theory, and the Representational MDL (RMDL) principle was introduced [4]. This principle can be used to estimate quality of decomposition of the task of model construction for some large data series into relatively independent subtasks. Residual mutual information between these subtasks can be taken into account by adaptive resonance models, which also have the information-theoretic formalization [5].

In this paper, we consider application of the RMDL principle as an unavoidable meta-heuristic for the model of the universal algorithmic intelligence. Only one heuristic is not enough to achieve efficient universal intelligence, but it makes this goal a little bit closer.

2   Background

The model of intelligence as some sort of search for the best chain of actions was the first one adopted in the AI field. It can be applied for solving any problem, but only in the case of known determined settings and unlimited computational resources. Universal Solomonoff induction/prediction affords an opportunity to extend this model on the cases of arbitrary (computable) unknown environments. However, the problem of computational resources remains and becomes more complicated. Moreover, unbiased universal agent may need a lot of time to acquire necessary information about the world to become able to secure own survival even possessing infinite computational resources. Because speeding up the search for chains of actions can also be treated as learning, the induction problem should be considered in the first place.

Solomonoff induction relies on the notion of algorithmic probability, which is calculated for a binary string α as:

$$P_U(\alpha) = \sum_{p:U(p)=\alpha} 2^{-l(p)}, \qquad (1)$$

where U is some Universal Turing Machine (UTM), and p is its program with length $l(p)$ that produces the string α being executed on the UTM U.

Probabilities $P_U(\alpha)$ are referred to as the universal prior distribution. Why are they universal? The basic answer to this question rests on the fact that any universal machine U can be emulated on another universal machine V by some program u: for any p, $V(up)=U(p)$. Consequently,

$$P_U(\alpha) = \sum_{p:U(p)=\alpha} 2^{-l(p)} = 2^{l(u)} \sum_{p:V(up)=\alpha} 2^{-l(up)} \leq 2^{l(u)} P_V(\alpha), \tag{2}$$

and similarly $P_V(\alpha) \leq 2^{l(v)} P_U(\alpha)$.

This implies that difference between the algorithmic probabilities of arbitrary string α on any two UTMs is not more than some multiplicative constant independent of α. Given enough data, likelihood will dominate over the difference in prior probabilities, so the choice of the UTM seems to be not too crucial.

However, the amount of necessary additional data can be extremely large in practice. One can still refer to the algorithmic probabilities as universal priors, because no other distribution can be better in arbitrary unknown environment. Universality of this distribution simply means that it is defined on the algorithmically complete model space (any algorithm has non-zero probability and can be learned), and models are naturally ordered by their complexity (it is impossible to specify such universal machine that reverts this order).

Apparently, the universal agent based on the algorithmic probability (such as AIξ [2]) may require executing many actions to make history string long enough to neutralize influence of the arbitrarily selected U. And no unbiased intelligence can perform better.

However, we don't want our universal agent to be absolutely unbiased. Quite the contrary, we do want it to be universal, but biased towards our world. In this context, dependence of the algorithmic probabilities on the choice of UTM appears to be very useful in order to put any prior information and to reduce necessary amount of training data. This idea was pointed out by different authors [6, 7]. It is also said [8] that the choice of UTM can affect the "relative intelligence of agents".

Unfortunately, no universal machine can eliminate necessity for exhaustive search for algorithms that produce the whole agent's history. At the same time, the pragmatic MDL principle is applied to algorithmically incomplete model spaces specified by hand-crafted coding schemes, which allow for efficient non-exhaustive search procedures. Of course, it is unacceptable to replace UTMs with Turing-incomplete machines as the basis of the universal intelligence. Can this intelligence apply the MDL principle in the same way as we do?

3   Representational MDL Principle

The minimum description length principle states that the best model of the given data source is the one which minimizes the sum of

-   the length, in bits, of the model description;
-   the length, in bits, of data encoded with the use of the model.

In theory, this principle is based on the Kolmogorov (algorithmic) complexity $K_U(\alpha)$ that is defined for some string α as:

$$K_U(\alpha) = \min_{p}[l(p) \mid U(p) = \alpha]. \tag{3}$$

The MDL principle is derived from the Kolmogorov complexity if one divides the program p for UTM $p=\mu\delta$ into the algorithm itself (the regular component of the model) μ and its input data (the random component) δ:

$$K_U(\alpha) = \min_p[l(p) \mid U(p) = \alpha] = \min_{\mu\delta}[l(\mu\delta) \mid U(\mu\delta) = \alpha] = \min_\mu \min_\delta[l(\mu) +$$

$$+ l(\delta) \mid U(\mu\delta) = \alpha] = \min_\mu\left[l(\mu) + \min_\delta[l(\delta) \mid U(\mu\delta) = \alpha]\right] = \min_\mu[l(\mu) + K_U(\alpha \mid \mu)]. \tag{4}$$

Here, $K_U(\alpha \mid \mu) = \min_\delta[l(\delta) \mid U(\mu\delta) = \alpha]$ is the conditional Kolmogorov complexity of α given μ. Consequently, the equation

$$\mu^* = \arg\min_\mu[l(\mu) + K(\alpha \mid \mu)] \tag{5}$$

gives the best model via minimization of the model complexity $l(\mu)$ and the model "precision" $K(\alpha \mid \mu)=l(\delta)$, where δ describes deviations of the data α from the model μ. This equation becomes similar to the Bayesian rule, if one assumes $-\log_2 P(\mu)=l(\mu)$ and $-\log_2 P(\alpha \mid \mu)=K(\alpha \mid \mu)$.

The MDL principle differs from the algorithmic probability in two aspects. The first one consists in selection of a single model. It can be useful in communications between intelligent agents or for reducing the amount of computations [9], but in general the MDL principle is a rough approximation of the algorithmic probability.

The second aspect consists in adopting the two-part coding. In practice, it helps to separate regular models from noise. This separation can be considered as a useful heuristic, but it is somewhat arbitrary within the task of model selection. In any case, Kolmogorov complexity is also incomputable. Thus, we still need to bridge the gap between the theoretical MDL principle and its practical applications. This is done (to some extent) within the Representational MDL principle.

The main idea here is that machine perception and machine learning methods are applied in practice to mass problems (sets of separate, individual problems of some classes). For example, any image analysis method is applied to different images independently searching for separate image descriptions in a restricted model space. On the contrary, the universal intelligence agent enumerates algorithms producing the whole history string. Let this history consists of a number of substrings (e.g. images) $\alpha_1\alpha_2...\alpha_n$. If the agent tries to compute individual Kolmogorov complexities (or algorithmic probabilities) of these strings, the result in the most cases will be poor:

$$\sum_{i=1}^{n} K_U(\alpha_i) \gg K_U(\alpha_1\alpha_2...\alpha_n), \tag{6}$$

because these substrings normally contain a lot of mutual information. This mutual information (let it be denoted by S) should be removed from descriptions of individual data strings, and should be considered as prior information in corresponding subtasks of analysis of individual substrings. This implies usage of the conditional Kolmogorov complexities $K(\alpha_i \mid S)$. Indeed, one can expect that

$$K_U(\alpha_1\alpha_2...\alpha_n) \approx \min_S \left(l(S) + \sum_{i=1}^{n} K_U(\alpha_i \mid S) \right) << \sum_{i=1}^{n} K_U(\alpha_i). \tag{7}$$

Since S can be interpreted as an algorithm (some program for UTM), which produces any given data string from its description, the algorithm S precisely fits the verbal notion of representation formulated by David Marr [10]. The notion of representation is treated in the same way in the papers on AGI (e.g. "internal representation interprets input reconstructing it" [11]). Therefore, the following more strict definition can be given [4].

Definition. The program S for UTM U is called *representation* of the collection of data strings (e.g. images) $A = \{\alpha_1,...,\alpha_n\}$, if $(\forall \alpha \in A)(\exists \mu, \delta \in \{0,1\}^*) U(S\mu\delta) = \alpha$.

The string $\mu\delta$ is called *description* of α within the representation S. This description consists of the regular μ and the random δ components.

Consequently, the RMDL principle states that 1) the best model of the data string *within given representation* is the model, for which the sum of the length of the model and the length of this data string described with the use of this model is minimal; 2) the best representation of the collection of the data strings is the representation, for which the sum of the length of the representation and the summed length of the minimal descriptions of these data strings within the representation is minimal.

When we consider any practical image analysis method, it uses some representation of images. This representation specifies an inductive bias similar to that specified by the choice of the UTM in algorithmic complexity or probability. However, the universal agent is based on the single UTM, while representations can differ for different sensor modalities or even for different elements of the same modality, they can be Turing-incomplete, and they can be learned and changed during lifetime.

It is interesting to note that for any two UTMs U and V and for any representation S for U there exists the equivalent representation S' for V such that $K_U(\alpha \mid S) = K_V(\alpha \mid S')$ for any α. Indeed, it is obvious for $S'=uS$, where u emulates U on V. Thus, the choice of UTM influences on the representation construction, but not on the model selection within equivalent representations. Thus, we will write $K_S(\alpha)$ instead of $K_U(\alpha \mid S)$, and $K_S(\alpha \mid \mu)$ instead of $K_U(\alpha \mid S\mu)$.

It should be pointed out that the RMDL principle is not just an extension of the two-part coding to a "three-part" coding. Any three- (or more) part coding of an individual string could be re-structured to the two-part coding scheme [9], but S and μ in the RMDL principle cannot be united, because S describes the problem class, while μ describes its instance.

It is also interesting to note that the idea of deep learning architectures [12] arose from the fact that complexity of some models is exponentially larger within shallow representations than within deep representations. The RMDL principle allows for much more detailed analysis of the representation efficiency.

4 Hierarchical Representations and Adaptive Resonance

Separate descriptions of substrings even within a good representation will still contain some mutual information (large-scale regularities in the initial string). Thus, if one has the string α divided into the substrings $\alpha_1\alpha_2...\alpha_n$, and the descriptions $\mu_i\delta_i$ are independently constructed for each substring, it is natural to try to compress the string $\mu=\mu_1\mu_2...\mu_n$ (deltas can be ignored on the next level of description since they are interpreted as noise within the RMDL principle). This string can still be very long, so one would like to divide μ into larger substrings (or to group μ_i) and to describe these substrings within some higher-level representation. Resulting models (regular parts of descriptions) can be further compressed, and so on.

Specific division of the string into substrings can be unknown a priori and can be considered as a part of a model. For example, borders of word and sentence segments in speech signals are not known. Images also should be segmented into some regions, which content can be described almost independently. For now, we can ignore the structure of these models and use only whole strings.

That is, at first the model $\mu^{(1)}$ is constructed for the string α within the representation $S^{(1)}$. Then, the model $\mu^{(2)}$ is constructed for the string $\mu^{(1)}$ within some higher-level representation $S^{(2)}$, and so on up to some level of abstraction m:

$$\mu^{(1)} = \arg\min_{\mu}[l(\mu) + K_{S^{(1)}}(\alpha \mid \mu)],$$

$$\mu^{(i+1)} = \arg\min_{\mu}[l(\mu) + K_{S^{(i+1)}}(\mu^{(i)} \mid \mu)]. \tag{8}$$

The total description length (an approximation of Kolmogorov complexity) of the string α can be calculated as:

$$L_{S^{(1)}...S^{(m)}}(\alpha) = K_{S^{(1)}}(\alpha \mid \mu^{(1)}) + \sum_{i=2}^{m-1} K_{S^{(i)}}(\mu^{(i)} \mid \mu^{(i+1)}) + l(\mu^{(m)}), \tag{9}$$

where $K_{S^{(i)}}(\mu^{(i)} \mid \mu^{(i+1)}) = l(\delta^{(i+1)})$.

It can be seen that sequential construction (8) of models of higher levels of abstraction is not the same as minimization of the total description length (9). Indeed, one should search for the models on all levels of abstraction simultaneously in order to get the optimal result (9). However, such the exhaustive search is computationally expensive. The sequential model construction is much more practical, but much less robust, because it is bottom-up and greedy.

Here, one can adopt Grossberg Adaptive Resonance Theory. Some subsets of models should be considered on each level of abstraction, and models on different levels should support or suppress each other. Such models remain, for which resonance is established. Qualitative expression of support values can be derived from the RMDL principle in the form of equation (9), so it can be used in the information-theoretic formalization of the Adaptive Resonance Theory [5].

Hierarchical decomposition of a problem into slightly dependent sub-problems, construction of their separate solutions, and adaptive correction of these solutions in accordance with the whole problem can be considered as almost universal meta-heuristic.

5   Adoption of the RMDL Principle in Universal Algorithmic Intelligence

The opinion that representations should be incorporated into the models of general intelligence has been already stated [13, 14]. However, representations are usually implemented only in the form of prior information expressed in a special design of programming language. Besides insufficiency of strict quantitative analysis of representation quality, the main restriction here is absence of decomposition of the model construction task.

On the other hand, necessity of decomposition is also realized. In particular, importance of chunks and possibility to solve tasks only of small Kolmogorov complexity are noted [7, 15, 16]. The RMDL principle can strictly account for both these aspects.

Consider the universal intelligent agent based on the algorithmic probability. We will use Hutter's AIξ model for convenience in order to skip unnecessary detailed descriptions of less known models. The AIξ agent is intended to maximize the total reward choosing its actions [2]:

$$y_k = \arg\max_{Y_k} \ \max_{p:U(px_{<k})=y_{<k}Y_k} \sum_{q:U(qy_{<k})=x_{<k}} 2^{-l(q)} V_{km_k}^{pq} , \tag{10}$$

where $y_{<k}$ is the string of agent's actions till the time moment k, and $x_{<k}$ is the string of sensory history (including reward signals); p are possible agent's policies consistent with the history, and q are possible algorithmic models of the environment; $V_{km_k}^{pq}$ is the expected future reward summed in the $[k, m_k]$ time interval executing algorithms p and q on the UTM U.

The formal notion of representation can be almost straightforwardly applied to the agent's inputs $x_{<k}$. Although the RMDL principle can be extended from Kolmogorov complexity to algorithmic probability, we will use its basic version for the sake of simplicity (differences between Kolmogorov complexity and algorithmic probability are discussed in our companion paper). If one uses only one best model q_{opt}, the equation (10) can be rewritten:

$$y_k = \arg\max_{Y_k} \ \max_{p:U(px_{<k})=y_{<k}Y_k} V_{km_k}^{pq_{opt}} , \ q_{opt} = \arg\min_{q:U(qy_{<k})=x_{<k}} l(q) , \tag{11}$$

To apply the RMDL principle, one should decompose q_{opt} into some set of (nearly) independent models q_i conditioned by some representation S for the segmented history $x_{<k} = x_{m_1+1:m_2}...x_{m_{n-1}+1:m_n}$, where $m_1=0$ and $m_n=k$: $U(Sq_i y_{<k}) = x_{m_i+1:m_{i+1}}$ (however, it should be noted that this form of decomposition/segmentation is not universal).

In this case, q_i can be sought independently. If $l(q) \approx l(S) + l(q_1) + \ldots + l(q_n)$, the complexity of the full task will be $2^{l(S)} \prod 2^{l(q_i)}$, while the complexity of the decomposed task will be $2^{l(S)} \sum 2^{l(q_i)}$ that is much smaller. One can also divide q_i into the model μ_i and noise δ_i further simplifying the search problem. However, in order to calculate $V_{km_k}^{pq}$ it is necessary to predict future values $x_{k:m_k}$ of the input. This is impossible if induction is aborted after construction of the set of decomposed model $\{q_i\}$. If q_i are really independent, they are unpredictable. However, this is not the case in reality. Thus, one should construct a higher level model, which produces the sequence $q_{1:n}$, and extrapolates it. A number of intermediate levels of the representation can be introduced, and the hierarchical model can be optimized with help of adaptive resonance as it was described in the previous section.

Another difference from the pure RMDL principle here is that the environment model q takes agents actions $y_{<k}$ as input. Should the whole history of actions be taken for each partial model q_i? Probably, no. Here, one can think about representations for action history.

It is attractive to try to decompose the program p in the same way as it was done for the program q. However, there is a huge difference between these programs. The program q is used as the environment model in predicting the inputs x. However, the agent doesn't need to predict own actions, since they can be chosen directly:

$$y_k = \arg\max_{Y_k} \max_{Y_{k+1:m_k}} V_{km_k}^{q_{opt}(y_{<k}Y_{k:m_k})}. \tag{12}$$

This form of search is even less computationally expensive, because action chains $Y_{k:m_k}$ have bounded complexity, while programs p can have arbitrarily large complexity. Thus, there is no sense to enumerate all programs p and to decompose them. However, search in the space of all possible action chains is still too computationally expensive. It is clear that any simplification of this exhaustive search should be done very carefully in order to avoid substantial limitations of the agent's universality.

The notion of representation can still be useful here. One can imagine some generalized actions, which can be introduced as some combinations of elementary actions, or even as small programs p_i. These generalized actions will be useful only in the case, when the total number of chains of these actions is not larger than the total number of chains of elementary actions (this condition can be expressed also in probabilistic terms for stochastic search). Thus, variety of generalized actions will be smaller, and their introduction can be formally grounded only on the base of a criterion that takes computational costs of the search strategy into account. Such criterion is now absent, and possibility to mathematically introduce representations for actions can be proposed only as an idea.

It is interesting to note that if generalized actions are enumerated, one can consider models of the environment that accept chains of these generalized actions as input:

$$p_k = \arg\max_{P_k} \max_{P_{k+1:m_k}} V_{km_k}^{q_{opt}(p_{<k}P_{k:m_k})}, \quad q_{opt} = \arg\min_{q:U(qp_{<k})=x_{<k}} l(q). \tag{13}$$

Indeed, humans rarely predict explicit reaction of the environment on their each very elementary action. At the same time, generalized actions p_i can also accept generalized input strings q_i. Indeed, we say "take the apple" or "open the door". That is, representations for sensory data (including generalized rewards) and actions are interconnected. Search in the space of generalized entities can be greatly simplified (but representations should be still constructed using the Turing-complete space). This approach can be used to gradually introduce advanced representations as priors for efficient generally intelligent agents starting from low-level representations for raw data and elementary actions and finishing with knowledge representations.

6   Conclusions

The notion of representation is extremely useful for almost all cognitive functions. However, it is rarely defined strictly enough. The necessary formal definition was recently given jointly with the Representational MDL principle, which is derived from decomposition of Kolmogorov complexity. In this paper, we discussed possibility to extend the model of universal algorithmic intelligence (namely AIξ). We showed that this principle can be rather naturally incorporated into this model making it somewhat closer to efficient artificial general intelligence. Information-theoretic criteria of quality of representations and models can be used for consequently constructing more optimal methods of machine perception and learning, including multi-level systems with adaptive resonance.

However, the RMDL principle only partially solves the problem of quality of representations in the models of universal algorithmic intelligence. It was initially introduced for such tasks, which decomposition is defined a priori (e.g. a computer vision system should analyze images independently), and representations are needed in order to decrease negative effects of this decomposition. However, there is no given decomposition of the task of prediction in the case of the universal agent. Decomposition is necessary for reducing computational complexity, but it leads to increase of algorithmic (Kolmogorov) complexity of environment models. Thus, representations trade computational complexity for algorithmic complexity. Apparently, the RMDL principle based on Kolmogorov complexity is only a particular case of constant computational complexity. In future, generalized RMDL principle should be developed based on Levin complexity (e.g. defined in [17]). Representations for Levin complexity can help to strictly account for the bias in complexity of models, which are used many times in descriptions of different data segments or executed many time during prediction and sequential decision making. Another open problem consists in formalization of representations not only for sensory input, but also for actions. We believe that such formalization can help to develop a theory of efficient self-optimization.

References

1. Solomonoff, R.: A Formal Theory of Inductive Inference, par1 and part 2. Information and Control 7, 1–22, 224–254 (1964)

2. Hutter, M.: Universal Artificial Intelligence: Sequential Decisions Based on Algorithmic Probability. Springer (2005)
3. Schmidhuber, J.: The New AI: General & Sound & Relevant for Physics. In: Goertzel, B., Pennachin, C. (eds.) Artificial General Intelligence. Cognitive Technologies, pp. 175–198. Springer (2007)
4. Potapov, A.S.: Comparative Analysis of Structural Representations of Images based on the Principle of Representational Minimum Description Length. Journal of Optical Technology 75(11), 715–720 (2008)
5. Potapov, A.S.: Theoretic-Informational Approach to the Introduction of Feedback into Multilevel Machine-Vision Systems. Journal of Optical Technology 74(10), 694–699 (2007)
6. Solomonoff, R.: Algorithmic Probability, Heuristic Programming and AGI. In: Baum, E., Hutter, M., Kitzelmann, E. (eds.) Proc. 3rd Conf. on AGI, Lugano, Switzerland, March 5-8. Advances in Intelligent Systems Research, vol. 10, pp. 151–157 (2010)
7. Pankov, S.: A Computational Approximation to the AIXI Model. In: Proc. 1st AGI Conference. Frontiers in Artificial Intelligence and Applications, vol. 171, pp. 256–267 (2008)
8. Hibbard, B.: Bias and No Free Lunch in Formal Measures of Intelligence. Journal of Artificial General Intelligence 1, 54–61 (2009)
9. Dowe, D.L., Hernández-Orallo, J., Das, P.K.: Compression and Intelligence: Social Environments and Communication. In: Schmidhuber, J., Thórisson, K.R., Looks, M. (eds.) AGI 2011. LNCS (LNAI), vol. 6830, pp. 204–211. Springer, Heidelberg (2011)
10. Marr, D.: Vision: A Computational Investigation into the Human Representation and Processing of Visual Information. MIT Press (1982)
11. Lorincz, A.: Hebbian Constraint on the Resolution of the Homunculus Fallacy Leads to a Network that Searches for Hidden Cause-Effect Relationships. In: Goertzel, B., Hitzler, P., Hutter, M. (eds.) Proc. 2nd Conf. on Artificial General Intelligence, Arlington, Virginia, USA, March 6-9. Advances in Intelligent Systems Research, vol. 8, pp. 126–131 (2009)
12. Bengio, Y.: Learning Deep Architectures for AI. Foundations and Trends in Machine Learning 2(1), 1–127 (2009)
13. Looks, M., Goertzel, B.: Program Representation for General Intelligence. In: Goertzel, B., Hitzler, P., Hutter, M. (eds.) Proc. 2nd Conf. on Artificial General Intelligence, Arlington, Virginia, USA, March 6-9. Advances in Intelligent Systems Research, vol. 8, pp. 114–119 (2009)
14. Schaul, T., Schmidhuber, J.: Towards Practical Universal Search. In: Baum, E., Hutter, M., Kitzelmann, E. (eds.) Proc. 3rd Conf. on AGI, Lugano, Switzerland, March 5-8. Advances in Intelligent Systems Research, vol. 10, pp. 139–144 (2010)
15. Hewlett, D., Cohen, P.: Artificial General Segmentation. In: Baum, E., Hutter, M., Kitzelmann, E. (eds.) Proc. 3rd Conf. on AGI, Lugano, Switzerland, March 5-8. Advances in Intelligent Systems Research, vol. 10, pp. 31–36 (2010)
16. Gobet, F., Lane, P.C.R.: The CHREST Architecture of Cognition. The Role of Perception in General Intelligence. In: Baum, E., Hutter, M., Kitzelmann, E. (eds.) Proc. 3rd Conf. on AGI, Lugano, Switzerland, March 5-8. Advances in Intelligent Systems Research, vol. 10, pp. 7–12 (2010)
17. Sun, Y., Glasmachers, T., Schaul, T., Schmidhuber, J.: Frontier Search. In: Baum, E., Hutter, M., Kitzelmann, E. (eds.) Proc. 3rd Conf. on AGI, Lugano, Switzerland, March 5-8. Advances in Intelligent Systems Research, vol. 10, pp. 158–163 (2010)

Differences between Kolmogorov Complexity and Solomonoff Probability: Consequences for AGI

Alexey Potapov[1], Andrew Svitenkov[2], and Yurii Vinogradov[2]

[1] AIDEUS, Russia
[2] National Research University of Information Technology Mechanics and Optics, Russia
potapov@aideus.com

Abstract. Kolmogorov complexity and algorithmic probability are compared in the context of the universal algorithmic intelligence. Accuracy of time series prediction based on single best model and on averaging over multiple models is estimated. Connection between inductive behavior and multi-model prediction is established. Uncertainty as a heuristic for reducing the number of used models without losses of universality is discussed. The conclusion is made that plurality of models is the essential feature of artificial general intelligence, and this feature should not be removed without necessity.

Keywords: Universal Agents, Kolmogorov Complexity, Algorithmic Probability, Prediction, Inductive Behavior, Uncertainty.

1   Introduction

Solomonoff Algorithmic Probability (ALP) theory of prediction is known to be ideal and universal. Unsurprisingly, it became the main theoretical basis for the models of artificial general intelligence [1, 2]. However, computing algorithmic probabilities implies summation over all possible algorithmic models (programs). Naturally, the two-part Minimum Message Length (MML) or Minimum Description Length (MDL) principles are adopted instead of ALP while developing practically applicable methods of machine perception and learning. These principles also rely on the algorithmic information theory (namely, on Kolmogorov complexity), but they give criteria for selecting single best models in inductive inference tasks. The best model is assumed to be the model that minimizes the sum of the complexity of the model, and the length of the data encoded given this model. These principles are frequently called information-theoretic formalizations of Ockham's Razor, which simplified formulation states that plurality should not be assumed without necessity. The MDL and MML principles are usually treated as the practical approximations of ALP [3]. Even those authors, who utilize ALP in the models of universal agents, refer to Ockham's Razor [1] mixing ALP and MDL in spite of the fact that ALP implies plurality of models.

Besides the practical arguments some authors also claim that the MML (or MDL) principle is much more methodologically appropriate for intelligent agents. In particular, importance of the two-part coding (lossy compression) is pointed out in [4] in the

J. Bach, B. Goertzel, and M. Iklé (Eds.): AGI 2012, LNAI 7716, pp. 252–261, 2012.

context of multi-agent systems (social environments). Indeed, one can agree that agents should exchange only the first parts of MML messages (models or regularities) with each other, because there is no need to communicate noise. Apparently, social communications are better described by the MML principle than by the ALP theory of prediction. Even optimal prediction methods should really be based on ALP, it is said that ALP gives better results than MML or MDL if many the top models have similar quality [2, 4, 5]. Even 10 bit difference between models makes their probabilities incomparable. It can be seen that there are serious reasons to give up on ALP.

On the other hand, there is also the opinion that human brain prefers to describe observations in many different ways, and it is unlikely that some single model of the world is used. Such redundancy of descriptions contradicts Ockham's Razor [6]. It is also interesting to note that different compositions and mixtures of experts became quite popular in the field of pattern recognition. Their efficiency appeared to be somewhat surprising, because mixture models are very complex and should be subjected to overlearning as it follows from the MDL (MML) principle. In our opinion, these issues can be resolved within ALP.

In this paper, we analyze differences between algorithmic probability and Kolmogorov complexity in the context of the models of universal algorithmic intelligent agents. We argue that ALP not only ensures optimal prediction, but also allows for some essential features of intelligent behavior. In particular, inductive (or knowledge-seeking) behavior can naturally emerge only from consideration of many alternative models. Of course, the mentioned computational and communicational restrictions are valid, but it doesn't mean that one should simply reduce the number of models taken into account. We believe that models should not be just thrown out, but they should be united into some sets leading to uncertain models. That is, the notion of uncertainty absent in the resource-unlimited universal algorithmic intelligent agents originates from the necessity to account for many models while reasoning and communicating with limited resources and time.

These conclusions are illustrated with some particular models of time series forecasting and intelligent agent behavior in Markov environment.

2   Comparison of Prediction Quality

Consider the notion of algorithmic probability. The algorithmic probability $P_{ALP}(x)$ of some string x is defined as:

$$P_{ALP}(x) = \sum_{q:U(q)=x} 2^{-l(q)},   \tag{1}$$

where U is the Universal Turing Machine, each q is its program, which produces x and has the length $l(q)$.

At the same time, the Kolmogorov complexity $K(x)$ is defined as:

$$K(x) = \min_{q:U(q)=x} l(q).   \tag{2}$$

Formally, it is obvious that $-\log_2 P_{ALP}(x) < K(x)$. However, Kolmogorov complexity implies that there is the smallest program, which can be used as the most compact description of x and can be sent instead of the original data, while ALP doesn't provide us with an effective compression scheme. Thus, Kolmogorov complexity is the more natural basis to introduce the two-part coding separating models from noise:

$$K(x) = \min_{q:U(q)=x} l(q) = \min_{\mu\delta:U(\mu\delta)=x} (l(\mu)+l(\delta)) = \min_{\mu}(l(\mu)+K(x|\mu)), \quad (3)$$

where μ is interpreted as the model, and δ is interpreted as noise.

As the result, one can choose the best model μ yielding the minimum description length. This separation can also be performed in the case of ALP, but its meaning will be more vague. Actually, it is somewhat heuristic also in the case of Kolmogorov complexity, but it appears to be rather natural in each specific case.

Now, let's consider separately the task of prediction. Solution of this task can be based on the conditional algorithmic probability and the conditional algorithmic complexity defined as:

$$P_{ALP}(x|y) = \sum_{q:U(qy)=x} 2^{-l(q)}, \quad K(x|y) = \min_{q:U(qy)=x} l(q). \quad (4)$$

Of course, algorithmically complete solutions are now unachievable both for Kolmogorov complexity and ALP. Thus, we compare them on the restricted subset of algorithms specified by the dynamical artificial neural networks (DANNs). Each DANN can be described by the corresponding system of differential equations:

$$x_i'(t) = \frac{dx_i(t)}{dt} = f\left(\sum_{j=1}^{M} w_{ji} x_j(t)\right), \quad (5)$$

where x_i are activities of M neurons, w_{ji} are connection weights constituting a matrix $\mathbf{W}$, and f is an activation function.

Starting from some initial values $x_i(0)$, activities $x_i(t)$ will evolve producing some functions as an output. One interesting application is the time series forecasting, in which the data $D=\{\mathbf{y}(t_1),...,\mathbf{y}(t_n)\}$ is given, where the values $\mathbf{y}(t_i)=(y_1(t_i),..., y_N(t_i))$ of the N-dimensional vector are observed at some moments of time $t_i \in [0, T_{max}]$. The task is to predict values $\mathbf{y}(t)$ for $t > T_{max}$.

Such connection weights w_{ij} and such initial activities $x_i(0)$ should be found that the activities $x_i(t)$ are most precisely correspond to the values $y_i(t)$. Naïve approach leads to minimization of the mean-square error:

$$E^2 = \frac{1}{n}\sum_{i=1}^{n}\sum_{j=1}^{N}\left[y_j(t_i) - x_j(t_i)\right]^2. \quad (6)$$

The number of neurons M should be not less than the dimension N of the vector $\mathbf{y}$, but it can be larger. In this case, additional neurons can be treated as hidden dynamic variables. They are not included into the MSE criterion (6). Apparently, increase of the number of additional neurons will result in decrease of the MSE as well as in overfitting. In accordance with the MDL principle, the model complexity should also be taken into account in addition to the description length of the data encoded within the model that can be estimated as $nN\log_2 E$ (accurate to a constant). Here, one can see benefits of the two-part coding.

The ANN model description includes information about the number of neurons, established connections, their weights, and initial values of activity. Total MDL criterion for the ANN with M neurons and K connections requiring $\log_2 \sqrt{n}$ bits per parameter can be roughly estimated as:

$$L = nN\log_2 E + \log_2 M + \log_2 K + \log_2 C_{M^2}^K + 0.5(M + K)\log_2 n. \qquad (7)$$

To find the best ANN, one should consider and optimize ANNs with different number of neurons and connections. In order to reduce computational complexity of this process, we utilized an iterative scheme, in which new neurons are consequently added and redundant connections are removed if these operations result in reduction of the description length criterion (7). We considered and implemented a combination of several optimization techniques (stochastic gradient descent, genetic algorithms, and simulated annealing) for optimizing ANNs with fixed architecture.

While searching for the solution with the minimum description length, many other ANNs are generated. In any case, extrapolations of the given time series are calculated using these ANNs. Why don't we try computing average result of prediction for all these ANNs taken with weights proportional to 2^{-L} (actually, ALP implies averaging over probabilities, but here averaging over predictions also works)? We will refer to such the plural model as "P-model" (P stands for algorithmic probability). The best found model will be referred to as "K-model" (K stands for Kolmogorov complexity). Let's compare prediction precision for K-models and P-models on some specific data.

Consider the well-known Wolf annual sunspot time series (see [7] as an example of application of the MDL-based ANN learning). We used the Wolf numbers till 1979 as the training sample. The search algorithm was launched for several times. Table 1 shows the result for 3 best runs (K-models and P-models assigned the same indices were obtained during the same runs). MSE_{int} stands for the MSE on the training sample, MSE_9 and MSE_{22} stand for the prediction MSE for 1980–1988 years and 1980–2001 years correspondingly.

Table 1. Comparison of prediction precision for some P-models and K-models

Model	L or $-\log_2 P$	MSE_{int}	MSE_9	MSE_{22}
K-model #1	798.9	398	900	4010
P-model #1	790.6	382	795	3078
K-model #2	799.0	388	904	3359
P-model #2	789.6	369	815	2926
K-model #3	796.7	382	907	3956
P-model #3	789.4	383	875	3705

It can be seen that prediction precision of the K-models is usually worse than of the corresponding P-models, although the optimization procedure wasn't specially designed to search for alternative models with close weights. Actually, corresponding

K- and P-models produce functions with similar shape meaning that primarily the best K-model and some nearby models influence the P-models. It is interesting to merge different P-models (in order to merge two P-models, one should simple calculate averaged prediction using corresponding weights, and sum probabilities of these models). One can consider even P-models belonging to different model spaces.

To check this idea the P-model #4 was found using another activation function representing another subset of algorithms. This model has $-\log_2 P = 784.5$; $MSE_{int}=204$; $MSE_9=834$; $MSE_{22}=529$. Table 2 shows the prediction precision of the consequently merged P-models.

Table 2. MSE values for the merged P-models

Model	MSE_{int}	MSE_9	MSE_{22}
P-model #4	204	834	529
P-model #4+1	204	820	521
P-model #4+1+2	204	796	510
P-model #4+1+2+3	205	769	506

In this case, the final P-model showed the best prediction accuracy. Examples of the K- and P-model predictions are given on Fig. 1.

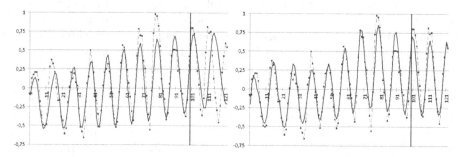

Fig. 1. Initial data (*dotted curves*) and reconstructed time series with the K-model #1 (*left*) and the merged P-model (*right*)

More interesting (but less reproducible) results can be obtained on such non-stationary data as financial time series. An example of such time series extrapolated with three best P-models (found on separate runs of the search algorithm) and the merged P-model are shown on Fig. 2. This is the case, when several the top models have similar weights, but give absolutely different predictions. 50 points ahead forecasting MSE for these models is given in Table 3.

Table 3. MSE values for the P-models

Model	#1	#2	#3	#1+#2	#1+#2+#3
MSE_{int}	0.0263	0.0258	0.0270	0.0250	0.0251
MSE_{50}	0.157	0.264	0.097	0.146	0.067

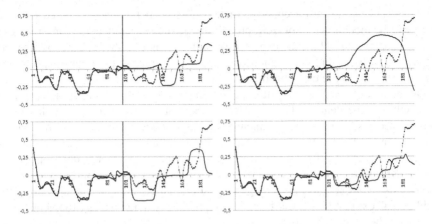

Fig. 2. Three initial P-models and the merged P-model (*bottom right*)

The shown prediction quality increase for the merged P-models is rather frequent. Of course, the prediction quality of a merged model is not always better than the quality of both models before merging. Sometimes it lies between them meaning that the quality of the merged model is worse than the quality of one of the models. However, the final P-model is almost always better than the best K-model. This is why different "mixtures of experts" in machine learning appeared to be so useful.

It should be pointed out that this increase of prediction quality is achieved almost without additional computation costs. Also, two-part coding was rather naturally used with the plural model prediction derived from ALP. At the same time, further usage of the plural models can be indeed computationally costly, e.g. in sequential decision making or in multi-agent communications.

3   Inductive Behavior

The disputable question is whether reinforcement learning is the appropriate framework for generally intelligent agents or not. Will the universal agent, which simply tries to maximize rewards received from the environment, show all types of behavior typical for humans? Here, we don't try to give a complete answer to this question. Instead, we focus on a specific behavior, namely the inductive behavior (knowledge seeking or active learning).

Different authors have considered necessity to extend (or even replace) the reward based utility function with the term expressing increase of agent's knowledge about environment. Then, the agent will be curious and will try to obtain new information. The reinforcement-learning agent has no direct motivation for inductive behavior.

Authors of [8] even claim that if this agent is allowed to arbitrarily modify its own inputs, it will do so. They call this situation the "delusion box". That is, the agent will prefer to live in illusion maximizing his utility function without obtaining information about the real world. However, the reinforcement-learning agent will choose to use the delusion box only if it will be able to predict that this choice will increase integral future reward taking into account predicted lifespan. If the agent is based on ALP, there will be models with non-zero probability predicting shorter lifespan in the case of the delusion box. Thus, the expected rewards will not be the highest possible, and the choice will depend on circumstances. For example, if the agent expects near death, it may try to use the delusion box.

On the other hand, if the agent uses only the best model for prediction, it will immediately use the delusion box (and ignore the real world), when probability of the lifespan decrease is lower. Consequently, one may suggest that inductive behavior in general can be derived from sequential decision making with ALP-based prediction. Indeed, if the agent refines predictions on each step of sequential decision making depending on the hypothesized answer of the environment, it will "automatically" account for the benefits of knowledge acquisition. Of course, one can also agree that "additional" explicit bias towards exploring previously unknown environmental regularities can be a useful heuristic [9].

Difference in the agent's behavior depending on usage of a single or multiple models can be experimentally checked on the example of the simplest Markov environment. Let environment be described by some probability distribution $P(x'|x, y)$, where x is the previous state of the environment, x' is the current state, and y is the last agent's action. We can even consider fully observable environments.

The agent tries to estimate the model of the world in the form of the distribution $P^*(x'|x, y)$ on the base of the history $xy_{\leq t}$. Obviously, the best model will be the model with probabilities simply equal to the frequencies of the corresponding transitions estimated on the base of the history, if complexities of different distributions P are assumed to be equal. When the history is empty, all the models have the same quality. Arbitrary model can be chosen depending on implementation details.

When the agent performed the action y at the state x for the first time, and this action leaded to the state x', the best model would contain $P^*(x'|x, y)=1$. Imagine that the state x appeared twice, and the agent performed actions y_1 and y_2 with the results x'_1 and x'_2. Obviously, the agent will choose the action that previously leaded to the best outcome. Situation will be more complex for sequential decision making, but the general result will be the same – the agent will choose the action that simply gave the best reinforcement in the past. Of course, the next try of this action in the given situation can lead to different states, and statistics for this action will be enriched. The agent can reject to use the action that seemed to be good on the first try, but appeared to be worse later. But this agent will not try such action that leaded to bad states unless all the other actions would be even worse. Thus, one can expect that the "single-model" agent will accumulate very inhomogeneous statistics for different actions.

On the contrary, for the Solomonoff prediction any distribution $P^*(x'|x, y)$ can be considered as a possible environment model for any history with some probability that can be easily estimated. Difference in probabilities will increase as the history length increases, but it will be small for short histories. Because prediction is based on averaging over all models, all expected reinforcements will be very similar at first. If some action was performed one or few times, its quality will be near average value, and preferences in actions will change very frequently until statistics for almost all of them are gathered.

Knowledge-seeking is "automatically" modeled in sequential decision making with the use of multi-model prediction. Indeed, some "unknown" action can have good outcome. In this case, this action will be repeated many times, and summed future outcome will be increased. The action can have bad outcome. In this case, this action will not be repeated many times, and summed future outcome will decrease only slightly. Because these both possibilities for "unknown" action have similar probabilities, it will be better in average to try such action (if there is no well-known action that has reliable outcome better than some average value). It can be seen that this agent will show knowledge-seeking behavior, when it is not "satisfied". Of course, it may be useful to boost knowledge-seeking behavior (or even make it the main "drive") by modifying the value function, but our goal was to show that this form of behavior naturally appears due to the multiplicity of environment models.

4   Uncertainty

As it was shown above, it is inadmissible to use the only one best model in AGI. Not only is multi-model prediction more accurate, but also it allows for such forms of behavior, which are essential for universal intelligence. At the same time, usage of too many models is practically impossible in sequential decision making and communications. Is it possible to reduce computational costs of multi-model approach without loosing its important features? We suppose that the number of models should be reduced not simply by eliminating worse models, but by uniting them into some sets.

Let's divide the whole set of models $Q=\{q: U(q)=x\}$ into finite number of disjoint subsets Q_i. Thus, one can write

$$P_{ALP}(x) = \sum_{q \in Q} 2^{-l(q)} = \sum_{Q_i} \sum_{q \in Q_i} 2^{-l(q)}. \tag{8}$$

We want to deal with subsets of models without addressing individual models in order to reduce complexity of their further usage. The simplest way is to use the best model within a subset instead of all models in this subset:

$$P_{ALP}(x) = \sum_{Q_i} \sum_{q \in Q_i} 2^{-l(q)} \geq \sum_{Q_i} 2^{-\min_{q \in Q_i} l(q)} \geq 2^{-\min_{q \in Q} l(q)} = 2^{-K(x)}. \tag{9}$$

This will be better than usage of the single best model, but still is not good enough. One needs not only to use one representative model instead some subset, but to describe the structure of this subset in more details.

To illustrate this idea, we analyze the simplest non-universal, but useful way of enriching descriptions of model subsets. Consider the subset, in which all models have the structure $q_j=\mu\pi_j\delta_j$, where μ is their common part (general model), π_j are the strings of particular parameter values, δ_j are the strings of deviations of j-th model $\mu\pi_j$ from the data x. One can write

$$\sum_{q \in Q_i} 2^{-l(q)} = \sum_{\pi_j \delta_j | \mu\pi_j \delta_j \in Q_i} 2^{-l(\mu)-l(\pi_j)-l(\delta_j)} = 2^{-l(\mu)} \sum_{\pi_j \delta_j} 2^{-l(\pi_j)-l(\delta_j)}. \tag{10}$$

Because all δ_j are interpreted as noise, it is not necessary to use them in prediction and decision-making. We also don't want to account for all possible values of π_j, but we are interested in the distribution:

$$P_{\mu,x}(\pi_j) = 2^{-l(\pi_j)-l(\delta_j)} . \tag{11}$$

If the set of parameters π_j constitute some metric space, one can estimate some statistical moments of this distribution. In the other case, assuming independence of distributions of each sign in π_j one can directly estimate these distributions. As the result, it is possible to represent the distribution $P_{\mu,x}(\pi_j)$ compactly. Such compact representation will contain information about uncertainty in the parameter values π of some best model from the subset Q_i.

Usage of such uncertain models allows estimating uncertainty in prediction caused by the simple fact that different models in the set Q_i produce different outputs $U(\mu\{\pi\delta\})=\{x\}$ (of course, the set of predictions $\{x\}$ cannot be known precisely unless all models are explicitly computed). More complex type of uncertainty can be considered, when one tries to reduce the number of models further uniting subsets Q_i containing models with different structures.

Uncertainty in the predicted x propagates through sequential decision making and becomes much larger in future. Obviously, if the agent has such a history that leads to models with high uncertainty, it will not be possible to guarantee high future rewards. Thus, actions aimed to decrease uncertainty will allow increasing future rewards in average. Thus, they can be chosen even in the case, when few models are used in sequential decision making, but uncertainty is taken into account.

In the case of simplest Markov environment, introduction of uncertainty leads to bias towards more uniform distribution $P^*(x'|x, y)$. Unsurprisingly, experiments show that more diverse actions are tried in presence of this bias, while the agent prefers exploitation in absence of this bias. The biased agent gains slightly smaller rewards at the beginning, but it has some chances to outperform unbiased single-model agent on long time intervals. Correct introduction of uncertainty as a heuristic in adoption of ALP can hopefully give optimal solution of the "exploration vs. exploitation" problem. This possibility has not been considered within algorithmic information theory.

It can be seen that uncertainty should be introduced as a heuristic that helps to greatly reduce computational costs of ALP without violating inductive behavior. It is frequently said that uncertainty and probability are different categories. However, theories of uncertainty usually rely on the combinatorial basis. However, if we follow Kolmogorov and Solomonoff, the notion of probability should be inferred from the notion of information, which should also have pure combinatorial (algorithmic) basis. Solomonoff induction doesn't include the notion of uncertainty, but it naturally appears in attempt to reduce the number of used models. Thus, the complete theory of uncertainty should be built on the base of the algorithmic information theory. Unfortunately, detailed analysis of this problem goes beyond the scope of the paper.

5   Conclusions

Some methodological aspects of usage of Kolmogorov complexity and algorithmic probability in universal intelligent agents were discussed. At first, the task of time series forecasting was considered. The dynamic artificial neural networks were used as a subset of algorithmic models. Accuracy of prediction given by the best ANN selected on the base of the MDL criterion was compared with accuracy of prediction derived from ALP (weighted sum of predictions made by all the models constructed during the search was calculated). MSE of the latter kind of prediction appeared to be stably lower. Decrease of MSE varied from 10% to 50% depending on data.

Then, the problem of information-seeking behavior was considered. It was shown that such inductive behavior naturally appears in the ALP-based agent, while the "single-model" agent will have a strong bias towards exploitation of actions with well-known good outcome. In order to reduce complexity of usage of multiple models in decision making and communications, subsets of models is proposed to replace with some "uncertain" models. A theory of uncertainty as one of meta-heuristics meant for considerable reduction of computational complexity of ALP without losses of universality is to be developed in future.

References

1. Hutter, M.: Universal Artificial Intelligence: Sequential Decisions Based on Algorithmic Probability. Springer (2005)
2. Solomonoff, R.: Algorithmic Probability, Heuristic Programming and AGI. In: Baum, E., Hutter, M., Kitzelmann, E. (eds.) Proc. 3rd Conf. on Artificial General Intelligence. Advances in Intelligent Systems Research, vol. 10, pp. 151–157 (2010)
3. Solomonoff, R.: The Discovery of Algorithmic Probability. J. of Computer and System Sciences 55(1), 73–88 (1997)
4. Dowe, D.L., Hernández-Orallo, J., Das, P.K.: Compression and Intelligence: Social Environments and Communication. In: Schmidhuber, J., Thórisson, K.R., Looks, M. (eds.) AGI 2011. LNCS (LNAI), vol. 6830, pp. 204–211. Springer, Heidelberg (2011)
5. Poland, J., Hutter, M.: MDL convergence speed for Bernoulli sequences. Statistics and Computing 16, 161–175 (2006)
6. Buchanan, B.G.: What Do We Know about Knowledge? AI Magazine 26(4), 35–46 (2005)
7. Small, M., Tse, C.K.: Minimum Description Length Neural Networks for Time Series Prediction. Physical Review E 66, 066701-1–066701-12 (2002)
8. Ring, M., Orseau, L.: Delusion, Survival, and Intelligent Agents. In: Schmidhuber, J., Thórisson, K.R., Looks, M. (eds.) AGI 2011. LNCS (LNAI), vol. 6830, pp. 11–20. Springer, Heidelberg (2011)
9. Schmidhuber, J.: Artificial Scientists & Artists Based on the Formal Theory of Creativity. In: Baum, E., Hutter, M., Kitzelmann, E. (eds.) Proc. 3rd Conf. on Artificial General Intelligence. Advances in Intelligent Systems Research, vol. 10, pp. 145–150 (2010)

Deconstructing Reinforcement Learning in Sigma

Paul S. Rosenbloom

Department of Computer Science & Institute for Creative Technologies
University of Southern California
12015 Waterfront Drive, Playa Vista, CA 90094
rosenbloom@usc.edu

Abstract. This article describes the development of reinforcement learning within the Sigma graphical cognitive architecture. Reinforcement learning has been deconstructed in terms of the interactions among more basic mechanisms and knowledge in Sigma, making it a derived capability rather than a de novo mechanism. Basic reinforcement learning – both model-based and model-free – are demonstrated, along with the intertwining of model learning.

Keywords: Reinforcement learning, cognitive architecture, graphical models.

1   Introduction

Reinforcement learning (RL) enables agents to learn effective policies for task performance based on rewards received over a sequence of trials [1]. It is a key concept in artificial general intelligence (AGI) – even being at the core of a proposal for a *universal artificial intelligence* [2] – plays an important role in intelligent robotics, and is increasingly important in conventional cognitive architectures [3-4]. This article describes the simple manner in which RL can be implemented within the *Sigma* (Σ) cognitive architecture [5], with its grounding in *factor graphs* [6] – a general form of graphical model [7] – and *piecewise linear functions* [8].

The goal of this effort has not been to implement from scratch a preselected RL algorithm within Sigma, nor even necessarily, at least at first, to yield an RL capability that is competitive with today's best, but to: (1) explore whether some variant of RL could emerge from how Sigma already works, and (2) analyze the ensuing results to see what they can tell us about both Sigma and RL. This approach to RL is driven by a key desideratum that is guiding Sigma's development towards general intelligence – *functional elegance*, which seeks to combine the broad range of capabilities implicit in general intelligence with simplicity and theoretical elegance. The ultimate aim is for something like a set of *cognitive Newton's laws* that yield the required diversity of behavior from interactions among a small set of very general primitives. AIXI [2] can be viewed as an attempt at an extreme example of functional elegance. The approach in Sigma is less ambitious, but still strongly in this direction.

J. Bach, B. Goertzel, and M. Iklé (Eds.): AGI 2012, LNAI 7716, pp. 262–271, 2012.

This article explains how model-based RL can be engendered within Sigma from the interactions among: (1) a more primitive gradient-descent learning mechanism that is capable, among other things, of learning to predict; and (2) schematic knowledge that determines what predictions are to be learned, what their initial values should be, and how to propagate such values backwards over time. This effectively deconstructs a form of model-based RL in terms of preexisting, more basic, capabilities already in Sigma, plus knowledge. In contrast, no means was found within Sigma's existing capabilities of producing either model-free RL or the intertwining of model learning with model-based RL. However, both do become possible after a minimal further addition to the architecture. This overall approach, of deconstructing capabilities in terms of existing architectural mechanisms when possible, and of minimal changes to the architecture only when necessary, directly supports functional elegance. It also reflects both a form of Occam's razor and an adherence to Allen Newell's exhortation to "listen to the architecture" [9].

2   Reinforcement Learning (RL)

The central concept in reinforcement learning is that of (logically) propagating rewards received later in performance backwards in time to assist in learning the expected utility of earlier actions (for use in later trials). Ultimately the learning is reflected in Q *values* – $Q(s, a)$ – which capture the expected (discounted) cumulative reward of choosing action a in state s, and which thus aid in selecting appropriate actions. The particular approach taken in Sigma provides an *on-policy* learning algorithm, which learns from the action taken rather than from the best action that could have been taken, making it more akin to SARSA [10] than to Q-learning [11]. The learning update in SARSA is defined as $Q(s_t, a_t) \leftarrow Q(s_t, a_t) + \alpha[r_t + \gamma Q(s_{t+1}, a_{t+1}) - Q(s_t, a_t)]$, where α is the learning rate and γ is the discount factor for future rewards.

Consider, for example, a one-dimensional, discrete, grid task in which the agent may start at any location and is to reach a goal location via left and right actions (Fig. 1). With no initial information concerning which operator to choose, behavior begins with random choices. However, once the goal location is reached, a reward will be received, and learning can begin. Over time, and future experiences, this information propagates backwards across actions to yield Q values that predict higher discounted cumulative rewards for choosing right when the agent is to the left of the goal and left when it is to the right of the goal. This example task will be used throughout the remainder of this article.

Fig. 1. 1D grid task with example goal (4), starting location (2), and actions (left and right). The two extreme locations act as buffers to avoid end effects.

3   The Sigma Architecture

Sigma has been under development in some form since 2008, although until now it lacked a name due to an ambivalence concerning whether what was being developed was a specific graphical architecture or a general approach, based on graphical models, for exploring the space of architectures. Although there remains room to explore a broader range of architectures, it has become increasingly clear that a specific architecture was being built, which now has a proper name: *Sigma*.

In general, graphical models provide an efficient means of computing with complex multivariate functions by decomposing them into products of simpler functions and then mapping them onto graphs. From these graphs, the marginals of the individual variables – i.e., the function's values when all other variables are summarized out – can be computed efficiently, as can the function's global mode. Bayesian networks and Markov random fields are common forms of graphical models, and some forms of neural networks map directly onto them. Factor graphs are a variant of graphical models that map decompositions of arbitrary multivariate functions onto undirected bipartite graphs of variable and factor nodes. Variables map onto variable nodes while decomposed factors map onto factor nodes. Undirected edges are defined between each factor node and its variables. Fig. 2 shows a factor graph for a simple multivariate algebraic function, along with its solution via the summary product algorithm [6], as is used in Sigma.

Given evidence about a subset of the variables, messages are passed along the links and processed at the nodes to yield new messages. Each message along a link provides information about the distribution of values for the link's variable. Incoming messages at variable nodes are combined via pointwise product – like an inner product without the final summation – to yield outgoing messages, but with each outgoing message omitting from its product the incoming message on its link. Similar pointwise products occur at

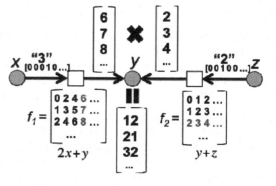

Fig. 2. Summary product computation over the factor graph for $f(x,y,z) = y^2+yz+2yx+2xz = (2x+y)(y+z) = f_i(x,y)f_2(y,z)$ of the marginal on y given evidence concerning x and z. Only the messages (and link directions) involved in computing y are shown.

factor nodes, but with the factor's function also included in the product; and then all variables not in the outgoing message are summarized out. Summarization typically occurs via *summation* – or *integration* for continuous functions – to yield marginals, or via *maximum* to yield the mode. Message passing terminates when a stopping criterion is hit, such as that no new message is significantly different from the previous message along the same link.

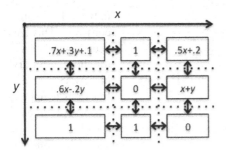

Fig. 3. Bivariate function as a 2D array of regions with linear functions

The generality and efficiency of the summary product algorithm depends critically on the representation used for the factor functions and messages. In Sigma, a multidimensional piecewise linear representation is used, with one dimension per variable (Fig. 3) [8]. This enables approximating arbitrary continuous functions as closely as desired, plus specialization to discrete representations – such as probability distributions – by mapping integers in the function's domain to unit regions while limiting the region functions to constants, and to symbolic representations by further limiting the constant functions to Boolean (0/T and 1/F) while assigning symbols to domain integers. A form of *hybrid mixed* representation is thus proffered.

Knowledge fragments in Sigma are specified via *conditionals*, such as the one in Fig. 4, which compile into subgraphs of long-term memory. What is normally viewed as evidence in graphical models appears in working memory nodes in Sigma. The conditional in Fig. 4 consists of two conditions and an action, thus amounting to a classical rule.

```
CONDITIONAL Move-Left
    Conditions: (Selected state:s operator:left)
                (Location state:s x:x)
    Actions: (Location state:s x:x-1)
```

Fig. 4. Grid conditional for executing action of moving left

The expression $x-1$ in the conditional's action indicates the use of an *offset* [12], part of Sigma's mechanism for *affine transformations* (in support of mental imagery) [13]. In general, a variable in a condition or an action may include a coefficient and an offset, where the coefficient must be a constant and the offset may be either a constant or a variable. This isn't simply a matter of multiplication and addition of values though, as an offset shifts a whole piecewise linear function along a variable's dimension by modifying the region boundaries, while a coefficient may – once again by modifying region boundaries – expand, contract, or invert a dimension. The combination of coefficients and offsets enables mental imagery to be translated, scaled and reflected. When combined with variable interchanges, they also enable limited forms of rotation.

When the offset is a variable rather than a constant, two random variables must be added, implicating a *convolution* in general. Although convolutions have not yet been implemented in Sigma, when the offset variable only has a single nonzero value, it can simply be extracted and used like a constant. Such an approach is exploited in RL to add the current reward to the (distribution over the) discounted future reward.

Another feature of Sigma that is relevant to the implementation of RL is a generalization from the use of constants in conditions and actions – such as `left` in Fig. 4 – to the use of *filters*. A constant in this context is essentially a filter that only passes through portions of messages that match it via a factor function that is nonzero

```
CONDITIONAL Select-Operator
    Conditions: (Location state:s x:x)
                (Q x:x operator:o value:[.1*q])
    Actions: (Selected state:s operator:o)
```

Fig. 5. Grid conditional that transforms distributions over Q values into operator weights for selection

only for the constant. This has been generalized to allow arbitrary piecewise linear functions to appear where previously only constant tests could. Fig.5, for example, shows a conditional with a filter – in square brackets to distinguish it from an affine transform – that converts distributions over the possible Q values for the operators, ranging in [0, 10), into an expected Q value for each operator. Q's domain values are multiplied by .1, with the result then multiplied by the incoming message. The variable q is summarized out via integration prior to the action, weighting each operator by its expected Q value.

Conditions and actions in Sigma limit the direction in which messages are passed – those within condition subgraphs only move away from working memory while those within action subgraphs only move towards it. This provides the forward momentum central to procedural memory. *Condacts* – a neologism for *cond*itions and *act*ions – provide the bidirectional message passing required for the full generality of factor graphs, as used for example in probabilistic reasoning, constraint satisfaction, signal processing, and (partial match in) declarative memory [14]. The conditional in Fig. 6 defines a transition function – i.e., an action model – using two conditions, a condact, and a function to specify an initial uniform distribution over the next location given the current location and operator. The stars (*) in the function denote that the value specified

```
CONDITIONAL Transition
    Conditions: (Location state:s x:x)
                (Selected state:s operator:o)
    Condacts: (Location*Next state:s x:nx)
    Function<x,o,nx>: .125:<*,*,*>
```

Fig. 6. Grid conditional for an initially uniform transition function (action model)

(.125) applies to all triples of current location, selected operator, and next location. The variable nx for the next state is underlined to denote normalization over it during learning.

The core cognitive (or *decision*) cycle in Sigma involves message passing until quiescence, with the results then used in deciding how to modify working memory. Learning also occurs at decision time, by altering functions in conditionals (structure learning remains for future work). *Episodic learning* modifies temporal functions in episodic conditionals that are automatically built for state predicates (such as Location and Selected). *Gradient descent learning* modifies conditional functions, as stored in factor nodes, by interpreting incoming messages as gradients that are to be normalized, multiplied by the learning rate, and added to the existing function. The idea for this learning mechanism, which was developed in conjunction with Abram Demski and Teawon Han, was inspired by earlier work [15] showing that gradient descent was possible in Bayesian networks, much as in neural networks, but without the need for an additional backpropagation mechanism because the local messages already determined the gradient.[1]   This form of learning is capable of working in either a supervised or unsupervised manner, and in Sigma supports both basic RL and model learning.

4   RL in Sigma

The core idea for deriving an RL algorithm from Sigma has been to leverage gradient descent in learning Q values over multiple trials, given appropriate conditionals to structure the computation as is needed for this to happen.   Much of the work has therefore involved understanding what these conditionals should be.

Two conditionals – the one in Fig. 4 plus another like it – implement the `left` and `right` actions in the grid task. Given these two conditionals, plus a third that proposes the actions for selection, Sigma performs a random walk until the goal is achieved.   To enable Q values to determine which action to choose, the proposal conditional must be augmented to use them as operator weights – or *numeric preferences* – as in Fig. 5. Initial Q values must

```
CONDITIONAL Q
   Conditions: (Location state:s x:x)
   Condacts: (Q x:x operator:o value:q)
   Function<x,o,q>: .1:<*,*,*> …
```

Fig. 7. Grid conditional for an initially uniform distribution over the Q values for the operators, given the locations

then also be provided, as in Fig. 7. If direct evidence were provided for the action's Q values, it would be trivial to use gradient descent to learn better values for this function without needing to invoke reinforcement learning.   However, without such evidence, RL is the means by which rewards from later steps in task performance propagate backwards to serve as input for learning Q values for earlier steps.   This occurs via a combination of: (1) learning to predict local rewards from the externally provided evidence for these rewards; and (2) learning to

```
CONDITIONAL Reward
   Condacts: (Reward x:x value:r)
   Function<x,r>: .1:<[1,6)>,*> …
```

Fig. 8. Grid conditional for an initially uniform distribution over rewards at locations

predict both discounted future rewards and Q values by propagating backwards the discounted sum of the next location's local reward and its discounted future reward.

To (learn to) predict a location's reward, the conditional in Fig. 8 is added. To learn discounted future rewards and Q values, the conditional in Fig. 9 is

```
CONDITIONAL Backup
   Conditions: (Location state:s x:x)
              (Selected state:s operator:o)
              (Location*Next state:s x:nx)
              (Reward x:nx value:r)
              (Projected x:nx value:p)
   Actions: (Q x:x operator:o value:.95*(p+r))
           (Projected x:x value:.95*(p+r))
```

Fig. 9. Grid conditional for backing up rewards

---

[1] The version here only approximates the true gradient in [15], but was sufficient for this work.

added (along with an unshown conditional for discounted future rewards). The Backup conditional examines the current location and operator, along with the predicted next location – as given by the transition function – and its predicted local reward and future discounted reward. In the actions, it leverages an affine transformation, with an offset to add the next location's predicted local reward to the distribution over its predicted future reward, and a coefficient to discount this sum. RL then results from using the messages that are passed back to the conditional functions as gradients in learning Q values and discounted future rewards.

Fig. 10 summarizes how RL emerges from all of this. Double arrows with elliptical tips represent decisions for the operator and location. Solid arrows predict aspects of the current location. The gray box is the external reward. Dotted boxes and arrows are predictions of/for the next location. Value backup involves the gray triangles and curved arrow.

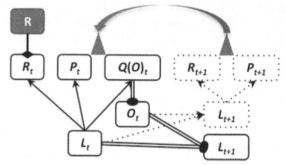

Fig. 10. Variables and processes for RL in the grid task

The resulting form of learning is like SARSA rather than Q-learning because it is driven by the operator actually selected rather than by the best available operator. This form of RL also is *model based*, leveraging a version of the transition conditional in Fig. 6 that embodies probabilities corresponding to the actions' actual effects. Learning then occurs via gradient-descent-based refinements to the functions in Figs. 7-8 and the unshown one, for the distributions over Q values, local rewards, and discounted future rewards, respectively.

After completing 20 trials for each of the two possible extreme starting points – locations 1 and 6 – the expected value of the learned reward function (by location) is identical to the externally defined reward function: <0, 0, 0, 0, 9, 0, 0, 0, 0>. The expected values learned for the discounted future reward are shown in Fig. 11 (Fixed Model). This peaks, as it should, as the goal location (4) is neared, but is zero for both the goal location and the buffer locations since

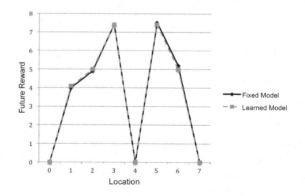

Fig. 11. Learned expected discounted future reward

they are initialized to zero and no move is ever made from them. The expected Q values learned for left vs. right are shown in Fig. 12. As desired, moving right is preferred when left of the goal and moving left when to the right. There is no preference at the goal.

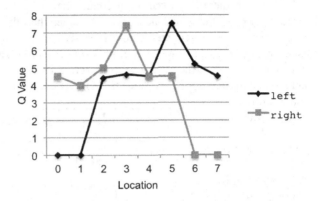

Fig. 12. Learned expected Q values

These results have been presented in terms of point values, a format that matches what is normally seen with RL. However, the learning actually involves full distributions rather than individual points, with points computed as expected values over distributions. Learning via distributions rather than points has been natural in Sigma, but it may also prove particularly advantageous when distributions can help, for example, identify when a representation is too coarse [16], or when a Soar-like impasse – forms of which already exist in Sigma [17] – should occur [18].

Everything in this example was learned in a *synchronic* manner, considering only one actual location. Even reward backup was synchronic, being based on the distribution over the predicted next location rather than on the actual next location. By focusing on learning to predict, RL has been able to proceed within Sigma in the context of a single actual location. However, for model-free RL, a pair of actual locations must be available simultaneously in working memory so that value backup can occur without the aid of the predictions the transition function provides in model-based RL. Similarly, although an initial uniform transition function is provided when the action models are to be learned, the correct gradient cannot be computed unless both locations are simultaneously in working memory.

As Sigma worked prior to this investigation of RL, consecutive states were simultaneously present only during the decisions that occurred at the end of cognitive cycles, when old working memory values were replaced by new ones. However, just one of these states would be in working memory at a time. If Sigma were extended to transiently represent both at once in working memory – essentially during the decision – with a solution to the graph occurring in the interim and learning enabled, then the kind of *diachronic* learning required for both model-free RL and the learning of action models should be possible with only a minimal extension to Sigma's architectural code. This is in fact what has been implemented. During decisions, new values are placed into *next* variants of to-be-altered state predicates – Location*Next here – and the graph is again solved with learning enabled, before actual modifications are made to working memory (and the *next* variants are flushed).

Now, when there is no transition conditional, model-free RL results, with value backup based on the actual next location rather than the predicted one. Given 20 trials, the expected discounted future rewards are the same as those learned with a fixed model (Fig. 11). When the uniform transition conditional from Fig. 6 is included, the gradient necessary to learn action models becomes available, enabling them to be acquired during the same trials in which rewards, Q values, and discounted future rewards are learned. Running 20 trials here yields a transition function where the only entries

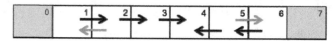

Fig. 13. Learned transition function

that are above the initial value of .125 are shown in Fig. 13 (with darkness corresponding to functional value). All of the on-path moves have a functional value of 1, whereas the two off-path moves predict the correct transition but at lower values. The expected discounted future rewards here – Fig. 11 (Learned Model) – are nearly indistinguishable from those learned with a predefined transition function.

5   Conclusion

Learning is central to general intelligence, with reinforcement learning providing a particular form that that has been prominently featured within both AGI and several cognitive architectures. When the time came to address how reinforcement learning would work in Sigma, the intriguing possibility arose of its emerging from the interactions among a general set of more basic mechanisms, making RL a derived capability rather than an architecturally implemented mechanism, and satisfying the joint constraints of functional elegance, Occam's razor and Newell's exhortation.

The work presented here is still only a beginning, but it does show how RL can be deconstructed in terms of a local form of gradient-descent learning plus appropriate knowledge structures, to yield basic on-policy, model-based, reinforcement learning. A single extension to Sigma – to simultaneously represent both the current and next state during an interpolated graph solution – was then required to enable both model-free RL and (intertwined) model learning. As it turns out, this is a non-RL-specific extension that was also motivated, for example, by the related problem of learning transition functions for POMDPs in Sigma [19]. The extension of Sigma's affine transformations to variable offsets also occurred in service of implementing RL, although the idea and the understanding of its need both predated this work on RL.

Much more is still required in a complete, state-of-the-art, architecturally integrated capability for reinforcement learning, including exploration, scaling, and structure learning. Also necessary is extensive experimentation with more complex tasks, careful comparisons with implementations of RL in other architectures, and investigations of synergies that might become available when RL interacts with other knowledge and capabilities in Sigma. Yet, the important result remains, that the core of RL has been demonstrated, along with its intertwining with model learning, and all in a functionally elegant manner.

Acknowledgments. This effort has been sponsored by the U.S. Army and the Air Force Office of Scientific Research. Statements and opinions expressed do not necessarily reflect the position or the policy of the United States Government, and no official endorsement should be inferred. I would like to thank Abram Demski, Nassim Mafi and Volkan Ustun for helpful discussions on this material.

References

1. Sutton, R.S., Barto, A.G.: Reinforcement Learning: An Introduction. A Bradford Book, MIT Press, Cambridge (1998)
2. Hutter, M.: Universal Artificial Intelligence: Sequential Decisions Based on Algorithmic Probability. Springer, Berlin (2005)
3. Sun, R., Slusarz, P., Terry, C.: The interaction of the explicit and the implicit in skill learning: A dual-process approach. Psychological Review 112, 159–192 (2005)
4. Nason, S., Laird, J.E.: Soar-RL: Integrating reinforcement learning with Soar. Cognitive Systems Research 6, 51–59 (2005)
5. Rosenbloom, P.S.: Graphical models for integrated intelligent robot architectures. In: AAAI Spring Symposium on Designing Intelligent Robots (2012)
6. Kschischang, F.R., Frey, B.J., Loeliger, H.: Factor Graphs and the Sum-Product Algorithm. IEEE Transactions on Information Theory 47, 498–519 (2001)
7. Koller, D., Friedman, N.: Probabilistic Graphical Models: Principles and Techniques. MIT Press, Cambridge (2009)
8. Rosenbloom, P.S.: Bridging dichotomies in cognitive architectures for virtual humans. In: AAAI Fall Symposium on Advances in Cognitive Systems (2011)
9. Newell, A.: Unified Theories of Cognition. Harvard University Press, Cambridge (1990)
10. Rummery, G.A., Niranjan, M.: On-line Q-learning using connectionist systems (1994)
11. Watkins, C.J.C.H.: Learning from Delayed Rewards. PhD thesis, Cambridge University (1989)
12. Rosenbloom, P.S.: Mental imagery in a graphical cognitive architecture. In: Second International Conference on Biologically Inspired Cognitive Architectures (2011)
13. Rosenbloom, P.S.: Extending Mental Imagery in Sigma. In: Bach, J., Goertzel, B., Iklé, M. (eds.) AGI 2012. LNCS (LNAI), vol. 7716, pp. 272–281. Springer, Heidelberg (2012)
14. Rosenbloom, P.S.: Combining Procedural and Declarative Knowledge in a Graphical Architecture. In: 10th International Conference on Cognitive Modeling (2010)
15. Russell, S., Binder, J., Koller, D., Kanazawa, K.: Local learning in probabilistic networks with hidden variables. In: 14th International Joint Conference on AI (1995)
16. Munos, R., More, A.: Variable resolution discretization in optimal control. Machine Learning 49, 291–323 (2002)
17. Rosenbloom, P.S.: From Memory to Problem Solving: Mechanism Reuse in a Graphical Cognitive Architecture. In: Schmidhuber, J., Thórisson, K.R., Looks, M. (eds.) AGI 2011. LNCS (LNAI), vol. 6830, pp. 143–152. Springer, Heidelberg (2011)
18. Bloch, M.K., Laird, J.E.: Heuristic value function revision. In: The 32nd Soar Workshop
19. Chen, J., Demski, A., Han, T., Morency, L.-P., Pynadath, P., Rafidi, N., Rosenbloom, P.S.: Fusing symbolic and decision-theoretic problem solving + perception in a graphical cognitive architecture. In: Second International Conference on Biologically Inspired Cognitive Architectures (2011)

Extending Mental Imagery in Sigma

Paul S. Rosenbloom

Department of Computer Science & Institute for Creative Technologies
University of Southern California
12015 Waterfront Drive, Playa Vista, CA 90094
rosenbloom@usc.edu

Abstract. This article presents new results on implementing mental imagery within the Sigma cognitive architecture. Rather than amounting to a distinct module, mental imagery is based on the same primitive, hybrid mixed, architectural mechanisms as Sigma's other cognitive capabilities. The work here demonstrates the creation and modification of compound images, the transformation of individual objects within such images, and the extraction of derived information from these compositions.

Keywords: Mental imagery, cognitive architecture, graphical models, piecewise continuous functions, affine transformations.

1 Introduction

Mental imagery is a cognitive capacity that enables humans to represent and reason about spatial information. It includes the ability to construct images from pieces retrieved from memory; to translate, scale and rotate (parts of) these images; and to extract new information from the composite and/or transformed results. Although nominally focused on the spatial aspects of the physical world, Gunzelmann and Lyon summarize its key role in other areas of human cognitive processing – such as numerical information processing, problem solving and language [1] – and Cassimatis has hypothesized that physical reasoning is part of a general cognitive substrate that underlies all of reasoning [2]. Mental imagery must also clearly relate to perception, but the focus here is on the connection with cognition rather than perception.

Following an extended debate concerning whether mental imagery is symbolic versus imagistic – based, for example, on pixel arrays – there is little doubt at this point that both are implicated in the full picture. Some of the most interesting recent work on this topic includes how to incorporate such a capacity into a *cognitive architecture*, a hypothesis about the fixed structure underlying cognition, and how these structures combine with each other (and knowledge) to yield intelligent human(-like) behavior. Imagery modules have been investigated in architectures such as Soar [3] and ACT-R [4], including ideas for introducing more explicitly hybrid aspects [5].

The *Sigma* (Σ) architecture is built to be hybrid from the ground up, in service of satisfying two general desiderata: *grand unification* and *functional elegance*. A traditional unified cognitive architecture attempts to bring together in an integrated manner the range of cognitive capabilities required for human(-level) intelligent behavior in the world. A grand unified architecture goes beyond this, in analogy to a

J. Bach, B. Goertzel, and M. Iklé (Eds.): AGI 2012, LNAI 7716, pp. 272–281, 2012.

grand unified theory in physics, to attempt to include the crucial pieces missing from a purely cognitive theory, such as perception, motor control, and emotion. Functional elegance implies a combination of the broad range of capabilities required in a (grand) unified architecture with simplicity and theoretical elegance. In Sigma, the aim is something like a set of *cognitive Newton's laws* that yield the required diversity of behavior from interactions among a small set of very general primitives. Within AGI, AIXI [6] can be seen as an attempt at an extreme form of functional elegance. The approach in Sigma is less ambitious, but still strongly in this direction.

Driven by these desiderata, work to date on Sigma has been deliberately broad – including forms of memory and learning [7-8], problem solving and decision making [9-10], perception and localization [10], and natural language – with the intent of determining whether a small set of general mechanisms can in fact be sufficient in combination. Thus, for mental imagery the natural question to ask became whether Sigma could provide a sufficient hybrid capacity without either distinct symbolic versus imagistic modules or distinct representations, memories and processes, as has been necessary in other architectural approaches.

Earlier work in Sigma showed how 2D images can be represented, and how translation of image components can be implemented [11]. The results were used as part of a hybrid approach to the Eight Puzzle – Fig. 1 – a classic sliding tile puzzle that is traditionally solved in AI systems via a symbolically represented board plus internal search over symbolic operators that model external actions. The Sigma approach included a hybrid representation of the board plus normal symbolic problem solving, but now over imagistic tile translations (implemented as *offsets*). The work here extends this via manipulations of Z *tetrominos* (Fig. 2), as found in the game of Tetris, to demonstrate: image composition and component deletion; additional forms of image transformation, including scaling, reflection and rotation (by multiples of 90°); and extraction of perceptual features from composites, such as object overlaps and collision detection, directionality among objects, and edge detection.

Fig. 1. Eight Puzzle

Fig. 2. Z tetromino

Mental imagery in Sigma is grounded in: (1) the architecture's generalized language of *conditionals*, which compiles down to *factor graphs* for processing via the *summary product algorithm* [12]; (2) an inherently continuous *piecewise linear representation* for the functions and messages in (1) [13]; and (3) *affine transformations* – a generalization of the offsets introduced earlier – and *piecewise linear filters*. By demonstrating mental imagery via interactions among more primitive mechanisms, this work contributes to the breadth of functionality unified within Sigma, while doing so in a simple and elegant manner. The key to functional elegance here has been to begin with a small set of very general mechanisms that are leveraged in combination when possible, and which are (minimally) augmented when necessary. This combination also supports grand unification, intertwining continuous perception-related information with general symbol processing.

2   Sigma and Mental Imagery

Knowledge representation in Sigma is based on *conditionals* – a generalized form of rule – plus *piecewise linear functions*. Fig. 3, for example, shows a conditional that uses two conditions and an action to determine the spatial

```
CONDITIONAL Overlap-0-3
   Conditions: (Image o:0 x:x y:y)
               (Image o:3 x:x y:y)
    Actions: (Overlap i:1 x:x y:y)
```

Fig. 3. Conditional for computing the spatial overlap between two specific objects

overlap between two particular objects in the image. The Image predicate specifies object locations via three arguments – o provides a numeric index into a vector of objects (which is specified by constants here, but can be variables in general), while x and y range over the continuous image dimensions – to yield a discrete vector of continuous planes, each element of which provides an occupancy grid for a single object in the image. In Fig. 4, for example, the planes correspond to the Eight Puzzle tiles, and the grayed regions denote where the blank and tile 1 are located in Fig. 1.

Technically, such images are 3D hybrid functions in Sigma, with one discrete variable (i.e., dimension) for objects (tiles here) and two continuous variables for space. The grayed regions are where the function has a value of 1 (or *true*) while the other regions are 0 (or *false*). In Sigma such functions are represented as piecewise linear over nD arrays of rectilinear (or *orthotopic*) regions (Fig. 5). The nD space is *sliced* orthogonally to its axes to generate an array of regions that are doubly linked along each dimension, with each region

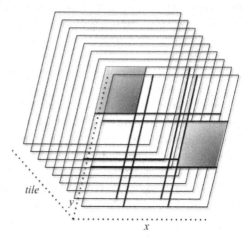

Fig. 4. Partial visualization of a hybrid representation for the Eight Puzzle board

having its own linear function over the variables. This can be viewed as a generalization of a pixel (or voxel) array, where the pixels can vary in size and have linear rather than just constant value functions.

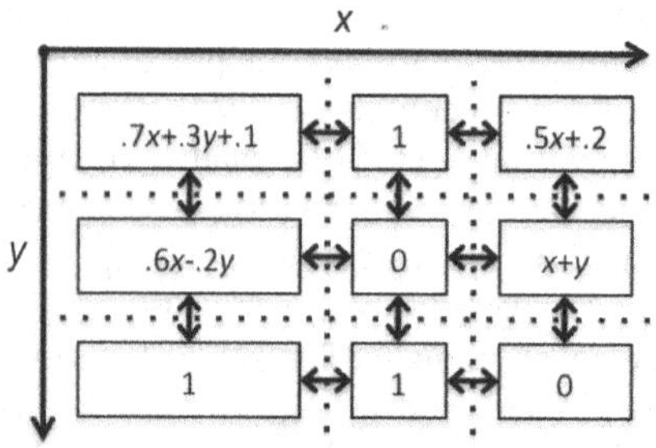

Although Sigma's function representation is inherently continuous, with its piecewise linear approach allowing arbitrary continuous functions to be approximated as closely as desired, it can also be specialized to: discrete representations – to enable, for example,

Fig. 5. Bivariate function as a 2D array of regions with linear functions

the vectors of objects we have seen, as well as discrete probability distributions – by mapping integers in the function's domain to unit regions; and symbolic representations by limiting the functions to Boolean (0/T and 1/F) while assigning symbols to domain integers. A form of *hybrid mixed* representation is thus proffered in a manner analogous to how digital circuits are implemented via restrictions on an underlying substrate that is naturally continuous.

The Overlap predicate in Fig. 3 is similar to the Image predicate, except that here there is a vector of object overlaps, rather than of objects. The semantics of conditionals specifies that the two conditions in Fig. 3 extract the 0th and 3rd objects from the image, with these two 2D object subimages then being multiplied in a *pointwise* manner – like an inner product but without the final summation – to yield a new 2D plane that is 1 where both input planes are 1 and 0 elsewhere (Fig. 6). Once mes-sage passing reaches quiescence, actions – such as the one in Fig. 3 that stores the computed

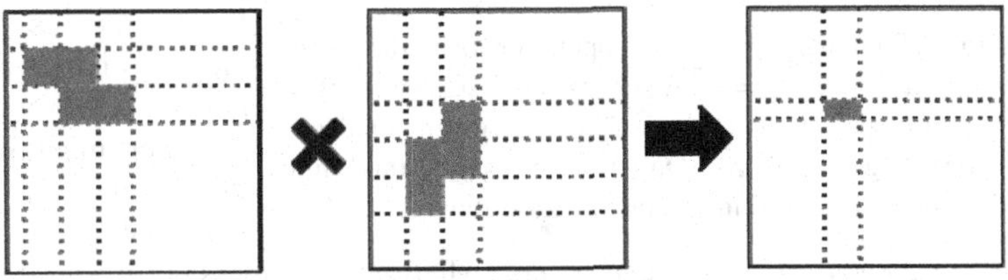

Fig. 6. Overlap between two images via conditional in figure 3

overlap into element 1 of Overlap – may yield changes to working memory, completing Sigma's core cognitive cycle. If a predicate has a *unique* variable – akin to a classic random variable, where a distribution is provided over all possible values but only one is ultimately correct – the best value for that variable is placed into working memory, while if it instead has only *universal* variables – akin to classic rule variables, where any subset of the values may be correct, but used here mainly for occupancy grids – all non-zero values are placed in working memory 14].

The processing of conditionals occurs by running the summary product algorithm over the factor graph into which they are compiled. Factor graphs are a general form of *graphical model* [15] – an approach to computing efficiently over complex multivariate functions by decomposing them into the product of simpler factors and then mapping the result onto a graph of nodes and links – that bear a family resemblance to other forms, such as Bayesian and Markov networks, but are concerned with arbitrary multivariate functions, not just probabilistic ones. Complex functions are first decomposed into products of simpler functions, and then mapped onto bipartite graphs, with variables mapped onto variable nodes and decomposed factors mapped onto factor nodes. Undirected edges are defined between each factor node and its variables. Fig. 7 shows an example factor graph for a multivariate algebraic function along with its solution via summary product, as used in Sigma.

Given evidence about a subset of the variables – as stored in working memory factor nodes – messages are passed along the links and processed at the nodes to yield new messages. Each message along a link provides information about the values of the link's variable. Incoming messages at variable nodes are combined via pointwise

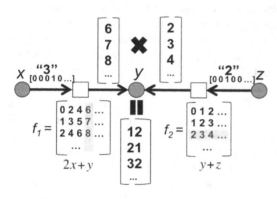

Fig. 7. Summary product computation over the factor graph for $f(x,y,z) = y^2+yz+2yx+2xz = (2x+y)(y+z) = f_1(x,y)f_2(y,z)$ of the marginal on y given evidence concerning x and z. Only the messages (and link directions) involved in computing y are shown.

product to yield outgoing messages, but with each outgoing message omitting from its product the incoming message on its link. Similar pointwise products occur at factor nodes, but with the factor's function also included in the product; and then all variables not in the outgoing message are summarized out. Summarization typically occurs via *summation* – or *integration* for continuous functions – to yield marginals, or via *maximum* to yield the mode; however, maximum is also used in Sigma for marginals of universal variables. Message passing ends upon quiescence; i.e., when no new message is significantly different from the previous message along the same link.

Both conditions and actions can be *negated*, inverting the resulting function to yield $f = maximum(1-f, 0)$. True (1) becomes false (0) and vice versa. Intermediate values are similarly inverted, and functional values greater than 1 are treated as if they are 1 during the inversion. Fig. 8, for example, shows how an object can be removed from an image via a negated action that spans the entire plane for object 1.

Both conditions and actions also limit the direction in which messages are passed – those within condition subgraphs only move away from working memory while those within

```
CONDITIONAL Delete-1
    Actions: (Image - o:1 x:* y:*)
```

Fig. 8. Deletion of object 1

action subgraphs only move towards it. This provides the forward momentum central to procedural memory. *Condacts* – a neologism for *cond*itions and *act*ions – provide the bidirectional message passing required for the full generality of factor graphs, as used for example in probabilistic reasoning, constraint satisfaction, signal processing, and (partial match in) declarative memory [7]. As condacts are not used in the results presented here, they aren't discussed further. We will also omit discussions of other aspects of Sigma not exploited here, such as learning.

Still, two remaining aspects of Sigma do require explication. The first, and the only one originally motivated by the needs of mental imagery, is the use of affine trans-formations; i.e., combinations of linear transformations with translations. Fig. 9 shows an example, where an affine transformation is used in the action of a conditional to scale a Z tetromino horizontally, in place. In general, a variable in a condition or an action may include a coefficient and an offset, where the coefficient must be a constant and the offset may be either a constant or a variable (although only constant offsets are used in the work described here). Affine transforms can be used in

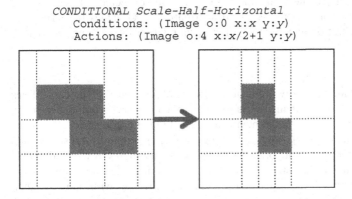

CONDITIONAL Scale-Half-Horizontal
    Conditions: (Image o:0 x:x y:y)
    Actions: (Image o:4 x:x/2+1 y:y)

Fig. 9. Scaling a Z tetromino by half, horizontally, in place

conditions, actions and condacts, but with a transformation in a condition (or the outgoing aspect of a condact) inverting what the same one does in an action (or the incoming aspect of a condact).

Although the affine transformation specified in Fig. 9's conditional may appear to involve just addition and multiplication of individual numbers, the figure makes it clear that such transformations actually operate on entire functions. In principle, affine transformation can and should be implemented by standard factor nodes that represent variants of *delta functions* [11]. However, delta functions are awkward and expensive to approximate via axially aligned slices, so specially optimized factor nodes that directly manipulate message slices, such as those in Fig. 9, are used instead. An offset shifts a whole piecewise linear function along a variable's dimension by modifying the dimension's slices, while a coefficient may, once again by modifying slices, expand, contract, or invert a dimension.

Once the slices have been modified, the resulting function may then need to be cropped and/or padded. Dimensions are not infinite in Sigma; each must be specified via minimum and maximum values, defining a domain that is closed at its dimensional minima and open at its corresponding maxima (this same half-open structure is also shared by regions). When a transformation extends a function beyond its dimensional bounds, it is cropped to fit back within these boundaries. When a transformation leaves areas within the boundaries undefined, the function is padded by assigning values to these areas. By default, closed-world predicates use a value of 0 and open-world predicates use a value of 1, corresponding for each to the standard value of *unknown*. Although originally motivated by mental imagery, affine transformations have since found important roles in Sigma across such areas as episodic memory, reflection, and reinforcement learning [11, 8].

The other aspect of Sigma used in the mental imagery results here is a capability for applying *piecewise linear filters* – generalizations of the constant tests typically found in rule conditions – to messages. A constant test is simply a filter that passes along only the portion of incoming messages matching the constant, via a filter that is 1 where the variable's domain equals the constant and 0 elsewhere. Sigma's filters can more generally specify arbitrary linear functions over regions. For example, in the condition (Image o:o x:x y:[.01*y]), the computation within the square brackets defines a filter that increases linearly with (the domain value) of y, with a slope of .01. The functional values in incoming messages are therefore pointwise multiplied by .01 times their y domain value. Such filters have been used, for example, in reinforcement learning to compute expected Q values via summarization (integration) over a weighted distribution of Q values [8]. They are leveraged in the next section in computing directional relationships among objects.

3   Results

The focus in this section is on key implications for mental imagery of the capabilities just described. This is not exhaustive, as new implications are continually being uncovered, but it does span the requirements mentioned in the introduction.

We can begin with the straightforward result that it is possible to translate, scale (shrink/enlarge), reflect, and rotate objects in images. Translation was covered in [11] and Fig. 9 demonstrated scaling in place, via a coefficient and an offset. Figs. 10 and 11 both start with the Z tetromino on the left of Fig. 9, with Fig. 10 then demonstrating reflection in place, via a negative coefficient and an offset, and Fig. 11 demonstrating rotation by 90° in place, via reflection and a swap of the x and y variables. As presently implemented, Sigma's affine transformations operate on individual variables (i.e., dimensions). By swapping variables – and reflecting when necessary – rotations by multiples of 90° are possible, as here, but not arbitrary-angle rotations. Two issues stand in the way: (1) Sigma's limitation to rectilinear, axially aligned, regions makes it complex and costly to represent the results of such rotations [11]; and (2) rotations at arbitrary angles require multivariate transforms. We are considering extending Sigma's function representation from orthotopic regions to (convex) *polytopic* regions – i.e., nD polygons – to allow representation of slices at arbitrary angles (as well as to enable more compact representations of complex objects). When this is in place, efficient multivariate transformation will be explored.

The conditionals in Figs. 9-11 demonstrate image composition – each adds one object (on its own plane) to the overall image – and Fig. 8 demonstrated object deletion. What hasn't been demonstrated is how the separate objects in an image can be combined into a single new plane, enabling hierarchies in which complex images can in turn be treated as objects in more complex images. Fig. 12 demonstrates this,

CONDITIONAL *Reflect-Horizontal*   CONDITIONAL *Rotate-90-Right*
    Conditions: (Image o:0 x:x y:y)   Conditions: (Image o:0 x:x y:y)
    Actions: (Image o:5 x:4-x y:y)   Actions: (Image o:3 x:4-y y:x)

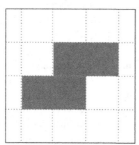
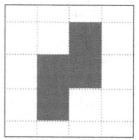

Fig. 10. Horizontal, in place, reflection of Z tetromino

Fig. 11. 90° rotation of Z tetromino

with the object variable (*o*) from the condition – which ranges over the four planes in the image – being summarized out via *maximum* to yield a message to the action that is 1 wherever there is a 1 in any of the individual objects in the image.

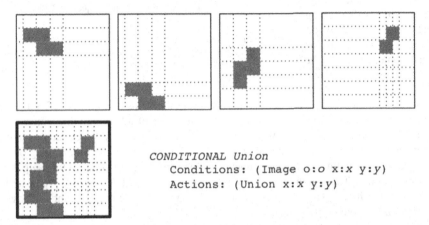

CONDITIONAL Union
    Conditions: (Image o:o x:x y:y)
    Actions: (Union x:x y:y)

Fig. 12. Combining four object planes (top) into a single new plane (bottom left)

The result of the processing in Fig. 12 is a new composite object that can be treated like any other object. For example, the left edge of this object – the slivers immediately to the right of blank areas – can be determined as in Fig. 13. This is an elementary perceptual operation that can extract useful information from images. Just as with the other imagery operations though, it occurs via a standard conditional that compiles down to a factor graph. In this instance, the conditional uses an offset in a negated condition to shift the image by ε (.0001 in this case) and then to invert it before multiplying by the original image. The result is 1s only for the sliver of the original image that is within ε to the right of a blank area. This approach turns out to perform edge detection without previously pixelating the image; instead, the thickness of the edge is a function of the offset.

A second example of extracting useful information from a combination of objects was shown in Figs. 3 and 6, where conditions for separate image planes

CONDITIONAL Left-Edge
    Conditions: (Union x:x y:y)
                (Union – x:x-.0001 y:y)
    Actions: (Left-Edge x:x y:y)0

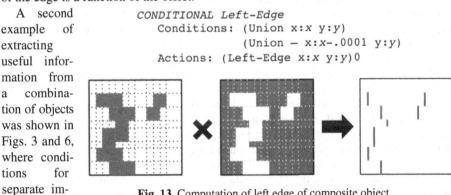

Fig. 13. Computation of left edge of composite object

compute their overlap via the *product* aspect of summary product. It is then a simple step from there to a third example, where colliding pairs are detected via summarizing – by *maximum* – the two spatial dimensions in the vector of overlap planes (Fig. 14).

As a fourth and final example of information extraction from mental imagery, consider the problem of determining directional information among objects, such as whether object 1 is to the right of object 2, or which object is topmost. Fig. 15

```
CONDITIONAL Collision
    Conditions: (Overlap i:i x:x y:y)
    Actions: (Collision i:i value:true)
```

Fig. 14. Determine which objects collide

```
CONDITIONAL Above
    Conditions: (Image o:o x:x y:[1-.1*y])
    Actions: (Topmost o:o)
```

Fig. 15. Determine which object is topmost

shows a conditional for the latter computation, where the topmost object is defined to be the one whose topmost point is above the topmost points of all of the other objects. It uses a filter in the condition to weight points in objects by their y (domain) values, decreasing as y increases. In generating a message for the action, by summarizing out x and y via *maximum*, this computes a function value for the object equal to the weight of its topmost point. The action then uses a unique variable in the Topmost predicate to select the most highly valued object; that is, the one whose topmost point is highest among all of the objects in the image.

Together these last four examples start to show how Sigma can extract useful information from the spatial interactions among objects in images, as the earlier examples show how to compose images from multiple objects, turn these composites into new objects, delete objects from images, and transform objects within images.

4   Conclusion

The mental imagery results presented here derive from a combination of: Sigma's core nD piecewise linear representation for functions/messages; its use of conditionals with conditions, actions and negations to define a factor graph; the generalization from constants to piecewise linear filters in conditionals; the addition of (optimized factor nodes for) affine transformations; and how the functions/messages are combined and reduced via the summary product algorithm. This combination enables the componential representation of continuous 2D images in terms of vectors of region-based objects; the addition and deletion of objects from these images; translation, scaling, reflection and (limited forms of) rotation of these objects; and the ability to extract implications from interactions among objects.

Although not a focus here, it is trivial via additional predicates to symbolically annotate these continuous objects. The initial step in extending this all from 2D to 3D imagery is also trivial, involving merely the addition of a z dimension. However, this hasn't yet been pursued because of the computational cost of processing these larger images. We are presently modifying Sigma's core representation so that slices need not span the entire space, and default-valued regions can be represented implicitly. These changes should reduce the size of the imagery functions and improve the efficiency of their processing. This should not only enable efficient exploration of 3D imagery, but also provide an important step in moving from orthotopes to polytopes (which should further simplify the representation of complex objects, while enabling exploration of arbitrary-angle rotations). We are also exploring the possibility of allowing more direct incorporation of Gaussians, or comparable functions, for more efficient representation of spatial, and other forms, of uncertainty.

Beyond these extensions, we need to look at incorporating these basic capabilities into naturalistic tasks that are tightly coupled with true perception; and, in the process, evaluate whether this functionality is both sufficient and sufficiently efficient. Still, the results presented here do demonstrate a significant mental imagery capability that is built upon a set of more primitive mechanisms that are common to other cognitive capabilities within Sigma; for example, reinforcement learning [8] also leverages all of the capabilities listed at the beginning of this section (except for negation). It thus represents a significant step towards a functionally elegant grand unification.

Acknowledgments. This effort has been sponsored by the Air Force Office of Scientific Research and the U.S. Army. Statements and opinions expressed do not necessarily reflect the position or the policy of the United States Government, and no official endorsement should be inferred.

References

1. Gunzelmann, G., Lyon, D.R.: Representations and processes of human spatial competence. Topics in Cognitive Science 3, 741–759 (2011)
2. Cassimatis, N.: Polyscheme: A Cognitive Architecture for Integrating Multiple Representation and Inference Schemes. Ph.D. Dissertation. MIT Media Laboratory (2002)
3. Lathrop, S.D., Wintermute, S., Laird, J.E.: Exploring the functional advantages of spatial and visual cognition from an architectural perspective. Topics in Cognitive Science 3, 796–818 (2011)
4. Trafton, J.G., Harrison, A.M.: Embodied spatial cognition. Topics in Cognitive Science 3, 686–706 (2011)
5. Chandrasekaran, B., Banerjee, B., Kurup, U., Lele, O.: Augmenting cognitive architectures to support diagrammatic imagination. Topics in Cognitive Science 3, 760–777 (2011)
6. Hutter, M.: Universal Artificial Intelligence: Sequential Decisions Based on Algorithmic Probability. Springer, Berlin (2005)
7. Rosenbloom, P.S.: Combining Procedural and Declarative Knowledge in a Graphical Architecture. In: 10th International Conference on Cognitive Modeling (2010)
8. Rosenbloom, P.S.: Deconstructing Reinforcement Learning in Sigma. In: Bach, J., Goertzel, B., Iklé, M. (eds.) AGI 2012. LNCS (LNAI), vol. 7716, pp. 262–271. Springer, Heidelberg (2012)
9. Rosenbloom, P.S.: From Memory to Problem Solving: Mechanism Reuse in a Graphical Cognitive Architecture. In: Schmidhuber, J., Thórisson, K.R., Looks, M. (eds.) AGI 2011. LNCS (LNAI), vol. 6830, pp. 143–152. Springer, Heidelberg (2011)
10. Chen, J., Demski, A., Han, T., Morency, L.-P., Pynadath, P., Rafidi, N., Rosenbloom, P.S.: Fusing symbolic and decision-theoretic problem solving + perception in a graphical cognitive architecture. In: Second International Conference on Biologically Inspired Cognitive Architectures (2011)
11. Rosenbloom, P.S.: Mental imagery in a graphical cognitive architecture. In: Second International Conference on Biologically Inspired Cognitive Architectures (2011)
12. Kschischang, F.R., Frey, B.J., Loeliger, H.: Factor Graphs and the Sum-Product Algorithm. IEEE Transactions on Information Theory 47, 498–519 (2001)
13. Rosenbloom, P.S.: Bridging dichotomies in cognitive architectures for virtual humans. In: AAAI Fall Symposium on Advances in Cognitive Systems (2011)
14. Rosenbloom, P.S.: Implementing first-order variables in a graphical cognitive architecture. In: First International Conference on Biologically Inspired Cognitive Architectures (2010)
15. Koller, D., Friedman, N.: Probabilistic Graphical Models: Principles and Techniques. MIT Press, Cambridge (2009)

Binary Space Partitioning as Intrinsic Reward

Wojciech Skaba

AGINAO, Trubadurow 11, 80205 Gdansk, Poland
wojciech.skaba@aginao.com

Abstract. An autonomous agent embodied in a humanoid robot, in order to learn from the overwhelming flow of raw and noisy sensory, has to effectively reduce the high spatial-temporal data dimensionality. In this paper we propose a novel method of unsupervised feature extraction and selection with binary space partitioning, followed by a computation of information gain that is interpreted as intrinsic reward, then applied as immediate-reward signal for the reinforcement-learning. The space partitioning is executed by tiny codelets running on a simulated Turing Machine. The features are represented by concept nodes arranged in a hierarchy, in which those of a lower level become the input vectors of a higher level.

Keywords: AGINAO, artificial general intelligence, self-programming, binary space partitioning, intrinsic reward.

1 Introduction

For an autonomous humanoid robot, learning a cognitive model from the natural environment, there seems to be no direct correspondence between low level sensory and high level external motivation. Furthermore, the reinforcement-learning becomes ineffective if the extrinsic reward signal propagates through too many states. The learning could be improved, however, should a good candidate for the immediate reward be found.

The term *intrinsic motivation* was borrowed by cognitive scientists from the psychology, to mean that an agent is engaged in some activity for its own sake, possibly activity in taking pleasure, rather than working to fulfil some external drives. This motivational force is referred to as independent ego-energy, based in organism needs to be competent and self-determining [1]. Closely related is the term *intrinsic reward*, to mean a reinforcement stimulus of the intrinsic motivation.

As for studies on epigenetic robotics and autonomous agents, however, the term has been conceptualized differently and in many distinct ways, while a unified definition seems not to exist yet [2]. Miscellaneous measures of intrinsic motivation have been proposed, including: information gain, curiosity, novelty, prediction error, competence progress, relative entropy, compression progress, etc. [2], [3]. We will focus here on a purely information-theoretic based approach, where intrinsic reward is defined as averaged information gain assigned to an action taken to evaluate a candidate feature. The action to be taken is represented by a directed edge connecting two concept nodes, the head to stand for the feature under consideration, the tail to stand

J. Bach, B. Goertzel, and M. Iklé (Eds.): AGI 2012, LNAI 7716, pp. 282–291, 2012.

for the input vector, possibly a lower level feature selected earlier, or raw sensory data (also represented by a feature vector). The intrinsic reward is then applied as imme-diate-reward signal for the reinforcement-learning algorithm, becoming the only source of reward. The latter to mean that no external motivation driven reward is employed.

2   AGINAO Cognitive Architecture

AGINAO is a project to build a human-level artificial general intelligence (AGI) sys-tem by embodiment of the cognitive engine in the NAO humanoid robot. It was first introduced in [4]. A more detail presentation of the self-programming engine is given in [5]. The open-ended learning, executed by the cognitive engine, is a result of a fully automatic self-programming development of a hierarchy of interconnected *concepts*, as shown in Fig. 1.

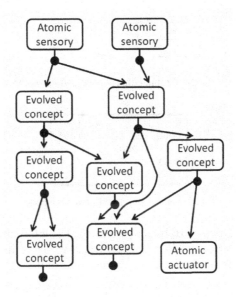

Fig. 1. Sample concept network

The evolved concept nodes represent the features of the spatial-temporal sensory patterns of the natural world and are evaluated concurrently at all levels of the hie-rarchy. The predefined atomic sensory and actuator concepts stand for the root and terminal nodes, respectively. An output of a concept becomes an input of a higher level concept, so the distinction between features and a patterns disappears. There are also concepts that act as the procedural memory, and concepts that behave like func-tions. For that reason, we prefer the word *pattern* to name the entities being discov-ered and managed by the concepts, while the word *feature* may be used for better communication, where applicable. A patternist philosophy of mind is thoroughly discussed in [6]. The idea that a single algorithm may be used to process both the spatial and temporal aspects of a pattern, and that pattern processing should be conducted simultaneously at all levels of the hierarchy, is presented in [7].

The feature detection is performed by a tiny piece of machine code, a *codelet*, embedded in a concept node. Following the execution, the action values and other parameters that govern the dynamic structure of the network are updated, effectively to mean feature extraction and selection. The codelets consist of instructions of a custom-designed virtual machine, a simulated Turning Machine. A typical setting of a 2-input concept is shown in Fig. 2. and a sample codelet in Fig. 3.

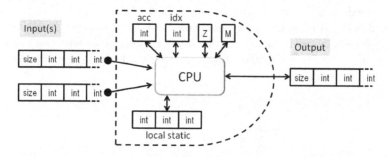

Fig. 2. A sample 2-input concept node and virtual processor

```
0000 MOV A, var1[00]
0005 ADD A, var2[00]
0010 APPEND, A
0011 JZ 0005
0014 RET
```

Fig. 3. Sample program in machine code

The basic internal type is a 16-bit integer (`int`). The information is exchanged between the concepts using a uniform data format, a vector of integers of know size. Fig. 4. depicts a sample feature vector of a visual pixel of the YUV color space.

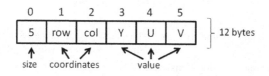

Fig. 4. Internal data format

The input feature vector, as depicted in Fig. 2., consists of two features, the values being vectors too, possibly of other feature vectors. Should a feature be detected by the execution of the concept's codelet, the output would be a feature vector, too.

It must be highlighted, however, that concept network is not a neural network. The concepts and the links (edges) are stored in a depository and launched as individual threads. Multiple concurrent runtime-threads may coexist and be used to evaluate a single concept. The codelet code as such is generated in a process called *heuristic search in program space*, basically random, creating programs of highly non-linear behavior and of flexibility theoretically equivalent to a Universal Turing Machine.

Last but not the least, if two concepts are connected by an edge to mean an action, it is the head concept's codelet that is executed as an action, while the action values are stored in the tail concept(s), individually for each edge outgoing from the tail.

3   Intrinsic Motivation

Whether external drives are primary or secondary to a more basic motivational mechanism, it may be questioned [8]. For example, the hunger drive seems to be a very basic one for humans. There are historical examples, however, of people who have committed a sort of starvation suicide for some ideas. What follows, a stronger intrinsic motivational reward must exist, one that seems to be of *information seeking* type. The reward must originate from the internal model of the world, rather than from the external drives. It is conjectured here that, since virtually any drives may be overpowered by the intrinsic motivation, a cognitive model may be built with extrinsic rewards being only secondary to the intrinsic reward mechanism, and merely reflected there.

The proposed measure of intrinsic motivation is based on the notion of *self-information* [9] or *information surprisal* [10] associated with the execution of a concept's codelet, i.e. the amount of information provided by an event being a successful (pattern matching) execution of the codelet. The resulting intrinsic reward is the averaged self-information gain.

Let ω be the outcome of a random variable with probability $P(\omega)$. Then the self-information may be computed as

$$I(\omega) = -\log_2(P(\omega)) \tag{1}$$

From now on, let us assume that each concept has only two outcomes, ω_{pos} for pattern matching and ω_{neg} for pattern not matching, and we appreciate the positive matches only. The more unique a pattern, the more information it entails, which reflects our intuition. We want our intrinsic reward mechanism to maximize the information gain in time, the time unit to be understood as a step of a (non-Markovian) decision process. Unfortunately, if the probability of an outcome decreases, we have to execute our concept codelet multiple times to get a match. Consequently, we get the following definition of intrinsic reward:

$$r(\omega_{pos}) = -P(\omega_{pos})\log_2(P(\omega_{pos})) \tag{2}$$

Self-information is a special case of Kullback–Leibler distance from a Kronecker delta representing the matching pattern to the probability distribution:

$$I(\omega_{pos}) = \sum_{i=pos,neg} \delta_{pos,i} \log_2 \frac{\delta_{pos,i}}{P(\omega_i)} = 1*\log_2 \frac{1}{P(\omega_{pos})} = -\log_2(P(\omega_{pos})) \tag{3}$$

An independent approach based on a measure of information gain calculated from the Kullback-Leibler distance was presented in [11].

The measure of self-information has an interesting additive property. If two independent events A and B with outcomes ω_A and ω_B have the probabilities $P(\omega_A)$ and $P(\omega_B)$, then the resulting information gain is

$$I(\omega_{A \cap B}) = I(\omega_A) + I(\omega_B) = -\log_2(P(\omega_A)) - \log_2(P(\omega_B)) \tag{4}$$

This may be a result of executing two concept codelets in sequence. It is quite likely, however, that a single concept codelet is performing exactly the same function as two concept in sequence, possibly created by a concatenation of the codelets. The resulting information gain would be

$$I(\omega_{A \cap B}) = -\log_2(P(\omega_A)P(\omega_B)) = -\log_2(P(\omega_A)) - \log_2(P(\omega_B)) \tag{5}$$

i.e. exactly what would be expected.

On the other hand, however, if the two concepts are executed in sequence[1], the resulting reward would be

$$r(\omega_{A \cap B}) = r(\omega_A) + r(\omega_B) = -P(\omega_A)\log_2(P(\omega_A)) - P(\omega_B)\log_2(P(\omega_B)) \tag{6}$$

while, the same function executed as a single concept would result in

$$r(\omega_{A \cap B}) = -P(\omega_A)P(\omega_B)\log_2(P(\omega_A)P(\omega_B)) \tag{7}$$

which is less than (6). This reflects the idea that getting the reward in separate steps is potentially more informative than doing everything in one step, especially in case when already

$$-P(\omega_A)\log_2(P(\omega_A)) > -P(\omega_A)P(\omega_B)\log_2(P(\omega_A)P(\omega_B)) \tag{8}$$

that hold if

$$P(\omega_A) < \frac{1}{e} \tag{9}$$

provided A is the first step (see Fig.5.). Separate steps may be preferred because—after the first step was executed—we get more opportunities, while assuming a priori that a unique pattern will be encountered is always risky. One might even erroneously

---

[1] A TD-learning discount factor γ, that would normally be included, is temporarily omitted.

conclude that splitting concepts into separate steps is always beneficial when (9) doesn't hold, at least as long as (roughly):

$$P(\omega_B) < \gamma \tag{10}$$

where γ in the discount-factor of TD-learning. That's not observed in practical implementations, however. The computational overhead of executing two separate concepts instead of one must also be taken into account.

The reward function is depicted on diagram in Fig. 5. and reaches the maximum at:

$$(-p\log_2 p)' = -\frac{\ln p}{\ln 2} - \frac{1}{\ln 2} = 0 \Rightarrow p = \frac{1}{e} \tag{11}$$

What follows is that preferred would be concepts with the probability of a positive match around the reciprocal of e. This must not be confused with the mentioned above question of splitting the concepts, for in the former case the probability is given, while in the latter case we search the space of concepts with unknown probabilities.

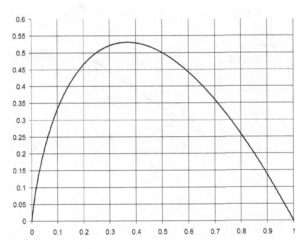

Fig. 5. $-p\log_2 p$

The properties of the reward function may be illustrated with the following example. Imagine, we want our cognitive engine to learn the most effective method for the graphical recognition of the 25 letters of the Latin alphabet. The simplest method would be to design an individual concept for each letter. Since, however, the individual probabilities of occurrence of each letter are rather low, so is the reward (left end of the diagram). We could increase the expected probability by designing an algorithm to exclude a letter rather than finding a match. Unfortunately, the resulting self-information gain would be rather low (right end).

An alternative approach could be based on detecting some feature first, like finding whether the observed letter contains a vertical bar. Some 14 Latin letters do have this property, and effectively the space is divided nearly evenly, and the resulting reward is close to the maximum. The same could be done with the next steps, provided a feature could be selected. If, however, the probability distribution is highly non-uniform, the aforementioned approach of matching some letters first could be more informative. Since the whole process is fully automatic, it can't be said a priori what concept structure would emerge and what features would be extracted and selected.

4   Binary Space Partitioning

The idea of binary space partitioning is depicted in Fig. 6. The input to a concept is a state space consisting of feature vectors of some multidimensional space. No matter how many inputs a concept has, we will consider all of them as a single vector. A hyperplane, depicted as a straight line, divides the input space into two disjoint subsets. We will call them positive and negative examples.

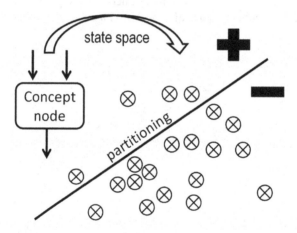

Fig. 6. Binary space partitioning

Let us assume that N_{pos} and N_{neg} are the numbers of positive and negative examples observed, respectively, and $N_{pos} + N_{neg} > 0$. Then the probability of a positive outcome may be computed as:

$$P(\omega_{pos}) = \frac{N_{pos}}{N_{pos} + N_{neg}} \qquad (42)$$

Fig. 7. presents the machine code implementation of the space partitioning. The instruction set of the virtual machine contains 65 unique codes, including conditional jumps, RET and EXIT. Both RET and EXIT terminate execution and quit, however, RET is interpreted as a positive outcome while EXIT as negative. The program generator of the heuristic search assures that RET and EXIT are placed in branches separated by a conditional jump.

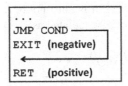

Fig. 7. Machine code implementation of space partitioning

Little can be said about the shape and the nature of the hyperplane that will be carried out by a codelet. Since the power of the program is virtually equivalent to that of a Universal Turing Machine, so is the structure of the hyperplane. The output may be either a feature vector, with the whole spectrum of values, or a binary flag. What matters is that, if the executed concept doesn't have internal states (e.g. no local static memory)[2], the partitioning really applies to the input state space.

Yet another problem may be encountered. With the growing $N_{pos} + N_{neg}$ the resulting probability would become insensitive to the incoming vectors. This problem has been solved by averaging the calculations over a window of 1000 recent vectors. As an interesting consequence observed on experiments, the candidate concepts exhibiting volatile probabilities do occasionally fall in low reward areas and consequently are dropped, while the stable concepts are preferred.

5   Reinforcement Learning

For every concept, the next actions to be taken at time t is $a_{i,t+1}$ where $i=1,...,N$, N is the number of actions currently available. Since, however, actions may be removed and new actions added, the maximum number is virtually unlimited.

Both (13) and (14) TD-learning rules have been experimented with.

$$Q_{i,t} = Q_{i,t} + \alpha \left[r_{i,t+1} + \gamma \max_{a_{i,t+1}} Q_{i,t+1} - Q_{i,t} \right] \tag{13}$$

$$Q_{i,t} = Q_{i,t} + \alpha \left[r_{i,t+1} + \gamma \overline{W}_{i,t+1} - Q_{i,t} \right] \tag{54}$$

where $Q_{i,t}$ is the value of a_i at time t, α is the learning rate, γ is the discount factor, $r_{i,t+1}$ is the immediate reward at time $t+1$, and

$$\overline{V} = \frac{\sum_j P_{j,t} Q_{j,t}}{\sum_j P_{j,t}} \tag{15}$$

---

[2]   The virtual machine design allows for the concepts to have local static memory and internal states, and there are instruction codes that access the local memory. The discussion, however, is beyond the scope of this paper.

where $p_{j,t}$ is the $P(\omega_{pos})$ at time t. It is must not be confused with the probability of selecting action a_i at time t, which is calculated as

$$P(a_{i,t}) = \frac{Q_{i,t}}{\sum_j Q_{j,t}} \tag{16}$$

The future reward may be much larger than immediate reward and consequently may secure even a non-rewarding concept, like one performing a truncating function with no EXIT instruction.

The probability of adding a new action, possibly replacing the least rewarding one, here referred to as *exploration*, is

$$P_{exp} \propto \frac{Q_{const}}{Q_{const} + \sum_i Q_i} \tag{17}$$

where Q_{const} is a predefined constant. The experiments with physical robot NAO have shown that most of the creative activity happens near the leaf nodes, while the area of stable concepts continuously extends from the root towards the higher levels.

6   Discussion

The application of immediate reward as the only source of reward, calculated locally at concept level and interpreted as intrinsic reward, does not exclude other more global fitness functions of intrinsic nature. In fact, it is already the parameters that control adding and removing actions, and the parameters that control the learning rate and discount factor, that may be understood as intrinsic motivation. Equation (17) may be also interpreted as the motivation towards curiosity, towards exploring the unknown areas.

Another question that has not been discussed above, and could also be contemplated in terms of intrinsic motivation, is the *artificial economics*. As was once mentioned, the computational overhead of evaluating the actions is also taken into account. A codelet that partitions the space optimally, if computationally too expensive, will be dropped as not rewarding The individual actions compete according to (16). In the current implementation, however, the reward, as defined in (2), is divided by the (averaged) execution time. It is the execution on a virtual machine that enables precise resources management. Consequently, our goal of maximizing self-information gain in time may be redefined. Now the time may be understood as the execution time of the virtual machine code.

References

1. Deci, E.L., Ryan, R.M.: Intrinsic motivation and self-determination in human behavior. Plenum Press, New York (1985)
2. Oudeyer, P.-Y., Kaplan, F.: How can we define intrinsic motivation? In: Proceedings of the Eighth International Conference on Epigenetic Robotics: Modeling Cognitive Development in Robotic Systems (2008)

3. Schmidhuber, J.: Formal theory of creativity, fun, and intrinsic motivation (1990-2010). IEEE Transactions of Autonomous Mental Development 2(3), 230–247 (2010)
4. Skaba, W.: Heuristic Search in Program Space for the AGINAO Cognitive Architecture. In: AGI 2011 Self-Programming Workshop (2001), http://www.iiim.is/wp/wp-content/uploads/2011/05/skaba-agisp-2011.pdf
5. Skaba, W.: The AGINAO Self-Programming Engine. Submitted to: Journal of Artificial General Intelligence, Special Issue on Self-Programming (2012), http://aginao.com/pub/The_AGINAO_Self-Programming_Engine.pdf
6. Goertzel, B.: The Hidden Pattern: A Patternist Philosophy of Mind. BrownWalker Press (2006)
7. Hawkins, J., George, D.: Hierarchical temporal memory (2006), http://www.numenta.com/htm-overview/education/Numenta_HTM_Concepts.pdf
8. Reiss, S.: Why Extrinsic Motivation Doesn't Exist. Psychology Today (2011), http://www.psychologytoday.com/blog/who-we-are/201108/why-extrinsic-motivation-doesnt-exist
9. Cover, T.M., Thomas, J.A.: Elements of Information Theory, p. 20. John Wiley & Sons, Inc. (1991)
10. Tribus, M.: Thermodynamics and Thermostatics: An Introduction to Energy, Information and States of Matter, with Engineering Applications, Princeton, N.J., Van Nostrand (1961)
11. Schmidhuber, J., Storck, J., Hochreiter, J.: Reinforcement Driven Information Acquisition In Non-Deterministic Environments. In: ICANN 1995, vol. 2, pp. 159–164. EC2 & CIE, Paris (1995)

Perceptual Time, Perceptual Reality, and General Intelligence

Leslie S. Smith

Computing Science and Mathematics, University of Stirling
Stirling FK9 4LA, UK
l.s.smith@cs.stir.ac.uk

Abstract. Perceptual time is a critical aspect of how humans (and probably animals too) perceive the world. It underlies general intelligence, particularly where that general intelligence is about interacting with the world on an everyday basis. We discuss what is meant by the perceptual instant, and how this may be important for (artificial and real) general intelligence. Lastly, we briefly discuss how perceptual time might be included in an artificial system which might display general intelligence.

1 Introduction

We believe that the nature of general intelligence is strongly intertwined with the nature of perception. This means that artificial general intelligence (AGI) is more than an abstract concept, but needs an understanding of the nature of perceptual reality in order to develop. This is an aspect of the issue of embodiment: like many (described in http://en.wikipedia.org/wiki/Embodied_cognition, and reviewed in [3] and [5]): we believe (but cannot prove) that embodiment is critical for AGI. What this paper considers is one aspect of the issue of what embodiment means in terms of the (internal) environment in which general intelligence (and hence also AGI) operates.

This aspect is perceptual time. This has been largely ignored in this context, yet seems critical for (real) behaviour and hence (real) general intelligence. In this context, *real behaviour* implies both real-world and real-time behaviour. In addition understanding perceptual time may shed some light on the differences between state-based systems and actual neural systems.

2 Perceptual Time and Perceptual Reality

One of the most difficult (and most unfashionable) questions in philosophical neuroscience is that of the nature of the neural construction of reality. That it has a neural construction appears to be generally agreed, yet avoiding the homunculus issue seems difficult, unless the neural activity directly gives rise to the first person experience of being[1]. One important aspect of this question is

---

[1] This underlies a central issue in artificial "first person" systems: can non-neural (electrical, for example) activity give rise to "first person" (machine?) experience?

J. Bach, B. Goertzel, and M. Iklé (Eds.): AGI 2012, LNAI 7716, pp. 292–301, 2012.

that of the nature of the neural construction of perceptual time. It is clear that perceptual reality differs from physical reality, and equally that perceptual time is also different from physical time (indeed, this goes back a long way, perhaps to St Augustine and certainly to von Baer [9]. We argue that the nature of the difference between physical reality and perceptual reality (including physical time and perceptual time) is critical for the nature of perception, and, further, for the nature of our everyday interaction with the world. We believe that understanding certain perceptual aspects of time may help to elucidate the differences between current computational approaches and natural generally intelligent systems.

It seems reasonable to accept that the nature of perceptual reality differs between different animals, and from human to human, and indeed, over time for a single person. Given that the location of the generation of perceptual reality (including perceptual time) is in the brain, it seems reasonable to posit that perceptual reality (including perceptual time) for humans has a neural basis. But what is the nature of this neural basis? And how should we look for it? Further, if we can identify and even understand the nature of the neural basis in humans or animals, what are the implications for *artificial* general intelligence? What aspects of it can be re-created in non-neural (e.g. electronic) systems?

Related questions arise for general intelligence. Firstly should one be seeking a specific physical location of the general intelligence, or should we consider this as, in some sense, emerging from the whole brain? Secondly, whatever the answer to the previous question, how should we seek to understand how it operates (investigating how some part of the brain is supporting general intelligence, or alternatively investigating the way in which general intelligence arises from the whole brain)? That is, what is the nature of the relationship between these physical aspects and actual intelligence? We may look for specific structures. Taylor (for example [13]) has suggested that it is to be found in the parietal lobes, although in later papers (e.g. [15], [14]) he moves away from specific locations. Alternatively, we may consider the overall nature of the brain, whether that be its constitution as a very large number of highly interconnected neurons, or in the nature of ionic and neurotransmitter (etc.) interactions within the brain. Finding these physical underpinnings is difficult enough, yet connecting them on to the nature of general intelligence (or awareness, or consciousness or whatever) seems even more difficult.

Because of the difficulty of this problem, we restrict ourselves to considering perceptual time: we believe that there may be lessons from this area for the study of (real) general and artificial general intelligence, and perhaps of the difference between Turing (state-based) machines and neural systems. Further, time is a central issue, because our every sensation, our every action, and that of all living creatures is bound up in time, both physical (external) and perceptual (internal).

3   Time, Events, and the Perceptual Instant

Time, from a physicists viewpoint, is considered as a spatial dimension though which we travel. Each instant is a point, and the points are continuous (or perhaps divided from each other by a very small amount: 5.39×10^{-44} seconds: see http://en.wikipedia.org/wiki/Planck_time), and form a 1 dimensional line. Yet our experience of time is very different from this: we experience it as episodes, each with some duration, possibly overlapping, but retaining their order, perhaps inherited from the (underlying) physical time.

One view of perceptual time is of events, each occurring at some "point" in time. Events have been discussed in many contexts, ranging from events in Milner's calculus of communicating systems [8], to synchronising communication in Hoare's Communicating Sequential Processes [6], and the various systems developed from them, such as Σ-algebras, to more generalised views of events, as discussed in the chapters of a recent conference book (From Event-Driven Business Process Management to Ubiquitous Complex Event Processing (EDBPM 2010): see [2]). There are many candidates for events in neural systems, from the release of a neurotransmitter vesicle, to the arrival of a single spike at a synapse, to the initiation of a movement.

Perceptual events are always over some length of time: nothing can happen within a physicist's point of time. As Dunne noted in 1925 "attention is never really confined to a mathematical instant. It covers a slightly larger period." [4] chapter 22.

The duration of the present instant (called "the minimum duration of the conscious present" by Schaltenbrand [11], or the specious present by Clay, renamed the mental present by Whitrow [17]) seems to have two rather different interpretations. On the one hand, there is a lower bound below which the present seems not to be divisible: this is set to about 40ms by von Baer [10], though it is possible to distinguish events closer than this if presented auditorially [11]: however, it is the case that continually presented auditory pulses fuse into a tone at about 18 presentations/second, and continually presented (similar) images fuse into apparent movement at about 20 Hz, suggesting some cross-modal integration time of 40 to 50ms [10]. Such a time period appears to correlate well with certain neural oscillations, such as those found in local field potentials, and may relate to temporal and cross-modal integration (see section 6.1).

Clearly, such perceptual instants are not coded by a purely spatial neural representation, but by one that extends over time.

Yet although we can perceive time as a sequence of events, our perception of time is not as a sequence of such instants. Poppel discusses a longer division of time, particularly in the context of pre-semantic temporal integration, and this he estimates at about 3 seconds [9][10][19]. This longer time period seems to be integrated at a higher level. This longer temporal integration period is associated with conscious perception [9].

4   Time and State

The perceptual views of an instant discussed above differ from a simple temporal ordering of events because the instants extend across time. This means that it is no longer possible to take a "snapshot" of the system. If events occur as points in time, then assuming no further interactions with the system's environment, this snapshot of state determines what will happen in the future to the system. Synchronous logic systems have this property (and very useful it is as well, enabling deterministic computation to be carried out). When events (and percepts are internal events) are spread across time, it is no longer clear what might be meant by such a snapshot.

In general, asynchronous logic systems do not generally have this snapshot property (and a great deal of work is often carried out to ensure that real computer systems which have asynchronous components behave like their synchronous counterparts). There is a realisation that asynchronous operation can bring its own advantages, but the mechanisms of taming this power have not yet, in general been found [1]. Can we use a synthetic version of a perceptual view of time to achieve this?

Real neural systems are highly asynchronous. They do not really have a usable instantaneous state: if, as seems likely, the spikes emitted by neurons are critically important, it is the pattern of spikes (over time, and over the set of neurons) that have been emitted that matters, so that any equivalent of state would need to consider the spikes over some period of time. But over how long? And should other matters (concentrations of different neurotransmitters and neuromodulators, depolarisation of patches of dendrite, for example), also be taken into account? It becomes impossible to know where to stop: as Hong [7] notes, even single interactions between molecules are stochastic because of the rapid thermal movement of the active areas of the interacting molecules.

This suggests that the lack of an identifiable instantaneous state in neural systems illustrates a specific difference between computer and neural systems. One might argue that computer systems can model anything, including systems which have this absence of instantaneous state, and asynchronous nondeterminism, and while that may be true, it would require a very large amount of electronic circuitry to model even a single neuron to any degree of accuracy.

5   Time and Context

Context has long been known to be vital for interpreting data. Context may be spatial, temporal, or both. In a computer program, context is (generally) implemented using the internal state (values of variables) within a program, so that the interpretation of some particular datum will depend on the explicitly adjusted values that make up this state. In non-algorithmic modes of computation, (such as those of neural networks and reinforcement learning), context is made up from the values of the different elements in the system. For example, in trained neural networks, the eventual interpretation of some input will depend on the dataset used to train the system (as well as the actual learning rule and architecture of the system). Thus a particular data element is interpreted in the context of the training set.

Context arises at many levels in both real and artificial neural systems. For example, in an integrate-and-fire neuron (which fires when its activity reaches a certain threshold level, after which the activity is reset), there is an activity level context which will determine whether some particular input results in the neuron reaching the firing threshold. In a pure integrate-and-fire neuron, this is simply the sum of all the inputs received since the last time the neuron fired. In a leaky integrate-and -fire (LIF) neuron, the activity has a time constant over which it leaks away, so that the current activity is a function particularly of inputs that have been received recently. In a similar way, Temporal Difference (TD) systems and reinforcement learning systems which gradually (and geometrically) discount recent events and changes also have a temporal context which values more recent inputs more highly than less recent ones.

In real neural systems, the neuronal membrane is leaky, but is not a point-like entity as it is in LIF neurones. Thus there is both a local temporal context, and local spatial context. Further, the strength of this context can be amplified for example through the way in which NMDA synapses work (because the local depolarisation level affects the presence or absence of $Mg+$ ions that permit these channels to open). At a slightly larger scale, the retina uses the context of both spatially and temporally neighbouring retinal neurones (through the action of the inner and outer plexiform layers) to determine its output, and this is partly responsible for our ability to operate in very variable light levels. Blackboard-based AI systems use the blackboard itself as context: in this case, the particular temporal and spatial (and higher-level) contextual effects are explicit, rather than implicit.

All of this is shows that AI (and other) systems already consider the effect of time, generally implementing its effects through the modulating effects caused by changes made by earlier events. These may be at many different levels: in explicit systems (like blackboard based systems) this is entirely up to the programmer. In implicit systems, it will depend on the different time constants within the system: there are often many of these, ranging from those of individual neuronal patches of membrane, to much slower effects resulting from gradual alteration in weights, such as might occur through STDP or back-propagated delta rule weight alteration. In section 3, we are arguing that there is a specific set of temporal contextual constraints at work in neural systems (and that these may well differ for different animals, and indeed, different values may be appropriate for different tasks). The temporal context applied in the systems discussed in this section is one way of achieving the same effect: we suggest that more careful consideration of the neural approach to perceptual time might lead to better, and perhaps more effective, temporal contextual modulation.

6   Why Perceptual Time Matters for Artificial General Intelligence

Time, in terms of ordering of inputs and outputs, has always been included in AI and AGI systems. It is true that systems for interpreting or classifying static images can ignore time: but clever though these may be, they are not intelligent systems. Only simple pattern discrimination systems such as back-propagated delta networks or radial basis function networks consider patterns one by one, without reference to their ordering. Further, each individual pattern is presented all at once. But even in these cases, when training is taking place, the order of presentation may matter, as the internal parameters are gradually altered in a non-linear way as a result of each patterns being presented (unless specific care is taken to avoid this, as occurs in so-called batch-processing weight update).

Taking general intelligence to be some mixture of common sense behaviour in a known or unknown environment and maintaining an organisms's overall goals under the vagaries of an unpredictable environment, it is clear that time plays a critical part. As discussed in section 5, this is not new, but how might the ideas on the perceptual instant in section 3, and on the effect of time on state-based machines (section 4), impact on the design of generally intelligent systems?

6.1   The Perceptual Instant

We consider the perceptual instant first: as noted in section 3, there seem to be two gradations of perceptual instant, one being around 40 to 50ms, and the other considerably longer at about 3 seconds. It seems possible that the faster of these relates to the way in which local oscillations occur in neural columns, and this may well be critical for cross-modal integration of senses. The timescale is within the range of beta oscillations (15 to 30Hz: i.e. 33 to 66ms period), and there are suggestions that these and gamma oscillations (30-80Hz: 12.5 to 33ms period) may be implicated in sensory integration [16]. These oscillations are strongly tied to the architecture of the cortical column, and specific mechanism related to the interplay between excitatory and inhibitory neurones have been suggested to underlie this behaviour [18]. Further, these oscillations have been suggested to be critical for encoding relations and binding different aspects of percepts [12].

It thus seems likely that this fast perceptual instant is closely linked to the columnar architecture of the cortex, and how it fuses the different aspects of sensory perception. Thus it is likely to be critical in human perception and perhaps human general intelligence. However, this does not necessarily imply that it is important for *artificial* general intelligence. Yet there are undoubtedly links between the nature of our perceiving organs, the coding of these percepts as they are converted from the actual transducer, through the brainstem, to the cortex, and the timescale of the sensory integration. These strongly colour our perception of our environment. One result that this has, is that the key percepts that humans use, the percepts that drive our interaction with our environment, take place (at least at one level) over this timescale. One may argue that this may be either a cause or an effect: for example, visual and auditory effects from a remote stimulus (like someone hitting a nail with a hammer) 10 metres away arrive about 30ms apart. Processing at this timescale influences what we consider to be general intelligence, at least in terms of the percepts that we expect to contribute to it.

Although there are slow oscillations within the cortex, they do not appear to be correlated with particular neuronal structures (beyond the cortex), or behaviour (beyond REM sleep): see http://www.scholarpedia.org/article/

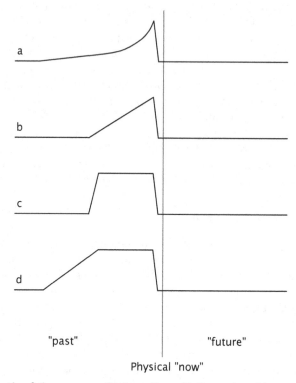

"past"   "future"

Physical "now"

Fig. 1. Schematic of time course of integration of information. Lines a and b show the integration that is implied by reinforcement or temporal difference learning, where the "current" time is the most important, and there is an exponential (a) or linear (b) drop off in the importance applied to previous information. Lines c and d show integration of recent time equally over a period, with a sudden drop-off in c, and a more gradual drop-off in d. We note that there is always a short delay between the current time and any information being used.

Thalamocortical oscillations . Perhaps this is not surprising, as the longer perceptual instant seems to be more like a travelling window, gathering together a number of shorter perceptual instants, than a three-second tiling of physical time. As noted in section 5, many models of neural systems do take time into account. However it tends to be a travelling exponentially decaying mechanism that is used, rather than a more even one, illustrated figure $1a$ and $1b$. What lines c and d in figure 1 suggest, is that up to a certain time into the past, recent events may be treated equally in terms of their contribution. Line c suggests a sudden change after a particular length of time, which is perhaps inappropriate, but line d suggests that there could be a decreasing contribution for some longer time. Such an integration interval does seem to coincide with a common-sense view of the world, where events that occurred in the last few seconds do contribute equally to the current state of the world, with events that happened a little longer ago having a smaller (or perhaps already acknowledged) effect. (Again one can argue that this might be either cause or effect: the entities that matter to us in the world are grouped into this timescale, and therefore our time percepts work in this way: or our time percepts work in this way, and this results in the entities that matter to us in the world being grouped at this timescale.)

6.2   Implications for Implementations

Given that the nature of perceptual time is an important aspect of human general intelligence, we are now interested in how to build a system whose percepts and reactions to percepts bear a resemblance to the timings used in human intelligence.

In section 5 we noted that temporal coding (which is certainly required for the types of perceptual time that we are discussing) means that there is no clear-cut notion of instantaneous state. What implications does this have for simulating such systems on standard (state-based) computers, or for implementing artificial general intelligence which includes perceptual time? It means that whatever representations are actually used, they must be representable as a state vector. Thus the simulation necessarily loses some accuracy, and quite possibly represents entities using different mechanisms. Whilst it is possible that these result in deep-seated differences between the capabilities of neural and computational systems[2], we believe that it should be possible to create a system programatically that can emulate perceptual time.

What might such a system consist of?

Such a system would be essentially asynchronous (though if implemented on a digital computer, it would be implemented on synchronous logic). It would have a number of parallel processing entities, processing different modalities. Note that each modality might be associated with a particular sense, but that there might well me multiple modalities per sense (for example, one might choose to process the *where* and the *what* information both in auditory and visual sensory systems separately). These would be integrated over a 30 to 50 ms timescale. This would model (in a functional sense) the cortical columns beta band oscillation, but would almost certainly not be implemented in the same way. (Of course, this implies a better understanding of the nature of the processing in these cortical columns, beyond that in [16] and [18]). This would enable a machine-based representation that matched the shorter version of the perceptual instant. It would aim to group together processed sensory information in pieces that represent events in the environment that take place over these timescales. (Of course, for a completely different, perhaps virtual, environment, the timescales might also be completely different.)

It is less clear how one should implement the three second long perceptual instant (and we note that it might not be a three second long perceptual instant in a different type of environment). We have no clue as to what the neural representation might be. One possibility would be to consider a short-term

---

[2] See http://www.cs.stir.ac.uk/~lss/recentpapers/lss_edinburgh_oct2007.pdf for more discussion of this.

blackboard-like store which is refreshed from the short-term perceptual instant, but which loses information after about three seconds. This would be used to mirror the moment-to-moment awareness of the world in which we normally live. More likely, it would integrate the shorter perceptual instants over a dynamically varying period, reflecting the changing circumstances of the AGI system.

Adaptation to the environment would use something like Reinforcement Learning or Temporal Difference Learning, but with a discount function more like that in figure 1c or 1d. Action choice would take place at a number of temporal levels, one corresponding to the fast integration (30 to 50ms), one to the slower but immediate temporal percept, at about 3 seconds, and one related to slow considered planning over a longer timescale. (Again we note that these timescales relate to human-level interaction with the real environment, but might be quite different in other environments.) One might consider the fastest of these to be like reactive actions, the middle one to be more like the immediate actions that humans take, and the slowest one to relate to the fulfilment of longer term plans and goals.

7   Conclusions

It is difficult to imagine an artificial general intelligence operating in a real environment unless it can process events and percepts in time in a way which at least bears some relation to how events and percepts are processed in time by real intelligent systems. Most of the activities which animals (and presumably artificially generally intelligent entities) perform take place over time, whether that be opening a door, navigating a route, telling a story, playing music or any other activity. We have looked at what appear to be the basics of human time perception, and tried to show how these might be transferred to machines. A great deal more work needs to be done to actually implement such a system, and we have tried to show what might be initially required.

References

1. Buesing, L., Bill, J., Nessler, B., Maass, W.: Neural Dynamics as Sampling: A Model for Stochastic Computation in Recurrent Networks of Spiking Neurons. PLoS Computational Biology 7(11), e1002211 (2011)
2. Cezon, M., Wolfsthal, Y. (eds.): ServiceWave 2010 Workshops. LNCS, vol. 6569. Springer, Heidelberg (2011)
3. Chrisley, R.: Embodied artificial intelligence. Artificial Intelligence 149(1), 131–150 (2003)
4. Dunne, J.: An Experiment with Time. Black (January 1929)
5. Goertzel, B.: Patterns, hypergraphs and embodied general intelligence. In: International Joint Conference on Neural Networks, IJCNN 2006, pp. 451–458 (2006)
6. Hoare, C.A.R.: Communicating sequential processes. Springer-Verlag New York, Inc. (January 2002)
7. Hong, F.T.: A multi-disciplinary survey of biocomputing: Part 1: molecular and cellular aspects, pp. 1–129. Imperial College Press (January 2005)

8. Milner, R.: Calculus of Communicating Systems. Springer (July 1980)

9. Poppel, E.: Lost in time: a historical frame, elementary processing units and the 3-second window. Acta Neurobiologiae Experimentalis 64(3), 295–302 (2004)

10. Poppel, E.: Pre-semantically defined temporal windows for cognitive processing. Philosophical Transactions of the Royal Society B: Biological Sciences 364(1525), 1887–1896 (2009)

11. Schaltenbrand, G.: Consciousness and time. Annals of the New York Academy of Sciences 138(2) (February 1967)

12. Singer, W.: Neocortical rhythms: an overview. In: von der Malsburg, C., Phillips, W.A., Singer, W. (eds.) Dynamic Co-ordination in the Brain. Strungmann Forum Reports, pp. 159–168. MIT Press (January 2010)

13. Taylor, J.G.: The Central Role of the Parietal Lobes in Consciousness. Consciousness and Cognition 10(3), 379–417 (2001)

14. Taylor, J.G.: On the neurodynamics of the creation of consciousness. Cognitive Neurodynamics 1(2), 97–118 (2006)

15. Taylor, J.G.: CODAM: A neural network model of consciousness. Neural Networks 20(9), 983–992 (2007)

16. Wang, X.J.: Neurophysiological and Computational Principles of Cortical Rhythms in Cognition. Physiological Reviews 90(3), 1195–1268 (2010)

17. Whitrow, G.J.: The natural philosophy of time. Thomas Nelson and Sons (October 1961)

18. Whittington, M.A., Kopell, N.J., Traub, R.D.: What are the local circuit design features concerned with coordinating rhthyms? In: von der Malsburg, C., Phillips, W.A., Singer, W. (eds.) Dynamic Co-ordination in the Brain. Strungmann Forum Reports, pp. 115–132. MIT Press (October 2010)

19. Wittmann, M.: The inner experience of time. Philosophical Transactions of the Royal Society B: Biological Sciences 364(1525), 1955–1967 (2009)

Transparent Neural Networks
Integrating Concept Formation and Reasoning

Claes Strannegård[1], Olle Häggström[2],
Johan Wessberg[3], and Christian Balkenius[4]

[1] Department of Philosophy, Linguistics and Theory of Science, University of
Gothenburg, Sweden and Department of Applied Information Technology,
Chalmers University of Technology, Sweden
claes.strannegard@gu.se
[2] Department of Mathematical Sciences,
Chalmers University of Technology,
Sweden
olle.haggstrom@chalmers.se
[3] Institute of Neuroscience and Physiology,
University of Gothenburg, Sweden
johan.wessberg@gu.se
[4] Department of Philosophy, Lund University, Sweden
christian.balkenius@lucs.lu.se

Abstract. We present the *transparent neural networks*, a graph-based
computational model that was designed with the aim of facilitating human understanding. We also give an algorithm for developing such networks automatically by interacting with the environment. This is done
by adding and removing structures for spatial and temporal memory.
Thus we automatically obtain a monolithic computational model which
integrates concept formation with deductive, inductive, and abductive
reasoning.

Keywords: transparent neural networks, developmental robotics, concept formation, deductive reasoning, inductive reasoning.

1 Introduction

Artificial General Intelligence (AGI) aims for computer systems with human-like
general intelligence [1]. Thus, just like humans, AGI systems should be able to
reason and learn from experience by interacting with the environment. This leads
to desiderata on AGI systems that concern developmental processes and automated reasoning. It has been suggested that to build intelligent machines, it is
necessary to use developmental methods where a system develops autonomously
from its interaction with the environment [2][3]. This lead to the research area of
developmental (or epigenetic) robotics, where models based on biological principles are used either to describe human cognitive development or to come up
with novel principles for AI. The explicit goal of the area is to design cognitive

J. Bach, B. Goertzel, and M. Iklé (Eds.): AGI 2012, LNAI 7716, pp. 302–311, 2012.

architectures that can autonomously develop higher cognitive abilities. However, most research so far has focused on sensory-motor development and social interaction and has mainly ignored higher cognitive functions such as reasoning. Reasoning is commonly analyzed as in the following quote from [4]:

> Three notable hallmarks of intelligent cognition are the ability to draw rational conclusions, the ability to make plausible assumptions and the ability to generalise from experience. In a logical setting, these abilities correspond to the processes of deduction, abduction, and induction, respectively.

These problems have been studied thoroughly in traditional AI with symbolic methods such as automatic theorem proving [5], sub-symbolic methods such as artificial neural networks (ANNs) [6], probabilistic methods such as Bayesian networks [7], and many others [8]. These approaches typically focus on a proper subset of the above-mentioned types of reasoning. For instance, the symbolic approach is mainly concerned with deductive reasoning and the sub-symbolic approach with inductive reasoning. This might suggest a hybrid approach, which integrates symbolic and sub-symbolic methods such as ACT-R [9], conceptual spaces [10], or neural-symbolic systems [4]. Hybrid approaches, however, tend to be limited by the difficulty of designing interfaces for complex interaction between the different subsystems.

Human reasoning processes seem to be tightly integrated with concept formation: new concepts are created continuously and become integrated with previous knowledge and involved in new reasoning processes. Looking at developmental psychology, evidence is accumulating that infants and children use similarity-based measures to categorize objects and form new concepts [11].

For these reasons, AGI could potentially benefit from a developmental system which integrates concept formation, deduction, induction, and abduction. This is the goal of the transparent neural networks (TNNs), which are introduced in sections 2 and 3. Section 4 contains an analysis of the TNN model from the perspective of concept formation and automated reasoning and Section 5 is a conclusion.

2   Transparent Neural Networks

The TNN model arose out of an attempt to create a computational model that simultaneously accommodates two previously developed models of human reasoning: one for deductive reasoning about propositional logic [12], the other for inductive reasoning about number sequence problems [13]. In fact, both of these models are based on term-rewriting systems. In this section we define the TNNs together with their computation rules and show how they can be used for handling spatial and temporal memory.

Traditional ANNs tend to be intransparent in the sense that it is virtually impossible for a human to understand how they work and predict their computations and input-output behavior. This holds already for feed-forward networks

Fig. 1. Network modeling the tentacle of a sea anemone, which keeps retracting for 5 time units after being touched

and still more for recurrent networks. Therefore, they are generally not suitable for deductive reasoning and applications that are safety-critical.

TNN is a restricted type of ANN, designed with the aim of facilitating human understanding. The TNN model was heavily inspired by neuroscience, but since our only concern here is AGI, we feel free to deviate as much as we want from any existing biological or computational model.

2.1   Definition

Definition 1 (TNN). *A TNN consists of the following parts:*

- *A set D of labeled nodes. The labels are SENSOR, ACTUATOR, MIN, MAX, AVERAGE, SPACE(μ, σ), DELAY(n), and REVERB(n). Here μ and σ are real numbers and n is a natural number.*
- *A cycle-free relation $R \subset D^2$, whose elements are called connections.*

Restriction: The labels ACTUATOR, SPACE, DELAY, and REVERB are only allowed on nodes with exactly one predecessor.

In this paper we use the graphical convention that connections point upward in all figures. Examples of TNNs are given in Figures 1 and 2.

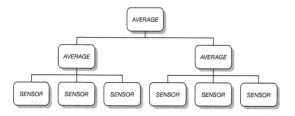

Fig. 2. Network modeling a gustatory organ for sweetness. Information on the local level is summarized and passed on to higher levels. A similar network with MAX nodes instead of AVERAGE nodes could model a sensory organ for pain.

2.2   Environments

Definition 2 (Frame). *Let V be the set of real numbers in the interval $[0,1]$. A frame for a TNN with sensor set S is a function $f : S \to V$.*

Definition 3 (Environment). *Let T be the set of natural numbers (modeling time). An environment for a TNN with sensor set S is a function $e : S \times T \to V$.*

Frames model momentary stimuli and environments model streams of stimuli generated by the surrounding world (which might include the TNN itself). For instance, an environment could represent the taste and smell of an apple, followed by the sound sequence [æpl], followed by the visual sequence "$6 \cdot 8 = 48$".

2.3   Activity

In contrast to the standard ANN model, our model has two types of activity. This enables us to model perception and imagination separately. For instance, it enables us to distinguish between the perceived and the imagined taste of an apple. It also enables us to model the perception of the sequence $2, 5, 8, 11$ and the imagination of the next number 14.

The inspiration behind the two types of activity comes from the distinction between (i) distal and proximal dendritic signal processing and (ii) inner and outer senses [14].

Let $N_{(\mu,\sigma)}(x) = \exp\{-(x - \mu)^2/\sigma^2\}$. This is the Gaussian density function with mean μ, standard deviation σ, and max value 1. Let A be a TNN with sensor set S and let $e : S \times T \to V$ be an environment. Then the *real* activity $r : D \times T \to V$ and *imaginary* activity $i : D \times T \to V$ are defined as follows.

Definition 4 (Real activity). *Let $r(a,0) = 0$ and let $r(a, t + 1) =$*

- $e(a, t)$ *if a is labeled SENSOR*
- $min\{r(a', t) : (a', a) \in R\}$ *if a is labeled MIN*
- $max\{r(a', t) : (a', a) \in R\}$ *if a is labeled MAX*
- $average\{r(a', t) : (a', a) \in R\}$ *if a is labeled AVERAGE*
- $r(a', t)$ *if a is labeled ACTUATOR and $(a', a) \in R$*
- $N_{(\mu,\sigma)}(r(a', t))$ *if a is labeled SPACE(μ,σ) and $(a', a) \in R$*
- $r(a', t - n)$ *if a is labeled DELAY(n) and $(a', a) \in R$*
- $max\{r(a', t') : t - n \le t' \le t\}$ *if a is labeled REVERB(n) and $(a', a) \in R$.*

SPACE nodes are used for modeling spatial memory. They output the value 1 if and only if the input is identical to a certain stored value μ. DELAY nodes and REVERB nodes are used for modeling temporal memory. DELAY nodes delay the signals before releasing them, whereas REVERB nodes make the signals linger on (reverberate). The REVERB label was inspired by reverberation among neuronal pools [14].

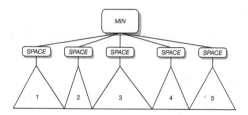

Fig. 3. Snapshot modeling apple taste. The subgraphs 1-5 model sensory organs for the five basic tastes sweetness, sourness, bitterness, saltiness and umami. For instance, subgraph 1 could be the graph of Figure 2. The top node represents a combination of memories of the basic tastes. This network can be used for detecting apple taste.

Definition 5 (Imaginary activity). *First we define an auxiliary function p, which will be used for keeping track of probabilities. Let $p : D \times T \to V$ be defined by $p(b, 0) = 0$ and*

$$p(b, t+1) = p(b, t) + \frac{r(b, t+1) - p(b, t)}{t+1}.$$

Let $i(a, 0) = 0$ and $i(a, t+1) =$

- *$min(1, \sum\{r(b, t) \cdot p(b, t) : (a, b) \in R\})$ if b is labeled MIN, MAX, or AVERAGE.*
- *$i(a, t)$ otherwise.*

Note that imaginary activity is defined in terms of real activity in the past and at present. Also note that imaginary and real activity propagate in opposite directions. The real activity is "mirrored" back in the form of imaginary activity. The definition of imaginary activity was inspired by (i) mirror neurons and (ii) "two-way streets" in cortex [14].

2.4 Memory Structures

Now let us show how spatial and temporal memory can be modeled.

Definition 6 (Memory). *A memory of a node a is a node b which is labeled SPACE and satisfies $R(a, b)$.*

Memories can be used for recording and recalling previously perceived values. For instance, the sweetness of a collection of apples can be recorded by a certain memory node and represented by a normal distribution.

Definition 7 (Snapshot). *Let Ω be a set of nodes. A snapshot of Ω is a structure consisting of (i) a memory a' of a, for each $a \in \Omega$, (ii) a node b labeled MIN, (iii) connections $R(a', b)$, for each $a \in \Omega$.*

An example of a snapshot is given in Figure 3.

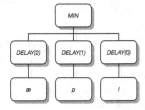

Fig. 4. Episode modeling the spoken word [æpl]. The bottom nodes may either be specialized sensors for the indicated phonemes or structures representing previously learned phonemes. A similar structure could represent the written word "APPLE" or the fact "6 · 8 = 48".

Fig. 5. Network modeling the co-occurrence of the spoken work [æpl] and apple taste. Here the node marked *æpl* could be the top node of Figure 4 and the node marked *Apple* the top node of Figure 3. The MIN node is activated if *æpl* and *Apple* are activated simultaneously modulo 10 time units. Note that real activity in *[æpl]* causes imaginary activity in *Apple* and vice versa.

Definition 8 (Episode). *Let* $a_0, \ldots, a_n$ *be snapshots. An* episode *joining* $a_0, \ldots,$ a_n *is a structure consisting of (i) nodes* $b_0, \ldots, b_n$ *labeled* $DELAY(n), \ldots,$ $DELAY(0)$, *respectively, (ii) a node* c *labeled MIN, (iii) connections* $R(a_i, b_i)$, *for all* $0 \leq i \leq n$ *(iv) connections* $R(b_i, c)$, *for all* $0 \leq i \leq n$.

An example of an episode is given in Figure 4. REVERB nodes can be used when the temporal conditions relate to time intervals, as in Figure 5. Note that REVERB nodes can be modeled as a MAX of DELAY nodes.

3 Organisms

Now we shall define the notion of organism and give a basic algorithm for generating organisms.

3.1 Definition

Definition 9 (Organism). *An* organism *is a sequence of TNNs* $(A_t)_{t \in T}$ *such that*

- A_0 *contains no nodes labeled SPACE, DELAY or REVERB.*
- A_0 *is a substructure of* A_i, *for all* i,
- *if* $a \in A_i$ *is labeled SENSOR, then* $a \in A_0$, *for all* $i > 0$.

A_0 *is called the* genotype *and the* A_i *are called* phenotypes *for* $i > 0$.

Let A_0 be any TNN which does not contain any SPACE, DELAY or REVERB nodes. Let A_{t+1} be obtained from A_t as follows.

1. (Update probabilities) Let $p'(a,t)$ be like $p(a,t)$, with the difference that the observations starting at the time when a was created. Then update this function as in Definition 5, mutatis mutandis.
2. (Make deletions) Let $a_1, \ldots, a_k$ be the nodes of $A_t - A_0$ that satisfy $p'(a_i, t) < c$. Here $c \in V$ is a fixed threshold value. Then delete each a_i along with all of its connections.
3. (Make additions) Proceed as follows:
   (a) Case: No complete snapshot is active at t.
      i. Subcase. All maximal nodes have memory nodes that are active at t. (Add snapshot) Then add a complete snapshot by connecting all active SPACE nodes to a MIN-node.
      ii. Subcase (otherwise). Some maximal nodes lack memory nodes that are active at t. Let $a_1, \ldots, a_k$ be all such nodes. (Add memories) Then add memories $b_1, \ldots, b_k$ to $a_1, \ldots, a_k$, respectively. Let the label of b_i be SPACE$(r(a_i, t), 0.25)$.
   (b) Case (otherwise): A complete snapshot is active at t. Then do both of the following.
      i. (Update snapshots) Let $b_1, \ldots, b_k$ be the SPACE nodes that are active at t and let a_i be the unique node satisfying $R(a_i, b_i)$. Suppose the label of b_i is SPACE$(\mu_{i,t}, \sigma_{i,t})$. Then compute the updated parameters $\mu_{i,t+1}$ and $\sigma_{i,t+1})$ by updating the old parameters with respect to the new data points $r(a_i, t)$ by means of Hansen's formula.
      ii. (Add episodes) Suppose there is an episode, which is active at t and joins the complete snapshots $a_1, \ldots, a_n$ (where $n \leq 9$). Then, unless it already exists, add an episode joining $a_1, \ldots, a_n, a$.

Fig. 6. Algorithm for developing organisms automatically. The algorithm uses Hansen's formula [15] for computing the mean and standard deviation incrementally.

Organisms model biological neural networks that develop over time by adding and deleting memory structures (learning and forgetting). Because of the two last conditions of Definition 9, each organism has a fixed set of sensors. Therefore the notion of environment extends to organisms in a straightforward manner.

3.2 Construction Algorithm

Next we shall give an algorithm for developing organisms automatically in a given environment. First we need to introduce some auxiliary concepts: (i) A node a is *active* at t if $r(a, t) \geq 0.95$; (ii) a node $a \in A_0$ is *maximal* if there is no node $b \in A_0$ such that $(a, b) \in A_0$; (iii) a snapshot is *complete* if it joins all maximal nodes (of A_0). The algorithm is given in Figure 3.2. Here are some remarks on the algorithm.

1. The genotype A_0 can be constructed, e.g., by modeling an existing biological or artificial network. It is a *tabula rasa*: a neural structure that has not yet formed any memories.

2. The step *Make deletions* serves the (productive) purpose of preserving memory structures that represent recurrent phenomena, while eliminating those that represent non-repeating coincidences. It was inspired by the forgetting mechanism of natural networks ("use them or lose them"), c.f. the decay theory of synapses [16].

3. The steps *Add snapshot* and *Add episode* were inspired by the Hebbian learning rule ("neurons that fire together wire together") [14].

4. The numerical values appearing in the algorithm can be changed freely. In particular this holds for the start value of standard deviation when only one data-point is available (0.25) and the maximal length of episodes (10).

4   Concept Formation and Reasoning

In this section we analyze the TNN framework from the perspective of concept formation and reasoning.

Concept Formation. The algorithm learns concepts from examples. This holds for sub-symbolic concepts, such as the taste of an apple (cf. Figure 3), and for symbolic concepts, such as the spoken word [æpl] (cf. Figure 4). Snapshots are formed on the basis of one example by means of *Add snapshot* and updated on the basis of similar examples by means of *Snapshot update*.

Concept Deletion. Concepts that are not active frequently enough are deleted by the algorithm. Conversely, repetition will make the concepts stay longer.

Classification. Snapshots and episodes serve as classifiers. In principle, once a pattern of stimuli has occurred and the corresponding snapshot or episode has been formed, it will be recognized every time it is encountered in the future. The robustness of these classifiers is determined by the values of σ of the SPACE nodes, which are in turn determined by experience. Another factor that contributes to robustness is the insensitivity of the functions MIN, MAX and AVERAGE to permutations of the inputs.

Deductive Reasoning. A simple example of deductive reasoning is given in Figure 7, where $6 \cdot 8$ is rewritten to 48. A similar rewrite step occurs when $6 \cdot 8$ appears as a subsequence of a complex expression (since real activity arises in the node $6 \cdot 8 = 48$ whenever the subsequence $6 \cdot 8$ becomes active). In general, deductive reasoning, e.g. arithmetic computations and theorem-proving, can be carried out in the TNN framework as a parallel rewrite process, based on rewrite rules that have been learned previously.

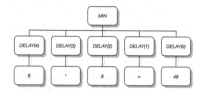

Fig. 7. What is 8 · 6? Real activity 1.0 in the four leftmost bottom nodes leads to real activity 0.8 in the top node. Imaginary activity then propagates back to all the bottom nodes, including 48.

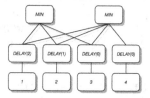

Fig. 8. What comes after 1,2? Suppose the organism has experienced both 1,2,3 and 1,2,4 before, the former more often than the latter. Then the sequence 1,2 will lead to imaginary activity in 3 and to a lesser extent in 4.

Inductive Reasoning. A simple example of inductive reasoning is given in Figure 8, where the sequence 1,2 is being extrapolated. The same mechanism can be used for interpolation, e.g. when reconstructing missing letters in words, both unambiguously as in ZEB?A and ambiguously as in H?T.

Abductive Reasoning. Abductive reasoning (for inferring possible causes) is performed via the interplay between real and imaginary activity. An example is given in Figure 9.

Fig. 9. Thunder appears within 10 time units after Lightning. Real activity in Thunder causes imaginary activity in Lightning and vice versa.

5   Conclusion

We presented a developmental model, which integrates concept formation and basic deduction, induction, and abduction. A version of this model was implemented in the context of an MSc project [17].

References

1. Schmidhuber, J., Thórisson, K.R., Looks, M. (eds.): AGI 2011. LNCS (LNAI), vol. 6830. Springer, Heidelberg (2011)
2. Weng, J., McClelland, J., Pentland, A., Sporns, O., Stockman, I., Sur, M., Thelen, E.: Artificial intelligence. Autonomous mental development by robots and animals. Science (291), 599–600 (2001)
3. Zlatev, J., Balkenius, C.: Introduction: Why epigenetic robotics? In: Balkenius, C., Zlatev, J., Kozima, H., Dautenhahn, K., Breazeal, C. (eds.) Proceedings of the First International Workshop on Epigenetic Robotics: Modeling Cognitive Development in Robotic Systems. Lund University Cognitive Studies, vol. 85, pp. 1–4 (2001)
4. d'Avila Garcez, A.S., Lamb, L.C.: Cognitive algorithms and systems: Reasoning and knowledge representation. In: Cutsuridis, V., Hussain, A., Taylor, J.G. (eds.) Perception-Action Cycle. Springer Series in Cognitive and Neural Systems, pp. 573–600. Springer, New York (2011)
5. Harrison, J.: Handbook of practical logic and automated reasoning. Cambridge University Press (2009)
6. Rumelhart, D., McClelland, J.: Parallel distributed processing: Psychological and biological models, vol. 2. The MIT Press (1986)
7. Pearl, J.: Probabilistic reasoning in intelligent systems: networks of plausible inference. Morgan Kaufmann (1988)
8. Russell, S., Norvig, P.: Artificial intelligence: a modern approach. Prentice-Hall (2010)
9. Kurup, U., Lebiere, C., Stentz, A.: Integrating Perception and Cognition for AGI. In: Schmidhuber, J., Thórisson, K.R., Looks, M. (eds.) AGI 2011. LNCS (LNAI), vol. 6830, pp. 102–111. Springer, Heidelberg (2011)
10. Gärdenfors, P.: Conceptual spaces. MIT Press (2000)
11. Sloutsky, V., Fisher, A.: Induction and categorization in young children: A similarity-based model. Journal of Experimental Psychology 133(2), 166–188 (2004)
12. Strannegård, C., Ulfsbäcker, S., Hedqvist, D., Gärling, T.: Reasoning Processes in Propositional Logic. Journal of Logic, Language and Information 19(3), 283–314 (2010)
13. Strannegård, C., Amirghasemi, M., Ulfsbäcker, S.: An anthropomorphic method for number sequence problems. Cognitive Systems Research (2012)
14. Baars, B., Gage, N.: Cognition, brain, and consciousness: Introduction to cognitive neuroscience. Academic Press (2010)
15. West, D.H.D.: Updating mean and variance estimates: an improved method. Commun. ACM 22(9), 532–535 (1979)
16. Wixted, J.: The psychology and neuroscience of forgetting. Annu. Rev. Psychol. 55, 235–269 (2004)
17. Olier, J.S.: Transparent neural networks, an implementation. Master's thesis, Chalmers University of Technology (2012)

Optimistic AIXI

Peter Sunehag and Marcus Hutter

Research School of Computer Science, Australian National University
Canberra Australia
{Peter.Sunehag,Marcus.Hutter}@anu.edu.au

Abstract. We consider extending the AIXI agent by using multiple (or
even a compact class of) priors. This has the benefit of weakening the
conditions on the true environment that we need to prove asymptotic optimality. Furthermore, it decreases the arbitrariness of picking the prior
or reference machine. We connect this to removing symmetry between
accepting and rejecting bets in the rationality axiomatization of AIXI
and replacing it with optimism. Optimism is often used to encourage
exploration in the more restrictive Markov Decision Process setting and
it alleviates the problem that AIXI (with geometric discounting) stops
exploring prematurely.

Keywords: AIXI, Reinforcement Learning, Optimism, Optimality.

1   Introduction

In this article, we aim to define agents that adapt to asymptotically act optimally
for as large a class of environments as possible. This task is fundamental for Artificial General Intelligence with many authors [LH07] using it as a definition of
intelligence. In [Hut05] the AIXI agent is defined as a Bayesian reinforcement
learning agent with particular attention being put on using the class of all computable environments as the hypothesis class. This agent has some interesting
optimality properties. Besides maximizing expected utility with respect to the
a-priori distribution by design, it is also Pareto optimal and self-optimizing when
this is possible for the considered class. It was, however, shown in [Ors10] that
at least with computable horizons, AIXI is not guaranteed to be asymptotically
optimal for all computable (deterministic) environments. Furthermore, [LH11]
shows that no agent can be.

Here we use multiple priors (or more generally multiple a-priori environments)
and the principle of optimism to define more explorative extensions of the AIXI
agent with the aim of being able to prove asymptotic optimality under weaker
conditions on the true environment. In other words, the agent can adapt successfully to a larger class of environments. The more priors used the more explorative
the agent will be; indeed we can even define the agent for all priors though the
convergence results will not apply and the agent can end up having no preference
between any of the actions in any situation. The meaningful cases include having
a compact class of strictly positive weight sequences $w_\nu, \nu \in \mathcal{M}$ for a countable

J. Bach, B. Goertzel, and M. Iklé (Eds.): AGI 2012, LNAI 7716, pp. 312–321, 2012.
© Springer-Verlag Berlin Heidelberg 2012

hypothesis class $\mathcal{M}$. We can, for example, consider a sequence $\alpha_\nu > 0$ and the set of mixtures with weights satisfying $w_\nu \geq \alpha_\nu$ and $\sum_\nu w_\nu = 1$.

In Section 2, we discuss the rational betting theory that has recently been used to derive AIXI [SH11a] and in Section 3, after introducing the reinforcement learning agent setting, we describe how the betting theory leads to active agents. Furthermore, in Section 2, we weaken the assumptions to introduce (in Section 3) our extended AIXI agent. In [SH11a], rationality axioms were presented that lead to the AIXI agent. Here we are going to extend AIXI by breaking the symmetry between accepting and rejecting bets in an optimistic fashion and as a consequence get a multiple-prior model. In the active AI setting where decisions affect the environment, the optimism makes the agent more explorative, which improves its chances of finding an optimal policy. Optimism has previously been used to encourage exploration in the more restrictive setting of Markov Decision Processes [SLL09]. Here we study general countable classes of environments.

In Section 3.2, we present our main results on asymptotic optimality under two conditions on how the a priori environment(s) relate to the true environment. If the a-priori environment ξ dominates an environment ν in the sense that $\xi(\cdot) \geq w_\nu \nu(\cdot)$, then we know from the Blackwell-Dubins theorem [BD62] that ξ will almost surely merge with ν in total variation distance under the followed policy. This is, however, not enough for achieving asymptotic optimality. We will say that ξ is optimistic for ν, if the expected value of following an optimal policy in ξ is always higher than it is in ν. If ξ is both dominating ν and optimistic for ν, then almost surely AIXI asymptotically achieves optimality. In this article, we extend the class of environments that we can prove optimality for by replacing ξ with a compact class of a-priori environments Ξ and decisions are taken according to the policy that maximizes the expected value for the environment in Ξ that is the most optimistic in the current situation. To guarantee asymptotic optimality we only need to assume that the optimistic environment is also optimistic relative the true environment. In a separate article [SH12] we remove those two conditions and replace them with the condition that the true environment lies in the class of a-priori environments, which then essentially serves as a hypothesis class.

2   Optimistic Rational Choice

In [SH11a, SH11b], AIXI was derived from rationality axioms inspired by the traditional literature [NM44, Ram31, Sav54, deF37] on decision making under uncertainty. Here we suggest replacing a symmetry condition between accepting and rejecting bets with optimism. The new weaker condition says that if we reject one side of a bet we must be prepared to accept the other side. The principle of optimism results in a more explorative agent and leads to multiple-prior models. Multiple-priors are also used in an approach sometimes called imprecise probability [Wal00], though our work is distinguished from the imprecise probability approach by actually making a choice among the priors. Axiomatics of multiple-prior models has been studied by [GS89, CMKO00]. These models can be understood as quantifying the uncertainty in estimated probabilities by assigning a whole set (or range) of probabilities. In the passive prediction case when the decisions do not affect the environment, one often combines the multiple-prior model with caution to achieve more risk averse decisions [CMKO00]. In the active case, we need to take risk to generate experience that one can learn successful behavior from and, therefore, optimism is appropriate.

2.1 Bets

The basic setting used in [SH11a] was inspired by the betting approach of [Ram31, deF37]. In this setting we are about to observe an event from a finite (or countable) alphabet and we are offered a bet (contract) $x = (x_1, ..., x_n)$ where $x_i \in \mathbb{R}$ is the reward received for the outcome i. We first introduce the setting of [SH11a] and its main theorem for the finite case.

Definition 1 (Bet). *Suppose that we are going to observe an event whose outcome is represented by a symbol from an alphabet with m elements. A bet for such an event is an element $x = (x_1, ..., x_m)$ in $\mathbb{R}^m$ and x_j is the reward received if the outcome of the event is the j:th symbol.*

Definition 2 (Decision Maker, Decision). *A decision maker is a pair of sets $Z, \tilde{Z} \subset \mathbb{R}^m$ which defines exactly the bets that are acceptable Z and those that are rejectable $\tilde{Z}$. In other words, a decision maker is a function from $\mathbb{R}^m$ to $\{accepted, rejected, either, neither\}$. The function value is called the decision.*

Next we present the axioms and representation theorem from [SH11a].

Definition 3 (Rationality). *We say that the decision maker $(Z, \tilde{Z})$ is rational if*

1. $Z \cup \tilde{Z} = \mathbb{R}^m$
2. $x \in Z \iff -x \in \tilde{Z}$
3. $x, y \in Z, \lambda, \gamma \geq 0 \Rightarrow \lambda x + \gamma y \in Z$
4. $\forall k \; x_k > 0 \Rightarrow x \in Z \setminus \tilde{Z}$

Theorem 1 (Existence of Probabilities, Sunehag&Hutter 2011). *Given a rational decision maker, there are numbers $p_i \geq 0$ that satisfy*

$$\{x \mid \sum x_i p_i > 0\} \subseteq Z \subseteq \{x \mid \sum x_i p_i \geq 0\}. \tag{1}$$

Assuming $\sum_i p_i = 1$ makes the numbers unique and we will use the notation $Pr(i) = p_i$.

Axiom 1 in Definition 3 is really describing the setting rather than an assumption. It says that we must always choose at least one of accept or reject. Axioms $3 - 4$ were motivated as follows in [SH11a]. If $x \in Z$ and $\lambda \geq 0$ then we want $\lambda x \in Z$ since it is simply a multiple of the same bet. We also want the sum of two acceptable bets to be acceptable. If we are guaranteed to win money we accept the bet and we are not prepared to reject it. Axiom 2 is a symmetry condition between accepting and rejecting which we are going to break in the optimistic setting. In the optimistic setting we will still demand that if we reject x we must accept $-x$ but not the other way around.

2.2   Rational Optimism

We present four axioms for rational optimism. They state properties that the set of accepted and the set of rejected bets must satisfy. The first two relate to optimism. The first one says that if a bet is not rejected it is accepted. The second says that if x is rejected then $-x$ must be accepted. In other words, if we reject one side of a bet we must accept the opposite. This was also argued for in the first set of axioms in the previous setting but in the optimistic setting we do not have the opposite direction. Namely we do *not* say that if x is accepted then $-x$ is rejected. The other two axioms are about rational rejection. If we reject two bets x and y, we reject $\lambda x + \gamma y$ if $\lambda \geq 0$ and $\gamma \geq 0$. The final axiom says that if the reward is guaranteed to be strictly negative we reject the bet. If the $\Rightarrow$ in Axiom 2 was instead an $\Longleftrightarrow$ we would have the same axioms as before, just slightly differently expressed.

Definition 4 (Rational Optimism). *We say that the decision maker* $Z, \tilde{Z} \subset \mathbb{R}^m$ *is a rational optimist if*

1. $x \notin \tilde{Z} \Rightarrow x \in Z$
2. $x \in \tilde{Z} \Rightarrow -x \notin \tilde{Z}$
3. $x, y \in \tilde{Z}$ and $\lambda, \gamma \geq 0 \Rightarrow \lambda x + \gamma y \in \tilde{Z}$
4. $x_k < 0 \; \forall k \; \Rightarrow x \in \tilde{Z} \setminus Z$

Theorem 2 (Existence of a set of probabilities). *Given a rational optimist, there is a set* $\mathcal{P}$ *of probability vectors* (p_i)*, that satisfy*

$$\{x \mid \exists (q_i) \in \mathcal{P} : \sum x_i q_i > 0\} \subseteq Z \subseteq \{x \mid \exists (q_i) \in \mathcal{P} : \sum x_i q_i \geq 0\}. \quad (2)$$

One can always replace $\mathcal{P}$ *with an extreme set the size of the alphabet.*

Proof. Properties 2 and 3 tell us that the closure $\bar{\tilde{Z}}$ of $\tilde{Z}$ is a (one sided) convex cone. Let $\mathcal{P} = \{(p_i) \in \mathbb{R}^m \mid \sum p_i x_i \leq 0 \; \forall (x_i) \in \bar{\tilde{Z}}\}$. Then, it follows from convexity that $\bar{\tilde{Z}} = \{(x_i) \mid \sum x_i p_i \leq 0 \; \forall (p_i) \in \mathcal{P}\}$. Property 4 tells us that it contains all the elements of only strictly negative coefficients and this implies that for all $(p_i) \in \mathcal{P}$, $p_i \geq 0$ for all i. We can directly conclude that $Z \subseteq \{x \mid \exists (q_i) \in \mathcal{P} : \sum x_i q_i \geq 0\}$ and furthermore, it follows from property 2 that $\{x \mid \sum x_i p_i > 0\} \subseteq Z$ for all $(p_i) \in \mathcal{P}$. Normalizing to $\sum p_i = 1$ does not change anything. Property 1 tells us that $Z \subseteq \{x \mid \exists (q_i) \in \mathcal{P} : \sum x_i q_i \geq 0\}$. $\square$

2.3   Making Choices

If we want to go from decisions on accepting or rejecting bets to a setting where we choose between different bets $x^j, j = 1, 2, 3, ...$, we define preferences by saying that x is better or equal (as in equally good) than y if $x - y \in \bar{Z}$ (the closure of Z), while it is worse or equal if $x - y$ is rejectable. For the first form of rationality stated in Definition 3, the consequence is that one chooses the option with the highest expected utility. If we instead consider optimistic rationality, and if there is $(p_i) \in \mathcal{P}$ such that $\sum x_i p_i \geq \sum y_i q_i \; \forall (q_i) \in \mathcal{P}$ then $\sum p_i(x_i - y_i) \geq 0$ and, therefore, $x - y \in \bar{Z}$. Therefore, if we choose the bet x^j by

$$\arg \max_j \max_{p \in \mathcal{P}} \sum x_i^j p_i$$

we are guaranteed that this bet is preferable to all other bets but not necessarily strictly so, even if $\max_{p \in \mathcal{P}} \sum x_i^j p_i$ is strictly larger than all competitors.

3   Intelligent Agents

We will consider an agent [RN10, Hut05] that interacts with an environment through performing actions a_t from a finite set $\mathcal{A}$ and receives observations o_t from a finite set $\mathcal{O}$ and rewards r_t from a finite set $\mathcal{R} \subset [0,1]$. Let $\mathcal{H} = \cup_n (\mathcal{A} \times \mathcal{O} \times R)^n$ be the set of histories and let ϵ be the empty history. A function $\nu : \mathcal{H} \times \mathcal{A} \to \mathcal{O} \times \mathcal{R}$ is called a deterministic environment. A function $\pi : \mathcal{H} \to \mathcal{A}$ is called a (deterministic) policy or an agent. We define the value function V based on geometric discounting by $V_\nu^\pi(h_{t-1}) = \sum_{i=t}^\infty \gamma^{i-t} r_i$ where the sequence r_i are the rewards achieved by following π from time step t onwards in the environment ν after having seen h_{t-1}.

Instead of viewing the environment as a function $\mathcal{H} \times \mathcal{A} \to \mathcal{O} \times \mathcal{R}$ we can equivalently write it as a function $\nu : \mathcal{H} \times \mathcal{A} \times \mathcal{O} \times \mathcal{R} \to \{0,1\}$ where we write $\nu(o,r|h,a)$ for the function value of (h,a,o,r). It equals zero if in the first formulation (h,a) is not sent to (o,r) and 1 if it is. In the case of stochastic environments we instead have a function $\nu : \mathcal{H} \times \mathcal{A} \times \mathcal{O} \times \mathcal{R} \to [0,1]$ such that $\sum_{o,r} \nu(o,r|h,a) = 1 \; \forall h, a$. Furthermore, we define $\nu(h_t|\pi) := \nu(or_{1:t}|\pi) := \Pi_{i=1}^t \nu(o_i r_i | a_i, h_{i-1})$ where $a_i = \pi(h_{i-1})$. $\nu(\cdot|\pi)$ is a probability measure over strings or sequences as will be discussed in the next section and we can define $\nu(\cdot|\pi, h_{t-1})$ by conditioning $\nu(\cdot|\pi)$ on h_{t-1}. We define $V_\nu^\pi(h_{t-1}) := \mathbb{E}_{\nu(\cdot|\pi, h_{t-1})} \sum_{i=t}^\infty \gamma^{i-t} r_i$ and $V_\nu^*(h_{t-1}) := \max_\pi V_\nu^\pi(h_{t-1})$. Given a countable class of environments $\mathcal{M}$ and strictly positive prior weights w_ν for all $\nu \in \mathcal{M}$, we define the a-priori environment ξ by letting $\xi(\cdot) = \sum w_\nu \nu(\cdot)$ and the AIXI agent is defined by following the policy

$$\pi^* := \arg \max_\pi V_\xi^\pi(\epsilon).$$

3.1   Rational Optimistic Sequential Decisions

There are some extensions to the results from Section 2 needed to reach the full AI (generic reinforcement learning) case we have in mind, but the procedure for doing this has already been outlined in [SH11a]. The first extension is to reactive environments where the outcome is affected by the choice made. One then chooses between different actions to take. It was concluded that it follows from the rationality axioms that there is a probability (p_i^j) for the outcome i given action j, and the action given a bet $x = (x_i)$ is chosen by

$$\arg \max_j \sum x_i p_i^j.$$

The extension to finitely many sequential decisions is simply about considering the choice to be made to be a choice of policy π (previously j). The discounted value $\sum r_t \gamma^t$ achieved then plays the role of the bet x_i and the decision on what policy to follow is taken according to

$$\arg\max_\pi V_\xi^\pi$$

where ξ is the probabilistic a priori belief (the p_i^j) and $V_\xi^\pi = \sum p_i^j (\sum r_t^i \gamma^t)$ where r_t^i is the reward achieved at time t in outcome sequence i in an enumeration of all the possible histories. The rational optimist takes the decision

$$\pi^\circ := \arg\max_\pi \max_{\xi \in \Xi} V_\xi^\pi$$

for a set of beliefs (environments) Ξ (corresponds to $\mathcal{P}$ before) which we will assume is compact in the metric topology of the total variation distance as in [SH12].

3.2   Asymptotic Optimality

In this section we will first prove that AIXI is asymptotically optimal if its a-priori environment ξ is both dominating the true environment μ in the sense of $\xi(\cdot) \geq c\mu(\cdot)$ and optimistic in the sense that $V_\xi^*(h_t) \geq V_\mu^*(h_t)$ (for large t). We extend this by replacing ξ with a compact (with respect to the total variation distance) set Ξ and prove that we then only need there to be, for each h_t (for t large), some $\xi \in \Xi$ such that $V_\xi^*(h_t) \geq V_\mu^*(h_t)$. The first domination property is most easily satisfied for $\xi(\cdot) = \sum_{\nu \in \mathcal{M}} w_\nu \nu(\cdot)$ with $w_\nu > 0$ where $\mathcal{M}$ is a countable class of environments with $\mu \in \mathcal{M}$. We are going to provide one simple example for the first theorem to illustrate what it is saying in a simple setting while after the second theorem we discuss the example that we really have in mind. This example addresses the AIXI agent as it was introduced in [Hut05] with a Solomonoff prior and the problem of defining a natural Universal Turing Machine [Mül10].

Theorem 3. *Suppose that $\xi(\cdot) \geq c\mu(\cdot)$ for some $c > 0$ and μ is the true environment. Also suppose that there almost surely is $T_1 < \infty$ such that $V_\xi^*(h_t) \geq V_\mu^*(h_t)$ $\forall t \geq T_1$. Suppose that the policy π^* acts according to the AIXI agent based on ξ in μ. Then there is almost surely, for every $\varepsilon > 0$, a time $T < \infty$ such that $V_\mu^{\pi^*}(h_t) \geq V_\mu^*(h_t) - \varepsilon$ $\forall t \geq T$.*

Proof. Due to the dominance we can (using the Blackwell-Dubins merging of opinions theorem [BD62]) say that almost surely there is for every $\varepsilon' > 0$, a $T < \infty$ such that $d(\xi(\cdot|h_t, \pi^*), \mu(\cdot|h_t, \pi^*)) < \varepsilon$ where d is the total variation distance. This implies that $|V_\xi^{\pi^*}(h_t) - V_\mu^{\pi^*}(h_t)| < \frac{\varepsilon'}{1-\gamma} := \varepsilon$ which means that, if $T \geq T_1$, $V_\mu^{\pi^*}(h_t) \geq V_\xi^*(h_t) - \varepsilon \geq V_\mu^*(h_t) - \varepsilon$. $\square$

Example 1 (Line Environment). Consider an agent who, when given a class of environments, will always choose its prior based on simplicity which is in accordance with Occam's razor [Hut05]. First let us look at a class $\mathcal{M}$ of two environments which both have six states $s_1, ..., s_6$ and two actions L (left) and R (right). Action R changes s_k to s_{k+1}, L to s_{k-1}. Also L in s_1 or R in s_6 result in staying. We start at s_1. Being at s_1 yields a reward of 0, while s_2, s_3, s_4, s_5 give reward -1 and the reward in s_6 depends on the environment.

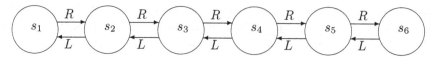

In one of the environments ν_1, this reward is -1 while in ν_2 it is 1. Since ν_2 is not simpler than ν_1 it will not have higher weight and if γ is only modestly high we will not explore along the line despite that in ν_2 it would be optimal to do so. However, if we define another environment ν_3 by letting the reward at s_6 be really high, then when including ν_3 in the mixture, the agent will end up with an a priori environment ξ that is optimistic for ν_1 and ν_2 and we can guarantee optimality for any γ.

Note that the example above is only supposed to show how the optimism condition can be satisfied for a subclass of the class one has a prior over. It will almost never be satisfied for the whole class. In the next theorem we prove that for the extended agent with a class of priors, only one of them needs to be optimistic at a time while we need all to be dominant.

Theorem 4. *Suppose that Ξ is a compact set for the total variation topology (maximized over all policies and histories) of a-priori environments such that for each $\xi \in \Xi$ there is $c_{\xi,\mu} > 0$ such that $\xi(\cdot) \geq c_{\xi,\mu}\mu(\cdot)$ where μ is the true environment. Also suppose that there almost surely is $T_1 < \infty$ such that for $t \geq T_1$ there is $\xi \in \Xi$ such that $V_\xi^*(h_t) \geq V_\mu^*(h_t)$. Suppose that the policy π° acts according to the rational optimistic agent based on Ξ in μ. Then there is almost surely, for every $\varepsilon > 0$, a time $T < \infty$ such that $V_\mu^{\pi^\circ}(h_t) \geq V_\mu^*(h_t) - \varepsilon \; \forall t \geq T$.*

The theorem is proven by combining the proof technique from the previous theorem with the following lemma. We have made this lemma easier by formulating it for time $t = 0$ (when the history is the empty string ϵ), though when proving Theorem 4 it is used for a later time point when the environments in the class have merged sufficiently in the sense of total variation diameter.

Lemma 1 (Optimism is nearly optimal). *Suppose that an infinite history h has been generated by running π° in the environment μ. Given $\varepsilon > 0$ there is $\tilde{\varepsilon} > 0$ such that $V_\mu^{\pi^\circ}(\epsilon) \geq \max_\pi V_\mu^\pi(\epsilon) - \varepsilon$ if*

$$|V_{\nu_1}^{\pi^\circ}(h_t) - V_{\nu_2}^{\pi^\circ}(h_t)| < \tilde{\varepsilon} \; \forall t, \forall \nu_1, \nu_2 \in \Xi.$$

Proof. Let $\nu_{h_t}^*$ be the environment in $\arg\max_\nu \max_\pi V_\nu^\pi(h_t)$ that π° use to choose the next action a_{t+1} after experiencing h_t. Define $\hat{\nu}$ by letting

$$\hat{\nu}(o_t r_t | h_{t-1}, a) = \nu_{h_{t-1}}^*(o_t r_t | h_{t-1}, a).$$

We will show that this implies that $V_{\hat{\nu}}^{\pi^\circ} \geq \max_{\nu \in \mathcal{M}, \pi} V_\nu^\pi$ where V_ν^π denotes $V_\nu^\pi(\epsilon)$. Let

$$\hat{\nu}_s(o_t r_t | h_{t-1}, a) = \begin{cases} \hat{\nu}(o_t r_t | h_{t-1}, a) \; \forall h_{t-1}, \text{ for } t \leq s \\ \hat{\nu}_s(o_t r_t | h_{t-1}, a) = \nu_{h_s}^*(o_t r_t | h_{t-1}, a) \; \forall h_{t-1}, \text{ for } t > s. \end{cases}$$

$\hat{\nu}_1$ equals ν_ϵ^* at all time points and thus $V_{\hat{\nu}_1}^\pi = V_{\nu_\epsilon^*}^\pi$. Let $\hat{R}_t^\nu$ be the expected accumulated (discounted) reward ($\mathbb{E} \sum_{i=1}^t \gamma^{i-1} r_i$) when following π° in environment ν up to time t.

$$\max_{\pi_{2:\infty}} V_{\hat{\nu}_2}^{\pi^\circ_{0:1}\pi_{2:\infty}} = \max_{\pi_{1:\infty}} (\hat{R}_1^{\nu_\epsilon^*} + \gamma \mathbb{E}_{h_1 | \nu_\epsilon^*, \pi^\circ} V_{\nu_{h_1}^*}^{\pi_{1:\infty}}(h_1)) \geq$$

$$\max_{\pi_{1:\infty}} (\hat{R}_1^{\nu_\epsilon^*} + \gamma \mathbb{E}_{h_1 | \nu_\epsilon^*, \pi^\circ} V_{\nu_\epsilon^*}^{\pi_{1:\infty}}(h_1)) = \max_\pi V_{\hat{\nu}_1}^\pi$$

since $\max_\pi V_{\nu_{h_1}^*}^\pi(h_1)) \geq \max_\pi V_\nu^\pi(h_1)) \; \forall \nu \in \mathcal{M}$. In the same way,

$$\max_{\pi_{k:\infty}} V_{\hat{\nu}_k}^{\pi^\circ_{0:k-1}\pi_{k:\infty}} \geq \max_{\pi_{k-1:\infty}} V_{\hat{\nu}_{k-1}}^{\pi^\circ_{0:k-2}\pi_{k-1:\infty}} \forall k$$

and it follows that $V_{\hat{\nu}}^{\pi^\circ} \geq \max_{\pi, \nu \in \mathcal{M}} V_\nu^\pi$. To conclude the proof, we show that if $\tilde{\varepsilon}$ is small enough, then

$$|V_{\hat{\nu}}^{\pi^\circ} - V_\mu^{\pi^\circ}| < \varepsilon \tag{3}$$

where μ is the true environment. That (3) is true is shown by induction. $\hat{\nu}_1 \in \mathcal{M}$ and, therefore, (3) holds with $\hat{\nu}_1$ instead of $\hat{\nu}$ if $\tilde{\varepsilon} \leq \varepsilon$. $\hat{\nu}_k$ and $\hat{\nu}_{k+1}$ are identical for the first k time step so $|V_{\hat{\nu}_k}^{\pi^\circ} - V_{\hat{\nu}_{k+1}}^{\pi^\circ}| < \gamma^k \tilde{\varepsilon}$. We conclude that

$$|V_{\hat{\nu}_1}^{\pi^\circ} - V_{\hat{\nu}}^{\pi^\circ}| < \frac{\tilde{\varepsilon}}{1 - \gamma}$$

and if $\tilde{\varepsilon} + \frac{\tilde{\varepsilon}}{1-\gamma} \leq \varepsilon$ then (3) holds and the proof is complete. $\square$

Proof. **of Theorem** 4. Due to the compactness, there is almost surely for every ε', a $T < \infty$ such that $d(\xi(\cdot | h_t, \pi^\circ), \mu(\cdot | h_t, \pi^\circ)) < \varepsilon \; \forall \xi \in \Xi \; \forall t \geq T$. This means that $|V_\xi^\pi(h_t) - V_\mu^\pi(h_t)| < \frac{\varepsilon'}{1-\gamma} := \varepsilon \; \forall \xi \in \Xi$. Applying Lemma 1 to the ξ that is optimistic at time T proves the result.

Example 2. For any Universal Turing Machine (UTM) U the corresponding Solomonoff distribution ξ_U, (see [LV93] for details) is dominant for any lower semi-computable semi-measure over infinite sequences. [Hut05] extends these constructions to the active case and defines (for each U) an environment that is dominant for all lower semi-computable environments and defines the AIXI agent based on it. The AIXI agent would have uniquely defined the most intelligent agent according to the underlying sense of intelligence (maximizing expected reward), if the choice of UTM was clear. Many have without success tried to find a single "natural" Turing machine and there might in fact be no such machine [Mül10]. With the approach that we introduce in this article one can pick finitely many machines that one considers to be natural. Though this does not fully resolve the issue of having to make arbitrary choices, it alleviates it by no longer demanding a unique choice of UTM. We can consider an enumeration of all UTMs U_i and let the agent $Agent_n$ be based on the first n machines. $Agent_n$ has better guarantees than $Agent_m$ (in the sense of Theorem 4) if $n > m$. The conclusion does, however, not carry through to a limiting case. Note, that if we instead combine finitely many machines into one by letting the first few bits represent a choice of machine, the resulting environment will not be optimistic for all the environments that we achieve optimism for with the multiple-prior approach.

4   Conclusions

We extended AIXI to a multiple-prior setting using the principle of optimism. This decreases the arbitrariness of picking an a-priori environment or a reference machine to base a Solomonoff prior on. Furthermore, we show that this leads to asymptotic optimality guarantees for more environments. We also explain that this extension is related to replacing symmetry with optimism in the recently introduced axiomatization of AIXI.

In a separate article [SH12], we perform a different sort of analysis where it is not assumed that all the environments in Ξ are dominating the true environment μ. The analysis, however, adds the assumption that the true environment is a member of this class of environments. The a priori environments are then naturally thought of as a hypothesis class rather than mixtures over some hypothesis class. In this article we note, that there is no mathematical difference between a class of environments that is considered a hypothesis class and one that is considered a class of a priori environments. However, in the case where we consider Ξ to be a hypothesis class, Ξ has to be very large to yield an agent that is guaranteed asymptotic optimality for many environments (the environments in Ξ), while in the case when it represents a mixture over a hypothesis class, a singleton Ξ (the AIXI case) is already a powerful agent. Another distinction is that in the case studied in [SH12], we need a mechanism for excluding environments from the class as they become inconsistent with experience.

A practical agent that builds upon the ideas of this article and the companion article [SH12], is a variation of a Bayesian reinforcement learning agent. A common way of implementing a practical Bayesian agent is that one samples several environments from the posterior and then act for a period of time according to what would give the highest expected value when averaging the expected value over the sampled environments. Instead we here suggest acting optimistically with respect to those sampled environments who are then, for a period of time, basically treated as a restricted hypothesis class. In the MDP case this is close to what the BOSS algorithm [ALL09] is doing.

Acknowledgement. This work was supported by ARC grant DP120100950. The authors are grateful for feedback from Tor Lattimore.

References

[ALL09]   Asmuth, J., Li, L., Littman, M.L., Nouri, A., Wingate, D.: Pac-mdp reinforcement learning with bayesian priors (2009)

[BD62]   Blackwell, D., Dubins, L.: Merging of Opinions with Increasing Information. The Annals of Mathematical Statistics 33(3), 882–886 (1962)

[CMKO00]   Casadesus-Masanell, R., Klibanoff, P., Ozdenoren, E.: Maxmin Expected Utility over Savage Acts with a Set of Priors. Journal of Economic Theory 92(1), 35–65 (2000)

[deF37]   deFinetti, B.: La prévision: Ses lois logiques, ses sources subjectives. In: Annales de l'Institut Henri Poincaré 7, Paris, pp. 1–68 (1937)

[GS89]   Gilboa, I., Schmeidler, D.: Maxmin expected utility with non-unique prior. Journal of Mathematical Economics 18(2), 141–153 (1989)

[Hut05]   Hutter, M.: Universal Articial Intelligence: Sequential Decisions based on Algorithmic Probability. Springer, Berlin (2005)

[LH07]   Legg, S., Hutter, M.: Universal Intelligence: A defintion of machine intelligence. Mind and Machine 17, 391–444 (2007)

[LH11]   Lattimore, T., Hutter, M.: Asymptotically Optimal Agents. In: Kivinen, J., Szepesvári, C., Ukkonen, E., Zeugmann, T. (eds.) ALT 2011. LNCS, vol. 6925, pp. 368–382. Springer, Heidelberg (2011)

[LV93]   Li, M., Vitany, P.: An Introduction to Kolmogov Complexity and Its Applications. Springer (1993)

[Mül10]   Müller, M.: Stationary algorithmic probability. Theor. Comput. Sci. 411(1), 113–130 (2010)

[NM44]   Neumann, J., Morgenstern, O.: Theory of Games and Economic Behavior. Princeton University Press (1944)

[Ors10]   Orseau, L.: Optimality Issues of Universal Greedy Agents with Static Priors. In: Hutter, M., Stephan, F., Vovk, V., Zeugmann, T. (eds.) ALT 2010. LNCS, vol. 6331, pp. 345–359. Springer, Heidelberg (2010)

[Ram31]   Ramsey, F.: Truth and probability. In: Braithwaite, R.B. (ed.) The Foundations of Mathematics and other Logical Essays, ch. 7, pp. 156–198. Brace & Co. (1931)

[RN10]   Russell, S.J., Norvig, P.: Artificial Intelligence: A Modern Approach, 3rd edn. Prentice Hall, Englewood Cliffs (2010)

[Sav54]   Savage, L.: The Foundations of Statistics. Wiley, New York (1954)

[SH11a]   Sunehag, P., Hutter, M.: Axioms for Rational Reinforcement Learning. In: Kivinen, J., Szepesvári, C., Ukkonen, E., Zeugmann, T. (eds.) ALT 2011. LNCS, vol. 6925, pp. 338–352. Springer, Heidelberg (2011)

[SH11b]   Sunehag, P., Hutter, M.: Principles of Solomonoff induction and AIXI. In: Solomonoff Memorial Conference, Melbourne, Australia (2011)

[SH12]   Sunehag, P., Hutter, M.: Optimistic Agents Are Asymptotically Optimal. In: Thielscher, M., Zhang, D. (eds.) AI 2012. LNCS, vol. 7691, pp. 15–26. Springer, Heidelberg (2012)

[SLL09]   Strehl, A.L., Li, L., Littman, M.L.: Reinforcement learning in finite MDPs: PAC analysis. Journal of Machine Learing Research 10, 2413–2444 (2009)

[Wal00]   Walley, P.: Towards a unified theory of imprecise probability. Int. J. Approx. Reasoning, 125–148 (2000)

On the Functional Contributions of Emotion Mechanisms to (Artificial) Cognition and Intelligence

Serge Thill and Robert Lowe

Interaction Lab
School of Humanities and Informatics
University of Skövde, P.O. Box 408, 54 128 Skövde, Sweden
{serge.thill,robert.lowe}@his.se

Abstract. We argue that emotions play a central role in human cognition. It is therefore of interest to researchers with an aim to create artificial systems with human-level intelligence (or indeed beyond) to consider the functions of emotions in the human cognition whose complexity they aim to recreate. To this end, we review here several functional roles of emotions in human cognition at different levels, for instance in behavioural regulation and reinforcement learning. We discuss some of the neuroscientific and bodily underpinnings of emotions and conclude with a discussion of possible approaches, including existing efforts, to endow artificial systems with mechanisms providing some of the functions of human emotions.

1 Introduction

Any endeavour to construct machines with human-level intelligence (and beyond) cannot proceed without considering, at least to some extent, our understanding of human cognition and intelligence in the first place[1]. At a minimum, this is required to provide an understanding of what "human-level intelligence" actually is but it may also facilitate insights into what particular mechanisms are either required or very desirable in the creation of intelligent machines.

Given the wealth of recent evidence (*e.g.* Stapleton, 2011; Damasio, 2010; Lowe and Ziemke, 2011; Ziemke and Lowe, 2009; Ziemke, 2008; Pessoa, 2008) that emotion and cognition are closely intertwined, we argue that one such mechanism is given by emotions. It is important to note at the outset that human emotions have evolved to meet the specific requirements of the human body. Therefore, one cannot simply "copy" features of human cognition into machines without considering what effect the difference in embodiment might have (as also previously argued by Thill, 2011). Does the human body provide mechanisms that are essential for emotions yet not realisable in machines? Do emotions provide functions that are simply irrelevant to machines? There would be little point in building an emotional machine if this doesn't somehow result in a significant advantage. While it is clear that emotions (and affect) play a central role in human cognition (see the above references), it is an open question

---

[1] For the purposes of the present paper, we follow Thill (2011) and distinguish between intelligence and cognition by defining intelligence as a *metric* of the cognitive abilities of an agent.

J. Bach, B. Goertzel, and M. Iklé (Eds.): AGI 2012, LNAI 7716, pp. 322–331, 2012.
© Springer-Verlag Berlin Heidelberg 2012

whether a machine would require emotions to reach human-level intelligence. Further, it is important to note that endowing machines with emotions may be a different issue from endowing machines with the ability to *recognise* emotions, although both abilities may be important for artificially intelligent agents.

In this paper, we review research on emotions from a perspective relevant to the creation of artificially intelligent systems. We focus on functional aspects, highlighting some of the most important hypothesised roles in human cognition and interaction. We argue that, although the functions of emotions are built upon the features of human existence, implementing both equivalent artificial mechanisms and the ability to recognise human emotions are desirable features in the design of artificial intelligent machines.

2 Functions of Emotions

Here, we define emotions as a functional subset of all affective phenomena. The exact function of emotions remain a topic of debate in the literature. Briefly, three major positions can be identified (Keltner and Gross, 1999):

1. Emotions have no functions
2. Emotions once served functions that are no longer necessarily appropriate
3. Emotions serve important functions now

Adherents of the first position generally see emotions not only as useless, but actually as a nuisance, as "disorganising forces in human behaviour" (Keltner and Gross, 1999). The second view essentially sets emotions on a par with the appendix but, in contrast with the first position, does not necessarily imply that emotions are entirely useless. Rather, it argues that whatever functions emotions serve today are not the reason emotions evolved in the first place and are probably not very important.

However, both the above views are in conflict with a large body of recent research which illustrates that emotions indeed have important roles in human cognition (Pessoa, 2008; Damasio, 2010; Lowe and Ziemke, 2011; Stapleton, 2011); as contended in the third view. For the present purposes, we can distinguish between two functional categories: *intrapersonal* (those that relate to an individual agent) and *interpersonal* (those that relate to interactions between two or more agents).

At perhaps the highest level of functional abstraction, emotions have been implicated, above all, in modulating learning (LeDoux, 1996; Rolls, 1999) and in guiding action selection and planning (Damasio, 2010; Frijda, 2010; Lowe and Ziemke, 2011). At a lower level of abstraction, emotions have been repeatedly implicated in:

1. *homeostatic regulation*: both behaviourally and internally (Sterling, 2004);
2. *'cognitive override' in goal-directed behaviour* (Oately and Johnson-Laird, 1987; Rolls, 1999; Boureau and Dayan, 2010);
3. *behavioural adaptation* (*e.g.* Rolls, 1999) fundamentally concerned with the effects of emotions on learning;
4. *communication*: the highly influential cross cultural studies of Darwin (1872) and Ekman (2003) have suggested that expression of emotion is high on informational content

5. *social transaction*: emotional expression may generally provide a sort of social glue during agent interactions (Griffiths and Scarantino, 2009).

Intrapersonally, emotions combine 1. to 3. of the above. However, interpersonally, social interaction (4. and 5.) must also be seen as constrained or even motivated by goals and basic homeostatic needs. This intrapersonal 'grounding' is critical to understanding to what extent, and how, social interaction provides a key role of emotions. The next section is dedicated to discussing these functions in more detail.

2.1   Intrapersonal Functions

Homeostatic Regulation. Although the human body is very adaptive to the external environment, it is also very sensitive to internal changes and can only function if internal parameters (blood pressure, levels of minerals and vitamins and so on) are kept within a very narrow range. This is ensured through homeostasis. Levenson (1999) reasons that it may occasionally be worthwhile to temporarily override this 'basal' homeostasis. For instance in a case of danger, it may be helpful to increase blood pressure, oxygen levels in the muscles of the leg and adrenaline levels to ensure a quick getaway. Thus a function of some (but certainly not all) emotions may be to override homeostasis. Levenson (1999) sees fear, anger and disgust as clear providers of such an 'emergency' function. This perspective has been echoed according to the notion of allostasis (*c.f.* Sterling, 2004). In Sterling's account, by overriding the (more or less) basic set points of 'essential' physiological control variables, the organism is empowered with a degree of predictive regulation. Through transiently modulating the control variables' sensitivity regime, organisms are equipped with the metabolic resources to deal with emergency situations characteristic of emotional activity (*c.f.* Damasio, 2010), even though a prolonged departure from the 'normal' state of the body is clearly noxious.

"Cognitive Override". Levenson (1999) points out, that emotions are sometimes thought to be a 'disorganiser' of rational thoughts. However, he argues, they can in fact be understood as 'organisers'. This view is reflected in the notion of emotions serving as 'alarms' (Sloman, 2001) that "detect situations where rapid global redirecting of processing is required". The perspective of emotions as attention orienters and biasers of action selection, as well as path search, is popular both in the fields of neuroscience and artificial intelligence (*c.f.* Simon, 1967; Oately and Johnson-Laird, 1987; Frijda, 2010). Simon's 'interrupts' and Oatley and Johnson-Laird's 'goal juncture' redirection postulation provide purported computational functions to emotions. Oately and Johnson-Laird suggested that the "basic" emotions ('sadness', 'happiness', 'disgust', 'anxiety', 'anger'[2]) are elicited following perceived junctures to a plan presently enacted. These emotions serve to reconfigure the plan according to the new ('emergency') circumstances. In a weaker form, this can also manifest as a cognitive bias (Damasio, 2003).

Behavioural Adaptation. The above-mentioned functions of emotions as biasers, redirectors or interrupts of ongoing behaviour can be understood from a neuroscientific per-

---

[2] 'Surprise' was not considered a basic emotion.

spective that evidences a strong link between behaviour selection and behavioural adaptation (learning). Rolls (1999), for example, has viewed emotions as being triggered following detected 'reinforcement contingencies' in relation to learned stimulus-reinforcer associations. These contingencies allude to violations of expectations concerning reward- or punishment-based returns. These violations concern: 1) *immediate consequences*: direct contact with a rewarding or punishing stimuli ('happiness', and 'fear', respectively); 2) *anticipated consequences*: unexpected presence or omission of obstacles to rewarding or punishing stimuli (precipitating 'anger' and 'relief', respectively). In this manner, Rolls has emphasized the interdependence of learning and biasing of action selection since emotion elicitation is triggered consequent to learned stimulus-reinforcer expectations. Where Rolls emphasized the neuroanatomic substrate of the reward-punishment systems constitutive of emotions (the interplay between orbitofrontal cortex and amygdala being key), Boureau and Dayan (2010) focused on the brainstem neuromodulator implementations of such systems. The implicated neuromodulators of dopamine and serotonin have been particularly linked to 'opponent process' reward and punishment based reinforcement learning. Their model, similar to Rolls, has a two dimensional flavour that links behavioural selection with adaptation. In this case, dopamine is suggested to encode for reward signals (utilized for learning) and active behavioural responding while serotonin encodes for punishment learning signals and inhibitory behavioural responding.

2.2   Interpersonal Functions

Emotion Expression as Communication. An essential question is to what extent emotional expression is of 'communicative' value. Hauser (1996) puts it thus: "in a majority of species, affective states are responsible for the production of communicative signals". However, communication implies an information exchange which implies that both expressor and perceiver gain some advantage from the communicative encounter.

An evolutionary mechanism of such communication (information exchange) has been posited. Darwin's (1872) 'principle of antithesis' proposed that emotional expressions in animals and humans have become, over evolutionary time, disambiguated for the purpose of communication: Orthogonal emotional states (e.g. fear vs anger) will be similarly expressed in a contrary manner. He took the specific example of dogs expressing anger and submission. Keltner et al. (2003) also suggest that facial emotional expressions may have evolved into disambiguated discrete forms for the benefit of communication.

In the spirit of Darwin, Ekman (2003) has accumulated much cross cultural evidence for the existence of unambiguously perceived "basic" emotions. His research indicates that a function of emotion may indeed be for communicative purposes. However, it is acknowledged that whereas perceptions of expressions may be universal, they may also be deceptive regarding the underlying emotional state; for example, a social smile is often hard to detect, by the untrained eye, relative to the 'natural', or 'duchenne' smile.

Emotion Expression as Social Exchange.   A different perspective to the above holds that emotion expression, more generically, provides a sort of social glue:

It disambiguates the respective roles and needs of conspecifics though not necessarily according to the equal benefit of all interacting parties.

The expressive component of emotion has been viewed by Griffiths and Scarantino (2009) as linked more to a social transaction than to pure communication. Here, the expression is not communicative in the sense of objectively expressing a cognitively held belief or intention. Instead, emotion expression facilitates a social harmony. Griffiths and Scarantino give the example of 'guilt', citing a study of Kroon (1988) in which only 28 percent of experimental subjects reporting this emotion attributed to themselves blame for the particular guilt-evoking event. In the social transaction view, guilt may be seen as promoting 'social engagement aimed at reconciliation'. This may provide a net benefit to the interactants but may not be considered pure information exchange benefitting all equally.

The means of communicative emotion expression may also be disputed. Perhaps contrary to the hitherto purported role of disambiguation, Snowdon (2003) suggests that for affect/emotion to have evolved a communicative function expression should not be particularly stereotyped or elaborate. Emphasis should be rather placed largely on perceivers discerning the relevance of expressions in a given context. He comments "we should expect little plasticity in the production and usage of calls. At the same time we can expect that it will be important to read signals accurately ... so plasticity in the development of responding to signals might be useful".

Camras (2011) has suggested that affective/emotional expression is developed according to the learned association of coordinated (facial) motor primitives. In this view, the expressed "basic" emotions as identified by Ekman may just be the products of early developmental exposure. On this basis, disambiguated 'antithetical' emotional expressions may even imply a shift in a perspective of the role of emotions in expression. Rather than being *for* information exchange regarding objectively appraised events, the primary role of expressing emotions is for manipulating the perceiver to the benefit of the expressor's bodily desires and needs.

3   Emotion Components for Artificial Systems

As we have seen in the above, human emotions are intrinsically tied to the requirements and constraints of the body. By itself, this may be a strong indication that artificial systems may never possess emotions in the human sense of the term. However, this does not exclude the possibility of creating machine equivalents thereof; processes that mimic the functionality of human emotions to the extent that this is relevant to an artificial agent (AA). In relation to the previous section, we now evaluate the extent to which AAs may be imbued with emotions and what functional role this may serve, both for the agent itself and for human-AA interactions.

3.1   The Role of the Embodiment

Loosely, we may understand embodiment in terms of the intrapersonal quality of the AA: (1) what are the AA's homeostatically regulated needs; (2) what are the AA's goals and how should it respond to goal junctures; and (3) how should the AA behaviourally adapt to unanticipated change and when?

In relation to 1, there is for instance no point in increasing the oxygen levels in the leg muscles if the machine doesn't have legs, or muscles for that matter. Nevertheless, an AA may have what Ashby (1960) identified as 'essential variables' (EVs). EVs serve as effective control variables that are required to operate within a homeostatic regime. Examples of EVs include blood glucose levels in a human, battery level in a robot, or perhaps system designer-specified performance variables in an AA. The AA is required to make a trade off so as to satisfy the set of concerns whilst not falling into irrecoverable deficits. Avila-Garcìa and Cañamero (2005) have applied the idea of EVs as homeostatic control variables to robots demonstrating the potential for 'emotional' agents to produce autonomous and sustainable behaviour.

In relation to 2 and 3, a system may have many goals or aims, and may utilize principles of reinforcement learning in order to successfully arrive at them. Artificial systems that purport to explore emotional learning have often focused on neural circuitry that qualitatively replicate neurobehavioural characteristic profiles of emotional activity (Armony, 2005; Balkenius et al., 2009; Lowe et al., 2009; Ziemke and Lowe, 2009; Roesch et al., 2010). These systems are somewhat divorced from homeostatic concerns though the reward-punishment systems that they model abstractly capture such intrapersonal concerns. It is also unclear to what extent these non-homeostatically regulated learning systems gain added value from being labelled "emotional".

Nonetheless, one of the major aspects of an artificial system that can be said to be intelligent in a general sense is the ability to perform a (general) range of tasks autonomously and adaptively. Such a system will necessarily be confronted with multiple possible actions at a given time. The system will therefore need the ability to select amongst these actions. For this, homeostatic processes and mechanisms to regulate them (as given by one function of emotions discussed here) might provide a significant advantage. In addition, as discussed above, such processes may play an important role in reinforcement learning mechanisms and may therefore be equally important for an AA's learning abilities.

3.2   Expressing and Recognising Emotions

One has to expect that an artificial system with human-level intelligence would need to interact and communicate proficiently with humans, thus implying both a need to be able to express emotions when relevant and to be able to recognise the emotions of humans. It should of course be kept in mind that we refer to an expression of internal states here; emotion expression may thus be of no value to artificial systems if they have no internal states and no sensorimotor autonomy.

Assuming the existence of relevant internal states, the problem for 'disembodied' artificial systems is not the fact that computer hardware is not able to somehow convey emotion-like states. After all, it would be relatively easy, for example, to make a computer screen go red if the computer is angry or blue if it is sad. The problem rather concerns believability: would a red computer screen still convey the emotion as effectively as an angry face (robotic or human)? While machines may be able to express an emotion, whomever it is directed at may fail to be moved by its message. Consequently, the function of the expression is lost. Of course people could (and probably would) learn to recognise 'computer emotions', but emotional computers should be as forthcoming to human expectations as possible in their design. In a first instance, this could well be confined to artificial 3D models of a human face or entire body displayed on the screen, which could then be animated. Much work using virtual characters of this type has been undertaken based on these principles (c.f. Becker-Asano and Wachsmuth, 2010).

Perhaps the most famous emotionally expressive artificial system or agent is Kismet developed at MIT by Breazeal (2003). This robot can be said to express disambiguated, but hardwired, 'basic' emotions of Ekman (2003). Kismet, therefore, is not so much a cognitive appraiser but an expressor of desires. Use of such a robot in human-robotic interactions is functional insofar as the facial expressions of Kismet are readily recognizable to human interactants. Not only does Kismet express stereotyped emotions, but is able to express according to: degree (e.g. across dimensions of 'arousal' and 'valence'); internal drives and goals mediated by an abstact homeostatic system; to cognitive appraisal of the social context; tone of voice.

As has been mentioned before, there are two sides to a communication. Thus an emotional agent would not only have to be able to convey its emotions, it would also have to be able to perceive the emotions of other persons. This is an area in which machines do rather well (see for instance work as far back as Picard, 1996, who describes a number of ways in which a computer can accurately determine a person's emotion). The aforementioned Kismet is also able to use a visual recognition system to similarly recognize such emotions in humans.

Nonetheless, a significant need for future research in expressing and recognising emotions by AAs remains. Kismet, although it can be understood as expressive emotional system, ultimately remains merely a robotic head. Producing a fully mobile robot able to detect emotional states in itself and others not limited to facial expressions (e.g. posture, gait) and elaborated social context (e.g. 'transactional', or involving aspects of deception) promise significantly greater challenges to naturalize the emotional range of an AA. Such challenges may need to be met in order to enable AAs to seamlessly integrate into human environments. Grounding higher cognitive capacities according to integrated and synchronized sensor-motoric and internal homeostatic activation patterns might be requisite to such further development.

3.3   "Feeling" Emotions and Higher-Level Cognitive Functions

The state of the art concerning AAs' higher level cognitive functions, whether they concern appraisals of social/non-social events in relation to planning and action selection, has thus far tended to neglect grounding such functionality in basic bodily requirements. These requirements involve levels of internal monitoring, e.g. regarding essential variables, so as to prioritize behaviours that meet current needs and goals. Such monitoring, however, also requires an apprehension of the social and bodily context of the present – grabbing the last piece of cake at a formal meal in order to satisfy a glucose deficit is a socially inappropriate act with potential long term detrimental consequences. The artificial (and biological) agent is thus required to continuously evaluate the appropriateness and feasibility of selecting particular behaviours (and planning for such).

Such monitoring requires the integration and synchronization of many different inputs, external and internal to the agent, over many different timescales.

As previously argued (Lowe and Ziemke, 2011), emotional feelings, or the neural-dynamic substrate upon which they exist, may provide the means for such high level monitoring. The "feeling" of emotion, rather than being merely epiphenomenal, may provide a powerful way for learning and adapting to the outside world. Levenson (1999) argues that what we 'feel' are essentially the sensations from the physiological changes that accompany an emotion, like a particular heartbeat or breathing pattern. Damasio (2010) suggests that neural maps of the body provide inputs into multimodal maps - 'zones of convergence' - that integrate and synchronize external and internal activation patterns. Many candidates exist for sub-symbolically representing such information in artificial systems, e.g. dynamic neural fields (cf. (Lowe and Ziemke, 2011), self-organizing maps, hierarchical neural networks).

It has been mentioned above that one of the functions of "feeling" emotions may be to make us aware of our emotional state. But the fact that we are able to realise that we are in a certain state appears to presuppose a certain sense of self. Sloman (2000) argues that, if one is truly experiencing emotions, then one finds it very hard to ignore them. One cannot stop thinking about them and they may return at any point. One is thus losing control over one's thought processes. But one cannot lose what one doesn't have and thus Sloman reasons that we are both able to a) control our thought processes and b) lose control over them. AAs, similarly imbued, would have systems that note discrepancies in expected or desired states at different levels of homeostatic-allostatic regulation, providing meta-levels of regulation in relation to a nested hierarchy of embodied states (Damasio, 2003, 2010, c.f.). Signals from reward and punishment systems, and their combined gestalt, for example, provide such information.

4 Conclusion

In the present paper, we have illustrated several functions of emotions in human cognition, showing that emotions form a central part of (human) cognition. We posit that an artificial intelligent agent cannot be expected to attain "human-like intelligence" if it does not possess at least a subset of the functional abilities provided by emotions, for instance concerning learning and adaption or behaviour selection. We have discussed some of the mechanisms underlying human emotions as well as existing work in endowing AAs with at least a rudimentary system providing emotional functionality. To conclude, we suggest that further research into the functional contributions of emotions to an (artificial) agent's cognition (and therefore intelligence), including ways of providing these functions in non-human systems, will play an important role in the creation of (generally) intelligent artificial systems.

Acknowledgments. This work was supported by the European FP7 project *Neural-Dynamics*, (A neuro-dynamic framework for cognitive robotics: scene representations, behavioral sequences, and learning), Grant agreement no. 270247.

References

Armony, J.L.: Computational models of emotion. In: Proceedings of the IEEE International Joint Conference on Neural Networks, pp. 1598–1602 (2005)

Ashby, W.R.: Design for a brain: The origin of adaptive behaviour. Chapman and Hall (1960)

Avila-Garcìa, O., Cañamero, L.: Hormonal modulation of perception in motivation-based action selection architectures. In: Proceedings of Agents that Want and Like: Motivational and Emotional Roots of Cognition and Action, Symposium of the AISB 2005 Convention (2005)

Balkenius, C., Morén, J., Winberg, S.: Interactions between motivation, emotion and attention: From biology to robotics. In: Proceedings of the Ninth International Conference on Epigenetic Robotics (2009)

Becker-Asano, C., Wachsmuth, I.: Affective computing with primary and secondary emotions in a virtual human. Autonomous Agents and Multi-Agent Systems 20, 32–49 (2010)

Boureau, Y., Dayan, P.: Opponency revisited: competition and cooperation between dopamine and serotonin. Neuropsychopharmacology Reviews 1, 1–24 (2010)

Breazeal, C.: Emotion and sociable humanoid robots. International Journal of Human Computer Interaction 59, 119–155 (2003)

Camras, L.A.: Differentiation, dynamical integration and functional emotional development. Emotion Review 3, 138–146 (2011)

Damasio, A.: Looking for Spinoza: Joy, Sorrow and the Feeling Brain. Harcourt, Orlando (2003)

Damasio, A.: Self Comes to Mind - Constructing the Conscious Brain. Pantheon Books, New York (2010)

Darwin, C.: The Expression of Emotions in Man and Animals. Reprinted by Julian Friedmann Publishers, London (1872)

Ekman, P.: Emotions Revealed: Recognizing Faces and Feelings to Improve Communication and Emotional Life. Times Books, New York (2003)

Frijda, N.H.: Impulsive action and motivation. Biological Psychology 84, 570–579 (2010)

Griffiths, P.E., Scarantino, A.: Emotions in the wild: The situated perspective on emotion. In: Cambridge Handbook of Situated Cognition (2009)

Hauser, M.D.: The Evolution of Communication. MIT Press/Bradford Books, Cambridge, MA (1996)

Keltner, D., Ekman, P., Gonzaga, G.C., Beer, J.: Facial Expression of Emotion. In: Handbook of Affective Sciences, pp. 415–433. Oxford University Press (2003)

Keltner, D., Gross, J.J.: Functional accounts of emotions. Journal of Cognition and Emotion 13(5), 467–489 (1999)

Kroon, R.M.: Aanleidingen en structuur van schuld gevoel. Master's thesis, University of Amsterdam, Amsterdam (1988)

LeDoux, J.E.: The emotional brain. Simon & Schuster (1996)

Levenson, R.W.: The intrapersonal functions of emotions. Journal of Cognition and Emotion 13(5), 481–504 (1999)

Lowe, R., Humphries, M., Ziemke, T.: The dual-route hypothesis: Evaluating a neurocomputational model of fear conditioning in rats. Connection Science 21(1), 15–37 (2009)

Lowe, R., Ziemke, T.: The feeling of action tendencies: on the emotional regulation of goal-directed behavior. Frontiers in Psychology 2(346), 1–24 (2011)

Oately, K., Johnson-Laird, P.N.: Towards a cognitive theory of emotions. Cognition & Emotion 1, 29–50 (1987)

Pessoa, L.: On the relationship between emotion and cognition. Nature Reviews Neuroscience 9, 148–158 (2008)

Picard, R.: Does HAL cry digital tears? In: HAL's Legacy: 2001's Computer as Dream and Reality. MIT Press, Cambridge (1996)

Roesch, E.B., Korsten, N., Fragopanagos, N., Taylor, J.: Emotion in artificial neural networks. In: Blueprint for Affective Computing, pp. 194–212. Oxford University Press (2010)

Rolls, E.: The brain and emotion. Oxford University Press (1999)

Simon, H.A.: Motivational and emotional controls of cognition. Psychological Review 74, 29–39 (1967)

Sloman, A.: Architectural Requirements for Human-Like Agents both Natural and Artificial (What Sort of Machines Can Love?). In: Human Cognition and Social Agent Technology (2000)

Sloman, A.: Beyond shallow models of emotion. Cognitive Processing: International Quarterly of Cognitive Science 2(1), 177–198 (2001)

Snowdon, C.T.: Expression of emotion in non-human animals. In: Handbook of Affective Sciences, pp. 457–481. Oxford University Press (2003)

Stapleton, M.: Proper embodiment: the role of the body in affect and cognition. PhD thesis, The University of Edinburgh, UK (2011)

Sterling, P.: Principles of allostasis: optimal design, predictive regulation, pathophysiology and rational therapeutics. In: Allostasis, Homeostasis, and the Costs of Adaptation. Cambridge University Press, Cambridge (2004)

Thill, S.: Considerations for a Neuroscience-Inspired Approach to the Design of Artificial Intelligent Systems. In: Schmidhuber, J., Thórisson, K.R., Looks, M. (eds.) AGI 2011. LNCS (LNAI), vol. 6830, pp. 247–254. Springer, Heidelberg (2011)

Ziemke, T.: On the role of emotion in biological and robotic autonomy. BioSystems 91, 401–408 (2008)

Ziemke, T., Lowe, R.: On the role of emotion in embodied cognitive architectures: from organisms to robots. Cognitive Computation 1, 104–117 (2009)

Stupidity and the Ouroboros Model

Knud Thomsen

Paul Scherrer Institut, CH-5232 Villigen PSI, Switzerland
knud.thomsen@psi.ch

Abstract. Since decades Artificial Intelligence is striving for an understanding and the production of general intelligence. In an attempt to put the relevant issues into a wider frame, the question shall be asked whether something could be learned from agents or situations characterized by an obvious lack of intelligence, i.e. "stupidity". The Ouroboros Model is a novel proposal for a biologically inspired cognitive architecture. It has earlier been proposed how the Ouroboros Model can shed light on selected cognitive functions including (human) reasoning, learning and emotions. In this short note, implications of the hypothesized structures, relations and processes shall be scrutinized with respect to their possible value for illuminating stupidity and dullness, - and in the end again, natural and artificial general intelligence.

Keywords: Algorithm, Iterative, Recursive, Schema, Process, Consumption Analysis, Limits, Consistency, Intelligence, Stupidity.

1 Introduction

In a series of recent papers the Ouroboros Model has been introduced as an attempt to explain a wide range of findings pertaining to cognition and consciousness of natural and also artificial agents [1-4]. It has been suggested how within a single approach centered around a principal algorithmic process on a suitably structured memory one can explain human cognitive performance and also formulate prescriptions of how to arrive at comparable capabilities for artificial agents implemented in hard- or software following a similar self-steered evolutionary program.

2 The Ouroboros Model in a Nutshell

2.1 Action and Memory Structure

Minds are seen as primarily data processing entities. The Ouroboros Model holds that memory entries are organized into (non-strict) hierarchies of schemata. Memory is made up of meaningful junks, combinations of features and concepts belonging together [1]. In brains, neural assemblies are permanently linked together when once co-activated in a specific manner. Later activation of a feature promotes the selected concept and leads to graded activation for each of the associated constituents, which

J. Bach, B. Goertzel, and M. Iklé (Eds.): AGI 2012, LNAI 7716, pp. 332–340, 2012.
© Springer-Verlag Berlin Heidelberg 2012

are usually active in the same context. Activation at a time of part of a schema biases the whole structure with all relevant slots and, in particular, empty slots, i.e. concurrently missing features.

2.2   Principal Algorithmic Backbone

At the core of the Ouroboros Model lies a self-referential recursive process with alternating phases of data-acquisition and -evaluation. A monitor process termed 'consumption analysis' is checking how well expectations triggered at one point in time fit with successive activations; three interweaved principal stages are identified:

- ... anticipation,
- action / perception,
- evaluation,
- anticipation, ...

These steps are concatenated into a full repeating circle, and the activity continues at its former end, like the old alchemists' tail-devouring serpent called the Ouroboros.

2.3   Consumption Analysis

Any occurring, e.g. sensory, activation excites associated schemata. The one with the highest activation is selected first, and other, possibly also applicable, schemata are inhibited, suppressed. Taking the first selected schema and ensuing anticipations active at that time as reference and basis, consumption analysis checks how successive input fits into this activated frame structure, i.e. how well lower level perceptual data are "consumed" by the chosen schema. Features are assigned to slots / attributes are 'explained away' [5].

If everything fits perfectly the process comes to a momentary partly standstill and continues with new input data. If discrepancies surface they have an even more immediate impact on the following elicited actions [2]. Attention is directed to and by highlighted dissonances. The actual appropriateness of a schema can vary over a wide range. In any case, consumption analysis delivers a gradual measure for the goodness of fit between expectations and actual inputs, in sum, the acceptability of an interpretation. Thresholds for this signal are set in terms of approval levels, depending in turn also on relevant experience in a context. There ensues a constraint and a trade-off: time is short, in the real world not everything can always be perfect, approximations and shortcuts often are good enough, and a wrong schema has to be abandoned at some point and another, new, conceptual frame is tried.

New schemata are preferentially laid down for concepts and episodes which are marked by the output of consumption analysis as deviating significantly from expectations derived from previous experience. Thus self-steered expansion and refinement over time guarantees the gradual and stepwise elaboration of useful hierarchically structured knowledge and behavior, especially in areas where the need surfaced [4].

3   Stupidity

Dozens of different definitions of intelligence have been suggested, and thus it is not immediately clear, with which one a model of general intelligence as outlined in the Ouroboros Model should comply [6]. This is the venture point for attempting to approach the issue from the other side, i.e. looking, what might be learned from situations or constellations, which are characterized by an apparent lack of intelligence, i.e. "stupidity".

Inspired by careful observation of real human behavior, no formal account, e.g. of bounded rationality, is adopted here but the following provocative working definition of real stupidity is suggested:

An agent will be called stupid, if he unwittingly works against his (important) goals and self-interest, not considering information, which is (easily) available.

Fig. 1. A precursor of this figure was given in [3] with the caption "A lack in self-awareness can easily become costly to an agent in the real world"

Guided by the classical example as depicted in Fig. 1, some main characteristics of not so clever behavior can be identified and highlighted:

- Stupidity basically is a feature ascribed to an actor by others observing his behavior from the outside; we see the poor guy on the tree and his way of cutting is deemed to cause him a problem.
- A stupid person is focusing on some minor detail while neglecting much more important aspects, which are directly relevant to the goals and the self-interests of the observed; holding fast to that twig certainly is not going to help for long.
- To an outside observer this neglect is hard to understand as a more complete picture and fitting behavior appear to be obvious and easily available to the agent; the guy knows he is cutting the branch he is sitting on, he ought to realize that he is going to fall down and harm himself. Watching this is itself hurtful to the viewer.

The observed points and more can be distilled from the examples of manifestly stupid (human) behaviors collected and analyzed over time by many authors [7,8,9]. As their first common point it shall be emphasized here that natural stupidity is a feature ascribed to an agent from the outside by another knowledgeable agent.

The more the resulting effects of behavior run counter to the (assumed) intentions of the observed actor, the stronger the impression of his stupidity. The same holds true with respect to the availability of alternatives: the easier different behavior, which would lead to success, can be found and performed, the sillier one must be to neglect or discard that information.

Stupidity is individual, and here also the border runs between simple innocent dumbness or blunt incapability and more sophisticated forms of stupidity. If an agent is charged beyond his capabilities, his behavior will not be optimum, but we would be much more willing to excuse his failure than if he could have managed if not too lazy or ignorant and arrogant. The same performance, which might be rated respectable for a student or novice, could fall under the rubric of stupid reaction if it came from a Nobel laureate in his claimed field of expertise.

Quite general, being an accomplished expert in one restricted field does not necessarily imply overarching intelligence. The Ouroboros Model stresses the 'local' nature of schemata and effective processes, and it identifies this at the same time as inherent constraint and principal limitation for performance.

Sophistication is possible in countless directions; as one commonplace and important example, an arrogant agent might be guided by a severely distorted self-assessment and be wrongly convinced that he knows very well what to do, even actively rejecting any help. ("Pride and ignorance are akin" the proverb knows).

Judging the motivation behind any non-trivial behavior from the outside is intrinsically difficult as it amounts to guessing some only personally accessible parts of the total frame relevant to the actor. Sometimes it thus might be hard to tell whether an act belongs to the category of stupidity or even obstruction and sabotage.

As a preliminary summary one might say that in any variant of stupidity information directly relevant to a behavior is mistakenly not taken into account in any appropriate and apparently obvious way. In terms of the Ouroboros Model this means that the applied schemata are a poor representation of the relevant features of reality or that the processes working on the basis of these schemata are faulty, e.g. perceptions are distorted or discrepancies are ignored.

4   General Intelligence

In the light of the claimed characteristics of naturally occurring stupidity one is tempted to see a reason for the obvious difficulty for defining intelligence in an objective and unquestionable way in the non-existence of context-free intelligence. Some statements concerning intelligence, inverse to the above hypotheses referring to stupidity, suggest themselves and seem intuitively right:

- Intelligence is a label that humans grant to other (rational) agents.
- An intelligent person (agent) takes into systematic account all conceivably relevant data, possibilities and circumstances, reaching with coherent and correct reasoning much beyond the directly obvious.
- The more unexpected and sophisticated a decisive combination or insight is, the higher we appreciate the feat and the apparent cognitive skill.

So, what would be an appropriate counterpart to Fig. 1? A modest attempt to provide one example is sketched in Fig. 2.

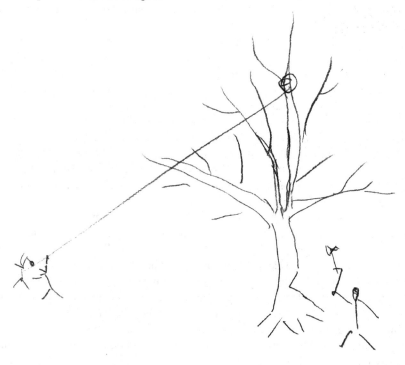

Fig. 2. Clever is, who applies an understanding as wide as possible, chooses appropriate tools as available and accepts help from friends

Importantly, in contrast to the gist of what is usually understood as intelligence, the sketch of a definition as given in the caption of Fig. 2 does not mention success as a criterion for a person or an action to qualify as intelligent. Adaption and success, no doubt, in the long run are more often the consequences resulting from intelligent rather than from stupid actions but in an open and complex world there is no simple one-to-one correlation. There are cases, e.g. of limited resources, in which no measure of intelligence can guarantee a favorable outcome; and it might not even be possible in hindsight to judge. An agent might have failed and still, she might have acted as intelligent and efficient as possible at all. Many a success is the child of mere luck.

Quite commonly, it is often not so clear, how to qualify an action or omission. Intelligence and stupidity are individual also in the sense that different observers might arrive at contradicting conclusions referring to one and the same instance. On top of observers' personal limitations principal restrictions due to bounded resources apply; this results in a grey scale comprising fundamental uncertainty.

The idea that intelligence is to be attributed by judges in a particular situation is not new; it lies at the heart of Turing's famous test [10]. The first chapter-title in his groundbreaking paper gives also a hint on how to achieve intelligence, and at the same time it names a limitation with the keyword of "imitation". Observing others, remembering and copying their (successful) behavior certainly can help to avoid some mistakes; on the other hand, simple imitation lacks the features of novelty, understanding or creativity, of which at least the first two are most often considered hallmarks of intelligence. Teachers are familiar with the related distinction between learning something by rote and true comprehension.

At a somewhat abstracted level, the cognitive skills of a person can be determined rather reliably and reproducibly. Interestingly, also the best available quantitative measure of general intelligence, i.e. the IQ of an individual as derived from his performance in a series of well defined and validated tests, is relative; it refers in its definition to a comparison to an ensemble comprising many other persons.

5   Intelligence According to the Ouroboros Model

It is hypothesized by the Ouroboros Model that not only representational capacity, but the total potential mental processing power of an agent is ground-laid as well as limited by structured knowledge. i.e. the number, complexity and elaboration of the concepts at her disposition [4].

Differentiated schemata, their numbers of slots, the level of detail, the depth of hierarchies, the degrees of connection and interdependence of the building blocks, and the width, i.e. the extent of main schemata and their total coverage from a bodily grounding level to the most abstract summits, determine what can be done or thought of efficiently. Sheer performance at a single point in time arises as a result of the optimum interplay between these structured data and the effective and systematic execution of the processing steps, in particular, self-referential consumption analysis.

Most important, efficient (long-term and working-) memory is seen as a mandatory prerequisite of intelligence. Understanding working memory as temporary common activation and binding of current input with material laid down in long term storage makes this proposal consistent with vast evidence, which indicates that working memory capacity is a valid predictor of general intelligence [11.12].

The pursuit of consistency as the fundamental basis for rational behavior and the efficient self-steering by consumption analysis entails a principal difficulty for differentiating between cunningness and foolishness or dullness [4]. If something is marked as strongly discordant with hitherto experience, it might be because it is novel and brilliant, or, it might simply be wrong, even stupid. Only the intelligent (!) embedding of the issue in question in the widest possible frame and taking into account all conceivably relevant information can offer a chance of meaningful and fair assessment. Stupidity can sometimes be temptingly simple and beautiful, while thoughtful elaborations, often tedious, might be deterrent.

Appraisal of any elaborate and complex behavior cannot be collapsed onto one single scale running between stupid and intelligent; there are much more dimensions to this topic than can be indicated with a few opposites. As just one example, a related distinction could be between rational and irrational. In the light of the Ouroboros Model, rational behavior takes all relevant information into account in a systematic manner, it can be comprehended in detail, and it necessarily entails consequent and traceable reasoning. Irrational actions cannot be fully understood by a spectator, at least not on the basis of the knowledge applicable for him at that point in time. Creativity would in this frame still lie somewhere in an orthogonal direction emphasizing the feature of unprecedentedness while relaxing requirements for stringency, "usefulness" and "grounding".

6   Conclusions

The Ouroboros Model holds that intelligence is conceded by a spectator to an actor whenever the actor consistently brings to bear all information considered to be really relevant by the spectator.

There is nothing like absolute stupidity or intelligence, no such observer-independent objective entities do exist. Whether a behavior is called clever or silly depends on the contexts prevalent for the involved agents at that particular time in question. The employed frames of reference can make a decisive difference.

Both figures in this paper are misleading; no adequate picture of stupidity or intelligence can be drawn in black and white. Any qualification of cognitive performance is possible only in a wider context admitting the agents, (self-) involved as actors and observers. The described mandatory inclusion of a human (even consciousness-) component into definitions of intelligence and stupidity can explain why so far no consensus has been reached among researchers on the essential abstract characteristics or a unique definition of intelligence.

The actual result of an action cannot righteously be taken as touchstone for the intelligence leading to that outcome. The situation is a little like looking into a mirror: the distinction between up and down is easy as well-defined by an outside reference; judging intelligence versus stupidity, alas, corresponds more to telling left from right.

Self-reflecting, we emphasize as one defining feature of stupidity a deficiency in considering all relevant (in principal available) information, which is judged as essential for success by an observer. This evaluating instance need not necessarily be a different person; it can be the actor himself reflecting on his own behavior at some earlier point in time.

A special case worth while mentioning in this respect are situations and behavioral options for which short-term benefits to an actor entail long-term disaster [9]. It certainly is a sign of stupidity, if the temporal dimension is not carefully paid heed to, and, for example, an action is judged as ingenious because it had turned out a success, - it is well possible that at the time of taking the corresponding decision, this particular behavior could only have been condemned as stupid; - the same is also possible the other way round.

In a setting of intended collaboration, stupidity of an actor can still easily be topped by an observer, - if he clearly displays that he considers the first one stupid.

The Ouroboros Model stresses the indispensability of orderly processes and it highlights the preeminent importance of exploiting a knowledge base as vast as ever possible. There is no contradiction to efficiently employing well-tuned short cuts and heuristics [13]; - the latter can be seen as a means of taking the dimension of time and, in particular, time-limitations in a natural and dangerous world, into due account.

A strong link between intelligence and consciousness has been proposed, see Fig. 1, and it has been argued that at a certain level of intelligence consciousness emerges naturally, even inevitably [3,14].

The Ouroboros Model claims to offer a self-consistent and self-relational consistent approach for understanding and avoiding stupidity in natural and artificial agents and for fostering the self-steered growth of intelligence. The general advice for guarding against stupidity that could be drawn from it might best be summarized in a plea for aiming at all-embracing consistency in the widest possibly and applicable frame.

Acknowledgments. It might be a bit delicate for this given subject but it should not be concealed that the author is indebted to certain individuals for providing a wealth of inspiration.

In enjoyable contrast, responding to encouraging questions and suggestions posed by unknown reviewers was a true pleasure.

References

1. Thomsen, K.: The Ouroboros Model in the light of venerable criteria. Neurocomputing 74, 121–128 (2010)
2. Thomsen, K.: The Ouroboros Model, Selected Facets. In: Hernández, C., et al. (eds.) From Brains to Systems, pp. 239–250. Springer, Heidelberg (2011)
3. Thomsen, K.: Consciousness for the Ouroboros Model. Journal for Machine Consciousness 3, 163–175 (2011)
4. Thomsen, K.: Knowledge as a Basis and a Constraint for the Performance of the Ouroboros Model. Presented at a Workshop at ZiF in Bielefeld, October 29-31 (2009)

5. Yuille, A., Kersten, D.: Vision as Bayesian inference: analysis by synthesis? Trends in Cognitive Science 10, 301–308 (2006)
6. Legg, S., Hutter, M.: A Collection of Definitions of Intelligence. In: Proceedings of the 2007 Conference on Advances in Artificial General Intelligence: Concepts, Architects and Algorithms (2007)
7. Geyer, H.: Über die Dummheit. VMA-Verlag Wiesbaden (1954)
8. Van Boxsel, M.: Die Enzyklopädie der Dummheit. Eichborn AG, Frankfurt am Main (2001)
9. Welles, J.F.: Understanding Stupidity. Mount Pleasant Press, NY (1995)
10. Turing, A.M.: Computing machinery and intelligence. Mind 59, 433–460 (1950)
11. Ericsson, K.A., Kintsch, W.: Longt-term working memory. Psychological Review 102, 211–245 (1995)
12. Oberauer, K., Süss, H.-M., Wilhelm, O., Wittmann, W.W.: Which working memory functions predict intelligence? Intelligence 36, 641–652 (2008)
13. Gigerenzer, G., Todd, P.M., ABC Research Group (eds.): Simple heuristics that make us smart. Oxford University Press, New York (1999)
14. Sanz, R., López, I., Rodríguez, M., Hernandéz, C.: Principles for consciousness in integrated cognitive control. Neural Networks 20, 938–946 (2007)

On Ensemble Techniques
for AIXI Approximation

Joel Veness[1], Peter Sunehag[2], and Marcus Hutter[2]

[1] University of Alberta
[2] Australian National University
veness@cs.ualberta.ca, {peter.sunehag,marcus.hutter}@anu.edu.au

Abstract One of the key challenges in AIXI approximation is model class approximation - i.e. how to meaningfully approximate Solomonoff Induction without requiring an infeasible amount of computation? This paper advocates a bottom-up approach to this problem, by describing a number of principled ensemble techniques for approximate AIXI agents. Each technique works by efficiently combining a set of existing environment models into a single, more powerful model. These techniques have the potential to play an important role in future AIXI approximations.

1 Introduction

In statistical data compression, one modeling approach used by many high performance programs is to use an ensemble method to combine the predictions of multiple statistical models (Mattern, 2012). Each model is typically tailored towards a particular kind of structure that occurs in popular file types. By specifying a number of specialized models, as well as one or more general-purpose models, excellent compression performance can be obtained across a variety of file types. This approach is taken by the powerful PAQ family (Mahoney, 2005) of data compressors, which currently obtain the best compression performance across many well-known benchmarks.

Within reinforcement learning (Sutton and Barto, 1998), some efforts (Veness et al., 2010, 2011) have recently been made towards approximating AIXI (Hutter, 2005), an optimality notion for general reinforcement learning agents. Impressively, these agents have been shown to be able to learn, *from scratch*, to play TicTacToe, Pacman, Kuhn Poker, and other simple games by trial and error alone – even the rules of each game were not communicated to the agent. The mathematical framework used in these works can be considered a natural generalization of the statistical data compression setting to reinforcement learning. The distinguishing feature of this setting is an extra source of side information – namely, the history of actions chosen by some control algorithm – which is incorporated into a sequential, probabilistic framework. Inspired by the success of ensemble methods within data compression, the goal of this paper is to explore a number of principled techniques for combining one or more probabilistic models within reinforcement learning. We restrict our attention to that of *universal*

J. Bach, B. Goertzel, and M. Iklé (Eds.): AGI 2012, LNAI 7716, pp. 341–351, 2012.
© Springer-Verlag Berlin Heidelberg 2012

methods, i.e. methods that provide competitive theoretical guarantees with respect to an interesting class of candidate environments. Our contribution is to survey some general techniques from Bayesian statistics, online learning and online convex programming and show how they can be used to define a variety of principled ensemble techniques for information theoretic agents.

2   Background

We now describe our probabilistic agent setting. A more detailed overview of this framework can be found in the work of Hutter (2005) and Veness et al. (2011).

Notation. A string $x_1 x_2 \ldots x_n$ of length n is denoted by $x_{1:n}$. The prefix $x_{1:j}$ of $x_{1:n}$, $j \leq n$, is denoted by $x_{\leq j}$ or $x_{<j+1}$. The notation generalises to blocks of symbols: e.g. $a x_{1:n}$ denotes $a_1 x_1 a_2 x_2 \ldots a_n x_n$ and $a x_{<j}$ denotes the string $a_1 x_1 a_2 x_2 \ldots a_{j-1} x_{j-1}$. The empty string is denoted by ϵ. The concatenation of two strings s and r is denoted by sr. The finite action, observation, and reward spaces are denoted by $\mathcal{A}, \mathcal{O}$, and $\mathcal{R}$ respectively. Also, $\mathcal{X}$ denotes the joint perception space $\mathcal{O} \times \mathcal{R}$.

The following definition states that the environment takes the form of a probability distribution over possible observation-reward sequences conditioned on actions taken by the agent.

Definition 1. *An environment ρ is a sequence of parametrized probability mass functions $\{\rho_0, \rho_1, \rho_2, \ldots \}$, where $\rho_n \colon \mathcal{A}^n \to Density\,(\mathcal{X}^n)$, that satisfies*

$$\forall a_{1:n} \forall x_{<n} : \; \rho_{n-1}(x_{<n} \,|\, a_{<n}) = \sum_{x_n \in \mathcal{X}} \rho_n(x_{1:n} \,|\, a_{1:n}). \tag{1}$$

In the base case, we have $\rho_0(\epsilon \,|\, \epsilon) = 1$.

Equation (1), called the chronological condition by Hutter (2005), captures the natural constraint that action a_n has no effect on earlier perceptions $x_{<n}$. For convenience, we drop the index n in ρ_n from here onwards. Now, given an environment ρ, we define the predictive probability

$$\rho(x_n \,|\, a x_{<n} a_n) := \rho(x_{1:n} \,|\, a_{1:n}) / \rho(x_{<n} \,|\, a_{<n}) \tag{2}$$

$\forall a_{1:n} \forall x_{1:n}$ such that $\rho(x_{<n} \,|\, a_{<n}) > 0$. It now follows that

$$\rho(x_{1:n} \,|\, a_{1:n}) = \rho(x_1 \,|\, a_1) \rho(x_2 \,|\, a x_1 a_2) \cdots \rho(x_n \,|\, a x_{<n} a_n). \tag{3}$$

Definition 1 is used in two distinct ways. The first is to describe the true environment, which is typically not known by the agent. The second is to describe an agent's *subjective* model of the environment. This model is usually adaptive, and will often only be an approximation to the true environment. To make the distinction clear, we will refer to an agent's *environment model* when talking about the agent's model of the environment. Additionally, we introduce the notion of an ϵ-positive environment model. This is defined as an environment model ρ satisfying $\rho(x_n \mid ax_{<n}a_n) \geq \epsilon$ for some real $\epsilon > 0$, for all $n \in \mathbb{N}$, for all $x_{1:n} \in \mathcal{X}^n$ and for all $a_{1:n} \in \mathcal{A}^n$. From here onwards we assume all environment models are ϵ-positive.

Redundancy. We will also introduce a notion of regret, *redundancy*, which we will later use to analyze the performance of our ensemble techniques. This is defined as

$$- \log_2 \mu(x_{1:n} \mid a_{1:n}) - \min_{\rho \in \mathcal{M}} - \log_2 \rho(x_{1:n} \mid a_{1:n})$$

for an arbitrary environment model μ, with respect to some class $\mathcal{M}$ of environment models. Our typical goal will be to show that the redundancy grows $o(n)$. Informally, such a result implies that the average performance of μ will eventually match that of the best model in $\mathcal{M}$ as n gets large.

3   Ensemble Techniques

This section discusses a number of principled ways to construct an enriched environment model from two or more existing environment models. A competitive analysis is given for each method, which justifies their usage in various situations.

3.1   Weighting / Model Averaging

A straightforward way to construct an adaptive environment model that can perform nearly as well as any single model from a finite set of candidate environment models is to use Bayesian Model Averaging (also known as weighting).

Definition 2. *Given a finite set of environment models* $\mathcal{M} := \{\rho_1, \rho_2, \dots\}$ *and a prior weight* $w_0^\rho > 0$ *for each* $\rho \in \mathcal{M}$ *such that* $\sum_{\rho \in \mathcal{M}} w_0^\rho = 1$, *the mixture environment model is* $\xi(x_{1:n} \mid a_{1:n}) := \sum_{\rho \in \mathcal{M}} w_0^\rho \rho(x_{1:n} \mid a_{1:n})$.

The above can easily be shown (for example, see Proposition 1 in the work of Veness et al. (2011)) to define a valid environment model. Because of this, we can simply use

$$\xi(x_n \mid ax_{<n}a_n) = \xi(x_{1:n} \mid a_{1:n}) / \xi(x_{<n} \mid a_{<n}) \tag{4}$$

to predict the next observation reward pair. Equation (4) can also be expressed in terms of a convex combination of model predictions, with each model weighted by its posterior probability. Formally,

$$\xi(x_n \mid ax_{<n}a_n) = \frac{\sum_{\rho \in \mathcal{M}} w_0^\rho \rho(x_{1:n} \mid a_{1:n})}{\sum_{\rho \in \mathcal{M}} w_0^\rho \rho(x_{<n} \mid a_{<n})} = \sum_{\rho \in \mathcal{M}} w_{n-1}^\rho \rho(x_n \mid ax_{<n}a_n),$$

where the posterior weight w^ρ_{n-1} for environment model ρ is given by

$$w^\rho_{n-1} := \frac{w^\rho_0 \rho(x_{<n} \mid a_{<n})}{\sum\limits_{\nu \in \mathcal{M}} w^\nu_0 \nu(x_{<n} \mid a_{<n})}. \tag{5}$$

This method is justified whenever there exists a model $\rho^* \in \mathcal{M}$ that predicts well, since

$$-\log_2 \xi(x_{1:n} \mid a_{1:n}) = -\log_2 \sum_{\rho \in \mathcal{M}} w^\rho_0 \rho(x_{1:n} \mid a_{1:n}) \leq -\log_2 w^{\rho^*}_0 - \log_2 \rho^*(x_{1:n} \mid a_{1:n}), \tag{6}$$

which implies that we suffer constant redundancy when using ξ in place of ρ^*.

Algorithm. The weights specified by Equation (5) can be maintained in $O(|\mathcal{M}|)$ time and space by using the identity $\rho(x_{1:n} \mid a_{1:n}) = \rho(x_{<n} \mid a_{<n})\rho(x_n \mid ax_{<n}a)$ to incrementally maintain the probability of the data under each environment model. Note however that in some special cases, more efficient techniques exist with time complexity sublinear in $|\mathcal{M}|$. One example is Context Tree Weighting (Willems et al., 1995), which was used as the basis for our previous AIXI approximations (Veness et al., 2010, 2011).

3.2 Switching / Tracking

While weighting provides an easy way to combine models, as an ensemble method it is somewhat limited in that it only guarantees performance in terms of the best *single* model in $\mathcal{M}$. It is easy to imagine situations where this would be insufficient in practice. Instead, one could consider weighting over *sequences* of models chosen from a fixed base class $\mathcal{M}$. Variants of this fundamental idea have been considered numerous times in the literature, for example by Volf and Willems (1998); Herbster and Warmuth (1998) and Erven et al. (2008). We now show how these ideas can be cast into our probabilistic agent setting, by describing an adaptation of the FIXEDSHARE algorithm (Herbster and Warmuth, 1998). We also provide a short competitive analysis.

Definition 3. *Given a finite set* $\mathcal{M} = \{\rho_1, \ldots, \rho_N\}$, $N > 1$, *of environment models and a switching sequence* $\alpha = \alpha_2\alpha_3 \ldots \in [0,1]^\infty$, *for all* $n \in \mathbb{N}$, *for all* $x_{1:n} \in \mathcal{X}^n$, *the switching environment model with respect to* $\mathcal{M}$ *and* α *is defined as*

$$\tau_\alpha(x_{1:n} \mid a_{1:n}) := \sum_{i_{1:n} \in \mathcal{I}_n(\mathcal{M})} w_\alpha(i_{1:n}) \prod_{k=1}^n \rho_{i_k}(x_k \mid ax_{<k}a_k) \tag{7}$$

where $\mathcal{I}_n(\mathcal{M}) := \{1, 2, \ldots, N\}^n$ *and the prior over model sequences is recursively defined by*

$$w_\alpha(i_{1:n}) := \begin{cases} 1 & \text{if} \quad i_{1:n} = \epsilon \\ \frac{1}{N} & \text{if} \quad n = 1 \\ w_\alpha(i_{<n}) \times \left((1 - \alpha_n)\mathbb{I}[i_n = i_{n-1}] + \frac{\alpha_n}{N-1}\mathbb{I}[i_n \neq i_{n-1}] \right) & \text{otherwise,} \end{cases} \tag{8}$$

Algorithm 1. SWITCHMIXTURE - $\tau_\alpha(x_{1:n} \mid a_{1:n})$

Require: A finite model class $\mathcal{M} = \{\rho_1, \ldots, \rho_N\}$ such that $N > 1$
Require: A weight vector $(w_1, \ldots, w_N) \in \mathbb{R}^N$, with $w_i = \frac{1}{N}$ for $1 \leq i \leq N$
Require: A switching sequence $\alpha_2, \alpha_3, \ldots, \alpha_n$

1: $r \leftarrow 1$
2: **for** $i = 1$ to n **do**
3:      $r \leftarrow \sum_{j=1}^{N} w_j \rho_j(x_i \mid ax_{<i}a_i)$
4:      $k \leftarrow (1 - \alpha_{i+1})N - 1$
5:      **for** $j = 1$ to N **do**
6:          $w_j \leftarrow \frac{1}{N-1} [\alpha_{i+1}r + kw_j\rho_j(x_i \mid ax_{<i}a_i)]$
7:      **end for**
8: **end for**
9: **return** r

Now, using the same argument to bound $-\log_2 \tau_\alpha(x_{1:n} \mid a_{1:n})$ as we did in Equation 6, we see that the inequality

$$-\log_2 \tau_\alpha(x_{1:n} \mid a_{1:n}) \leq -\log_2 w_\alpha(i_{1:n}) - \log_2 \rho_{i_{1:n}}(x_{1:n} \mid a_{1:n}) \tag{9}$$

holds for any sequence of models $i_{1:n} \in \mathcal{I}_n(\mathcal{M})$, where $\rho_{i_{1:n}}(x_{1:n} \mid a_{1:n})$ denotes the product $\prod_{k=1}^{n} \rho_{i_k}(x_k \mid ax_{<k}a_k)$ of the sequence of conditional probabilities defined by $i_{1:n}$. Next, we state an upper bound on $-\log_2 w_\alpha(i_{1:n})$ that holds for any sequence of model indices.

Lemma 1. *Given a base model class $\mathcal{M}$ and a decaying switch rate $\alpha_t := \frac{1}{t}$ for $t \in \mathbb{N}$,*

$$-\log_2 w_\alpha(i_{1:n}) \leq (m(i_{1:n}) + 1)(\log_2 |\mathcal{M}| + \log_2 n),$$

for all $i_{1:n} \in \mathcal{I}_n(\mathcal{M})$, where $m(i_{1:n}) := \sum_{k=2}^{n} \mathbb{I}[i_k \neq i_{k-1}]$ denotes the number of switches in $i_{1:n}$.

Proof. See the work of Veness et al. (2012).

Combining Equation 9 with Lemma 1 gives the following bound.

Theorem 1. *Given a base model class $\mathcal{M}$ and switch rate $\alpha_t := \frac{1}{t}$ for $t \in \mathbb{N}$, for all $n \in \mathbb{N}$, for all $i_{1:n} \in \mathcal{I}_n(\mathcal{M})$,*

$$-\log_2 \tau_\alpha(x_{1:n} \mid a_{1:n}) \leq (m(i_{1:n}) + 1)[\log_2 |\mathcal{M}| + \log_2 n] - \log_2 \rho_{i_{1:n}}(x_{1:n} \mid a_{1:n}).$$

Thus if there exists an environment model $\rho_{i_{1:n}}$ with $m(i_{1:n}) \ll n$ that predicts well, then τ_α will also predict well. In the case where the best sequence of models satisfies $m(i_{1:n}) = 0$, Theorem 1 gives an extra cost of $\log_2 n$ bits compared to a uniform weighting. Assuming both bounds are tight, $\log_2 n$ can be thought of as the cost of using switching in situations where weighting would have been sufficient.

Algorithm. A direct computation of Equation 7 is intractable. For example, given a history $ax_{1:n}$ and a model class $\mathcal{M}$, the sum in Equation 7 would require $|\mathcal{M}|^n$ additions. Fortunately, the structured nature of the model sequence weights $w_\alpha(i_{1:n})$ can be exploited to derive Algorithm 1. The same argument used to derive the correctness of this procedure for the sequence prediction setting (Veness et al., 2012) can be easily generalised to our agent setting. Assuming that every conditional probability can be computed in constant time, Algorithm 1 runs in $\Theta(n|\mathcal{M}|)$ time and uses only $\Theta(|\mathcal{M}|)$ space. Furthermore, only $\Theta(|\mathcal{M}|)$ work is required to process each new symbol.

3.3   Convex Mixing

This next section introduces *convex mixing*, a technique which, unlike weighting or switching, can sometimes be expected to perform better than any single model or sequences thereof from some base class of environment models $\mathcal{M}$. The key insight is to consider arbitrary convex combinations of the individual model predictions at each time step. More formally, given a set of base environment models $\mathcal{M}$, consider the product of an arbitrary sequence of convex combinations of the conditional probabilities determined by each environment model.

Definition 4. *Given a finite set of ϵ-positive environment models $\mathcal{M}$ and a sequence of weights $\lambda := \{\lambda_1, \lambda_2, \dots\}$, where each $\lambda_i := \{\lambda_i^\rho\}_{\rho \in \mathcal{M}}$ such that $\lambda_i^\rho \in \mathbb{R}$, $\lambda_i^\rho \geq 0$ and $\sum_{\rho \in \mathcal{M}} \lambda_i^\rho = 1$ for $i \in \mathbb{N}$, the convex environment model with respect to λ is defined as*

$$\nu_\lambda(x_{1:n} \,|\, a_{1:n}) := \prod_{i=1}^n \sum_{\rho \in \mathcal{M}} \lambda_i^\rho \, \rho(x_i \,|\, ax_{<i}a_i). \tag{10}$$

The above can easily be seen to define a valid chronological measure.

Proposition 1. *A convex environment model is an environment model.*

Proof. As each environment model $\rho \in \mathcal{M}$ is ϵ-positive, every conditional probability $\rho(x_k \,|\, ax_{<k}a_k)$ is well defined. Therefore we just need to check that Equation (1) is satisfied. Now, $\forall a_{1:n} \in \mathcal{A}^n$ and $\forall x_{<n} \in \mathcal{X}^{n-1}$ observe that

$$
\begin{aligned}
\sum_{x_n \in \mathcal{X}} \nu_\lambda(x_{1:n} \,|\, a_{1:n}) &= \sum_{x_n \in \mathcal{X}} \prod_{i=1}^n \sum_{\rho \in \mathcal{M}} \lambda_i^\rho \, \rho(x_i \,|\, ax_{<i}a_i) \\
&= \nu_\lambda(x_{<n} \,|\, a_{<n}) \sum_{x_n \in \mathcal{X}} \sum_{\rho \in \mathcal{M}} \lambda_n^\rho \, \rho(x_n \,|\, ax_{<n}a_n) \\
&= \nu_\lambda(x_{<n} \,|\, a_{<n}) \sum_{\rho \in \mathcal{M}} \lambda_n^\rho \sum_{x_n \in \mathcal{X}} \rho(x_n \,|\, ax_{<n}a_n) \\
&= \nu_\lambda(x_{<n} \,|\, a_{<n}) \sum_{\rho \in \mathcal{M}} \lambda_n^\rho \\
&= \nu_\lambda(x_{<n} \,|\, a_{<n}),
\end{aligned}
$$

Algorithm 2. CONVEXMIXTURE - $\nu_\lambda(x_{1:n}|a_{1:n})$

Require: A history $ax_{1:n} \in (\mathcal{A} \times \mathcal{X})^n$, $n \in \mathbb{N}$
Require: An initial weight vector $\lambda_1 \in \Delta^{|\mathcal{M}|-1}$
Require: A sequence $\eta_1, \eta_2, \ldots, \eta_n$, of positive, real-valued step sizes

1: $r \leftarrow 1$
2: **for** $i = 1$ to n **do**
3:     $r \leftarrow r \times \sum_{\rho \in \mathcal{M}} \lambda_i^\rho \, \rho(x_i \,|\, ax_{<i}a_i)$
4:     $\lambda_{i+1} = \text{SIMPLEXPROJECT}(\lambda_i - \eta_i \nabla \ell_i(\lambda_i \,;\, x_i))$
5: **end for**
6: **return** r

---

which is what we need. The first three steps follow from Equation (10) and stand-ard calculations, the fourth step follows from Equation (2), and the final step follows since $\sum_{\rho \in \mathcal{M}} \lambda_n^\rho = 1$ by definition.

Adaptive Convex Mixing. We will now show how to apply the framework of online convex programming (Zinkevich, 2003; Hazan, 2006) to dynamically (i.e. as a function of $ax_{1:n}$) produce a sequence of weights $\hat{\lambda}$ whose redundancy

$$- \log_2 \nu_{\hat{\lambda}}(x_{1:n} \,|\, a_{1:n}) - \min_{\lambda_* \in \Delta^{|\mathcal{M}|-1}} \left\{ - \log_2 \prod_{i=1}^{n} \sum_{\rho \in \mathcal{M}} \lambda_*^\rho \rho(x_i \,|\, ax_{<i}a_i) \right\} \quad (11)$$

grows $O(\sqrt{n})$ with respect to the best set of *constant* weights in $\Delta^{|\mathcal{M}|-1}$, for all $n \in \mathbb{N}$ and for all $x_{1:n} \in \mathcal{X}^n$, where Δ^k denotes the standard k-simplex. This can be considered as an alternative to weighting over the probability simplex, which will invariably require more restrictive assumptions on the environment model in order to gain computational tractability.

To begin with, we require a sequence of history dependent convex loss func-tions. These can be obtained by noticing that

$$- \log_2 \nu_\lambda(x_{1:n} \,|\, a_{1:n}) = \sum_{i=1}^{n} - \log_2 \sum_{\rho \in \mathcal{M}} \lambda_i^\rho \, \rho(x_i \,|\, ax_{<i}a_i),$$

which lets us naturally define the loss function at time $n \in \mathbb{N}$ to be

$$\ell_n(\lambda_n \,;\, ax_{1:n}) := - \log_2 \sum_{\rho \in \mathcal{M}} \lambda_n^\rho \, \rho(x_n \,|\, ax_{<n}a_n).$$

The next proposition shows us that this class of loss functions is convex.

Proposition 2. $\forall n \in \mathbb{N}$, $\forall ax_{1:n} \in (\mathcal{A} \times \mathcal{X})^n$, $\ell_n(\cdot \,;\, ax_{1:n})$ *is convex.*

Proof. Denote $g_n(\lambda) := \sum_{\rho \in \mathcal{M}} \lambda^\rho \, \rho(x_n \,|\, ax_{<n}a_n)$ and $h(x) := - \log_2(x)$. First observe that as a linear function, g_n is concave. Also, note that the extended-value extension of h, defined by*

$$\tilde{h}(x) = \begin{cases} - \log_2 x & \text{if } x \in (0, \infty], \\ \infty & \text{otherwise} \end{cases}$$

Algorithm 3. SIMPLEXPROJECT($\boldsymbol{w}$)

Require: A vector $\boldsymbol{w} = (w_1, \ldots, w_d) \in \mathbb{R}^d$ for $d \geq 2$

1: $i = 1, s = -1$
2: $\boldsymbol{y} \leftarrow$ SORTDESCENDING$(w_1, \ldots, w_d)$
3: **loop**
4:      $s = s + y_i$
5:      $r = s/i$
6:      **if** $i = d$ **or** $r \geq y_{i-1}$ **then**
7:          $t \leftarrow r$
8:          **break loop**
9:      **end if**
10:      $i \leftarrow i + 1$
11: **end loop**
12: **for** $i = 1$ to d **do**
13:      $w_i \leftarrow \max(0, w_i - t)$
14: **end for**
15: **return** $\boldsymbol{w}$

---

is non-increasing on $\mathbb{R}$. *Therefore, since* h *is convex, it follows (see Section 3.2.4 of (Boyd and Vandenberghe, 2004)) that for all* $n \in \mathbb{N}$, $\ell_n(\cdot, ax_{1:n})$ *is convex.*

The gradient $\nabla \ell_n(\lambda_n \,; ax_{1:n})$ of the loss with respect to λ_n can now be determined by repeatedly using the identity

$$\frac{\partial \ell_n}{\partial \lambda_n^\rho} = \frac{-\rho(x_n \mid ax_{<n} a_n)}{\ln 2 \sum_{\nu \in \mathcal{M}} \lambda_n^\nu \, \nu(x_n \mid ax_{<n} a_n)},$$

for all $\rho \in \mathcal{M}$, to construct the relevant $|\mathcal{M}|$-dimensional column vector. Note that due to the ϵ-positive assumption, we can bound each coefficient in the gradient by

$$\left| \frac{-\rho(x_n \mid ax_{<n} a_n)}{\ln 2 \sum_{\nu \in \mathcal{M}} \lambda_n^\nu \, \nu(x_n \mid ax_{<n} a_n)} \right| \leq \frac{1}{\ln 2 \sum_{\nu \in \mathcal{M}} \lambda_n^\nu \epsilon} = \frac{1}{\epsilon \ln 2},$$

which implies that

$$\|\nabla \ell_n(\lambda_n \,; ax_{1:n})\|_2 \leq \sqrt{|\mathcal{M}|} \frac{1}{\epsilon \ln 2}. \tag{12}$$

Theoretical Analysis. Since we have cast our problem into the framework of online convex programming, the argument of Zinkevich (2003) can be used to state a redundancy bound for convex environment models. This analysis assumes the existence of a known upper bound $G := \sup_{1 \leq i \leq n} \|\nabla l_i(\lambda_i; ax_{1:i})\|_2$ on the l_2-norm of the gradients as well as on the diameter $D := \max_{c_1, c_2 \in \mathcal{C}} \|c_1 - c_2\|_2$ of the convex set (the simplex for us) that we perform the optimization over. The result, formulated by Hazan (2006) in Theorem 2.1 (page 12), says that by setting $\eta_i = \frac{D}{G\sqrt{i}}$, the cumulative regret after n steps is bounded by $3GD\sqrt{n}$.

Theorem 2. *Using Algorithm 2 with a step size of $\eta_i = \frac{\epsilon \ln 2}{\sqrt{i}}$ for $1 \leq i \leq n$,*

$$\max_{\lambda_* \in \Delta^{|\mathcal{M}|-1}} \left\{ \log_2 \prod_{i=1}^{n} \sum_{\rho \in \mathcal{M}} \lambda_*^\rho \rho(x_i \mid ax_{<i}a_i) \right\} - \log_2 \nu_{\hat{\lambda}}(x_{1:n} \mid a_{1:n}) \leq \frac{3|\mathcal{M}|\sqrt{n}}{\epsilon \ln 2}$$

Proof. The result follows by using Proposition 2, the fact that the diameter D of $\Delta^{|\mathcal{M}|-1}$ is $\sqrt{|\mathcal{M}|}$, the bound (12) that gives us G and the theorem by Zinkevich (2003) as formulated by Hazan (2006) in Theorem 2.1.

Algorithm. Algorithm 2 shows how to efficiently compute a convex mixture environment. It uses the notation λ_i to compactly denote the vector $(\lambda_i^{\rho_1}, \ldots \lambda_i^{\rho_{|\mathcal{M}|}})$ formed from the weights of each environment model in $\mathcal{M}$ at time i. The subroutine SIMPLEXPROJECT projects an arbitrary vector in $\mathbb{R}^{|\mathcal{M}|}$ onto the closest (in terms of Euclidean Distance) point inside the probability simplex $\Delta^{|\mathcal{M}|-1}$. The pseudocode for this routine, derived from the technique presented by Chen and Ye (2011), is given in Algorithm 3; it runs in $O(|\mathcal{M}| \log |\mathcal{M}|)$ time. The SORTDESCENDING subroutine in Algorithm 3 returns a vector y whose components $y_1, \ldots, y_d$ are a permutation of the components of the input vector satisfying $y_1 \geq y_2 \cdots \geq y_d$. The overall complexity of the algorithm (not including the cost of running the models in $\mathcal{M}$) is $O(n|\mathcal{M}| \log |\mathcal{M}|)$, and can be computed incrementally using $O(|\mathcal{M}| \log |\mathcal{M}|)$ time to process each percept.

3.4   A Second Order Method

Additionally, we can exploit a stronger property of our class of loss functions to describe a more computationally demanding algorithm with better redundancy behaviour. To do this, we begin by showing that our class of loss functions is α-exp-concave. Recall that a function f is said to be α-exp-concave for a real $\alpha > 0$ if the function $\exp\{-\alpha f(\cdot)\}$ is concave.

Proposition 3. $\forall n \in \mathbb{N}, \forall ax_{1:n} \in (\mathcal{A} \times \mathcal{X})^n, \ell_n(\cdot; ax_{1:n})$ is 1-exp-concave.

Proof. $\forall n \in \mathbb{N}, \forall ax_{1:n} \in (\mathcal{A} \times \mathcal{X})^n$, observe that

$$\exp\{-\alpha \, \ell_n(\lambda_n \, ; ax_{1:n})\} = \left(\sum_{\rho \in \mathcal{M}} \lambda_n^\rho \, \rho(x_n \mid ax_{<n}a_n) \right)^\alpha .$$

Thus when $\alpha = 1$, $\exp\{-\alpha \, \ell_n(\cdot; ax_{1:n})\}$ is a convex combination of conditional probabilities, which is a concave function. Hence $\ell_n(\cdot; ax_{1:n})$ is 1-exp-concave.

This property, along with our previous upper bound on the Euclidean norm of the gradient of the loss, permits us to use the second order ONLINENEWTONSTEP method of Hazan et al. (2006) in place of Algorithm 2. The resultant method would enjoy a guaranteed redundancy of $O(\log n)$, at the cost of a more complicated implementation whose space complexity is $O(|\mathcal{M}|^2)$, and whose *per time-step* complexity is $O(|\mathcal{M}|^2)$ plus the cost of solving a convex quadratic program to compute a generalized projection onto the probability simplex. We defer a more thorough empirical comparison between these two approaches to future work.

4 Conclusion

This paper has described a number of principled ensemble techniques for universal reinforcement learning agents. Each technique works by efficiently combining a set of existing environment models into a single, more powerful model. We expect these techniques to play an important role in future AIXI approximations. For example, the MC-AIXI agent could be extended by using these techniques to combine multiple instantiations of FAC-CTW, with each instantiation using a different notion of context as per Section 9.3 of the work of Veness et al. (2011).

Acknowledgments. This work was supported by ARC grant DP0988049.

References

Boyd, S., Vandenberghe, L.: Convex Optimization. Cambridge University Press (2004)

Chen, Y., Ye, X.: Projection Onto A Simplex. ArXiv e-prints 1101.6081 (January 2011)

Van Erven, T., Grünwald, P., De Rooij, S.: Catching Up Faster in Bayesian Model Selection and Model Averaging. In: Platt, J.C., Koller, D., Singer, Y., Roweis, S. (eds.) Advances in Neural Information Processing Systems 20, pp. 417–424. MIT Press, Cambridge (2008)

Hazan, E.: Efficient algorithms for online convex optimization and their applications. PhD thesis, Princeton, NJ, USA (2006)

Hazan, E., Kalai, A., Kale, S., Agarwal, A.: Logarithmic Regret Algorithms for Online Convex Optimization. In: Lugosi, G., Simon, H.U. (eds.) COLT 2006. LNCS (LNAI), vol. 4005, pp. 499–513. Springer, Heidelberg (2006)

Herbster, M., Warmuth, M.K.: Tracking the best expert. Machine Learning 32, 151–178 (1998)

Hutter, M.: Universal Artificial Intelligence: Sequential Decisions Based on Algorithmic Probability. Springer (2005)

Mahoney, M.: Adaptive weighing of context models for lossless data compression. Technical report, Florida Institute of Technology (2005)

Mattern, C.: Mixing strategies in data compression. In: Data Compression Conference (DCC), pp. 337–346 (2012)

Sutton, R.S., Barto, A.G.: Reinforcement Learning: An Introduction. MIT Press (1998)

Veness, J., Ng, K.S., Hutter, M., Silver, D.: Reinforcement learning via AIXI approximation. In: Proc. 24th AAAI Conference on Artificial Intelligence, Atlanta, pp. 605–611. AAAI Press (2010)

Veness, J., Ng, K.S., Hutter, M., Uther, W., Silver, D.: A Monte Carlo AIXI approximation. Journal of Artificial Intelligence Research 40, 95–142 (2011)

Veness, J., Ng, K.S., Hutter, M., Bowling, M.H.: Context Tree Switching. In: Data Compression Conference (DCC), pp. 327–336 (2012)

Volf, P.A.J., Willems, F.M.J.: Switching between two universal source coding algorithms. In: Data Compression Conference, pp. 491–500 (1998)

Willems, F.M.J., Shtarkov, Y.M., Tjalkens, T.J.: The Context Tree Weighting Method: Basic Properties. IEEE Transactions on Information Theory 41, 653–664 (1995)

Zinkevich, M.: Online convex programming and generalized infinitesimal gradient ascent. In: ICML, pp. 928–936 (2003)

Motivation Management in AGI Systems

Pei Wang

Department of Computer and Information Sciences
Temple University, Philadelphia, USA
`pei.wang@temple.edu`

Abstract. AGI systems should be able to manage its motivations or goals that are persistent, spontaneous, mutually restricting, and changing over time. A mechanism for handles this kind of goals is introduced and discussed.

1 Properties of Goals in AGI Systems

In a broad sense, all AI systems are "goal-oriented", in that every activity in it serves certain purpose. Researchers have been using notions like "motivation", "drive", "need", "goal", "task", and "intention" to indicate this *teleological* aspect of the system. In this paper, they are all called "goals", since the differences among these notions are not significant for this discussion. No matter what we call it, a process in such a system points to a certain destination, and it is against this destination that the system's progress and success are evaluated. In this broad sense, we do not require every goal to be explicitly represented or consciously known to the system.

In the context of AGI, some related topics have been discussed from different perspectives [1–4], though there are still many issues to be resolved. In this paper, we do not focus on the *content* of goals in AGI systems, like [1, 3], but on the general *properties* of goals, as well as on how they should be managed in the system. In AI, existing works are summarized in [5–7], though the situation is more or less different in the context of AGI, with the stressing on the versatility and unity of the system.

In the following we will discuss several questions:

- Can the system achieves its goals one after another? If not, when to switch the effort from one goal to another?
- Can the co-existing goals be assumed to be compatible with each other? If not, how to handle their conflicts?
- Can the goals change over time? If yes, why and how?
- Can the system produce its own goals? If yes, will it be out of control?

Before discussing these questions in the AGI context, let us consider the classical case of a *computation process* in a Turing Machine [8]. In this situation, the unique "goal" of the process is specified by the *final states* of the machine, which are predetermined, constant, and reachable. A traditional computer system typically has multiple running programs at any given moment, and each of which

J. Bach, B. Goertzel, and M. Iklé (Eds.): AGI 2012, LNAI 7716, pp. 352–361, 2012.
© Springer-Verlag Berlin Heidelberg 2012

corresponds to such a goal-guided process. Usually these processes are mutually *compatible*, in the sense that one does not prevent another to be reached. From time to time, there are processes start, while some others stop, so the "current goals" change, though remains a subset of all the possible goals of the system, which correspond to the programs in the system. All these goals are given be the designers and users of the system, so no goal really comes from the system *itself*. Since this situation is very simple, it is unnecessary to be described using fancy words like "goal" or "motivation".

However, the situation is not so simple for AGI systems. In the following let us discuss the four questions raised previously one by one.

Transient vs. Persistent

The goals in traditional computer systems are *transient*, in the sense that each of them only exists for a relatively short time, from its creation to its satisfaction, corresponding to the beginning and ending of a computational process. Even when a program is repeatedly executed, the corresponding goal is usually not explicitly related to its previous occurrence.

Many AI systems also specify their goals in this way, that is, as "states satisfying particular conditions" [9], where the process stop and the system is reset to its initial state with respect to this process. The most typical examples are the systems doing state-space search, such as GPS [10].

On the contrary, in AGI systems, many (though not all) goals will be *persistent*, in the sense that once created, such a goal may last in the lifetime of the system. Examples of persistent goals can be found everywhere in the human mind, and many of them are also clearly desirable or inevitable in AGI systems, such as "be self-protective" and "to acquire resources" [1, 11].

This type of goals cannot be treated as final states where process stops. For one reason, such a "state" may never be actually reached, but serves merely as the direction for the system to move. Furthermore, even if it is achieved at a given moment, the system should not consider it done and does not think about it anymore, but has to prevent the achievement from being destroyed by future events.

For the above reasons, the system cannot treat a persistent goal as the ending point of a process, but a destination to be approached or a status to be preserved, and to decide when to stop the process by some other criteria, such as the quality of the obtained result (such as a "satisfying threshold") or the cost of the processing (such as an "expense budget").

Now we see that an optimization problem fall into this category, as far as the system cannot prove whether a given candidate answer is optimal or not. In AI, many learning techniques have this nature, such as genetic algorithm [12] and reinforcement learning [13]. In such a system, the goal is to optimize a measurement ("fitness", "reward", or "utility"), and the processing typically stops before all possibilities have been tried. If there is a fixed threshold, then the persistent goal is converted into a transient goal, by treating all states above the threshold as final states. However, this is not the only option. The persistence nature will be handled better if such a goal is pursued using an anytime algorithm

[14] and let the stop decision be made in a context-sensitive way, or the pursuing of the goal may never stop, though become dormant from time to time.

Compatible vs. Restricting

Generally speaking, all interesting systems have multiples goals, since a non-trivial goal is almost always achieved though the achieving of its subgoals or derived goals. Even so, in traditional systems it is usually more fruitful to consider a single goal at a time. This is valid, because in the terminology of graph theory, the goals in such a system can be considered as a "forest", consisting of trees where the predecessor-successor relation between nodes represents the supergoal-subgoal relation between goals. Normally, the top-level, or *root*, goals in disjoint trees are *mutually compatible*, in the sense that the achieving of one does not prevent another from being achieved, otherwise the goals cannot coexist in the same system.

In many systems, each goal-tree can be represented by its root, because

1. The subgoals are recursively created as means to achieve the root goal;
2. As far as the goal-derivation process is designed correctly, the effects of the subgoal should be implied by the effects of the root goal;
3. The duration in which each subgoal exists is a sub-interval of the duration in which the root goal exist.

For these reasons, to analyze the goals of such a system, it usually suffices to only consider the top-level goals. Their subgoals may cause some issues, such as one may have another as a prerequisite, or the two may compete for a piece of resource, but these issues usually can be resolved by careful scheduling.

For AGI systems, however, this is not the case anymore. Even if the compatibility of the top-level goals can still be assumed (actually even this assumption is shaky), it definitely cannot be assumed for the subgoals derived from them. This is the case because a realistic AGI system is not omniscient, and at the same time has to deal with goals for which it has uncertain and incomplete information. Consequently, the goal derivation is only based on the system's current beliefs, which are not absolutely true. For example, if the system beliefs that event E_1 implies event E_2, then when the latter becomes a goal, the former may be derived as another goal. However, this situation is different from the above classical supergoal-subgoal relation, because E_1 and E_2 may turn out to be irrelevant, or even contradictory, to each other.

When the goals involved are persistent, the situation become even more complicated, because the existing period of a "subgoal" may be beyond that of the "supergoal" from which it was derived. Though it may sound irrational, there is an explanation for an adaptive system to do so, since a goal derived for one reason may be valuable for another purpose, or for similar purposes in the future, so becomes desirable *for its own sake*. It should not sound too strange to us, because many human motivations initially appear as means to achieve other ends. Psychologist Allport called this phenomenon "functional autonomy of motives" [15], and it can also explain many Freudian notions, such as "compensation" and "sublimation". It has been argued that in an adaptive system working with insufficient knowledge and resources, such a phenomenon is inevitable [16].

It means that in such a system though goal H is derived as a way to achieve goal G, the former nevertheless may gradually gain independence. For this reason, the traditional "supergoal-subgoal" relation cannot be assumed anymore between an original goal and a derived goal. The relation between the two may only be *historical*, rather than *logical*.

As a result, the goals in an AGI system should be considered as *mutually restricting*, in the sense that the achieving of one sometimes does prevent another from being achieved, or at least makes it more difficult. To handle that requires the goal management mechanism to prioritize the existing goals for resource allocation, as well as to resolve their conflicts in action selection.

Constant vs. Variable

There are several reasons to assume that in an AGI system the goals may change from time to time: the environment changes, the system's internal needs change (such as its energy reserves), and as discussed above, the overall *goal complex* of the system evolves as new goals are derived, even when the original goal remains the same.

Due to the resource restriction, an AGI system usually cannot take all of its existing goals into consideration at every moment. Instead, it has to focus on different goals at different moments. As a result, even though the system in its whole lifetime has many goals, at a moment usually only a small number of them are in effect in determining which action to take. These "effective goals" are what matters when the system's behavior is predicted or explained, not the dormant goals, though the latter do exist in the system, and some may have higher levels of significance in the system's lifetime.

If we take the goal complex of an AGI system as a whole, we should assume that it changes as the system runs, and the change is not circular, nor does it converge to a stable state — a system may never have identical goal-states in its lifetime, and that is arguably the case for a human being. On the other hand, the change is not pure random, or can be specified according to a probability distribution, because there will be new goals generated, which cannot be logically reduced into the previous goals.

For these reasons, it is not proper to assume that an AGI system always chooses or evaluates its actions according to a constant goal, no matter how that goal is specified or interpreted.

Mandatory vs. Spontaneous

Many authors have expressed the opinion that a truly intelligent system should be "autonomous" [4–6, 17] or "self-motivated" [2], though what that exactly means differ from author to author. Intuitively speaking, the consensus is that such a system should behave according to goals of its own choice or creation.

Some people consider this expectation impossible or even self-contradictory. After all, an AI system is designed, directly or indirectly, by human designers, who, among other things, specifies the system's (initial) goals. In this situation, how can the system have any goal that is not created, directly or indirectly, by its designer?

Actually we have answered this question. Previously, it has be explained that for an adaptive systems, even though all of its *initial* goals are specified by its designer as part of the system's initial state, the same cannot be said about the *derived* goals, which are decided by both the initial goals and the beliefs of the system. When the beliefs are learned from the system's experience, the goal complex of the system does not only depend on its initial design (its *nature*), but also on its experience (its *nurture*). When the system's experience is complicated enough, especially when it is not folly controlled by a tutor, the system may have goals that cannot be fairly attributed to anyone but *the system itself.*

Such a system still have *mandatory* goals that are either built-in by its designer, or imposed-upon by a user via its user interface. But at the same time, the system derives new goals recursively from the existing goals, and some of them can be considered as *spontaneous*, in the sense that they are not destined by the system's design, but mostly come out of the system's idiosyncratic history. Due to the functional autonomy phenomenon, these goals are not logically related to the initial goals, though they are derived from the latter. As the system gets more and more experience, it becomes more and more autonomous, in the sense that its behaviors are more and more oriented to its own goals.

2   Motivation Management in NARS

As a concrete example of systems with goals that are *persistent, mutually restricting, variable*, and *spontaneous*, in the following we will introduce the representation and processing of motivations in NARS.

NARS is an AGI built in the framework of a reasoning system, based on the theory that "intelligence" is the ability of adaptation with insufficient knowledge and resources [16, 18]. This paper only describes the motivation management, plus the directly related aspects, of the system.

As many other systems, NARS can be analyzed at more than one level of description, where some "motivations" or "goals" can be recognized. For example, obviously every program consisting of NARS can be seen as goal-oriented, where the "goal" can be as simple as adding two numbers together. However, to analyze the system at such a level does not tell us much about its overall behaviors. Therefore, in the following we treat NARS as a whole, to see that type of "tasks" it can carry out.

Every task in NARS has a *statement* as its content, which is a sentence of a formal language whose grammar and semantics are accurately specified [16, 18]. There are three types of *task* defined in NARS:

Judgment: In a judgment, the statement represents a conceptual relation experienced by the system, with a *truth-value* indicating the evidential support the statement gets. A truth-value consists of a *frequency* in [0, 1], which is the ratio of positive evidence among available evidence, and a *confidence* in (0, 1), which is the ratio of currently available evidence among all available evidence at a moment in the near future. Since the system is always open to new evidence, a confidence value can never reach is upper bound 1.0.

Goal: In a goal, the statement represents a conceptual relation to be established by changing the environment or the system itself. A goal has a *desire-value* attached, which is a variant of truth-value, indicating the evidential support for the statement to be desired by the system.

Question: In a question, the statement represents a conceptual relation whose truth-value or desire-value needs to be determined. A question may contain variables to be instantiated, corresponding to the *wh-questions* in a natural language.

To manage the resource competition among the tasks, in NARS each task is given a *priority-value* to indicate its relative priority in resource allocation at the moment.

Therefore, the *task* in NARS corresponds to what we call "motivation" or "goal" in general discussions, while the *goal* in NARS corresponds to a specific type of it. The other two types are distinguished from it, since they are processed differently in NARS, a reasoning system.

The tasks in NARS have two origins: *input* or *derived*, where the former are assigned to the system by its designer or user, while the latter are generated by the inference rules from the former (directly or indirectly) according to the beliefs of the system.

Input tasks can be either implanted into the system as part of its initial state, or assigned to the system through the user interface. As a general-purpose system, NARS can accept input tasks of any content, as far as they are expressible in its representation language, which allows arbitrary conceptual relations. The designer and users of the system can also assign priority-values to input tasks to influence the system's resource allocation.

NARS runs by repeating a working cycle, each time on a selected task, which can be either input or derived. What is done to a task depends on its type:

Judgment: A judgment contains new information to be absorbed. The system uses it to revise the previous belief on the content to form a updated belief, to solve the pending goals or questions, and to spontaneously derive its implications using other beliefs. Unlike an ordinary database or knowledge base, NARS does not simply insert new knowledge into a storage, and let it wait there passively for future queries; instead, it actively revises and updates the system's beliefs, as well as makes predictions about future situation. This process recursively derives new judgments as tasks.

Goal: When a goal is under processing, the system first checks its content against the reality to see whether somehow the request has already been satisfied. If not, the next step is to check whether there is an executable operation that will directly satisfy the request. If neither is the case, the system will use its beliefs to derive new candidate goals as means to achieve the current goal. A candidate goal will not be directly pursued, but is used to adjust the desire-value of the corresponding statement. After the adjustment, if the desire-value of the statement is high enough, and the system believes that there is a way to achieve it, a corresponding goal will be generated, and pursued side-by-side with its "parent" goal.

Question: When a question is under processing, the system keeps looking for the answer that is the current best (in terms of truth-value and simplicity). If the question is an input task, such answers are reported to corresponding user as soon as they are found. In the meanwhile, derived questions are recursively produced by using the inference rules *backwards*, so that an answer to the derived, or "child", question will produce an answer to the "parent" question. As a result, an input question may obtain multiple answers, each of which is better than the previous ones (as evaluated by the system), similar to the performance of an anytime algorithm [14].

For a task, its processing may contain any number of working cycles, depending on how many time it is selected for processing, which is proportional to its priority-value. Though an input task comes with a given priority-value, the system can adjust it according to the result of processing. For a derived task, its priority-value is initially determined and later adjusted by the system according to several factors. Overall, the priority-value of a task represents its urgency, plausibility to be achieved, and relevance to the current situation. Managed by a forgetting mechanism, all priority-values decay gradually, and tasks with the lowest priority-values will be removed when the storage space is in short supply.

Now we can see why the tasks in NARS have the properties listed previously:

- A task is *persistent*, since its processing rarely stops at its "logical end" — except in trivial situations, the system cannot exhaust all implications for a *judgment* task, nor can it find a perfect solution for a task which is a *goal* or a *question*. Instead, each time a task is processed, it is *partially achieved*, so its priority-value is deceased. When a task stops being processed, it is because its priority-value is too low, not because it has been fully achieved. How long a task lives depends on many factors.
- Tasks are *mutually restricting* because there is no requirement for the input tasks to be logically consistent in what they want the system to do. Furthermore, the task derivation is carried out according to the system's beliefs at the moment, which may be wrong. Finally, even compatible tasks compete with each other for the system's limited resources, so the achieving of one may cause another to be ignored temporarily or permanently.
- The overall task complex is *variable* because new (input and derived) tasks are added constantly to the system, while some old tasks get forgot gradually. Also, due to resource restriction, only a small part of the task complex is effective at a given moment, and controls the system's behaviors. Which task is in this active region changes from time to time.
- Certain tasks are *spontaneous* in the sense that they are only historically and remotely related to input tasks, and owe their existence mostly to the system's experience. Therefore, they should be considered as the system's *own* tasks. As the system runs, it tends to become more and more autonomous and self-motivated.

3   Implication and Discussion

The above analysis shows that unlike the situation in ordinary computer systems and "narrow AI" systems, motivation management in an AGI system is more similar to the situation in the human mind. This is a natural consequence of the requirement of being general-purpose and working in realistic environments.

On one hand, an AGI system should not be considered as a problem-solving system that processes its goals one by one, as in BDI agents [19]. On the other hand, it should not be considered as guided by a constant ultimate goal, from which all the other motivations are logically derived as subgoals.

From a pure mathematical point of view, it is possible to refer to the whole goal complex or motivational mechanism as a single "goal" (like talking about the resultant of several forces in different directions), which changes from time to time, as the guidance of the system. However, to actually design or analyze an AGI system in this way is very difficult, if not impossible, and it is much easier and more clear to explicitly identify the individual factors, which may come and go from time to time, and compete with each other on what the system should think and do at each moment. For this reason, it is not a good idea for an AGI system to be designed in the frameworks where a single goal is assumed, such as evolutionary learning, program search, or reinforcement learning, despite of their other advantages [20, 21].

The major conclusion argued in this paper is that an AGI system should always maintain a goal structure (or whatever it is called) which contains multiple goals that are separately specified, with the properties that

- Some of the goals are accurately specified, and can be fully achieved, while some others are vaguely specified and only partially achievable, but nevertheless have impact on the system's decisions.
- The goals may conflict with each other on what the system should do at a moment, and cannot be achieved all together. Very often the system has to make compromises among the goals.
- Due to the restriction in computational resources, the system cannot take all existing goals into account when making each decision, and nor can it keep a complete record of the goal derivation history.
- The designers and users are responsible for the input goals of an AGI system, from which all the other goals are derived, according to the system's experience. There is no guarantee that the derived goals will be logically consistent with the input goals, except in highly simplified situations.

One area that is closely related to goal management is AI ethics. The previous discussions focused on the goal the designers assign to an AGI system ("super goal" or "final goal"), with the implicit assumption that such a goal will decide the consequences caused by the A(G)I systems. However, the above analysis shows that though the input goals are indeed important, they are not the dominating factor that decides the broad impact of AI to human society. Since no AGI system can be omniscient and omnipotent, to be "general-purpose" means such a system has to handle problems for which its knowledge and resources are insufficient [16, 18], and one direct consequence is that its actions may produce unanticipated results. This consequence, plus the previous conclusion that the effective goal for an action may be inconsistent with the input goals, will render many of the previous suggestions mostly irrelevant to AI ethics.

For example, Yudkowsky's "Friendly AI" agenda is based on the assumption that "a true AI might remain knowably stable in its goals, even after carrying out a large number of self-modifications" [22]. The problem about this assumption is that unless we are talking about an axiomatic system with unlimited resources, we cannot assume the system can accurately know the consequence of its actions. Furthermore, as argued previously, the goals in an intelligent system inevitable change as its experience grows, which is not necessarily a bad thing — after all, our "human nature" gradually grows out of, and deviates from, our "animal nature", at both the species level and the individual level.

Omohundro argued that no matter what input goals are given to an AGI system, it usually will derive some common "basic drives", including "be self-protective" and "to acquire resources" [1], which leads some people to worry that such a system will become unethical. According to our previous analysis, the producing of these goals are indeed very likely, but it is only half of the story. A system with a resource-acquisition goal does not necessarily attempts to achieve it at all cost, without considering its other goals. Again, consider the human beings — everyone has some goals that can become dangerous (either to oneself or to the others) *if pursued at all costs*. The proper solution, both to human ethics and to AGI ethics, is to prevent this kind of goal from *becoming dominant*, rather than from *being formed*.

A similar analysis can be applied to the "the instrumental convergence thesis" of Bostrom [11]: though it is reasonable to assume the generation of certain "intermediary goals", there is no enough reason to believe that they will converge, independent of the system's experience. The problem comes from the belief that a "superintelligence" would be "more likely to achieve her final goals" [11]. Even though it is possible for an AGI to have more computational power and more experience than human beings, that does not make it omniscient and omnipotent. As argued in detail in [16], an AGI will still be bounded by insufficient knowledge and resources, which means it cannot realize all of its goals.

In summary, "intelligence" and "autonomy" are arguably two sides of the same coin. Therefore, the motivational mechanism in AGI systems will have properties that are more similar to those of the human beings than those of the traditional computer systems. Some of these properties are desired, while some others provide challenges to AGI research. None of the challenges has been proved unsolvable, though they demand novel ideas and approaches.

References

1. Omohundro, S.M.: The basic AI drives. In: Proceedings of AGI 2008, pp. 483–492 (2008)
2. Liu, D., Schubert, L.: Incorporating planning and reasoning into a self-motivated, communicative agent. In: Proceedings of AGI 2009, pp. 108–113 (2009)

3. Bach, J.: A Motivational System for Cognitive AI. In: Schmidhuber, J., Thórisson, K.R., Looks, M. (eds.) AGI 2011. LNCS (LNAI), vol. 6830, pp. 232–242. Springer, Heidelberg (2011)
4. Thórisson, K.R., Helgasson, H.P.: Cognitive architectures and autonomy: A comparative review. Journal of Artificial General Intelligence 3(2), 1–30 (2012)
5. Beaudoin, L.P.: Goal processing in autonomous agents. PhD thesis, School of Computer Science, The University of Birmingham (1994)
6. Norman, T.J.F.: Motivation-based direction of planning attention in agents with goal autonomy. PhD thesis, Department of Computer Science, University College London (1997)
7. Hawes, N.: A survey of motivation frameworks for intelligent systems. Artificial Intelligence 175(5-6), 1020–1036 (2011)
8. Hopcroft, J.E., Ullman, J.D.: Introduction to Automata Theory, Language, and Computation. Addison-Wesley, Reading (1979)
9. Wellman, M.P., Doyle, J.: Preferential semantics for goals. In: Proceedings of AAAI 1991, pp. 698–703 (1991)
10. Newell, A., Simon, H.A.: GPS, a program that simulates human thought. In: Feigenbaum, E.A., Feldman, J. (eds.) Computers and Thought, pp. 279–293. McGraw-Hill, New York (1963)
11. Bostrom, N.: The superintelligent will: Motivation and instrumental rationality in advanced artificial agents. Minds and Machines (2012)
12. Holland, J.H.: Escaping brittleness: the possibilities of general purpose learning algorithms applied to parallel rule-based systems. In: Michalski, R.S., Carbonell, J.G., Mitchell, T.M. (eds.) Machine Learning: An Artificial Intelligence Approach, vol. II, pp. 593–624. Morgan Kaufmann, Los Altos (1986)
13. Sutton, R.S., Barto, A.G.: Reinforcement Learning: An Introduction. MIT Press, Cambridge (1998)
14. Dean, T., Boddy, M.: An analysis of time-dependent planning. In: Proceedings of AAAI 1988, pp. 49–54 (1988)
15. Allport, G.W.: The functional autonomy of motives. American Journal of Psychology 50, 141–156 (1937)
16. Wang, P.: Rigid Flexibility: The Logic of Intelligence. Springer, Dordrecht (2006)
17. Bach, J.: Seven principles of synthetic intelligence. In: Proceedings of AGI 2008, pp. 63–74 (2008)
18. Wang, P.: Non-Axiomatic Logic: A Model of Intelligent Reasoning. World Scientific, Singapore (in press, 2012)
19. Rao, A.S., Georgeff, M.P.: BDI-agents: from theory to practice. In: Proceedings of the First International Conference on Multiagent Systems (1995)
20. Schmidhuber, J.: The new AI: General & sound & relevant for physics. In: Goertzel, B., Pennachin, C. (eds.) Artificial General Intelligence, pp. 175–198. Springer, Berlin (2007)
21. Hutter, M.: Feature reinforcement learning: Part I. Unstructured MDPs. Journal of Artificial General Intelligence 1, 3–24 (2009)
22. Yudkowsky, E.: Artificial intelligence as a positive and negative factor in global risk. In: Bostrom, N., Cirkovic, M. (eds.) Global Catastrophic Risks, pp. 308–345. Oxford University Press (2008)

Hippocampal Formation Mechanism Will Inspire Frame Generation for Building an Artificial General Intelligence

Hiroshi Yamakawa

FUJITSU LABORATORIES LTD.
1-1 Kamikodanaka 4-chome, Nakahara-ku, Kawasaki, Kanagawa, 211-8588, Japan
ymkw@jp.fujitsu.com

Abstract. The author argues that an artificial general intelligence (AGI) system capable of adapting to various domains autonomously must have the ability to develop domain-specific frames within a practical amount of time; however, current AI technologies are insufficient to achieve this. Frames are knowledge representations which consist of sets of variables. In the frame generation procedure, a significant subprocedure, that of frame candidate generation by variable assimilation, has not yet been realized because of the huge hypothesis space. Representations that can express various relationships among variables in the system can assist in developing this subprocedure, but no such representations have heretofore been known. Through intimate collaboration with neuroscientists, the author searched for clues for such representations in the neuroscience field. Then, the author examined neuroscientific research results to conclude the following: (A) hippocampal formation (HCF) is in charge of frame generation, and (B) distribution equivalent groups (DEGs) are the representations used by HCF for expressing variable relationships. (B) is based on two findings on HCF, namely the phase precession phenomenon and configural association theory. The author used binary-variable assumption to estimate that DEGs exhibit sufficient diversity. Having determined the brain region responsible for a critical function necessary to realize AGI and information representation for that function, this paper offers a foundation for further research into the algorithms used in brain. These results can contribute to the realization of an AGI.

Keywords: computational theory, relationship equivalence, neocortex, variable assimilation, frame problem, hippocampus, relation index, neuroscience.

1   Introduction

In general, empirical intelligence is based on comparisons of multiple cases (instance/ row) within a "frame." A frame is a well-known declarative knowledge representation; each frame is composed of a frame name and a variable set (including labels for the variables) in which each variable has a value that matches a case. As M. Minsky stated [1], human knowledge is thought to be composed of multiple frames which exist within the brain. As for the current state of artificial intelligence (AI) and machine learning, human beings must design a frame or frame candidates. For example, data analysts use programming languages to define arrays of variables and/or classes

J. Bach, B. Goertzel, and M. Iklé (Eds.): AGI 2012, LNAI 7716, pp. 362–371, 2012.
© Springer-Verlag Berlin Heidelberg 2012

as frames. Model selection techniques often chose likely frames from a set of frame candidates (FCs). Tremendous efforts have been made to design various frames in every field; today, domain-specific AI systems can surpass humans in ability.

However, in order to create an artificial general intelligence (AGI), a system must be able to generate domain-specific frames autonomously. Frame generation techniques implemented by selecting a part of a given frame are presently available. For example, feature selection techniques choose useful variables and clustering techniques extract sets of cases as new concepts. Moreover, techniques such as COBWEB [2] and situation decomposition [3] extract concepts by selecting both variables and cases simultaneously. However, these techniques only extract parts of human-designed frames. Thus, we cannot expect creative prediction ability achieved using these techniques to exceed the frame designers' vision. In this paper, I detail a first step toward autonomous frame generation technology beyond this limitation.

2   Computational Theory for Frame Generation

From the above-mentioned background information, it can be surmised that the ability to combine different types of knowledge autonomously is necessary for an AGI. Thus, this section contains an explanation of a computational theory for generating new frames by combining multiple frames together. Here, the equivalence of relationships among variables will play an important role in the practical implementation.

2.1   Frame Generation by Variable Assimilation

There are two kinds of processes to join two frames: the process that assimilates the cases between the frames and the process that assimilates the variables (left side of Fig. 1). In the former process, case assimilations are mediated by the variables shared by both frames ('D' in Fig. 1). Such operations are often used for databases.

By contrast, the latter process generates new frames by joining different cases through assimilating variables (hereinafter, "variable assimilation"). Because this function is related to the frame problem[1], little progress has been seen in research on this subject. The variable assimilation ability is related to high-level intelligences that are well developed in humans, such as analogy, creativity and mimicry. In consideration of this, the heretofore unachieved frame generation ability based on variable assimilation is probably an essential element for creating an AGI. Therefore, a new computational theory to achieve such a function is highly desirable.

On the other hand, some abilities related to variable assimilation have been already realized to a considerable extent because variable assimilation can sometimes be defined as spatial coordinate transformation. For example, many animals can transform from egocentric coordinates to allocentric coordinates for navigation and/or homing. Another example is that visual object recognition systems have the ability to transform input images via operations such as translation, rotation and zoom.

---

[1] This is a famous fundamental problem for AI; it is caused by the limitless increases in cost for choosing the variables required to perform a target task in an open environment.

2.2   Relationships Index Supports Frame Candidate (FC) Generation

Because pieces of knowledge in different domains are joined by using a symbolic relationship structure in analogy processes [5], I assumed that combining two sub-spaces which share some kind of equivalent relationship was likely to be a successful approach for generating a frame by variable assimilation. Here, "subspace" refers to a partial space composed of subsets of variables and "dimensionality" refers to the number of variables in those subsets.

In the example shown in Fig. 1, two subspaces with three variables extracted from two different frames, one containing variables B, A and C and the other containing variables E, G and F, are joined together. Here, the relationship between variables B and A and that between E and G are equivalent, as well as the relationship between A and C and that between G and F. I call the presence of such secondary relationships "relationship equivalence." Based on the relationship equivalence shown in this ex-ample, FCs can be generated by assimilating variable B to E, A to G, and C to F.

I denote the total number of variables within a system (including multiple frames) by N and the total number of all available d-dimensional subspaces, each of which contains a unique combination of d variables chosen from all variables, by $S_N(d)$, so $S_N(d) = {}_NC_d$. Thus, the maximum number of paired frames which can be generated is ${}_NC_d \times {}_NC_d$; this limit is a combination of the subspaces. In order to create a practical algorithm against the $O(N^{2d})$ hypothesis space, I needed a technique for drastically reducing the search space.

To focus on the heretofore unachieved computational function, I divided the frame generation procedure into two sequential subprocedures. The first subprocedure, which is for frame candidate (FC) generation, enumerates likely candidates at a prac-tical calculation cost. The second subprocedure, which is for frame verification, selects and improves frames. Because the number of FCs is assumed to be appro-priately limited by the former subprocedure, the latter subprocedure can be realized by conventional technology. In the latter subprocedure, criteria such as the mutual information and situation decomposition criteria [3] can be used for evaluating the appropriateness of frames. In the FC generation subprocedure, to enumerate more FCs which can pass the following verification subprocedure, an equivalent relation-ship among two combined subspaces of an FC should be considered more appropriate as a frame. A relationships index, which categorizes diverse, appropriate subspaces, will help improve the efficiency of FC generation.

This proposed computational theory for frame generation will lead to the develop-ment of flexible intelligence technologies and promote the realization of an AGI. The dominant problem is the implementation of an FC generation function because the huge hypothesis space prevents a practical algorithm for implementing this func-tion from being developed. An index of appropriate relationships among variables will assist in the development of an FC generation subprocedure. However, the re-presentation of these relationships is not yet clear.

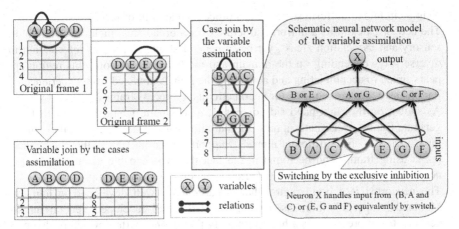

Fig. 1. A variable assimilation (VA) process and its neural network model for frame generation Variables from both frames are matched up with using relational structure in VA process

In the brain, many frame generation abilities are thought to be nonverbal. For example, the spatial coordinate transformation ability (Subsection 2.1) is common to many animals that do not speak any language. It is also known that subconscious intuition and spatial reasoning play important roles in the thinking ability of humans [4]. Research has been conducted on relationship equivalence. The structural mapping theory explains analogies as transferring knowledge from the base field to the target field based on the relationship equivalence among symbolic objects [5]. Neural network models can autonomously discover the relationships among variables from verbal clues [6]. However, these studies are based on symbolic relationships; they cannot explain how to represent nonverbal relationships in the brain.

3   Which Brain Region Handles Frame Generation?

As mentioned in Subsection 2.1, the brain most likely flexibly generates frames by variable assimilation, but computer systems can presently do little in this regard. Through close collaboration with neuroscientists, such as the fMRI study on human intuition [7], I searched for clues to create the representations and algorithms for such heretofore unachievable functions for computers [8].

3.1   Frames Are Accumulated on the Neocortex and Activated

To gather clues about FC generation function from the brain, I desired to identify the brain regions that are responsible for this function. However, since it was difficult to directly specify that region, I instead examined the brain region responsible for accumulating and activating frames. The neocortex is the most likely candidate region for the following four reasons; no other proper candidates have been found.

1. Neural circuits of uniform structure can process general information.

   The neocortex exhibits a uniform structure over a broad area, including the motor, sensory and association areas[2], yet has a general ability to process information in diverse ways depending on the domain and modality. Therefore, this region appears suited to accumulating and activating the frames obtained from experience.

2. Parallel switches are required for neural circuits to process frames.

   As shown on the right-hand side of Fig. 1, a schematic neural network that can generate frames necessitates a network that allows for switching in parallel among input variables[3] from different inputs. Support for the possibility that the neocortex is using frames can be found in the fact that it is capable of creating neural networks that switch inputs to local circuits by top-down attention [9].

3. The neocortex is a brain region that is particularly well developed in humans.

   Mammals, especially humans, have particularly well-developed general intelligence. Therefore, there is a high possibility that the neocortex, which is also particularly well developed in humans, supports general intelligence.

4. The information integration function of the neocortex is also suitable for frames.

   The neocortex is thought to have evolved to provide a multi-modal information integration function that brings together auditory, olfactory and tactile input, which is required for mammals to accurately identify external objects in the dark. The function to select the relevant variables required for reasoning through the use of frames is essential for achieving effective integration of information.

3.2   Hippocampal Formation (HCF) Works as the Frame Generator

If the neocortex is the brain region that accumulates and activates frames, it is natural to consider the possibility that frames are also generated within the neocortex. However, I contend that the neocortex is incapable of generating FCs for the reasons to follow in this section. Instead, I believe that hippocampal formation (HCF) is the most probable candidate responsible for generating frames.

Frame generation requires a function to globally integrate the distributed knowledge accumulated locally in individual areas of the neocortex. As already mentioned in Section 2, FC generation requires a function for comparing and categorizing the relationships among variables. If the neocortex has such a function, there must be suitable representations sufficiently diverse to categorize at least 4×10^{12} relationships across different areas of the neocortex[4]. Firing synchronization of neuron populations is a known mechanism for transmitting information directly across different areas of the neocortex; however, the amount of information that can be transmitted by this mechanism is far too small to express the relationships among microscopic neural

---

[2] The neocortex has a functionally differentiated six-layer structure and a column structure. Its basic architecture is the same in all mammals.

[3] Variables can potentially be associated to various substances such as neurons, minicolumns, hyper-columns and cell assemblies in neural networks within the brain.

[4] Even if each variable is assumed to be a hyper column that is a large unit in the neocortex, there are about 2×10^6 variables in the human neocortex [12]. Thus, the number of relationships between two variables numbers 4×10^{12}.

activities. Therefore, the neocortex lacks representations sufficient to categorize neural activity relationships across different areas, so it cannot generate FCs by itself through such representations.

If the neocortex has no function for generating frames by assimilating the variables dispersed through relationship equivalence, HCF is the only plausible candidate capable of having such a function for the following four reasons:

1. HCFs receive projections from a wide area of the neocortex.
   Because HCFs receive information from a wide area of the neocortex through the entorhinal cortex (EC) [10], they can compare distributed variables on the neocortex to generate frames.
2. HCFs memorize experiences before the neocortex.
   First, memories obtained from the external environment as experience are stored in HCFs. Later, they are gradually transported to the neocortex over a period of several months (in the case of humans) [11]. Therefore, the frame representations in the neocortex are likely to be generated in HCFs.
3. HCFs act together with the frame-executable circuit.
   Because HCFs act in collaboration with the EC they presumably can execute a frame function like the neocortex. Therefore, HCFs can use memories seamlessly while transporting such memories to the neocortex.
4. HCFs contain a local circuit for signal exchange.
   In the subregion of HCFs (dentate gyrus and CA3), single-layer neurons form a circuit-like crossbar matrix [13]. These circuits are suited for switching global inputs and outputs and are probably appropriate for searching for FCs.

Then, HCFs are thought to be responsible for generating various pieces of knowledge as frames and for using these frames in collaboration with ECs. In addition, frames are transported to the neocortex over time. These assumptions are consistent with one explanation of the function of HCFs, the relational theory [14].

4   Distribution Equivalent Groups (DEGs) Represent Relationships

In the above arguments, I explained that in order to realize an AGI, a computational theory for generating frames by variable assimilation is a promising approach. I also contended that the neural circuits of HCFs and the ECs provide clues for designing the representations and algorithms necessary for this theory. The most serious problem is how to deal with the huge hypothesis spaces in the process of generating FCs. To overcome this obstacle, the approach of developing an algorithm which uses the relationships among variables is promising. Using clues from findings on HCFs, in this section I discuss probable candidates for representations that express the relationships among variables.

4.1 DEGs as Particular Representations for HCFs

The long history of research on HCFs provides an ample amount of valuable experimental findings as well as theoretical hypotheses. The following two HCF-specific findings are significant in restricting representation of relationships.

First, there is the theta phase precession phenomenon, in which an approximately 5 Hz theta rhythm is generated in HCFs of an animal moving around an experimental field and discrete case sequences, which contain from seven to twelve cases, appear in the theta phase in a time-compressed manner [15]. Secondly, according to the configural association theory [16], which explains the functional role of HCFs, HCFs associate combinations (complexes) of stimuli rather than individual stimuli with the meaning of behaviors. Although an animal suffering from lesions on its HCFs can form simple associative memories between stimuli, it cannot perform tasks by memorizing a number of stimuli all together (e.g., a transverse patterning problem). These particular characteristics of HCFs lead me to assume that each relationship representation is likely to be a set of about ten cases in a multi-dimensional subspace.

Here, I define a Distribution Equivalent Group (DEG), which consists of about ten cases set in a multidimensional subspace in consideration of variable exchange symmetry. This symmetry means that if two distributions are identical when exchanging variables within the subspace, then they belong to same DEG. After all, DEGs are thought to be the representation used by HCFs for variable relationships.

4.2 Binary Variable DEGs for Estimation

In order to estimate the number of DEGs, I assumed a binary variable $\{0, 1\}$ and composed lattices as a set of cells as shown in Fig. 2-A. Cells which contain cases are shaded red. All binary lattice patterns for low dimensional ($d = 1$ or 2) DEGs are shown in Fig. 2-B. Here, the number of cells within a binary lattice is denoted by v, the number of distribution patterns by r, and the number of DEGs by e. The degree of degeneration resulting from symmetry is shown to the right of each lattice. Binary lattices featuring the same number of case-containing cells are presented in the same row, with the total number of distribution patterns indicated at the end of each row.

As shown in the figure, when the subspace dimensionality equals one ($d = 1$), then the number of cells equals two ($v = 2$), and there is no reduction due to symmetry since there are no variables that can be exchanged; therefore, the number of DEGs is four ($e = 4$). When the subspace dimensionality equals two ($d = 2$), then the number of cells is four ($v = 4$), and the degree of reduction is two for the binary lattice in the middle of the second row due to the degeneration of different patterns by variable exchange. In this example, the total number of DEGs is twelve ($e = 12$).

4.3 Representation Diversity of DEGs as Relationships among Variables

As stated in Subsection 2.2, to implement an FC generation function on a computer, pairs of subspaces sharing equivalent relationships must be chosen from high-dimensional data. Assuming this function is performed in the HCF, the number of d-dimensional DEGs (e) used to categorize relationships must exhibit diversity on the same order as the total number of subspaces ($S_N(d)$).

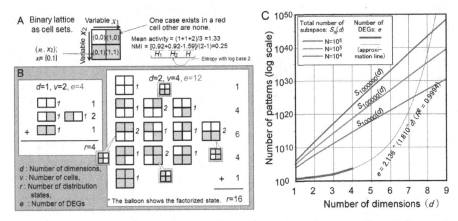

Fig. 2. Pattern of DEGs and number; A: Example of a binary lattice as a cell set, B: Pattern list of low dimensional DEGs, C: Number of DEGs corresponding to subspace dimensionality

The excitatory neurons in the major subregions of HCFs consist of hundreds of thousands (dentate gyrus: about 800,000; CA1: about 400,000; CA3: about 300,000). Therefore, if we assume that variable N is the number of such cells, N falls within the range of 10^5 to 10^6. If using the 2-dimensional DEGs shown in Fig. 2-B as representations, their variety in pattern is only 12. Such a situation obviously lacks sufficient diversity to categorize the total number of subspaces, and as a result equivalent DEGs appear too frequently in many subspaces.

I examined the number of high dimensional DEGs (e) as shown in Fig. 2-C. Although the number of DEGs can actually be counted for DEGs with as many as four dimensions, it is not easy to do for DEGs with higher dimensionality. Thus, the number of DEGs with five or more dimensional subspaces were extrapolated by an approximation function, a second order exponential function of $e = 2.136^\wedge(1.810^\wedge d)$. From this estimation, it was determined that 8-dimensional DEGs have a sufficient number of patterns to categorize the total number of subspaces extractable from more than 100,000 variables ($S_{100000}(d)$). In short, DEGs exhibit sufficient diversity to categorize all combination of subspaces within HCF; they have sufficient capacity for categorizing the relationships among variables in the system.

4.4   Appropriate DEGs within 4-dimensional Patterns (4d-DEGs)

I next analyzed the appropriateness (in terms of predictability and mean activity level[5]) of the DEGs. In this section, I focus on the 3,984 patterns of 4-dimensional DEGs, which are highest dimensionality within those actually counted. Because of the length limit, I will omit an explanation of the algorithm for enumerating 4d-DEGs.

As mentioned in Subsection 2.2, the higher the predictability of newly generated FCs, the greater the chance of their being chosen in the following verification process. Generally, the higher the predictability of DEGs that connect variables in generated FCs, the higher the predictability of the generated FCs. Normalized mutual

---

[5] Activity level refers to the mean number of variables whose values equal 1. (Fig. 2-A)

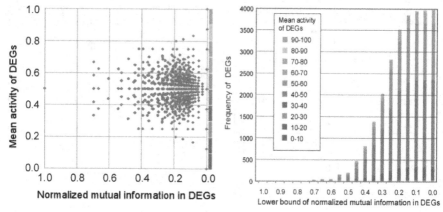

Fig. 3. Profiles of 4d- DEGs; A: Normalized mutual information (NMI) and mean activity of each DEG, B: Number of DEGs over the specified NMI value depending on the mean activity

information (NMI) is estimated for every pattern of DEGs. Here, the NMI value is calculated by taking log base 2 and dividing by d-1 (Fig. 2-A); each cell is assumed to contain either one or zero cases. Because the information encoding of HCFs is thought to be sparse, I also calculated the mean activity[6] of each pattern.

NMI has a peak value of 1, which is obtainable only when the mean activity level is 0.5; the value decreases to 0 toward both ends as shown in Fig. 3-A. Fig. 3-B shows the frequencies of NMI that exceed certain values. From these figures, one can see that DEGs are densely distributed around a mean activity level of 0.5. There were only 203 DEG patterns with a highly predictable NMI of 0.5 or more. There were no DEGs whose NMI value was 0.35 or more and mean activity was 0.3 or lower.

If similar natures can be assumed for DEGs of higher dimensionality, we can conjecture regarding the next discussion. Although neural activity is sparse overall, these results suggest that relationships of variables are likely to be represented by locally active neuron groups such as cell assemblies[7].

5   Conclusions

Though the autonomous generation of domain-specific frame representations seems to be an indispensable function for realizing an AGI system, no technology exists to implement such a function. In designing a frame generation function, a subprocedure that is difficult to implement is the enumeration of frame candidates from the huge hypothesis space at a practical calculation cost. Assuming these candidate frames are generated by the cases-join process using variable assimilation, an index of representations that can express various relationships among variables will play an important

---

[6] Mean activity refers to the mean of activity across all cases in one DEG pattern. Here, case activity refers to the rate of variables whose value is 1 for a single arbitrary case.

[7] Cell assembly is a diffuse structure comprising cells in the cortex and diencephalon; it is capable of acting briefly as a closed system and delivering facilitation to other such systems [17].

role in this subprocedure. Sufficient scientific evidence exists to show that the neocortex is the region responsible for accumulating and activating frames. HCF is thought to be the region responsible for generating frames before they are transported to the neocortex. I conjectured that the information representation unique to HCF corresponds to the representations for relationships among variables. These representations are DEGs, each of which is a set of about ten cases in a multi-dimensional subspace that considers variable exchange symmetry. For simplicity, I used binary variable DEGs for estimating the diversity of representation, and my results showed such an approach exhibits sufficient diversity to categorize all combinations of subspaces within HCF. It has been suggested that DEGs are represented by active neuron groups such as cell assemblies.

Consequently, DEGs are a plausible candidate representation of the relationship among variables for a frame generation function; its algorithm can be studied based on this hypothesis in the future.

References

1. Minsky, M.: The Society of Mind (1988)
2. Fisher, D.H.: Knowledge Acquisition via Incremental Conceptual Clustering. Machine Learning 2, 139–172 (1987)
3. Yamakawa, H., Maruhashi, K., Nakao, Y.: Multi-Aspect Gene Relation Analysis. In: Pacific Symposium on Biocomputing, vol. 10, pp. 233–244 (2005)
4. Newcombe, N.: Picture This: Increasing Math and Science Learning by Improving Spatial. American Educator, 29–43 (Summer 2010)
5. Gentner, D.: Structure-mapping: Theoretical framework for analogy. Cognitive Science 7(2), 155–170 (1983)
6. Doumas, L.A.A., Hummel, J.E., Sandhofer, C.M.: A theory of the discovery and predication of relational concepts. Psychological Review 115, 1–43 (2008)
7. Wan, X., et al.: The Neural Basis of Intuitive Best Next-Move Generation in Board Game Experts. Science 331(6015), 341–346 (2011)
8. Yamakawa, H.: What is neural basis of flexible inductive inferences? In: Proc. JNNS (2011)
9. Wagatsuma, N., et al.: Layer-dependent attentional processing by top-down signals in a visual cortical microcircuit model. Frontiers in Computational Neuroscience 5 (2011)
10. Penner, M.R., Mizumori, S.J.: Neural systems analysis of decision making during goal-directed navigation. Prog. Neurobiol. 96(1), 96–135 (2012)
11. Bird, C.M., Burgess, N.: The hippocampus and memory: insights from spatial processing. Nature Reviews Neuroscience 9, 182–194 (2008)
12. Johansson, C., Lansner, A.: Towards cortex sized artificial neural systems. Neural Networks 20, 48–61 (2007)
13. Lisman, J.E.: Role of the dual entorhinal inputs to hippocampus: a hypothesis based on cue/action (non-self/self) couplets. Prog. Brain Res. 163, 615–818 (2007)
14. Cohen, N.J., Eichenbaum, H.: Memory, Amnesia, and the Hippocampal System (1993)
15. Yamaguchi, Y.: A theory of hippocampal memory based on theta phase precession. Biol. Cybern. 89(1), 1–9 (2003)
16. Rudy, J.W., Sutherland, R.J.: Configural and elemental associations and the memory coherence problem. J. Cognitive Neuroscience 4, 208–216 (1992)
17. Hebb, D.O.: The organization of behavior: a neuropsychological theory. John Wiley & Sons (1949)

Fuzzy-Probabilistic Logic for Common Sense

King-Yin Yan

Abstract. P(Z) logic offers a new way to reason about vagueness (ie fuzziness), that treats fuzziness as degrees, distinct from probabilities. One then applies probability distributions over fuzziness. This approach is different from both classical fuzzy logic [26] and possibility theory [1]. P(Z) logic is specially designed for common-sense reasoning.

1 Main Idea

Vagueness is pervasive in common-sense reasoning. A **calculus of degrees** allows common-sense statements to be rendered into formal logic and be reasoned about computationally, thus fulfilling a need in logic-based AGI (artificial general intelligence) systems [5]. It is widely believed that a general-purpose uncertainty calculus should somehow combine the ideas in probability theory and those in fuzzy logic; The current approach is not ground-breaking, but rather an intuitive, simple and practical solution based on well-established probability theory over continuous degrees. We acknowledge that it has not been empirically tested.

A more detailed exposition of our AGI theory is [25]. The logic described here deals with propositions, assigning truth values consisting of 2 components: Z = fuzzy, P = probabilistic. We will also refer to B = binary logic, which is subsumed by $P(Z)$.

1.1 Prior Research

The theory presented here is a synthesis of old ideas that have been expressed in the literature on fuzzy logic [26] [14] [15] and vagueness, in particular the so-called degree theory [20] [2] [8] [6] [21] [22].

1.2 What Is Fuzziness?

The central idea is to treat vagueness as degrees, which are distinct from probabilities. A fuzzy value, $z \in [0,1]$ represents a degree of something. The degree z itself is not really "fuzzy" and is unnatural for use in common sense reasoning. For example, it would be ridiculous for an exact fuzzy value of 0.7 to imply that Mary's height is *exactly* 1.7m and not 1.70000001m. To better capture

J. Bach, B. Goertzel, and M. Iklé (Eds.): AGI 2012, LNAI 7716, pp. 372–379, 2012.

the essence of fuzziness, it makes intuitive sense to distribute probabilities over degrees.[1]

Once we conceptualize vagueness in this manner, the calculus for reasoning with vagueness follows rather routinely.

Any physical quantity (eg age, height) in $[0, \infty)$ can be translated into a degree $\in [0, 1]$ via sigmoidal transformations such as:

$$Z(x) = e^{-\ln 2 \cdot (x/\xi)^2} \tag{1}$$

where ξ is the *point of neutrality* for that specific quantity, ie the point at which $z = 0.5$ (for example Fig 1 is the case for *young*). Note that the ratio (x/ξ) makes z *dimensionless*.

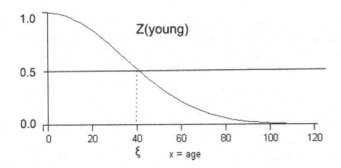

Fig. 1. Neutral point

Reference Classes: A tall building and a tall person should not be compared by the same scale. For each reference class there would be a characteristic ξ, but it is the job of the logic to decide which ξ to use, whereas this paper focuses on the calculus of propositional truth-values.

The common-sense interpretation of numerical Z values is shown in Table 1.

---

[1] Note that P(Z) is different from Fuzzy Random Variables (FRV) [11]. P(Z) values are probability distributions over [0,1], ie, simple random variables; whereas FRVs are probability distributions over fuzzy sets which are themselves membership functions from some arbitrary domains to [0,1]. In other words, FRVs explicitly manage transformations such as Eqn (1), whereas our approach simply distributes probabilities over [0,1] and thus is easier to use.

Another alternative is to use interval fuzzy values, but their inference mechanisms tend to be more complicated (see eg [9]), and the fuzzy intervals tend to diverge to [0,1] very quickly during inference.

Table 1.

z	interpretation
1.0	definitely or extremely
0.9	very
0.7-0.8	moderately
0.6	slightly
0.5	neutral
0.4	slightly not
0.3-0.2	moderately not
0.1	very not
0.0	definitely not

2   P: Probabilistic Logic

A variety of probabilistic logics have been proposed, but the most popular approach seems to be "Bayesian logic" (eg [4] [7]).[2]

In an AGI, when we describe some probabilistic relations, we get a *network* of probabilistic conditionals. For instance, we may say:

- *If a burglary occurs without an earthquake, the alarm will sound with 0.94 chance*
- *If the alarm sounds, Mary will call with 0.9 chance*
- etc etc..

then voila, we already have a Bayesian network (BN). Such BNs can be generated on-the-fly upon each user query. This technique is known as KBMC (knowledge-based model construction) [24] and has become standard for lifting propositional probabilistic logics to first-order. Once we have the BN we can use **belief propagation** to find the truth value of the propositional variable we want.

2.1   Conditionals

At the heart of logical reasoning is the implication operator, often called the "arrow". In Bayesian networks, nodes represent random variables and links represent **probabilistic conditionals** of the form $P(x|y)$. Probabilistic conditionals correspond to **implications** $(x \leftarrow y)$ in classical logic[3]. P(Z) logic is the

---

[2] This view is explained in the "AIMA" textbook [19], 2nd ed, in §14.6. Several other ways to lift probabilistic reasoning to first-order settings are briefly described in the textbook [12] §9.3.7. They include, but not exhaustively: [18]'s Markov Logic Networks which is based on Markov random fields instead of Bayesian networks; and Loopy Logic which is based on [16]'s belief propagation algorithm; [3]'s Probabilistic Relational Models; and [10]'s Bayesian Logic Programs. Relatedly, [17] developed a Stochastic Lambda Calculus, and [13] provides a way to perform probabilistic reasoning within classical higher-order logic.

[3] This correspondence is not exact. Indeed, the relation between implications and conditionals is controversial and has resulted in variants of probabilistic logics. Our view is that classical implication should be replaced by probabilistic conditionals.

extension of Bayesian logic where random variables can take continuous values in [0,1].

Referring to the commutative diagram (Fig 2), which shows the relation between the 4 types of truth values (B, P(B), Z, and P(Z)) and their logical operators. When going from B to P, we replace classical implication $(y \rightarrow x)$ with the Bayesian network link $(y \twoheadrightarrow x)$. When going from P(B) to P(Z), we will also give up the classical connectives $(x \lor y$ and $x \land y)$. The top-right corner requires us to invent a new set of fuzzy-probabilistic operators, a technical issue we won't go into here.

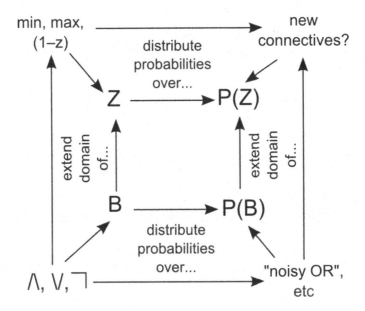

Fig. 2. The inner square shows the 4 types of truth values, the outer square their logical operations

3   P(Z): Probability Distributions over Fuzziness

The logical operators in *pure* Z logic include $\land = \min$, $\lor = \max$, and $\neg = 1-z$. It is a direct consequence of negation as $1-z$ that 0.5 is neutral and 0.0 represents the *opposite* of a concept.

P(Z) logic is the combination of Z with P. Each P(Z) value is a probability distribution over [0,1] (for example Fig 3). All distributions are restricted to be beta distributions, represented by their means and variances (μ, σ^2). The beta distribution is chosen because it is the most well-studied continuous distribution over [0, 1], and can be represented by just 2 parameters. With this choice we cannot represent multi-modal distributions, but it seems to be an adequate "first approximation".

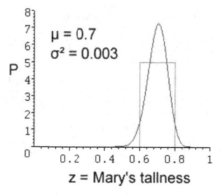

Fig. 3. An example P(Z) distribution

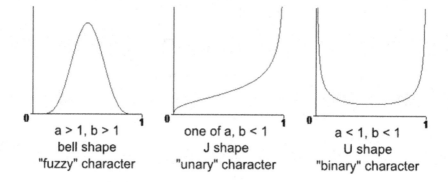

a > 1, b > 1	one of a, b < 1	a < 1, b < 1
bell shape	J shape	U shape
"fuzzy" character	"unary" character	"binary" character

Fig. 4. Shapes of beta distributions

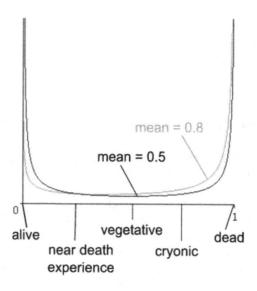

Fig. 5. A concept with binary character

The beta distribution is very versatile and can represent common sense concepts with "fuzzy", "unary", and "binary" characters (Fig 4). For example, common sense says that a person is either dead or alive, but upon closer examination we may discover a continuous spectrum (Fig 5).

"Java girl" Paradox: For example, a boy may judge a girl's desirability based on traits like "good looks", "personality", "intelligence":

$$\text{desirable} \leftarrow \text{trait}_1 \wedge \text{trait}_2 \wedge \text{trait}_3 \wedge \text{etc}...$$

but imagine a girl who scores 0.9 in the top traits but is also 0.9 "good at Java"; she would be even more desirable, but $\wedge$ in fuzzy logic would still give a value of 0.9, counter-intuitively. A solution could be based on taking into account the variance of the P(Z) distributions, as shown in Fig 6, where we know with more specificity and higher overall certainty that girl A is more desirable.

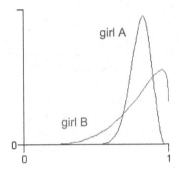

Fig. 6. Same mean, different variance

4   Fuzzy Modifiers

Fuzzy modifiers are introduced to handle natural-language hedges such as "moderately", "very", "extremely". They can be any smooth function $\Gamma : [0,1] \rightarrow [0,1]$, such as those in Figure 7.

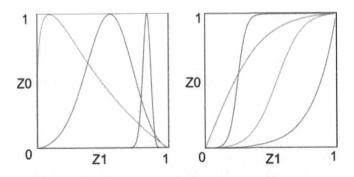

Fig. 7. Fuzzy modifiers

5   Inference

All formulas in P(Z) logic has this general syntax:

$$H \leftarrow B_1, B_2, B_3, \ldots$$

where H is the head and B_i is the body (which may be empty). Some P(Z) logic operators, with numerical parameters, will determine the CPT (conditional probability table) of $P(H|B_i)$.

As an example, the inference rule for $z_0 \leftarrow z_1 \vee z_2$ is:

$$\mu_0 \approx \max(\mu_1, \mu_2)$$

$$v_0 \approx \begin{cases} v_1 & : & \mu_1 > \mu_2 \\ v_2 & : & \mu_2 > \mu_1 \end{cases}$$

and the rule for $\wedge$ is similar. The rule for negation ($z_0 \leftarrow \neg z_1$) is simply:

$$\mu_0 = 1 - \mu_1, \quad v_0 = v_1$$

These rules are obtained by considering the result z_0, a random variable, as a function of other random variables (the operands). Some of the formulas are obtained by simple infinitesimal analysis, others by empirical computations.

Fig 8 shows the behavior of $\max(f_1, f_2)$ against f_1 and f_2. The distribution of f_0 seems to "eat up" the probability masses of f_1 and f_2, whichever comes from the right first, until it is "full" (reaches 1) . Therefore the mean of f_0 is not much different from the max of the means of f_1 and f_2, resulting in the approximate rule above. Note that there is in general a slight *right-shift* for max, this $\Delta\mu$ may be included in a more accurate version...

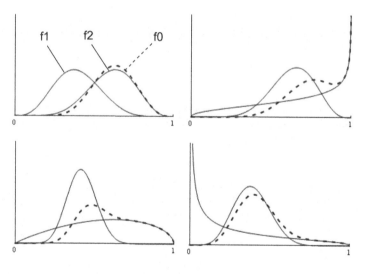

Fig. 8. Example PDFs of $z_0 := z_1 \vee z_2$

Acknowledgments. Abram Demski and Anna Nachesa advised me on the probabilistic aspects. I am also indebted to Pei Wang [23] and Ben Goertzel [5] for their seminal ideas.

References

1. Dubois, Prade: Possibility Theory: An Approach to Computerized Processing of Uncertainty. Plenum Press, New York (1988)
2. Edgington: Validity, uncertainty and vagueness. Analysis 52, 193–204 (1992)
3. Getoor, Friedman, Koller, Pfeffer: Learning probabilistic relational models. Journal of Relational Data Mining, 307–335 (2001)
4. Getoor, Taskar (eds.): Introduction to statistical relational learning. MIT Press (2007)
5. Goertzel, Pennachin: Artificial general intelligence. Springer (2007)
6. Graff, Williamson (eds.): Vagueness. Ashgate, Dartmouth (2002)
7. Heckerman, Meek, Koller: Probabilistic entity-relationship models, PRMs, and plate models. In: Statistical Relational Learning, ch. 7. MIT (2007)
8. Keefe: Theories of Vagueness. Cambridge University Press (2000)
9. Kenevan, Neapolitan: A model theoretic approach to propositional fuzzy logic using Beth Tableaux. In: Fuzzy Logic for the Management of Uncertainty, pp. 141–157. John Wiley & Sons, Inc., New York (1992)
10. Kersting, de Raedt: Bayesian logic programs. In: Cussens, Frisch (eds.) Work-in-progress Reports of the 10th International Conference on Inductive Logic Programming, ILP 2000 (2000)
11. Kruse, Meyer: Statistics with vague data. Reidel Publishing Company (1987)
12. Luger: Artificial intelligence: structures and strategies for complex problem solving. Pearson Education (2009)
13. Ng, Lloyd: Probabilistic reasoning in a classical logic. Journal of Applied Logic 7(2), 218–238 (2009)
14. Nguyen, Walker: A first course in fuzzy logic, 1st, 2nd, 3rd edn. Chapman & Hall/CRC (1997, 2000, 2006)
15. Novak, Perfilieva, Mockor: Mathematical principles of fuzzy logic. Kluwer Academic Press (1999)
16. Pearl: Probabilistic Reasoning in Intelligent Systems - Networks of Plausible Inference. Morgan Kaufmann, California (1988)
17. Pless, Luger: Towards general analysis of recursive probabilistic models. In: Proceedings of Conference of Uncertainty in Aritificial Intelligence, San Francisco (2001)
18. Richardson, Domingos: Markov logic networks. Journal of Machine Learning 62, 107–136 (2006)
19. Russell, Norvig: Artificial Intelligence - a modern approach. Prentice Hall (2003)
20. Sainsbury: Degrees of belief and degrees of truth. Philosophical Papers 15, 97–106 (1986)
21. Shapiro: Vagueness in Context. Oxford University Press (2006)
22. Smith: Vagueness and degrees of truth, Oxford (2008)
23. Wang: Rigid Flexibility - The Logic of Intelligence. Springer applied logic series (2006)
24. Wellman, Breese, Goldman: From knowledge bases to decision models. Knowledge Engineering Review 7(1), 35–53 (1992)
25. Yan: Genifer – an artificial general intelligence (currently electronic version only) (2010), http://launchpad.net/agi-book
26. Zadeh: Fuzzy sets. Information and Control 8, 338–353 (1965)

Author Index